MACROECONOMICS

Private Markets and Public Choice

Fifth Edition

MACROECONOMICS

Private Markets and Public Choice

Robert B. Ekelund, Jr.
Auburn University

Robert D. Tollison
George Mason University

 ADDISON-WESLEY

An imprint of Addison Wesley Longman, Inc.

Reading, Massachusetts • Menlo Park, California • New York • Harlow, England
Don Mills, Ontario • Sydney • Mexico City • Madrid • Amsterdam

Library of Congress Cataloging-in-Publication Data

Ekelund, Robert B. (Robert Burton), 1940–
    Macroeconomics : private markets and public choice /
Robert B. Ekelund, Jr., Robert D. Tollison. -- 5th ed.
        p.   cm.
    Includes bibliographical references and index.
    ISBN 0-201-91897-8 (soft cover bound). --
ISBN 0-201-85318-3 (unbound)
    1. Macroeconomics.   I. Tollison, Robert D.   II. Title.
HB172.5.E42   1996
339--dc20   96-38799
                                                    CIP

Printed in the United States of America.

1 2 3 4 5 6 7 8 9–DOW–99989796

Senior Sponsoring Editor:	Denise J. Clinton
Associate Editor:	Lena Buonanno
Editorial Assistant:	Thomas Park
Managing Editor:	James Rigney
Senior Production Supervisor:	Loren Hilgenhurst Stevens
Cover Designers:	Diana Coe & Regina Hagen
Cover & Interior Illustrator:	Eileen Hoff
Photo Researcher:	Kathy Smith
Prepress Buyer:	Caroline Fell
Copyeditor:	Kathy Smith
Production Services:	Kathy Smith
Indexer:	Alexandra Nickerson
Manufacturing Supervisor:	Hugh Crawford
Executive Marketing Manager:	Beth Toland
Composition & Prepress:	Pre-Press Company, Inc.
Printer:	R. R. Donnelley & Sons Company

For My Mother, Anna Mae Ekelund

RBE

For Willa and Joe

RDT

PREFACE

Economic issues dominate the world we live in, affecting our perceptions about ourselves and our futures. Like it or not, we are faced with economic issues on television, in newspapers, in the voting booth, in career choice, and, perhaps most significantly, in balancing our checkbooks every month! Will persistent federal deficits and more than $5 trillion of debt saddle future generations, and very possibly ourselves, with high taxes, slow growth, and stagnation? Put another way, can we expect the children of our generation to be better off than our generation or that of our parents? Do federally guaranteed entitlements—such as Medicare, Social Security, and welfare—have a future? Will international trade agreements, such as the North American Free Trade Association (NAFTA) or the General Agreement on Tariffs and Trade (GATT), have a positive or negative impact on the economic well-being of Americans? Should government play a large, small, or negligible role in providing the groceries we buy in the store or in the health insurance we buy every year?

A solid foundation in economics helps us answer such questions. In this fifth edition of our introduction to macroeconomics, we again present economic ideas in a policy-real-world context that students—both those who continue the study of economics and those for whom this is the first and last class—can master and understand. Since our approach stresses the relationship between theory and policy, the technical presentations in this book are concise and straightforward. We rely heavily on examples to illustrate abstract theory, and describe graphs and graphical relationships in patient detail.

Our approach to economic study is "market oriented." It stresses that, in general, society's welfare is maximized when markets are used to allocate resources to their most desired private uses. Our approach goes further, however, to show (as early as the first chapters) how our public choices working through a political process can have a number of effects, not all of them desirable from the perspective of society. Democratic politics (as we make clear in Chapter 4) and interest groups may actually reduce society's welfare. In short, our approach to basic macroeconomics is underscored by the integration of politics and markets—and by the new subtitle to the fifth edition of *Macroeconomics: Private Markets and Public Choice*. The fifth edition again covers macroeconomics in clear and student-friendly prose with:

- Renewed emphasis on the use of markets to solve the basic economic problems created by scarcity;

- New and interesting examples of how economic and political markets interact and affect economic efficiency;
- Coverage of recent and continuing global events, particularly those that have created new "free-trade" alliances between the United States and other nations of the world;
- Clear analysis of important domestic policies and proposals relating to such issues as tax reform, deficits, the mega-debt, and monetary policy.
- Targeted, but streamlined discussions of theory and policy in a shorter presentation than the fourth edition.

New to the Fifth Edition

The fifth edition of *Macroeconomics* contains many changes, including new topics, examples, and applications. While structural changes requiring a fundamental revision of instructor's lectures and assignments have been held to a minimum, there are some important differences from the fourth edition, in addition to those listed above.

The public choice theme (present in all previous editions) has been clarified and expanded. In spite of the supposed public choice emphasis of other texts, we have found that the critical issue of how politics affects markets is not integrated into discussions of standard economic issues. In addition to a new Chapter 4 dealing with public choice, we provide in-text and "application-style" examples integrating public choice with discussion of basic economic issues. Thus, the student is introduced to issues such as why joining a health club is different from being a member of the student government at a university (Chapter 3) and how peanut and auto quotas are related to politics (Chapter 16).

There is renewed emphasis on the importance of all trade, including international trade. The principles of specialization, opportunity cost, and trade run throughout the book and are explicitly introduced to the student in Chapter 2, which explains the role of free trade associations such as NAFTA in producing greater economic welfare and integrates international trade and interest group considerations right from the beginning. The emphasis on the importance of international trade and markets is carried throughout the text. See, for example, discussions of how the macroeconomy is related to international trade in Chapter 10, the discussions of international counterfeiting or monetary control institutions in Chapter 12, and the new discussions of property rights arrangements and their relation to growth in China, Korea, and other nations in Chapter 14.

Organization

Our presentation is provided in five parts:

Part One—The Power of Economic Thinking

Part Two—The Fundamentals of Macroeconomics

Part Three—Money

Part Four—Macroeconomic Policy and Economic Growth

Part Five—The Global Economy

We have found that many books attempting to provide an "orderly" and simple presentation of macroeconomic theory actually do the opposite. Students taking the "macro half" of principles of economics who are barely conversant with supply and demand are overwhelmed by "three-sector equilibrium" models of macroeconomic theory with short-run/long-run aggregate supply distinctions. We take a different approach—one that presents a smooth, logical, and historical transition from classical economics (Chapter 7) to Keynesian economics (Chapter 8) to aggregate demand and supply (Chapter 9). Our remaining chapters in macroeconomics then develop macroeconomic and monetary policies in the context of this progression (Chapters 10–13). This logical approach permits instructors to spend as much time emphasizing their own views of "key issues" while maintaining an orderly approach to macroeconomic theory. Those wishing to elongate the discussion of macroeconomic policies and their relation to U.S. and global growth may then go on to Chapters 14 and 15.

Two major alterations have been made in our structuring of macroeconomics. The first is that Keynesian economics, which was developed in two chapters in previous editions (Chapters 23 and 24 in the fourth edition), is now streamlined to one chapter (Chapter 8). We find this treatment—and the treatment of classical macro principles—to be logical and pedagogically sound. Most texts "hide" the nature of Keynes's contribution, giving Keynes and his "rejection" of the classical ideas short shrift. Keynes thus appears as a minor figure; in fact, his ideas were the most important source of the "debate" that rages within macroeconomic theory and policy—the question of whether "activist" or "non-activist" policies have the greatest effect on overall growth of GDP in the United States or internationally. We assert that the source of these ideas continues to rest upon a sound understanding of both classical and Keynesian ideas and believe our in-depth treatments (in Chapters 7 and 8) promote this understanding.

A second major change in our presentation of macroeconomics is that we have streamlined an over-long basic money, banking, and Federal Reserve discussion from two chapters (Chapters 28 and 29 of the fourth edition) to one chapter (Chapter 12). Moreover, Chapter 32 on business cycles in the fourth edition has been eliminated, and the most relevant and interesting materials from that chapter are now included in other chapter discussions.

Part Five—The Global Economy, includes Chapters 16 and 17, which are devoted to issues relating to international trade and finance. A number of instructors have told us that they prefer to teach these issues as a special unit or topic. These chapters have been streamlined and completely updated for that purpose. However, international trade issues and their relation to our economy and well-being are an integral part of our entire book. Our view is that these issues are not separate from trade issues in general. We therefore begin, in Chapter 2, with matters of specialization, comparative advantage, and trade from an international perspective. These ideas and applications are then carried throughout the book.

Features of the Fifth Edition

We have designed the fifth edition of *Macroeconomics* solely with the learning objectives of the student-reader in mind. The most successful pedagogical features of all earlier editions have been maintained and several innovative ideas have been added. Each chapter opens with an overview of the topics covered and a bulleted list of chapter objectives.

- Figures are drawn with consistent use of color, helping students understand key concepts and the direction and magnitude of changes in economic behavior.
- Key concepts and terms are boldfaced when first mentioned in the text, with definitions appearing in the margin.
- Reader-friendly Focus boxes—at least one per chapter—provide interpretations and perspectives on critical or illustrative ideas or policies mentioned in the text. Many of the Focus features are new to the fifth edition. Examples include: "Scarcity, Economizing, and the College Student's Time" (Chapter 1); "Is Student Government Different from Joining a Health Club?" (Chapter 4); "Do Politicians Create Ups and Downs in the Business Cycle?" (Chapter 5); "How the Political System Helps Create Deficits" (Chapter 8); "Did Keynesian Economics and World War II Save Us From the Depression?" (Chapter 10); "Can a Pub Become a Bank? The Modern Case of Ireland" (Chapter 12); and "Counterfeiting and the Quantity Theory of Money" (Chapter 13).
- Applications of key text material are again included in our presentation. These are in-depth discussions of issues or policies brought up in the text. Many of these features are new to the fifth edition. A sample includes: "When a Rose is Not a Rose: Interest Groups and Shifting Comparative Advantage in the Flower Industry" (Chapter 2); "Why Are There So Many Restaurants and Golf Courses in State Capital Cities?" (Chapter 4); "Beating the IRS: How Big is the Underground Economy?" (Chapter 6); "Mortgaging Your Future: The Government and Your Incentive to Save" (Chapter 8); "The Impact of Freer Trade on the Macroeconomy" (Chapter 10); "Moral Hazard and the Savings and Loan Crisis" (Chapter 12); "Politics and Inflation: A Global Perspective" (Chapter 13); and "NAFTA: Free Trade or Free-For-All?" (Chapter 16).
- Every chapter contains a concluding summary of the major ideas and concepts of the chapter, a list of key terms, questions for review and discussion, and, where applicable, problems for the student to solve.
- Point/Counterpoint features containing biographies of great economists, past and present, along with their contrasting ideas, conclude each book part.
- A glossary of terms, including text page references, is provided at the back of the book, together with a useful and thorough index.

PRINT SUPPLEMENTS

The *Study Guide* by John Keith Watson of the University of Southwestern Louisiana is a comprehensive learning package containing chapter overviews; learning objectives; helpful hints; fill-in, true/false, multiple-choice, and short-answer questions, and "Something to Think About" segments.

The *Instructor's Resource Manual* by John Keith Watson of the University of Southwestern Louisiana is coordinated with the text and contains chapter overviews and outlines, learning objectives, answers to text questions, extra problems and essays with solutions, "One Step Further" segments and suggestions for additional readings.

The *Test Bank* by Frank Mixon of the University of Southern Mississippi contains over 3,400 multiple-choice questions coded by level of difficulty. Ten percent of the questions are new to this edition and are identified with a margin icon.

Color acetates of main figures and tables in the text are also available.

SOFTWARE SUPPLEMENTS

For the Student
Economics Tutor by Daniel K. Benjamin of Clemson University is a Windows-compatible DOS tutorial program with three distinct features. First, it employs a graphical user interface that can be driven by either a mouse or a keyboard. Second, it goes beyond the conventional "textbook on a screen" approach by involving the student in a fully interactive way. Finally, the program's architecture recognizes that students who enjoy what they are doing are likely to do more of it, so *Economics Tutor* brings the "feel" of computer games into a college-level economics tutorial program for the first time.

For the Instructor
TestMaster, a computerized test generator that allows you to construct tests by choosing questions from the test bank, is available in IBM and Windows versions. If desired, test questions can be viewed on the screen, edited, saved, and printed. Instructors can also add or create their own questions. A *TestMaster User's Guide* provides comprehensive instructions.

Acknowledgments
No book of this size and structure could be developed without the help of friends, colleagues, friendly critics, not-so-friendly critics, and editors. This book, both in its former editions and in the new fifth edition, is no exception. We gratefully acknowledge the following colleagues, friends, users, and students (past and present) whose generosity and advice fill these pages: John Allen, Gary Anderson, Leonardo Auernheimer, Andy Barnett, Raymond Battalio, Randy Beard, Richard Beil, Don Boudreaux, the late Katherine Boudreaux, Bill Briet, Butch Browning, Steve Caudill, Roy Cordato, Audrey Davidson, Elynor Davis, Charles DeLorme, David Gay, Kathie Gilbert, Cary Heath, Bob Hebert, Elmer Holt, John Jackson, Dave Kaserman, Roger Koppel, Dave Laband, Dwight Lee, Bobby McCormick, Charles Maurice, Francois Melese, Margaret O'Donnell, Karen Palasek, Chris Paul, Phil Porter, Ed Price, Rand Ressler, Morgan Reynolds, Richard Saba, Tom Saving, Bill Shughart, John Sophocles, Chris Thomas, Henry Thompson, John Wells, and David Whitten. For special help and assistance on this edition we want to thank Roy Gilbert of Texas A&M University, Rand Ressler of the University of Southwestern

Louisiana, and Bill Breit of Trinity University. Frank Mixon of the University of Southern Mississippi has offered valuable advice and provided an excellent and streamlined *Test Bank* for the fifth edition.

Several individuals deserve very special gratitude for helping us improve the quality and direction of *Macroeconomics* in both this edition and previous ones: Frank Adams, Gustavus Adolphus, Richard Ault, Auburn University; Paula Gant, University of Louisville; David Saurman, San Jose State University; Keith Watson, University of Southwestern Louisiana; and Mark Thornton, Auburn University.

Past and present graduate assistants—many of whom are now professors and productive contributors to economic research—were of help with all five editions of *Macroeconomics*: Manisha Perrera, Bharat Vijayan, Brian Goff, Ladd Jones, Dan Berry, George Ford, Yvan Kelly, Paul Gentle, Dwight Nystrom, Shawn Rittenour, Ken Somppi, Jim Tillery, Marc Ulrich, Deborah Walker, Doug Walker, and Biff Woodruff. Of special help in helping us gather and check data and materials for the fifth edition was Keith Reutter of Auburn University.

Thomas Park—our developmental editor—did much to improve this book as did our production editors, Loren Hilgenhurst Stevens and Kathy Smith. Denise Clinton, our editor at Addison Wesley, could not have been more supportive of this project, and we owe her a profound debt of gratitude. The cliche that "this book would not have been possible without her help" is very true here.

Official reviewers for this edition were Douglas Agbetsiafa, Indiana University; Richard F. Gleisner, St. Cloud State University; Cary Heath, University of Southwestern Louisiana; George Hoffer, Virginia Commonwealth University; David MacPherson, Florida State University; James N. McGowen, Jr., Belleville Area College; Rand Ressler, University of Southwestern Louisiana; and Phil Sorenson, Florida State University.

Official reviewers and contributors for the earlier editions were Douglas K. Agbetsiafa, Indiana University; Ralph E. Ancil, Southwestern Missouri State University; Robert A. Baade, Lake Forest College; Dean Baim, Pepperdine University; Richard O. Beil, Jr., Auburn University; J. Lloyd Blackwell, IV, University of North Dakota; Robert Carbaugh, Central Washington University; Albert Celoza, Phoenix College; John Dennis Chasse, State University of New York-Brockport; George Shih-Fan Chu, University of Nevada at Reno; Paul A. Cleveland, University of Central Florida; Cheryl Cohen, Millikin University; Barbara Craig, Oberlin College; Robert D. Crofts, Salem State College; Steve Cunningham, University of Connecticut; William W. Davis, Western Kentucky University; David Denslow, University of Florida; Carl E. Enomoto, New Mexico State University; Donald H. Farness, Oregon State University; Arthur A. Fleisher III, Metropolitan State College of Denver; Andrew W. Foshee, McNeese State University; Robert Gillette, Texas A&M University; Jack Goddard, Northeastern State University; Anthony Greco, University of Southwestern Louisiana; Carole A. Green, University of South Florida; William B. Green, Sam Houston State University; Edward Greenberg, Washington University; Anthony O. Gyapong, Wayne State University; Jan M. Hansen, University of Wisconsin-Eau Claire; Steven C. Hine, State University of New York-Binghamton; James H. Holcomb, Jr., University of Texas-El Paso; John B. Horowitz, Ball State University; Arthur Kartman, San Diego State University; Philip King, San Francisco State

University; Gary F. Langer, Roosevelt University; Stephen E. Lile, Western Kentucky University; Marvin S. Margolis, Millersville University; Lawrence W. Martin, Michigan State University; Warren Matthews, Texas A&M University; Mary Ann Meiners, Middle Tennessee State University; Charles C. Milliken, Siena Heights College; Khan Mohabbat, Northern Illinois University; Dan Myers, Western Kentucky University; Emmanuel Nnadozie, Northeast Missouri State University; Edd Noell, Westmont College; Terry Olsen; Don Owen, Ottawa University; Elliot Parker, University of Nevada at Reno; Ken Patterson, Oregon State University; Gerald Pelovsky, College of the Sequoias; Steven C. Pitts, Houston Community College; J. M. Pogodzinski, San Jose State University; Munir Quddus, University of Southern Indiana; Farhad Rassekh, University of Hartford; Doralia Reynolds, Seward County Community College; Peter Rupert, West Virginia University; Carlos E. Santiago, State University of New York-Albany; Gerald W. Sazama, University of Connecticut; Chaitram J. Talele, Columbia State Community College; Steven G. Thorpe, University of Colorado at Boulder; H. Bruce Throckmorton, Tennessee Technological University; Abraham Usumang, Bowling Green State University; James VanBeck, Blinn College-College Station Campus; John Wakemann-Linn, Williams College; Harold Warren, East Tennessee State University; Walter J. Wessells, North Carolina State University; Darrell Young, University of Texas-Austin; and Mahmood Yousefi, University of Northern Iowa.

CONTENTS

xix

CHAPTER 11

Taxes. Deficits, and the Debt

245

PART 4

MACROECONOMIC POLICY AND ECONOMIC GROWTH   327

CHAPTER 14

Macroeconomic
Theory and Policy
328

CHAPTER 15

Global Economic Growth and Development 349

MACROECONOMICS
Private Markets and Public Choice

PART 1

THE POWER OF
ECONOMIC THINKING

CHAPTER 1
ECONOMICS IN PERSPECTIVE

Economics is the study of human behavior as we go about "the ordinary business of life."[1] As such, it offers a way of thinking about how the world works and a framework for making choices and decisions of all kinds. These choices may be private choices about such issues as how much you should invest in higher education, or they may be public choices about which candidate to vote for or which public policy is most desirable. Close study of economics gives us a new perspective on a wide variety of human activities and institutions. When you finish Chapter 1 you should understand

- how individuals, societies, and nations solve the basic economic problem caused by scarce resources and unlimited wants.

- the functions of prices and how they act as signals to producers, consumers, and governments in any economy.

- the basis on which all individuals actually make economic decisions.

- how economics gives insight into human behavior with respect to the private and public choices that individuals must make.

[1] Alfred Marshall, *Principles of Economics* (London: Macmillan, 1920), p. 1.

WHAT ECONOMICS IS

Most people would say that economics deals with the stock market or with how to make money by buying and selling gold, land, or some other commodity. This common view contains a grain of truth but does not touch on the richness, depth, and breadth of the matter. Economics is a social science—the oldest and best developed of the social sciences. As such, it studies human behavior in relation to three basic questions about an economy: What **goods** and **services** are produced? How are goods and services produced? For whom are goods and services produced?

For at least 200 years, economists have tried to analyze how individuals and societies answer these insistent questions. Complicating their task is the tendency of individuals and societies to change their minds. Communism, for example, appeared to be a viable answer to the questions *what*, *how*, and *for whom* in many countries throughout much of the twentieth century, but today it has largely been abandoned.

Economics, particularly the study of markets, has much to say about the link between the amount of government economic control and personal freedom and democracy. It deals with countless other important issues, such as health care, inflation, and the availability of jobs as well. The tools of economics may be applied to each of these matters, and the skill of analyzing such issues is a characteristic of an informed person. The insistent questions—What? How? and For whom?—must be asked; for at least two centuries, economists have tried to analyze how individuals and societies answer them.

Economics: A Working Definition

A common thread runs through all definitions of economics. Each definition emphasizes the inescapable fact that **resources**—the wherewithal to produce goods and services—are not available in limitless quantities and that people and societies, with their unlimited desires for goods and services, must make some hard choices about what to do with the resources that are available. Our working definition of economics may be expressed as follows:

> Economics is the study of how individuals and societies, experiencing virtually limitless wants, choose to allocate scarce resources to best satisfy their wants.

Unlimited wants, scarcity, and the choices they force on us are thus the key elements in understanding economics. Consider the nature of scarcity.

The Economic Condition: Scarcity

What, exactly, is **scarcity**? More to the point, what are scarce resources? Dorothy Parker, an American humorist, once said, "If you can't get what you want, you'd better damn well settle for what you can get." The entire study of economics amplifies and expands on Parker's proposition. As individuals and as a society, we cannot get all of what we want because the amount of available resources is limited. The role of the economist and of economics in general is to explain how we can make the most of this problem of scarcity—in Parker's terms, how to get as much as we can of what we want.

Goods
All tangible things that satisfy people's wants and desires.

Services
All forms of intangible but useful activities that are valued by people.

Resources
Those things used to produce goods and services. These include land, machines, energy, and human labor and ingenuity. Resources are also called factors of production.

Scarcity
The condition whereby the resources, goods, and services available to individuals and society are limited relative to the wants and desires for them.

The most important problem in economics is that while the wants of individuals and societies must be satisfied by limited resources, the wants themselves are not limited; they are endless. We are never satisfied with what we have. Individuals will forever be lured by more tempting foods, more cleverly engineered computers, more up-to-date fashions. Societies continually desire safer highways, more national security, greater Social Security benefits, or more cancer research. Problems of scarcity and unlimited wants—economics itself—apply to all nations, regardless of political, social, and religious orientation. Moslems, Jews, and Christians all face the eternal problem of satisfying limitless wants with limited means. Methods of dealing with scarcity, of course, differ from society to society, depending on cultural differences and on particular endowments of resources within political boundaries, but the fundamental problem is the same everywhere.

Scarcity is independent of time and fortune. Our generation has many more services and goods to choose from than our parents and grandparents did. The quantity and quality of goods and services may have grown from primitive to modern times, but the supply of resources needed to produce them is limited, and human wants are not.

Scarcity affects both private and public choices. We must choose virtually every day among items that we commonly purchase, such as food, transportation, and clothing, and we surely cannot have all of the things that we would like to have. How about a new Mercedes? And in our public choices as well, scarcity dictates that we must choose. Do we want to support candidates who want to spend more resources on public programs or less? How about increased space missions?

Economic goods and services
Goods and services that are scarce.

All scarce goods—from television to chlorinated water—are called **economic goods**. Their scarcity leads to **costs**. While it is customary to associate cost with the money price of goods, economists define cost as the value of the good or activity given up in place of the good or activity actually chosen. Since all unlimited wants cannot be met with scarce resources, individuals have to make choices—between, for instance, more steaks and more computer games. Public choices have to be made between safer highways and more accurate missiles. Cost is, therefore, the direct result of the scarcity of resources. Scarcity of resources means that individuals both in their public and private choices must endure the costs of acquiring more of any good or service. That cost is the value of the good or activity given up in place of the good chosen.

Costs
An implication of scarcity; the necessary sacrifices associated with making any choice.

Think for a moment about that scarce resource time. Being absolutely limited in supply for each of us, time—or rather, the use of time—bears a definite cost. No college student, certainly, has escaped being confronted with economic decisions arising from the need to allocate this costly resource. (See the Focus "Scarcity, Economizing, and the College Student's Time.")

Free goods and services
Things that are available in sufficient amounts and provide all that people want at zero cost.

You may feel that some things are not scarce and that some things—such as love, sunshine, and water—are free. In economic terms, **free goods and services** are goods that are available in sufficient amounts to satisfy all possible demands. But are many things truly free? Surface water is usually unfit for drinking except in areas far from human habitation. Water suitable for drinking must be raised to the surface from deep wells or piped from reservoirs and treatment plants, operations involving resources that are scarce even when water itself is not. Scarcity of win-

Cooollege students know the principle of scarcity all too well. Indeed, a successful student needs an ability to make sound and efficient economic decisions not only in the case of scarce monetary resources but in the allocation of scarce time resources as well. Time is a valuable resource to all human beings, but it exists in finite quantities of 24 hours a day, 168 hours a week, and (approximately) 720 hours a month.

Every student knows that he or she cannot have and do everything and that economic decisions, whether they are recognized as such or not, must be made every day. A student's time often must be allocated over a day or a week. A weekend trip to an out-of-town football game must be "paid for" not only in monetary terms but also in less time to work on the English paper due on Wednesday. The end of a term always necessitates economizing: Given the limited time available, should an additional two hours be di-

rected to chemistry or art history? Actual choices will depend on perceived net gain or potential net gain from the array of alternatives. Ordinarily, most activities or goods and services selected, if they are divisible, will be combined by the choice-maker to maximize satisfaction (for example, one hour spent on chemistry and one hour spent on art history).

College students are not alone, of course. For anyone, the choice may be between attending a rock concert or a Bach organ recital. We may have chosen a career in acting or dance instead of law or computer programming. A retiree may choose to return to the classroom rather than to spend time fishing or playing bridge. Economizing—maximizing the value of monetary or time resources under conditions of scarcity—forms the foundation of human behavior. Students, workers, politicians, philanthropists, business executives—all must make choices, and an analysis of these choices forms the basis of the social science of economics.

ter sun in the North leads many people to seek costly winter vacations in the snowbird states. And if you think love is free. . . .

Scarce Resources and Economic Problems

There are basically two categories of scarce resources: human resources and nonhuman resources. **Human resources** encompass all types of labor, including specialized forms of labor such as management or entrepreneurship. **Nonhuman resources** include land, natural resources such as minerals and water, and capital.

Examples of human resources abound. By definition, all human resources apply talent and energy to produce goods and services. The cook at the Chicken Shack, the hairstylist at the Mad Hacker, the chief executive of a computer firm, and the assembly-line worker at a General Motors plant all represent human resources. Obviously, labor includes a huge variety of skills, both general and precise. Knowledge, or know-how, is also part of human resources. Economists are interested not only in the scarcity of labor but in its quality. The quality of human resources can be enhanced through investments in education and training.

Economists view *entrepreneurship* as a special form of labor. An entrepreneur is a person who perceives profitable opportunities and who combines resources

Human resources
All forms of labor and skill used to produce goods and services.

Nonhuman resources
All resources other than human resources, such as machines and land.

to produce goods or services. Entrepreneurs attempt to move resources from lower- to higher-valued uses in the economy and take the risk that they can make profits by doing so. Inventors, such as Thomas Edison, are good examples of entrepreneurs. *Management*, a second special form of labor, guides and oversees the process by which separate resources are turned into goods or services.

Human resources utilize nonhuman resources such as land, minerals, and natural resources to produce goods and services. A commercial lot in Manhattan, an acre in Iowa, a coal deposit in Pennsylvania, a uranium mine in South Dakota, and a timber stand in Oregon are all scarce nonhuman resources. New deposits of minerals can be discovered, forests can be replanted, and agricultural land can be reclaimed from swamps. But at any one time, the available supply of nonhuman resources is limited.

Capital, another category of nonhuman resources, comprises all machines, implements, and buildings used to produce goods and services either directly or indirectly. A surgeon's scalpel, a factory, an electric generator, and an artist's brush are all used to produce goods and services and, thus, are considered capital.

Many different forms of capital may be needed to produce a single economic good. With a wheat harvesting machine, a South Dakota farmer can reap a huge crop. But the wheat must also be milled into flour and transported from South Dakota to bakeries in, say, California. Once the wheat has arrived, bakeries must utilize brick or convection ovens to produce bread. The harvesting and milling machines, the railroad, and the baker's ovens are all capital goods, created to increase the amount of final production.

Capital—and the resources used to produce it—is scarce. To create capital, we must sacrifice consumer goods and services because the production of capital takes time away from the production of goods that can be consumed in the present. Societies and individuals must therefore choose between immediate consumption and future consumption. That choice is crucial to economic growth and ultimate economic well-being. We return to this important issue in Chapter 2.

Other Factors Affecting Resources and Growth

Quantities of human and nonhuman resources are only one prerequisite for economic growth and well-being in an economy. The institutional framework of an economy, such as the nature of its legal system and its form of government, is also critical for economic growth and development, as are factors such as technology and information. Consider, first, the nature of technology and information.

Technology and information assist resource utilization in a modern, functioning economy. **Technology**, in general, is composed of know-how, inventions, and innovations that help us get more from scarce resources. An improvement in technology implies that we can produce more from a given amount of resources. Existing technology is the outcome of many inventions, some of which were the invention of new resources—such as aluminum and hybrid plants. All inventions that increase the productivity of labor and capital can be considered improvements in technology. Innovation is the application of technology to the production of goods and services. Technology, then, helps make other resources less scarce.

Information is a scarce and costly ingredient in the economic process. The acquisition of information for economic decision making has never been free. In the

Technology
Knowledge of production methods associated with producing a particular good.

Information
A scarce and important element in the process of economic exchange and growth.

nineteenth and early twentieth centuries, businesses hired armies of bookkeepers to provide sufficient information for managers to make decisions. The development of the digital computer in the mid-twentieth century made the storage and retrieval of information less costly. Technology has progressed so rapidly that the quantity of information that could be stored in a warehouse-sized computer in 1950 can now be placed on a chip the size of a fingernail. Information, then, helps us economize on the use of scarce resources.

Resources, both human and nonhuman, never operate in a vacuum; they always exist in some real-world setting that includes government, a legal system, and a structure of property rights. **Property rights** are those rules that establish and govern the ownership and control of resources. Property rights are established by laws developed within a society's traditions and social relations. Institutions are the sum total of the traditions, mores, laws, and governmental structures of an economy. **Institutions** in the United States include the Constitution and the laws of the states. Some of these institutions restrict and define the rights to own and use resources. Others enhance the flow of resources among individuals and states. The U.S. Constitution, for example, guarantees the free movement of resources from state to state.

These institutions represent a type of capital that is the result of public choices that citizens and leaders in a society make. We live in a world filled with many governments representing many different institutional structures. Some countries are blessed with huge quantities of land and natural resources but still do not manage to achieve economic growth and development beyond the barest minimum. Prior to the 1980s, China's communist government directed almost all human and nonhuman resources from the highest levels of bureaucracy. Despite China's huge resource base, these institutions reduced the country's ability to achieve economic development. More recently, and in spite of periodic political repression, the Chinese government has tentatively embraced some elements of a Western-style free market system, in which some areas of the economy, such as agriculture, are given over to self-interested production, distribution, and exchange. However slowly, Western institutions and technology are being adopted in China because they have encouraged a more efficient use of human and nonhuman resources in producing goods and services.

When property rights are not assigned to scarce resources, the resources tend to be wasted. The old adage "What is owned by all, is cared for by none" means the failure to legally assign property rights to specific resources will ensure that the resources will not be utilized in the most efficient fashion. Most Western economists believe that private rights over property—combined with free and unregulated private markets for human and nonhuman resources—are essential to growth in any nation. The success stories of relatively free and unrestricted economies such as Hong Kong, Taiwan, and Singapore—each endowed with very modest quantities of resources—are often presented as evidence that noninterventionist institutions contribute greatly to economic development. The shift in New Zealand's economy from more to less regulation of resources has produced heightened growth there, while the coexistence of private property and extensive controls on resource use in the Indian economy has produced stagnation. The lesson to be learned from these cases is that institutions—especially the form of government

Property rights
Any legal and/or enforceable rights to the use of resources of any kind.

Institutions
The sum total of the traditions, mores, laws, and governmental structures of an economy.

and the nature of controls over resources and resource utilization—are keys to productivity and economic growth in any society.

When it comes to material goods, most people throughout history have believed that more is better than less. Accordingly, economic growth has been defined as *more* housing, *more* food, *more* health care, *more* leisure, *more* of everything. Growth, however, may be defined to include the attainment of less tangible environmental goals as well as an increase in the output of physical goods and services. Today, some people prefer the kinds of "goods" associated with a simpler, safer, and cleaner life for society. The acquisition of these goods also requires public decisions and public choices about the expenditure of resources.

Scarcity of resources and scarcity of imagination in designing institutions to facilitate resource use are at the heart of all economic problems. Resources can be augmented over time; indeed, we are much better off materially than our grandparents, and our grandparents were better off than their grandparents. At any one time, however, individuals and societies cannot get all of what they want. Given scarcity, individuals and societies must make choices, and a primary role of economists is to analyze scarcity and the process of choosing.

KEY PRINCIPLES OF ECONOMIC THINKING

All economists share certain ways of thinking. These perspectives, which form the core of the science of economics, appear many times throughout this book. A look at these economic perspectives in simple, commonsense language should convince you that economics and economic reasoning are closely related to the private and public decisions you make every day.

Resources and Activities Cost More Than You Think

What does it cost you to take a skiing weekend in the mountains or to make a trip to the beach during spring break? Your reply might include the costs of gasoline, auto depreciation, airfare, lift tickets, food, drink, entertainment, and a motel room. These money expenditures are called **accounting costs**, or explicit money costs.

Accounting costs
Actual money expenditures associated with any activity; out-of-pocket costs.

Explicit costs
Accounting costs.

Implicit costs
Nonpecuniary costs associated with the consumption of a good or service.

Opportunity cost
The highest-valued alternative forgone in making any choice.

Economists define *costs* more broadly than accountants do. In addition to the **explicit** (money) **costs** considered by accountants, economists consider additional **implicit costs** associated with an action. In the case of a ski trip, an economist would recognize that an additional implicit cost of a ski weekend is the forgone opportunity of using the time in its next most valuable use when all viable alternatives are considered. For example, if the student who goes skiing would otherwise have spent the weekend working at a part-time job, an implicit cost of skiing is the income that would otherwise have been earned, if working is the highest-valued alternative. Therefore, the full economic cost of the ski weekend—the **opportunity** cost—equals the explicit money costs (that money does have an alternative use) plus the implicit costs of forgone income. Opportunity costs always include all accounting costs.

Consider the case of Greg, a self-employed lawyer who charges $125 per hour for his services. His next-door neighbor owns four large cats, whose nighttime howling disturbs Greg's sleep. Unable to convince his neighbor to quiet the cats, Greg spends 10 work hours preparing a lawsuit to demand satisfaction. Greg bears an opportunity cost, although he paid no lawyer to handle his case. If Greg's next-best alternative was to work for a client (and we assume that it is), he could have earned $1250. An economist would say that his opportunity cost of the lawsuit against his neighbor was $1250, for that is what his choice to prepare the lawsuit cost him in terms of forgone legal billings. Therefore, bringing the suit is costly to the lawyer even though no explicit costs are incurred.

Such opportunity costs also exist for public choices. Use of government lands in Wyoming and Montana as national forests entails a cost. Through lease or purchase, these lands could be used as a source of oil, minerals, and timber. Such use would contribute to society's well-being, but park land serves the recreational needs of society as well. Whatever public choice society makes for the use of land will imply a cost in economic terms. An opportunity must be forgone when the land is used in either manner.

A favorite saying of economists is "There is no such thing as a free lunch." The first fundamental principle of economics is that most things in life come at the opportunity cost of something forgone. They are never free. For many activities, out-of-pocket costs understate opportunity cost. In economics, opportunity cost is the true, total measure of the costs of anything.

Economic Behavior Is Rational

Rational self-interest
The view of human behavior espoused by economists. Given circumstances and preferences, people weigh the costs and benefits of choices in order to do the best they can for themselves.

A second fundamental principle of economics is that people behave according to **rational self-interest**. Economists selected from a number of alternative views of human behavior and settled on a very simple one—that of *homo economicus* (economic man or woman). Economists argue that human behavior is predictably based on a person's weighing the costs and benefits of decisions. Simply stated, individuals pursue their goals, whether public or private in nature, in a purposeful fashion. A student will choose to eat lunch at the local health-food restaurant rather than the fast-food cafeteria on campus if the perceived personal benefits of doing so—eating nutritious food in a pleasant atmosphere, say—outweigh the perceived costs, such as longer lines and greater distance to be walked. A student will choose to vote on the same basis—do the perceived benefits (voting for a favorite candidate) exceed the costs (the time and effort to go to the polls)?

The view of the individual espoused by economists has always been subject to misinterpretation. When economists say that humans are self-interested, they do not mean that other views of human behavior and motivation are unimportant or irrelevant. Altruistic or charitable behavior, for example, is perfectly compatible with *homo economicus*. If a person values altruism, then an act that benefits others will carry personal benefits and will therefore be in that person's rational self-interest. Economists simply maintain that people consider the costs and benefits of their decisions and act in their own self-interest.

If the IRS were to quadruple the income tax deduction for charitable contributions, economists would predict an increase in charity. No economist would deny that love, charity, and justice are important aspects of human behavior. Economists have merely advanced the simple but powerful proposition that, given personal tastes, values, and social philosophy, rational self-interest is a better guide to predicting behavior than any other assumption about why people act as they do.

The economist's view of the rational self-interested individual applies not only to economic behavior but also to other realms of behavior. Economics as a social science includes observations of what people, motivated by self-interest, actually do. Politicians maximize their self-interest by wooing voters to elect and reelect them. Since politicians face periodic elections, political behavior such as garnering support from particular voters can be predicted using the economic self-interest assumption. Even activities such as dating, marriage, and divorce have been analyzed using the self-interest assumption! After more than 200 years of economic theorizing, rational self-interest remains a most powerful predictor of behavior.

Choices Are Made at the Margin

Margin
The difference between costs or benefits in an existing situation and after a proposed change.

Economists are typically concerned with decisions made at the **margin**—the additional costs or benefits of a specific change in the current situation. An individual consumer, for example, does not spend his or her entire budget solely on food, cassette tapes, or weekends at the beach. Consumers purchase hundreds of goods and services. Their choice to purchase or not purchase additional units of any one good is based on the additional (or marginal) satisfaction that that single unit would bring to them.

Marginal analysis
Looking at changes in the costs and benefits of a change from the status quo to a proposed new situation. These marginal changes in the costs and benefits are the basis for rational economic choice.

Marginal analysis is a method of finding the optimal, or most desirable, level of any activity—how much coffee to drink, how much bread to produce, and so on. In an economic sense, every activity we undertake involves both benefits and costs, so an optimal level of an activity is the point at which the activity's total benefits outweigh its costs by the greatest amount. For example, the optimal level of coffee drinking is reached when coffee's total benefits (its taste and stimulating effects, perhaps) exceed its costs (the expense, the health risks, the acid indigestion) by the greatest degree.

Students make marginal decisions all the time, whether studying for exams, purchasing a new sweater, or voting. Clearly, additional study for a mathematics examination will improve the grade you receive. But doing your best will not mean devoting all available time to the project. The total gain in terms of grade achieved will rise, but the total costs due to the opportunity cost of time will rise also. Additional hours spent studying math may require forgone activities such as work, sleep, studying history, or even recreation. The rational student will stop studying for an examination when the marginal benefits from another hour of study equal the marginal costs of study. Beyond this point, additional study hours would likely raise the exam grade by a few more points, but the additional study would not be worth the additional cost in terms of other activities given up. The net benefits of studying math (net benefits = total benefits – total costs) are always maximized where the marginal benefits equal the marginal costs.

The marginal principle in economics adds new meaning to the familiar statement "Whatever is worth doing, is worth doing well." We never want to maximize the total benefit or return from an activity—studying for an examination, purchasing and eating hamburgers, or voting—without weighing the cost. We "do well" by maximizing the net benefits from purchases or activities, which means that we follow the marginal principle. Rational self-interest requires isolating and considering the specific effects of specific changes—of choices at the margin—in the area of change.

Marginal analysis also breathes life into the familiar adages "Don't cry over spilt milk" and "Never throw good money after bad." Previously incurred costs—sunk, historic, or fixed costs—do not ordinarily enter into future decisions, but marginal costs do. Should one stay through a dreadful movie simply because the ticket cost six dollars?

Prices Are Signals to Producers and Consumers

What products and services are produced in our economic system, and how are they produced? Consumers decide what is to be produced—TVs, automobiles, public parks —with the scarce resources in our society. Economists say that consumers transmit their desires through **markets**, which are simply arrangements where buyers and sellers exchange goods or services for money. Buyers and sellers can be physically together in a market, as in a livestock market, or they can be separated by geographic distance or by wholesalers and other intermediaries, as when the buying and selling of a company's stock is carried out through stockbrokers. The prices established in these markets (through mechanics to be explored in Chapter 3) are the key to understanding what gets produced and how much is produced in our economic system. Economists, therefore, give a great deal of attention to the role and function of prices and markets in explaining how things get done.

In a market economy **prices** are the essential signals that tell producers and resource suppliers what and how much to produce. Take, for example, a fairly new product, the compact disc (CD) player. Scarce resources—integrated circuits, electronic components, lasers, and fabricated metals—are used in producing CD players, and someone finds it profitable to do so.

What happened when consumers suddenly wanted more CD players than cassette decks or turntables in their homes and automobiles? Consumers expressed this desire by buying many more CD players and leaving cassette decks and turntables to gather dust on store shelves. Meanwhile, the relative unavailability of CD players caused their price to rise, because, temporarily, there were insufficient resources and production to meet the new demand. Manufacturers observed the increased sales and rising prices and realized that producing more CD players would be profitable. They reacted by producing more players, which meant ordering more electronics and circuitry and plastics, and hiring more labor and machinery. Higher prices for integrated circuits, fabricated metals, and wiring gave producers in Silicon Valley and other resource suppliers a signal to supply more of their inputs and services. Why did they do it? Because higher prices mean greater profitability to resource suppliers as well. Resources were diverted to CD players as both demand for and production of cassette decks and turntables declined.

Consumers also view prices as signals that help them decide what, and how much, to buy. Prices are both a mechanism that signals the degree of scarcity of

Market
A collection of buyers and sellers exchanging resources, goods, or services.

Prices
The market-established opportunity costs of goods and services obtained through exchange.

goods and services to consumers and an allocator of the available quantities of goods and services among consumers.

Shortages developed in the former Soviet Union, for example, because the production of consumer goods was given low priority. These shortages meant that goods such as sausage and potatoes had to be rationed in the marketplace. Low controlled prices were a signal to consumers to buy more, but low prices were just as much a signal to suppliers to produce less. When the former Soviet republics and Eastern European countries began to lift controls, prices rose dramatically, informing consumers of the scarcity. The signal to consumers was to buy less. In a true free market system, the scarcity would be temporary. High prices and the potential for profits would signal producers to produce more, which (ultimately) would have the impact of lowering prices.

Prices serve two basic functions in an economy. They serve to determine how much and what goods and services are produced by producers. They also serve to ration available commodities among different consumers and competing end uses.

Public Choices Are Different from Private Choices

Private choice
Choices made through private (non-governmental) markets.

Public choice
The economic analysis of political decision making, politics, and the democratic process.

As we have studied, individuals make private and public choices. Their **private choices** are made through markets, and involve the supply and demand of cars, housing, and other private goods. **Public choices** must also be made by that individual with respect to the things that he or she wants government to do. How much should we spend on national defense versus national parks, for example?

The individuals who make public choices are the *same* individuals who make private choices. We thus make the same assumption about their behavior—that is, they act in their self-interest, broadly defined as before, when they make public choices. The person who buys carrots at the grocery store is the same person who votes or works for a government agency.

What is different about public choices is that the setting or constraints that affect public choices are different than those that affect private choices. Public decisions in democracies are made by voting, and voting does not work in the same way as markets. To understand how voting and the market differ is to study public choice. This is the study of the behavior of self-interested political actors—voters, politicians, bureaucrats, regulators, judges—as they go about their "ordinary" business of governing. Economics is concerned with both private and public choices and how they are made, and with the consequences of allocating resources through markets and voting. Throughout this book, we will discuss both public and private choice.

Economists Do Not Decide Who Gets What

Economists study poverty and wealth, but as economists they have no unique knowledge to make judgment about how rich people should be or how much poverty is tolerable. Economists do not decide whether a college football coach deserves $16 million on a five-year contract or whether a Nobel Prize winning physicist deserves more. Economists basically explain that the economic value of all individuals—expressed as their income—is determined by the relative desires for their services and by the relative scarcity of their talents and abilities.

Most products and services—such as food, vacations, and domestic help—are allocated to those with the greatest desire and ability to pay for them. Our ability to pay is determined by the economic value of our own particular services or resources in the marketplace. This value depends on our education, on-the-job training, health, luck, inheritance, and a host of other factors.

The distribution of publicly provided goods and services—such as highways and bridges and space weapons—is conducted by governments through the filter of politics and voting. A decision whether to add seating capacity to the football stadium or to double the size of the English department at a public university may be made by a university committee appointed by the president and board of trustees, who may be appointed by the governor, who is elected by the citizens of the state. Ultimately, therefore, decisions on how resources are to be distributed are made by voter choices. If voters do not like the decisions made in the political process, they have a right to change the decision-makers. Chosen by voters, politicians make economic decisions based on their perceptions of costs and benefits to the public—as well as to their own chances of reelection. In government, as in the workings of the market, the chief role of economists is not to say who should get what, but to describe and analyze the process—the costs, benefits, and incentives—through which the distribution of all products and services takes place.

We All Want Money, But Not Too Much

Economists also place a special significance on the role of money in our lives. The trade of goods for goods, called **barter**, will not work in any economy that completes billions of transactions every day. Barter may have been sufficient in primitive societies where few things were produced and traded, but as individuals became specialized, using more and more of their talents and skills, the number and kinds of traded commodities and services grew. As the number of commodities grew, the cost of transacting by barter grew enormously. Low-cost trade demanded a double coincidence of wants—you had to demand the corn I produced at the same time and place that I demanded the baskets you produced. A common denominator, acceptable to all, developed within economic societies to reduce the costs and inconveniences of barter. That common denominator is **money**, which serves as a medium of exchange.

Money is not limited to coins and paper dollars. Throughout history many things—shells, feathers, paper, gold, and cattle, for instance—have served as money. The important point to economists is that money, whatever it is, reduces the costs associated with barter and increases specialization and trade. At the same time, economists are concerned that money should not be available in such quantities as to become unacceptable and valueless to people who produce, buy, and sell. For society, at least, huge increases in the money supply may be too much of a good thing. For example, in post–World War I Germany the government attempted to solve the nation's economic problems by printing more money. Eventually, money was worth more as paper than as a medium of exchange; buying a loaf of bread required a wheelbarrow full of money.

When the quantity of money increases beyond its use as a means of making transactions, confidence in the medium of exchange and its value (in terms of the

Barter
Direct exchange of one good or service for another without the use of money.

Money
A generally accepted medium of exchange.

Inflation
A sustained increase in the general level of prices; inflation reduces the purchasing power of money.

quantity of goods and services a unit of it can purchase) deteriorates. Economists call this phenomenon **inflation**. Inflation was a fact of American life during the 1970s, and it is a persistent element in nations around the world, as in the republics of the former Soviet Union. Inflation, if left untamed, can result in the collapse of entire economies, with reversion to primitive barter conditions. Economists therefore are very concerned with the relation between the production and trade of goods and the quantity of money available to facilitate these crucial activities.

Voters Choose the Role of Government— The Economist Analyzes

In a functioning democratic system, society chooses an economic role for government by electing politicians. In general, that role has included such activities as taxation for and provision of collective goods such as national defense, highways, and education; the regulation of monopoly; pollution control; control of the money supply; and alleviation of poverty through welfare programs. In its economic role of taxing and spending, government can affect economic factors such as inflation, the degree of unemployment, economic growth, and international trade.

Economists have always been concerned with the effects of government activity in these areas. In the United States, economists are in the thick of government policy-making. Since 1946 an official Council of Economic Advisers has been appointed by the president to aid in the formulation and implementation of economic policy. Almost every agency of government employs economists to provide analysis in their areas of expertise.

In their role as advisers, economists primarily evaluate, from the perspective of economic theory or analysis, the effects of proposals or, more correctly, of marginal changes in economic policies. Economists do not argue, for example, that additional funds should be allocated to Social Security and taken away from water reclamation projects. They simply evaluate and communicate the costs and benefits of such proposals.

Economists are not confined to giving advice on specific issues such as the Social Security program or the effects of advertising regulation by the Federal Trade Commission. Larger issues are within economists' purview as well. Predicting the effects of government taxing and spending policies on employment, interest rates, and inflation is a very large part of economists' role. Economists might predict, for example, the impact of a tax cut on private spending, interest rates, the private production of goods and services, and inflation. As such, economists are concerned with economic stabilization.

Despite economists' influence, however, the economic role of government is ultimately decided by voters in periodic elections. Specific budgetary decisions are not decided in elections, but politicians run on platforms pledging to "increase social welfare spending," "increase defense spending," "reduce the debt," "balance the budget," and "increase environmental regulation." In a loose sense, then, voters decide economic policies. Economists evaluate the implications of government's economic policies. Economists advise. They do not make ultimate decisions about what the government should do.

THE ROLE OF THEORY IN ECONOMICS

Economists organize their thoughts about human behavior and its results through models. Economists, like all scientists, construct models to isolate specific phenomena for study. Constructing a **model** requires assumptions and abstractions from the real world.

Model
A simplified abstraction of the real world that approximates reality and makes problems easier to analyze; also called a theory.

Economists must *abstract* from extraneous factors to isolate and understand some other factor because, as one economist has put it, people's minds are limited and nature's riddles are complex. Economists must assume that the extraneous factors are constant—that "other things are equal"[2]—or that, if altered, they would have a predictable effect on the relations or model under consideration. Humanity has never progressed very far in understanding anything—be it chemistry, astronomy, or economics—without abstracting from many factors that are not central to a given problem. *Thus, all economic models are of necessity abstractions. Good models, those that perform and predict well, use relevant factors; poor models do not.*

An economic model (or, essentially the same thing, a theory) can be expressed in verbal, graphical, or mathematical form. Sometimes verbal explanation is sufficient, but graphs or algebra often serve as convenient shorthand means of expressing models. Economics is like other sciences in this regard. A complicated chemical or physical process can be described in words, but it is much more convenient to use mathematics. All methods of expressing models will be used in this book, but we rely primarily on words and graphs. The appendix to this chapter explains how to read and interpret graphs.

In recognizing the regularities of human behavior and in committing them to a model, economists or scientists do not have to rethink every event as it occurs. Theory saves time and permits useful predictions about future events based upon regularities of human behavior.

Since a complex world is the economist's workshop, economic theory cannot be tested in the way chemical or physical theories can. The accuracy of economics is like that of meteorology. Total accuracy is not within the meteorologist's abilities. At least, total accuracy is not worth what it would cost to obtain in either weather forecasting or economics.

In economics, the problem of imperfect conditions for testing is a limitation to theory, but theory is essential nonetheless. Nothing can substitute for the usefulness of theory in organizing our thoughts about the real world and in describing the regularities of economic behavior.

THE ROLE OF ECONOMICS AND ECONOMISTS

Economics—and its practice by economists—permeates society. University-trained economists wear many hats and perform diverse roles within the profession. Most

---

[2]The Latin phrase *ceteris paribus*, meaning "other things being equal," is common economic shorthand for this assumption about human behavior.

economists specialize in some area of particular concern. Some economists work as researchers in think tanks, such as the Hoover Institution at Stanford University or the Brookings Institution in Washington, D.C. Others serve as corporate forecasters for private businesses. Every conceivable area of the economy—health, energy, agriculture, research on the role of particular technologies—is part of the research program of these economists. Many economists don policy hats and advise federal, state, and local governments on a huge variety of matters—including budgets, taxes, government spending, and policies toward business. Last, but not least, economists teach economics. In virtually every college and university in America, economists perpetuate their field by teaching undergraduate and graduate courses and conducting research. Since 1969, a Nobel Prize has been awarded in economics, underlining the special prestige of the discipline as a social science. The Nobel Prize has been awarded to an impressive number of economists at American universities. Consider some other aspects of the role of economics and economists.

Positive and Normative Economics

Positive economics
Observations, explanations, or predictions about economic life; scientific economics.

Normative economics
Value judgments based on moral principles or preferences about how economic life should be.

Economics is a positive rather than a normative science. **Positive economics** describes what is or predicts what will be under certain circumstances, whereas **normative economics** entails value judgments about what should be. For the most part, economists confine themselves to positive statements. This does not mean that economists as individuals act always as pure scientists. They most certainly do arrive at normative positions based on their own personal values in addition to their positive analyses. But their value judgments about policy should carry no more weight than those of any other citizen.

Consider U.S. welfare programs. To say that additional tax dollars should be spent on welfare would involve a normative (or value) judgment on the part of economists. Once society has decided to spend more on welfare, however, economists can make positive statements about the effects of such spending. Or economists may observe the welfare system and analyze how the system could work more efficiently in achieving its goals. In other words, economic analysis can show, once society has decided on a welfare system and on some dollar amount to be devoted to welfare, how alternative systems of welfare distribution would alter the effectiveness of the program. Economists make positive statements in presenting alternatives and their effects so that society might get the most for the dollars spent.

Microeconomics and Macroeconomics

Microeconomics
Analysis of the behavior of individual decision-making units, including individuals, households, and business firms.

The first half of this book concerns what economists call microeconomics, while the second half deals with macroeconomics. **Microeconomics**, like microbiology, concerns the components of a system. Just as a frog is made up of individual cells of various kinds, individual sales and purchases of commodities from potatoes to health care are the stuff of which the whole economy is composed. Microeconomists are thus concerned with individual markets and with the determination of relative prices within those markets. Supply and demand for individual goods, services, and factors of production are the subject matter of microeconomics. Microeconomists address questions such as the following: Will the use of larger quantities of solar energy reduce the total energy bill of Americans? Will an increased tax on cigarettes increase or decrease federal revenues from the tax? Will the quality and quantity of nursing services in the state of Wyoming be changed by the licensing of nursing in that state?

Macroeconomics is the study of the economy as a whole. The overall price level, inflation rate, international exchange rates, unemployment rate, economic growth rate, and interest rate are issues of concern to macroeconomists. Macroeconomists analyze how these crucial quantities are determined and how and why they change. The most common measures of macroeconomic well-being are **gross domestic product (GDP)** and **gross national product (GNP)**.

Some issues contain elements of both microeconomics and macroeconomics— for instance, a proposed U.S. tariff on Japanese auto imports. Microeconomists would be interested in the effects of the tariff on auto prices, on the American auto industry, and on the quantity of cars bought by U.S. consumers. Macroeconomists would be primarily interested in the effects of the tariff on economic growth, employment, international trade, the balance of payments, and total spending.

Let's Get to Work

Economics, like meteorology, is an inexact science, and it is likely to remain so. But economic theory and prediction are accurate and testable enough to provide extremely important insights into numerous issues that touch our lives. And the science of choice and scarcity is constantly being improved from both theoretical and empirical perspectives. The well-established power of economic thinking is the result of 200 years of such continuing improvements. Sound understanding of the principles of economic thinking will improve your understanding of the world.

Macroeconomics
Analysis of the behavior of an economy as a whole.

Gross domestic product (GDP)
A measure of the final goods and services produced by a country with resources located within that country.

Gross national product (GNP)
The value, measured at market prices, of all final goods and services produced in an economy in one year.

SUMMARY

1. Economics is basically concerned with three questions: What goods and services are produced? How are goods and services produced? For whom are goods and services produced?
2. Economics is the study of how individuals make private and public choices to allocate scarce resources given unlimited wants.
3. Scarce resources include human and nonhuman resources as well as time, institutions, and technology. Human resources consist of labor, including entrepreneurship and management. Nonhuman resources include land and all natural resources, technology, information, and capital.
4. All scarce resources bear an opportunity cost. This means that individuals or societies forgo other opportunities whenever scarce resources are used to produce specific goods and services.
5. Economic behavior is rational. Human beings are assumed to behave predictably by weighing the costs

and benefits of their decisions and their potential actions.
6. Economic choices are made at the margin—that is, they take into account the additional costs or benefits of a change in the current situation. Prices are the signal that indicates individual choices for goods and services as well as the relative scarcity of the resources necessary to produce the goods and services.
7. Private and public choices are made by the same rational persons, but public choices are made by voting while private choices are made in markets.
8. The study of prices of individual products and inputs is called *microeconomics*, and the study of inflation, unemployment, economic growth, and related problems is called *macroeconomics*.
9. Economics is a more inexact and imprecise science than chemistry or physics. It is accurate enough to predict much economic behavior, however, and to provide insight into a large number of important problems.

KEY TERMS

goods	institutions	barter
services	accounting costs	money
resources	explicit costs	inflation
scarcity	implicit costs	models
economic goods	opportunity cost	positive economics
costs	rational self-interest	normative economics
free goods	margin	microeconomics
human resources	marginal analysis	macroeconomics
nonhuman resources	markets	gross domestic product (GDP)
technology	prices	gross national product (GNP)
information	private choice	
property rights	public choice	

QUESTIONS FOR REVIEW AND DISCUSSION

1. What problem creates the foundation of economic analysis? Is this problem not restricted to the poor?
2. Can wants be satisfied with existing resources?
3. What are resources? How is the resource capital different from the resources land and labor?
4. What is the difference between behaving in one's self-interest and behaving selfishly?
5. What functions do prices have in the economy? Why were goods and services rationed during World War II?
6. You have already paid your tuition. What does it cost you, at the margin, to attend your afternoon economics class on Friday? On Tuesday? (Remember: The margin refers to the additional cost of attending one additional class.)
7. Is air a free good? Is clean air a free good? Is cleaner air a free good?
8. Why do economists abstract from reality when formulating theories? Does this imply that their theories have no relevance in the real world?
9. Describe as many ways as you can how the choices you make in shopping for groceries differ from voting in a presidential election.
10. "The distribution of income in the United States is not fair." What type of statement is this? Can "fair" be used to describe something without being normative?
11. To what extent can we say that economics is an accurate science?
12. What is the role of economists in society?
13. John gives an annual contribution of $500 to his church. By doing so, he is acting in his own self-interest. Explain.
14. Would you expect a discussion of the Great Depression of the 1930s or the 1996 budget talks to be covered in a macroeconomics class or a microeconomics class?

WORKING WITH GRAPHS

Economists frequently use graphs to demonstrate economic theories or models. This appendix explains how graphs are constructed and how they can illustrate economic relations in simplified form. By understanding the mechanics and usefulness of graphs, you will find it much easier to grasp the economic concepts presented in this book.

The Purpose of Graphs

Most graphs in this book are simply pictures showing the relation between economic variables, such as the price of a good and the quantity of the good that people are willing to purchase. There are many such pairs of variables in economics: the costs of production and the level of output, the rate of inflation and the level of unemployment, the interest rate and the supply of capital goods, for example. Graphs are the most concise means of expressing the variety of relations that exist between such variables.

Many of the graphs in this book use the Cartesian coordinate system, which consists of points plotted on a grid formed by the intersection of two perpendicular lines. See Figure 1.1. The horizontal line is the *x*-axis, and the vertical line is the *y*-axis. The intersection of the two lines is the point 0, called the *origin*. Above the origin on the vertical axis, all values are positive. Below the origin on the vertical axis, all values are negative. Values to the right of the origin are positive; values to the left are negative. The economic variables we use in this book are usually positive; that is, to plot economic relations we will usually use the upper-right portion, or quadrant, of a graph such as the one in Figure 1.2.

How to Draw a Graph

Suppose you wish to graph the relation between two variables. Variable *y* is the number of words memorized, and variable *x* is the number of minutes spent memorizing words. Table 1.1 presents a set, or schedule, of hypothetical data for these two variables.

We can plot the data from Table 1.1 on a graph using points in the upper-right quadrant formed by the *x*-axis and the *y*-axis. See Figure 1.2. The variable, number of words memorized, is measured along the *y*-axis and is considered the *y* value. The variable, number of minutes spent memorizing, is measured along the *x*-axis and is the

FIGURE 1.1

A Grid for Plotting Graphs

Any pair of numerical values can be plotted on this grid. The upper-right quadrant, shaded here, is the portion of the graph most often used in economics.

FIGURE 1.2

A Simple Line (or Linear) Graph

Curve *AE* shows the essential relation between two sets of variables: the number of words memorized and the number of minutes spent memorizing. The relation is positive; as the variable on the *x*-axis increases or decreases, the variable on the *y*-axis increases or decreases, respectively. A positive relation is shown by an upward-sloping line tracing the intersection of each pair of variables.

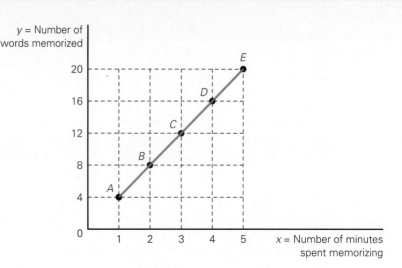

ative, or **inverse, relation,** the two variables change in opposite directions. An increase in *y* is paired with a decrease in *x*. Or a decrease in *x* is paired with an increase in y. Figure 1.3 shows a negative, or inverse, relation on a graph. The curve for a negative relation slopes downward from left to right—the opposite of a positive relation.

x value. From the data in Table 1.1 we see that each increase of 1 minute of memorizing resulted in 4 more memorized words. The graph in Figure 1.2 illustrates this relation.

The points marked as large dots in Figure 1.2 represent pairs of variables. Point *A* represents the pair on the first line of Table 1.1: 4 words and 1 minute. Point *B* represents 8 words and 2 minutes, and so on. When we connect the points, we have a straight line running upward and to the right of the origin. Lines showing the intersection of *x* and *y* values on a graph are referred to as **curves** in this book, whether they are straight or curved lines.

Curves show two types of relations between variables: positive and negative. The relation between the *x* and *y* values in Figure 1.2 is positive: As the *x* value increases, so does the *y* value. (Or, as the *x* value decreases, the *y* value decreases as well. Either way, the relation is positive.) On a graph, a **positive,** or **direct, relation** is shown by a curve that slopes upward and to the right of the origin. In a neg-

GENERAL RELATIONS

Throughout this book, some graphs display general relations rather than specific relations. A general relation does not depend on particular numerical values of variables, as was the case in Figure 1.2. For example, the relation between the number of calories a person consumes per week and that person's weight (other things being equal) is positive. This suggests an upward-sloping line, as shown in Figure 1.4a, with calories on the *x*-axis and weight on the *y*-axis. Figure 1.4a represents a general relation, so it does not need numerical values on either axis. It does not specify the particular number of calories required to maintain a particular body weight; it simply shows that an increase in the number of calories consumed increases body weight. Figure 1.4b shows an inverse relation between body weight and the amount of exercise per week, again a general relation. Sometimes two variables are not related. Figure 1.4c shows that a person's weight is independent of a neighbor's caloric intake. Thankfully, no matter how much your neighbor eats, it has no effect on your weight.

At this point you should be able to construct a graph showing simple relations. For example, graph the relation between the weight of a car and the miles per gallon it achieves or between the length of the line at the school cafeteria and the time of day. If the relationship between any two variables you select is represented by a straight

TABLE 1.1

Schedule of Hypothetical Data

Number of Words Memorized (y)	Number of Minutes Spent Memorizing (x)
4	1
8	2
12	3
16	4
20	5

FIGURE 1.3

A Negative Relation Between Two Variables

As the price of a cup of coffee increases, the number of cups drunk each day decreases. When variables move in opposite directions, their relation is negative, or inverse. Negative relations are shown by a curve that slopes downward and to the right of the origin.

line, it is said to be **linear**. A linear relationship means that for every unit change (increase or decrease) in one of the variables (the weight of a car), the other variable (miles per gallon of gasoline) changes (increases or decreases) by some fixed amount.

NONLINEAR RELATIONS

Often, relations between two variables are not the simple linear relationships depicted in Figures 1.2, 1.3, and 1.4. For example, unlike in Figure 1.2, where each additional minute spent studying enables one to memorize 4 additional words, it may be that the number of additional words memorized changes as the number of minutes

changes. Such a **nonlinear** relationship is depicted in Figure 1.5. There, 1 minute of studying enables a student to memorize 6 words, but 2 minutes of studying enables a student to memorize only 11 words—the second minute adds only 5 additional words to the total. Additional minutes of studying beyond 2 lead to even smaller increases in the total number of words memorized. Therefore, there is a positive relationship between the two variables, but the relationship is *nonlinear*.

Occasionally, nonlinear relations are more complex than the one depicted in Figure 1.5 and do not fall into the simple categories of positive or negative. A U-shaped curve, as graphed in Figure 1.6, shows that the *x* value is

FIGURE 1.4

General Graphical Relations

General relations are (a) positive, (b) inverse, or (c) independent. General relations are not measured numerically on the *y*- or *x*-axis.

(a)

(b)

(c)

FIGURE 1.5

A Nonlinear Graph

Curve *AE* shows the nonlinear relation between the number of minutes spent studying and the number of words memorized.

at first inversely related to the *y* value and then positively related. After some critical value, *x**, the *y* value begins to rise as the *x* value increases. The *y*-axis in this example might represent the probability of having an accident on an interstate highway, and the *x*-axis might show the miles per hour at which a car travels. To avoid accidents, *x** is the optimal, or "best" speed. Driving at speeds lower than *x** increases the probability of an accident, but rates faster than *x** mph also increase the chances of an accident.

Slope of the Curve

In graphical analysis the amount by which the *y* value increases or decreases as the result of an increase or decrease in the *x* value is the **slope** of the curve. The slope of the curve is an important concept in economics. Much economic analysis studies the margin of change in a variable or in a relation between variables, and the slope of a

curve measures the marginal rate of change. In Figure 1.2, for example, every change in the *x* value—every increase of 1 minute—is associated with an increase of 4 words memorized. The slope of the curve in Figure 1.2 is the rate of change. Economists express the concept "change in" with the symbol Δ. So in Figure 1.2 the slope of the line *AE* is $\Delta y / \Delta x = -4/1 = -4$.

For the straight-line curves in Figures 1.2 and 1.3 the slope is constant. Along most curves, however, the slope is not constant. In Figure 1.6, an increase in driving speed from 55 to 60 mph may increase the probability of an accident only slightly, but an increase from 60 to 65 mph may increase the probability by a greater amount. Not only does the probability increase for each mile-per-hour increase in driving speed, but it increases by a greater amount. This indicates that the slope not only is positive but also is increasing.

FIGURE 1.6

A U-shaped Curve

Some relations yield a U shape. Variables along the *x*- and *y*-axes are inversely related at first, but after some critical value, here shown as *x**, they become positively related.

FIGURE 1.7

Slope Along a Curve

The slope of a curve at a particular point is the slope of a straight line tangent to the curve at that point.

The slope of a curved line is different at every point along the line. To find the slope of a curved line at a particular point, draw a straight line tangent to the curve. (A tangent touches the curve at one point without crossing the curve.) Consider point A in Figure 1.7. The slope at A on the curved line is equal to the slope of the straight line tangent to the curved line. Dividing the change in the y variable (Δy) by the change in the x variable (Δx) yields the slope at A. In Figure 1.7, every change in x from 0 to 1, 1 to 2, and so on, results in a change in y along the curve. At point A, y = 4. So $\Delta y/\Delta x$ = -4/1 = -4. At lower points along the curve, such as B, the curve is flatter—that is, less steep. The line tangent at B has a slope of -1. As we move from point A to point B, equal increases in x result in smaller and smaller decreases in y. In other words, the *rate* at which y falls decreases as x increases along this particular curve.

Other relations lead to different slopes and different changes in the slope along the curve. Along the curve in Figure 1.8, not only does the y value increase as the x value increases, but the slope increases as the x value increases. For equal increases in the x value, the incremental changes in the y value become larger.

Interpreting the essential concepts illustrated in graphs is a necessary part of learning economic principles. Should you encounter difficulty in interpreting any of the graphs in later chapters, a brief review of this Appendix will prove helpful.

FIGURE 1.8

A Curve with an Increasing Slope

As the x variable increases, the change in the y variable increases.

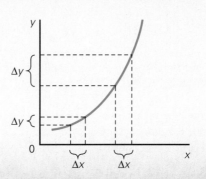

SUMMARY

1. Graphs are a concise expression of economic models, or theories. Graphs usually show the relation between two variables, such as price and quantity.
2. Linear graphs are drawn with two perpendicular lines, called axes. The *x*-axis is a horizontal line. Variables measured along the *x*-axis are called *x* values. The *y*-axis is a vertical line. Variables along it are called *y* values.
3. Lines showing the correlation between *x* and *y* values are called curves. An upward-sloping curve indicates a positive, or direct, relation between variables: As the *x* value increases or decreases, the *y* value increases or decreases. A downward-sloping curve indicates a negative, or inverse, relation between variables: As the *x* value increases, the *y* value decreases, and vice versa.
4. Relations between variables may be specific or general. Specific relations are based on numerical quantities measured on either the *x*- or *y*-axis or both. General relations are not based on specific numerical quantities.
5. Relations between two variables can be either linear (straight lines) or nonlinear (curved lines).
6. Variables can be both positively and negatively related over certain ranges. In such complex relations, a curve is either bow-shaped or U-shaped.
7. The slope of a curve measures the ratio of change in the *y* value to change in the *x* value, expressed as $\Delta y/\Delta x$. Along a straight-line curve, the slope is constant. Along a curved line, the slope is different at every point.

KEY TERMS

x-axis, *y*-axis
curve
positive, or direct, relation

negative, or inverse, relation
linear relation

nonlinear relation
slope

QUESTIONS FOR REVIEW AND DISCUSSION

1. Explain how the slope of a line tells you whether the relation between the two variables illustrated is direct or inverse. If you drew a line illustrating your score on a history test as you study more hours, what would its slope be?
2. Plot the following points on a graph with *X* on the horizontal axis and *Y* on the vertical axis. Connect the dots to show the relation between *X* and *Y*.

	X	Y
A	0	2
B	2	4
C	4	8
D	6	14
E	8	22

What is the slope of the line between points *A* and *B*? What is the slope between *C* and *D*? Is this a straight line?

3. Curves can be represented in algebraic form by an equation. For example, the points along a certain line can be demonstrated by the equation

$$Y = 10 - 2X.$$

The value of *Y* can be found by inserting different values of *X* and solving the equation for *Y*. Some of the values of *Y* for different values of *X* are shown in the following table. Fill in the blanks by solving the equation for the values of *Y* for each value of *X* given.

X	Y
0	10
2	6
4	—
6	—
8	—
10	—
12	—

Draw this set of points on a graph. Does this show a direct or inverse relation between *X* and *Y*? What is the slope of this line between the first and second points? Between the second and third? Is this a straight line?

4. If you measured body weight on the horizontal axis and the probability of dying of heart disease on the vertical axis, what would be the slope of a curve that showed the relation between these two variables?

OPPORTUNITY COST, SPECIALIZATION, AND TRADE

T he essence of the economic problem is how to get as much value as we can from limited and costly resources. To do so, we constantly make choices. Economists emphasize that decisions to use scarce resources bear an opportunity cost. The opportunity cost of a decision is the next most preferred or next-best alternative to a good or activity that one must forgo in order to obtain some other good. Economists have developed tools for expressing that choice and opportunity costs are central to all decisions. After reading Chapter 2 you should understand

- the role of specialization and trade for individuals and societies.

- how individuals and societies actually make decisions given that they are always costly.

- how specialization and trade increase quantities of output for parties who exchange goods and services.

- how exchange, transaction costs, and certain public choices to erect barriers to trade reduce the benefits from specialization and trade.

SPECIALIZATION AND TRADE: A FEATURE OF ALL SOCIETIES

Opportunity cost
The highest-valued alternative forgone in making any choice.

Specialization
An economic entity producing only one good or service or the performance of a single task in a production process by an individual.

Division of labor
Individual specialization in separate tasks involved with a production process; the result of specialization.

Specialization refers to a situation in which the tasks associated with the production of a product or service are divided—and sometimes subdivided—and performed by many different individuals to increase the total production of the good or service. Virtually all known peoples have engaged in specialization and trade, and theories and principles related to specialization and trade have been part of economists' tool kits for more than 200 years. Adam Smith (1723–1790), the Scottish philosopher and recognized founder of economics, published his great work *An Inquiry into the Nature and Causes of the Wealth of Nations* in 1776 (a year of declarations). It formally established the science of what we now call economics. (For more information about Adam Smith, see Point/Counterpoint, pp. 111–112.)

At the very core of economics, according to Smith, is the ability of individuals and societies to deal with the facts of scarcity through specialization and trade. In the *Wealth of Nations,* Smith used the example of a pin factory, a seemingly trivial manufacturing activity he had observed directly, to evaluate specialization. Smith observed that pin making was no longer a trade peculiar to a single individual but instead was "divided into a number of branches, of which the greater part are likewise peculiar trades."[1] Straightening wire, cutting it, putting a point on it, constructing a head to the pin, and inserting the pins into paper for ease of handling were all separate "trades" performed by individuals.

How does Smith's description of a pin factory promote an understanding of output growth? Smith's point is that when tasks are divided, permitting each individual to concentrate on a single element in the production of a good, output increases over what it would be if each individual produced the entire good. Specialization and the **division of labor** led to increased output. As a result, people became more dependent on one another for all goods. We may work in an automobile plant, for example, but we still want eggs for breakfast. Smith recognized that mutual dependence could be a problem, but thought that the potential for increased output with given resources was well worth the cost.

If an analysis of a pin factory does not stir your imagination, think of any organization and try to list the number of distinct divisions of labor in it. Think of a larger factory, a steel mill, a football team, a fraternity, a church. Specialization exists in almost everything we do. (See the Focus "Economic Specialization in Everyday Life: Marriage and Roommate Selection" for illustrations.)

All modern nations, states, firms, and individuals specialize in the production of economic goods and services, in varying degrees. The individual, the most basic economic entity, specializes to the greatest extent. Your teacher for this course specializes in economic research and teaching. Other people specialize in mechanical engineering services or in breeding thoroughbred racehorses. Some businesses produce only one product, whereas others offer a multitude. One very critical point must be made about all specialization and trade—it is as significant as having more and better resources or improved production techniques. As Smith noted, specializa-

---

[1] Adam Smith, *An Inquiry into the Nature and Causes of the Wealth of Nations,* ed. Edwin Cannan (1776; reprint, New York: Modern Library, 1937), pp. 4–5.

focus Economic Specialization in Everyday Life: Marriage and Roommate Selection

Specialization and trade has increased economic welfare and human progress from the very beginning of time. These gains have depended on the diverse talents of individuals as well as the different resources of great nations. Consider two examples that do not often come to mind when considering the economic principles of specialization: the selection of a marriage partner and selection of a roommate.

Although relationships like marriage have many bases—love, security, and so on—one of them is surely economic. The greatest gains from trade occur when individuals (or countries) with widely differing skills or resources trade. In a society in which males and females acquire widely different skills, the incentive to marry is quite strong. If, as in primitive society, women do not know how to hunt or fish and men cannot prepare food or make clothing, the gains to both partners in a marriage relationship are immense. In fact, survival outside of a marriage-type relationship may be impossible. In such societies, nearly everyone would marry, and individuals would abandon a marriage relationship only to enter another one. In societies where men and women acquire similar skills, the gains from exchange between marriage partners are much smaller. Individuals, therefore, have a weaker incentive to marry or to remain married. The slowing marriage rate

and the growing divorce rate in Western societies in recent decades may partly be attributed to greater occupational equality. As the incomes of women rise (and the opportunity cost of child rearing), a lower birth rate may be expected. Specialization may even be reversed, with men taking more active roles in raising children. "Mr. Mom" may become more common due to economic specialization and trade.

Roommate selection, an activity perhaps closer to your experience, also takes place, in part, on the basis of economic specialization and trade. Students room together to save money, but they also do so, in part, because of the gains from specialization and trade. Communal arrangements ranging from fraternities and sororities to clubs and study groups work best when the participants have tradable skills. Ideally, then, one roommate would be an excellent cook, say, while another roommate would be an expert carpenter, and yet another would be adept at yard work. Even if individuals' skill levels are pretty much the same, trade is still profitable when roommates' tastes and preferences for specific jobs differ and trade is possible. Problems and disputes arise most often between roommates when trade agreements or "contracts" are not enforceable. You may do the cooking, but can you "force" your roommate to clean up the kitchen—assuming you both agreed she would?

The benefits of specialization and trade are not just of academic interest, nor do they pertain only to trade in goods and services between nations such as Japan and the United States. As workers, club members, marriage partners, roommates, or friends, these principles affect us every day.

tion and division of labor lead to increased output without any additional resources. The gains from specializing in and exchanging goods and services are, in effect, equivalent to acquiring or developing additional natural resources or capital.

The notion of specialization can also be applied to entire nations. Table 2.1 shows that many of the goods consumed by Americans are obtained largely from other countries. In 1994, the value of goods imported from other countries into the United States was $658 billion, up from $490 billion in 1990. (As shown in Table 2.1, the United States also exports huge quantities of goods to other nations, amounting to $374 billion in 1990 and $482 billion in 1994.) For certain commodities—crude rubber and diamonds, for example—there is no domestic production; the entire supply is imported. While there is a very active import and export trade in finished goods between the United States and other nations, patterns of specialization across countries in particular goods may be observed nonetheless. Exotic spices are not commercially grown in Canada, for example, although they

TABLE 2.1

U.S. Exports and Imports, 1990 and 1994

The table shows the value and relative importance of major exports and imports in 1990 and 1994 by category. Agricultural products accounted for a smaller percentage of U.S. exports in 1994 than in 1990. The United States is *both* an important exporter and an important importer of machinery (electrical and nonelectrical) and transportation equipment.

| | MAJOR EXPORTS | | | |
| | 1990 | | 1994 | |
Category	Value (in billions)	Percentage of Total	Value (in billions)	Percentage of Total
Agricultural products	$22.6	6.0	$22.1	4.6
Coal	4.5	1.2	2.9	0.6
Food	16.2	4.3	23.1	4.8
Tobacco	5.0	1.3	5.4	1.1
Textiles	3.6	0.9	5.1	1.0
Apparel	2.8	0.7	6.1	1.3
Lumber	6.5	1.7	7.3	1.5
Paper products	8.6	2.3	11.0	2.3
Chemicals	37.8	10.1	49.0	10.2
Petroleum and coal products	6.8	1.8	5.5	1.1
Rubber and plastic products	6.4	1.7	9.9	2.1
Stone, clay, and glass products	3.3	0.9	4.2	0.9
Primary metal products	13.1	3.5	16.3	3.4
Nonelectrical machinery	61.2	16.3	82.1	17.0
Electrical machinery	39.8	10.6	63.8	13.2
Transportation equipment	68.1	18.2	85.1	17.7

could be grown there with greenhouses, sufficient heating expenditures, and so on. Canada does produce a fair proportion of the world's wheat. Likewise, no fine silk is produced on the tiny Caribbean island of Grenada, but nutmeg and other spices are. The explanation for such general production patterns across countries and more complete patterns of specialization among individuals resides in concepts that are at the very core of economics—comparative advantage, specialization, and trade.

OPPORTUNITY COST: THE INDIVIDUAL MUST CHOOSE

Suppose that a student is trying to decide what to do with 4 hours of time on a Sunday evening. One alternative is to work at the library, where the student earns $4 per hour. The other choice is to study for an economics quiz to be given Monday morning. The student views these two activities as the highest-valued uses of the 4 hours of time on Sunday evening. Table 2.2 depicts five different ways the student can allocate the 4 hours of time. Also depicted are five different combinations of income earned and percentage quiz scores the student could "produce" with the five different allocations of time.[2] Choice (1), no work and 4 hours of

[2]The student's expectations may be based on grades up to this point in the class or on past performance in this and other classes or on some other basis. The manner in which the student forms expectations is not relevant to our example.

TABLE 2.1 (Continued)

| | MAJOR IMPORTS | | | |
| | 1990 | | 1994 | |
Category	Value (in billions)	Percentage of Total	Value (in billions)	Percentage of Total
Agricultural products	$ 5.9	1.2	$ 8.7	1.3
Fish and marine products	4.4	0.9	5.5	0.8
Petroleum and natural gas	48.9	10.0	44.9	6.8
Food	16.6	3.4	17.3	2.6
Textiles	6.8	1.4	6.5	1.0
Apparel	24.6	5.0	38.6	5.9
Lumber	5.4	1.1	10.5	1.6
Furniture	5.2	1.1	7.2	1.1
Paper products	11.7	2.4	11.8	1.8
Chemicals	21.6	4.4	31.7	4.8
Petroleum and coal products	14.5	1.1	9.5	1.4
Leather and leather products	10.9	2.2	13.0	2.0
Primary metals	23.2	4.7	30.1	4 6
Nonelectrical equipment	55.0	11.2	89.7	13.6
Electrical machinery	55.7	11.4	94.3	14.3
Transportation equipment	89.6	18.2	116.0	17.6

SOURCE: 115th Edition *Statistical Abstract of the United States,* 1995 (Washington, D.C: U.S. Government Printing Off1ce, 1995), p. 824.

study, yields the student a perfect quiz score but no income. Choice (2), allocating 1 hour to library work and 3 hours to study, produces an income of $4 and a score of 90 percent. The third, fourth, and fifth alternative choices mean still more income but lower quiz scores. In choice (5)—no study time at all and a score of 0 percent—the student earns the highest income possible for the evening's work, $16.

Table 2.2 sets forth an important point. The student must spend time working and studying to obtain some income and an acceptable quiz score. The student's scarce resource, time, is used to produce two economic goods, grades and income.

Consider the two right-hand columns in Table 2.2. These show the five different combinations of income and grades that the student can obtain from allocating the evening's available 4 hours of time five different ways. In Figure 2.1 these combinations are plotted as dots and are connected with a smooth curve. Choice (3) from Table 2.1, $8 of income and a score of 75 percent, is shown as point (3) in Figure 2.1. This particular combination of goods produced implies 2 hours of time allocated to library work and 2 hours to study.

Several aspects of Figure 2.1 are important. First, all possible combinations of income and quiz scores that the student could conceivably earn are represented by the curved line. This means that the choices between working and studying are *continuous.* Continuous choice implies that the five combinations in Table 2.2 are not the only ones available with 4 hours time. The student could choose any combination of income and quiz score that together required 4 hours of time to produce—say, $2 of income for ½ hour worked and a score of 95 percent with 3½ hours of study. If choices were *discrete,* the student would be limited

TABLE 2.2

The Individual Chooses: Working or Studying

Individuals must make choices from many alternatives available. In this example, the individual has choice options involving various combinations of studying and working in the library. These options range from no studying and all work to no work and all studying, with various other options in between these two. The trade-off involved in these choices is clear—more work (and more income) comes at the expense of less study time and a lower grade, and vice versa.

Choice of Time Allocation	Income Earned (dollars)	Grade Earned (percent)
(1) 0 hours working, 4 hours studying	0	100
(2) 1 hour working, 3 hours studying	4	90
(3) 2 hours working, 2 hours studying	8	75
(4) 3 hours working, 1 hour studying	12	55
(5) 4 hours working, 0 hours studying	16	0

to the five choices labeled (1) through (5). (Discrete choices are fixed in number.) For convenience, economists ordinarily assume that economic relations are continuous.

A second crucial point is that Figure 2.1 and Table 2.2 constitute what economists call a *model*. Economists construct models to isolate specific phenomena for study. The model summarized in Figure 2.1 and Table 2.2 assumes a number of things about the student in the example. First, as just explained, the choices are continuous rather than discrete. Second, we assume as given that the total amount of time that the student has available for both activities combined is fixed—in this case, 4 hours. The general relationship governing the amount of time put into an activity and the resultant amount of the activity produced is also assumed given. Each hour worked yields $4 and only $4 of income. The first hour of study always yields a score of 55 percent, never 60 or 50 percent. Two hours of study produce a grade of 75 percent, not 74 or 76 percent. Other factors, such as the total amount of time the student has already put into the course before Sunday evening, are assumed given. Does the student have the flu, a factor that would detract from performance on the quiz? Is the income more important to the student than the economics quiz? Are there other alternatives, such as washing a car or spending time in language lab? Is the fact that one alternative has a future payoff, such as a job, relevant to the choice? Certainly matters such as these are significant, but we assume them as given with respect to the choice at hand. The value of abstraction is that it permits us to focus on the essentials of interest to the economic analyst.

Economists also emphasize that the decision to study or to work is made at the margin. Practically, making decisions at the margin means that we are not generally faced with all-or-nothing choices but with degrees of balancing units of one choice against another. Each choice would be made in terms of the costs of an additional

FIGURE 2.1

The Individual Chooses: Income or Grades

As the hours spent working increase, the score on the economics quiz falls.

Choices at the margin
Decisions based on the additional benefits and costs of small changes in a particular activity.

hour of study or work forgone. Satisfactions from both activities are thus balanced **at the margin.** For example, suppose the student had originally planned on working 2 hours and studying 2 hours. This division of the evening's time would produce $8 of income and a grade of 75 percent on the economics quiz. Suppose the student considers choosing to earn $4 more income. This would entail working 1 additional hour, which means studying 1 less hour. A reallocation of the time resource means that a quiz grade of 55 percent will be earned rather than 75 percent. The student must make a decision at the margin. Does the additional satisfaction of the extra $4 of income outweigh the quiz score falling by 20 percentage points? The drop of 20 points is the opportunity cost of choosing to earn an additional $4.

In making decisions at the margin we assume that all other factors are equal, or fixed. Each time we make a decision, some fixed or given factors resulting from previous decisions come into play. In our example, the student would weigh, for instance, the amount of previous study, a fixed factor in choosing work or study on the evening in question.

Previous decisions cannot be changed and are gone forever, but that does not mean that they have no impact on current choices. It simply means that we make choices in the present with unchangeable past choices as given and unalterable. This is another aspect of making choices at the margin.

OPPORTUNITY COST AND PRODUCTION POSSIBILITIES: SOCIETY MUST CHOOSE

So far we have focused on individual choices, but the same principles apply to public choices. Just as an individual is limited by the scarcity of time in choosing among options, society is constrained by scarce resources in producing and

TABLE 2.3

Society Decides: Cheeseburgers or Automobiles

Society must choose among many alternative combinations of goods to produce. The cost of one good is the lost production of other goods.

Choice	Cheeseburgers (millions)	Automobiles (millions)
A	100	0
B	90	4
C	75	8
D	50	12
E	0	16

consuming alternative goods. And just as it was necessary to make certain assumptions and abstractions from the real world when considering the choices made by an individual college student, it is necessary to eliminate nonessential details when examining society's choices. Imagine a society in which the following things are true:

1. Only two goods are produced;
2. Supplies of resources are fixed; and
3. Technology is held constant, and no economic growth occurs.

Our hypothetical (theoretical) society can produce cheeseburgers and/or automobiles.

Given the state of technology and assuming that the society uses all its resources, the society could produce either 100 million cheeseburgers or 16 million automobiles (see Table 2.3). Or the society may choose to devote some of its resources to producing cheeseburgers and some to producing automobiles. These choices, called society's *production possibilities,* are listed *A–E* in Table 2.3. From this information a production possibilities curve can be constructed (see Figure 2.2). A production possibilities curve depicts the alternatives open to society for the production of two goods, given full utilization of all existing resources, human and nonhuman, and an existing state of technology at some point in time. When resources are fully employed, moreover, society is said to be producing on its **production possibilities frontier.**

At choice *A* in Figure 2.2, society produces 100 million cheeseburgers and no automobiles, while at choice *E* society uses all its resources in automobile production. Choices in between, with some of both commodities produced, are shown at points *B, C,* and *D.* Continuous choices of all other possible combinations are shown along the curve; resources are assumed to be fully employed at all points on the curve. The curve therefore shows all of the possibilities for the production of automobiles and cheeseburgers, assuming resources are fully employed at present or at some given point in time. Points such as *G* lie beyond the production possibilities frontier. The country's resources and technology do not permit it to produce at points such as *G* that lie outside the frontier.

Production possibilities frontier

The curve that graphs all the possible combinations of two goods that an economy can produce given the available technology, the amount of productive resources available, and the fact that these resources are fully utilized.

FIGURE 2.2

Production Possibilities Curve

As more and more automobiles are produced, the opportunity cost per automobile increases. The opportunity cost of producing the first 4 million automobiles is 10 million cheeseburgers. The opportunity cost of producing the next 4 million automobiles is an additional 15 million cheeseburgers, and so on.

Law of increasing costs
As more scarce resources are used to produce additional units of one good, production of another good falls by larger and larger amounts.

The Law of Increasing Costs

Just as there was an opportunity cost to the student in choosing to study for the quiz or to work in the library, there is an opportunity cost for society in any choice between producing cheeseburgers and automobiles.

Consider a society that produces nothing but cheeseburgers, choice *A* in Figure 2.2. The opportunity cost of that choice is that no automobiles can be produced. A move to choice *B,* representing a movement of some resources from cheeseburger production to automobile production, means a sacrifice of 10 million cheeseburgers, but society gains 4 million automobiles. Thus the opportunity cost of producing the first 4 million automobiles is 10 million cheeseburgers. To get the second 4 million automobiles, however, a larger quantity of cheeseburgers must be given up—15 million. Thus as society becomes more specialized in production of either automobiles or cheeseburgers, the opportunity cost per unit of the good rises. This effect is called the **law of increasing costs.**

Why does the law of increasing costs hold? Resources, training, and talents are not all alike and are not perfectly adaptable to alternative uses. Capital suited to cattle raising or dairy farming is not equally suited to steel making or automobile manufacturing, and vice versa. Cowboys and farmers are not equally adept at the manufacture of seat covers for automobiles or metal fabricating without additional training. The most-suited human and nonhuman resources are moved into production first, but as production of a good increases and becomes more specialized, less-adaptable resources must be used to produce it. The costs of producing additional units of the good rise because larger amounts of these increasingly less-adaptable resources are required to produce each successive unit. This means that greater quantities of another good do not get produced and must therefore be sacrificed in the process.

Unemployment of resources
A situation in which some human and/or nonhuman resources that can be used in production are not used.

The law of increasing costs always applies when resources are fully employed. When there is a degree of **unemployment of resources,** however—such as a certain amount of land lying idle—society finds itself producing at a point within the production possibilities curve. Point *F* in Figure 2.2 represents such a situation. From point *F* to the curve, additional cheeseburgers or automobiles can be produced without any increase in opportunity costs until resources become fully employed. The production possibilities curve is thus referred to as a *frontier* because it represents full employment of resources. Full employment means that society is realizing its maximum output potential.

WHY THE PRODUCTION POSSIBILITIES FRONTIER SHIFTS

If we keep in mind the meaning and assumptions of the production possibilities frontier, we will also understand that an increase or decrease in society's human or nonhuman resources can shift society's output potential. An understanding of such changes is central to an understanding of economic growth—or the lack of it.

The Shifting Frontier

The production possibilities frontier can shift leftward or rightward in response to any change in the quantity of human resources, any change in the quantity of nonhuman resources, or any change in technology. Changes in these factors shift the production possibilities frontier because we previously assumed they were constant.

Suppose a technological improvement in dairy production increases the productivity of cheese making. In such a case, society's production possibilities relating to cheeseburgers are increased without a similar increase in automobile production. The result is a shift rightward on the cheeseburger section of the production possibilities curve. Such a change is shown in Figure 2.3a as a shift from the PP_1 curve to the PP_2 curve.

In Figure 2.3b, a productivity change brought about by technological improvement occurs in automobile production. Here the production possibilities curve shifts rightward on the automobile end; if society prefers, additional automobiles can be produced without any sacrifice of cheeseburgers.

In Figure 2.3c, a general change in productivity, technology, or resource supply is assumed. An increase in the quantity of labor (through a simple growth in population), for example, shifts the entire production possibilities frontier rightward from PP_1 to PP_2. Suppose society now chooses the cheeseburger/automobile combination A_1. More of both goods are produced and consumed as a result of the technological improvement. But society faces new trade-offs once it is producing on its new frontier. Opportunity costs arise again in resource utilization, just as they did at combination *A* on production possibility curve PP_1. Society cannot escape scarcity, yet it can improve its production possibilities through growth in technology, quantity of human or nonhuman resources, or resource productivity.

FIGURE 2.3

Shifting the Production Possibilities Frontier

(a) A technological improvement in cheeseburger production shifts the production possibilities curve outward at the cheeseburger end. (b) A technological improvement in automobile production shifts the production possibilities curve outward at the automobile end. (c) A general increase in technology or resource supply shifts the entire production possibilities curve outward.

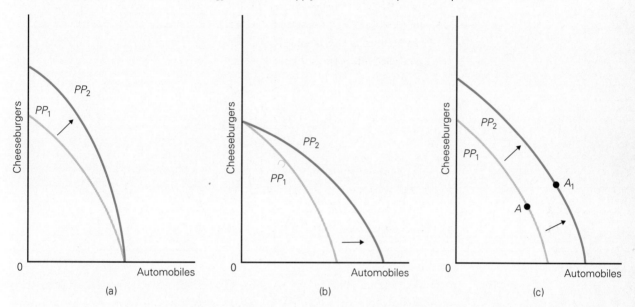

Economic Growth: How Economies Progress

We can understand the nature of economic growth with the aid of the production possibilities curve model. The key to economic growth in society is related to the growth or change in capital stock and other crucial resources.

Capital stock

The amount of nonhuman resources available in the economy. These include tools, land, machinery, equipment, and so on.

The creation of **capital stock** (a supply of items used to produce other items) takes time and bears an opportunity cost in present consumption. The benefits of creating capital, however, are in increased amounts of future consumption. In other words, forming new capital stock requires that people save–that is, abstain from consuming in the present. When investment in capital stocks results from this saving, capital formation and growth occur. The formation of capital goods–tools, tractors, computers and so on–requires a redirection of resources from consumption of goods to production of capital goods. The opportunity cost of acquiring capital is thus consumption goods forgone, but the reward for society is an increase in future productive capacity in consumption goods, capital goods, or both.

We can illustrate this phenomenon with the production possibilities curve. Figure 2.4 shows two production possibilities frontiers that contrast capital goods production (the vertical axis) with consumption goods production (the horizontal axis) for two hypothetical societies with initially similar production possibilities curves. Consider society A's choice of consumption and capital goods in 1997, represented by point E_A in Figure 2.4a. Clearly, society A devotes a larger proportion of its resources to capital goods production than to consumption goods production. Saving (abstaining from current consumption), investing, and capital formation are all

FIGURE 2.4

Growth Choices on the Production Possibilities Curve

(a) By producing more capital goods, K_A in 1997, society A can produce more consumption goods in the future than (b) society B, which produces only K_B capital goods in 1997.

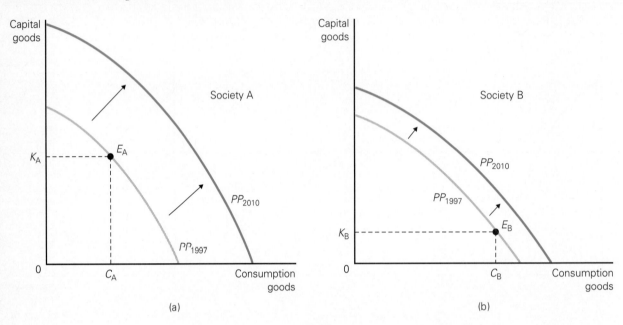

(a)   (b)

Economic growth

A permanent increase in the productive capacity of the economy.

high in that society. The payoff for society A will come later, say in 2010, with vastly enlarged productive capacity, designated by the shift of the production possibilities curve to PP_{2010} in Figure 2.4a.

Society B chooses to use almost all of its resources in 1997 for consumption goods, with only a small quantity of resources devoted to capital goods, a combination represented by point E_B in Figure 2.4b. The consequence of this choice is low economic growth over the following decade. By 2010, the production possibilities of that society have grown by only a small amount, as curve PP_{2010} in Figure 4b indicates. Thus **economic growth** in the future is largely determined by current decisions about production. Technological changes are important factors in the progress of society, but to take advantage of technology, society must sacrifice some present consumption. With reductions in human or nonhuman resources, societies can actually regress. After World War II, for example, the production possibilities of Germany and Japan were virtually smashed, leading to a massive shift to the left of their relevant production possibilities curves.

And keep in mind something we have not done so far. We have discussed trade-offs and opportunity costs, but we have not told you how individuals make private choices about these trade-offs or how societies make public choices about them. In short, where on the production possibilities curve does one end up or choose to be? Individuals make these choices in both private and public settings and we will explore how they do this throughout the rest of the book.

In addition to making choices between consumption now and later, both individuals and societies can increase their output by specializing in and trading, or ex-

TABLE 2.4

Production Possibilities in Canada and Mexico

Canada has a comparative advantage in lumber. If Canada were to move to producing combination *A* instead of *B,* 300,000 board-feet of lumber could be had at an opportunity cost of 30,000 ounces of silver. Each board-foot of lumber has a marginal opportunity cost $1/10$ of an ounce of silver going unproduced. If Mexico were to move from *B* to *A,* 40,000 more ounces of silver could be had at an opportunity cost of 40,000 board-feet of lumber. Each ounce of silver costs Mexico 1 board-foot of lumber. Likewise, Mexico has a comparative advantage in producing silver. In Canada an extra ounce of silver costs 10 board-feet of lumber.

	Canada's Production Possibilities			Mexico's Production Possibilities		
	A	*B*	*C*	*A*	*B*	*C*
Silver (ounces)	0	30,000	100,000	0	40,000	80,000
Lumber (board-feet)	1,000,000	700,000	0	80,000	40,000	0

changing, goods and services. The manner in which both individuals and societies specialize is related to an important principle—the law of comparative advantage.

COMPARATIVE ADVANTAGE

While Adam Smith developed the fundamentals underlying specialization and trade, it was left to his English followers, David Ricardo (1772–1823) and Robert Torrens (1780–1864), to develop the critically important principle of specialization—the theory of comparative advantage. Comparative advantage (and its relation to specialization and trade) is best understood with a simple, hypothetical example. Table 2.4 describes three combinations of silver and lumber production for two different countries, Canada and Mexico. The production possibilities information in Table 2.4 is reproduced graphically in Figure 2.5. The production possibilities curves of Figure 2.5 do not look exactly like the production possibilities curves we have discussed so far. For simplicity, we have temporarily assumed that the law of increasing costs does not hold in the two countries—at least not where lumber and silver production are concerned. Instead, we assume that in each country both silver and lumber production are subject to constant opportunity costs of production. This means that the production possibilities curves are straight lines instead of curves.

Table 2.4 indicates that production of the first 30,000 ounces of silver in Canada means 300,000 board-feet of lumber do not get produced. Moving from point *A* to point *B* on Canada's production possibilities curve reduces the production of lumber from 1 million to 700,000 board-feet. In such a move, each additional ounce of silver produced has an opportunity cost of 10 board-feet of lumber. If Canada is producing 30,000 ounces of silver and shifts productive resources from the lumber industry to produce 70,000 more ounces of silver (for a total of 100,000 ounces), lumber production drops by 700,000 board-feet. Each additional ounce of silver produced has a constant opportunity cost of 10 board-feet of unproduced lumber, regardless of how many ounces of silver are already being produced.

FIGURE 2.5

Canada's and Mexico's Production Possibilities Curves

Both countries agree that each 1000 ounces of silver trades for 5000 board-feet of lumber, or a board-foot of lumber for ⅕ of an ounce of silver. Each agrees to trade on these terms because obtaining a good through trade is less costly than obtaining the good by producing it at home. After specialization and trade, each country will consume combination *D*, a combination that lies beyond each country's production possibilities curve.

(a)

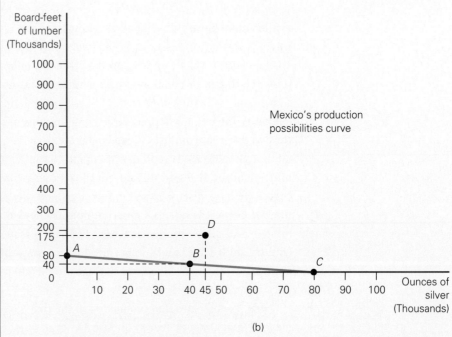

(b)

Marginal opportunity production cost
The number of units of one good that do not get produced when one additional unit of another good is produced.

The same information may be expressed in a different manner. In Canada, the additional cost, or **marginal opportunity production cost**, of 1 board-foot of lumber is constant and equal to ¹⁄₁₀ of an ounce of silver. Silver and lumber production in Mexico are also subject to constant (marginal opportunity) production costs. For each additional ounce of silver produced, only 1 board-foot of lumber goes unproduced. The marginal opportunity cost of producing 1 ounce of silver in Mexico, 1 board-foot of lumber, is *less* than it is in Canada, where it is equal to 10 board-feet of lumber. Mexico is said to possess a comparative advantage over Canada in producing silver. A comparative advantage exists because the marginal opportunity cost of producing an ounce of silver in Mexico (1 board-foot of lumber) is less than it is in Canada (10 board-feet). So, any locale with a lower marginal opportunity cost of producing a good possesses a comparative advantage over some other locale in producing that good.

Canada has a comparative advantage over Mexico in lumber production, as indicated in Table 2.4. Canada can produce lumber at a lower marginal opportunity cost ($\frac{1}{10}$ of an ounce of silver) than can Mexico (1 ounce of silver). If Canada has a comparative advantage in lumber production, this necessarily means that Mexico has a **comparative advantage** in silver production. One ounce of silver costs Mexico only 1 board-foot of lumber, whereas in Canada the cost is 10 board-feet. Each country has a comparative production advantage over the other, but in a different good.

Suppose that both Mexico and Canada are initially self-sufficient in silver and lumber. That is, each country produces and consumes some of both goods and does not trade with the other nation. Specifically, suppose that both countries produce and consume the combination of silver and lumber labeled *B* in Table 2.4 and Figure 2.5. We assume that combination *B* represents the most desirable consumption combination for both Canada and Mexico that is attainable from self-production.

How might Mexicans and Canadians be made better off economically? Excluding economic growth, residents of each country could improve their economic situation through specialization and trade. Each could specialize in producing the good for which that locale has a comparative advantage and then trade some of its output for the other good. The residents could consume more of both goods or more of one good and the same quantity of the other good.

Specialization

Suppose that Mexico and Canada happen to hire the same economic consultant to help them improve their respective economic fortunes. After a study of each economy, the consultant brings representatives of both countries together and suggests a plan that will leave each better off economically: Specialize according to comparative advantage and trade with each other.

The benefits of specialization and trade are shown in the four parts of Table 2.5. Table 2.5a shows the situation in each country before specialization and

Comparative advantage
An economic entity's ability to produce a good at a lower marginal opportunity production cost than some other entity.

TABLE 2.5A

Canada and Mexico before Specialization and Trade

The amounts actually produced and thus consumed in Canada and Mexico are the combinations labeled B in Table 2.4. Amounts of each good for the "world" are the sums of the two countries' production.

	Canada Produces and Consumes	+	Mexico Produces and Consumes	=	World Produces and Consumes
Silver (ounces)	30,000		40,000		70,000
Lumber (board-feet)	700,000		40,000		740,000

TABLE 2.5B

Canada and Mexico after Specialization But before Trade

Specialization in production according to comparative advantage yields a world gain in the output of both goods.

	Canada Produces	+	Mexico Produces	=	World Produces	World Gains
Silver (ounces)	0		80,000		80,000	+10,000
Lumber (board-feet)	1,000,000		0		1,000,000	+260,000

trade occur. Specifically, it reproduces combination *B* from each locale's production possibilities curves shown in Figures 2.5a and 2.5b. Combination *B*, recall, is assumed to be the most desirable consumption combination for each country. Also shown in Table 2.5a is the sum total of both countries' production and consumption of each good. It is assumed that Canada and Mexico constitute the "world."

Table 2.5b depicts the production situation in each country, and, therefore, the world, after Canada and Mexico have specialized in production according to comparative advantage. After specialization, total world output of silver is 10,000 ounces greater than it was at combination *B* on the production possibilities curve in Figure 2.5. World production of lumber has also increased. It is 260,000 board-feet more than before specialization. The world is better off economically (more of both goods), but we have yet to show that each individual country is made better off as a result of specialization according to comparative advantage. There is one more step to the process, that of trade.

Trade: The Fruits of Specialization

Our consultant realizes that neither Canada nor Mexico would voluntarily agree to an exchange that would leave them worse off (than before trade). For voluntary exchange to take place, each nation must end up better off economically. With this in mind, the consultant proposes that Canada trade 175,000 board-feet of lumber to Mexico in exchange for 35,000 ounces of silver, or 5 board-feet of lumber for each ounce of silver. The Canadians would agree to this trade since domestic production of the 35,000 ounces of silver would cost them 10 board-feet of lumber each, for a total of 350,000 board-feet. This exchange allows the Canadians to obtain silver from the Mexicans more cheaply than it costs to produce it themselves.

The Mexicans would also agree to the proposed trade. Each board-foot of lumber costs them 1 ounce of silver to produce, but the proposed trade allows them to obtain each board-foot for $1/5$ of an ounce of silver. The trade with Canada enables Mexico to obtain 175,000 board-feet of lumber for 35,000 ounces of silver. The opportunity cost to Mexico of producing 175,000 board-feet of lumber would be 175,000 ounces of silver. It is less costly for Mexico to obtain lumber through trade than through self-production. This trade is depicted in Table 2.5c.

TABLE 2.5C

The Trade Between Canada and Mexico

Canada and Mexico agree that each ounce of silver trades for 5 board-feet of lumber, or a board-foot of lumber trades for $\frac{1}{5}$ of an ounce of silver. Each agrees to trade on these terms because obtaining a good through trade is less costly than obtaining it by producing it at home.

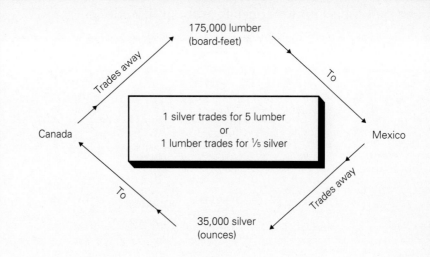

Terms of trade
The number of units of one good that exchange in the market for one unit of some other good. Although not expressed in terms of money, it is a price nonetheless.

The number of board-feet of lumber that trade for an ounce of silver is called the **terms of trade.** The terms of trade is really a price that is not measured in terms of either country's money. In this example, Canada pays Mexico 5 board-feet of lumber for each ounce of silver. Mexico pays $\frac{1}{5}$ ounce of silver for each board-foot of lumber. The terms of trade is a price that defines the number of units of one good that exchange for one unit of some other good. The terms of trade will always fall somewhere between the marginal opportunity production costs of a given good in each of the two countries. In this case, an ounce of silver has an opportunity cost of 10 board-feet of lumber in Canada and 1 board-foot of lumber in Mexico, so the terms of trade will be at least 1 board-foot of lumber for 1 ounce of silver and at most 10 board-feet of lumber for 1 ounce of silver. Terms of trade outside these limits would cause trade to be counter to the interests of citizens in one of the countries—for instance, Canadians would be better off producing their own silver than paying more than 10 board-feet per ounce for Mexican silver.

Table 2.5d summarizes the economic positions of Canada and Mexico after specializing in production and trading. Most important, both countries end up with more of both goods to consume than before trade. Canada consumes 125,000 more board-feet of lumber than it did initially; Mexico, an additional 135,000 board-feet. Both enjoy 5000 more ounces of silver than in the prespecialization and trade period. In Figures 2.5a and 2.5b, both countries are consuming combination *D*—combinations of goods that lie beyond the respective production possibilities curves. Without specialization and trade, these combinations could only be attained through economic growth. It is as if additional resource quantities of silver and lumber were actually created through specialized production and division of labor. Residents in each country are better off economically. Specialization according to comparative advantage and trade has led to increased living standards in both parts of the world.

TABLE 2.5D

Canada and Mexico after Specialization and Trade

Specialization in production according to comparative advantage and trading yields a world gain and a gain for each country.

		CANADA			
	Produces	Trades For (+) Away (−)	Consumes After Trade	Produced and Consumed Before Trade	Gains from Trade
Silver (ounces)	0	+35,000	35,000	30,000	+5,000
Lumber (board-feet)	1,000,000	−175,000	825,000	700,000	+125,000
		MEXICO			
	Produces	Trades For (+) Away (−)	Consumes After Trade	Produced and Consumed Before Trade	Gains from Trade
Silver (ounces)	80,000	−35,000	45,000	40,000	+5,000
Lumber (board-feet)	0	+175,000	175,000	40,000	+135,000

Factors Explaining Comparative Advantage

There are basically two reasons why a locale would have a comparative advantage over some other locale in producing any given good relative to other goods—differences in technology or differences in the quantities of productive inputs in the two locales. Relative differences in production technologies of the goods in the two locales can lead to a comparative advantage for each locale. With a given level of productive resources, Mexico might be able to produce an ounce of silver relatively more cheaply than Canada owing to technological differences in the production process in the two countries. Lumber production technology may be identical in each locale, but the technical know-how of making silver may be more advanced in Mexico. Certain institutional factors can also affect both the level of technology utilized and costs. One country may impose minimum wage laws on employers. Another may contain effective environmental laws which create different costs to producers.

Alternatively, if production technologies are identical in both locales, an abundance of the productive resources used in producing lumber in Canada compared to Mexico's amounts of these resources could exist. This would give Canada a comparative advantage in lumber. But a relative abundance of lumber-producing trees in Canada implies a relative abundance of silver inputs in Mexico. These relative, or comparative, differences in the amounts of productive resources in the two countries can produce the pattern of comparative advantage described earlier. Patterns of comparative advantage may, of course, shift over time with either natural or artificially induced changes in resource prices and supplies or with changes in technology.

Consider another aspect of the situation in Mexico and Canada. Table 2.4 indicates that Canada has the ability to produce more lumber in absolute terms than

Mexico if each country produces only lumber (1 million board-feet versus 80,000 board-feet). Canada also has the capacity to produce absolutely more silver (100,000 ounces versus 80,000 ounces) than Mexico. Canada has what economists call an absolute advantage in production of both goods. That is, Canada can specialize in silver production and simply produce more silver than Mexico. The same holds for lumber production. Any time a country can specialize in producing a good and produce absolutely more of it than some other country, the first country has an absolute advantage over the second. An absolute advantage can arise because of technological factors or because one country possesses a larger quantity of productive resources. Although Canada has an absolute advantage in producing both goods, it has a comparative advantage only in lumber. Mexico has an absolute disadvantage in both goods, but it still can produce silver at a lower marginal opportunity cost than Canada. Both countries still benefit from specialization and trade according to comparative advantage.

It is important to understand the simplification attached to the preceding discussion of comparative advantage. Differences in marginal opportunity costs explain comparative advantages, but the economic system does not actually require an "economic consultant" to tell countries (or businesses or individuals) about the potential gains from specialization and trade. Relative scarcities based on differences in marginal opportunity costs are transmitted to producers and consumers through the price system. Prices "inform" producers and consumers about what, how much, and when to supply and consume millions of goods and services. The details of how prices are formed through the interaction of supply and demand are reserved for Chapter 3. Nonetheless, it is useful to remember that prices, not hypothetical economic consultants, "discover," signal, and reflect the comparative advantages that exist between nations, businesses, and individuals.

Exchange Costs

The model of comparative advantage and trade—along with all other economic models—is a simplification of reality. A number of important assumptions hide behind our simple discussions. But there are also costs to the process of exchange that must be accounted for when calculating the benefits of specialization and trade. We classify these **exchange costs** as transaction costs, transportation costs, and artificial barriers to trade.

Exchange costs
The opportunity costs of the resources used in making trades; includes transaction costs, transportation costs, and artificial barriers to trade.

Transaction costs
The opportunity costs of the resources directly associated with trade; includes time costs, brokers' fees, and so on.

TRANSACTION COSTS   Transaction costs are all the resource costs (including time-associated costs) incurred because of exchange. Transaction costs occur every time goods and services are traded, whether exchanges are simple (purchase of a pack of gum) or complex (a long-term negotiated contract with many contingencies). Here's a simple example: Gwen goes to the supermarket to purchase a pound of coffee. What are the costs of the transaction? Gasoline and auto depreciation must be considered as resource costs, of course, but the principal cost is the opportunity cost of Gwen's time. Gwen might have spent this time working or playing tennis instead of grocery shopping. Gwen's wage rate might then serve as her opportunity cost. If the shopping trip takes 30 minutes and if Gwen's wage rate is $15 an hour, the time part of her transaction costs is $7.50.

In this simple case the contracting and negotiating are instantaneous—Gwen simply gives the money to the checkout person, takes her coffee, and the transaction is complete. In other, more complex exchanges—such as the purchase of a house, a car, or a major appliance or the negotiation of a long-term labor contract—contracting and negotiating costs can be substantial. Think of the time and other resource costs associated with long-term supply contracts such as U.S. arms deals with allies or negotiations for ammonia plants in China. Every detail must be studied, formulated, and then spelled out.

The important point is that transaction costs include resources used by each party to the exchange. The higher the resource costs, the lower the benefit that comes from specialization and trade. Institutions—new legal arrangements, new marketing techniques, new methods of selling—have emerged, and are continually emerging, to reduce all forms of transaction costs. Gwen could have purchased coffee at a convenience store nearer to her house. The price of the coffee might have been somewhat higher, but Gwen's time costs, and therefore her total transaction costs, would have been lower. In a broader sense, laws about contracts, and law itself, are means by which transaction costs are reduced. The invention of money and the development of various forms of money and financial instruments are responses to transaction costs associated with barter and more primitive means of exchange.

In addition to money, intermediaries such as wholesalers and advertisers developed over the ages to facilitate exchange. The creative marketing of goods and services from bazaars to discount stores to media advertising has increased consumer information and thus reduced the costs of making transactions. Middlemen have lowered transaction costs by decreasing the risk of exchange. The production of some goods entails some risk and uncertainty on the part of buyers and sellers. Planting wheat in the spring for sale in the fall obviously entails some uncertainty about what prices will be at harvest. Middlemen-speculators who deal in futures provide sellers and buyers assurance of prices in the future. This type of middleman makes profits on the miscalculations of buyers and sellers but reduces uncertainty and thereby increases trade and specialization.

Transportation costs
The value of resources used in the transportation of goods that finalize any trade.

TRANSPORTATION COSTS   Transportation costs, resource costs associated with the physical transport of products from place to place, are also an impediment to trade. The higher these resource costs are, the lower the benefits from specialization and trade.

We did not include transportation costs in our initial examples of comparative advantage with Canada and Mexico. Let's do so now. Suppose that transportation costs associated with the trade amounted to 10,000 board-feet of lumber to each country. Even after paying these transportation costs, Canada and Mexico still enjoy more lumber than they did before specializing and trading (see Table 5d). Even if the "consultant," or the intermediary who organized trade, also charged a fee of 5000 board-feet of lumber to each country, both would still gain from specialization and trade. However, if transportation costs were high enough, possible advantages to specialization and trade could be wiped out completely. Cheaper transportation costs permit more trade and open up opportunities for new forms of and increases in specialization. The invention of the railroad in the nineteenth century, the spread of the automobile and the truck, and the dawning of air freight transport in the twentieth century were all boons to specialization and increased output.

Artificial barriers to trade
Restrictions created by the government that inhibit or prevent trade; includes import quotas and tariffs.

Tariff
A tax or levy on imported goods.

Quota
A restriction or limit on the quantity of an imported good.

ARTIFICIAL BARRIERS TO TRADE   The final impediments to specialization and trade are government-imposed restrictions such as tariffs, quotas, and outright prohibitions on the import or export of goods. **Tariffs** are taxes or levies on imported goods. **Quotas** are quantity limitations on imports of products purchased from abroad. More localized restrictions include minimum-wage laws and specific restrictions on an industry or in an area. Such impositions, known as artificial barriers, either reduce or eliminate the benefits of specialization and trade.

Governments always have reasons for these restrictions, but the reasons must be closely scrutinized because the benefits from international and domestic specialization and trade are potentially huge for all consumers. Artificial barriers have the power to reduce economic welfare by reducing or eliminating the benefits of specialization according to the law of comparative advantage.

The possible effects of restrictions on trade can be seen in the growing volume of trade between Japan and the United States in commodities such as TVs, automobiles, stereo equipment, and musical instruments. Special-interest groups—such as American autoworkers and manufacturers—have lobbied for import tariffs and other trade restrictions to protect their own interests, which include increased demand for American-made products and therefore increased domestic production. Government-enforced tariffs make Japanese goods more expensive, however, causing a reduction in the general well-being of Americans. Artificial restrictions on trade, whatever their purpose, reduce the advantages of specialization and trade. As a matter of economic principle, therefore, most economists generally advocate free trade over any type of trade restriction. Further, any institution or mechanism that reduces the costs of exchange usually gets the support of economists because greater specialization permits better utilization of scarce resources. Specialization, in other words, helps us get more of what we want, given a limited amount of resources.

TARIFFS, TRADE, AND TRADE ZONES   In both the modern and ancient worlds, trade and specialization take place when countries agree to special trade arrangements. Fine details of free trade zones differ, but the basic idea is that certain nations agree to have free trade with each other while continuing to have trade barriers—tariffs or quotas, for example, against other countries. Currently the best known, but by no means the only, free trade association affecting the United States is the North American Free Trade Association or NAFTA. It is composed of the countries of Mexico, Canada, and the United States. NAFTA went

Mexican workers assembling shoes at a plant in Guadalajara, Mexico.

into effect on January 1, 1994, creating the largest free trade association in the world and affecting more than 360 million consumers. (See Focus: "Free Trade Associations, Past and Present" for details about these important international trade organizations.) We will have more to say about such associations in this book, but a simple example will help you understand how tariffs and trade agreements affect the quantity and directions of trade. Consider a simple example of computer trade between three countries, the United States, Mexico, and Taiwan.

Table 2.6 illustrates several points concerning real-world patterns of trade. It shows the potential effects of a free trade zone on Mexican consumers. Assume that Mexico, the United States, and Taiwan are all able to produce computers, and that computers are subject to a Mexican tariff rate of 40 percent. The Mexican

TABLE 2.6

Example of Potential Effects of a Free Trade Zone on Mexican Computer Consumers

Producer of Computers	Domestic Price of Computers		
	MEXICO'S TARIFF RATES ON COMPUTERS		
	0%	20%	40%
Mexico	$2000	$2000	$2000
U.S. before NAFTA	$1800	$2160	$2520
U.S. after NAFTA	$1800	$1800	$1800
Taiwan	$1600	$1920	$2240

Free Trade Associations, Past and Present

Economic unions, taking advantage of the principles of specialization and trade, have been common since ancient Greek and Roman times and even before. As such, the North American Free Trade Agreement is only the latest in a long list of arrangements for economic gain. All unions—for economic betterment and growth, for defense, or for any political purpose—presuppose that mutual gain can be had by enacting policies that are beneficial to all parties. However, the extent of the union may vary from full political and economic unification, where separate countries may in fact become one, to far less extreme agreements on tariffs and other trade restrictions.

The prototype for a popular form of modern union was the Zollverein or customs union of the last century. The name was given by the Prussians to a union established in 1833 to set uniform tariffs among separate German states (initially comprising Hesse Cassel, Hesse Darmstadt, Bavaria, and Wurtemberg) and the rest of the world. The agreement specified no tariffs or trade restrictions among these states. The Zollverein was the nineteenth century model for many other unions. Many small states, for example, grouped themselves with larger states for customs and free trade purposes. Examples abound: San Marino developed a customs union with Italy in 1862, Monaco with France in 1865, Liechtenstein with Austria in 1875, and Portuguese India with British India in 1878. Some of these nineteenth century unions survive today.

These nineteenth century agreements provided models for contemporary trade blocs in North America and Western Europe. The most famous economic union in the post–World War II period is the European Economic Community or Common Market, which forms the basis for the new European Community of today. Before the end of the century (if all goes well), the EC will become a unified market of twelve member-nations (the United Kingdom, France, Denmark, Belgium, Greece, Italy, Luxembourg, the Netherlands, Portugal, Ireland, Spain, and a unified Germany). The union will make trade within Europe as regulation-free among the countries of Europe as it is between the states of Massachusetts and New Hampshire. Eventually, all tariff and non-tariff barriers will fall to zero and the EC will, after the NAFTA countries, become the largest and most populous trading area of the world. But unlike the union between Mexico, Canada, and the United States, the EC is expected to evolve into a proposed monetary and political union with common legal rules and a common currency.

Many unanswered questions accompany this new-world scenario of "competing Zollvereins." Not to be minimized is the potential for dissolution of any trade bloc from internal disagreements and dissension. For example, the debate over the net benefits of NAFTA within the United States did not end with its passage in January 1994. Financial problems in Mexico, U.S. loans to bolster Mexico's currency, and the (inevitable) adjustments in domestic employment in some fields have led to much dissension in the political arena.

There are other problems. Free trade will promote economic growth *within* these blocs, but a unified front on the part of trading areas with the *outside world* may in fact encourage new levels of protection and trade wars. But negotiating costs between groups of nations are lowered by such unions. This means that negotiated settlements between blocs of nations may create freer trade. It is impossible to predict the exact impact on the welfare of the world's consumers, but economists are in virtual agreement that more trade is preferred to less.

producers can make a computer for $2000 and do not pay a tariff. U.S. producers can make a computer for $1800. With a 40 percent tariff, their price is $2520 in the Mexican market. Taiwanese producers can make a computer for $1600 and, under the same tariff rate, their price is $2240 in the Mexican market. Mexican firms emerge, as a result of the 40 percent tariff, as the low-cost producers in their domestic market and supply the entire market demand; thus, there is no international trade.

Now consider the trade-creating effects of the North American Free Trade Agreement (NAFTA). The fundamental premise behind NAFTA is the creation of a free trade zone (no tariffs) between Mexico, the U.S. and Canada *only*. In other words, the agreement establishes a system of preferential treatment for particular trading partners. If Mexican tariff rates on imported computers are 20 percent, the United States will emerge as the low-cost producers ($1800) following the implementation of the Agreement. This result emerges from tariff-free trade between the United States and Mexico while trade in computers between Mexico and Taiwan would still be subject to a 20 percent tariff and, thus, a higher price ($1920). In this example, NAFTA's creation of a free trade zone diverts trade from the low-cost producer, Taiwan, to a relatively higher-cost producer, the United States.

Notice that only when tariff rates are 0 percent between all three countries will an efficient pattern of production and trade result with the low-cost producer, Taiwan, supplying the Mexican (and the American) market. Trade diversion is not a problem for the member nations, but from a global perspective trade diversion results in inefficient production, because the more efficient producer loses sales to a less efficient producer. Thus a key feature in the debate over free trade zones is the debate over whether the free trade zone results more in trade creation or more in trade diversion. But economists are almost uniform in their support of free trade and would almost unanimously support a worldwide reduction in tariff and nontariff barriers to trade. For the United States there are many benefits from the creation of free trade zones such as NAFTA. One is the reduction in the prices of imports to U.S. consumers because of reduced tariffs. Another benefit is the increased efficiency of production and the increased competition that comes from a larger market. Some estimate that after the ten- or fifteen-year phase-in period, NAFTA could yield additional trade of $1 to $2 trillion. But there will be winners and losers as free trade becomes a reality between the United States, Mexico, and Canada. Over the fifteen or so years of adjustments, some U.S. business owners and employees of those businesses that cannot compete with Mexican and Canadian producers will lose. Some business owners will lose their investments and some workers will lose their jobs. Some textile firms, for example, will lose their production facilities to Mexico since labor is cheaper there.

Economists argue that the *net effects* of tariff reduction through free trade associations and other means is positive. But even if economists condemn tariffs and quotas, they also recognize how individuals in their public choices may be able to convince government to pass a tariff. Think of it. The benefits of the tariff to a domestic industry may be highly concentrated on the workers and owners in the industry. New trade agreements that lower tariffs and quotas ordinarily create jobs and destroy other jobs. The costs of the tariff in terms of higher prices and costs are spread across the general public so that they may not even notice the effects. Government decision makers respond to this concentrated benefit-diffused cost condition by "supplying" a tariff to the industry. We will have a great deal more to say about this process later in this book. For

TABLE 2.7

Leading Trading Partners of the United States

In terms of exports, Canada is the biggest customer of the United States. In terms of imports, Canada is also the biggest supplier of the United States.

Country	Value of U.S. Imports (billions)	Value of U.S. Exports (billions)
All countries, total	$663.7	$512.7
Canada	128.9	114.4
Japan	119.1	53.4
Germany	31.7	19.2
United Kingdom	25.1	26.8
Mexico	49.5	50.8
France	16.8	13.6
South Korea	19.7	18.0
Hong Kong	9.6	11.4
Singapore	15.4	13.0

SOURCE: U.S. Bureau of the Census, *Statistical Abstract of the United States,* 1995 (Washington, D.C.: U.S. Government Printing Office, 1995), pp. 819–822.

now, we raise the issue, and illustrate it with an examination of the domestic flower industry. (See the Application, "When a Rose Is Not a Rose: Interest Groups and Shifting Comparative Advantage in the Flower Industry," at the conclusion of this chapter for details.) The point is that government can and often does override comparative advantage in order to respond to political pressures for protection.

REAL-WORLD PATTERNS OF TRADE   The previous sections suggest that trade occurs between two countries when the countries have differences in opportunity costs of producing various goods (when comparative advantages exist), when transaction costs and transportation costs are small, and when the countries promote free trade. Real-world evidence reported in Table 2.7 and Figure 2.6 supports these arguments. For example, Canada is the leading trade partner of the United States. Transportation costs between the two countries are very low, and the two countries have one of the freest trade relationships in the world. In contrast, the United States trades substantially less with the United Kingdom because its trade policies are more restrictive and transportation costs are much greater than those with Canada.

Other factors explain the relative importance of foreign trade in the economies of different nations. Foreign trade is relatively more important to the Jordanian and Malaysian economies than to the German or Canadian economies. Geography and transport costs are part of the explanation, but the resource endowments (or lack thereof) is another principal explanation for larger volumes of trade. Further, nations pursuing less restrictive trade policies may, other things being equal, be expected to engage in more foreign trade.

FIGURE 2.6

Exports and Imports as a Percentage of Gross Domestic Product (1994) in Various Countries

International trade is clearly more important in percentage terms to some countries— Jordan or Malaysia—than to others, such as the United States and Japan.

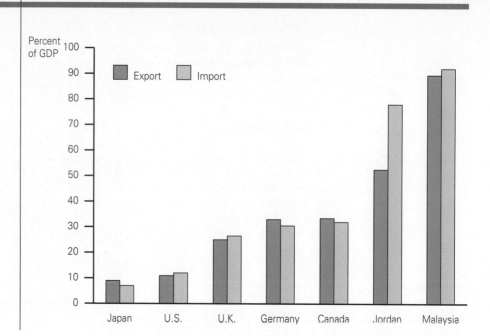

The tremendous volume of trade between the United States and other nations is best explained by strong comparative advantages. Because the types of productive resources found in the countries differ greatly, certain goods that have high opportunity costs elsewhere have low costs in the United States, and vice versa. A huge trade volume, therefore, exists between nations of the world despite transportation costs and the fact that many nations pursue policies to restrict trade. The gains to specialization and trade are enormous, no less between nations as between individuals and all other trading units.

APPLICATION
When a Rose Is Not a Rose: Interest Groups and Shifting Comparative Advantage in the Flower Industry

Changes in technology, in capital investment, and in resource prices will often alter comparative advantage and trade in surprising ways. Consider conditions in the American flower industry, particularly among flower and plant growers.

Imported plants and cut flowers were a mere trickle in the early 1970s compared to recent years. Colombia, Mexico, Australia, the Netherlands, and Israel have made huge incursions into U.S. wholesale and retail markets for fresh cut flowers (especially roses, carnations, and chrysanthemums), and Belgium, Canada, Denmark, the Netherlands, Israel, and Costa Rica have done the same in the plant market. Colombia, one of the leading foreign suppliers of cut flowers and plants to the United States, exported over $240 million in flowers and plants to the United States in 1994. Between 1990 and 1994, imports of fresh roses grew 19 percent to $124.4 million and imports of miniature carnations increased about 58 percent to $25.9 million.[a] In fact, cut flowers have been second only to coffee as Colombia's leading legal export item in recent years.

A number of reasons related to shifting comparative advantage can be offered for the lower prices and increased supplies of cut flowers and plants from foreign sources. The energy crisis of the 1970s raised the price of heating greenhouses, putting a cost squeeze on many domestic growers, especially those in the colder climates of North America. In 1986, according to U.S. Department of Agriculture (USDA) estimates, the states of Florida and California combined accounted for approximately half of the entire U.S. greenhouse and permanent-cover growing area. Under the high energy price conditions of the 1970s and early 1980s, nations such as Colombia had a new source of comparative advantage in flower growing—no heating of greenhouses is necessary in these nations.

While higher energy prices might help explain the initial shift in comparative advantage from the United States to Colombia and other nations in flower and plant growing, it does not explain why comparative advantage has not been regained by the United States since the weakening of OPEC and lower energy prices in recent years. Other factors related to comparative advantage are clearly relevant. Most important, perhaps, is the fact that significant technological advances occurred in flower growing and transportation during the 1970s, 1980s, and 1990s. Growers in such nations as Colombia started up with state-of-the-art capital and growing techniques. Modernization of greenhouses and equipment together with a willingness to risk capital will be required before the United States can recapture its comparative advantage.

Predictably, efforts to institute artificial barriers to trade, such as tariffs and quotas, were made by lobby groups and trade organizations of the various segments of the American flower industry in the late 1980s and 1990s. Protectionists, especially those representing flower growers, drew battle lines, declaring "cheap foreign labor," "inferior-quality products," "unemployment in the flower industry," "foreign government subsidies," and "health hazards through damaging insect pests." Leading the fight has been the Washington-based lobby group of the industry called the Society of American Florists (SAF). Roses, Inc., a floral trade association, called for legislation against countries who supposedly sell ("dump") flowers in the United States below their costs of production.

These groups have had a measure of success since the late 1980s. In 1987, a thinly disguised protectionist "Anti-Dumping Duty" was imposed on U.S. importers of carnations and pompom chrysanthemums from several Latin

American countries, and duties were imposed on flower containers and silk flowers imported from South Korea, Taiwan, Hong Kong, and Singapore (all formerly duty-free nations) in 1989. As a result of these measures, flower costs to American consumers rose by an estimated $4 million in 1987, and the price of floral arrangements to American consumers rose by approximately 33 percent in 1989.

In September 1994 the Commerce Department levied tariffs of 22.7 percent on the wholesale price of roses—representing an amount of money that must be paid to the government in taxes (another name for a tariff). Prices will either be raised to rose consumers and/or profits will fall to rose importers. It is as yet unclear how much more protection will be supplied to the flower industry. Not all interests in the U.S. flower business are the same. Flower growers and groups such as container manufacturers favor protection, while flower importers are, in general, fighting it. Politicians and government agencies have demonstrated that they will respond to protectionist pleas from the industry. A small increase in the price of roses to consumers will probably not elicit a "political response," whereas the lobbying of concentrated interest groups (such as domestic flower producers) tends to rule policy. Unfortunately, the economic principles of comparative advantage, specialization, and trade suggest that gains to one small group of producers would be more than offset by higher prices and welfare losses to other industry segments and to flower consumers as a whole.

QUESTION

How do tariffs and quotas distort the comparative advantage of a country?

[a]*National Trade Data Book*, U.S. Department of Commerce, 1995.

SUMMARY

1. Economic choices, both for the individual and for society, always involve an opportunity cost.
2. Opportunity cost is the highest-valued alternative forgone in the decision to engage in a particular activity.
3. The law of increasing costs means that as more of one good is produced by a society, the opportunity costs of obtaining additional units of that commodity rise. The increase in cost is the result of resources becoming less adaptable as production becomes more specialized.
4. Specialization—the division of tasks to produce goods and services—takes place in all known societies. The principles of specialization are thus related to the decisions all societies and economic organizations face in trying to overcome the basic problem of scarcity.
5. The production possibilities curve shows the possible quantities of two goods that could be produced given the state of technology and society's scarce resources.
6. Changes in technology or increases (or decreases) in the amount of resources cause rightward (or leftward) movements in the production possibilities frontier.
7. Greater quantities of output can be obtained with society's scarce resources when people specialize and trade. Trade takes place according to the principle of comparative advantage.
8. Trade can take place between two individuals or economic entities even if one of the entities is more efficient at producing all goods. All that is required is that each entity be relatively more efficient than the other in some production.
9. Transaction costs, transportation costs, and artificial trade barriers such as tariffs and quotas reduce the benefits obtainable from specialization and trade.

KEY TERMS

opportunity cost
specialization
division of labor
choices at the margin
production possibilities frontier
law of increasing costs
unemployment of resources

capital stock
economic growth
marginal opportunity
    production cost
comparative advantage
terms of trade
exchange costs

transaction costs
transportation costs
artificial barriers to trade
tariffs
quotas

QUESTIONS FOR REVIEW AND DISCUSSION

1. What did reading this chapter cost you? Did you include the price of the book? What will reading the next chapter cost? Does that include the price of the book?
2. Do government-sponsored financial aid programs for college students influence the amount of education produced? Do these programs shift the production possibilities curve?
3. What does a movement along the production possibilities frontier suggest? What does a point inside the curve suggest?
4. A subsidy to farmers who purchase combines and tractors increases the production of this farm machin-
ery. Does this cause an increase in the production possibilities curve or just a movement along the curve? Can subsidies cause economic growth?
5. Why would a country with an absolute advantage in the production of all goods be willing to trade with other countries?
6. Alpha can produce 60 bottles of wine or 40 pounds of cheese. Beta can produce 90 bottles of wine or 30 pounds of cheese. Both have constant costs of production. Draw their production possibilities curves. What is Alpha's costs of 1 bottle of wine? What is Beta's cost of 1 pound of cheese? If they trade, who should specialize in cheese?

7. What are the costs of going to college? Does the marginal benefit outweigh the marginal cost?

8. Is the lost present consumption associated with the production of capital goods worth the benefit of the new capital?

9. Does Japan have an absolute advantage over the United States in the production of televisions and stereo equipment, or is it just a comparative advantage?

10. Who is hurt by and who benefits from an import quota on foreign beef?

11. How does the cost of purchasing a loaf of bread at a supermarket compare with the cost of purchasing a loaf of bread at a convenience store?

12. What is the law of increasing costs and why does it hold?

13. When the gains from specialization and trade are assessed, exchange costs must be considered. What are these costs?

14. If the United States opened its border with Mexico and lowered all tariffs and quotas, what would happen to the production possibilities frontier of the United States?

PROBLEMS

1. Countries A and B both produce golf balls and golf clubs. The table shows what each country can produce at full employment.

A		B	
Golf Balls	Golf Clubs	Golf Balls	Golf Clubs
1200	0	900	0
1000	50	750	25
800	100	600	50
600	150	450	75
400	200	300	100
200	250	150	125
0	300	0	150

a. Graph the production possibilities curve of each country.

b. Do both production functions exhibit constant costs?

c. Who has the absolute advantage in both golf ball and golf club production?

d. Who has the comparative advantage in the production of golf balls?

e. Who has the comparative advantage in the production of golf clubs?

2. Consider the following data concerning the production possibilities of the countries Alpha and Beta.

ALPHA		BETA	
X	Y	X	Y
0	20	0	60
20	15	10	45
40	10	20	30
60	5	30	15
80	0	40	0

a. Which commodity, X or Y, does Alpha have a comparative advantage in producing?

b. Where does Beta's comparative advantage lie?

c. Show the results in a graph.

PRIVATE MARKETS AND PRICES: LAWS OF DEMAND AND SUPPLY

Simple specialization began to take place in primitive cultures as individuals recognized unique abilities in themselves and in others. As we have seen, increasing specialization led to organized markets where people bought and sold goods, to the use of money, and to increasingly large groups of buyers and sellers. Economists define these organized markets—such as bazaars, the stock exchange, or Saks Fifth Avenue—as places or circumstances that bring together demanders (buyers) and suppliers (sellers) of any goods or services. After reading Chapter 3 you should understand

- the motivations of demanders and suppliers in the exchange of goods and services in markets.

- how and why some goods and services get produced and sold at certain prices while other items are not produced or sold at all.

- what happens to demand and supply when governments or other agencies institute price or rent controls.

- that the full price we pay for goods and services includes the money price and such things as time and the other costs involved in a transaction.

AN OVERVIEW OF THE PRICE SYSTEM

Every day the news media provide dramatic evidence of the workings of the market system. The price of silver rises by 45 percent in one day as massive investments in silver futures by two of the world's richest oil magnates trigger a bandwagon effect. Leak of a technological breakthrough by a certain computer firm creates a frenzy of stock buying, driving up the price of the firm's stock overnight. Crude oil prices rise sharply when Iraq invades Kuwait.

In the familiar economic transactions of everyday life, we too enter markets where buyers and sellers congregate to buy and sell a great variety of products and services. The typical American supermarket sells thousands of products, and as we wander through the store we can view a price system in action. In the produce section, for instance, quantities and prices of fruits and vegetables depend on the quantities consumers want and on the season. Early crops usually bring in the highest prices. Watermelon may sell for more than $2 per pound in March but only $0.15 per pound by the Fourth of July.

What determines who will get the early melons or how they will be rationed among those who want them? Why are prices and quantities constantly rising and falling for millions of goods and services in our economy? How do new products find their way to places where buyers and sellers congregate? The answers are simple. In a market society, the self-interest of consumers and producers, of households and businesses, determines who gets what and how much. To paraphrase Adam Smith, it is not to the benevolence of the butcher and the baker that we owe our dinner but to their self-interest. The primary way that consumers and producers express their self-interest is through the economic laws of supply and demand. Sticking a price tag on a product does not imply price-setting power, as anyone who has run a garage sale knows. In a market system, demand and supply determine prices, and prices are the essential pieces of information on which consumers, households, businesses, and resource suppliers make decisions. High melon prices in March will encourage suppliers and discourage demanders, whereas low prices in July will encourage demanders and discourage suppliers. Before investigating the mechanics of these laws of supply and demand, we consider a simple overview of the price system.

As market participants, households and businesses play dual roles. Businesses supply final output of products and services—rock concerts, bananas, hair stylings—but also must hire or demand resources to produce the outputs. Households demand rock concerts, bananas, and hair stylings for final consumption. But they also supply labor and entrepreneurial ability, as well as quantities of land and capital to earn income for the purchase of products and services.

The Circular Flow of Products and Resources

As Figure 3.1 shows, businesses and households are interconnected by the **products (outputs) market** and by the **resources (inputs) market**. Each market depends on the other; they are linked by the prices of outputs and inputs. The particular mix of goods and services exchanged in the products market depends on consumer demands in that market plus the cost and availability of necessary resources. For example, which bands are featured at an outdoor music theater will depend on

Products market
The forces created by buyers and sellers that establish the prices and quantities exchanged of goods and services.

Resources market
The forces created by buyers and sellers that establish the prices and quantities exchanged of resources such as land, labor services, and capital.

FIGURE 3.1

The Product and Resource Markets: A Circular Flow

Businesses play a dual role in the market economy: They are the suppliers of goods and services as well as the demanders of resources. Households also have a dual role. They are both demanders of goods and services and suppliers of resources.

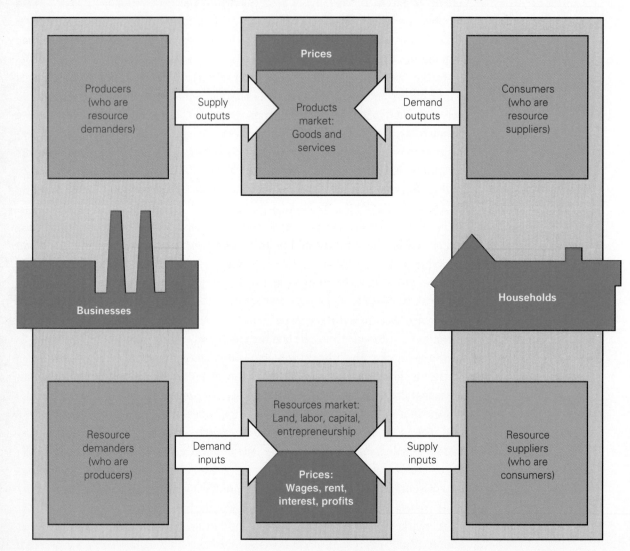

what the targeted audience wants to hear plus the ability of that audience to pay the price asked by the groups and the groups' availability on particular dates. Similarly, the particular mix of resources available at any one time or through time is determined by what households are demanding—subject also to the availability of the resources. If land suitable for banana growing is available, it is most likely to be sold for banana plantations if households are demanding a lot of bananas, thereby making it possible for banana growers to pay landowners for their land.

Prices are the impulses of information that make the entire system of input and output markets operate. Take the prices of fad goods: At times, certain goods or services—such as hula hoops and Nintendo video games—have quickly appeared and then disappeared. When a fad begins to catch on, prices tend to be high because there is a high and rapidly growing demand and because resources necessary to produce the good may be scarce and command a high price. It takes time to adapt resources to the production of the fad good. Labor must be drawn from other uses and trained in the new production techniques. Marketing channels must be established so that sellers and buyers can converge at convenient points of trade. Demand for the fad good is transmitted through businesses to the factors of production through a system of prices. Initially high prices signal the scarcity of goods and resources. As more entrepreneurs and businesses perceive the profit opportunities associated with the fad and as more resources are discovered or developed to produce it, prices of both the inputs and the outputs change accordingly.

The price system reacts similarly with goods that remain in the market for a longer time. Consider the development of computers and computer technology in the 1960s. Initial investments by producers were substantial, as businesses rushed to introduce computer systems. In particular, the wages of computer programmers and technicians were high because there was a relative scarcity of workers possessing the skills necessary to use and produce computers. High demand and relative scarcity mean high wages. However, high wages are also an excellent piece of information that may encourage changes that ultimately lower wages. From the 1960s to the present, many schools teaching computer technology have emerged, reducing the scarcity of this resource. Demand for computer technology, however, has grown over time. The wages for people supplying services essential to production depend on consumers' demand for computers and on price(wage)-signaled supply conditions in the market for these services.

The informative signals of a price system work whether goods have short or long lives. The prices formed in both product and resource markets reflect the relative desires of consumer-demanders for particular goods and services as well as the relative scarcity of the resources required to produce them. The very fact that a product or service bears a price means that scarcity exists. Supply and demand in all markets is at the core of scarcity and, therefore, of economics.

Full versus Money Prices

A distinction must be made about prices resulting from the forces of supply and demand: There is a difference between the **money price** of a product or service and the **full price**. Consider the money price of a haircut for which the customer pays $12.50 in cash. Is this the full price of a haircut?

Money price is often not the only cost to consumers. In the case of a haircut, we must account for the time spent traveling to and from the salon, the time spent waiting, and the time spent with the hairdresser. The economist accepts the truth of the adage "time is money." Time, like diamonds, is a scarce resource, and it bears an opportunity cost. Time costs are often estimated in terms of the wage rate forgone, the leisure time forgone, or, generally, as the opportunity cost of the consumer's next-best alternative. Thus the full price of a haircut or any other good or service includes the price in money terms plus any other resource costs required in the purchase of the commodity. (See the Focus "Full Price and a New Orleans Restaurant.") Prices as interpreted in the simple model of demand and supply of this chapter are to be regarded as full prices. Consumers react to full prices, not

Money price
The dollar price that sellers receive from buyers; a price expressed in terms of money, not in terms of an amount of another good.

Full price
The total opportunity cost to an individual of obtaining a good; includes money price and all other costs, such as transportation costs or waiting costs.

fOcus
Full Price
and a New Orleans Restaurant

New Orleans is considered a restaurant town by gourmets. Restaurants such as Le Ruth's, Antoine's, Brennan's, and Commander's Palace consistently offer some of the best cuisine to be found anywhere. One of our favorite French Quarter restaurants, however, is Galatoire's. Galatoire's has earned a reputation for producing some of the highest-quality meals in the city. Menu prices, however, have remained low relative to other famous establishments over the past several decades.

Have both menu prices and full prices remained low at Galatoire's? If not, why not? Finally, what evidence might be offered for a real price increase? How would an economist view the matter?

The economist would focus on elements in the full price of a meal at Galatoire's. The restaurant has not enlarged its classic physical plant over the years but, over time, longer and longer lines form outside the door during the day and evening. Galatoire's, unlike most of its competition, does not take reservations and has only recently begun accepting credit cards. Moreover, Galatoire's enforces a dress code—ties or coats for men (evenings and all day on Sundays) and, until a few years ago, dresses (no pants) for women.

All these factors would tend to increase the full price of dining at Galatoire's. There are opportunity costs to waiting for a table (time is a scarce resource); the time and resources spent dressing for dinner are also applicable to the full price. The length of the line at the restaurant can also make the real price higher or lower than anticipated, although diners can form hunches about when the line is apt to be shortest.

These additional costs mean that the full price exceeds the money price printed on the menu. However, the economist must calculate all benefits as well as all costs associated with purchasing products or services. Consider the possibility that some customers get positive benefits from dressing for dinner and from being surrounded by those similarly attired. Others may value the prestige or satisfaction of dining at the legendary restaurant. Such factors would tend to increase the benefits to these consumers. The full price paid for a meal at Galatoire's varies among consumers, depending on opportunity cost. However, all consumers marginally balance the perceived costs of buying products and services with the perceived benefits associated with consumption. When price or price formation is discussed in this book, it is therefore the full price, not the nominal or money price, that is being considered.

money prices. No one, for example, should take an advertisement for "free puppies" or "free kittens" literally. There is no such thing! Do consumers react to the money price of products and services or to what economists call the full price? The theory of supply and demand discussed in this chapter does not explicitly stress the distinction between money prices and full prices. But it is important to interpret even basic supply and demand theory as a theory of full, not money, prices. With this distinction taken into account, the theory of supply and demand forms the foundation for understanding how markets function and, therefore, for understanding the whole science of economics.

THE LAW OF DEMAND

Relative price
The price ratio or "trade-off" in consumption between one product (or service) and another product (or service) or between one good and other goods taken as a whole.

The concept of demand is intuitive. The notion that the amount of goods sold depends on the prices charged seems to "just make sense." The amount of any one good bought during a sale, for example, depends upon the **relative price** of the good on sale—the price in relation to the price of some other good or of goods as a whole. The actual money price of the good in isolation does not determine what

Fast food restaurants reduce the full cost of meals by saving time for college students.

we purchase. If the relative price of a particular pair of shoes declines—that is, the item is put "on sale"—the price has fallen relative to other shoes, shirts, or camcorders. Intuitively, we understand that more of these shoes will be purchased.

Students often complain that explicit treatment of the law of demand in textbooks is absurd because it is so intuitively appealing. But because virtually all analyses of markets are supported by a formal treatment of the law of demand, a formal understanding of what lies behind individuals' demand curves is required. Intuition concerning this critically important idea is not enough. The concept of demand must be made rigorous and scientific.

What determines how much of any good or service—camcorders, compact discs, or hair styling—consumers will purchase during some period of time? Economists have answered that question for hundreds of years in the same manner—by formulating a general rule, or law, of demand. The **law of demand** states that, other things being equal or constant, the quantity demanded of any good or service increases as the price of the good or service declines. In other words, **quantity demanded** is inversely related to the price of the good or service in question.

The relation between price and quantity demanded is a fact of everyday experience. The reaction of individuals and groups to two-for-the-price-of-one sales, cut-rate airline tickets, and other bargains is common proof that quantities demanded increase as prices decrease. Likewise, gas price hikes will lower the quantity of gasoline demanded. The formalization of the inverse relation between price and quantity demanded is called a law because economists believe it is a general rule for all consumers in all markets. Imagine a graphic representation of the law of demand—called a **demand curve**—for two hypothetical consumers.

The Individual's Demand Schedule and Demand Curve

Suppose that we observe the behavior of Dave and Marcia over one month. These two music lovers own compact disc players and are willing and able to purchase,

Law of demand
The price of a product or service and the amount purchased are inversely related. If price rises, then quantity demanded falls; if price falls, quantity demanded increases, all other things held constant.

Quantity demanded
The amount of any good or service consumers are willing and able to purchase at all various prices.

Demand curve
A graphic representation of the quantities of a product that people are willing and able to purchase at all possible prices.

TABLE 3.1

Two Consumers' Demand Schedules

While individuals' demand schedules may differ, they do not violate the law of demand. For both people, the quantity demanded increases as the price falls.

Price of Compact Discs (dollars)	QUANTITY DEMANDED (PER MONTH)	
	Dave	Marcia
20	0	0
19	1	0
18	2	0
17	3	1
16	4	2
15	5	3
14	6	4
13	7	5
12	8	6
11	9	7
10	10	8

or demand, CDs. To determine Dave's and Marcia's demand for CDs, we need only vary the price of discs over the month, assuming that all other factors affecting their decisions remain constant, and observe the quantities of CDs they would demand at the various prices. This information is summarized in Table 3.1.

Table 3.1 shows a range of CD prices available to Marcia and Dave over the one-month period and the quantities (numbers) of discs that each would purchase, all other things being equal. Given factors such as their income and the availability of other forms of entertainment, neither person would choose to purchase even a single CD at $20 per disc. Dave, however, would buy one CD per month at $19 and two at $18. Marcia would not buy her first CD until the price was $17. Each would purchase more discs as the price falls. Thus, Dave's and Marcia's CD-buying habits conform to the law of demand.

We obtain the individuals' demand curves by plotting or transferring the information from Table 3.1 to the graphs in Figure 3.2. The prices of CDs are given on the vertical axis of each graph, and the quantities of CDs demanded per month are given on the horizontal axis. The various combinations of price and quantity from Table 3.1 are plotted on the graphs. Each demand curve is then drawn as the line connecting those combinations of price and quantity. For both Dave and Marcia, the demand curve slopes downward and to the right (a negative slope), indicating an increase in quantity demanded as the price declines and a decrease in quantity demanded as the price rises.

Factors Affecting the Individual's Demand Curve

Factors affecting demand Anything other than price, such as consumer income and preferences, that determines the amount of a product or service that consumers are willing and able to purchase.

In addition to the price of a good or service, there are dozens, perhaps hundreds, of other factors and circumstances affecting a person's decision to buy or not to buy. These **factors affecting demand** include income, the price of related goods, price expectations, income expectations, tastes, the number of consumers, and time.

FIGURE 3.2

Demand Curves for Two Consumers

A consumer's demand for a product is the quantity that he or she is willing to purchase at each price. The demand curve is downward-sloping for both Dave (a) and Marcia (b). As the price falls, the quantity demanded increases; and as the price rises, the quantity demanded decreases.

(a)

(b)

Ceteris paribus
The Latin phrase for "all other things held constant."

HOLDING FACTORS OTHER THAN PRICE CONSTANT To isolate the effect of price on quantity demanded, essential factors must be held constant. We want to know what quantity of CDs Dave and Marcia would choose to purchase in a month at various possible prices, given that other factors affecting their decision do not change. This condition is called **ceteris paribus** ("other things being equal") by economists. It is essential to the development of any economic theory or model dealing with real-world events since all events cannot be controlled. Economists hold factors such as income and the price of related goods constant when constructing a demand schedule or curve.

This does not mean that these factors cannot change, but if they do change, the demand schedule or curve must be adjusted to account for them. Laboratory scientists are in a better position than economists to hold conditions constant. Chemists can perform controlled experiments, but economists, like weather forecasters, deal with a subject matter that can rarely be controlled. Economics, after all, is a social science; it deals with human nature and with people in society. The very subject matter of economics makes most factors affecting demand difficult to control. But like their scientific counterparts, economists must use scientific methods to organize real-world events into theories of how things work. The economist can use these theories to predict some of the effects on the demand schedule of changes in factors other than price.

Change in quantity demanded
A change in the amount of a good a consumer is willing and able to purchase that is caused by a change in the price of the good or service.

CHANGES IN DEMAND VERSUS CHANGES IN QUANTITY DEMANDED
A simple but crucial distinction exists between a change in Dave's or Marcia's demand for CDs and a **change in quantity demanded** of CDs for Dave or Marcia. Other things being equal, a change in the price of CDs will change the quantity

FIGURE 3.3

Increase in Quantity Demanded

Holding Marcia's demand constant, a decrease in the price of CDs from $14 to $13 will lead to an increase in the quantity of CDs demanded from 4 to 5 per month.

FIGURE 3.4

Decrease in Quantity Demanded

Holding Marcia's demand constant, an increase in the price of the CDs from $14 to $16 will cause Marcia to decrease the quantity of CDs demanded from 4 to 2 per month.

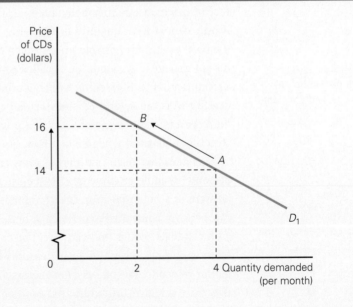

demanded of CDs, as we have seen. Figures 3.3 and 3.4 illustrate an increase and a decrease in quantity demanded, respectively. The graphs illustrate a movement along a single demand curve, indicating that factors like buyers' incomes and preferences are held constant. Figure 3.3 shows that a decrease in the price of discs leads to an increase in the quantity demanded. Figure 3.4 shows that an increase in the price of discs reduces the quantity demanded. A change in any factor other

FIGURE 3.5

Increase in Demand

A change in any factors affecting demand causes a shift to the right or left in the demand curve. In this case, Marcia's income increases, causing an increase in her quantities demanded for CDs at every price. The demand curve shifts to the right. At a price of $14 per disc, Marcia previously would purchase 4 CDs, but given her increased income, she would now purchase 8 CDs.

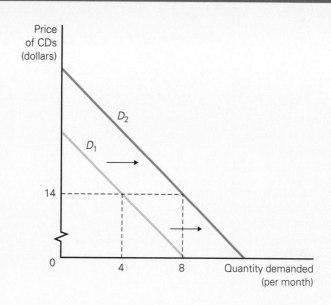

Change in demand
A shift of the entire demand curve to the right or left.

Normal good
A good that a consumer chooses to purchase in smaller (larger) amounts as income falls (rises).

Inferior good
A good that a consumer chooses to purchase in smaller quantities as income rises or in larger amounts as income falls.

than the price will shift the entire demand curve to the right or left. Economists call this a **change in demand**. An increase in demand is shown as the rightward shift of the entire demand curve in Figure 3.5. A decrease in demand, shown in Figure 3.6, is a leftward shift of the entire demand curve.

CHANGE IN INCOME   Marcia's or Dave's income may change, and such a change would necessitate a redrawing of the entire demand curve for CDs. For most goods, a rise in income means an increase in demand. For instance, if Marcia's income increases from $1500 to $2000 a month, she will demand more CDs at every price because she can afford more. Figure 3.5 shows that, given a new, higher income, Marcia's demand curve shifts to the right for every price of CDs. When demand increases, quantity demanded increases at every price.

Although the theory that rising income means greater demand for goods holds true for most goods, it does not apply to all goods. Economists distinguish between normal goods and inferior goods. **Normal goods** are those products and services for which demand increases (decreases) with increases (decreases) in income; the demand for **inferior goods** actually decreases (increases) with increases (decreases) in consumers' income. Joe's demand for Honda automobiles may decrease as his income increases; a Honda automobile is an inferior good to him. Beth purchases less Haagen-Dazs vanilla ice cream as her income falls, indicating that Haagen-Dazs ice cream is a normal good for her.

The terms *normal* and *inferior* contain no implications about intrinsic quality or about absolute standards of goodness or badness. Indeed, a good or service that is normal for one consumer in a given income range may be inferior for another consumer in the same income range. It is even possible for a good to be normal for an individual consumer at certain levels of income and inferior at

FIGURE 3.6

Decrease in Demand

A leftward shift of the demand curve indicates a decrease in demand. In this case, the price of a substitute good decreased, causing Dave to demand fewer discs at every price. The demand curve shifts to the left. Before the price change in the substitute good, Dave would purchase 5 CDs at $15 each, but given the change in the substitute good's price, he would purchase only 2 CDs at $15 each.

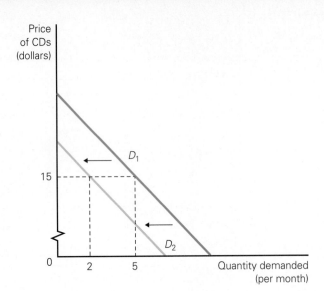

other levels. As one's income rises, for example, hamburgers or compact cars may change from normal to inferior. We will discuss this distinction in more detail later, but it is important to note that a change in income will produce a shift in the demand curve.

PRICES OF RELATED GOODS   Suppose that the price of a good closely related to CDs—such as cassette tapes or CD players—changes during the month for which Dave's and Marcia's demand curves are drawn. What happens? Clearly, one of the assumptions about other things being equal has changed, and the demand curve will shift right or left depending on the direction of the price change and on whether the closely related good is a **substitute** for or a **complement** to the product under consideration.

Suppose that other forms of entertainment can substitute for CDs in Dave's or Marcia's budgets. If ticket prices for movies or tape prices decline during the month, the demand curve for CDs for both consumers would shift to the left; that is, the demand for CDs would decline. For every price of CDs, the quantity demanded would be lower. This shift is represented in Figure 3.6. If the price of a substitute good increased during the month, the demand for CDs would increase.

If the price of a good or service complementary to CDs rises or falls, the demand curve for CDs would shift. Such a complementary good or service might be compact disc players for home or auto. If the price of the complement increases, the demand for CDs would decrease (shift left). If the price of the complement decreases, demand for CDs would increase (shift right).

OTHER FACTORS SHIFTING THE DEMAND CURVE   A number of factors other than income and the price of related goods can cause a shift in the demand

Substitutes
Products that are related such that an increase in the price of one will increase the demand for the other or a decrease in the price of one will decrease the demand for the other.

Complements
Products that are related such that an increase in the price of one will decrease the demand for the other or a decrease in the price of one will increase the demand for the other.

curve. Among these are consumers' price and income expectations and consumers' tastes. If the price of CDs or the income of consumers is expected to change in the near future, the demand for CDs during the month will be altered. Marcia may discover during the month that she will receive an inheritance. The basis under which her original demand curve was derived changes because she anticipates a change in income. Or back-to-school CD sales might be announced for August during the middle of July, causing a decrease in demand during July. Likewise, any alteration in the time period under examination—changing from a month to a day, week, or year—will alter the construction of the demand curve. A purchase of four pizzas per month at a price of $6.95 each would be represented differently than a weekly consumption of one pizza. A change in the time period requires a redrawing of the demand curve. Also held constant is the quality of the good or service. Changing the amount of ice in a 10-ounce soft drink, for example, will alter the quality of the drink. The change in quality will alter quantity demanded at any price.

Reviewing the Law of Demand

The demand curve expresses an inverse relation between the price of a good and the quantity of the good demanded, assuming that a number of factors affecting demand are held constant. As price rises, quantity demanded falls; as price falls, quantity demanded rises. When any of the other factors affecting demand change, we must reevaluate the demand schedule and curve. In general, we identify only the most important factors affecting demand curves. If we have missed some important factor affecting demand—the muffler on Dave's car unexpectedly falls off in the middle of the month, for example—that factor must be accounted for in analyzing demand.

Economists predict that individuals (and collections of individuals), all things being equal, will purchase more of any commodity or service as its price falls. To verify this prediction, the individuals in question do not even have to be fully aware of their behavior; they need only act in the predicted manner. Individuals' response to sales of any kind—they buy more when price declines—is evidence that a general and predictable law of demand exists. That law is a fundamental tool of economists' analyses of real-world events.

From Individual to Market Demand

Market demand

The total amount consumers are willing and able to purchase of a product at all possible prices, obtained by summing the quantities demanded at each price over all buyers.

While an individual's demand curve is sometimes of interest, economists most often focus on the **market demand** for some product, service, or input such as automobiles, intercontinental transport, or farm labor. Market demand schedules are simply the summation of all individual demand schedules at alternative prices for any good or service. An increase in the number of consumers increases the market demand curve and a reduction decreases market demand. The key is to add up the quantities demanded by all consumers at alternative prices for the good or service in question.

We can use the CD demand example to understand market demand. We constructed individual demand schedules for Dave and Marcia by varying the price and observing the quantities of discs that they would buy at those prices, other

TABLE 3.2

Market Demand Schedule

The total market demand for a product is found by summing the quantities demanded by all consumers at every price.

Price of CDs (dollars)	QUANTITY DEMANDED (PER MONTH)			
	Dave	Marcia	All Other Consumers	Total Market Quantity Demanded
20	0	0	0	0
19	1	0	39	40
18	2	0	78	80
17	3	1	116	120
16	4	2	154	160
15	5	3	192	200
14	6	4	230	240
13	7	5	268	280
12	8	6	306	320
11	9	7	344	360
10	10	8	382	400

things being equal. To determine the market demand schedule we simply observe the behavior of all other consumers in the same market situation.

Table 3.2 begins with the data on Dave's and Marcia's demand from Table 3.1. The table also contains a summary of quantity demanded for all other consumers at every price and, finally, the total quantity demanded for all consumers, or the total market demand. At a price of $20 no one, including Dave and Marcia, wants to buy CDs. At a slightly lower price, $19 per disc, Marcia does not choose to buy, but Dave and 39 other consumers buy 1 disc. The total market demand is, therefore, 40 discs at a price of $19. (Note that actual numbers of discs sold to all consumers would be much higher. We use low numbers for simplicity. The important point is that the market demand schedule for CDs or any other privately produced product or service is constructed in precisely this manner.)

The market demand schedules can be represented graphically as market demand curves (see Figure 3.7). Dave's and Marcia's demand curves are repeated from Figure 3.2. The demand of all other consumers, taken from Table 3.2, is plotted in Figure 3.7c. The total market demand, shown in Figure 3.7d, is simply the horizontal addition of the demand curves of Figures 3.7a, 3.7b, and 3.7c.

As in the case of individual demand curves, the market demand curve is downward-sloping (negatively sloped) and drawn under the assumption that all factors other than the price of CDs remain constant. If the incomes of consumers change, or the price of goods or services closely related to CDs is altered, the market demand would shift right or left, as in the case of individuals' demand curves. Economists must focus closely on these related factors in any real-world application. Changes in the demand for any product—compact cars, energy, crude

FIGURE 3.7

Market Demand Curve

The total market demand curve for a product is obtained by summing the points on all the individual demand curves horizontally. This is accomplished by selecting prices and summing the quantities demanded by all individuals to obtain the total quantity demanded at each price.

oil—will be closely related to factors such as income changes and the price of substitutes and complements.

The important concept of market demand summarizes only half of the factors determining and affecting prices. Like the cutting blades of a pair of scissors, two sets of factors—demand and supply—simultaneously determine price.

THE LAW OF SUPPLY AND FIRM SUPPLY

Law of supply
The price of a product or service and the amount that producers are willing and able to offer for sale are positively related. If price rises, then quantity supplied rises; if price decreases, then quantity supplied decreases.

Quantity supplied
The amount of any good or service that producers are willing and able to produce and sell at some specific price.

Supply curve
A graphic representation of the quantities of a product or service that producers are willing and able to sell at all possible prices.

The **law of supply** states that, other things being equal, firms and industries will produce and offer to sell greater quantities of a product or service as the price of that product or service rises. There is a direct relationship between price and quantity supplied: As price rises, **quantity supplied** increases; as price falls, quantity supplied decreases. The assumption of other things being equal is invoked, as in the case of demand, so that the important relation between price and quantity supplied may be specified exactly. This relation, called a **supply curve**, shows the quantities of any good that firms would be willing and able to supply at alternative prices over a specified time period.

The method for constructing an individual firm's (and the market's) supply schedule is identical to the method we used for individual and market demand. All factors affecting supply except the price of the good or service are held constant. The price of the good or service is varied and the quantities that the firm or the industry will supply are specified.

To see how the supply curve is drawn, we turn to the supply side of CDs. Suppose that there are a number of firms supplying CDs in a given geographic area and that the output per month of two typical firms (Oranges Inc. and Joe's Audio)

TABLE 3.3

Individual Firm and Market Supply Schedules

Individual firms' supply schedules follow the law of supply: As the price of the product increases, the quantity supplied increases. The total market supply is obtained by summing the quantities supplied by all firms at every price.

	QUANTITY SUPPLIED (PER MONTH)			
Price of CDs (dollars)	Oranges Inc.	Joe's Audio	All Other Firms	Total Market Quantity Supplied
20	24	16	410	450
19	21	14	365	400
18	18	12	320	350
17	15	10	275	300
16	12	8	230	250
15	9	6	185	200
14	6	4	140	150
13	3	2	95	100
12	0	0	50	50
11	0	0	0	0
10	0	0	0	0

and all other firms combined is as shown in Table 3.3. The supply schedules of Oranges Inc. and Joe's Audio are given in the table by the combination of price and quantity supplied. That is, given alternative prices of CDs and the assumption that all other things are equal, Oranges Inc. and Joe's Audio specify the quantity of CDs that they would be willing to supply during a one-month period. At a price of $20 per disc, Oranges Inc. would be willing and able to supply 24 discs, but if the price falls to $13 per CD, Oranges Inc. will supply only 3 discs.

As in the case of demand schedules, the information from supply schedules can be graphically expressed as supply curves (see Figure 3.8). The individual supply curves for Oranges Inc. and Joe's Audio conform to the law of supply—other things being equal, as price rises, the quantity supplied increases and as price falls, quantity supplied decreases. Note that the supply curve for the individual firm is sloped upward and to the right. This is because the marginal opportunity cost of resources used for increased CD production rises as more discs are produced. As more CDs are produced, less-adaptable resources are drawn into disc production. To increase the quantity of CDs supplied, a firm may have to enlarge its quarters by buying and converting buildings formerly used for other purposes, incur the costs of hiring and training workers who have never made CDs before, and perhaps redesign its product to use alternative materials as original materials become more scarce. These increases in marginal costs may make it unprofitable for the firm to supply more CDs unless the price of CDs rises.

Change in quantity supplied
A change in the amount of a good a producer is willing and able to produce and sell that is caused by a change in the price of the good or service.

Changes in Quantity Supplied and Shifts in the Supply Curve

As in the case of demand, a change in price will cause a **change in quantity supplied**, indicated by a movement along a given supply curve, and a change in

FIGURE 3.8

Market Supply Curves

The market supply curve of a product is obtained by summing the quantities that will be supplied by the two individual firms and by all other firms at every price. For example, at a price of $17 the total quantity supplied is 300 (15 + 10 + 275).

Change in supply
A shift of the entire supply curve to the right or left.

Factors affecting supply
Anything other than price, such as technology or input costs, that determines the amount of a product or service that sellers are willing and able to offer for sale.

any other factor will cause **a change in supply**, indicated by a shift in the supply curve either right or left. An increase in price will increase the quantity supplied, but a decrease in price will reduce the quantity supplied. The supply curve is positively sloped—upward and to the right—and, as we saw, the demand curve is negatively sloped—downward and to the right. When **factors affecting supply**—that is, factors other than the price of the good—change, the whole supply curve shifts.

CHANGES IN COST OF PRODUCTION   The most important influence on the position of the supply curve is the cost of producing a good or service. The price of resources—labor, land, capital, managerial skills—may change, as may technology or production or marketing techniques peculiar to the product. Any improvement in technology or any reduction in input prices would increase supply; that is, it would shift the supply curve to the right.

Suppose that the price of plastic materials used in compact disc construction falls or that the wages of salespeople available to CD stores decline. As the production or sales costs to firms producing and selling CDs decline, the quantity supplied increases and the supply curve shifts to the right for every price of CDs. An increase in supply is shown in Figure 3.9a. At price P_0, the firm was willing to supply quantity Q_0 of discs when the supply curve was S_0. After the firm (and all other firms) experiences a reduction in costs, the supply curve shifts rightward to S_1, indicating a willingness to supply a quantity Q_1 at price P_0. An improvement in production or sales techniques or a reduction in the price of some resource shifts the supply curve to the right. A decline in production or sales or an increase in any input cost shifts the supply curve to the left, as shown in Figure 3.9b.

FIGURE 3.9

A Shift in the Supply Curve

As factors other than price change, the supply curve shifts. When input costs fall, the quantity supplied increases from Q_0 to Q_1 at the price P_0, shifting the supply curve to the right from S_0 to S_1. An increase in input costs causes a decrease in quantity supplied from Q_0 to Q_2 and the supply curve shifts to the left, from S_0 to S_2.

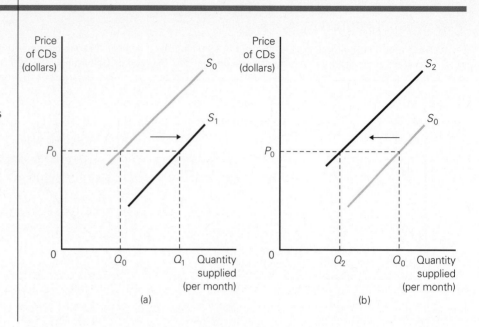

OTHER DETERMINANTS OF SUPPLY   Factors other than cost of production changes can affect the location of the supply curve. One such factor is changes in producer-seller price expectations. The supply curve, like the demand curve, is drawn for a certain time period. If expectations of future prices change drastically in a market—for example, prices of the good or service are expected to rise suddenly—suppliers would withhold current production from the market in anticipation of higher prices. The current supply would be reduced, causing the supply curve to shift to the left, as in Figure 3.9b.

One other factor deserves mention. The supply curve is drawn for a given time period. A change in the time period (from one month to one week or one year) will alter the dimensions of the supply curve; it must be redrawn if the time period changes.

Market Supply

Market supply
The total amount producers are willing and able to offer for sale of a product at all possible prices, obtained by summing the quantities supplied at each price over all producers.

Market supply is simply the addition of all firms' quantities supplied for every price. If the number of firms in a given market increases or decreases, the supply curve would increase or decrease accordingly because the market supply curve is constructed by adding all the supply curves of individual firms. The market supply of CDs represented by the price-quantity combinations of the first and last columns of Table 3.3 is plotted in Figure 3.8d. The market supply curve is obtained by plotting the total quantities of CDs that would be produced and sold at every price during the time period. Note that market supply is simply the horizontal summation of all of the individual supply curves. For example, at a price of $14, quantity supplied would be 6, 4, and 140 units of CDs, respectively, from the three suppliers depicted in Table 3.3 and Figure 3.8. Thus the market supply of CDs at a price of $14 is 6 + 4 + 140 = 150.

The market supply curve is positively sloped—that is, total quantity supplied increases with increases in price—because the real marginal opportunity cost of CD production rises as more discs are produced. Resources become more costly as more and more inputs are diverted from other activities into CD production.

MARKET EQUILIBRIUM PRICE AND OUTPUT

Market
The interaction of buyers and sellers producing and buying goods and services. Prices tend toward equality in a market through the continuous exchange between suppliers and demanders.

Perfect market
A market in which there are enough buyers and sellers that no single buyer or seller can influence price.

Law of one price
In perfect markets, the market forces of supply and demand produce a single, equilibrium price for a good or service.

We now put the concepts of supply and demand together to understand how market forces work to establish a particular price and output. A **market** is any area in which demand and supply prices of products or services tend toward equality through the continuous interactions of buyers and sellers. Competitive (self-interested) forces of both buyers and sellers guarantee this result. All other things being equal, a buyer of dog food will always choose the seller with the lowest price, whereas a seller will choose if possible to sell at higher prices. Buyers will not pay more than price plus transportation costs, and sellers will not take less. There will always be a tendency to one price.

In a **perfect market**, both buyers and sellers are numerous enough that no single buyer or seller can influence price. In addition, buyers and sellers are free to enter or exit the market at any time. In this case of perfect competition, no single seller sells enough of the commodity and no buyer buys enough of the product or service to influence price or quantity. Each party to exchange has complete information. In a perfect market the **law of one price** holds: After the market forces of supply and demand, of buyers and sellers, are at rest or in equilibrium, a single price for a commodity (accounting for transportation and other costs) will prevail. If a single price did not prevail, someone could get rich by buying low and selling at a higher price, thereby driving prices to equality. The self-interested, competitive forces of buyers and sellers acting through supply and demand guarantee this important result.

The Mechanics of Price Determination

Price and output are determined in a market by the simple combination of the concepts of supply and demand already developed in this chapter.

TABULAR ANALYSIS OF SUPPLY AND DEMAND   Table 3.4 combines the data on the market supply and demand for compact discs and contrasts the quantities supplied and quantities demanded at various prices. The numbers used in Table 3.4 come from Tables 3.2 (market demand for CDs) and 3.3 (market supply of CDs). The principles discussed here apply to supply and demand functions in any market.

Consider a price of $20 for CDs in Table 3.4. At the relatively high price of $20, the quantity of discs supplied would be 450 while quantity demanded would be zero. That is, suppliers would be encouraged to supply a large number of CDs at $20, but consumers would be discouraged from buying CDs at that high price. If a price of $20 prevailed in this market, even momentarily, a **surplus** of 450 CDs would exist and would remain unsold on the sellers' shelves.

Surplus
The amount by which quantity supplied exceeds quantity demanded at a price above the equilibrium price.

These unsold inventories of CDs would create a competition among sellers to rid themselves of the unsold discs. In this competition sellers would progressively lower the price. Consider Table 3.4 and assume that the price is lowered to $17. At $17 the quantity supplied of discs is 300, while the quantity demanded is

TABLE 3.4

Market Supply and Demand

The equilibrium price is established when quantity supplied and quantity demanded are equal. Prices above equilibrium result in surpluses; prices below equilibrium result in shortages.

Price (dollars)	Quantity of CDs Supplied (per month)	Quantity of CDs Demanded (per month)	Surplus (+) or Shortage (−)
20	450	0	450 (+)
19	400	40	360 (+)
18	350	80	270 (+)
17	300	120	180 (+)
16	250	160	90 (+)
15	200	200	0
14	150	240	90 (−)
13	100	280	180 (−)
12	50	320	270 (−)
11	0	360	360 (−)
10	0	400	400 (−)

120—a surplus of 180. Only when the price falls to $15 per CD is there no surplus in the market.

Now consider a relatively low price: $13 per CD. As the hypothetical data of Table 3.4 tell us, the quantity demanded of CDs at $13 would far exceed the quantity that sellers would willingly sell or produce. There would be a **shortage** of 180 CDs—that is, 280 minus 100. Clearly some potential buyers would be unable to buy CDs if CD prices remained at $13. However, some buyers would be willing to pay more than $13 per CD rather than go without music. These buyers would bid CD prices up—offer to pay higher prices—in an attempt to obtain the product.

As the price bid by buyers rises toward $15, sellers will be encouraged to offer more CDs for sale; simultaneously, some buyers will be discouraged (will buy fewer CDs) or drop out of the market. For instance, at a price of $14 per disc, sellers would sell 150 CDs while buyers would demand 240, creating a shortage of 90 CDs. The shortage would not be eliminated until the price reached $15.

Equilibrium price in this market is $15; equilibrium quantity is 200 compact discs supplied and demanded. At this price there is neither a shortage nor a surplus. A price of $15 and a quantity of 200 is the only price-output combination that can prevail when this market is in equilibrium—that is, where quantity demanded equals quantity supplied. The very existence of shortages or surpluses in markets means prices have not adjusted to the self-interest of buyers and sellers. Equilibrium means "at rest." In economic terms, equilibrium is that price-output combination in a market from which there is no tendency on the part of buyers and sellers to change. It is the price-output combination that clears the market. The free competition of buyers and sellers leads to this result.

Shortage
The amount by which quantity demanded exceeds quantity supplied at a price below the equilibrium price.

Equilibrium price
The price at which quantity demanded is equal to quantity supplied; other things being equal, there is no tendency for this price to change.

FIGURE 3.10

Equilibrium Price and Quantity

The equilibrium price is established at the point where the demand and supply curves intersect. At this price, quantity demanded equals quantity supplied. At prices below equilibrium, the quantity demanded exceeds the quantity supplied, and the price is bid upward. At prices above equilibrium, the quantity supplied exceeds the quantity demanded, and the price is bid downward.

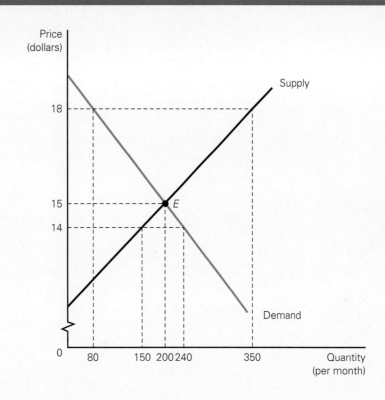

GRAPHIC REPRESENTATION OF SUPPLY AND DEMAND   The most common and useful method of analyzing the interaction of supply and demand is with graphs. Figure 3.10 displays the information of Table 3.4 in a graph that combines the market demand curve of Figure 3.7d with the market supply curve of Figure 3.8d.

The interpretation of Figure 3.10 is identical to the interpretation of Table 3.4, but the point of equilibrium is pictured graphically. Equilibrium price and quantity for CDs is established at the intersection of the market supply and demand curves. The point where they cross is labeled E for *equilibrium.* At equilibrium, both demanders and suppliers of CDs are mutually satisfied. Any price higher than $15 causes a surplus of CDs; that is, a higher price eliminates some demanders and includes more suppliers. Any price below $15 eliminates some suppliers and includes more demanders, resulting in a shortage of CDs.

The theory of supply and demand is one of the most useful abstractions from the world of events that is available to economists. Here we will discuss a few of the implications of supply and demand for society and for public policy.

Price Rationing

Prices, which are formed through the interaction of supply and demand, are **rationing** devices. Scarce resources are channeled to those who can produce a desired product in the least costly fashion for the demanders who most desire the product. Another way of saying this is that resources flow to their most highly valued uses.

Rationing
The allocation of goods among consumers with the use of prices. The equilibrium price rations the limited amount of a good produced by the most willing and able suppliers, or sellers, to the most willing and able demanders, or buyers.

Consider our hypothetical market for compact discs again. Suppliers who are able and willing to produce or sell CDs at a cost below $15 (including a profit) are "successful" in that their discs will be purchased. Demanders who are willing and able to purchase CDs at a price at or above $15 are the successful buyers of CDs. Only the most able sellers and buyers of CDs are successful in this market. High-cost producers (above $15) and buyers with a low preference for CDs (below $15) are eliminated from the market. CDs and all other goods are rationed by a price system—by the free interplay of supply and demand. In such a theoretical system no conscious attempt is made by any organization (such as government) to allocate scarce resources on the basis of factors such as presumed need, eye color, morals, skin color, or ideas of justice. As such, the market system plays no favorites. A price rationing system ensures that only the most able suppliers and demanders participate in markets. All consumption decisions are made by individuals themselves.

Effects on Price and Quantity of Shifts in Supply or Demand

Both individual and market supply and demand functions are constructed by assuming that other things are equal. What happens if other things do not remain equal? We can summarize these other factors and indicate their influence on equilibrium price and quantity in any market obeying the law of one price.

DEMAND SHIFTS   Any change in a factor other than the price of a good will alter the basis on which a demand curve is drawn; that is, it will shift the curve left or right. (Remember the difference between a change in demand, which is caused by a change in other factors, and a change in quantity demanded, which is caused by a change in price.) When demand changes, equilibrium price and quantity move in the same direction.

These facts can be seen graphically in Figure 3.11. Factors causing an increase in demand will have the effects on price and quantity shown in Figure 3.11a. An increase in demand shifts the whole demand curve rightward from D_0 to D_1. A shortage appears at price P_0. All the self-interested market forces that we discussed earlier now come into play. Demanders bid price up to P_1, where additional quantities are supplied by firms and where a new equilibrium, E_1, is established. Thus, an increase in demand has the effect of increasing the equilibrium price and the quantity of the product demanded and supplied. A decrease in demand causes the demand curve to shift leftward (Figure 3.11b). This has the effect of reducing equilibrium price and quantity demanded.

SUPPLY SHIFTS   Any increase or decrease in a factor such as resource prices or price expectations will cause increases or decreases in the whole supply schedule. Effects of such changes are shown graphically in Figure 3.12.

Figure 3.12a shows the effects on price and quantity of an increase (rightward shift) in the supply schedule. At price P_0 a surplus is created and self-interested competitive firms and buyers bid price down to P_1. Note, however, that while equilibrium price decreases, equilibrium quantity increases from Q_0 to Q_1. A price decline from P_0 to P_1 means that an additional quantity of the product or service will be demanded by consumers. Figure 3.12b shows the effects on price and quantity

FIGURE 3.11

Shifts in the Demand Curve

(a) An increase in demand from D_0 to D_1 will increase equilibrium price and equilibrium quantity. (b) A decrease in demand from D_0 to D_1 will decrease both equilibrium price and quantity.

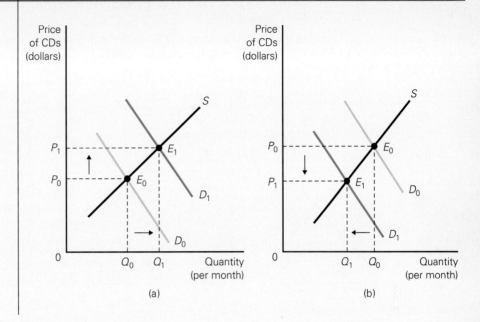

(a)   (b)

FIGURE 3.12

Shifts in the Supply Curve

(a) An increase in supply from S_0 to S_1 will lower the equilibrium price and increase the equilibrium quantity. (b) A decrease in supply from S_0 to S_1 will increase the equilibrium price and lower the equilibrium quantity.

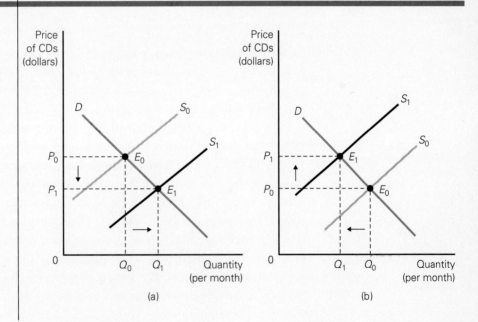

(a)   (b)

of a factor that decreases the supply curve (shifts it leftward). A decrease in supply has quantity-decreasing (from Q_0 to Q_1) but price-increasing (P_0 to P_1) effects, as Figure 3.12b shows. With supply shifts, unlike demand shifts, equilibrium price and quantity change in opposite directions.

SHIFTS IN BOTH SUPPLY AND DEMAND   In the previous two sections, we have examined the effects of shifts in either the demand curve or the supply curve. We now consider the effects of simultaneous shifts in both curves. If both

FIGURE 3.13

Simultaneous Demand and Supply Increases

An increase in demand and supply will result in an increase in equilibrium quantity, but could cause an increase, a decrease, or no change in equilibrium price. Thus the price change is said to be indeterminate.

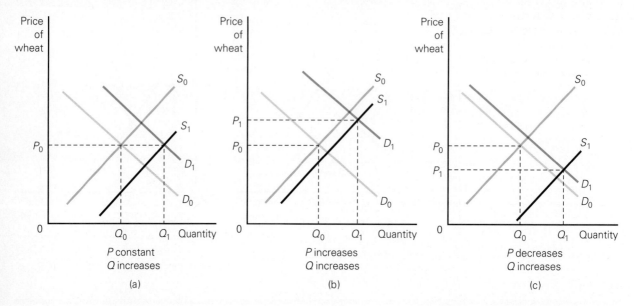

curves shift simultaneously, changes in both equilibrium price and quantity are possible, but the direction of change for only one of the two can be predicted. To see why this is true, we turn to a new example. Each of the three parts of Figure 3.13 shows the initial positions of demand (D_0) and supply (S_0) of U.S. wheat. The initial equilibrium price in each part is P_0. An increase in the number of U.S. farmers who grow wheat would cause the supply curve in each part to shift from S_0 to S_1. If demand for wheat remained unchanged, the increase in supply would unambiguously lead to a decline in the equilibrium price to some level below P_0. Suppose, however, that during the same time period that supply increases, Russia arranges to purchase a large amount of U.S. wheat, which leads to increased demand. In each part of Figure 3.13, the increase in demand is depicted as a shift from D_0 to D_1. The new equilibrium points occur where D_1 intersects S_1. Comparing each new equilibrium with each old one reveals that the equilibrium quantity has increased in each case. Since both increases in demand and increases in supply lead to higher equilibrium quantities, simultaneous increases in supply and demand also lead to higher equilibrium quantities. However, it is impossible to predict what will happen to the equilibrium price when both supply and demand increase. The increase in demand will raise the equilibrium price, but the increase in supply will lower it. The final result depends on the relative size of the change. As shown in Figure 3.13b, the equilibrium price will increase if the increase in demand is greater than the increase in supply. The equilibrium price will decrease, however, if the increase in demand is smaller than the increase in supply (see

FIGURE 3.14

A Simultaneous Increase in Demand and Decrease in Supply

An increase in demand and a decrease in supply will always produce an increase in equilibrium price. Quantity change, however, will depend on the relative sizes of the shifts.

Figure 3.13c). Figure 3.13a shows that no change at all in the equilibrium price occurs when supply and demand increase by the same amount.

Because both decreases in demand and decreases in supply tend to lower equilibrium quantities, simultaneous decreases in supply and demand will also lead to lower equilibrium quantities. As is true with simultaneous increases in supply and demand, the effect of simultaneous decreases in supply and demand on equilibrium price depends on the sizes of the changes.

Suppose an increased demand for U.S. wheat occurs simultaneously with a decreased supply of U.S. wheat—perhaps due to a drought in the Midwest or a rise in the price of inputs used in wheat production. The decrease in supply is shown in each part of Figure 3.14 as a shift from S_0 to S_1; the increase in demand, as a shift from D_0 to D_1. Since an increase in demand (with no change in supply) will always have a price-increasing effect and a decrease in supply (with no change in demand) will always have a price-increasing effect, equilibrium price will always rise with increased demand and decreased supply. However, the equilibrium quantity may remain constant (Figure 3.14a), rise (Figure 3.14b), or fall (Figure 3.14c), depending on the relative sizes of the shifts. If the decrease in supply is large relative to the increase in demand, equilibrium output declines; if the decrease in supply is small relative to the demand increase, equilibrium output increases.[1]

---

[1] Note that it is also possible for demand decreases to be accompanied by supply increases. In such cases, the equilibrium price declines. The change in the equilibrium quantity, if any, will be determined by the relative sizes of the supply and demand shifts.

Milk price floors and subsidies established by dairy interests in Congress have long kept the price of milk above equilibrium in the United States.

SIMPLE SUPPLY AND DEMAND ANALYSIS: SOME FINAL CONSIDERATIONS

Many real-world events—new entrants into markets, oil price increases, new computer technology—can be analyzed using the simple laws of supply and demand. Some seemingly unrelated events also affect supply and demand. The theory of supply and demand is one of the most powerful tools the economist has to analyze the real world. It is important to understand some limitations and some possible applications and extensions of the simple mechanics described in this chapter.

Price Controls and Public Choice

As we have seen, a major effect of the free interplay of supply and demand is the rationing of scarce goods by a system of prices. One of the best ways to understand price rationing and its usefulness is to examine what happens when government intervenes with regulation in freely functioning markets. One such intervention into the natural functioning of supply and demand is called a **price control**. Rent controls, price controls, agricultural price supports, usury laws (controls on interest rates), and numerous other policies are examples of such tinkering in free markets. The expression "government intervenes" in markets is, of course, an expression for "self-interested groups intervene." In reality the principles of public choice explain how all of these interventions take place within our economy at various levels of government. Self-interested groups vie for such regulations which may be set up at any level of government. Rent controls, which in most countries are an urban phenomenon, are created when some groups—those that would benefit from legally controlled rents—are strong enough politically to have them enacted. Farm subsi-

Price control

The setting, by government, of a price in a market different from the equilibrium price.

FIGURE 3.15

A Shortage Caused by a Price Ceiling

When the price of wheat is not allowed to rise above $5 per bushel, quantity demanded exceeds quantity supplied, creating a shortage of wheat.

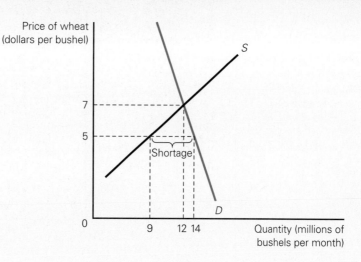

Price ceiling

A form of regulation in which a maximum legal price is established by government above which exchange between buyers and sellers is illegal.

dies or protective tariffs (as we saw in Chapter 2) are enacted at the national level to benefit politically powerful special interests—sugar, peanut, or wheat farmers or steel manufacturers, for example. The basic elements of how this takes place within the political process are discussed in Chapter 4 and we deal with many of these matters elsewhere in the book. But simple supply and demand analysis provides the basis for an initial discussion of the rationing of goods and services by non-price means.

PRICE CEILINGS AND PRICE FLOORS   Imagine a hypothetical market for wheat. The market demand and supply curves are depicted in Figure 3.15. Without government interference, the equilibrium price of $7 per bushel would be reached with 12 million bushels of wheat being bought and sold each month. Government officials could become concerned about the high price of food and impose a **price ceiling** of, say, $5 per bushel. The government is declaring that wheat can be sold only at prices of $5 per bushel or less. While the intent of the legislation is to enable buyers to obtain all the wheat they want at a lower price, Figure 3.15 shows that at the ceiling price of $5 per bushel, the number of bushels that buyers would like to buy (14 million bushels) exceeds the quantity that sellers are willing to sell (9 million bushels) by 5 million bushels. In other words, at the $5 price, there will be a shortage of wheat equal to 5 million bushels. Clearly, the desires of buyers and sellers are not synchronized at that price. Wheat buyers who cannot obtain desired quantities of wheat will offer to pay more than $5 per bushel (in some cases even more than $7 per bushel) rather than go without.

To prevent the price from rising above legal levels, the government must engage in potentially costly enforcement activities. If the government succeeds in preventing illegal price increases, some other means will be used to determine which buyers get wheat. Any number of allocation plans could be used. Sellers could make the wheat available on a first-come, first-served basis, in which case

FIGURE 3.16

A Surplus Caused by a Price Floor

When a price floor above equilibrium price is placed on any commodity, quantity supplied exceeds quantity demanded, creating a surplus of wheat.

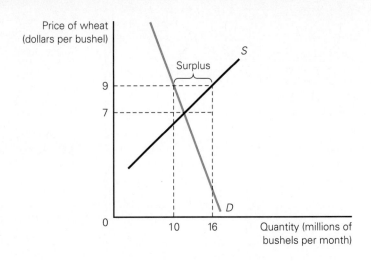

Price floor

A form of regulation in which a minimum legal price is established by government below which exchange between buyers and sellers is illegal.

long lines would form. Consumers could buy wheat at a reduced dollar price, but they would also pay with their time. Alternatively, the government could impose rationing so that each consumer is restricted to buying a fraction (nine-fourteenths) of their desired quantity of wheat. Other possibilities would be for government to establish priority schemes, with some consumers being permitted to buy and others being denied that opportunity. At any price below the equilibrium level there is an insufficient amount of wheat to meet demand, and some non-price rationing scheme must be used to determine who does and does not obtain wheat.

Alternatively, given the same circumstances, government officials might decide that the equilibrium price of $7 per bushel is too low to assure prosperity to wheat growers. They might decide to keep the price of wheat up by imposing a **price floor**—a minimum legal price of perhaps $9 per bushel—on the sale of wheat. Figure 3.16 shows that at $9 per bushel, the quantity supplied of wheat (16 million bushels) exceeds the quantity demanded (10 million bushels) by 6 million bushels. In this case, a surplus of wheat of 6 million bushels exists. Wheat producers would find it difficult to locate buyers at the legal price, and they would have an incentive to reduce the price (in the absence of government enforcement). With effective enforcement, only 10 million bushels will be purchased at $9 per bushel; the government would be forced to use taxpayers' money to buy the surplus.

The U.S. government has supported prices of products such as milk, cheese, and peanuts, and these purchase and storage programs can be costly. This experience also shows why world trade of agricultural products has caused serious disputes among countries. For a variety of reasons, governments in Great Britain, Japan, the United States, and several Western European countries have imposed price floors on various agricultural products. As a consequence, the cost of storing surpluses has grown dramatically. Each of the governments, therefore, is eager to get rid of domestic surpluses by selling in world markets. Simultaneously, each government wants to prevent the inflow of foreign agricultural products. An inflow will force the government to purchase larger quantities of its own product in order to keep the price of the product from falling below the price floor. For example, the Japanese government has a strong incentive to prevent American rice from entering the Japanese market; the U.S. government has an equally strong motive for providing American growers access to Japanese markets.

PRICE CONTROLS AND QUALITY CHANGES   An additional implication of price controls is interesting and relevant to understanding the competitive market process. We have assumed in the foregoing that the quality of goods and services produced remains the same when price controls are established. This is not generally the case.

Consider the deregulation of the U.S. airline industry. Prior to deregulation in the late 1970s, airline fares were controlled (regulated) by the Civil Aeronautics Board, a government agency, at levels above equilibrium. This price floor created a surplus of passenger seats and unfilled airplanes. The reaction of the airlines, since they were by law forbidden to lower airfares, was to alter the quality of passenger air service in an effort to compete. Higher quality is more costly to suppliers, in effect shifting the supply curve to the left. Higher quality is, at the same time, more valuable to consumers, shifting the demand curve to the right. Both effects tend to eliminate the surplus. In the case of airlines, gourmet meals, more frequent flights, and other extras were offered to a pampered flying public. These activities increased the quality of air travel at the controlled fares. Quality competition, which eventually became too costly for airlines and contributed to their deregulation, sidestepped the money price control imposed by the government and effectively lowered the price of air services to customers through increased quality.

Price ceilings also may be avoided through quality changes. New York, Washington, D.C., Los Angeles, and a host of other U.S. cities impose rent controls on apartments and other rental housing. This means that the rental price of these apartments is fixed by law. While such price controls are often enacted to "protect" low-income families, quality changes may often mean lower quality to these groups over time. In some cases, available housing goes to upper-income and well-connected individuals rather than to the poor. When landlord-owners cannot by law raise rents as the demand for housing increases or as the cost of supplying housing rises, equilibrium rents rise above the controlled ones. If these rates are adequately enforced, the available housing will be rationed to housing demanders as a result of the shortage. Since some of the demanders will be willing to pay higher prices than the controlled rate for the lower available quantity of housing, black markets (extralegal markets) may develop. Illegal side payments to landlords, known as "key money," are common in rent-controlled cities.

Another possibility exists, however. If controls are effectively enforced and black markets are prohibited, landlords have little incentive to maintain rental

property. Excess demand for apartments at the controlled price makes it possible to obtain tenants even if the unit deteriorates. Regulations that prevent prices from adjusting to equilibrium levels cause predictable changes in quality. Experience with rent controls in cities as diverse as New York City; Lisbon, Portugal; and Berkeley, California, shows that such programs produce low prices, substandard housing, and the allocation of rent-controlled housing to the well connected and well-to-do. (For a discussion that relates rent controls to student voter activism, see the Application: "Students' Public Choice: The Effects of Rent Controls in College Towns" at the conclusion of this chapter.) Markets can clear at very low prices if quality can be reduced to a sufficiently low level. This type of non-price competition has thwarted the best intentions of many regulators.

APPLICATION
Students' Public Choice: The Effects of Rent Controls in College Towns

Rent controls are a form of price ceiling. They have been a feature of urban life in large cities for many years, but rent controls have also been the result of student participation in the political life of college towns.[a] Imagine that student activists—believing that rents are "too high"—energize the vote in your college town. Let us suppose that market rental rates of $500 per two-bedroom apartment of given quality are considered exorbitant by students. After marches on the mayor's office and a voter registration drive, an election results in council members pledged to enacting rent controls of no more than $350 per two-bedroom apartment. What effect would these controls have on student housing immediately and in the future?

First, suppose that the demand and supply for that type of apartment unit is depicted in Figure 3.17. The equilibrium rent is $500 per month in the figure but, as described above, the city council passes a law prohibiting rents in excess of $350 per month. At a rental rate of $350, quantity demanded exceeds the quantity supplied by Q_d minus Q_s. It is important to note that prior to rent controls, land-

lords found it imperative to maintain the quality of their units at prevailing levels. At the market-clearing price of $500, there were just enough tenants to go around, so a landlord who allowed his units to become run down by lo-

FIGURE 3.17

Rent Controls on Two-Bedroom Apartments

A legal rate of $350 created an excess demand for two-bedroom apartments of quantity AF. The quantity demanded for student apartments at that rate exceeds the quantity supply. The results include a reduction in apartment maintenance and discrimination among prospective tenants.

[a] Rent controls have been a feature of urban life for more than 50 years in New York City, ever since a wartime rent control act was passed as an emergency measure to protect renters from being outbid by transient, high-income workers in war-related industries. The result has been a deterioration of New York's housing stock—especially in certain areas, such as Harlem. The city spends, on average, more than $1 billion each year to renovate dilapidated housing that has been confiscated for nonpayment of back taxes. Another effect of the controls is that rent-controlled housing in desirable neighborhoods—Greenwich Village, for example—tends to remain in the hands of upper-income individuals, whose influence and knowledge of the system allows them to aquire and maintain low rents.

cal standards would find it impossible to keep his units fully occupied unless the rent was reduced below $500.

After rent controls are imposed, it ceases to be necessary to maintain quality in order to prevent vacancies. At a price of $350, there are many prospective tenants seeking apartments, and landlords who allow their units to deteriorate can still obtain tenants. Over a longer time period, landlords have an incentive to allow deterioration—the costs of normal maintenance are high, and yet the unit can be rented at the same price ($350) whether or not it is well maintained. Therefore, we would expect a general decline in the level of maintenance under rent control.

Aspects of this quality adjustment are very relevant for students and other groups rent controls supposedly help. When rent controls are initially imposed, landlords find themselves able to exploit the shortage by picking and choosing among prospective tenants. Therefore, to the extent that the law allows, we would expect certain types of tenants to be excluded—tenants who have pets, tenants who have children, and tenants who are young and unmarried. No landlord wants to rent to four young beer-drinking undergraduates if other tenants are available. Under free-market conditions, many landlords accept such tenants because the alternative is vacant apartments.

The effects of rent control are actually observable in university towns such as Cambridge, Massachusetts, and Berkeley, California. In an attempt to seek revenge on "rent-gouging" landlords, a large student-voter population in Berkeley helped institute rent controls in 1979. Since the controls were put into effect, the population of Berkeley has shifted; there are now fewer blue-collar, older, and poorer people and more upper-income professional and white-collar people than there were prior to rent controls. Although such a demographic shift might have occurred anyway, it seems fairly certain that rent controls accelerated the process. Today's Berkeley students have a difficult time finding apartments because the Class of '79, which helped vote rent controls in, has proved to be extremely skillful at finding and holding onto rent-controlled units as "thirtysomething" professionals. The effects of rent controls have been devastating in many cities—not least because they have greatly damaged the kinds of people they were designed to protect.

SOURCE: William Tucker, "A Model for Destroying a City," *Wall Street Journal* (March 12, 1993), p. A8.

QUESTION

Rent controls are often offered as a solution to the high cost of housing in many cities. How do rent controls damage the people they were designed to help?

SUMMARY

1. The extension of specialization from earlier societies is the modern market society, where individuals and collections of individuals buy and sell—demand and supply—millions of products and services.
2. Demand can be expressed as a schedule or curve showing the quantities of goods or services that individuals are willing and able to purchase at various prices over some period of time, all other factors remaining constant.
3. Supply can be expressed as a schedule or curve showing the quantities that individuals or businesses are willing and able to sell at different prices over a period of time, other factors remaining constant.
4. Equilibrium prices and quantities are established for any good or service when quantity supplied equals quantity demanded. In equilibrium, there is no tendency for price to change.
5. A change in the price of a good or service changes the quantity demanded or quantity supplied along a given demand or supply curve. A change in demand or supply occurs when some factor other than price is altered. When these factors change, the demand or the supply curve shifts to the right or left, either raising or lowering equilibrium price and quantity.
6. Simultaneous shifts of the supply and demand curves have predictable effects on either equilibrium price or equilibrium quantity but not on both.
7. The market system, through supply and demand, rations scarce resources and limited quantities of goods and services among those most willing and able to pay for them. Products and services, moreover, appear and disappear in response to the market system of supply and demand.
8. Price controls instituted by governments tend to create shortages or surpluses of products. Market forces usually result in some form of rationing other than price rationing under such circumstances.
9. Public choice principles suggest that coalitions of interest groups create government regulations and other interventions for their own gain. Price controls of all sorts, including rent controls, subsidies, and protective tariffs are examples of these kinds of interventions.

KEY TERMS

products market	normal good	market
resources market	inferior good	perfect market
money price	substitutes	law of one price
full price	complements	surplus
relative price	market demand	shortage
law of demand	law of supply	equilibrium price
quantity demanded	quantity supplied	rationing
demand curve	supply curve	price control
factors affecting demand	change in quantity supplied	price ceiling
ceteris paribus	change in supply	price floor
change in quantity demanded	factors affecting supply	
change in demand	market supply	

QUESTIONS FOR REVIEW AND DISCUSSION

1. What happens to demand for a product if the price of that product falls? What happens to the quantity demanded?
2. What happens to the supply of coal if the wages of coal miners increase?
3. If income falls, what happens to the demand for potatoes? Are potatoes inferior goods?
4. If price is above equilibrium, what forces it down? If it is below equilibrium, what forces it up?
5. What is a shortage? What causes a shortage? How is a shortage eliminated?
6. If the demand for compact disc players increases, explain the process by which the market increases the production of CD players. What are the costs of CD players?
7. A price ceiling on crude oil has an effect on the amount of crude oil produced. With this in mind, explain what happens to the supply of gasoline if there is a price ceiling on crude oil.
8. What happens to the supply of hamburgers at fast-food restaurants if the minimum wage is increased?
9. What is the full price of seeing a movie? Is it the same for everyone?
10. "Lately the price of gold keeps going up and up, and people keep buying more and more. The demand for gold must be upward-sloping." Does this statement contain an analytical error?
11. What are price controls? When is a price floor imposed? What are some of the consequences of price controls?
12. Do the actions of self-interested coalitions of voters working through the political process help explain price controls? How? Can you think of an example?
13. What happens to the demand for pizza if the price of hamburgers increases? What happens to the demand curve for pizza? What are the effects on the equilibrium price and quantity of pizza?
14. If the price of sugar doubles, what will happen to the supply of regular (nondiet) colas? How will this affect the equilibrium price and quantity of regular colas?
15. Given the scenario in question 14, what will happen to the demand for diet colas? (Hint: Diet and regular colas are substitutes. What effect will this have on equilibrium price and quantity of diet colas?)

PROBLEMS

1. Use the data in the table to answer the following.
   a. Graph the supply and demand curves.
   b. What is the equilibrium price?
   c. What is the equilibrium quantity?
   d. At what price does a shortage of 280 exist?
   e. At a price of $19, how much of a surplus exists?

Price	Quantity Demanded (per month)	Quantity Supplied (per month)
$ 0	400	0
3	340	60
5	300	100
8	240	160
10	200	200
13	140	260
16	80	320
19	20	380

2. Disasters have a way of highlighting economic problems. Consider the hurricane that devastated South Florida in 1992. As Hurricane Andrew approached, the people of South Florida rushed to buy batteries, canned food, and other provisions. Afterward, a number of commodities, including ice, became extremely scarce. Assume that the price of ice was $50 per bag on the day after the storm and answer the following questions given the supply and demand schedule.

a. What is the result of a price ceiling on ice at $30 per bag? Does $30 represent the full price of ice?
b. If the mayor of Homestead, Florida, sets the minimum price of ice at $60 per bag, what type of price control is this?
c. What is the impact on quantities traded at a controlled price of $60 per bag?
d. Draw a graph of the price ceiling at $30 and indicate the shortage.

Price	Quantity Demanded (per month)	Quantity Supplied (per month)
$20	1600	250
30	1400	500
40	1200	750
50	1000	1000
60	800	1250
70	600	1500

CHAPTER 4

DEMAND AND SUPPLY: PROPERTY, MARKETS, AND PUBLIC CHOICE

Private markets, motivated by suppliers and demanders, work ceaselessly to see that some goods get produced and others disappear or never materialize. These markets, as we defined them in Chapter 3, are everywhere—in your local convenience store, when you buy a used car, or when you mail order a Christmas present for someone. These are private markets, not directly affected by government. We also saw, in Chapter 3, how government directly affects how certain markets work—how interferences with the free interplay of supply and demand affects the rationing of scarce goods such as rental housing or agricultural price supports for cotton or peanuts.

The present chapter extends your knowledge of supply and demand to show how government or "the public sector" interacts with and affects private markets. Clearly a role for government is critical in such areas as protecting property and establishing a rule of law. These institutions provide the very framework for free market functioning. Yet another concept—the idea of why economists believe free and competitive markets to be "efficient"—should be mastered before turning to the possible reasons why markets might "fail" or, alternatively, why additional roles might be provided for government. The political context of how decisions get made in the public sector will also help you understand the role and functions of government.

There are obviously many ramifications of government actions in the private economy and we will consider many examples later in this book. But after mastering this chapter you should understand:

- the basic institutions which facilitate markets.
- the nature and efficiency of competitive markets.
- why markets might not function in a competitive fashion, thereby providing a role for government.
- some reasons why public choice (through voting and politics) differs from market choices in affecting the supply of goods and services to people.
- how efficiency might be affected by transfers and regulations granted in political markets.

INSTITUTIONS ARE "RULES OF THE GAME" THAT FACILITATE MARKETS

Economic system
The part of the social system determining what, how, and for whom goods and services are produced.

Pure capitalism
An economic system in which most resources are owned, and most relevant decisions are made, by private individuals.

Pure communism
An economic system in which most productive resources, both human and nonhuman, are publicly owned.

Socialism
An economic system in which most nonhuman productive resources are owned by the state.

Economic efficiency
The allocation of resources that allows maximum benefit to be achieved at minimum cost.

All exchange takes place within the context of some economic system. An **economic system** is the particular form of social arrangements through which the "what to produce," "how to produce" and "for whom to produce" questions are answered. The economic system of any given country is based on the institutions surrounding property ownership, incentives, and decision making that underlie all economic activity in that country.

Systems differ among countries. The extremes are **pure capitalism** and **pure communism**, with **socialism** in between. A society organized along the lines of pure capitalism is one in which government economic control is minimal. Under pure capitalism most resources are privately owned and government's role in the economy is pretty much limited to protecting and enforcing private property rights and to providing national defense and other public goods. Common ownership of both human and nonhuman resources, at the other extreme, typifies pure communism. Socialism, in between these two extremes, is a system in which the state owns some nonhuman productive resources and makes production decisions by planning the economy's output. In reality, of course, all systems that we observe in the world today are "mixed" with elements of each other. The initial "rush to capitalism" in the Russian Republics (after the breakup of the Soviet Union) and in Eastern European countries such as Poland is being rethought, with some communist politicians (if not the system) making a resurgence. Institutions—such as enforceable property rights—must exist to support capitalism and such institutions have been lacking in many parts of Eastern Europe and Russia.

Institutions are therefore the key to understanding the conditions and incentives under which exchange takes place. **Economic efficiency**—producing goods and services at lowest cost and exchanging goods so as to maximize the advantage of all traders—can be discussed only under some given set of institutions. The basic economic "questions" of every society are answerable only under the legal rules that determine rights, ownership, and obligations. The forms of legal institutions regarding contracts, property rights, and their enforcement are central to the attainment of high or low economic efficiency. They virtually guide production, exchange, and consumption in all economies.

Some institutions are so fundamental that they are common to virtually all modern societies. Money and real goods circulate through both (predominately) market-capitalist economies and economies with greater socialist orientations like blood through the veins and arteries of the body. This is important: A common feature to all economic systems is the use of money. The alternative, barter—the exchange of goods for goods—is unbearably cumbersome and costly. For an economic system to take advantage of the kind of specialization discussed in Chapter 2, output must grow steadily. For output to expand, trade must take place at a low cost. The costs of bartering goods are numerous, because the value of each good must be recorded in terms of other goods traded. As the volume of goods traded increases, calculations become overwhelming. Money evolved as a medium of exchange and a unit of accounting. It is a good in terms of which the value of all other goods can be calculated. Money lowers the cost of transacting business and, therefore, is essential to any modern society.

Different societies, in past and present, have created different institutions for the *ownership* and *use* of property, including goods and money. A capitalist economy relies primarily on market forces and the profit motive for production, distribution, and consumption of goods and services. Capitalism is characterized by individual ownership of property, free enterprise, open competition, and (ideally) a minimal role for government. Let us consider each of these features briefly.

Property Rights and Contracts

We exchange property every day. Billions of exchanges—contracts between exchanging parties—take place in the United States alone. Explicitly or implicitly, we make a contract when we supply or demand labor. On the New York Stock Exchange, an average of 200 million shares of stock are traded daily. A purchase of cat food at the supermarket is as much a contract as the agreement by a New Jersey electrical utility to buy a five-year supply of coal from a Montana mine. Throughout the world, in stock and commodity markets, bazaars, shopping centers, and resource markets, literally trillions of contracts are made every day. Property, a bundle of rights, is transferred through contracts in all cases.

Private property

Property that an individual (as opposed to a government) holds the right to control.

In the United States economy the individual's right to own and dispose of property is regarded as basic. In a system of **private property**, the individual (as opposed to government) holds the right to control property. The individual receives the benefits and must pay the costs associated with the use of her property. Property here takes on a wide definition. It includes both physical property (such as houses and computers) and intellectual or intangible property. For example, the ownership of poems, songs, and books by their authors is protected by copyright laws. Inventions are protected by patents. The formal legal apparatus set up to protect such rights may even make a distinction between property and property rights. Rental of a carpet cleaner from U-Rent-Um gives the renter certain property rights over the cleaner but not ownership of the property itself. In all societies, rights to use property are limited. For example, the Environmental Protection Agency has used its legislatively derived power to limit the rights of businesses to pollute air and water and has established worker protection standards (such as

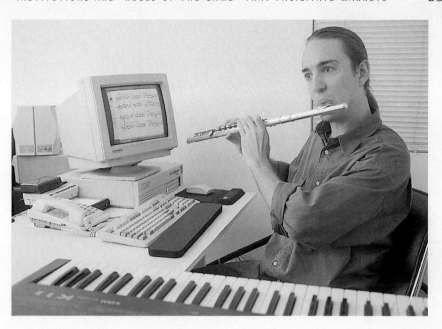

Individuals have rights to their own intellectual property, such as songs, poems, and books, in a market system.

those limiting the use of asbestos) that restrict individuals' free use of property. The real key to understanding the importance of property rights is their link to economic incentives.

Property Rights and Economic Incentives

When we consider the operation of large economies like those of the United States, Japan, Poland, or Russia, we can see how overwhelmingly complex it is to solve basic economic problems. Given the trillions of decisions that must be made and the informational demands of decision makers, it is clear that some kind of idealized economic efficiency in terms of *value produced for scarce resources expended* is unattainable for any kind of society. However, some practical "working" systems are clearly more efficient than others. To attain efficiency, decision makers must have the incentive to make correct economic decisions. That incentive is governed by the legal institutions surrounding property rights. To put the matter more clearly, the assignment of property rights is the key to economic efficiency.

The basic point concerning property and incentives is simple: When property, such as a meadow or whales or owls, is communally owned, no one can exclude others from its use. All members of the community regard the use of the meadow, whales, or owls as "free" and of zero opportunity cost. A rush will be on to exploit the resource, because the marginal opportunity cost and the price of using it is virtually zero. Maximum demand (at a zero price) leads to overutilization and ultimately ruination of the resources. Here private incentives (to get there first and to get as much as one can) conflict with socially desirable incentives (to conserve the resource). This so-called "tragedy of the commons," that is to say, of common property, exists today in the problems generated by common property resources such as fisheries, endangered species, and ill-defined water rights (see the discussion of "externalities" later in the chapter).

Private property, on the other hand, where each individual is permitted to own or exchange property rights as she sees fit, is the key to economic efficiency. You bear the full costs of your decision to use or trade property, but you also receive the full benefits that might result from your decision. Without some guarantees that property rights will be protected, there would be little incentive to accumulate capital stock and, therefore, to grow economically. Without government guarantees of rights to property, individuals would have to protect their own property at high personal cost. Indeed the higher opportunity costs of individual protection as one's property accumulates makes the collective enforcement of property rights through police, courts, and prisons less costly than the total costs of such enforcement to individuals acting separately (such as through the use of mercenaries or posses). In other words, the protection of property rights of citizens is naturally (in economic efficiency terms) a major function of government.

Given the costs and benefits of doing so, buyers and sellers in markets will find it profitable to make contracts and contract terms ever more perfect in terms of incentives and outcomes. A famous historical example drives this point home. One of the greatest reformers of nineteenth century England (akin to modern-day consumer activist Ralph Nader) was Sir Edwin Chadwick (1800-1890).[1] Chadwick once devised a plan for reducing the mortality of British criminals transported to Australia. He noted that the British government paid a flat fee to a ship's captain for each convict who boarded from a British port. The captains quickly discovered that they could maximize their profits by packing on as many prisoners as could be carried without endangering the ship and by minimizing expenditures on prisoner food, drink, and hygiene en route to the colony. The survival rates stood at 40 percent under this incentive system. Humanitarians were outraged at the state of affairs. After a quick assessment of the program, Chadwick changed the payment system so that the ship's captain received a fee for each *live* convict that *disembarked* in Australia. Soon the survival rate increased to 98½ percent. The rule change gave ships' captains incentives to protect the health of the convicts. A new contract arrangement rearranged incentives and created an identity of interest between the public interest (that is, the health and safety of the prisoners) and private interests (that is, the profit of the shipper). Similarly, the design of modern-day contracts in the purely private sector to transfer property rights works toward ever more efficient results—that is, toward more efficient use of scare resources in producing goods and services of highest value to consumers and society.

Private Competitive Markets

Contracting and the exchange of property rights takes place within private competitive markets. American capitalism approximates these conditions. Free competition or **free enterprise** is a primary feature of this world. It is the freedom to pursue one's economic self-interest, with few or no governmental restraints or subsidies and where resources may be combined by businesspeople to produce goods

Free enterprise
Economic freedom to produce and sell or purchase and consume goods without government intervention.

[1] See Edwin Chadwick, "Opening Address," *Journal of the Royal Statistical Society of London* 25 (1862), p. 12. Chadwick was also a pioneer contributor to the economics of crime, the courts, sanitation, and the public supply of utilities and other services. These and a number of other examples are discussed in Robert B. Ekelund, Jr., and Robert F. Hebert, *A History of Economic Theory and Method*, 4th ed. (New York: McGraw-Hill, 1997).

and services for profit. Businesses, consumers, laborers and input owners of all types are free to produce, purchase, and exchange property rights to any good or service provided that their activity does not infringe on others' rights. Individuals are of course constrained by the rule of law concerning the use of property—you cannot drive your auto on the sidewalk, for example. (Bear in mind that participants are also not free of the constraints of limited resources and unlimited wants.)

Within these limits, however, the American economic system is characterized by free competitive markets. This means that, as implied above, property rights are well-defined, enforceable, and tradable. But **competition** implies two other important conditions: There is no collusion among consumers or any other market participants (such as laborers) and all transactors are able to freely enter or exit the market. The self-interested behavior of buyers and sellers will tend to keep the prices of goods and services at a competitive level—that is at the costs of producing the good or service plus a normal profit for the entrepreneur—when these conditions are met.

Under the discipline of private competitive markets, non-collusion means that each seller and each buyer makes decisions about their willingness and ability to sell or buy that are completely independent of the decisions of other sellers or consumers. While this condition does not require large numbers of buyers and sellers, the existence of large numbers virtually guarantees that no individual buyer or seller can affect the market price of a product or service. Many millions of individuals purchase canned soup, for example, but not one buyer purchases enough to affect the market price of the soup. Likewise, the existence of competing suppliers means that no individual seller can acquire enough power to alter the market for his or her gain. Sellers of canned soup are numerous enough that no one seller can affect the price of soup by changing output.

Firms must also be free to enter and leave markets in response to profit opportunities or actual losses. But bankruptcies and business failures are expected consequences of a competitive system (yes, failure of some is an essential feature of competition). New fast-food restaurants open every day in anticipation of profits. Airlines declare bankruptcy and leave the industry—a sure sign of losses. Competition requires that entry and exit into business be free and unregulated.

Actually, coordination of the billions of individual decisions involved in competition is an interconnected system of prices for inputs and outputs that is so complex that no individual or computer can fully comprehend it. We began to study the intricacies of the price system in Chapter 3. Supply and demand explains much about how resources are "efficiently" allocated between the production of CDs, chiropractic services, and home computers. However, we must be able to explain exactly what is meant by economic efficiency.

WHY ARE PRIVATE COMPETITIVE MARKETS EFFICIENT?

Clearly, the protection of private property and a legal system that protects the assignment of property rights are key factors in permitting markets to function. Non-collusive behavior and freedom of entry and exit from the market are two others.

Competition
A market which functions under two conditions—no collusion among sellers or buyers (which occurs with a large number of buyers and sellers) and freedom to enter and exit the market. Competition results in prices equal to the costs of production plus a normal profit for sellers.

Other institutions, some of them provided by government, are critical as well. As we have seen, the provision of a stable money supply and the freedom to use resources in any way we please underlies free competitive markets. These and other factors define what we mean by competitive markets, but why should economists (or anyone else) champion private competitive markets? We must return to the principles of supply and demand learned in Chapter 3 in order to understand *why* private markets are considered "efficient" by economists.

Demanders Value Goods

Markets are the means through which individuals—self-interested demanders and suppliers—help relieve the problems brought on by the scarcity of resources. Economic efficiency means that total value is, in general, maximized in that goods are produced at least cost. Let us see how "value" is calculated and recorded by demanders.

Any demand curve—for an individual or for a whole market—may be given two different but equivalent interpretations. As you learned in Chapter 3, the demand curve indicates the specific amount of some good or service that consumers are both willing and able to purchase *at a given price* per unit of time (of course, holding all other factors affecting demand constant). Market demand is simply the summation of the quantities demanded by all consumers of the good or service at each price.

A demand curve, under certain conditions, may also measure the value that consumers place on a good because it expresses what they are willing and able to sacrifice to obtain it.[2] Consider Figure 4.1, which shows the market demand (taken from Table 3.4) for a competitively produced product—compact discs (CDs). The amount in terms of price that CD demanders are willing to sacrifice in order to obtain discs in Figure 4.1 is a measure of value. Specifically, the demand curve is equivalent to a **marginal private benefit curve**—which represents the value consumers place on the last (marginal) disc under consideration.

Marginal private benefit curve
A curve, equivalent to a demand curve, which represents the value that consumers place on marginal units of the good or service.

Continuing the numerical example from Chapter 3 (see Table 3.4), we may say that the value consumers place on the marginal disc—the 120th disc per month—is $17. The value that consumers would place on fewer discs per month, say the 40th, is $19. Looking at the areas under the demand curve, it is clear that the total expenditure is the quantity purchased times the price of discs (when each unit of discs is purchased at the same price). If the price of a disc, in Figure 4.1, was actually $17, consumers would buy 120 of them. Their total expenditure would be $17 times 120 or $2,040. (In our example, we are keeping numbers simple—a more realistic demand would simply multiply consumers and expenditure by 1,000.)

Clearly the figure—$2,040—represents consumer expenditures on discs. But does it represent value to consumers? The answer is no! The total valuation of the 120 discs is higher than the $2,040 that disc consumers must pay to get them. In fact, consumers are willing and able to pay a good deal more for a given quantity of

[2] This interpretation holds if we assume that consumers are buying a good or service that does not have any external or "third-party" effects, such as would take place if, for example, second-hand smoke had to be accounted for in the consumption of cigarettes. We consider the relevance of these external effects later in the chapter.

FIGURE 4.1

Demand and Marginal Private Benefit Curve

The market demand curve represents the value consumers as a whole place on marginal units of the good. The total value of any quantity produced is the area under the demand or marginal private benefit curve from zero up to that quantity. The difference between what consumers would be willing to pay for the good or service and what they actually pay is called *consumers' surplus*.

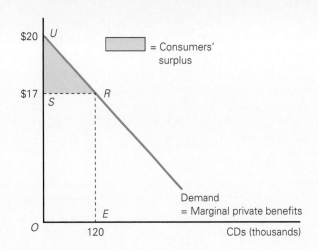

Total consumer valuation
The total amount that consumers are willing to pay for a given quantity of a good or service rather than go without it.

most goods and services rather than not get these goods or services at all. **Total consumer valuation**, is the total amount consumers in the market are willing and able to pay for a given quantity of a good or service rather than go without it. This total value may be shown graphically as the area under the demand/marginal valuation curve from zero quantity (0) out to the quantity under consideration (in this case 120 discs).

In effect, most consumers get a real bargain because they are willing and able to pay more for discs than they must pay for discs. This is *value received but not paid for* by consumers in association with a purchase. For more than a century and a half, economists have known about this surplus and by consensus call it *consumers' surplus*. **Consumers' surplus** is defined as the total valuation consumers place on a given quantity of a good or service *minus* the total cost or expenditure of obtaining the good or service in exchange. If the market demand curve for discs is the one identified in Chapter 3 (in Table 3.4), total expenditures on discs at a price of $17 is $2,040, but consumers get a surplus of the shaded area when they consume 120 of them—this is, the amount they would have spent less what they actually had to spend for 120 discs. The actual value of the surplus going to consumers may also be calculated—it is $180.[3] It is also equal to the shaded area of Figure 4.1 (triangle *SUR*). In general these surpluses exist in all markets for all goods and services—for airline travel, for broccoli, and for school tuition. Thus, the total valuation of consumers (area *OURE* in Figure 4.1) consists of two parts—total expenditures on the good or service (area *OSRE*) and consumers' surplus (area *SUR*). It is the total that consumers would be willing and able to pay for any good or service.

Consumers' surplus
The difference between what consumers are willing to pay for a given quantity of a good or service (the total consumer valuation) and what they have to pay (their total expenditure).

[3]The actual amount of consumers' surplus in dollars may be calculated in the following manner. Note from Table 3.4 that all consumers of discs disappear at a price of $20 per disc. The (shaded) area of Figure 4.1—consumers' surplus—is half a rectangle (that is, a triangle). The rectangle is calculated by the difference between the price consumers must pay ($17) and the price that eliminates consumption of discs altogether ($20) or $3 multiplied by the quantity consumed at a price of $17 or 120 discs. That value is $360 (the rectangle) and half of that—the consumers' surplus—is $180.

FIGURE 4.2

Supply and Marginal Private Costs

Market supply represents the marginal private cost curve showing the opportunity cost of producing additional units of the good or service. The total cost of producing any quantity of the good is equal to the area under the supply curve up to that point (that is, the alternative uses of opportunity cost in terms of resources forgone). Total receipts of sellers less this total cost results in a "producers' surplus" associated with the production of many goods.

Supply, Costs and Value

Recall now our conventional definition of *supply* from Chapter 3. A so-called "law of supply" is the assumption we make concerning the behavior of producers or sellers of some good or service. A seller will be willing and able to sell or produce a larger quantity of a good or service at a higher rather than at a lower price, given all other factors which influence his decision (the *ceteris paribus* assumption). Conversely, any producer or seller would be willing and able to produce and sell smaller quantities of a good or service at a lower price than at a higher price, given all other factors affecting the decision (the *ceteris paribus* assumption again). Other things being equal, as price rises, the quantity supplied of a good or service increases and, as price declines, the quantity supplied decreases. A supply curve, recall, is obtained by summing up the quantities supplied at each price over all producers. A market supply curve, such as the one for compact discs in Figure 4.2, can be thought of as a collection of price and quantity supplied combinations of many individual suppliers. At a price of $13 dollars per disc, suppliers will be willing to put 100 discs per month on the market.

There are other ways to view the supply curve which are correct and equivalent to that above. The market supply curve indicates the minimum price (per unit or per disc in our case) that sellers will be willing and able to receive in order to get them to produce and sell the units of the good or service under consideration. Sellers must receive $13 at a minimum in order to get them to sell 100 discs per month in the example above. We must now recall *why* this is so. Under competitive conditions the supply curve (for any individual seller) is also the marginal cost of the inputs or resources used to produce the discs. These costs are, as we noted in Chapter 3, the marginal opportunity costs associated with any given amount of discs produced. As the quantities of discs produced rises, resources that are less and less adaptable to disc production must be drawn into use, producers

Marginal private cost curve
A curve showing the marginal or additional cost to society—the opportunity cost of scarce resources—of producing additional units of a good or service.

Producers' surplus
The difference between the total revenue to producers from selling a given quantity of a good or service and the total cost to them and to society of using the scarce resources in that particular production.

must enlarge facilities and hire and train workers who have not produced CDs before, and marginal costs may be expected to rise. The opportunity cost of using resources in disc production rises and the rising supply curve reflects this fact. The production of more discs by sellers may become unprofitable if the market price of discs does not rise. When the production of a good or service (discs) does not create third-party or external effects (discussed below), the marginal or additional cost to society is the opportunity cost of the scarce resources used to produce discs. We may call the supply curve the **marginal private cost curve** of producing discs for society.[4]

These points about supply may be illustrated with Figure 4.2. Consider again the price of $13 for discs. At this price 100 discs are produced. The total revenue of all disc sellers is simply the quantity sold times the price, and when the price of discs is $13, total revenue is $1,300 or area *OGHM* in Figure 4.2. But these total revenues are not equivalent to total cost. Total costs are the opportunity costs of all of the productive resources used up in the production process. The total opportunity cost is the sum of all of the marginal opportunity costs of producing 100 discs. Graphically, it is the area under the supply or marginal private cost curve from 0 quantity up to the quantity under consideration. It is, in Figure 4.2, equal to $1,200 or to area *ONHM*.[5]

The difference between total revenue of the producers and the total cost to them (and to society) is called **producers' surplus** (or, sometimes, *factor surplus*). (In dollar terms, producer surplus is $100 in Figure 4.2.) The concept, analogous in some respects to consumers' surplus, is expressed from the point of view of the factors of production that are employed in producing and supplying a good or service (discs in our case). It is the payment received by a factor of production over and above the minimum payment just necessary to induce the factor into the particular use (producing discs). The producers' surplus is equal to the total revenue of the disc sellers minus the total opportunity cost of all of the scarce resources used in producing 100 discs. Through the exchange process, the total revenue of disc sellers is distributed among all of the factors used in making discs. The total revenue of the disc sellers thus represents the total payments to the factors of production in association with producing and selling 100 discs.

Producers' surplus is the difference between the total opportunity cost of all factors—the area under the supply curve—and the total payments received by all the factors of production or the total revenue of disc sellers. That surplus may be well understood by possibly considering your own labor supply. Suppose you work for a local manufacturer and earn $15 dollars per hour for 10 hours per week (a total of $150 per week). This $15 per hour wage is the competitively determined market price of your abilities in this line of work. But suppose that your next best or highest

[4] In the absence of third party effects, the marginal private costs of producing any good or service are also equivalent to the marginal social costs of production.

[5] Note that in Figure 4.2, the total cost of producing 100 discs can be calculated by dividing up the area under the supply curve into two portions—a rectangle with a height of $11 and base of 100 units plus a right triangle with a height of $2 ($13 minus $11) and base of 100. The money amount of producers' surplus is the area formed by the triangle GHN in Figure 4.2. Since the area of the triangle is one-half the area of the rectangle found by multiplying the base (100 units) times the height ($2), the amount of producers' surplus in the example shown in Figure 4.2 is $100.

valued alternative—your opportunity cost—is $8 per hour working 10 hours per week at a local pizza palace (a total of $80 per week). The opportunity cost of the 10 hours is $80 (10 hours times the value of your next best alternative, $8 per hour), but you are actually paid $150. Your producers' surplus is therefore $70 per week.[6]

Just like consumers, then, most producers receive a surplus from supplying production efforts in the marketplace. The marginal producer who produces the last CD in Figure 4.2 just covers his or her opportunity cost of production, which is obviously $13. Every other producer along the supply curve form N to H earns a producer surplus given by the difference that they are actually paid, $13, and their opportunity cost as read off the supply curve. The first resources committed to the production CDs are the most adaptable or lowest cost, and they therefore earn large producer surpluses. These lower cost producers earn a producer surplus up to GN or $2 in Figure 4.2.

And it should be kept in mind that both consumers' and producers' surplus represents wealth and wealth creation in the price system. Consumers' surplus in Figure 4.1 was $180, and producers' surplus in Figure 4.2 is $100. *This represents wealth that accrues to consumers and producers as a result of their market interactions.* The market system works to maximize the total of these surpluses and, what is the same thing, produces what economists call efficiency.

Competitive Equilibrium and Economic Efficiency

The efficiency of competitive markets may be analyzed with these simple tools. Recall from earlier in this chapter that competitive markets required certain conditions. They were that property rights were well-defined, enforced, and tradable; that sellers or buyers were not able to collude or to have an effect on the market-clearing price (large numbers of buyers and sellers tend to guarantee this); and that any firm willing and able to become a seller can enter the market without entry barriers. Under these conditions, which we assume hold in the production, sale, and purchase of compact discs, the market will be efficient! Figure 4.3 tells us what is meant by this concept.

Figure 4.3 (as in Figure 3.10) shows the market clearing price for compact discs. At $15 the market clears—that is, the quantity supplied (per month) of discs is 200 and the quantity demanded (per month) is 200. Alternatively, the quantity exchanged in the market is the amount that sellers produce (200 discs) and the amount that consumers buy at the market clearing price (200 discs). This is what is meant when we say "the market clears." In the case described in Figure 4.3, market equilibrium under competitive conditions means that just the right amount of discs—not too many or too few—are produced. Competitive markets, under the conditions described, are said to result in *allocative efficiency*. Those individuals who most demand the product get it at a price that exactly represents society's opportunity cost of resources in producing it. All but the very last consumers value discs higher than the equilibrium price of $15 and only the very last consumer(s) pay

---

[6] It is very tempting to interpret this surplus as "profit" to the firm. The surplus—interpreted as producers' or factor surplus—may actually be realized in part or in whole as profits to the firm *or* as payments to factors. The actual division requires more advanced economics than we go into at this point.

FIGURE 4.3

Allocative Economic Efficiency

The "market clears" where supply and demand (or marginal private benefit curve and marginal private cost curve) intersect. This means that the total net value of the good or service is maximized. At this point the *sum* of consumers' and producers' surplus is maximized.

the marginal opportunity cost of producing discs in terms of resources given up by society to produce discs.

The market clearance of Figure 4.3 is also critical to understanding economic efficiency. *Economic efficiency* means that, under competitive conditions, the net value of society's scarce resources is maximized. The *total value* produced by 200 discs to society (with reference to Figure 4.3) is equal to the area under the demand curve from 0 discs produced to 200. We may call that area the *total social value of consuming the scarce resources*. After subtracting the *total social cost* of using the scarce resource to produce discs—equal to the area under the supply curve from 0 to 200 discs—we arrive at the net social value of the scarce resource. If there are no third party effects, that is, if consuming or producing discs does not produce costs or benefits that are not borne by consumers or producers—a competitive market creates a maximum of *net* social value. This means that society's resources have been allocated in efficient fashion. The sum of consumers' surplus and factor or producers' surplus is maximized when net social value is maximized under competition.[7] Any attempt by producers or consumers to get a greater share of the surplus—such as through the political process—may result in a reduction in the sum of the total surplus produced (i.e., less consumers' + producers' surplus). We will soon see how this might well happen in the context of a democratic political system.

THE ROLE OF GOVERNMENT

Government has always played a critical role in the economies of all nations current and historical. We have seen, at the beginning of this chapter, how one

---

[7] In numerical terms, the net social value may be found by combining the procedures discussed in notes 3 and 5. You may verify that consumers actually pay $3,000 for discs, but that they would have been willing to pay $3,500 so that consumer surplus is $500. Sellers of discs receive $3,000 for 200 units (what the consumers actually pay), but of this $400 is producer surplus. Therefore, the total net value of disc production to society is $900.

Market failure
A situation in which the socially optimal (most economically efficient) amount of a good or service does not get produced by the private market; usually stems from unclear property rights assignment.

fundamental and essential role of government is to set the "rules of the game" for the economy. This means that, through government, a legal framework for the definition and enforcement of private property rights is established. Competitive markets function within these rules. But what if competitive markets fail to provide a maximum of total value to society; that is, what if society's assumed goal of maximizing the net social value of resources (described above) is not achieved? How might this **market failure** happen and what, if anything, can be done about it? Consider some possible market failures.

Externalities and Market Failure

The failure of markets to provide maximum economic efficiency is most often related to problems with property and the definition of rights over property. Owners of private property are free to hold, trade, or exchange rights, and they bear the full costs and benefits of their actions. Market failure most often occurs when the rights over resources are either ill-defined or not defined at all. These so-called common property resources, such as air, whales, underground pools of oil, and the atmosphere belong in specific quantities to no one. But when they belong to no one, no individual has an interest in conserving them. Indeed, self-interest and the goals of society often conflict so that individuals in the pursuit of their own self-interest damage the resource, sometimes irreparably, for society as a whole. You do not have to reach far to understand these cases—the "save the whale" and other endangered species campaigns or the "global warming problem" arising from the burning of fossil fuels are well known.

Markets may fail for other reasons, but these failures are most often related to ill-defined or nonexistent property rights. The active pursuit of self-interest by one person may impose costs or benefits on others. There might be, in other words, third-party effects from consuming or producing particular products. **Externalities**, therefore, are the costs and benefits of somebody's behavior or activity that that particular individual does not bear. Well-known examples come to mind. Second-hand smoke might injure people who do not do the smoking. A factory emits smoke or waste products to the detriment of the population in the area or downstream. Automobile exhaust creates smog for the population generally, especially in congested urban areas. Other examples are your roommate's loud stereo, airport noise, or obnoxious perfume or cologne worn by the student sitting next to you.

Externality
Benefits or costs of an individual's activity that the individual does not receive or bear.

But externalities may be positive as well as negative. Your neighbor may maintain a beautiful yard or garden, all of which pleases you and improves the value of your own property. This benefit—a positive externality—is (ordinarily) not compensated for by paying the neighbor for the benefits you receive. Smallpox vaccinations or flu shots provide other examples. The presence of externalities means that the marginal private costs or benefits of actions do not always equal the marginal social costs or benefits of consumer or producer behavior on the part of the whole society. This divergence between self-interest and society's overall welfare would have the effect of causing adjustments in the "efficiency"

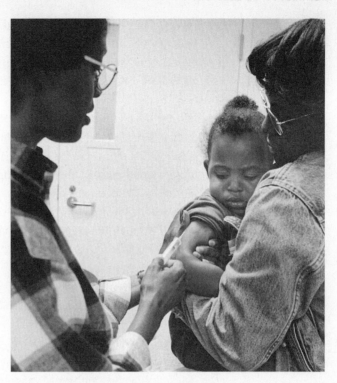

Vaccinations against communicable disease contitute a positive externality—others are protected when you protect yourself.

arguments developed in the preceding discussion in this chapter. When marginal social costs exceed marginal private costs, unfettered private competitive markets produce too much of a good or service. When, however, marginal social benefits from some consumption (a beautiful garden or a polio vaccination) exceed marginal private benefits, too little of a good or service is produced. Economic efficiency might be achieved in these cases, but some non-market adjustments might be necessary.

Obviously, a wise and efficient government would identify and address each of these situations. But there are enormous problems involved in identifying and addressing externalities on the part of government. Not all problems should be addressed. If the cost of adding noise control devices on airplanes landing at some specific airport exceeds the collective value that homeowners around the airport place on noise reduction or elimination, the costs of eliminating the externality would exceed the benefit and it would be "uneconomic" to proceed. Determining just what these costs and benefits are is of course a very difficult problem to begin with in particular situations.

Once relevant externalities have been identified, there are a number of approaches that might be taken, some of them involving government, some not. In general, when the costs of bargaining and transacting between the parties to an externality are low, simply assigning property rights to one or the other parties to the externality may do the trick. If smokers and "relevant" nonsmokers are able to freely transact with one another, a private solution may be possible. Other cases are of course far more difficult to handle and demand other solutions. Water rights or rights to whales can hardly be assigned to individuals. Governments therefore often resort to taxing or subsidizing externalities in order to "correct" "inefficient" markets. Another well-known solution is to use administrative regulations of all kinds to address negative externalities. The Environmental Protection Agency, administered by the federal government, is an example of a regulatory approach to externalities. Indeed, many kinds of policies, including the sale of "rights to pollute" with proceeds going to reducing the effects of pollution, have been and are being tried. All of these solutions are partial in effect and, sometimes to the detriment of all parties, must be filtered through a political process. We will have more to say concerning this critical matter later in this book. For now, however, it is useful to remember that there is a positive role for government in addressing externalities, be it through the definition and enforcement of property rights or through more direct means.

Public Goods and Market Failure

Public good

A good such that, once produced, one individual's consumption of the good does not reduce or exclude the ability of other individuals to consume the good.

Another and somewhat more obvious role for government is in the provision of public goods—goods that would not or could not be provided through free competitive markets. Public goods are another kind of "market failure." What economists call **public goods** are those which, once produced, cannot reduce or impede the ability of others to consume the good regardless of whether consumers are willing to pay or not. The most widely acknowledged public good is national defense. Why should I provide national defense (in the right amounts) if you and everybody else in society can "free ride" on my provision? If I could exclude you from receiving the benefits of my provision, I could charge you for "units" of defense (missile protection, jet carriers). But I cannot exclude you from protection and you have no incentive to reveal how much national defense you "demand." So, it is not in a private individual's self-interest to pay for defense. More specifically, your consumption of national defense does not compete with mine; we both "consume" each unit of defense that is provided. Since defense is necessary to protect the property of all individuals in society, a role for government is created.

Conceptually, the case of national defense is easily understood. Not so for many other candidates. Are lighthouses public goods? Would they not be produced at all or in the right numbers if not provided by governments? (It is a historical fact that many were created and maintained privately.) What about circuses or outdoor rock performances? Does one individual's consumption compete with or complement another's consumption at an outdoor Bruce Springsteen concert? These are difficult questions which await some answers later in this book.

One issue concerning the provision of public goods is worth noting at the outset. Just as it is difficult to determine costs and benefits in assessing the extent of "externalities," it is just as perplexing to determine, through a political process, how much of a public good would be "value maximizing" for society. Many smaller countries of the world have, for example, been "free riders" on U.S. investments in national defense. Further, certain features of the political process to be discussed later in this chapter bring into question the efficiency of national defense expenditures. What is indisputable, however, is that the government's provision of public goods, especially national defense, is a justifiable role for government.

Antitrust and Monopoly Regulation

Several other important problems in markets, in addition to externalities and public goods, have been put forward as justifying a role for government in markets. All of these reasons collapse into one—the existence of significant monopoly power. Monopoly (a single firm's control of a market) or oligopoly (the control of a market by a small number of firms), has justified government control over property rights through direct regulation of the activities of firms (over, for example, electric, water or communications utilities) or by enforcing a set of "rules" with which firms must comply at the risk of civil and criminal penalties (antitrust regulations).

Antitrust policies

Regulations established by laws and government agencies that attempt to preserve business competition.

Industry regulation has included, since the early decades of this century, **antitrust policies** prohibiting price discrimination, collusion among producers, and deceptive advertising practices all passed in an attempt to restore competition where it no longer existed. Even earlier, however, economists and politicians believed that government had a role whenever competition could not exist, perhaps because of economies of large-scale production, or what economists call natural monopolies. Such monopolies are created when each seller can produce more and more output at lower and lower costs. Eventually it becomes profitable for only one seller to supply the total quantity demanded of a good, thereby creating a monopoly. Federal, state, and local governments undertook the regulation—not the ownership or operation—of transportation, communications, energy, and many other industries that were regarded as natural monopolies. Government regulation, in this view, was regarded as a substitute for competition where viable competition could not exist because of industry production and cost conditions.

Some economists have strongly disputed this view and question the existence of large-scale economies (natural monopoly) in many of these regulated industries. Some economists believe, with some justification, that regulation of prices and profits must fail, either because regulation has been ineffective or because these industries are more competitive than previously thought. For example, since the early 1980s there has been significant deregulation affecting airlines, long-distance communications, and trucking. Questions have been raised concerning the self-interested supply of regulation by politicians combined with the self-interested demand for regulation by firms and industries. Do industries and other interest groups use the government regulatory apparatus for their own benefit? Should broad new areas of industry regulation, such as in telecommunications and public utilities, be reduced or eliminated? These and many other questions concerning the expanded role of government are in hot debate, and a firm foundation in economic theory will help you in providing answers to them.

PUBLIC CHOICE—THE RELATION BETWEEN POLITICS AND ECONOMIC EFFICIENCY

We live in a democracy with a particular set of political institutions. These include majority voting, the existence of political parties, a federal system or a hierarchy of representative governments, a huge administrative bureaucracy, and organized interests of all kinds. Public choice, as noted in Chapter 1, is the analysis of the political sector based on the economic notion that self interest guides public decision-makers (voters, politicians, bureaucrats) as well as private decision-makers (consumers, sellers, and market intermediaries). Obviously, the individual who buys a new automobile is the same individual who votes so that political and economic decision-makers are often one and the same person. Importantly, however, there are different institutions and constraints facing economic markets—the decision to buy a car—and political markets—the decision to vote or the decision to sponsor legislation as a politician.

A fundamental question that we answer later in this book is whether political processes are themselves efficient at reflecting the true preferences of voters. But political decisions also have enormous implications for the efficiency of private markets. Environmental regulations may benefit some firms at the expense of others. Entry restrictions in certain professions may be designed to benefit a few workers at the expense of many. Tariffs on imported sugar or peanuts may raise their price to consumers in order to benefit a few favored domestic producers. We must therefore understand a few basic reasons (a) why political markets do not work the same way that economic markets do, and (b) how special interests tend to dominate the political process, often reducing economic efficiency in the process.

Political versus Economic Markets

There are numerous differences between political and economic markets, although both are guided by *self-interested* behavior. Individuals make decisions in private markets in which *all* costs and benefits are borne by the decision maker. Suppose you decide to make an investment in a high-tech stock or in some rental property. If the stock or property fails to earn a competitive return, *you* will bear the full costs of your actions. Likewise, if the investment proves to be a bonanza, *you* receive the full benefits.

This complete internalization of costs and benefits does not take place in political markets. The politician does not bear the full economic consequences of his decisions or incentives to control costs. Politicians cannot personally recoup any savings they make for the public and they are only weakly controlled by voters when high costs are incurred.

The self-interest of politicians also explains an enormous amount of activity within legislatures. The phenomenon of vote-trading or **logrolling,** where you vote for my courthouse and I'll vote for your water reclamation project, is clearly understood by most of the voting public. (*Why* voters let it go on is a question we pose presently.) While economists generally regard exchange as efficient, logrolling in a political context may not be efficient behavior. Since politicians represent particular geographic areas and since politicians face a re-election con-

Logrolling
The exchange of votes by legislators, usually in order to gain support for particular legislation.

straint (two years for U.S. Congress, six years for U.S. Senate), bringing the "pork" back home improves re-election prospects. The problem is that logrolling is not generally efficient in reflecting the preferences of voters on national issues. Rather, it redistributes income toward certain regions and industries and generally does not lead to a more productive economy. We, as collective Americans, get more dams, military bases, and special-interest tax "reform" bills than we want. The political system, in short, tends to produce economic *in*efficiency.

Why Are Voters "Myopic"?

Clearly, the electorate is not made up only of fools or idiots. Why do they "let" politicians pursue their own self-interest at the expense of the common good expressed as the will and preferences of the people? It is because there are substantial and critical differences in the private market and the political market that facilitate logrolling and other nonefficiency producing political behavior. (For a campus example of such behavior see Focus: "Is Student Government Different from Joining a Health Club?".)

When you buy a second car, you buy only a second car. When you vote for your local congressional representative, you vote not for a single issue, but for a whole package of issues or a platform that she represents. We say that the consumer gets *marginal* choices in the private market, but only *all-or-none* decisions in the political market. Another point is that voting is irregular when compared to shopping in the marketplace. That feature of political markets makes it difficult to alter your "consumption" of policies and candidates. You can fairly quickly change grocery stores when you find inferior vegetables at one of your local markets, but it is more difficult to change elected officials.

Perhaps the greatest problems occurring in political markets stem from the fact that voters have weak incentives to inform themselves on the particular political choices their representatives are making. Do you really know or care how your representative feels about or votes on providing a new federally sponsored park in northern Oregon? Voters have few incentives to gather information concerning their public choices, whereas they have strong incentives to acquire information concerning market choices. The costs of staying informed on the hundreds (even thousands) of decisions made by all of your representatives is enormous. Therefore, as a rational voter—one calculating the direct costs and benefits of your representative's decisions—you stay rationally uninformed or rationally ignorant. This does not mean that voters are stupid or that they "don't care about government." Rational ignorance simply means that the costs of being fully informed on each and every decision made are prohibitively high. The *pro rata* share of the costs and benefits of so many of these decisions—the new Oregon park—are so low to individual voters that they are not concerned with how politicians vote in such cases.

Interest Groups Tend to Dominate

Since voters are rationally uninformed, they present serious difficulties for politicians. Naturally, elections do tend to generate some information for representatives, but that information is seldom direct and not very useful. Inasmuch as individual

ƒOcus   "Is Student Government Different from Joining a Health Club?"

When you decide to buy some private good, such as a health club membership, a new swim suit or a plate of Asian food, you do so with direct "dollar votes." Whether or not a formal contract exists—it might for the membership but might not for the dinner or the swim suit—property rights are directly traded in your purchase. You give rights over a certain amount of money and you obtain property rights over the good or service you have purchased. You incur the costs of the exchange and obtain all the benefits of the new property rights.

This is not the case for public choices. As noted in the text, public choices, like private choices, are self-interested, but differ in important aspects. Political decision makers do not bear the full costs of their decision, nor do they reap all of the benefits. They cannot capitalize on decisions and have no incentives to control costs. Such is the case for many student governments at colleges and universities across the country. You pay a fee for student government activities—akin to a tax—and you vote for representatives. How do the results of student government activities differ from your private market participation?

First, allocations for funding student groups are made by your representatives and committees composed thereof, but there is no reason to believe that such funding will accurately or even closely reflect your preferences. Who gets the money will depend on who can muster the strongest coalitions within the student government. On some campuses, Panhellenic (fraternity and sorority) interests will dominate. On others, athletic interests or the Society of Student Engineers or even minority group clubs will win larger allocations. Allocations, in other words, will be made on the basis of interest groups and the coalitions they form. You may want to add new journals to the school library or to expand aerobics classes in the student union with the fees collected, but your preferences might not be recognized.

Then there is the familiar problem of voter or student apathy. You may be so busy with classes, activities, or a job that you remain "rationally ignorant" of exactly what the student government is actually doing or what the candidates are like in the first place. Even if you were *acutely* interested in the outcomes of the political process at your university, it would be exceedingly costly to monitor your representatives once they are elected. And, since most office holders in student governments are only around for one or two years, it is highly unlikely that "turning the rascals out" would be a viable or effective option. You cannot change student representatives as you can brands of fast food hamburgers. In these senses, therefore, you are a captive (at least temporarily) of a political process not unlike that established for democratically elected officials at all levels of government.

Interest groups
Collections of individuals with one or more common characteristics, such as occupation, who seek collectively to affect legislation or government policy so as to benefit members of the group.

voters are rationally ignorant of voting on particular issues, politicians are uncertain about voter preferences. But some individuals and, particularly, blocs of voters—called **interest groups**—are clearly interested in particular outcomes.

Coalitions of particular interests—businesses surrounding the proposed Oregon park—are in a prime position to put pressure on politicians to vote their way. Politicians, ever mindful of promised votes, campaign contributions, and other perks, are all too eager to supply legislation. (See the Application at the end of this chapter: "Why Are There So Many Restaurants and Golf Courses in State Capital Cities?" for some insight into this issue.) Special-interest legislation at all levels of government—local, state, and federal—is therefore explained as the result of rational self interest on the part of voters at large (who are rationally ignorant), coalitions of particular interest groups directly affected by legislation, and by politicians who, in *their* own self interest, want to be re-elected. The problem, and it is a big problem, is that the demand and supply of such legislation within the political process reduces the economic efficiency of markets and thwarts the general will and preferences of the electorate. Let us see how with an example.

INTEREST GROUPS AND WEALTH TRANSFERS: THE CASE OF BARBERS

The behavior of interest groups explains much in the political arena. Concentrated interests on the part of particular groups of individuals—as against the wider public interest—are represented by lobbyists in all political venues. Lobbyists and political action committees (PACs) for particular groups cover every conceivable interest at one level of government or another. Examples include real estate, physicians (the American Medical Association), defense industries, teachers, postal workers, banking and financial institutions, textiles, petroleum, labor unions, and virtually any other interest for which legislation or regulation can affect economic benefits or costs in a positive or negative fashion. To see how interest groups affect government policy, consider the process by which a statewide group of barbers might organize to advance their interests. (We conclude this discussion with some real-world data on how hair styling fees are affected by state regulations.)

The most fundamental problem that barbers (or hair stylists or health professionals) face is how to get organized. Specifically, each barber has incentives to stay outside the interest group, for if the interest group is successful in, say, obtaining higher prices for haircuts, a free-riding barber—one who does not pay dues to the barbers' association—can benefit without incurring any costs. Free-riding behavior makes the formation of interest groups difficult, but by no means impossible. For such reasons, interest groups seek ways to limit the benefits of their activities to members only.

Assume that the barbers organize. The group's representatives go to the state legislature and seek a legally sanctioned barbers' monopoly. The purpose of this monopoly (actually a cartel or interest group) is to protect barbers from new competition by erecting barriers to entry into barbering, thereby allowing barbers to raise the price of a haircut above competitive levels—that is, above costs in terms of resources used in providing a haircut. In other words, the barbers petition the state government to raise their wealth at the expense of haircut consumers. Put another way, they are demanders of a wealth transfer from the state.

Who are the potential suppliers of wealth transfers? The suppliers are those—in this case, consumers of the barbers' product—who do not find it worthwhile to organize and to resist having their wealth taken away by the barbers. This is an unusual concept of supply, but it is a supply curve nonetheless. The attitude that will prevail among suppliers of wealth is that it would cost them more to protest the barbers' proposal than any benefits they would derive from protesting. For example, the average consumer might spend $100 to defeat the barbers' proposal,

FIGURE 4.4

How an Interest Group's Demands Are Met

P_c is the competitive price that the barbering industry charges per haircut, and P_m is the price established by the group after it is granted protected (cartel) status through the political process. After the cartel is formed, it stands to gain P_mABP_c in profit from consumers of haircuts. This transfer is from consumer surplus to profits, but society also loses a net amount ACB in welfare.

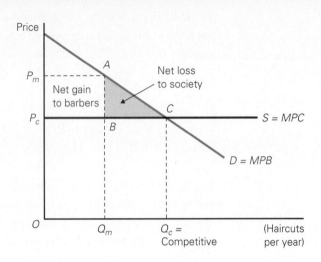

the net result of which would save $10 in haircut costs. Why spend $100 to save $10?

This example describes a "demand" and a "supply" of wealth transfers in the case of barbers. How does the market for wealth transfers work? Politicians are brokers in this market and in the market for legislation generally. The politician's job is to pair demanders and suppliers of wealth transfers. If they transfer too much or too little wealth, they will be replaced at the next election by more efficient politician-brokers.

The outcome for the barbers may be shown (in Figure 4.4) as an extension of our discussion on the meaning of competitive economic efficiency earlier in the chapter. The barbers start out as a purely competitive industry, producing Q_c haircuts per year at a price of P_c. When their interest group forms, they persuade the legislature to grant them special cartel status. This persuasion is not very difficult because the consumers who are harmed by the cartel do not find it worthwhile to protest to the legislators. The barbers are the only ones to be heard, and perhaps by putting their arguments for a cartel in public-interest terms ("higher prices mean higher quality," "barbers must be licensed to ensure an orderly marketplace," and so on), they carry the day with the legislature.

Legislators, for their part, assess the costs and benefits of creating a barber cartel. In Figure 4.4, the barbers seek P_mABP_c in cartel profits at the expense of consumers' welfare. (We assume, for simplicity and not unreasonably, that barbering services are produced at constant opportunity cost of resources and that the supply curve lies flat at the competitive price.) This means that an amount of consumer surplus (P_mABP_c) is transferred to barbers as profits. Area ACB represents a net welfare loss to consumers due to the legal monopoly supplied by legislators. The per capita gains to barbers, who are a relatively small number of producers, exceed the per capita costs to the more numerous haircut consumers. The result: The legislature passes a law giving the barbers a cartel (and, perhaps,

Legal licensing granted through the political process transfers gains to barbers and cosmetologists from consumers along with a net loss to society.

the barbers make campaign contributions to the legislators who supported their cartel bill). *The net value of society's resources is not maximized because of the transfer.*

There is actual evidence that state regulation of hair stylists has produced this result. A recent study of cosmetology regulation in the fifty states has shown that a variety of restrictions on entry into the market, including educational, age, and training restrictions have had the effect of increasing the price of hair style services across the United States.[8] The greater the degree to which the cosmetology profession in a particular state has attained political power and influence, the greater the benefit to the profession in the state and the greater the cost to consumers of these services. Even a modest average increase in price due to restrictions—say 50 to 75 cents per hair style—will reduce consumer surplus by an enormous amount—possibly by several billion dollars per year—over all consumers. *The moral*: An industry does not have to be vital to health or national defense to seek transfers in this case from consumers to suppliers of barbering and cosmetological services—through the political process.

Our discussion of barbers concerns a particular kind of restriction. Interest groups do not always work as producers versus consumers. Technically, any group can organize and act as an interest group, and we find that interest groups represent many overlapping segments of society. There are labor unions; women's rights groups; religious groups; trade associations; and organizations for doctors, nurses, and all health professionals, for lawyers, hunters, environmentalists, and farmers. Moreover, not all of these groups are small. Many large groups, such as farmers,

---

[8] See A. Frank Adams, III, Robert B. Ekelund, Jr., and John D. Jackson, "Occupational Licensing of a Competitive Industry: The Case of Cosmetology" (Manuscript: Auburn University, 1996).

are effectively organized as an interest group. The fundamental point is that you can begin to explain why a certain law is passed if you try to answer two questions: Who wins? and Who loses?

Another critical point is that the particular features of political markets—at least in a representative democracy—permit sanctioned and legal transfers of wealth from one group to another. Almost every policy you can think of has this effect. While transfers are not so important to the economists, overall economic efficiency—the maximization of the net value of all of society's resources—is of great concern. The differences between private markets and public choice practically guarantees that overall economic efficiency will not be attained.

Clearly, markets are excellent institutions through which to allocate resources. Markets, along with institutions such as private property and free contracting described in this chapter, give people in society the goods they value most. Indeed, they do this most of the time. When market activity creates third-party effects such as pollution or other externalities, government may step in to attempt to alleviate problems. In general, however, markets underlie wealth creation and wealth creation is about making society better off.

Market functioning, however, takes place with the context of democratic political institutions in a world of "public choice." When left alone, markets are unconcerned with "welfare triangles." But when politics and interest groups enter the picture, as we have seen in this chapter, society's wealth may be redistributed and the triangles under supply and demand curves become important. They showed, for example, how the barbers were able to increase their wealth at the general expense of the net wealth of society. When political participation in the economy is considered, the economist's emphasis turns from efficiency to distribution. Our discussion of public choices revealed that democracy and its institutions create the possibilities for losses through redistributions. This does not mean that democracy must be done away with or significantly altered, however. Democracy remains the best conceivable system in a world of imperfections.

APPLICATION

Why Are There So Many Restaurants and Golf Courses in State Capital Cities?

It is obvious that a lot of effective lobbying takes place. It would be difficult otherwise to explain many local, state, or federal allocations and subsidies, such as water subsidies in the West or inland waterways in the South. How much activity takes place is another question. If politicians are self-interested, as modern public-choice economists believe, they will always make policy with an eye to re-election and enrichment. Because the direct transfer of money for votes is fairly easy to detect, politicians must rely on other kinds of transfers and perquisites.

Interest groups are often able to deliver blocs of votes, as mentioned in the text, or to finance campaigns by a variety of means. Most proposed reform focuses on changing methods of campaign finance.

But there are numerous other ways to pay off politicians for economic interventions that benefit special interests. For example, it would be a rare representative or senator specializing in banking or transportation legislation who did not have opportunities to work for the industry he or she regulated after retiring from politics. Family members or business partners and associates of the politician, moreover, may be in position to accept payoffs.

Distortions (payoffs?) may take many other forms. Although most of the attention has been fixed on cash and other bribes, many forms of in-kind transfers (that is, not in money) are in fact used. Overt cash bribes attract attention and invite regulation, but lobbying efforts may be indirect, as when trips, fancy (or not-so-fancy) meals, transportation or limo services, employment of relatives or business associates, or golf rounds are provided for legislators.

Recent research into in-kind perquisites of state politicians has produced convincing results. When allowance is made for per-capita income and other key variables, state capital cities have been shown to contain a larger per-capita percentage of sit-down (non-fast food) restaurants than paired, randomly chosen same-state cities with similar income characteristics.[a] The bigger the budget of the state (the more opportunities for profit-seeking transfers by special interests) and the more full-time lobbyists in the state, other things equal, the more restaurants the city has. The same goes for golf courses.

What are the costs of such lobbying by special interests? First, there is the cost to society of skewing regulations and goods toward concentrated interests and not to the public interest as discussed in this chapter. But there is a direct cost as well. In the sample of 47 state capitals, there are a total of 9,635 additional restaurants for the capital cities solely because of their political status as capital cities. A lower-bound estimate of resource distortion from restaurant payoffs is suggested by multiplying 9,635 times the average start-up cost per restaurant. Then there are also 286 additional golf courses to consider.

There are many forms of political payoffs from special interests. More hidden in-kind payoffs may be expected where functions and funding are shifted away from the federal level and to cities and states. Cruder, lower-cost forms of payoffs may be expected where the gains from special treatment are lower. In smaller communities, lunch at McDonald's or Wendy's or a weekend fishing vacation may do the trick. Whatever the case, such special-interest legislation and regulation will likely have negative benefits for voter-consumer-taxpayers at large.

These negative benefits from lobbying may of course be resisted by the electorate at large. Voters at any level of government might demand lobbying restrictions by special interests, limits to campaign spending, and so on. In 1996, for example, the U.S. Congress placed a "gift ban" on its own members in response to criticisms from the media and the electorate. The "exemptions" that Congress passed along with the ban were interesting, however. Free meals are OK, it seems, if interest groups invite a "large group" to dine. And both major parties supported a total exemption on gift and party giving at the Republican and Democratic National Conventions held in August of 1996!

QUESTION
How can you explain the proliferation of sit down restaurants and golf courses in state capitals?

SUMMARY

1. All economies are characterized by institutions—the "rules of the game"—that shape and guide economic activity.
2. A key capitalist institution is private property. Private property, protected and enforced by government, permits and facilitates efficient contracting between individuals. It also encourages private incentives for long-term planning and investment, which promotes economic growth.
3. Private competitive markets exist when individuals are free to buy and sell resources, enter or exit business, and produce and consume goods and services with little or no government intervention.
4. Free and private competitive markets, in which there are no third-party effects to exchange, produce allocative efficiency. Such economic efficiency occurs at quantities where the demand curve or (what is the same thing) the marginal private benefit curve intersects the supply or marginal private cost curve. In different terms, maximum economic efficiency occurs where total *net* benefits are maximized, that is, where the difference between total value and total cost for producing some good or service is the greatest. Allocative efficiency is also (and equivalently) achieved when the *sum* of producer and consumer surplus is maximized.
5. Government's role in the economy, besides setting the institutional "rules of the game," is to address problems when markets and private exchange fails to produce allocative economic efficiency. Failures might occur when third party effects, such as externalities, are created through market exchange or when property rights are difficult or impossible to define. Water pollution, factory smoke, and noise around airports are possible examples of this phenomenon.

6. The provision of public goods such as national defense provide another rationale for the role of government. Once produced, a public good is provided at little or no cost to all.

7. The government also institutes industry regulation through the regulation of business practices and through anti-monopoly regulation (called *antitrust laws*).

8. Public choice is the study of political markets—how self-interested individuals and groups of voters, politi-cians, and bureaucrats guide public decision making. Organized interest groups are often able to use the political process to transfer wealth. Unorganized and myopic voters permit transfers as they remain "rationally uninformed" or "rationally ignorant" when the cost of being informed is high and the *pro rata* cost of the political decision is low.

KEY TERMS

economic system
pure capitalism
pure communism
socialism
economic efficiency
private property
free enterprise

competition
marginal private benefit curve
total consumer valuation
consumers' surplus
marginal private cost curve
producers' surplus
market failure

externalities
public goods
antitrust policies
logrolling
interest groups

QUESTIONS FOR REVIEW AND DISCUSSION

1. What is *capitalism* and what does it have to do with property rights and economic freedom?

2. What, exactly, is an *institution*? How do institutions help solve the basic economic "questions" in capital-ist societies?

3. What is private property? What is common property? How do incentives differ under such systems?

4. What are the conditions underlying private competi-tive markets? Why is "non-collusion" a necessary con-dition for the existence of free competition in markets?

5. What is a marginal private benefit curve and why is it equivalent to a demand curve for a good or service? What is a marginal private cost curve and why is it equivalent to a supply curve for a good or service?

6. Explain clearly why economic efficiency (without third-party effects) occurs when the marginal private benefits from producing a good equal the marginal private costs of producing that good. Is this equiva-lent to saying that economic efficiency occurs when the *sum* of producer and consumer surplus is maxi-mized? Why?

7. What are some of the roles of government in the U.S. economy?

8. What is an "externality"? Does cigar smoking on a crowded bus create an externality? Explain.

9. What is a public good? Explain whether or not the following items fit the definition of a public good: national defense, education, cable television.

10. Explain some of the differences between private choices and public choices. Why is a "vote" for a hamburger different from your vote for your congres-sional representative or city councilman?

11. Are voters "myopic" or shortsighted in permitting politicians to pursue their own interests? What does it mean to be "rationally uninformed" or "rationally ignorant"?

12. Explain the process by which special interests might be able to take over the political apparatus for their own gain and against economic efficiency or the "general welfare."

POINT COUNTERPOINT

ADAM SMITH

KARL MARX

Adam Smith and Karl Marx: Markets and Society

Adam Smith, one of the most important figures in the history of economics, actually began his career as a lecturer in moral philosophy at Scotland's Glasgow College in 1751. Moral philosophy in Smith's time encompassed a wide range of topics, including natural theology, ethics, jurisprudence, and economics. In 1776, Smith published *An Inquiry into the Nature and Causes of the Wealth of Nations,* known usually by the shorter title *Wealth of Nations.* The book won much attention from scholars of the day, and it brought together most of what was then known about the workings of the market system.

Smith was born in Kirkcaldy on the east coast of Scotland in 1723 and lived most of his life in his native country. Although known for his brilliant lectures (and for his many eccentricities), Smith did not devote his entire career to teaching. In 1778, he accepted a well-paying job as commissioner of Scottish customs, a post at which he remained until his death in 1790.

Karl Marx "looked like a revolutionary," writes Robert Heilbroner in *The Worldly Philosophers.* "He was stocky and powerfully built and rather glowering in expression with a formidable beard. He was not an orderly man; his home was a dusty mass of papers piled in careless disarray in the midst of which Marx himself, slovenly dressed, padded about in an eye-stinging haze of tobacco smoke."[a]

Marx wrote in response to the miseries of the European working class during the Industrial Revolution of the late eighteenth and nineteenth centuries. Coauthor with Friedrich Engels of the *Communist Manifesto,* which predicted the inevitable downfall of capitalism and the triumph of communism, Marx spent most of his life in difficult circumstances. His activities as a radical in the communist movement caused his exile from his native

Germany as well as from Belgium and France. In 1849, a year after the publication of the *Manifesto,* he settled in London, where he and his family survived through the benevolence of Engels and where Marx researched and wrote *Das Kapital,* a theory and history of capitalism and its ills. Marx died in 1883 in London.

The "Invisible Hand"

Smith's views of the free-market system are summarized in a passage from the *Wealth of Nations,* in which he writes that individuals pursuing their own self-interest are "led by an invisible hand to promote an end which was no part of [their] intention."[b] Smith believed that by freely exchanging goods and services across markets, individuals contribute to the public good—the aggregate wealth of society—even though they act from purely self-interested motives. In other words, markets cause individuals to benefit others when they intend only to benefit themselves.

To Smith, voluntary market exchange coordinated the decisions of consumers and producers and generated economic progress. Producers compete with one another to satisfy consumers with the most appropriate and cheapest goods and services, simply because they maximize their profits by doing so. Markets coordinate supply and demand by way of the price system. Consumers express their preferences in their decisions about what to buy; producers attract customers by producing goods at the least cost. In this system of coordination without command, individuals pursuing their own interests are led "as if by an invisible hand" to mesh their interests with those of other individuals trading across markets.

[a]Robert L. Heilbroner, *The Wordly Philosophers* (New York: Simon and Schuster, 1953), p. 131.

[b]Adam Smith, *An Inquiry into the Nature and Causes of the Wealth of Nations,* ed. Edwin Cannan (1776; reprint, New York: Modern Library, 1937), p. 423.

Smith was not opposed to government, but argued that its proper role in society was to provide a legal framework—police and courts—within which the market could operate, as well as to provide certain other services (including national defense, highways, and education) that the market itself would either not supply or would tend to supply in inadequate amounts. Smith also felt that government should provide welfare services for the poor. But he strongly believed that government could best assist the market economy achieve growth by stepping out of the way—that is, by not regulating and by not granting monopoly privileges to favored groups.

In Smith's view, income was distributed in a market economy by the production of wealth. An individual's income was a strict function of the value of his or her output. Smith did not feel that income inequality by itself was unfair, because he believed that anyone can increase his or her income in a free market by serving the consumers in a new, better, or faster way.

The "Anarchy of Production"

In *Das Kapital*, Karl Marx argued that Smith's writing represented merely the interests of the ruling capitalist class. To Marx, the market process was a system of exploitation by which owners of capital robbed their employees by paying them wages less than the worth of their labor (a situation he termed the *alienation of labor*).

The alternative social system that Marx thought would eliminate this exploitation and at the same time greatly increase the efficiency of production was a "general organization of the labor of society . . . [that] would turn all society into one immense factory."[c] He viewed the market economy as one of general disorganization. Its main feature was "the anarchy of production," where producers overproduced and consumers were forced to accept goods they neither wanted nor needed.

In Marx's view, Smith's "invisible hand" was a euphemism for describing the economic system in which "chance and caprice have full play in distributing the producers and their means of production among the various branches of industry . . . [T]he division of labour within the society [the theme of much of Smith's *Wealth of Nations*] brings into contact independent commodity-producers, who acknowledge no other authority but that of competition, of the coercion exerted by the pressure of their mutual interests . . . [T]he same bourgeois mind which praises division of labour in the workshop [as a conscious organization that increases productivity] denounces with equal vigour every conscious attempt to socially control and regulate the process of production."[d] Only the central planning of economic activity by society (government), which owned all means of production, could coordinate the needs of consumers and producers and eliminate the wastefulness of capitalism. To Marx, it was nonsense to describe the market as organized economic activity, because there was no organizer. Coordination of economic activity requires conscious, centralized control.

While Smith described the emerging market economy of his day and offered reforms, Marx offered a vision of economic organization that did not exist at the time he wrote but that he maintained was the inevitable wave of the future. In a sense he was proven correct. Followers of the teachings of Marx and his admirer Lenin (who filled in many details of what a central planning system would look like in practice) imposed avowedly Marxist-socialist, centrally planned economies on many countries, including Russia and China, in the first half of the twentieth century. However, without exception, the centrally planned economies seemed to function poorly—providing low per capita income and poor rates of economic growth—relative to the modern versions of the capitalist economies whose central principle of market organization was so clearly seen by Smith.

[c]Karl Marx, *Das Kapital*, ed. Max Eastman (1867; reprint, New York: Modern Library, 1932), p. 83.

[d]Marx, *Das Kapital*, p. 83.

PART 2

THE
FUNDAMENTALS OF
MACROECONOMICS

CHAPTER 5
CONTEMPORARY MACROECONOMICS

Today's local newspaper or the evening television newscast is likely to contain much economic news. There might be stories on conditions in microcomputer markets or on the migration of agricultural labor from Minnesota to South Dakota. By far the most consistently reported economic news relates to the overall health of the economy, and, especially, to employment conditions.

The media pay careful attention to monthly and quarterly statistics on such measures as the inflation rate, the unemployment rate, and the growth rate in gross domestic product (GDP). Government economic policies to remedy macroeconomic problems are also heavily reported.

Topics such as the real rate of growth in the economy may seem abstract and distant, but they do have an immediate and lasting impact on individual economic well-being. Economists have spent more than 200 years seeking to understand how the macroeconomy—the large-scale economy—shapes our lives.

Think for a moment about how the major macroeconomic issues—inflation, unemployment, and growth—are likely to influence your future. Will economic conditions affect your ability to repay your college loan? Will you enter the job market during a time of high unemployment? Will your hopes for a high-paying job, a comfortable home, a promising future for your children be realized? How will government deficits affect your future economic welfare? The study of macroeconomics certainly cannot answer these questions for you, but it can better equip you to plan for the future, whatever the future may hold. Likewise, this chapter is not intended to begin our formal study of macroeconomics. Instead, we present an overview of basic macroeconomic policy goals and introduce much of the terminology employed by macroeconomists. When you complete Chapter 5 you should understand

- the overall goals of macroeconomic policy and the trade-offs among goals.
- the nature of unemployment and inflation and their effects on economic growth.
- how, in general terms, fiscal and monetary policies are used to achieve the goals of macroeconomic policy.
- the essential tools of aggregate demand and aggregate supply that economists use to analyze the macroeconomy.

THE GOALS OF MACROECONOMICS

In Chapter 1 we defined *macroeconomics* as the analysis of the economy as a whole. When working with macroeconomic theory, the focus is on whole quantities, or what economists call aggregate quantities. Macroeconomics concerns not just one market but all markets; not just one price change but all price changes; not just one firm's employees but all employment.

As with any discipline, the field of macroeconomics is made up of many specialized areas, competing theories, and ongoing debates. Consistent throughout macroeconomics, however, is a shared set of goals. Both macroeconomists and the politicians who heed (or disregard) their advice are interested in achieving three separate, sometimes conflicting, objectives: full employment, price stability, and economic growth. We discuss each of these goals separately, but you will soon see that they are closely intertwined.

The Full-Employment Goal

Full employment is a primary goal of any economic society for obvious reasons. The more fully resources are employed, the greater the levels of output of goods and services, and the higher the prosperity.

SOCIAL CONCERN OVER UNEMPLOYMENT   Not only does high unemployment threaten to bring poverty to millions of citizens, but it also can lead to political upheaval. During the Great Depression of the 1930s, for example, signs of social and political unrest appeared in the United States. Farmers marched on Washington, D.C., makeshift camps of the poor and out-of-work dotted the nation's cities, and mass migrations of the jobless from the Dust Bowl of the Midwest to the Promised Land of California took place. When World War II mobilized the economy, full employment was restored before serious political and social upheaval could erupt.

Other nations of the world have experienced similar upheavals. Consider the frequent changes of government and political systems in developing nations, where poverty—much of it caused by widespread unemployment—is rampant. Increased crime and even violent revolution can result from failure to attain the macroeconomic goal of full employment.

The purely human costs of unemployment on individuals, families, and society itself can be devastating. Unemployment is a primary cause of poverty, dislocations of families, and, in extreme cases, homelessness. It puts extraordinary pressure on social and welfare services that are funded with taxes. More important, unemployment represents resources *not used* to produce goods and services—perhaps the ultimate inefficiency.

In recognition of the social and political implications of unemployment, the U.S. government passed the Employment Act of 1946 on the heels of the Depression and World War II. The act recognized and enshrined maximum employment as a macroeconomic goal of the federal government. The meaning of the term *maximum employment* has been modified in the intervening years, but policymakers still respect the intent, if not the letter, of the law. Unemployment rates of 10 percent and more, for example, which characterized the U.S. economy in 1982 and 1983, brought great concern to the U.S. Congress and to the Reagan administration. In 1992, unemployment rates of around 8 percent were a factor in the defeat of President George Bush by Bill Clinton. By 1996, the unemployment rate was hovering at about 5 percent. In all nations, however, the goal of full employment is critical. Social programs such as unemployment compensation and food stamps ease the burden of unemployment, but they cannot substitute for the economic benefits of full employment.

DEFINING THE LEVELS OF EMPLOYMENT AND UNEMPLOYMENT Some unemployment in specific markets is always expected. In a dynamic economy, demand grows for some goods and services and declines for others. In recent years, for example, the demand for high-technology outputs such as microcomputers, lasers, and fiber optics has outpaced demand for the products of heavy industry, and temporary unemployment in heavy industries such as steel and machine tools has been very high. Some workers may develop new skills, however, and temporarily unemployed resources may flow into new areas of production.

From an economic perspective, there is little reason to be concerned with the temporary periods of unemployment that workers in specific fields experience as the economy undergoes change. In such cases, **unemployed** workers generally remain out of work for relatively brief periods of time before they succeed in obtaining a job. However, there is reason for concern when numerous workers in many different industries simultaneously become unemployed. When this happens, output levels fall far below potential, and families of the unemployed workers experience real hardship over extended periods of time. For this reason, the federal government keeps close tabs on the **unemployment rate** each month.

The labor force is therefore defined as the total of employed and unemployed persons. To calculate the unemployment rate, the number of unemployed persons is divided by the total labor force. Table 5.1 presents data on the unemployment rate, the number of unemployed workers, and the size of the labor force for the period 1975–1995. The Bureau of Labor Statistics also breaks down the unemployment rate into rates for various demographic groups to show the *differing rates* of unemployment for particular groups in the economy. Figure 5.1 shows the total unemployment rate in the U.S. economy for the period 1960–1995 and the corre-

Unemployed
A labor-force status characterized by an individual who is actively seeking employment but is not working.

Unemployment rate
The percentage of the labor force without jobs.

TABLE 5.1

Unemployment, the Unemployment Rate, and the National Labor Force, 1975–1995

The number of unemployed persons, along with the unemployment rate, varies over time. Both the total number and the rate decreased between 1992 and 1995.

Year	Unemployment Rate (percent)	Unemployment (thousands of persons)	Civilian Labor Force (thousands of persons)[a]
1975	8.5	7,929	93,775
1976	7.7	7,406	96,158
1977	7.1	6,991	99,009
1978	6.1	6,202	102,251
1979	5.8	6,137	104,962
1980	7.1	7,637	106,940
1981	7.6	8,273	108,670
1982	9.7	10,678	110,204
1983	9.6	10,717	111,550
1984	7.5	8,539	113,544
1985	7.2	8,312	115,461
1986	7.0	8,237	117,834
1987	6.2	7,425	119,865
1988	5.5	6,701	121,669
1989	5.3	6,528	123,869
1990	5.5	6,874	124,787
1991	6.7	8,426	125,303
1992	7.4	9,384	126,982
1993	6.8	8,734	128,040
1994	6.1	7,996	131,056
1995	5.6	7,404	132,304

SOURCE: Council of Economic Advisers, *Economic Report of the President* (Washington, D.C.: U.S. Government Printing Office, 1996), p. 316.

[a]Age 16 and over

Full employment
A situation in which unemployment exists only because of normal market adjustments to changing demand or supply or to outmoded skills of workers; also a numerical federal government goal for the unemployment rate.

Natural rate of unemployment
A theoretical concept; the unemployment rate that coexists with macroeconomic stability or labor-market equilibrium in the long run.

sponding unemployment rates by race, sex, and age. Some facts about the composition of the unemployment rate are apparent: (1) Minority groups have experienced a higher unemployment rate than whites, (2) teenagers in the 16–19 age group have experienced a higher unemployment rate than any other age group, and (3) women over 20 years of age have generally experienced higher unemployment rates than men of the same age.

Despite the presence of unemployment, **full employment** remains a political goal. As we have seen, the Employment Act of 1946 charged the federal government with the responsibility of promoting maximum employment. In 1978, Congress passed the Full Employment and Balanced Growth Act, which committed the government to full employment, defined as an unemployment rate of 4 percent. The goals of the act have been modified (upward) in the intervening years.

How can full employment be defined as allowing for any unemployment? Some economists feel that there is a **natural rate of unemployment** (or employment), the rate that would exist under long-run equilibrium conditions because of the time

FIGURE 5.1

Unemployment Rates, 1960–1995

The unemployment rate (the number of persons unemployed divided by the labor force) rises and falls with other economic activity. However, African Americans and teenagers consistently have higher rates of unemployment than other groups.

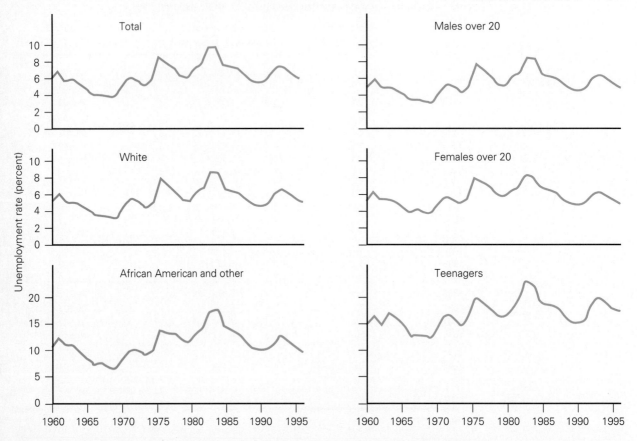

SOURCE: Council of Economic Advisers, *Economic Report of the President* (Washington, D.C.: U.S. Government Printing Office, 1996), p. 324.

needed for adjustments in the labor market, the lag in matching vacancies and workers, the costs of hiring and firing and of changing jobs, regulations affecting structural changes in labor markets, and so forth. Market forces and institutions, not individuals, determine the natural rate of unemployment at any given time. The actual rate of unemployment can be compared to the theoretical concept of the natural rate, as in Figure 5.2. Note that the actual unemployment rate has fluctuated around the natural rate, with cycles of business activity producing unemployment below the natural rate in some periods and above the rate in other periods. In the most direct sense, macroeconomics deals with why the actual rate of unemployment differs from the natural rate and with what might cause the natural rate to change over time.

Economists debate, sometimes hotly, what the appropriate level of full employment is. In fact, the unemployment rate has not fallen below 5 percent since 1973, and many economists now think that the "full-employment" unemployment rate

FIGURE 5.2

Rate of Unemployment, 1890–1995

The actual rate of unemployment has fluctuated widely since 1890. The unemployment rate rose to dangerous levels during the 1930s but has stayed within narrower limits since World War II. The actual unemployment rate has fluctuated around the natural rate of unemployment, a theoretical concept that depends on the situations and institutions surrounding the demand and supply of labor.

SOURCES: Robert J. Gordon, *Macroeconomics*, 5th ed. (Glenview, IL: Scott, Foresman, 1990), p. 14; and Council of Economic Advisers, *Economic Report of the President* (Washington, D.C.: U.S. Government Printing Office, 1996), p. 325.

should be in the 5–7 percent range, a range close to the theoretical concept of the natural rate of unemployment. From a practical and political viewpoint, politicians would be happy to speak "positively" by calculating an *em*ployment, rather than an *un*employment rate. But the unemployment rate has remained the primary focus of economists and analysts.

The Goal of Price Stability

Price stability

A situation of no inflation or deflation in the economy; no change in the overall level of prices of goods, services, and resources.

The second major macroeconomic goal is **price stability**—the absence of inflation or deflation in the overall level of prices. Inflation is a process of price level increases that take place over time. Inflation can be stable and predictable or unstable and unanticipated—in either case, bringing higher costs to consumers and producers, and to buyers and sellers. Inflation is far more disruptive when it arrives unannounced, however.

Inflation is not simply a rise in the price of gasoline or chicken. Rather, inflation is a macroeconomic situation characterized by sustained and continuous increases in the overall level or average of all prices. One way to measure inflation is to look at the average of prices for some representative collection, or market basket, of goods and services that people buy. An increase in this average, or general, level of prices over some given time period (a month or a year) indicates the presence of inflation in the economy.

Suppose that food was the only good people bought. A 2 percent increase in the average level of food prices during the month of March means that the consumer must spend $1.02 at the end of March to buy the same market basket of food items that $1.00 would purchase in February. Never mind that bacon prices actually fell in March and that potato chip prices rose by 10 percent. Inflation is measured by considering the average prices of some representative bundle of goods at some given level—such as the retail, wholesale, or producer level.

If the cost of some market basket of goods and services was, say, $200 in one month and $210 in the next month, then prices in general would have risen by 5 percent during the month. When the change in prices over any period of time (a month here) is expressed as a percentage, the number calculated is called the **inflation rate.** The inflation rate is the speed at which prices in general are increasing. In this example, the inflation rate calculated is 5 percent per month. If prices continued to increase at the same speed for an entire year, the inflation rate would be 80 percent per year (5 percent per month compounded for 12 months). A statistic calculated by the federal government's Bureau of Labor Statistics, called the consumer price index (CPI), is used to measure the overall average level of prices in the United States. By calculating the percentage changes in the CPI, the inflation rate in the U.S. economy can be measured. (The CPI will be explained and discussed fully in Chapter 6.)

Deflation is a decrease in the general price level. Since World War II, price instability has been due to inflation rather than deflation. During the 1970s, for example, the United States experienced double-digit inflation rates reaching almost 14 percent per year in 1980.

Certainly we have plenty of evidence that inflation can get out of hand. Like severe unemployment, runaway inflation can wreak havoc in a society, causing social and political disintegration. A classic example occurred in post–World War I Germany when the inflation rate was as high as thousands of percentage points *per day*. Eventually, the German mark was worth more as paper—it was actually used as wallpaper—than as money. As a result, goods disappeared from markets and people starved. Looking farther back in time, economic historians claim to have evidence that runaway inflation was partly responsible for the breakdown of the Roman Empire's economic and political institutions.

Many of the costs of inflation and deflation can be traced to the inability of various economic institutions to adjust quickly to unanticipated price changes. When inflation is fully anticipated, adjustments can be made in personal savings for education, retirement, or vacations; tax codes; and financial contracts. But when inflation is unanticipated, adjustments become costly and difficult. People who live on fixed incomes—many of them elderly and poor to begin with—are particularly hard hit by inflation, as we will see in Chapter 15.

Historically, inflation has been a problem in the United States during postwar periods. Even then, as Figure 5.3 shows, the inflation rate has seldom risen above 10 percent per year. In the period of inflation following the Vietnam War, the inflation rate rose to 13.5 percent in 1980, before falling sharply. Other countries have had much worse inflation problems in recent years. For example, the inflation rate in Argentina and Brazil reached annual levels in excess of 1000 percent

Inflation rate
The percentage change in the average level of prices over a period of time; the speed at which prices in general are rising.

Deflation
Sustained decreases in the average level of prices.

FIGURE 5.3

The Rate of Inflation, 1960–1995

The inflation rate is measured by calculating the yearly percentage change in the consumer price index. Inflation rates varied greatly over the period 1960–1995, although the trend since 1960 has been toward a higher average rate of inflation. Notice, however, the downward trend in the inflation rate since 1980.

SOURCE: Council of Economic Advisers, *Economic Report of the President* (Washington, D.C.: U.S. Government Printing Office, 1996), p. 348.

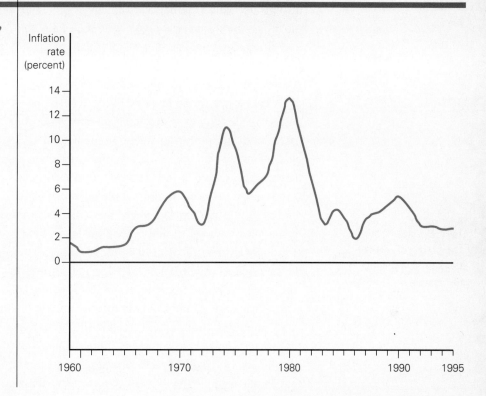

during the 1980s. In Bolivia, the annual inflation rate exceeded 20,000 percent in 1985. In the 1980s, Mexico had inflation rates in excess of 150 percent but has since adopted policies that sharply reduced the inflation rate to less than 25 percent per year. Inflation in the United States has remained generally low in the 1990s, approximating 3 percent in 1995.

Even when the rate of inflation stands at relatively modest levels, it can pose problems for the economy. First of all, inflation has peculiar redistributive effects. That is, it enhances some people's real incomes at the expense of others'. **Real income** is the quantity of goods and services that can be bought with an individual's **nominal,** or money, **income.** In other words, real income is the real purchasing power of one's nominal income. For example, if a person was earning $10,000 per year in 1975 and continued to do so in 1996, a modest inflation rate of 6 percent per year from 1975 to 1996 would mean that the person's real income, or purchasing power, would have fallen by more than 50 percent, despite the fact that his nominal income remained the same. This loss of real income is all too familiar to people on fixed money incomes—those on fixed pension plans, for example. When prices of the goods and services consumed by these groups rise, but their nominal incomes remain the same or do not rise as fast as prices, the real income of these consumers falls. Naturally, consumers whose income is rising at a faster rate than prices are better off during inflationary periods. Under such circumstances, arbitrary redistributions take place, with those on fixed incomes bearing the costs.

Uncertainty about future prices also results from price instability. Debtors and creditors, for instance, must guess at future prices and charge or pay interest rates

Real income
The purchasing power of money income; the quantity of goods and services that money income can buy.

Nominal income
Income measured in terms of money, not in terms of what the money can buy.

that may or may not cover the real change in the value of money. Inflation also disrupts decisions of producers and consumers. Consumers' expectations about future prices and future real incomes are especially important. Consumers may adjust to their expectations, buying today if they expect prices to push higher tomorrow or if they think that inflation will reduce purchasing power in the future. (Likewise, if consumers expect deflation at some point in the future—far less likely, given U.S. experience—they would be more likely to postpone purchases, especially of durable goods.) While fully expected inflation may cause some transaction costs, unanticipated inflation and an unstable, unpredictable inflation rate greatly disrupt the plans of buyers and sellers. Before 1981, consumers also faced the possibility of real income erosion due to the tax structure. When nominal income increased as a result of attempts to maintain real income, income earners were forced into higher tax brackets. This "bracket creep" occurred because tax rates have been levied on money income received, not on real income earned. **Tax indexation** is one way to curb this detrimental effect of inflation. Under tax indexation, the federal tax tables are tied to the inflation rate. Tax indexation was first implemented in 1981, was preserved in the Tax Reform Act of 1986, and continues in the 1990s.

Tax indexation
The basing of income taxes on real income instead of nominal income.

Producers are also profoundly affected by unanticipated inflation. With uncertainty about inflation, producers may withhold output of goods and services from the market. Under extreme uncertainty, the plans of investors and business entrepreneurs can be badly upset, causing postponement or abandonment of projects that enhance employment and economic growth. High, unpredictable rates of inflation help explain the low rates of capital formation and slow economic growth in some developing nations.

The Objective of Economic Growth

Economic growth
A sustained increase in the overall productive capacity of an economy over time.

The third major macroeconomic issue is growth in the economy. **Economic growth** refers to any increase in the productive capacities of the economy, whether as a result of an increase in the labor supply, an increase in the productivity of labor (the output per worker), or a net increase in the quality or quantity of the nation's capital stock, the wherewithal of production.

The labor supply grows through increases in population, immigration, or the number of people willing to work. Increased productivity of labor in output per worker is achieved through improvements in education and human capital or through a higher quantity and quality of capital stock supplied to labor. Writers and secretaries, for instance, may increase their productivity by switching from typewriters to word processing systems. Additions to the nation's capital stock are made through new investment in capital goods—word processors in offices, machines in factories. This investment arises from another macroeconomic variable, private saving. To save, individuals must forgo present consumption. Under favorable economic conditions, when the two goals of price level stability and full employment are achieved, any given rate of private saving is more likely to generate more new investment, capital formation, and economic growth than would otherwise be the case.

Gross domestic product (GDP)
A measure of the final goods and services produced by a country with resources located within that country.

Real economic growth, measured in terms of change in **gross domestic product (GDP)**, has averaged about 3 percent per year in the United States over the past hundred years. However, this rate of growth has slowed somewhat in the last two

FIGURE 5.4

Real and Nominal GDP

The black line shows the rising level of nominal GDP. Most of this increase is caused by rising prices. The colored line shows the trend in real GDP by removing the effects of inflation on prices. Real GDP, in other words, rises less rapidly in terms of constant 1992 dollars.

SOURCE: Council of Economic Advisers, *Economic Report of the President* (Washington, D.C.: U.S. Government Printing Office, 1996), p. 280, 282.

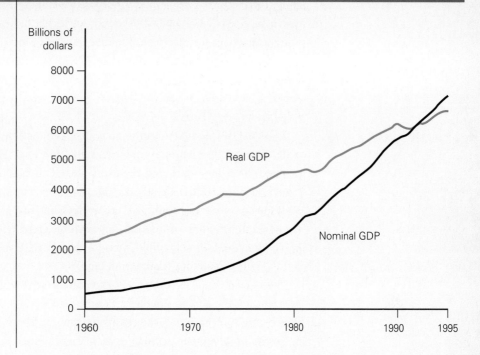

Nominal GDP

The total production of final goods and services within a country measured in monetary units that have not been adjusted for changes in the price level.

Real GDP

The total production of final goods and services within a country measured in monetary units that have been adjusted for changes in the price level.

decades. Another related problem in recent U.S. experience has been slowed growth in productivity—a reduction in the ratio of total output to the number of employed workers. While the reasons for a slowdown in productivity growth are complex—as are the relations between economic growth and changes in productivity—one major problem has been a reduced rate of technological development in the United States. Reduced productivity may translate into much slower economic growth in the future and a lessened standard of living for Americans.

The effects of these slower growth rates are not immediately apparent. However, the cumulative effect of a slower growth rate can become staggeringly large in just a generation. For example, if a country's rate of growth is 8 percent per year instead of 10 percent per year, real GDP will be only half as large within 36 years as it would have been at the slightly higher annual rate. Except for the period of the Great Depression, for over 100 years each generation of Americans has had reason to believe that it would have a markedly higher standard of living than the preceding generation. If U.S. productivity and economic growth fall to low levels, this expectation may no longer be realistic for many Americans. Figure 5.4 shows two measures of aggregate economic growth between 1960 and 1992. One line measures **nominal GDP**; the other line, **real GDP**. Nominal GDP for each of the years is measured in terms of prices that prevail in that year. Therefore, increases in nominal GDP can be caused either by increases in output or by increases in prices. Real GDP is a measure of the economy's output adjusted for general price level changes. The measures of real GDP in Figure 5.4 reflect the quantities of goods that are produced in the various years in constant dollars, or in prices that existed in some given year (1982 in Figure 5.4).

The distinction between real GDP and nominal GDP is important: Price changes cloud the picture of the value of output over time. Nominal GDP can increase between any two years even if production levels fall because the effect of rising prices can offset the effect on nominal GDP of falling levels of production. Therefore, we focus on real GDP, not nominal GDP, in measuring the rate of economic growth.

Global Objectives

A final goal of U.S. macroeconomic policy is to maximize domestic economic well-being through international trade. As noted in Chapter 2, international output can be maximized by employing the principles of specialization, comparative advantage, and trade. Under these principles, one macroeconomic goal—for the United States or for any other country—is to achieve balance between exports and imports. A huge and growing volume of trade will maximize domestic production for exports, increase domestic employment of labor, and create demands for all other resource inputs, including capital and land.

The United States is a relative newcomer on the trade scene. Countries such as Switzerland, the United Kingdom, France, and Germany have a great deal of experience with international trading arrangements. The vast size of the United States makes its involvement in trade of great significance, but until recently, the international sector (imports and exports) made up a relatively small portion of total economic activity in the United States. Only 30 years ago, less than 4 percent of all of the goods purchased by Americans were imported. In 1995, about 10 percent of all goods purchased by Americans were imported. Many more goods, including automobiles and computers, contain imported components.

Media coverage of trade "deals," free trade agreements, and the value of the dollar in relation to other currencies all suggest that trade relations have become important to the average American. Changes in technology, capital investments, and resource prices are constantly altering trade patterns. One goal of macroeconomic policy in the United States is to take maximum advantage of trade opportunities within an overall system of balanced world trade relations.

STABILITY, GROWTH, AND BUSINESS CYCLES

Economic stabilization
A situation in which the price level and the unemployment rate vary from desired levels only temporarily and by small amounts.

The overall goal of macroeconomic policy is to achieve **economic stabilization.** By stabilization, we do not mean *no* economic growth. Instead, the term describes an environment in which price changes (resulting either from inflation or from deflation) are moderate and in which the unemployment rate differs little from the full-employment level. In such an environment, the prices of individual goods will change, leading to changes in employment levels, as existing industries grow and contract and as new industries arise. However, neither a persistent change in the price level nor excessive unemployment will upset overall consumption and production and disrupt economic growth under stabilization.

Economic stability thus means the achievement of full employment under inflationless or near inflationless conditions to attain maximum economic growth in the

Business cycles
Recurrent, systematic fluctuations in the level of business
activity; usually measured
by changes in the level, or
rate of growth, of real GDP
over time.

present and future. Stabilization is a tall order in a modern economy, where economic activity is subject to fluctuations. These fluctuations, called **business cycles,**
are the result of severe variations in the plans of buyers and sellers beyond those
variations necessary for changes and improvements in production and consumption.

Business cycles are made up of, at one extreme, peaks and, at the other extreme,
recessions or depressions. At the peak of a business cycle, the economy is expanding rapidly, with employment at or near capacity. In a recession or depression, resources—especially human resources—are grossly underused. In the expansionary
phase of a cycle, increased demand for goods and services causes rapidly increasing demand for all resources, putting pressure on the supplies of labor, capital, and
raw materials. One signal that the economy is in the expansionary phase is that
business inventories are rapidly being depleted. This period of a business cycle is
often characterized by increased inflation, as business activity and employment
expand. After the peak of the cycle, the economy enters a contractionary phase. As
production of goods exceeds demand for them, inventories build up—one signal of
contraction. This phase is characterized by stable or falling prices, excess production capacities, and unemployment. When depression or recession is reached, the
economy experiences negative real economic growth rates and stagnation. When
recovery is relatively quick in arriving, the period of stagnation is termed a *recession.* A *depression* is a longer, more damaging period of stagnation. Eventually,
however, growing demand for goods and services will pull the economy out of any
slump. Figure 5.5 shows cycles of business activity as measured by real GDP
growth rates since 1960. Figure 5.6 illustrates a typical business cycle.

The goals of macroeconomic policy are to even out or counterbalance the opposing forces of the business cycle. Such policy is therefore called countercyclical

FIGURE 5.5

Cycles of Real Annual Growth Rate in GDP, 1960–1995

Periods of economic expansion and contraction have varied a great deal in this century. Note the roller-coaster path since 1960,
punctuated by sharp recessions in 1974–1975, 1980, 1981–1982, and 1990–1991.

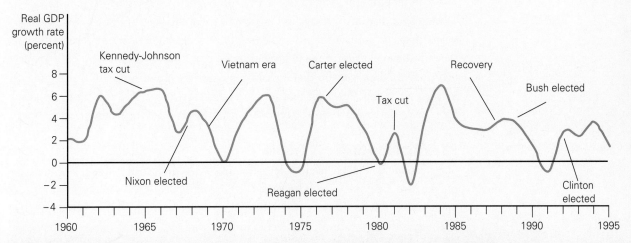

SOURCE: Council of Economic Advisers, *Economic Report of the President* (Washington, D.C.: U.S. Government Printing Office, 1996), p. 283.

FIGURE 5.6

A Typical Business Cycle

Business cycles vary in length and intensity. A typical cycle includes an expansionary phase of rising business activity and growth, a peak of activity, a contractionary phase of falling activity, and a low point, usually referred to as a trough.

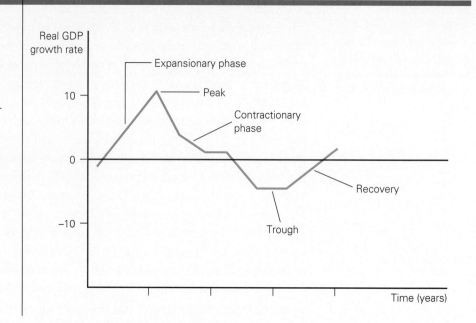

policy. Its role is to counter the business cycle to produce inflationless economic growth with full employment. The role of macroeconomic and monetary theory is to understand the causes of changes in business activity–that is, the causes of the business cycle.

Business Cycles in the United States

Using statistical analysis, researchers have identified numerous business cycles in U.S. economic history. Table 5.2 presents some data on business cycle activity in the United States since 1900. The statistics show that business cycles are recurrent but have different lengths. Twenty cycles were identified from 1900 to 1990. Measured peak to peak, the average duration of these cycles was approximately 55 months, or about four and a half years. The shortest business cycle (January 1980–July 1981) lasted 18 months. The longest (April 1960–December 1969) lasted 116 months.

Moreover, the business cycles exhibited varying degrees of intensity. In the two-year expansion from April 1958 to April 1960, real GNP rose by 8 percent. By contrast, in the expansion from July 1980 to July 1981, real GDP rose by only about 2 percent. And the recession that lasted from August 1990 to April 1991 was followed by such an anemic recovery that recession and recovery were almost indistinguishable. As of December 1996 the economy had not yet completed another cycle.

Forecasting Business Cycles

Some economists specialize in forecasting business conditions. These individuals are often called econometricians because they are highly trained in applying statistical methods to economic data, a subdiscipline of economics called **econometrics**. Econometrics is used to predict events in the economy.

Forecasting is both a science and an art. The science of forecasting involves the construction of statistical models of the operation of the economy and of economic

Econometrics
The combined use of economic theory and formal statistical techniques to analyze, explain, and predict economic phenomena.

TABLE 5.2

U.S. Business Cycles Since 1900

Trough	Peak	Length of Cycle (peak to peak in months)
December 1900	September 1902	39
August 1904	May 1907	56
June 1908	January 1910	32
January 1912	January 1913	36
December 1914	August 1918	67
March 1919	January 1920	17
July 1921	May 1923	40
July 1924	October 1926	41
November 1927	August 1929	34
March 1933	May 1937	93
June 1938	February 1945	93
October 1945	November 1948	45
October 1949	July 1953	56
May 1954	August 1957	49
April 1958	April 1960	32
February 1961	December 1969	116
November 1970	November 1973	47
March 1975	January 1980	74
July 1980	July 1981	18
November 1982	July 1990	108
April 1991		

SOURCE: Department of Commerce, Bureau of Economic Analysis, *Business Conditions Digest* (July 1986), p. 104; U.S. Bureau of the Census, *Statistical Abstract of the United States* 1995.

indicators that predict the future level of such variables as GDP or GNP. The art of forecasting is the use of past experience and commonsense judgment about what types of variables are important in predicting how the economy will behave, given that no two business cycles are precisely alike.

Who are some of the users of economic forecasts? Business decision-makers and government policymakers need reliable data on the future course of GDP to plan their activities. When business executives make decisions about investments in plant and equipment that will lead to increased output in the future, they need to have some idea of what the state of the economy will be when this output comes on the market. Overall tax revenues will usually depend on the level of national income and consumer spending in the future. To plan government spending, policymakers need estimates of future tax revenues.

To produce a forecast, the forecaster seeks information about what changes in the economy today are a good indication of what the state of the economy will be tomorrow. For this purpose economic forecasters have developed **economic indicators,** key economic statistics that provide clues about the future state of the economy. The news media regularly report on movements in these indicators.

The most commonly used indicators are listed in Table 5.3. Data on these statistics are published quarterly by the Department of Commerce, and the trend of

Economic indicators
Important data, or statistics, such as the money supply, investment spending, unemployment, and inventories that are used to help forecast economic activity and business cycles.

TABLE 5.3

Leading Economic Indicators

Indicator

New business orders
Unfilled orders
Construction approvals and starts
New company formation and vacancies
Average hours worked
Average profits
Inventory change and level
Production bottlenecks
Stock prices
Changes in raw materials prices
Tendency surveys of expected production

SOURCE: Department of Commerce, *Survey of Current Business* (August 1989), p. 24.

leading indicators is usually reported in the press. The leading indicators tend to change together over time, and a particularly useful summary statistic is the composite or combined index of leading indicators.

How reliable is the composite index of leading economic indicators in predicting downturns? Prior to each recession since World War II, the index of leading indicators dropped. Sometimes, however, it dropped more than a year before a recession started (as in the 1957–1958 recession), and at other times it dropped just months prior to a recession (as in the 1953–1954 recession). Moreover, the index dropped several times during the 1960s and no recession ensued. Economist Paul Samuelson once quipped that economic indicators "have correctly predicted nine of the last five recessions."

No predictive model of the future is perfect, but the fact that the leading indicators are widely used by economists, government officials, and businesspeople is a testimony to their usefulness as inputs to economic forecasts.

THE COSTS OF BUSINESS CYCLES

Business cycles have received much attention from economists and politicians because they entail genuine economic costs. When the economy goes into a recession or depression, the production of goods and services falls, causing living standards to fall. It may seem that these reductions in living standards are only temporary and that rapid increases in production during the recovery stage of the business cycle will counteract them. However, much of the lost production can never be regained. An economic downturn results in unemployment of economic resources of all types. Plants are closed down, farmland may lie idle, and workers with all types of labor skills remain out of work. Although all of the idle resources may become employed when the economy recovers, the lost production cannot be regained; a worker unemployed for a year cannot make up for lost production during the ensuing year. Production that is lost due to idle resources is production that is lost forever.

The second way in which business cycles reduce living standards is by depleting the capital stock. At any point in time, a society's ability to produce goods and services depends crucially on the size of its capital stock. As we saw in Chapter 2, a society's production possibilities curve is shifted rightward when capital accumulates and leftward when the capital stock declines. During an economic recession or depression, existing capital continues to depreciate, which lowers the capital stock. In a normal business environment, business firms have an incentive to replace and even add to depreciating plant and equipment; in a recession, firms are less likely to replace depreciating capital. Sales are so low that existing firms have idle capital and little incentive to replace equipment that becomes worn out. As a consequence, business downturns tend to erode the stock of productive capital and to reduce future production ability.

It is more difficult to predict how a downturn in the business cycle will affect the stock of human capital. In a recession, individuals have conflicting incentives to invest in human capital—that is, in education or on-the-job training. On the one hand, additional training or education may seem like a waste of time—why study to become a welder if there are no jobs for welders? On the other hand, unemployed persons may choose to get education or training because the opportunity cost of their time is low. If individuals consider their current level of training and skills inadequate, schooling may be a hope for a better life.

Government may step in to prevent the stock of human capital from declining. This is precisely what happened in the United States (and elsewhere) during the Great Depression of the 1930s. Programs such as the PWA and the WPA hired unemployed workers to construct bridges, highways, and public buildings. In doing so, they provided job skills for workers (human capital) and improved the nation's infrastructure. Despite these programs, the United States entered World War II with a greatly reduced stock of capital goods, which hampered U.S. military mobilization at the outset of the war.

Who Pays for Business Downturns?

In the preceding section we saw that business downturns are costly because they lower living standards both in the short run and in the long run. This does not mean that the burden is borne evenly by all citizens in terms of uniformly lower real incomes. Because U.S. firms tend to respond to downturns in business by laying off a portion of their labor force instead of reducing the hours of all workers (a practice common in Japan), the experiences of workers will vary. Workers who are laid off experience huge reductions in incomes, while other workers are barely affected.

Table 5.4 indicates that the overall unemployment rate has risen on average by more than two percentage points during each of the nine recessions since World War II. In a typical recession, the unemployment rate has risen from about 4 percent to just over 6 percent. While the unemployment rate for most types of workers rises during a business downturn, it rises much more for some types of workers than for others. The data in Table 5.4 indicate that, during recessions,

TABLE 5.4

Changes in Unemployment Rates During Recessions

During the nine recessions that have occurred in the United States since World War II, the overall unemployment rate increased by an average of more than two percentage points. However, increases in the unemployment rates for teenage workers and for black workers were substantially higher over the recession periods.

	UNEMPLOYMENT RATE			
Recession Year	All Workers	Females	Blacks	Teenagers
1947	3.8%	4.1%	5.9%	9.2%
1948	5.9	6.0	8.9	13.4
1952	2.9	3.6	5.4	8.5
1954	5.4	6.0	9.9	12.6
1957	4.2	4.7	7.9	11.6
1958	6.6	6.8	12.6	15.9
1960	5.4	5.9	10.2	14.7
1961	6.5	7.2	12.4	16.8
1969	3.4	4.7	6.4	12.2
1971	5.8	6.9	9.9	16.9
1973	4.8	6.0	9.0	14.5
1975	8.3	9.3	13.8	19.9
1979	5.8	6.8	11.3	16.1
1980	7.0	7.4	13.1	17.8
1981	7.5	7.9	14.2	19.6
1982	9.5	9.4	17.3	23.2
1990	5.4	5.4	11.3	15.5
1991	6.6	6.3	12.4	18.6

SOURCE: Council of Economic Advisers, *Economic Report of the President* (Washington, D.C.: U.S. Government Printing Office, 1993), p. 390.

unemployment rates for teenage workers and for black workers tend to rise about 60 percent more than the overall unemployment rate. However, the unemployment rate for female workers generally rises a little less than the overall rate. Statistics for workers in different industries or in different parts of the country also reflect the uneven burden of unemployment among workers. During recessions, sales of consumer durables like new homes and cars generally fall sharply, causing extremely high unemployment for workers in building trades and in the auto industry. Since automakers and their suppliers are concentrated in certain parts of the United States, some states—Michigan, in particular—are hit harder by economic downturns than states with more diversified economies.

The economic disadvantages of business cycles are not necessarily limited to the costs associated with high unemployment. There is also evidence that business cycles are a cause of inflation. During economic "booms," when demand for goods and services grows rapidly, bottlenecks in the production process are likely to arise. Rapid economic growth often frustrates the economy's ability to quickly match unemployed workers with job openings; the newly created jobs may arise in geographic areas or in industries with relatively few unemployed workers. The consequence of production bottlenecks is that wages and prices are bid up, causing inflation.

AGGREGATE DEMAND, AGGREGATE SUPPLY, AND MACROECONOMIC POLICY

Identifying goals is only the first step. Questions abound: How can full employment be reached? How can inflation be tamed? How can economic growth be sustained? Questions such as these require both theoretical and political answers. In this section we briefly introduce two of the most important macroeconomic theoretical tools—aggregate demand and aggregate supply—and the two most important types of macroeconomic policy.

Aggregate Demand and Aggregate Supply

Aggregate demand
The total spending that occurs in an economy at various price levels during a specified period of time.

Aggregate supply
The total output that will be produced by an economy at various price levels during a specified period of time.

In examining macroeconomic phenomena, it is often useful to conceive of aggregate demand and aggregate supply curves. In the abstract, **aggregate demand** represents all components of expenditure on domestically produced goods and services. Like an ordinary demand curve, which shows the quantity of a particular good or service that buyers as a group are willing to purchase at each possible price, an aggregate demand curve shows the value of all goods and services that buyers (domestic consumers, business firms, government agencies, foreign buyers) are willing to purchase at each price level over a specific period of time. Similarly, the **aggregate supply** curve shows the time-specific value of all goods and services that producers as a group are willing to offer for sale at each possible price level. In drawing an aggregate demand or supply curve, price level is measured on the vertical axis, and aggregate output is measured on the horizontal axis. Typical aggregate demand and supply curves are depicted in Figure 5.7.

Although the analogy between demand and supply in an individual market (such as the market for CDs) and the aggregate demand and supply of all goods and services is not perfect, the concepts are similar. Both the demand curve for an individual product and the aggregate demand curve are negatively sloped; as price declines, quantity of goods and services demanded rises. Several factors lead to larger aggregate demand at lower price levels. One of the most obvious is an increase in export sales to foreign buyers. A decrease in prices in this country is likely to make American goods more attractive to foreign buyers, causing the foreign component of aggregate demand to rise. Spending by domestic buyers is also likely to increase, for reasons we will detail in Chapter 10.

Like a typical supply curve in an individual market, the aggregate supply curve shown in Figure 5.7 is positively sloped. Producers as a group are revealed in Figure 5.7 to be willing to supply larger quantities of goods and services at higher price levels, presumably because higher price levels yield higher rates of profit. A detailed discussion of the forces underlying aggregate supply will also be presented in Chapter 10.

FIGURE 5.7

Aggregate Demand and Aggregate Supply Curves

Like the demand and supply curves for a single good, the aggregate demand and aggregate supply curves for all goods and services determine a price level and a level of output for all goods produced and consumed. Equilibrium is achieved at the point where aggregate demand equals aggregate supply.

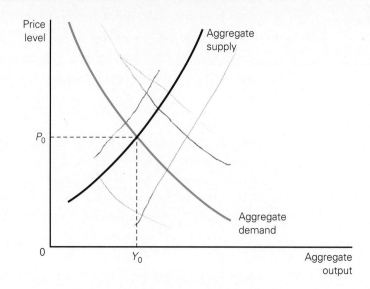

Equilibrium occurs where aggregate demand equals aggregate supply. This occurs at a price level of P_0 and an output level of Y_0 in Figure 5.7. At price levels above P_0, aggregate supply of goods and services exceeds aggregate demand. This surplus of goods and services in aggregate supply exerts downward pressure on prices, causing the price level to fall to P_0. At price levels below P_0, aggregate demand is greater than aggregate supply. General shortages of goods and services cause prices to rise, driving the price level up to the equilibrium at P_0.

Aggregate demand and supply curves are useful for examining the issues of unemployment, price stability, and economic growth. Depending on the positions of aggregate demand and supply, the equilibrium level of output can be at high or low levels. Unemployment becomes a serious problem when the equilibrium level of production is too low, causing many workers to lose their jobs.

To consider the goal of price stability, it is necessary to consider shifts in aggregate demand and supply over time. Such shifts can lead to price instability—changes in the equilibrium price level above or below P_0 in Figure 5.7. Price stability occurs if neither of the curves shifts or if both shift rightward or leftward at the same rate. However, suppose that aggregate demand increases more rapidly than does aggregate supply. In this case, the economy will experience inflation, as the price level rises to an equilibrium level above P_0. Similarly, the economy would experience deflation if aggregate supply rose relative to aggregate demand.

Comparisons of the equilibrium level of output at different points in time provide a picture of economic growth. Shifts to the right in either aggregate demand or aggregate supply will cause economic growth, the pace depending on the rate at which aggregate demand or supply increases.

MACROECONOMIC ISSUES: CAN GOALS BE MET IN A WORLD OF POLITICS?

Policy trade-off
A situation in which a policy that promotes the attainment of one macroeconomic goal necessarily implies that the attainment of another macroeconomic objective becomes more difficult.

Discretionary policy
A policy or change in policy that is determined by choices or decisions of policymakers.

Fiscal policy
The use of government spending and taxation to effect changes in aggregate economic variables.

Monetary policy
The use of money supply changes to effect changes in aggregate economic variables.

Unfortunately, policies to achieve full employment, price stability, and economic growth often fail. One explanation for this is that macroeconomic policies that might work beautifully in isolation sometimes can conflict with each other. For example, policies that shift aggregate demand rightward to attain full employment will tend to cause price increases rather than price stability. Also, certain policies to contain inflation will increase unemployment. In such cases, decision-makers are faced with a **policy trade-off;** they are forced to decide which of the economic goals is more important to attain.

Additional problems in implementing macroeconomic policy arise from political considerations. Certain policy changes, such as reductions in government spending or tax increases, are politically unpopular. Therefore, such policies tend not to be implemented or tend to be delayed, even when economically desirable.

Can Discretionary Macroeconomic Policy Work?

A more fundamental macroeconomic issue relates to the advisability of using **discretionary policies** (monetary or fiscal adjustments in the economy). Some economists question whether the economy can be managed at all by fallible public officials who possess imperfect information. **Fiscal policy**—taxing and spending policy—is controlled by Congress and the president. **Monetary policy**—control over the growth in the money stock—is controlled by the politically appointed Federal Reserve Board. The issue is whether these groups could ever know enough about

©1996 Joseph Farris from The Cartoon Bank™, Inc.

the economy or react quickly enough to disturbances to direct and control the economy in discretionary fashion. If mistakes are possible, could not discretionary policies create so much uncertainty and confusion that they might sometimes have the opposite effects to those intended?

Some contemporary macroeconomists believe that, for reasons such as conflicting goals and imperfect information, discretionary fiscal and monetary policies have built-in side effects that make them worse than useless. These economists call for the use of policy rules such as predetermined growth in the money supply and balanced federal budgets instead of discretionary control of the macroeconomy. Rules and balanced budgets would, in the view of some, take policy out of error-prone human hands, leading to more certain expectations among consumers, producers, and investors in the economy.

Underlying a faith in establishing rules rather than discretion in enacting policy is the belief, held by early classical economists and upheld by their followers today, that the economy, if left undisturbed by government, will automatically achieve the goals of full employment, price stability, and maximum economic growth. Much of the policy controversy discussed in ensuing chapters centers on issues such as these. Can discretionary policy work? How automatic are free-market forces in achieving macroeconomic goals? Are rules preferable to continual alterations in fiscal and monetary policies?

Demand-Side Versus Supply-Side Policies

Most contemporary macroeconomic theory and policy, originating in the 1930s in the writing of John Maynard Keynes, is directed toward manipulating aggregate demand, either in discretionary fashion or with rules designed to produce full employment, price stability, and growth. This approach is now referred to as **demand-side policy.**

Some economists, notably those associated with the Reagan administration, have focused instead on some of the factors related to output response or to aggregate supply changes. As noted earlier, output response is largely determined by factors related to resource supply and to investment and capital accumulation. **Supply-side policy** emphasizes the possible effects of taxes on work effort, labor supply, and investment. High tax burdens on consumer-workers and on investors mean that the economy's output response is constricted. A lower output response creates rigidities in the economy, limiting the attainment of macroeconomic goals. Indeed, one of the goals of most tax reform proposals of the 1980s was to stimulate output by lowering the federal income tax rates individuals and businesses face. Institutional changes surrounding the work decision—such as an increase in the number of women in the work force—plus government social programs and minimum-wage laws may also play a role in influencing aggregate supply. A focus on aggregate supply should not be taken to mean that aggregate demand theory or policy is unimportant. As we will see, both aggregate demand and aggregate supply play critical roles in explaining success or failure in obtaining macroeconomic goals.

In any discussion of macroeconomic policy, some allowance must be made for the possibility that policymakers will not make the "right" response—that is, the fis-

Demand-side policy
Fiscal or monetary policy intended to alter the overall level of spending, or aggregate demand.

Supply-side policy
Fiscal or monetary policy intended to alter the incentives to produce output; policies designed to shift the aggregate supply curve to the right.

fOcus
Do Politicians Create Ups and Downs in the Business Cycle?

Some economists have suggested that there is a political business cycle. Incumbent politicians pursue economic policies that promote their reelection, and, as a consequence, the economy goes through a business cycle every four years. In an attempt to enhance their reelection prospects, incumbent politicians promote expansionary policies prior to election day—tax cuts, increased government spending, and greater money supply growth. These policies have politically popular consequences in the short run: lower unemployment and interest rates, along with growth in real output of goods and services. Immediately after the election, the politicians reverse course. To limit the higher inflation rates that the reelection strategy fosters, they raise taxes and cut spending, and money supply growth is reduced. The result of these political moves is a business cycle whose length is roughly equal to the interval between elections.

Important objections have been raised to this idea. The model is said to be naive because it assumes that voters in a presidential election care only about inflation and unemployment. The critics note, correctly, that election results turn on a variety of issues, including foreign relations, income distribution, "family values," and the personalities of the candidates. Timing is also a problem—politicians cannot easily predict how particular policies might affect the economy or when. But the most important issue is whether voters can be systematically fooled. If individuals are actually short-sighted, then the political business cycle hypothesis would seem to be plausible. If people can actually and rationally predict the effects of polities, the political gain the incumbent politician had hoped for would vanish or be diminished.

There have been a number of attempts to test for various aspects of the political business cycle theory. Many of these tests consist of searches for patterns in unemployment rates or other macroeconomic variables during the periods surrounding congressional or presidential elections. The results are so far inconclusive, and there is evidence on both sides of this issue. But the idea continues to intrigue economists.

cal or monetary policy change consistent with accepted economic theory. Experience tells us that in the world of interest-group politics, economic considerations are not always uppermost in the minds of policymakers. There is every reason to believe that, like everyone else, elected politicians are self-interested individuals. What is it that the self-interested politician seeks to maximize? Is it the public interest or job security (the probability of future reelection by voters)? Many economists believe it is the latter, so they recognize that knowledge of economic theory on the part of government policymakers does not guarantee justifiable decisions. Political motives, in other words, frequently dominate fiscal policy decisions and in fact, may actually create a business cycle (see the Focus, "Do Politicians Create Ups and Downs in the Business Cycle?").

MODERN MACROECONOMICS: A MIXED APPROACH

Our brief look at the issues surrounding the attainment of macroeconomic goals suggests that modern economists can lay claim to a practical understanding of the basic functioning of the aggregate economy. Still, economists often take different policy positions based on alternative outcomes—and different magnitudes of outcomes—predicted by different theories. No single theory tells us everything we want to know. Rather, there are a number of theoretical approaches that may be viewed as alternative or complementary to each other in explaining developments in the macroeconomy. And, of course, one should never minimize the role of "politics" in macroeconomic analysis.

SUMMARY

1. Whereas microeconomics is concerned with the functioning of supply and demand in specific markets, macroeconomics studies the effects on inflation, unemployment, and economic growth of the interplay of aggregate demand and aggregate supply.
2. The overall goal of macroeconomic theory and policy is economic stabilization. Specifically, macroeconomic policy aims at an inflationless and fully employed economy with maximum economic growth. Some unemployment is expected in any fluid, dynamic economy, as individuals change jobs and other resources adapt to changing market conditions.
3. Inflation and unemployment are the enemies of economic growth because they create an environment within which private saving and new investment are reduced. A reduction in new investment means lower capital formation and reduced growth prospects.
4. Runaway inflation can have disastrous social and economic effects in an economy. Redistributions of real income from those on fixed incomes, often the poor and the elderly, extreme variations in buyers' and sellers' plans, and arbitrary increases in taxes required by government are among the problems created by inflation.
5. A business cycle is a recurrent but not predictable fluctuation in GDP. No two business cycles are exactly alike.
6. The four phases of a business cycle are expansion, peak, recession, and trough.
7. Economic forecasters try to predict economic upturns and downturns. Economic indicators are an integral part of the forecaster's tools. Leading economic indicators, economic variables that tend to turn up or down before a general business upturn or downturn, are key statistics for forecasters.
8. Trade-offs may exist in the pursuit of economic goals, such as decreased inflation and increased unemployment.
9. Fiscal policy and monetary policy are the two major means for manipulating aggregate demand and aggregate supply. Fiscal policy is the alteration in tax or spending activities by government. Monetary policy is control of the money supply and interest rates.
10. Economists have differing opinions about whether discretionary macroeconomic policy is stabilizing or destabilizing in promoting economic goals. In the view of some economists, rules should be substituted for authority in the quest for economic stabilization.
11. Supply-side economists have shifted attention to the factors affecting output response in the economy, such as the effect of taxation on work effort, new investment, and labor productivity.

KEY TERMS

unemployed
unemployment rate
full employment
natural rate of unemployment
price stability
inflation rate
deflation
real income
nominal income

tax indexation
economic growth
gross domestic product (GDP)
nominal GDP
real GDP
economic stabilization
business cycles
econometrics
economic indicators

aggregate demand
aggregate supply
policy trade-off
discretionary policy
fiscal policy
monetary policy
demand-side policy
supply-side policy

QUESTIONS FOR REVIEW AND DISCUSSION

1. What is price stability? Is a constant rate of inflation at 10 percent less harmful than an inflation rate that randomly fluctuates between 2 percent and 8 percent?

2. What are the three major goals of macroeconomic policy? Which of these goals are most politicians least concerned about achieving? Why?

3. Why do economists disagree on macroeconomic policies? Does this imply that economists do not understand macroeconomics?

4. What is discretionary-demand management policy? Can discretionary fiscal policy eliminate swings in the business cycle?

5. Suppose that the economy is experiencing less than full employment. Utilizing the aggregate demand and aggregate supply theory developed in this chapter, explain the possible trade-offs that would have to be made to attain full employment.

6. What is necessary to achieve economic growth? Do inflation and unemployment hinder this process?

7. Do changes in leading economic indicators actually cause the changes in GDP?

8. Can discretionary-demand management cause aggregate supply problems? What other trade-offs exist for policymakers?

9. Which do you suppose is better for the economy, an increase in aggregate demand or an increase in aggregate supply? What is the difference?

10. Why is the unemployment rate a less than perfect measure of the overall condition of the economy?

11. If the actual rate of unemployment exceeds the natural rate of unemployment, what happens to the production possibilities frontier?

12. What are some of the problems associated with unanticipated inflation?

CHAPTER 6
MEASURING THE MACROECONOMY

I n Chapter 5 we presented recent data on the American economy, including statistics on gross domestic product, unemployment, and inflation. In this chapter we look at these measures in more detail, examining the components of GDP, the relation between GDP and national income, and the methods through which economists derive these aggregate data. We also look at the methods for measuring inflation in the economy and at how a price index is compiled. Statistics such as GDP and the rate of inflation are the bread and butter of macroeconomic study and of policy debate. Price changes are revealed monthly and real GDP performance is revealed quarterly. Consumers and businesses, not to mention many world markets, react to each announcement of the data. When you complete Chapter 6 you should recognize

▪ what aggregate measures of economic well-being include (and what they do not include).

▪ why no measure of an economy's progress is perfect and why all measures must be qualified.

▪ the methods upon which economists and statisticians build the national income accounts.

▪ how price changes and inflation or deflation relate to aggregate measures of economic progress.

AGGREGATE ACCOUNTING AND THE CONCEPT OF GDP

National income accounting
The process of statistically measuring the nation's aggregate economic performance.

Gross domestic product (GDP)
A measure of the final goods and services produced by a country with resources located within that country.

Gross national product (GNP)
The value, measured at market prices, of all final goods and services produced in an economy in one year.

Final goods
Goods sold to the final consumers of the goods.

Economists have long been interested in aggregate economic statistics, but it was not until the 1930s in both the United States and Great Britain that economists and government agencies began to collect such data. At that time, Congress instructed the Department of Commerce to assemble and report on the national accounts. Modern **national income accounting,** or the statistical measuring of the nation's economic performance, was officially born.[1] These principles were, in large measure, the legacy of two Nobel Prize–winning economists—Simon Kuznets in the United States and Sir Richard Stone in Great Britain.

By now, you are familiar with one of the most common national income aggregates: **gross domestic product (GDP).** A more comprehensive national income statistic is **gross national product (GNP).** GNP is the total market value of all final goods and services produced over a given period in the United States. It is perhaps more helpful to define GNP as the total market value of final goods and services owned by U.S. residents. This is an important distinction in that there are foreign-owned U.S. factories and American-owned foreign factories. GDP measures total production of U.S. factories regardless of the nationalities of their owners. GNP adds to GDP the net investment income (profits) received by American owners of foreign factories. When Americans receive more income from their overseas investments than foreigners receive from their investments in the United States, GNP exceeds GDP. When the reverse is true, GDP exceeds GNP.

As we shall see in more detail later, the word *gross* means that the total market value of all goods produced in the domestic economy, including the production of capital goods, is included in GDP. GDP therefore does not account for the wear and tear on physical assets—called depreciation—that takes place during a given period. The word *product* refers to the market value of final goods and services. We are able to calculate the sum of the money or market values of different goods and services because businesses keep records of their receipts for tax purposes.

Two other elements of the definition are important. First, only sales of **final goods** and services are counted in GDP. To do otherwise would be to double-count. The value of McDonald's or Burger King's purchases of raw meat would be added to consumers' purchases of hamburgers and thus be double-counted if all purchases of goods and services sold in the domestic economy were used to calculate GDP.

A second point involves the time period. GDP ordinarily refers to final sales over the period of a year. GDP and other national income accounts, such as GNP, are measures of what economists call *flows.* Flows are processes taking place through time and, as such, are measured per unit of time. GDP is the total output of an economy *per year.* A stock, such as the capital stock of an economy, is the total amount of something in existence at a point in time. Additionally, economists also discuss the rates at which variables such as GDP are changing. These growth rates are measured by calculating percentage changes of the variables from one period to the next.

[1]Economists use the term *national income* both as a generic term encompassing *all* of the national income accounts and as a specific term referring to the total compensation of all the factors of production (labor, capital, and so on) in the economy over some period.

What GDP Does Not Count

Official statistics on GDP are far from perfect. The most serious shortcoming is that they fail to include the value of certain types of production. Goods and services produced for home consumption are omitted, for example. This category includes such activities as backyard vegetable gardens, do-it-yourself home repair, and the myriad services provided by homemakers. Since the value of such goods and services is so hard to estimate, national income accountants omit the value of this kind of production in their calculations of GDP.

A second category that does not appear in official GDP estimates is the underground economy. Various goods and many services, such as yard work or maid service, are paid for in cash and are not reported for tax purposes. Also, some firms avoid paying taxes by not recording all sales. GDP accountants elect to omit such transactions because it is so difficult to estimate their magnitude. (See the Application, "Beating the IRS: How Big Is the Underground Economy?" at the end of this chapter.)

The third major category of omitted production is illegal goods and services. As you know, profits from illegal drug sales run into the billions worldwide each year. These transactions are omitted from official statistics—again, because the magnitude of drug sales is difficult to judge, but also because there is a reluctance to view the production of illegal goods as an addition to national income.

Such glaring omissions caution against making sweeping statements about international comparisons of GDP. In developing countries, a huge percentage of all production may be used by the large rural population for home consumption. In other countries, a majority of all production may be sold in the underground economy. Official GDP statistics understate actual levels of production in all economies, though not necessarily to the same degree. Official statistics showing the GDP of the United Kingdom to be slightly larger than the GDP of Italy are not conclusive evidence that actual production is larger in the United Kingdom. It may simply be that a smaller proportion of Italian production is included in GDP statistics.

Other transactions are excluded from GDP calculations because they do not represent purchases of current goods or services. For example, the purchase of stock or other securities is not included because it represents a transfer of assets and not production of goods or services. Similarly, real estate transactions involving old homes are not counted. However, any fees paid to stockbrokers or real estate agents would be included, since they represent payment for current services.

GDP as a Measure of Economic Welfare

It is tempting to use readily available GDP statistics to measure economic welfare. Even if the problem of uncounted production were solved, however, GDP still would not accurately measure worldwide economic welfare. Raw GDP statistics do not include pollution and congestion costs, which go hand in hand with economic growth in most developed countries. Also, the average work week in industrial countries has declined markedly in this century, but GDP statistics do not capture the value of increases in leisure time. Actually, GDP never was intended to be a measure of economic welfare. GDP is a measure of production—without any indication of who gets the goods and services produced or what the goods and services are. GDP is indifferent between the provision of handguns or health care. Nonethe-

Measure of economic welfare (*MEW*)
A concept of social and economic well-being that accounts for the production of all goods and services, not just those transacted for in markets.

less, some economists have attempted to compute a **measure of economic welfare (MEW)** based on GDP statistics.

NATIONAL INCOME ACCOUNTING

We have thus far spoken only of the market value of goods, but aggregate value in the economy can actually be derived either by summing all expenditures for final goods or by summing all income received. Now, we will explain why these constructs should yield identical results and the factors to take into account to arrive at identical sums.

The Circular Flow of Economic Activity

National income (GDP) can be measured in two ways: the flow of expenditures approach and the flow of earnings, or income, approach. The **flow of expenditures** approach looks at national income as the total amount spent on final goods and services. The **flow of earnings,** or income, approach looks at national income as the amount earned by factors of production (land, labor, capital, and the entrepreneur).

Flow of expenditures
Total spending of consumers, businesses, and government on final goods and services during any given time period.

Flow of earnings
Total income received by resource suppliers during any given time period.

Logically, the two approaches have to yield the same figure for national income: All income earned by all factors in the production of goods and services is spent on those goods and services. Figure 6.1 is a circular flow diagram for an economy with only two sectors—a household, or consumer, sector and a firm, or business, sector. In the inner loop of the upper part of the diagram, firms (suppliers) produce goods for sale to consumers (demanders). The flow of goods to households is matched by a return flow of expenditures, indicated by the outer flow line. Businesses use the revenue from final sales to cover their costs of operation.

The inner part of the lower loop shows businesses or firms (demanders) employing factors of production from the household sector (suppliers). The factors of production are paid incomes that reflect their productivity in producing final output. Firm revenues are exhausted by factor payments because any leftover, or residual, portion accrues to the entrepreneur or owners of the firm in the form of profit, which is a type of income.

The upper and lower loops of the circular flow diagram illustrate the identity of the two approaches to measuring national income. The revenues from producing final goods and services are transformed into payments to cover the costs of producing the output. Total revenues from producing goods break down into profits, wage payments, interest, and land rent. By necessity, the dollar value of the expenditure flow on goods and services equals the dollar value of the income, or earning, flow to the factors of production. The important point is that national income can be measured with either approach, and the results will be identical. The flow of expenditures approach is formally identical to the flow of earnings, or income, approach.

Leakages and Injections: Some Complications

Before using these equivalent approaches to national income, consider some complications. The simple case described by Figure 6.1 excludes such features as saving and other important sectors of the economy such as government or the foreign sector. Without them, the flow of income to factors of production matches the flow of expenditures on final goods and services to firms. But since the excluded

FIGURE 6.1

The Circular Flow of Economic Activity

The circular flow diagram is portrayed with only a business and a household sector. The upper loop is the flow of final output and expenditures on final output. The lower loop is the flow of input factors of production and the return flow of factor incomes. By definition the value of the upper and lower loops must be equal. Therefore, GDP as measured by the flow of expenditures approach and GDP as measured by the flow of earnings approach must be identical.

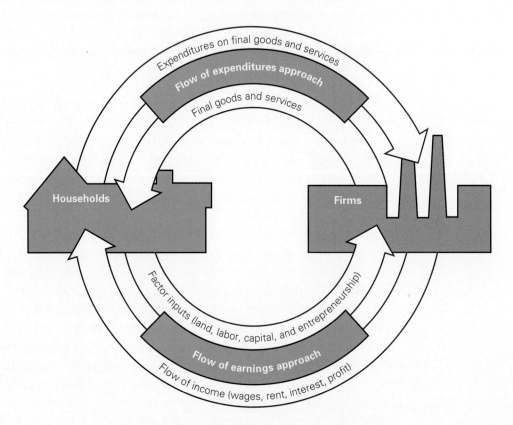

features and sectors are part of the economy, Figure 6.1 does not account for certain leakages out of and injections into the simple flow of expenditures and receipts. A leakage occurs when spending is diverted from the income stream. Household or business saving is a leakage from the expenditure stream. When processed through banks and other financial institutions or intermediaries, such saving becomes investment, an injection or addition to the expenditures flow.

Likewise, government expenditures are injections into the simple flow of expenditures, since the government, like households and businesses, makes expenditures on goods and services. Government transfers income to recipients through welfare and other programs as well. All such expenditures are injections into the circular flow. Financing such expenditures, however, requires the taxation of households and businesses. Taxation represents a leakage from the expenditure stream of the private economy.

The U.S. economy is also heavily involved in international trade and exchange, but the simple flows shown in Figure 6.1 do not include exports and imports. Exports—the sale abroad of goods and services produced in the United States—are an injection into the circular flow of expenditures and income, while imports—

FIGURE 6.2

Leakages From and Injections Into the Circular Flow

The simple two-sector economy portrayed in Figure 6.1 does not include the leakages represented by savings, taxation, and imports and injections represented by investment, government purchases, and exports. When these additional concepts are included, economists speak of a four-sector economy, including firms, households, government, and international markets.

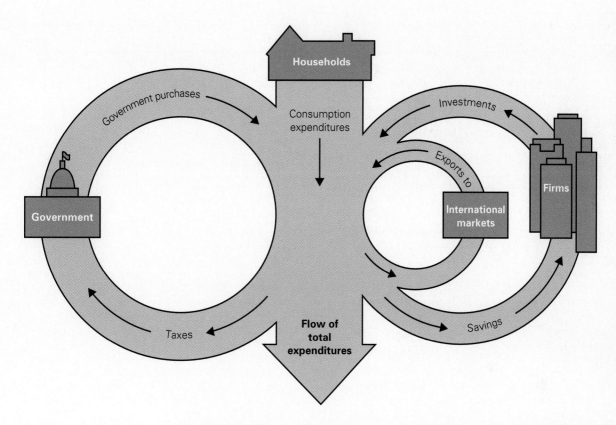

expenditures on goods and services produced abroad—are leakages from the simple income-expenditure flow.

In short, the simple income-expenditure model of Figure 6.1 does not account for certain leakages and injections. Government expenditures and exports must be counted as injections into the expenditure stream of private household and business spending. Likewise, household and business savings, along with government taxes and imports, are leakages from the simple circular flow of economic activity (see Figure 6.2).

The Flow of Expenditures Approach

National income accounting puts into practice the principles of the simple, two-sector circular flow diagram as amended by injections and leakages. The national income accountants apply the flow of expenditures approach to measuring GDP by breaking the economy down into four sectors: household, business, government, and foreign. Individuals in the economy are assigned among the four sectors, and GDP is estimated by adding the amount spent on final output by individuals in each sector. Table 6.1 gives the 1995 data on spending in each sector. Figure 6.3 compares the flow of expenditures to the flow of earnings.

TABLE 6.1

Gross Domestic Product, 1995: The Flow of Expenditures

Total expenditures in the economy are broken down into four basic groups: private consumption expenditures; private domestic investment expenditures by businesses; government expenditures; and net exports (foreign purchases of U.S. goods minus U.S. purchases of foreign goods).

	Expenditures (billions of dollars)
Personal consumption expenditures (C)	
Durable goods	604.3
Nondurable goods	1483.3
Services	2815.8
Total	4903.4
Gross private domestic investment (I)	
Fixed investment	1022.2
Change in business inventories	40.9
Total	1063.1
Government purchases (G)	
Federal	519.9
State and local	837.2
Total	1357.1
Exports and imports of goods and services	
Exports (X)	796.2
Imports (M)	906.0
Net total (X - M)	-109.8
Total expenditures on GDP	7213.8

SOURCE: Council of Economic Advisers, *Economic Report of the President* (Washington, D.C.: U.S. Government Printing Office, 1996), pp. 280–281.

NOTE: The above figures represent an annualized average over the first three quarters of 1995.

PERSONAL CONSUMPTION EXPENDITURES   Expenditures by individuals and nonprofit institutions are called **personal consumption expenditures (C)**. These expenditures are broken down into spending on durable goods, on nondurable goods, and on services. Durable goods are items such as refrigerators that are expected to last for more than three years. Nondurable goods are such things as food and clothes that are not expected to last for more than three years. Services are intangible items such as travel, car repair, entertainment, and medical care. Personal consumption expenditures represent the largest expenditure component of GDP ($4903.4 billion in 1995).

GROSS PRIVATE DOMESTIC INVESTMENT   Expenditures on final output by private business firms (including resource-owning households) are called **gross private domestic investment (I)**. Investment expenditures include spending on capital goods such as machinery and warehouses, new residential construction, improvements to existing houses, farm investments, and inventories. These expenditures were $1063.1 billion in 1995. The qualifier *gross* is used because these expenditures include spending on new plant and equipment as well as on the re-

Personal consumption expenditures (C)
Total spending by households on final goods and services.

Gross private domestic investment (I)
Total spending by private businesses on final goods, including capital goods and inventories.

FIGURE 6.3

Total Expenditures Equal Total Income Plus Adjustments

In any given year, total expenditures, composed of consumption, investment, government purchases, and net foreign spending, must equal the income to the factors of production plus corrections. This income is composed of wages, rents, interest, proprietor's income, and corporate profits. The flow of total expenditures must equal the flow of total earnings.

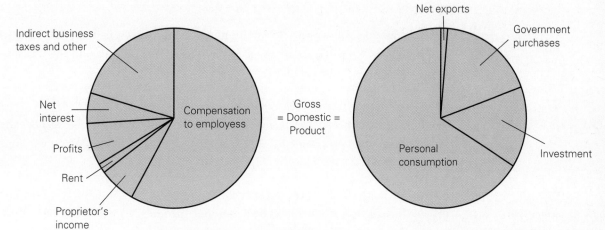

placement of worn-out plant and equipment. Business inventories are an investment in the holding of finished goods, semifinished goods, or raw materials by business firms. Investment in business inventories can vary greatly; that is, inventories can be built up or drawn down. For example, firms often draw down the level of their inventories in a period when business is bad, such as a recession. They hold fewer goods in inventory in the anticipation of decreased demand for the goods by consumers. Conversely, businesses will add to inventories in anticipation of sales increases and prosperous times.

Government purchases (*G*)
Total spending by federal, state, and local governments on final goods and services.

Net exports (*X - M*)
Total spending by foreigners on domestically produced goods and services minus total spending by domestic residents on foreign produced goods and services.

Exports (*X*)
Total spending by foreigners on domestically produced goods and services.

Imports (*M*)
Total spending by domestic residents on foreign produced goods and services.

GOVERNMENT PURCHASES The third component in the expenditure approach to GDP is **government purchases (*G*)** on final goods and services at the federal, state, and local levels. Government spending was $1357.1 billion in 1995. Government transfer payments, such as Social Security and veterans' benefits, are not included in this Figure because such payments are not made to individuals for current productive activities.

NET EXPORTS The final category of spending in the expenditure approach to GDP is **net exports (*X – M*)**. **Exports (*X*)** are domestic goods purchased by foreigners. **Imports (*M*)** are foreign goods purchased by U.S. citizens. The purpose of GDP accounting is to measure current production in the economy. Thus, we must add the value of domestic goods purchased by foreigners and subtract the value of foreign goods purchased by Americans in calculating GDP by the expenditures approach. In other words,

$$\text{Net exports} = \text{total exports } (X) - \text{total imports } (M).$$

Net exports can be negative or positive. Obviously, if we spend more on imports than we sell in exports, net exports are going to be negative. In 1995, net exports were negative. We imported more than we exported by $109.8 billion.

The flow of expenditures approach to measuring GDP is quite simple:

$$GDP = \text{personal consumption expenditures } (C)$$
$$+ \text{ gross private domestic investment } (I)$$
$$+ \text{ government purchases } (G)$$
$$+ \text{ net exports } (X - M),$$

or $$GDP = C + I + G + (X - M).$$

By this method, GDP was $7213.8 billion in 1995, as shown in Table 6.1. Keep in mind that the expenditures approach is the national income accounting measure of the upper loop in the circular flow model of economic activity.

The Flow of Earnings Approach

The flow of earnings approach should give us the same value for GDP as does the expenditures approach. Table 6.2 gives the categories used in the flow of earnings approach. (Refer also to Figure 6.3.)

National income (NI)
Total earnings of resource suppliers during a given period of time.

NATIONAL INCOME   The most inclusive figure in the flow of earnings approach to GDP is specifically called **national income (NI)**. NI is determined by adding the income earned by factors of production (land, labor, capital, and entrepreneurship) used to produce final goods and services during a given period. Table 6.2 shows national income of $5760.7 billion for 1995, the sum of income items 1 through 5: compensation of employees, proprietors' income, rental income of persons, corporate profits, and net interest.

Compensation of Employees.   Compensation of employees is the largest component of national income. It is the sum of wages and salaries paid to employees plus employer contributions to Social Security and employee benefit plans. In 1995, this category amounted to $4184.5 billion.

Proprietors' Income.   Proprietors' income is the net income earned by sole proprietorships and partnerships. Both proprietorships and partnerships are mainly small businesses that are not incorporated. This income in 1995 was $475.5 billion.

Rental Income of Persons.   Rental income of persons is the income of individuals from renting property, such as a house or a car, as well as returns to individuals who hold patents, copyrights, and rights to natural resources, such as an oil or timber lease. National income accountants also estimate a rental value to owner-occupied houses. In other words, home ownership is treated like a business that produces a service sold to the owner. All of these forms of rental income yielded earnings of $120.2 billion in 1995.

Corporate Profits.   Corporate profits are the net income of private corporations, including profits on foreign operations. The total of corporate profits was $578.4 billion in 1995.

Net Interest.   Net interest consists of the interest received by U.S. households and governments minus the interest paid by these households and governments. Some

TABLE 6.2

Gross Domestic Product, 1995: The Flow of Earnings

GDP can be calculated by summing the incomes received by suppliers of resources. Labor income, interest income, rental income, and profits are all summed—with adjustments for indirect business taxes and depreciation—to obtain the same level of GDP as found by the expenditures approach.

	Earnings (billions of dollars)
1. Compensation of employees	4184.5
2. Proprietors' income	475.5
3. Rental income of persons	120.2
4. Corporate profits	578.4
5. Net interest	402.1
National income (total of 1–5)	5760.7
6. Indirect business taxes and other adjustments	633.6
7. Capital consumption allowances (depreciation)	819.5
Gross domestic product (GDP)	7213.8

SOURCE: Council of Economic Advisers, *Economic Report of the President* (Washington, D.C.: U.S. Government Printing Office, 1996), pp. 306–307.

NOTE: GDP is in nominal 1995 dollars.

interest payments are not counted as a part of national income because they are not considered payment for current production. Net interest was $402.1 billion in 1995.

FROM NATIONAL INCOME TO GROSS DOMESTIC PRODUCT   The figure for national income in Table 6.2—the sum of income items 1 through 5—does not equal the 1995 figure for gross domestic product in Table 6.1 figured by the flow of expenditures approach. Yet we know by the principle of the circular flow model that both approaches to measuring GDP must yield the same result. The problem is that there are two items—items included in total expenditures that are not income to anyone—that must be added to national income to obtain GDP. Let us examine these adjustments.

Indirect Business Taxes and Other Adjustments.   Indirect business taxes and other adjustments must be added to national income to determine GDP because such taxes are part of the total expenditures on goods and services but are not received by anyone as income. These include sales and excise taxes paid by purchasers of goods and services; property taxes; business transfer payments such as corporate donations to charitable institutions; government subsidies; and other minor statistical adjustments.

Capital Consumption Allowances.   Capital consumption allowances, or depreciation, are an adjustment made for the wearing out of capital goods such as plant and equipment during the current production period. Capital consumption allowances, like indirect business taxes, enter the flow of earnings approach to calculating GDP even though they do not truly represent earnings. They do represent, however, part of the resource cost of producing GDP. Depreciation is not an expenditure on final output. For this reason, these items are included in the flow of earnings calculation of GDP. In Table 6.2, depreciation is equal to $819.5 billion. With adjustments for indirect business taxes and capital consumption allowances, GDP figured by the flow of earnings approach is $7213.8 billion, the same estimate derived from the flow of expenditures approach given in Table 6.1. Using the flow of earnings method of accounting, GDP is, in short, the sum of returns to the factors of production (wages, proprietors' income, rents, interest, and corporate profits) plus indirect business taxes and depreciation.

Other National Income Concepts

Macroeconomics is often concerned with the amount of income that goes to the household sector in an economy. By adjusting the figure in Table 6.2 derived for national income—income earned by factors of production—we can arrive at the concepts of personal income and disposable personal income.

Personal income (PI)
Total earnings resource suppliers actually receive during a given period of time plus transfer payments.

PERSONAL INCOME   **Personal income (PI)** is the amount of income that households receive during a certain period. There is a difference between income earned and income received. A writer, for example, may not receive royalties on the great American novel until years after writing the book because of the time lags in the production and marketing processes. Current production does not necessarily translate instantly into current income. The major categories of situations in which household earnings do not coincide in time with household income are given in items 1, 2, and 3 in Table 6.3.

To determine personal income, items 1, 2, and 3 must first be subtracted from national income because they represent income earned but not directly received by households in the current period. Corporate profits do not flow directly to individuals, but instead to firms. Net interest, because it refers to interest earned by businesses, also must be subtracted from national income in calculating personal income. Contributions for social insurance ($657.1 billion)—such as payroll deductions for Social Security—are also excluded from personal income because they are earned but not received by workers in the current period.

Items 4 through 7 are received by households in the current period and are therefore counted as part of personal income. These include government transfer payments, such as Social Security payments, personal interest income, dividends, and business transfer payments.

Depending on the magnitudes of the minuses and pluses, national income can be larger or smaller than personal income. In a period of declining business activity, for example, national income can fall below personal income because corporate profits go down while government transfer payments go up. Personal income in 1995 was $6063.7 billion, an amount greater than national income.

Disposable personal income
Personal income minus taxes; income available to spend.

DISPOSABLE PERSONAL INCOME   **Disposable personal income**—what income receivers have left to spend or save after taxes—is found in Table 6.3 by subtracting certain personal taxes (including income and property taxes) from personal income. In 1995, disposable personal income was $5272.8 billion.

TABLE 6.3

National Income, Personal Income, and Disposable Personal Income, 1995

National income minus income not received (items 1, 2, and 3) plus income received (items 4, 5, 6, and 7) yields personal income. Subtracting personal taxes from personal income yields disposable personal income.

	Value (billions of dollars)
National Income	5760.7
1. Minus: corporate profits[a]	-578.4
2. Minus: Net interest	-402.1
3. Minus: Contributions for social insurance	-657.1
4. Plus: Government transfer payments	+993.8
5. Plus: Personal interest income	+711.7
6. Plus: Personal dividend income	+212.5
7. Plus: Business transfer payments	+22.6
Personal income	6063.7
8. Minus: Personal taxes	-790.9
Disposable personal income	5272.8

SOURCE: Council of Economic Advisers, *Economic Report of the President* (Washington, D.C.: U.S. Government Printing Office, 1996), pp. 305, 310.

[a]Includes inventory valuation and capital consumption adjustments.

NOTE: Disposable personal income is in nominal 1995 dollars.

Personal Saving

Personal saving

Disposable personal income less personal consumption expenditures.

Personal saving, another important economic statistic, represents the funds provided for investment by the saving of individuals and unincorporated businesses in the economy. Their choice to refrain from spending all they receive is a crucial ingredient in economic growth. Table 6.4 shows personal saving as $229.2 billion in 1995.

THE MEASUREMENT OF PRICE CHANGES

Was GDP in 1995 greater than in 1980? To answer this question, we might simply compare GDP for 1980 and 1995. Yet changes in prices make such comparisons difficult. Think of a simple world in which only chocolate fudge is produced. The fact that total expenditures on fudge rose from $5 million in 1980 to $10 million in 1995 tells us very little. Total expenditures will increase if (a) more fudge is produced, (b) the price of fudge rises, or (c) both (a) and (b) happen at the same time. The same facts hold for changes in GDP. GDP can change over time because total output increases, prices increase, or both happen at the same time. Thus, because we are interested in comparing differences in aggregate output over time when using national income statistics, a means has to be found to adjust GDP data for changes in prices. (The more difficult issue of changes in the type and quality of goods over time is treated in the Focus "Should You Trust GDP as an Economic Measure?".) The **price level** is the average of the prices of all goods and services. It is not to be confused with relative prices, which show the price of one good in terms of another.

Price level

The average of the prices of all goods and services in the economy; used for calculating the inflation rate and for converting nominal into real values.

TABLE 6.4

Personal Saving, 1995

Disposable personal income may be saved or spent by households. In 1995, households chose to save $229.2 billion and spend $5043.6 billion of their disposable income.

	Value (billions of dollars)
Disposable personal income	5272.8
Minus: Personal outlays	−5043.6
Personal saving	229.2

SOURCE: Council of Economic Advisers, *Economic Report of the President* (Washington, D.C.: U.S. Government Printing Office, 1996), p. 310.

NOTE: Numbers are in nominal 1995 dollars.

Price index

A statistic used to calculate the price level and the rate of inflation.

Economists and national income statisticians approach the problem of detecting price level changes by constructing a **price index.** All indexes use a base year, against which subsequent changes in prices are measured. The most common method of measuring price change uses base-year quantities as weights for the price indexes of ensuing years. Any price index compares the average level of prices at a given point in time (be it today or 1947) to the average level of prices at some specific point in the past (the base year or period). If the ratio is greater than 1, then prices in general are greater at the time for which the index is calculated than they were in the base year. If the ratio is less than 1, then prices are generally lower than in the base period. (The consumer price index formula is multiplied by 100.)

Price indexes serve two very important functions. Above all, they give us a measure of what is happening to the overall level of prices. By calculating the percentage change in a price index, the inflation rate over any given time period is measured. Additionally, a price index can be used to convert nominal variables, such as GDP, to real variables. Suppose the price index is based in 1982. Dividing nominal GDP in 1995 by the price index in 1995 (based in 1982) gives a measure of the total output of the economy in 1995 measured in 1982 prices. This allows more accurate comparisons of GDP between years, comparisons that are not biased by price changes. This gives a more accurate picture of how aggregate output changes over time. Almost all nominal variables can be converted to real variables by dividing by a price index. Government statistics calculate several indexes for the American economy.

The Consumer Price Index

Consumer price index (CPI)

A price index that uses the prices of goods and services consumers generally buy to calculate the price level and the rate of inflation.

The **consumer price index (CPI)** measures price changes in a typical market basket of goods purchased by urban wage earners and clerical workers. This "market basket" was developed from a survey of about 20,000 families, who provided information on their buying habits. The market basket includes food, housing (rental costs), apparel, transportation, health and recreation, and miscellaneous services. To measure price changes in the market basket, the Bureau of Labor Statistics at the Department of Labor collects data every month from a wide variety of retail stores and service establishments. The CPI is issued monthly, and its base period is 1982–1984. Current prices are compared to average base-period prices. In the CPI, 1982–1984 = 100.

f O cus   Should You Trust GDP as an Economic Measure?

Comparisons of GDP over time are even more complicated than controlling for price changes with a price index. Such comparisons are fundamentally difficult because entrepreneurs introduce new and improved goods and services to the economy. For example, how useful is it to compare GDP in 1890 with GDP in 1996? The United States at these two time periods comprised two different economies. In 1996, there were cars, fast-food restaurants, televisions, computers, and liver transplants. These goods and services did not exist in 1890. On the other hand, there was a great deal of open land, a relatively low crime rate, and little or no acid rain in 1890.

The goods available to consumers—that is, the final outputs of the economy—change over time. Even someone with a lot of money in 1890 could not have purchased what the average middle-income family purchases today. The point is simple but profound. An economy changes across time, and comparisons of GDP therefore lose much of their relevance.

So, while we know that the U.S. economy has grown remarkably over its history, the fact that the bundle of goods available to consumers has changed over time makes the measurement of this growth difficult. For example, real per capita GDP in 1960 was $12,518. In 1995, it was $25,565. Does this mean that workers in the United States produced roughly twice the amount in 1995 as they produced in 1960? The problem is that GDP cannot give a clear answer to this type of question. (Remember: A change in GDP does not necessarily measure a change in welfare.) The goods produced in each period have changed. We do not now produce more of the same goods produced in 1960, or even in 1994. Our capacity to produce goods and services has increased, no doubt, but the exact amount of this growth is not measured by the growth of real GDP.

The farther apart in time that comparisons of GDP are made, the more severe is the problem caused by the differences in economies in the two periods. However, even over a short period, GDP comparisons are difficult because of changes in the quality of existing goods. In a span of a little more than ten years, consumers in the United States have gained access to improved goods such as cable television and more efficient computers. Do these improvements in quality mean growth in the value of the economy? If so, how could it possibly be measured? These complications indicate that GDP comparisons over time are useful, but not perfect.

Finally, exactly the same point can be made about the difficulty of comparisons of GDP across countries. Countries obviously produce different bundles of goods, and for the reasons just given, international comparisons of GDP are difficult and subject to interpretation. Different tastes for goods and services likely exist across countries, further complicating simple GDP comparisons intended to reflect differences in economic well-being. None of this argues that comparisons of GDP are meaningless. The point is that such comparisons should be made carefully and conclusions drawn about economic growth only after a careful study of all the relevant information about the economy or economies concerned. A healthy bit of skepticism should accompany all statistics!

The Implicit Price Deflator

Implicit price deflator
A price index that uses the most comprehensive set of prices to calculate the level of prices and the rate of inflation facing households, businesses, and government; also called the GDP deflator.

Another major index is the **implicit price deflator**, often called the GDP deflator. This index goes to the heart of the problem of measuring price changes over time. As we have seen, it is impossible to add the different outputs of goods over time. Rather, we add the dollar amounts spent on commodities. But since both prices and quantities of commodities can change over time, the comparison of GDP at different points in time is difficult. Remember that the economist is interested in measuring the economy's real output. Therefore, the GDP statistician must be careful to distinguish current or nominal GDP, which is evaluated in current dollars, from real or constant GDP, which is evaluated in constant dollars. The implicit price deflator is a means to convert nominal GDP values into real GDP values.

TABLE 6.5

Nominal GDP, GDP Deflator, and Real GDP, 1975–1995

The GDP deflator is used to convert nominal GDP into real GDP. By dividing any year's GDP by that year's GDP deflator, one can estimate real GDP in terms of 1992 dollars.

Year	Nominal GDP (billions of dollars)	GDP Deflator (1992 = 1)	Constant GDP (billions of 1992 dollars)
1975	1630.6	0.422	3865.1
1976	1819.0	0.446	4081.1
1977	2026.9	0.475	4279.3
1978	2291.4	0.509	4493.7
1979	2557.5	0.553	4624.0
1980	2784.2	0.604	4611.9
1981	3115.9	0.661	4724.9
1982	3242.1	0.702	4623.6
1983	3514.5	0.732	4810.0
1984	3902.4	0.759	5138.2
1985	4180.7	0.786	5329.5
1986	4422.2	0.806	5489.9
1987	4692.3	0.831	5648.4
1988	5049.6	0.861	5862.9
1989	5438.7	0.897	6060.4
1990	5743.8	0.936	6138.7
1991	5916.7	0.973	6079.0
1992	6244.4	1.000	6244.4
1993	6550.2	1.026	6383.8
1994	6931.4	1.050	6604.2
1995	7213.8	1.073	6724.7

SOURCE: Council of Economic Advisers, *Economic Report of the President* (Washington, D.C.: U.S. Government Printing Office, 1996), pp. 280, 282, 284.

The GDP deflator is similar to the CPI in that it is a price index. However, the GDP deflator is a broader index of prices than the CPI. The CPI pertains only to goods and services purchased by consumers; the implicit price deflator also takes into account goods and services generally consumed by producers and government. A major weakness of price indexes is the noncompatibility of base years. Government agencies that collect and publish various statistics often change the base year used, causing potential confusion. Nominal GDP is converted to real GDP by use of the GDP deflator—that is, by dividing nominal GDP by a constant GDP value for the same base-year prices. For example, Table 6.5 reveals that the GDP deflator was 1.073 in 1995. This number tells us that, on average, prices were 7.3 percent higher in 1995 than in 1992 (1992 being the base year). Nominal GDP for 1995, $7213.8 billion, divided by the GDP deflator for 1992 gives the real GDP for 1995: $6724.7 billion (7213.8/1.073). This number indicates what the value of GDP would have been in 1995 if prices had not changed since 1992. Thus, it measures the value of the output of goods and services in 1995 in terms of 1992 prices.

Table 6.5 shows GDP both in constant-dollar and current-dollar (or nominal) terms, using the varying price deflator for GDP for the period 1975–1995. One interesting aspect of these data is that between 1979 and 1980, 1981 and 1982, and 1990 and 1991, GDP in current terms was rising while real GDP was falling. In other words, growth in the GDP was due to inflation in prices rather than to increases in output. The proper measure of the real performance of the economy is the movement of real GDP over time.

We have talked a great deal in this chapter about the deficiencies of various measures of economic health. It should now be clear that no single measure of unemployment, inflation, or economic growth is a perfect indicator of economic well-being. Despite their limitations, however, such measures are useful: They form the basis for an understanding of the effects of macroeconomic and monetary policies.

APPLICATION

Beating the IRS: How Big Is the Underground Economy?

The underground economy refers to all the transactions between individuals and firms that are not officially recorded in the government's national income accounts. Unrecorded transactions are not limited to illicit transactions such as gambling, prostitution, and the drug trade. They also include the summer yard work that children and teenagers do for pay, babysitting and daytime childcare services that are paid for in cash and not reported to the Internal Revenue Service (IRS), the many kinds of barter transactions that occur, and a multitude of other exchanges that take place in economies that simply do not get entered on the official books.

One factor responsible for the existence of the underground economy is the income tax and all other taxes levied at all levels of government. Individuals act in their own self-interest, and some will choose to evade paying a portion of their taxes in order to increase their wealth. Some professionals simply do not declare all their earned income on their income tax forms. Waiters and waitresses occasionally underestimate their tips to the tax authorities. One result is that the value of these services does not enter the government's official income accounts. Nonetheless, the services these people perform make the economy wealthier and should be reflected in GDP. Quite often these unreported transactions are purely cash transactions. Checks or credit cards leave a paper trail, whereas cash is much harder for income tax auditors to trace.

Income tax rates have traditionally played a major role in determining the extent and size of the underground economy. When people barter or swap goods and services, the value of the transaction goes unreported in GDP but still enhances the barterer's economic welfare. When all relevant tax rates that individuals face are lower, the incentive to barter is diminished, and the underground economy will shrink in size. Indeed, this was one of the reasons that the top federal income tax rate was lowered in the late 1980s. (In 1991 and, more significantly, in 1993, the top marginal rate was raised, however; other taxes at all levels—including Social Security taxes—have also been rising in recent years.)

A third explanation for the existence of the underground economy is that artificial entry barriers exist in many occupations. Factors such as a person's age, immigrant status, union status, or other legal requirements may prevent employment in the regular economy. Illegal aliens may work as domestics for unreported income in order to avoid detection and deportation. Hundreds of "gypsy cabs" operate in New York City; these private automobiles that ferry passengers about the city are driven by people unable to obtain a license for an official taxicab. Other people work in the underground economy because they can earn larger incomes than they could by working in the official economy.

Just how big is the underground economy? No one knows for sure, and economists have used various techniques to estimate its size. One method is to compare Department of Commerce data on GDP to the IRS's income data. Another approach looks at government data concerning the proportion of the population that is officially reported as employed. This figure can be compared to the number that could reasonably be expected in calculating the size of underground income earned. A third method tracks the total amount of cash, including the amount in "large" bills, circulating in an economy and compares it with total checking accounts and credit pur-

chases. Unusually large amounts of cash or numbers of large bills indicate a large underground economy.

Estimates on the size of the underground economy in the United States for the late 1970s range from 4 to 25 percent of GDP. If 10 percent of all economic activity were hidden from official view in 1995, then underground GDP would total more than $500 billion. While this is large in absolute terms, some have estimated Italy's underground economy to amount to about 35 to 40 percent of that country's official GDP. Japan, however, appears to produce only about 1 to 2 percent of its total output in an underground economy. Clearly, such factors as tax rates, cultural attitudes, laws, and resources devoted to uncovering the underground economy will influence the extent of such activity across countries.

QUESTIONS

What measures can government take to reduce the size of the underground economy? Explain how underground markets may actually be more efficient than legal markets.

SUMMARY

1. National income accounting is concerned with the measurement of the aggregate performance of the economy.
2. Gross domestic product (GDP) is the market value of all the final goods and services produced in an economy during a given period. It includes only currently produced goods and services, and it excludes such items as illegal transactions and household production.
3. GDP is not a measure of economic welfare. It does not count social costs such as pollution, which lower economic welfare, or such goods as leisure, which raise economic welfare.
4. Gross domestic product can be computed in two ways: by adding expenditures on final goods and services produced during a given period or by adding the earnings or incomes of the factors of production used to produce final goods and services during the period. The two approaches, subject to a statistical discrepancy, yield the same result for GDP.

The Flow of Expenditures Approach

personal consumption expenditures		gross private domestic investment		government purchases of final goods and services		net exports		
(C)	+	(I)	+	(G)	+	(X - M)	=	GDP

The Flow of Earnings Approach

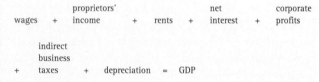

The flow of expenditures approach focuses on buyers' evaluations of goods produced during a year. The flow of earnings approach concentrates on the cost of production of goods and services. The circular flow of economic activity, therefore, ensures that the two approaches are identical. That is,

$$\text{Dollar spending on final outputs}$$
$$= \text{GDP} = \text{dollar costs of producing final outputs.}$$

5. Other important national income accounting concepts are personal income, disposable personal income, and personal saving. Each provides important information for the macroeconomist in analyzing economic stability and growth.
6. To compare GDP in different time periods, some method must be used to control for price changes. The government uses indexes, including the consumer price index and the implicit price deflator for GDP.

KEY TERMS

national income accounting
gross domestic product (*GDP*)
gross national product (*GNP*)
final goods
measure of economic
    welfare (*MEW*)
flow of expenditures
flow of earnings

personal consumption
    expenditures (*C*)
gross private domestic
    investment (*I*)
government purchases (*G*)
net exports (*X – M*)
exports (*X*)
imports (*M*)

national income (NI)
personal income (PI)
disposable personal income
personal saving
price level
price index
consumer price index (CPI)
implicit price deflator

QUESTIONS FOR REVIEW AND DISCUSSION

1. Why does GDP count only the production of final goods and services? Why aren't intermediate goods and services counted?
2. How is GDP related to national income, personal income, and disposable personal income?
3. List three reasons GDP should not be considered an overall indicator of society's well-being.
4. What are the three approaches used to estimate GDP?
5. American society has become more urbanized and industrialized since 1930. Other things being equal, do you think this means that our measurement of GDP is more or less precise? Why?
6. What is GDP in constant dollars? How is it calculated?
7. Why might GDP be a misleading statistic with which to compare the economy of the United States with that of China?
8. Which of the following are counted in the calculation of this year's GDP: (a) the services provided by a homemaker; (b) the wage paid to a maid; (c) Sam's purchase of an antique desk; (d) Joan's purchase of ten shares of stock; (e) Social Security checks received by the elderly; (f) Social Security taxes paid by workers?
9. In the former Soviet Union, black markets supplied final goods and services that the central government did not provide in adequate quantities. Were these final goods and services counted as part of the Soviet Union's GDP?
10. How are leakages transformed into injections?
11. Using the flow of expenditures approach, why are trade deficits detrimental to the economy?
12. If fewer final goods and services are produced this year than were produced last year, can GDP increase during the same time period? How?
13. Explain the differences between the consumer price index and the implicit price deflator.

PROBLEMS

1. Suppose that nominal GDP in 1995 totals $8475 billion and rises to $12.5 trillion ten years later. If the GDP deflator for 1995 is 1.85 and for 2005 is 2.75, in what year is real GDP greater? By how much?
2. Consider the following information for the country Alpha. During the past year, consumption expenditures increased by $13.5 billion, gross private domestic investment increased by $5.8 billion, and government purchases declined by $10.4 billion. In addition, the country experienced a trade deficit of $2.9 billion. Did Alpha's GDP increase or decrease? By how much?

CLASSICAL MACROECONOMIC THEORY

Measuring the rise and fall of macroeconomic variables such as the rate of inflation, GDP, and unemployment is only a first step toward understanding why these economic indicators fluctuate and what measures, if any, are needed to maintain stability and growth.

The next three chapters survey some of the major theoretical tools of macroeconomics to discover the conditions under which the economy can achieve stability and growth. We concentrate on both aggregate demand—the spending side of the economy—and aggregate supply—the producing side of the economy. This chapter and Chapter 8 develop economic principles pertaining to aggregate demand. Chapters 9 and 10 deal with the interaction of aggregate demand and aggregate supply.

Some simplifications are necessary to understand how aggregate demand and supply interact to sustain full employment, economic growth, and low levels of inflation. This chapter and the next concentrate on two views of consumer and business spending—the private or nongovernment part of aggregate spending. The first view is the classical notion of a self-regulating aggregate economy; the second is the perspective of John Maynard Keynes, who focused attention on how spending changes cause prosperity and depression. To simplify our development of aggregate demand and supply theories, we only briefly cover here important but complicating variables such as the money supply. We defer our in-depth analysis of money until Part Three.

The classical view sees the economy as self-regulating, without need of large-scale government intervention. A full appreciation of the classical view is the starting point for understanding how and why Keynes and others modified macroeconomic theory. When you complete Chapter 7 you should understand

- why the classical writers had faith that a nonregulated economy could fully employ all resources in the long run.
- the four essential components of the classical view that the economy would function at or near full employment over time.
- the basic classical view that government intervention should be minimized in the private economy.
- how classical macroeconomic theories and their policies interrelate.

CLASSICAL THEORY

Can the economy remain as close as possible to its production possibilities frontier? Can it manage to keep all resources, human and nonhuman, fully employed? More fundamentally, can the economy automatically produce full employment, a maximum GDP, and price stability? If not, what actions are necessary to maintain these important goals?

Historically, economists have given many different answers to these difficult questions. **Classical macroeconomic theory** stems from Adam Smith's pioneering work, *An Inquiry into the Nature and Causes of the Wealth of Nations*, published in 1776. Smith, and those who followed in the classical tradition, believed that given laissez-faire government policies and enough time, the economy would achieve the goals of price stability, full employment, and economic growth through its own ability to correct short-run unemployment and inflation. In other words, the classical theorists believed that unemployment and inflation were temporary phenomena. In the long run (a period of time that is hard to specify), the economy would remain close to or on its production possibilities frontier and enjoy a stable level of prices. The theory that grew from Smith's faith in a self-adjusting market mechanism was the work of many economists who wrote at different times in response to different conditions. The following simplified discussion of classical macroeconomics is a composite of various individual contributions. First, consider the classical engine of economic growth.

The Classical Blueprint for Economic Growth

The classical economists were writing at a time of rapid technological advance. Attitudes toward the Industrial Revolution—the catchphrase for the technological advances of the eighteenth and early nineteenth centuries—undoubtedly colored the classical economists' conception of how the economy works and grows. The **classical process of economic growth** conceives of a circular flow of human activities leading to growth in per capita output and economic well-being for the average citizen of the economy. The circular flow of this classical process of economic growth—like the one considered in Chapter 6—focuses on the real factors and activities leading to economic growth.

The heart of Adam Smith's view of economic progress is the natural tendency for society to divide tasks. The **division of labor** in producing output creates

Classical macroeconomic theory
A view of the macroeconomy as being self-adjusting and capable of generating full employment and maximum output in the long run without government intervention; dominant from the late eighteenth century through the early twentieth century.

Classical process of economic growth
A process based on the division of labor, but also involving increases in saving, investment, capital accumulation, and, ultimately, growth in real GDP.

Division of labor
An economic principle whereby individuals specialize in the production of a single good, service, or task, thereby increasing overall productivity and economic efficiency.

FIGURE 7.1

The Classical
Process of
Economic Growth

Enhanced division of labor
in the classical growth process
leads directly to increased output of goods and services.
The division of labor is directly
fueled by capital accumulation
in the circular flow.

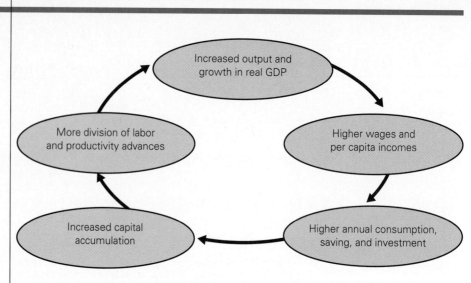

enormous advantages for society. A modern assembly line or fast-food production by McDonald's are excellent examples of the division of labor. Given enough
time, a single worker could certainly build an automobile from scratch. Only the
hobbyist would approach car building this way, however. Adam Smith hit on the
critical idea (from observation) that the division of tasks (in the context of automobile manufacturing, fitting parts, welding motor parts, installing windshields,
and the like) educates workers in some critically important ways. The repetition
of specific tasks in production leads to increased skill and dexterity in every
worker, thereby increasing human capital and productivity. The repetition of specific tasks also fosters invention and creativity in workers—an advantage encouraged by the narrow focus of the individual's attention on particular tasks.
Moreover, while training and retraining for specific tasks takes time, on balance
the application of the division of labor saves time in that workers need not move
from task to task.

Figure 7.1 shows, in simplified form, how the division of labor leads to the
growth of real output as it works its way through production processes in an economy. As the circular flow progresses, increased real GDP creates higher real wages
and higher per capita incomes. Higher wages and incomes permit individuals to
consume and save more annually. But, as we will see in more detail later in the
chapter, saving by some individuals is translated directly into investment by other
individuals. At low interest rates, individuals want to invest more, and savers want
to save less. High rates encourage savers and discourage investors. There is a point
at which the desires of savers and of investors are in equilibrium.

The process depicted in Figure 7.1 is continuous; there is no starting point.
Each element is equally important to the process, and each can serve as the "first
step." For ease in understanding, however, we may think of the process as beginning with increased demand (consumption) for goods. The saving of consumers
permits, through the link to investment, additional capital accumulation. An increase in the (net) capital stock raises the productivity of both labor and natural

resources, permitting more division of labor. The result of greater application of capital and enhanced division of labor is higher real GDP. Wages rise, as do per capita incomes, leading to more consumption, saving, and investment. The process continues until, in Adam Smith's words, the extent of the market is reached—that is, until domestic and international markets are saturated with goods and services.

It is worthwhile to remember that, in this simple process, savings are translated *automatically* into the exceptionally important mechanism of investment. Through investment, capital is accumulated. Capital—broadly defined to include factories, machinery, tools, and human skills—is a force for growth because it permits and facilitates the division of labor. Increased capital accumulation, as shown in the circular flow of Figure 7.1, allows increased division of labor and, along with it, increased *productivity of labor and capital*. Using Smith's words again, the "wealth of a nation"—GDP—is the annual product of the raw materials, land, and labor of a society, assisted, critically, by the accumulation of capital goods and the division of labor.

Many of the classical economists' predecessors equated the accumulation of gold and other precious metals with the wealth of a nation. Instead, according to the classical economists, human capital and resource development, assisted by growing capital and the division of labor, produced the wealth of the nation and contained the keys to economic growth. The division of labor gives rise to increased output and economic growth. Higher per capita wages and incomes result from increased real output. Higher incomes produce higher consumption and savings. Additional savings lead to additional investment in capital and in capital accumulation. Capital accumulation enhances and facilitates a greater division of labor, and the process continues.

LIMITS TO GROWTH   The process depicted in Figure 7.1 is neither instantaneous nor limitless. As we already mentioned, the growth process may be limited by the "extent of the market." Profitable investment outlets may dry up as demand, both foreign and domestic, for goods and services becomes saturated. The classicals knew that the economy's maximum attainable output is limited by its actual supply of human and nonhuman resources, the state of technology, productivity, and population. The classical view of the macroeconomy was a **long-run equilibrium** conception. In other words, classical theory was concerned with how an economy adjusts to some hypothetical equilibrium given some actual supply of resources, level of population, technology, or state of specialization.

Classical long-run equilibrium
The hypothetical adjustment of an economy to full employment given an actual supply of resources, population, technology, and degree of specialization.

The classicals believed that mechanisms within the economy were self-adjusting—in other words, that mechanisms automatically brought full employment in the long run. Full employment of resources in the long run is, of course, tantamount to being on the economy's production possibilities curve (see Figure 7.2a). Society's choice between capital and consumer goods in the present has an effect on future economic growth. In the classical context, a choice of more capital goods relative to consumer goods means more investment and capital accumulation, which produces a greater division of labor and more rapid future economic growth. The point to remember, however, is that the attainment of any point such as A on PP_0 in Figure 7.2a is the result of self-adjusting forces in the economy in the long run. The exact point chosen on any production possibilities

FIGURE 7.2

Production Possibilities and the Aggregate Supply Curve

In the long-run adjustment mechanism of classical economics, attainment of points such as A on production possibilities curve PP_0 of Figure 7.2a translates to a vertical aggregate supply curve such as AS_A and output level Y_0 in Figure 7.2b. In the classical model, there is no unemployment in the long run. Technological advances or discovery of new resources could be part of the long-run economy-wide adjustments that shift the production possibilities frontier and aggregate supply curve rightward.

(a)

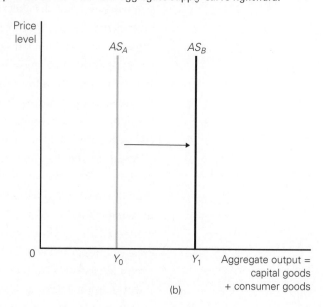

(b)

curve also depends on society's relative demands for present and future consumption. The society that chooses more capital goods at the expense of consumer goods will enjoy more future growth potential. The society that chooses more consumer goods in the present will enjoy more goods and services now but will have less growth potential.

Points such as A on PP_0 in Figure 7.2a also imply that all resources are fully employed in the economy. At the risk of getting a little ahead of ourselves, we should note that later economists, including Keynes, challenged the belief that automatic, self-adjusting forces could be relied upon to get the economy to points such as A on PP_0. They believed that certain short-run factors, such as wage and interest-rate inflexibility inhibited the classical mechanism. For now, just keep in mind that points such as A in Figure 7.2a are attained only after adjustments take place in the long run and full employment is reached in the entire economy.

ECONOMIC GROWTH AND AGGREGATE SUPPLY   Economic growth, as summarized by a production possibilities model, may also be related to the aggregate (economy-wide) supply curve developed in Chapter 5. If production possibilities curve PP_0 is drawn under assumptions of constant technology, possibilities for the division of labor and economic growth are limited. The attainment of point A in Figure 7.2a may be viewed as equivalent to a level of income, Y_0, that defines the aggregate supply curve AS_A in Figure 7.2b. At any given moment, then, the growth process is limited by, among other things, the state of technology. The maximum amount of output that can be had out of the economy, irrespective of the price level, is designated AS_A or Y_0. Note that the vertical supply curve of Figure 7.2b differs from the upward-sloping aggregate supply curve in Chapter 5 because the attainment of any point on production possibilities curve PP_0 means that consumer and capital goods production is maximized. The upward-sloping aggregate supply curve indicates that some unemployment of resources exists—in other words, that the outer limits of the production possibilities curve have not been reached.

A change in technology or the augmentation of resources (perhaps through international trade or through resource discoveries) would shift the production possibilities curve rightward. Attainment of a new equilibrium point such as B in Figure 7.2a through long-run, economy-wide adjustments would shift the aggregate supply curve rightward. All points on new production possibilities frontier PP_1 contain higher total production of consumer and capital goods than on PP_0. In terms of Figure 7.2b, aggregate supply shifts to AS_B at output level Y_1. In short, the aggregate supply curve of any economy is based on the "possibilities" of attaining maximum production. A vertical aggregate supply curve means that society has reached the production possibilities curve of the economy.

Aggregate Demand, Aggregate Supply, and the Macroeconomic Problem

The aggregate demand and supply apparatus developed in Chapter 5 may be used to show possible policy choices facing economic decision-makers. The impact of any change in aggregate demand created by fiscal or monetary policy will depend on the shape of the aggregate supply curve and on the initial point of intersection. The shape of the aggregate supply curve depends on the state of the economy—that is, on prevailing economic conditions. Consider Figure 7.3. The conditions described in this chapter—full employment of resources, an economy on its production possibilities frontier—are represented by the vertical portion of the aggregate supply curve in Figure 7.3 (the portion labeled "classical case"). When all available resources are employed, an individual producer can expand production only by bidding resources away from other competing producers. Under these conditions, any increase in aggregate demand will drive the price level up without increasing overall production.

Suppose, however, that the economy is merely producing fairly close to capacity. Under these conditions the aggregate supply curve will be steeply sloped, as depicted in Figure 7.3 by the portion of the curve labeled "intermediate range." In this case, any attempt to increase production leads to shortages of certain resources. The average cost of many productions of goods and services will rise with an increase in aggregate demand, as shown by the shift from AD_1 to AD_2 in Figure 7.3. Such an increase will inevitably increase prices from P_1 to P_2. Note, however, that aggregate output of goods and services, measured as real output on the horizontal axis of Figure 7.3, will rise from Y_1 to Y_F.

The existence of an intermediate case implies the existence of economic conditions that are the opposite of those represented by the vertical portion of the aggregate supply curve. Indeed, the horizontal portion of the aggregate supply curve,

FIGURE 7.3

Aggregate Demand, Aggregate Supply, and Policy Choices

The effects of changes in aggregate demand on prices and output will be determined by the shape of the aggregate supply curve. Given economic depression and widespread unemployment (the Keynesian case), an increase in demand will increase real income with no increase in the price level. With fully employed resources (the classical case), an identical increase in aggregate demand will simply cause inflation with no increase in income. In the classical case, output cannot increase in real terms; it can, however, increase in nominal terms—an outcome called *inflation*. In the intermediate case, both the price level and real income respond somewhat to aggregate demand increases, such as a shift from AD_1 to AD_2.

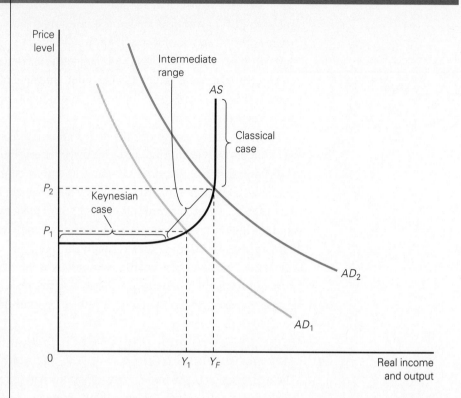

labeled "Keynesian case," represents a situation in which there are large quantities of unemployed resources available for work. (This portion of the aggregate supply is named for John Maynard Keynes, who paid a great deal of attention to the situation of massive unemployment in the economy.) When the economy is operating far below its capacity in this manner, production can increase without causing much of an increase in input prices. Not only is it possible to employ more labor without wage increases, all other kinds of resources (machinery, land, and capital) are readily available. Firms can hire more inputs without having to compete with other firms for them, thereby avoiding increased resource prices and higher average production costs. Small increases in aggregate demand would lead to large increases in national output.

The simple apparatus of aggregate demand and aggregate supply can show us the alternatives facing the economy, but a fuller understanding of economic policy can only be had with a closer analysis of each policy position. Keynesian and other newer views will be developed in future chapters. In this chapter we investigate how the classicals arrived at two startling conclusions: (1) that the aggregate supply curve was vertical and (2) that a self-adjusting mechanism virtually guaranteed that the economy would always tend toward full employment and full production in the long run if left unassisted by outside forces such as government.

FIGURE 7.4

Say's Law

In the circular flow of income and output, the act of supplying goods and services is necessarily equal to the act of demanding goods and services.

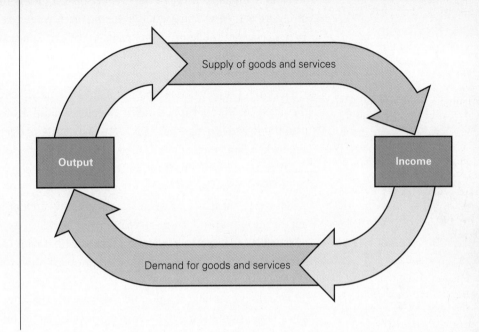

Cornerstones of Classical Macroeconomic Theory

Classical economic theory primarily concerned itself with how economies grow and prosper. Imbedded within the elements of economic progress they described, however, is a theory of the macroeconomy. Taken as a group, the classicals developed an exact theory of how the economy adjusts in the long run to reach a point on the production possibilities or aggregate supply curve. The classical economist's belief that the economy self-adjusts in response to short-run disturbances and produces full employment and economic growth without government interference rests on four cornerstones:

1. Say's law;
2. Interest rate flexibility;
3. Price-wage flexibility; and
4. The quantity theory of money.

The first three cornerstones deal with the flexibility of the macroeconomy in maintaining full employment. The fourth concerns the determination of the price level and the control of inflation.

Say's law

A proposition of the classical economists that the production of goods and services will generate incomes sufficiently large that those goods and services will be purchased.

SAY'S LAW   Say's law is an economic proposition first attributed to Jean-Baptiste Say (1767–1832). According to Say's law, diagrammed in Figure 7.4, the act of supplying goods, or total real output, is the equal but opposite side of demanding goods, or total real expenditures. Say's law implies that full employment is a permanent, built-in feature of the macroeconomy. Resource unemployment is impossible because the act of producing goods is the same act as demanding goods. In other words, supply creates its own demand.

Say believed that in a money economy the aggregate demand for goods and services is financed through the earning of income, as in the circular flow diagram in Figure 6.1. How do productive factors earn wages, rents, interests, and profits? They do so by producing goods and services. In this system, as in a barter system, the act of producing specific goods and services results in the demand for other goods and services.

According to Say, supply creates its own demand, since the income generated in the act of producing (or supplying) goods would always be used to buy (or demand) goods of equal value. Say's law may seem perfectly sensible, but what happens when consumers choose to save part of their income? The act of saving—the sacrifice of present consumption for larger future consumption—disrupts the perfect balance between income and output.

Saving is a leakage, or withdrawal, from the circular flow of income and spending. If this withdrawal from spending is not matched by an injection—another form of spending to compensate for the saving withdrawal—underconsumption and unemployment result and Say's law does not work. Investment spending is one form of injection into the circular flow to make up for a savings leakage. But how do private savings—the leakage—and investment—the injection—become linked? Can Say's law be vindicated? The answer, the classical economists thought, lay in the mechanism of interest rates.

INTEREST RATE FLEXIBILITY   People save, or postpone current consumption, because of a reward for doing so. Interest paid on savings is their reward, enabling savers to consume more goods later. This important relation may be expressed

$$S = s(r),$$

or saving (S) is a function of the real rate of interest (r). The rate of interest is both the percentage that savers earn annually on their savings and the percentage that borrowers must pay to use funds deposited in savings institutions. The **real rate of interest** is the nominal rate of interest minus the annual rate of inflation. The real rate reflects the fundamental forces of saving and investment in the economy.

Real rate of interest
The nominal interest rate minus the inflation rate; the interest rate that measures the true incentives and costs that savers and investors face.

Classical economists believed that saving was positively related to the real interest rate: A rise in the interest rate increased the amount saved. For example, when the real interest rate increases from r_0 to r_1, depicted in Figure 7.5, consumer-savers in the economy are encouraged to save more for future consumption. The higher the interest rate, the less you must sacrifice today in order to increase consumption by a given amount in the future for a new car, a college education, a new house. A high interest rate encourages savers to devote greater amounts to saving out of current income because future goods become *cheaper* relative to current consumption. Any increase in attitudes encouraging saving would cause the S curve in Figure 7.5 to shift to the right, indicating more saving at all rates of interest. If attitudes toward thrift become discouraged, of course, the whole curve would shift to the left.

FIGURE 7.5

The Classical Concept of Saving

Saving and interest rates are positively related. As the real rate of interest rises, from r_0 to r_1, the level of saving in the economy rises from S_0 to S_1. An increase in the amount saved means that present consumption, or demand, is diminished by an equal amount.

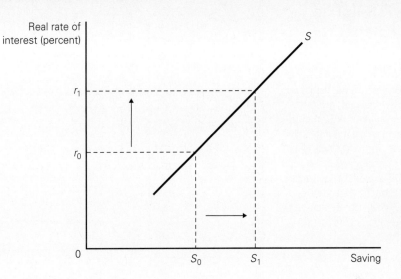

Keep in mind that increases in saving are accompanied by simultaneous decreases in current consumption. In other words, according to the classical model, aggregate demand falls by the amount that saving increases. Will an increase in saving mean that aggregate supply will not call forth enough aggregate demand? Will goods remain on shelves, inventories pile up, and thousands of workers be laid off? To both of these questions, the classical economists answered no—with the qualification that the economy must be allowed to reestablish its equilibrium. Not only does the interest rate paid to savers determine their choices, but the interest rate charged on loans determines the behavior of investors. Investment is a flow of expenditures to repair or replace capital goods or to make additions to the capital stock of the nation. Investment spending, just like consumption spending, generates income and employment.

In classical theory, a lower rate of interest makes more investment projects—such as expenditures for warehouses and machinery—profitable. Since interest payments factor into the cost of new investment, higher interest rates make new investment more costly, other things being equal. Investments become more attractive when the interest rate falls. The interest rate may be thought of as the price of loanable funds to investors. As this price (the interest rate) rises, investors are discouraged from engaging in new investment projects. As it falls, investors spend more on capital goods. Technically, this relation can be expressed

$$I = i(r),$$

or investment (I) is a function of the real rate of interest (r). However, unlike the relation between saving and interest, investment and the real rate of interest are negatively related. Rises in r cause declines in the amount of I, and reductions in r provoke increases in the amount of I.

FIGURE 7.6

The Classical Concept of Investment

The amount invested (I) and the real rate of interest (r) are negatively related, given a constant rate of return on investment in capital goods. As the rate of interest falls from r_0 to r_1, businesses invest more in capital goods. The increase in investment expenditures from I_0 to I_1 represents a net increase in demand.

This inverse relation is depicted in Figure 7.6. As the real rate of interest declines, the investment spending represented by curve I increases. Conversely, when the rate of interest rises, fewer and fewer investment projects become profitable, and investment spending declines. Increases in the productivity of capital–through inventions or improvements in technology–would increase the level of investment at every rate of interest, shifting the whole curve to the right.

According to the classical system, saving and investment are balanced by means of the interest rate. Figure 7.7 reproduces the saving and investment curves already discussed. An initial economy-wide equilibrium is established where saving equals investment at interest rate r_0. At interest rate r_0, in other words, the amount that individuals in society wish to direct from consumption to savings is S_0. Real interest rate r_0 is the savers' reward for their thrift. At interest rate r_0, moreover, investors find I_0 worth of investment projects to be profitable–no more, no less. Given curves S and I, no other interest rate is compatible with equilibrium. Why? Because an interest rate lower than r_0 would create a shortage of investment funds, and one higher than r_0 would mean a surplus of funds. In the former case, according to the laws of supply and demand, investors' demand would force the interest rate up to r_0; in the case of a surplus of funds, savers' demand would force the interest rate down to r_0. To put the matter formally, macroeconomic equilibrium requires that the amount of saving equal the amount of investment, or, in terms of the preceding equations, that

$$S = I.$$

What happens if the whole saving curve or investment curve shifts, reflecting a sudden change in society's underlying attitudes toward thrift (increased saving for retirement or expectations of hard times) or a technological breakthrough that increases the productivity of investments? Suppose, for example, that individuals

FIGURE 7.7

The Relation Between Rate of Interest, Saving, and Investment in the Classical System

Initial equilibrium E_0 is established at interest rate r_0 with saving and investment curves S and I. An increase in thrift will cause the saving function to shift rightward from S to S_1, lowering the rate of interest from r_0 to r_1. As the interest rate declines, the amount of investment spending increases. Reduction in the amount of consumption spending brought about by increased saving is therefore accompanied by a counterbalancing increase in the amount of investment spending.

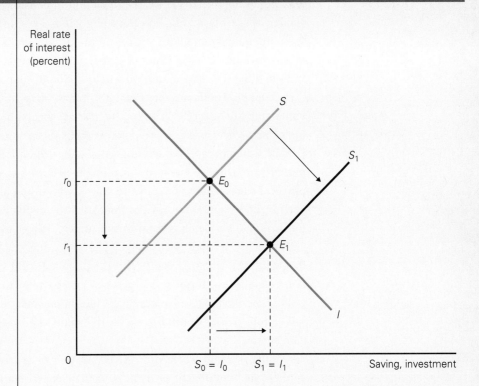

Price-wage flexibility
An economic principle whereby prices and wages can fluctuate with changing economic conditions; thus the economy will be self-adjusting toward full employment even in response to shocks in supply and demand.

wish to save more at every rate of interest, shifting the saving function rightward from S to S_1 in Figure 7.7. A surplus of saving develops at interest rate r_0, forcing the rate of interest down. As the rate falls, investors take advantage of new, profitable investments. Finally, at the new equilibrium interest rate, r_1, a new higher quantity of savings, S_1, equals a new, higher level of investment expenditures, I_1.

If Say's law is true, all leakages from the income stream must be replaced by injections. According to classical economics, increases in saving (leakage) are replaced by increases in investment (injection) through the mechanism of the real rate of interest. Aggregate demand for goods and services would fall short of aggregate supply were it not for the mechanism of interest rates. In other words, the classical economists believed that Say's law is valid if the interest rate is able to adjust freely upward or downward without regulations or restrictions. Consumption spending plus investment expenditures will be sufficient to purchase all of the output produced by the economy.

PRICE-WAGE FLEXIBILITY   The validity of Say's law requires another cornerstone of classical thought: **price-wage flexibility**. To understand this second concept, suppose that future economic conditions appear very uncertain. There might be expectations of war, of a coming depression, or even of an overall decrease in prices. In response to this uncertainty, individuals seek greater immediate economic security. A drastic increase in saving at such a time of crisis will have the effect of lowering the interest rate; the price of loanable funds is reduced to investors, encouraging more investment and additions to the capital stock and making up the difference for the reduction in consumption. But in the event of a sudden surge of saving, investors might not be able or willing to adjust their spending quickly enough to make up the difference in total spending. Aggregate demand would be insufficient to carry off the aggregate supply of goods and services and Say's law (temporarily) would not hold; supply would not be creating its own demand. Unemployment would increase disastrously, leaving the economy vulnerable to collapse. According to classical theory, however, any such reduction in demand would also provoke another mechanism—price-wage adjustment.

With a (temporary) reduction in total spending, prices and wages would be expected to fall in the economy in proportion to the size of the reduction. As the prices of shoes, computer software, hair stylings, and all other goods and services decline, additional quantities of goods will be demanded, and all excess production will quickly be bought up by consumers. Wages of laborers and the prices of all raw materials and other inputs will also decline, encouraging their employment by businesses. Nominal wages and the price level (for commodities) will both decline, helping to preserve the purchasing power of the new, lower nominal incomes. The flexibility of prices and wages in a competitive market helps guarantee full employment, even in the event of a sharp and protracted reduction in aggregate demand.

It must be emphasized that the classical cornerstone of price-wage flexibility applies when aggregate demand is insufficient to maintain full employment for *any* reason. Natural disasters and wars were thought to pose no threat to full employment in the long run, as long as prices and wages were allowed to adjust. The purely competitive market system—an assumption of classical economists—is the fail-safe mechanism through which unemployment over long periods of time was thought to be impossible. For the system to operate properly, of course, there could be no restrictions on prices (such as price controls) or wages (such as minimum wage) in either product or resource markets.

Quantity theory of money
A theory stating that in the long run with output and velocity fixed, changes in the money supply cause proportional changes in the price level.

THE QUANTITY THEORY OF MONEY   In the long run, real GDP and employment would be maximized in a laissez-faire economy. Thrift, the productivity of capital investment, and Say's law guaranteed maximum output in the classical economist's theoretical system. The price level and the nominal wage level were explained in the classical system by a theory that, in the long run, viewed output and employment as independent of the money supply—the **quantity theory of money**. The quantity theory of money simply states that, in the long run, there is a clear and proportional relation between the money supply and the price level in the economy.

While we postpone a detailed discussion of money and prices until later, it is useful at this point to understand some of the principles that underlie the formation of prices and inflation. The classical economists (like modern economists) used certain relationships in the real world to explain and predict how the price level is formed. They began their argument by noting that the following relationship existed:

Money supply × velocity = the price level × real GDP.

In symbols,

$$MV = PY,$$

where,

> M = the money supply, consisting of currency in the hands of the public plus all checkable deposits (all checkbook money) used in transactions by the public (in the U.S. monetary system, M is determined by the Federal Reserve System, an agency of the federal government);

> V = velocity, or the average number of times a unit of money changes hands per year (or other time period) in financing the purchase of real output by the public;

> P = the price level of all output (goods and services); and

> Y = the final real output of goods and services produced and sold in the economy over some time period. (Y, in other words, is real GDP.)

If money is defined as currency plus checkable deposits held by the public, the public, at any given time, will hold a certain portion of their wealth in the form of money, in addition to houses, goods, and other types of assets. They will demand money (currency and checkable deposits) to facilitate transactions as a proportion of their total income. For example, if income in the economy was $6 trillion in 1992 and the public demanded one-third of this amount to facilitate all transactions in the economy, the average dollar exchanged hands or "turned over" three times in the economy in 1992. This means that **velocity** (necessary to facilitate the purchase of yearly GDP) was 3. The classical economists thought that this proportion was a constant over specific time frames, such as a year, and that velocity changed slowly due to (slow-changing) institutions in the economy.

Velocity
The average number of times a unit of money changes hands per year in financing the purchases of GDP.

If we consider the above equation and believe, along with the classical economists, that money serves individuals only as a medium of exchange, we may understand that increases in the *supply* of money will cause the price level to rise in the same proportion. That is, by assuming velocity and real GDP are constant, the equation $MV = PY$ becomes an expression of the quantity theory of money. If the money supply, M, were to double, the equation indicates that the price level, P, also would double. More money in the hands of individuals means that too much is being held to facilitate their level of goods and services transactions. What will people do? They will increase their demands for these goods and services by offering larger amounts of money for them. But recall from the other three foundations of the classical system that *real* output of these goods and services is always (over the long run) at a maximum. When no more goods can be obtained, prices must rise. If the velocity of money, which is another way of expressing individuals' money demand behavior, is constant, and if real income is already at a maximum, the only possible effect of an increase in the money supply is to cause an increase in the price level.

If resources were for any reason unemployed in the short run, and if, as this implies, real output (real GDP) were not at a maximum, increases in M with constant velocity would imply that real output and employment could be brought to a maximum. New spending created by increases in *M* would increase society's real output of goods and services and employ the resources necessary to produce them. This means that velocity is a key to understanding why increases in the money stock could be used in a short-run situation of unemployment to return the economy to full employment. The classical economists assumed that the public's money demand (which determined velocity) was stable and did not change when the money supply was altered. Thus, the strict quantity theory relationship—for example, a doubling of *M* causing a doubling of *P*—held only in the long run, when real output and employment were at a maximum and velocity was constant.

Throughout the nineteenth century and into the twentieth, the size of the money supply was, in the main, determined by gold and silver stocks. The discovery (or hoarding) of precious metals had a profound impact on the price level at any time (and on the rates of inflation or deflation). In the modern U.S. system, the money supply is independent of the amount of gold or silver in the economy. It is controlled by the Federal Reserve System, an agency of the federal government. The Federal Reserve directs the money supply by regulating lending and other activities of banks in our economy. All of these matters will be carefully discussed in later chapters, but for now it is useful to remember that the classical writers thought that resources were fully employed and real output was maximized in the normal state of the world.

CLASSICAL THEORY AND POLICY: THE MEANING OF A SELF-ADJUSTING ECONOMY

Classical self-adjustment mechanism
The theory that, through Say's law, full employment will be reached given interest rate flexibility and price–wage flexibility.

The cornerstones of classical macroeconomic theory imply that self-adjusting forces in the economy will guarantee full employment. Long-run unemployment is simply not possible if the economy functions as the theory predicts. Consider the meaning of the **classical self-adjustment mechanism** in a real-world context.

The classical economists knew that adjustments due to supply "shocks" such as rapid technological change or new inventions, weather conditions, or wars were not instantaneous. Suppose, for example, that a drought occurs. A sharply reduced supply of grain and other foodstuffs means that the price of food will rise (given downward-sloping demand). But given the logic of the quantity theory of money, the prices of other goods that are consumed in the economy must fall! Adjustments of nominal prices in all of the various markets of the economy will be accompanied by changes in the nominal wage rates associated with each production. While all of these prices and wages are changing, the economic system will be in disequilibrium, with temporary surpluses and shortages of some goods and with excess demand for or supplies of labor in various markets. Unemployment of labor and other resources, as a temporary *and necessary* phenomenon, will take place, a fact the classical economists freely acknowledged. If wages and/or prices were "sticky"—that is, if they were not allowed to rise—unemployment would be more persistent. A critical question is: How long will the economy have to endure this temporary phenomenon in actual time? Two months? One year? Ten years?

While never directly answering this question, the classical economists did offer some important insights, based on the understanding that any interference by government or private coalitions would make the problem of adjustment worse. In other words, although natural and unfettered market forces would not restore equilibrium instantaneously, reliance on market forces was the best choice in an imperfect world. The setting of wage or price controls of any kind, such as minimum wages or union-controlled wage rates, would only impede flexibility in the marketplace. Market forces would eventually conquer the controls, extending the time period for adjustment. Unemployment would last longer if wages, prices, and interest rates were not permitted to adjust through unregulated market forces. The long run over which the market will adjust to changing underlying conditions in the economy (a drought, perhaps, or technological changes) was an indeterminate period of time that was minimized by the absence of controls in the economy.

John Maynard Keynes took exception to classical economic theory's conception of the nature of actual conditions in the economy—specifically, the issue of how rigid or flexible prices and wages are in the real world. The logic of classical economics led to the conclusion that market forces, in and of themselves, are the best means of providing adjustments in prices, wages, employment, and output. All adjustments take time, of course, but in the classical view free-market adjustments minimize the time necessary for full employment of resources to take place.

Classical Policies for Rapid Self-Adjustment

The classical economic policy recommendations fit hand in glove with the theoretical cornerstones. If the logic of their system required full flexibility of prices, wages, and interest rates—as well as the encouragement of industry—then their economic policy had to promote free markets. On practically every point of economic policy, the classicals supported economic freedom. Consider some of the chief tenets of their economic policy. (The Application, "How Classical Economics Affects You," considers similarities between classical economic policy prescriptions and recent economic policy in the United States.)

BALANCE THE BUDGET   Classical economists emphasized the need for a balanced government budget for a number of reasons. If government is allowed to spend more than it receives in taxes, the government will be forced to compete with investors to borrow available funds. Such competition will tend to increase real interest rates, choking off private investment, capital formation, and economic growth. Financing deficits by printing money—an attractive option when governments have access to the presses—would have equally bad effects on the private economy. As we will discuss in Chapter 14, increases in the money supply can create inflation, which is tantamount to a tax on the private sector.

KEEP GOVERNMENT SMALL   High levels of taxes necessary to finance big government reduce incentives to private saving from which new investments are made. Big government, in the classical view, short-circuits the mainspring to progress. Moreover, large-scale government includes domestic or international regulations that tend to reduce trade, productivity, and consumers' well-being. In the classical laissez-faire view, the government should be restricted to providing national defense, a legal system, and a few other functions.

LAISSEZ-FAIRE   Capitalism requires well-defined property rights. The classical economists underscored this belief by promoting policies that encouraged individual ownership and increased incentives to save and invest. These were primarily "hands-off" policies, or laissez-faire. The theory is that most regulation in the workplace, business, and in financial markets should be dismantled; also, all newly proposed regulations should be viewed with extreme skepticism. The classicals also adhered to the belief that much regulation was inspired by interest groups who wanted to capture the political process for their own gain. A good example of this is the factory legislation of early nineteenth-century England, which, supposedly, was passed to protect children from exploitation. (See the Focus "The Factory Acts and the Macroeconomy of Nineteenth-Century England.") Any laws or regulations that reduced saving, investment, or capital formation—domestic or international—were opposed by classicals.

FREE FOREIGN TRADE   The self-adjusting macroeconomy and economic growth were also believed to be fostered by international free trade. The free-trade philosophy espoused by nearly all classical economists brought about calls for the elimination of all barriers to free exchange, such as tariffs and quotas. A major strand of classical economic policy, then, was the removal or reduction of all impediments to both internal and external trade—anything, in other words, in the way of the gains from specialization and comparative advantage.

Classical Theory and Policy: Summary

The classical cornerstones of macroeconomic theory were part of a long-run view of economic activity. Yet the classical writers never stated the actual time period needed for the economy to self-adjust. They merely emphasized that any short-run government tinkering with the private economy in either a macroeconomic or a microeconomic sense would have negative long-run effects. In their view, the best long-run economic hope for all members of society—laborers, households, consumers, businesspeople, investors, savers—was to let unfettered market forces work in the private economy, unassisted by government.

Recessions, depressions, or periods of high unemployment caused by massive shifts in consumption spending, natural disasters, or wars all could wreak short-run havoc and temporary unemployment in the economy, as all classical economists knew. Society's members, however, would all be better off to suffer the temporary consequences rather than demand that government intervene. In the classical view, nearly all short-run actions of government in the aggregate economy only made problems worse, prolonged recessions or depressions, and created built-in instabilities in the macroeconomic system. Capitalism was not perfect, but society's inability to endure the short-run pains of recession and unemployment (reflected in demands for government to *do something*) meant that there would be greater economic pain in the long run.

focus

The Factory Acts and the Macroeconomy of Nineteenth-Century England

In general, policy recommendations of the classical economists were based on the notion of a self-adjusting economy. The vehemence of the classical economist Nassau Senior's (1790–1864) objections to factory legislation is not unusual.

The Factory Acts, enacted between 1833 and 1850, were a series of restrictions on the employment of women and children in the British textile industry. While many historians believe that these acts were passed for humanitarian reasons, Senior saw more rhetoric than genuine concern for working women and children. He identified an interest group—primarily, male workers—as the real agitator for factory legislation. If competing suppliers of labor—women and children—were eliminated from the work force and if hours of work were shortened or regulated, the wages of male workers would rise. Senior believed that the actual efforts to pass factory legislation had little to do with the "public interest."

Senior's second reason for opposing the Factory Acts rested on the impact on the macroeconomy of legislatively mandated reductions in work hours and labor participation in the textile industry. Senior interviewed mill owners on the matter of the proposed restrictions, quoting one as having said, "When a laborer lays down his spade, he renders useless, for that period, a capital worth eighteen pence. When one of our people leaves the mill, he renders useless a capital that has cost 100 pounds."[a] In other words, restrictions on labor contracts idled capital and reduced the marginal efficiency of capital, thereby reducing the efficiency of resource allocation. Senior knew that a legislated reduction in the efficiency of capital would lower the rate of return on capital investment in the textile industry below that which could be earned outside the industry. Higher-cost producers would leave the industry, reducing employment and granting a competitive advantage to foreign producers not subject to legislated restrictions on work hours and labor participation. Senior complained that "the English capitalist using his machinery for only 10 hours a day will be undersold by the German or the American who employs his for 12, 13, 14 and even 15," and that "the factories which work for the foreign market must be closed, and with them the means of clothing, feeding, and supporting many hundreds of thousands of workpeople [in England]."[b]

Senior's point, shared by most classical economists, was that regulations that had negative effects on investment, capital formation, and domestic employment were detrimental to maximizing society's total income. A modern parallel of this argument is the U.S. Environmental Protection Agency's regulations on the sulphuric content of coal. This legislation has adversely affected the demand for coal extracted in Appalachia by coal demanders such as electrical utilities in the northeastern United States. The response of these utilities has been to import coal (of lower sulphuric content) from western Canada (via the Panama Canal) and from Latin American countries. Economists, of course, do not dispute the fact that clean air has value or that some humanitarian purpose might have been accomplished by the Factory Acts. Rather, they point out that rules and regulations have costs—costs that are often ultimately reflected in the self-adjusting character of the economy and in the economy's attainable output and income potential.

[a]N. W. Senior, *Selected Writings on Economics* (New York: Augustus Kelley, 1966), p. 14.

[b]N. W. Senior, *Industrial Efficiency and Social Economy*, vol. 2 (New York: Henry Holt, 1928), p. 309. Also see Gary M. Anderson, Robert B. Ekelund, Jr., and Robert D. Tollison, "Nassau Senior as Economic Consultant: The Factory Acts Reconsidered," *Economica* 56 (February 1989), pp. 71–81.

Undeniable parallels exist between classical and modern macroeconomic theory and policy. In theory, many modern macroeconomists, including the monetarists and new classical economists (see Chapters 14 and 15) hold to the classical idea that government intervention in markets will, at best, do little good and could reduce output potential in the economy. While modern theories of economic functioning are much more complex than the classical theory, they share the underlying premise that maximum output results from free-market functioning with minimal government interference.

Especially on the campaign trail, Democrats and Republicans alike often appear to be in agreement with classical economists. Virtually all presidential candidates in 1996 pledged to make efforts to balance the federal budget and to reduce the federal debt. (As noted in the text, classical writers and policymakers insisted on balanced budgets because government borrowing tends to crowd out private saving and investment.) Judged by their records rather than by their rhetoric, however, Reagan and Bush would be regarded as disappointments by classical economists. Federal budget deficits ranged from $150 billion to over $250 billion throughout the 1980s. In 1992 the federal deficit reached an all-time high, $290.4 billion. Although the federal deficit has come down in recent years (estimated at $163.8 billion in 1995), the federal debt remains at a record-high $4.9 trillion. Recent attempts by Congress and the president to balance the federal budget would be looked upon favorably by classical economists.

It is interesting to contrast recent events with the more draconian policies of politicians in the classical era. Consider the policies of William Gladstone, who was appointed vice president of the Board of Trade in England under the Conservative government of Prime Minister Robert Peel in 1841. Gladstone aimed to eliminate as much government intervention in the private sector as possible. To this end, he removed import tariffs (a form of excise tax on imported goods and a major source of government revenues) from all but 15 of the 400 products subject to the tariffs. Gladstone's tariff reductions resulted in a temporary government deficit. To balance the budget, Gladstone called for a 10 percent income tax. The income tax rate was reduced in subsequent years, before being eliminated altogether. In other words, the income tax was a temporary measure and disappeared after its aims had been achieved.

Tariff reductions (and eliminations), one of the most treasured policy prescriptions of the classicals to promote economic growth, have also been part of contemporary macroeconomic policy. The United States, Canada, and Mexico have eliminated most of the existing trade barriers among the three nations and have become the world's largest free trade zone. The classical economists would clearly approve in spite of what are regarded as short-term financial and other problems within the Mexican economy! Modern economists, along with their classical counterparts, support *worldwide* reductions in tariff and nontariff barriers to trade. Consumers of all participating nations in a free-trade zone and consumers of other nations (if trade agreements can be made between zones) will gain from increased specialization and trade. (Chapters 2 and 32 explain in detail how specialization, comparative advantage, and trade increase net economic welfare.)

Deregulation—a classical tenet—has also characterized recent political administrations. President Jimmy Carter's administration (1976–1980) achieved significant deregulation in the economy—for example, in the airline industry. President Ronald Reagan's original economic proposals emphasized less total government spending and lower taxes to increase private saving and investment, although lower total spending proved to be infeasible politically. Reagan was more successful in continuing the trend toward deregulation, notably in the transportation and communications industries.

In general, Reagan's policies had a long-run orientation. Certainly, the Reagan administration's so-called trickle-down theory (the idea that prosperity follows a downward course from increased industry to the poor) is consistent with the tenets of classical macroeconomics. In the 1992 and 1996 campaigns, "trickle-down" economics was ridiculed by Bill Clinton, who argued that more government subsidies and spending are required to ensure jobs, growth, and prosperity. Clinton's campaigns focused on distinctly nonclassical themes: higher taxes on the "wealthy"; increased government spending on "infrastructure," such as highways, bridges, and public works; and government job creation reminiscent of the Depression-era Works Progress Administration. At times, however, Clinton has sounded a more classical tone, calling for limitations on welfare, support of freer trade, and (ultimately) a balanced budget.

Today, the role of government in the U.S. economy is so pervasive that even marginal changes are considered radical. The Reagan-Bush policies aimed at lowering the financial base of the federal government were less successful than those aimed at deregulating some critical industries and transferring control over resources from the public to the private sector and from federal to state and local governments. The so-called "Republican Revolution" inaugurated with the take-over of Congress in the midterm elections of 1994 has aimed at the decentralization of government championed by the classical economists. At the local level, shrinking tax revenues have made returning garbage collection, ambulance services, and many social services to the private sector more attractive. If nothing else, the return to private operation of such activities fits into the classical idea that government should only be responsible for those desired activities that private enterprise cannot perform, will not undertake, or does not do sufficiently well.

QUESTION

Which recent U.S. economic policies reflect the principles of the classical macroeconomists? Which policies deviate from these principles?

SUMMARY

1. The classical blueprint for economic growth consists of progressive extensions of the division of labor, private saving and investment, and capital accumulation.

2. Economic growth in any economy is limited by, among other things, the economy's actual supply of human and nonhuman resources, the state of technology, productivity, and population.

3. Given the factors that limit growth at any one point in time, the best the economy can attain is a point on the production possibilities curve. The point of attainable possibilities corresponds to a vertical aggregate supply curve for the economy.

4. Classical macroeconomics consists of four cornerstones: Say's law, price-wage flexibility, interest rate flexibility, and the quantity theory of money. From these foundations, classical economists concluded that the economy would self-adjust to reach a full-employment level of production and income.

5. Say's law states that the act of supplying goods creates an automatic demand for the goods. The act of saving or hoarding does not mean that overproduction will occur. If prices and wages are flexible downward, price and wage declines will ensure that all units of production will be sold. Further, the linkage between the rate of interest and saving and investment guarantees that what is removed from the income stream (saving) will be returned in a different form of spending (investment). The quantity theory of money indicates that the price level is proportional to the nominal money supply and suggests an avenue by which prices change when the money supply changes.

6. Classical economic policy, in the main, reflected the classical economists' theoretical view of the macroeconomy. Consequently, they supported policies that promoted the flexibility of prices, wages, and interest rates in the face of ever-changing conditions.

7. In the classical view, maximum price and wage flexibility would be promoted by the reduction both of internal and external regulations and by minimal government involvement in the economy and a balanced budget.

8. Classical macroeconomic theory was a long-run theory that emphasized the self-adjusting character of the economy as the least-cost means for arriving at the economy's production possibilities curve. In the classical view, all economies must go through adjustments, and the best way to let all markets adjust is through reduction or elimination of government interference.

KEY TERMS

classical macroeconomic theory
classical process of economic
   growth
division of labor

classical long-run equilibrium
Say's law
real rate of interest
price-wage flexibility

quantity theory of money
velocity
classical self-adjustment
   mechanism

QUESTIONS FOR REVIEW AND DISCUSSION

1. According to Say's law, under what circumstances would the quantity of goods demanded be less than the quantity of goods supplied?

2. Will people be willing to save money when the real rate of interest is equal to zero? What is the real rate of interest on a passbook savings account if the inflation rate is 7 percent and the bank pays 5 percent interest?

3. According to the classical view, why does an increase in savings not decrease the total level of spending? Would this be true if interest rates were not flexible?

4. What is the importance of price and wage flexibility under the classical system? What would be the consequence of rigid wages or prices if the macroeconomic system were disturbed by, say, poor grain crops?

5. Does the self-adjusting mechanism of classical economics indeed guarantee full employment of labor and other resources at all times? (Remember the distinction between the short run and the long run.)

6. How were classical macroeconomic theories and economic policy recommendations related?

7. Why did classical economists recommend small balanced budgets for government? Why did they suggest that large budget deficits would lead to lagging economic growth?

8. Why did the classical economists oppose regulations on business behavior? What did laissez-faire mean to classical economists?

9. How do flexible interest rates ensure that Say's law will hold even when consumers engage in saving?

10. If the money supply doubles while velocity and real GDP remain constant, will the economy experience inflation or deflation and to what degree?

11. In the classical framework, how does division of labor lead to growth in real GDP?

12. List three factors that limit economic growth according to classical theory.

13. In your opinion, would the classical economists approve of the degree to which our government and economy are related?

CHAPTER 8
KEYNESIAN MACROECONOMICS

$\mathbf{C}$ lassical economic theory, the topic of the previous chapter, dominated the economic debate until the early twentieth century, when a series of catastrophic events sorely tested economists' faith in a self-adjusting economy and the validity of Say's law. After the unevenly prosperous 1920s, the United States and the rest of the world fell into the deepest and most prolonged depression in modern history.

In September 1929, the market for stocks and other securities began to fail. On what has come to be known as Black Thursday, October 24, 1929, stock prices plummeted and thousands of investors lost hundreds of millions of dollars' worth of securities. The stock market crash was the most public indicator of steep declines in industrial production, real income, and civilian employment. For more than a decade, between 1929 and 1940, industrial production in the United States failed to exceed its 1929 level. Real economic output (expressed in 1982 dollars) was about $700 billion in 1929, a level unmatched until 1939. Most important, civilian unemployment rose to more than 30 percent by 1933.

The exact causes of the Great Depression are still a matter of debate among macroeconomists, but the prolonged economic chaos is a matter of fact. The Depression and the unemployment that accompanied it brought ruin for millions of Americans and similar hardships around the world. The classical self-adjusting macroeconomic system did not appear to work. In this chapter we present the theory of John Maynard Keynes, which was a reaction to the apparent failure of the macroeconomic system to adjust to the problems of the Depression. Modern macroeconomists, whether of a classical or a Keynesian stripe, all believe that the economy adjusts to some natural rate of full employment *in the long run*. Keynes and his modern followers part company with classical thinkers on how to achieve full employment without inflation *over shorter periods of time*. Thus, an understanding of basic Keynesian theory is absolutely necessary in order to appreciate the forces underlying economic fluctuations in our modern economy. After reading Chapter 8 you should understand

- Keynes's criticisms of the self-adjusting classical principles of macroeconomics.
- how total private expenditures by consumers and businesses form the basis for Keynes's model of income determination.
- how the impact of spending changes on income described by Keynes is important in explaining cycles of business and economic activity.
- how foreign trade and government act as components of spending in the economy.
- how government spending and taxation in a Keynesian system are called upon to alleviate downturns and to modify inflationary pressures in the private economy.

KEYNES AND THE CLASSICALS

Economists were among the first to recognize that the catastrophic events of the Great Depression appeared to overwhelm theory. J. M. Keynes (1883–1946) was particularly vocal. In open letters to President Franklin D. Roosevelt, published in the *New York Times*, Keynes advocated the use of government spending and taxation policies to supplement private spending as a cure for the ailing economy. (Roosevelt, clinging to more traditional thinking, heeded Keynes's advice guardedly and hesitantly.) Keynes was firmly convinced that, contrary to classical theory, private market forces would not be sufficient to regain full-employment equilibrium in the depressed economy. He dismissed the long-run self-adjustment theory of the classical economists with scorn. As he said in another context, "In the long run we are all dead." The economy could be stuck at some equilibrium characterized by high levels of unemployment for an extended period of time, as it seemed to be in the early 1930s.

Since the classical theory, in Keynes's view, did not offer rescue from the Depression, Keynes sought a better model from which to interpret events. In 1936, Keynes published his *General Theory of Employment, Interest and Money*, which established a new theory of how the economy functions—a new macroeconomics. In proposing this theory, Keynes had to counter the foundations of the classical macroeconomic system.

Recall that Say's law states that supply creates its own demand if savings (a leakage) can be transformed into investment expenditures (a compensating injection) through a flexible interest rate and if prices and wages are flexible when aggregate demand is exceeded by aggregate production. Keynes took exception to Say's law and to the two other cornerstones that support it—the belief that price-wage flexibility and interest rate flexibility will cure any temporary disruptions in the economy.

First, Keynes argued that saving and investment are determined by a host of forces in the economy in addition to the rate of interest. In Keynes's view, savers and investors are different groups with different sets of motivations and interests. Savers, he thought, are more responsive to their amount of personal disposable income than to the rate of interest in deciding how much to save.

Similarly, investment was not very responsive to the short-run interest rate, in Keynes's view. Much investment, especially in large projects, takes place over long periods. Once investment decisions are made, the investment is autonomous, unrelated to the interest rate or other variables. The point is that the different motivations of savers and investors mean that saving and investment plans could become unlinked. A flexible interest rate, responsive to the desires of savers and investors, would not guarantee that the saving leakage would automatically be turned into the investment injection. There was no built-in assurance that savings would equal investment at a full-employment, growth-maximizing level of economic activity.

Second, Keynes argued that in reality the internal structure of the economy was not competitive enough to permit prices and wages to fall in response to insufficient aggregate demand. To Keynes, the existence of monopoly and union pressures in the economy had to be taken into account. If demand fell off, monopolies would let output fall rather than accept price reductions. Workers, moreover, would refuse to take cuts in their money wages, thereby creating unemployment and layoffs by businesses. Even if workers did take money wage cuts, the reduction in income would further reduce the demand for goods and services, probably reducing output and employment even more. The conclusion: *Classical self-adjusting mechanisms in the private economy would not lift us out of a depression.*

THE INCOME-EXPENDITURES MODEL

Keynes believed that a prolonged depression proves that the economy can establish equilibrium at less than full employment. The classical economists, as we have seen, placed their confidence in a flexible price system—flexible prices, wages, and interest rates—as the self-adjusting mechanism that would assure full employment when aggregate demand got out of kilter with aggregate supply.

Keynes argued instead that aggregate demand and economic activity in general were determined by income and by changes in income. He thereby developed an **income-expenditures model** of macroeconomics. Keynes focused on aggregate demand or spending because he viewed rapid aggregate demand changes as the villain in recessions and depressions. Keynes believed that aggregate supply factors—large-scale changes in productivity, such as new technology and inventions and changing incentives to work and produce—changed slowly and could therefore be neglected when considering short-run macroeconomic problems. (Aggregate supply factors will be considered in Chapter 9.) In the short run, the time period most relevant to Keynesian macroeconomics, the economy's production or supply of goods and services is seen to react passively to changes in total expenditures.

Income-expenditures model
A theory suggesting that private expenditures are basically determined by the level of national income and that these expenditures in turn determine the levels of output and employment in the economy.

Private Consumption Expenditures

The classical writers, as we saw earlier, placed primary emphasis on the real rate of interest in determining the relation between savings (income reserved for future consumption) and expenditures (income used in current consumption). One of Keynes's basic criticisms of classical theory was that the rate of interest could not always enable us to predict how much of current income an individual would choose to save or to spend. Keynes believed that current income was the most reliable and predictable determinant of consumption expenditures. Private saving, the residual of income after consumption, was also a function of, or was explained by, income. The simple Keynesian model of consumption and saving, in other words, does not account for any factors other than current income. Consider how these relations between consumption and income and between saving and income might be expressed and analyzed.

Consumption and Saving Functions

Keynes constructed consumption and saving functions and schedules based on income. The consumption function and the saving function can be expressed simply as

$$C = C(Y) \text{ and } S = S(Y).$$

In other words, consumption (C) is a function of income (Y), and saving (S) is a function of income, which simply means that consumption and saving are related to income in some way. Both consumption and saving, as we will see, are positive functions of income, meaning that an income increase will increase both consumption and saving, and an income decrease will decrease both consumption and saving.

Planned consumption and saving relations can also be regarded as schedules. A consumption-income schedule shows the amount that households would desire or plan to consume at every level of income. Likewise, a saving-income schedule shows the desired or planned level of saving that households would undertake at various levels of income.

In the basic Keynesian model, income can be disposed of by households in only two ways: They may consume it or save it. This observation means that

$$Y = C + S,$$

and it also means that consumption and saving are related in a unique way.

Numerous studies have attempted to relate saving and consumption to family income. The evidence provided by these studies shows that as income increases, families increase both saving and consumption. Further, richer families tend to save a higher proportion of income than do poorer families.

Macroeconomists are often interested in knowing how consumption or saving will change with a change in income. The two concepts that give us this answer are the marginal propensity to consume and the marginal propensity to save. The **marginal propensity to consume (MPC)** is defined as the ratio of the change in

Marginal propensity to consume (MPC)
The percentage of an additional dollar of income that is spent on consumption; change in consumption divided by change in income.

consumption (ΔC) to the change in income (ΔY) that causes the change in consumption, or

$$MPC = \frac{\Delta C}{\Delta Y} = \frac{\text{change in consumption}}{\text{change in income}}$$

The **marginal propensity to save (MPS)** is the ratio of a change in saving (ΔS) to a change in income that causes the change in saving, or

$$MPS = \frac{\Delta S}{\Delta Y} = \frac{\text{change in saving}}{\text{change in income}}$$

Marginal propensity to save (MPS)
The percentage of an additional dollar of income that is saved; change in saving divided by change in income.

Since households in the simple Keynesian model dispose of income only by consuming or saving, any change in income will be completely exhausted by the resulting changes in consumption and saving. Because the *MPC* measures the change in consumption resulting from a change in income and the *MPS* measures the change in saving arising from the same change in income, the *MPC* plus the *MPS* must add up to 1:

$$MPC + MPS = 1.$$

Economists are also interested in how much, on average, households consume and save at various income levels. The **average propensity to consume (APC)** is the proportion of income consumed at any income level, or C/Y. Likewise, the **average propensity to save (APS)** is the ratio of saving to income at any level of income, or S/Y. Since consumption and saving are the only two ways that households can dispose of income, a unique relation exists between the *APC* and the *APS*:

Average propensity to consume (APC)
The percentage of a particular level of income that is spent on consumption; total consumption divided by total income.

Average propensity to save (APS)
The percentage of total income that is saved; total saving during any given period divided by total income in the same period.

$$1 = \frac{\text{consumption}}{\text{income}} + \frac{\text{saving}}{\text{income}}, \text{ or } 1 = APC + APS.$$

The Keynesian Model of the Private Economy

The features of actual household consumption and saving behavior can be translated into a theoretical model of consumption and spending for the entire economy—how the country as a whole would choose to spend or save at different levels of national income. To make this model easier to comprehend—with no important loss in accuracy—we will assume that the consumption-income and saving-income relations are in the form of straight lines. This assumption means that the *MPC* and the *MPS* are constant. No matter what the level of income, the *MPC* will be the same number. If, for example, the *MPC* were 0.8 at the $100 billion level of income, it would be 0.8 at the $300 billion and the $750 billion levels also. The same relationship holds for the *MPS*. This simplifying assumption does no damage to our conclusions, and it greatly facilitates understanding of these crucial ideas.

Hypothetical information about economy-wide consumption and saving is given in Table 8.1. The hypothetical data of Table 8.1 show, in billions of dollars, what private consumption and private saving would be at alternative levels of income. Consider, for instance, a year in which national income is $100 billion. How would households plan to divide this income between purchases of

TABLE 8.1

Hypothetical Consumption and Saving Data for the Economy

The economy consumes and saves more as income increases. Further, the average propensity to consume declines and the average propensity to save rises with increases in income. For the sake of simplicity, the *MPC* and the *MPS* are assumed to be constant.

National Income (billions of dollars) (*Y*)	Planned Consumption Expenditures (billions of dollars) (*C*)	Planned Savings (billions of dollars) (*S*)	Average Propensity to Consume (*APC* = *C* ÷ *Y*)	Marginal Propensity to Consume (*MPC* = Δ*C* ÷ Δ*Y*)	Average Propensity to Save (*APS* = *S* ÷ *Y*)	Marginal Propensity to Save (*MPS* = Δ*S* ÷ Δ*Y*)
0	40	-40	—	0.8	—	0.2
100	120	-20	1.2	0.8	-0.2	0.2
200	200	0	1.0	0.8	0	0.2
300	280	20	0.93	0.8	0.7	0.2
400	360	40	0.90	0.8	0.10	0.2
500	440	60	0.88	0.8	0.12	0.2
600	520	80	0.87	0.8	0.13	0.2
700	600	100	0.86	0.8	0.14	0.2

Dissaving
Occurs when consumption is greater than income; the use of previous years' savings or borrowing to finance consumption expenditures that are greater than current income.

Autonomous consumption
Consumption expenditures that are independent of the level of income.

consumption goods and saving? Consumption expenditures at a $100 billion level of national income would exceed income by $20 billion. This -$20 billion would be **dissavings**. To consume $120 billion at an income level of $100 billion, in other words, households would have to draw down $20 billion in previous savings. A special interpretation is given to dissaving at a zero income level. Note that all households would consume at the level of $40 billion even if no income were earned; this $40 billion is independent of income. Such **autonomous consumption** expenditures are independent of income. At levels of income higher than zero, consumption expenditures increase until they are equal to income. If national income were $200 billion, all income would be devoted to consumption. At income levels higher than $200 billion, consumption expenditures fall short of current income, and the remainder is devoted to saving.

CONSUMPTION AND THE 45-DEGREE LINE   An important method for understanding how consumption is related to income is to compare historical consumption levels with a hypothetical relation in which consumption spending is always equal to income. When consumption spending always equals income, graphing the two variables yields a straight 45-degree line like that in Figure 8.1. The positive slope of the consumption schedule graphed in Figure 8.1, *C*(*Y*), reflects Keynes's basic notion that the larger our income, the larger will be our consumption expenditures.

Consumption function
The positive relationship between levels of consumption expenditures and levels of income, holding all other relevant factors that determine consumption constant.

Examine Figure 8.1, on which national income levels are displayed on the horizontal axis and consumption expenditures on the vertical axis. At every point on the 45-degree line in Figure 8.1, total spending—in this case, consumption spending—*equals* total income. The extent to which actual consumption levels for particular periods differ vertically from this 45-degree line indicates the degree to which consumption does not equal income. Points along the **consumption function**

FIGURE 8.1

The Level of Consumption as a Function of the Level of Income

The consumption function, $C(Y)$, shows that the level of consumption expenditures rises as income rises. When income is $100 billion, consumption spending is $120 billion; when income is $200 billion, consumption is $200 billion; and when income is $300 billion, consumption is $280 billion. Along the hypothetical 45-degree line, consumption expenditures are exactly equal to income. The degree to which consumption differs from income indicates dissaving and saving by society as a whole. In this example, consumption spending is equal to income only at the $200 billion income level. Along the consumption function and above the 45-degree line, society dissaves; along the consumption function and below the 45-degree line, positive saving takes place.

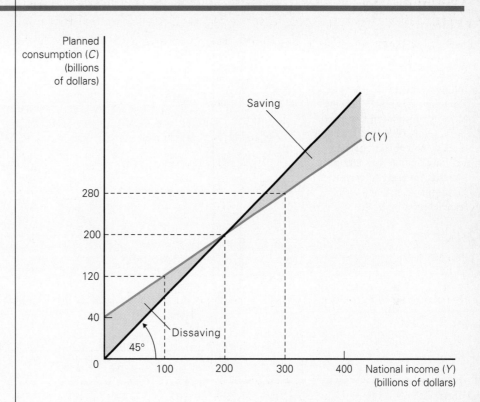

above the 45-degree line indicate dissavings; points below it indicate savings. In Figure 8.1, actual consumption is equal to income only at the $200 billion income level. At a national income below this break-even point, society would go into debt or dip into past savings; above it, society would save some of its income.

THE CONSUMPTION SCHEDULE Household consumption is the major factor in total spending, spending that creates jobs and production in the economy. Macroeconomists are therefore very interested in how much planned household consumption will change with changes in national income. The value of the marginal propensity to consume tells us how much more will be consumed out of an additional dollar—or an additional 100 billion dollars—in national income.

The marginal propensity to consume is of course different for different individuals and for different groups in society. Some of us are more likely than others to spend every dollar we have. In this example, we simplify the variations by choosing an *MPC* value of 0.8 for society as a whole and by holding this value constant across varying national income levels. In Figure 8.2, an increase in national income from $300 billion to $400 billion will increase the level of planned

FIGURE 8.2

Marginal Propensity to Consume

Along a straight-line consumption function, $C(Y)$, the MPC is constant. In this graph, MPC = 0.8. Each time income rises by $100 billion, the level of consumption rises $80 billion. Or, for every $1 increase in income, consumers increase expenditures by $0.80.

consumption spending from $280 billion to $360 billion, an increase of $80 billion. Likewise, an increase from $400 billion to $500 billion will cause planned consumption spending to increase by another $80 billion. The MPC is, therefore, the ratio 80/100 or 80 percent or 0.8, as indicated in Table 8.1.

Though the actual relation of the MPC to national income is a matter of debate, we know that the average propensity to consume changes as income levels change. In general, as income rises, the APC, or the ratio of consumption to income, falls. At a $300 billion income level, for instance, consumption expenditures are $280 billion and the APC equals 280/300, or 0.93. On average, the population would be spending 93 percent of its income. But if national income rose to $600 billion, households would spend only 87 percent of their income (520/600).

THE SAVING SCHEDULE   Like consumption, saving is a positive function of income. That is, the more income we have, the more we save; the lower our income, the less we are able to save. In the hypothetical **saving function** in Figure 8.3, at a national income level of $400 billion, desired saving is $40 billion. In fact, saving becomes positive rather than negative at all levels of income greater than $200 billion in this example.

The marginal and average propensity to save are also illustrated in Figure 8.3. Remember, the MPS is the ratio of a change in saving to a change in income. As shown in Figure 8.3, incremental changes of $100 billion change sav-

Saving function

The positive relationship between levels of current saving and levels of income, holding constant all other relevant factors that determine saving.

FIGURE 8.3

A Saving Function

The saving function, $S(Y)$, shows that the desired or planned saving is positively related to the level of national income. At a low level of income (below $200 billion), there is dissaving. As the level of income rises from $200 billion to $300 billion, the level of saving rises from $0 billion to $20 billion. At $Y = 400$, $S = 40$, and at $Y = 500$, $S = 60$. The figure also illustrates the marginal propensity to save. Along a straight-line saving function, the *MPS* is constant. Here the *MPS* is equal to 0.2. For each increase in income of $100 billion, the level of saving increases by $20 billion.

ing by $20 billion, so

$$MPS = 20/100 = 0.2.$$

The average propensity to save is the ratio of savings to income at any level of income. The *APS* rises as income rises, as you can see in Table 8.1, from which the data in Figure 8.3 are taken.

Assuming the straight-line consumption and saving functions and the use of all income as either saving or spending,

$$1 = MPC + MPS \quad \text{and} \quad 1 = APC + APS,$$

or

$$MPS = 1 - MPC \quad \text{and} \quad APS = 1 - APC.$$

The values of *MPC*, *MPS*, *APC*, and *APS* are very important for economic policy. A high *MPC* means that increases in income will generate a large amount of additional private spending. A low value for the *MPC* (or, exactly the same thing, a high *MPS*) means that increases in income will generate only small increases in consumption. (Keep in mind that the values of *MPC* and *MPS* given in Figures 8.2 and 8.3 are based on hypothetical data.) These features of the consumption function will have an extremely important impact on the model of total expenditures developed in the following chapters.

Nonincome Factors Influencing Consumption and Saving

Although Keynes's basic argument involved the effects of income levels, income is not the only factor affecting consumption expenditures. A host of nonincome

FIGURE 8.4

Shifts in the Consumption Function

Any change in nonincome factors affecting consumption spending will shift the consumption function, $C_0(Y)$, either upward or downward. An increase in consumption means that planned consumption spending rises for every level of income (from A to B); a decrease in spending creates a fall from A to D in the figure. By contrast, a change in income, all other factors being equal, moves consumers along a given consumption function. For example, increasing national income from Y_0 to Y_2 would move consumption from point A to point F in the figure.

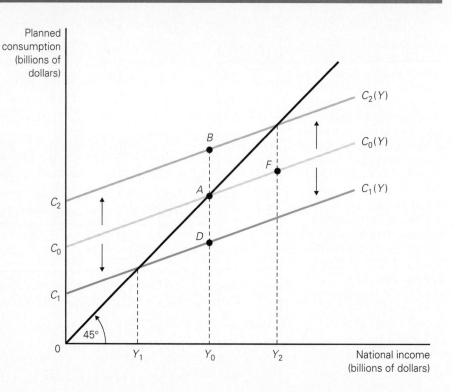

factors also determine the amount of planned consumption spending by all households. If any nonincome determinant of consumption spending changes, the entire consumption function shifts upward or downward. The amount of planned consumption changes at every income level when a nonincome element affects consumption changes. In contrast, a change in income simply changes the amount of income consumed, expressed graphically as a movement along a given consumption function.

In Figure 8.4, assuming an initial consumption function $C_0(Y)$, a change in any nonincome factor affecting consumption will shift the consumption schedule either upward to $C_2(Y)$ or downward to $C_1(Y)$. (The break-even level of income, where consumption spending equals income—on the graph, the point where the consumption function intersects the 45-degree line—also changes: to Y_2 with consumption C_2 or to Y_1 with consumption C_1.) By contrast, if income increases from Y_0 to Y_2, planned consumption increases along consumption function $C_0(Y)$ from point A to point F.

What are the nonincome factors that may affect consumption? Such factors are numerous, but the most important nonincome factors are thought to be (accumulated) wealth, the price *level*, price and income expectations, credit and the interest rate, taxation, age, and geographic location and population. Consumption and saving patterns will also change over your lifetime, some of them induced by government policies (see the Application at the end of this chapter entitled "Mortgaging Your Future: The Government and Your Incentive to Save").

Naturally, people consume on the basis of a previously accumulated stock of wealth. As the price level changes and the money value of items in that stock of wealth changes (the money value of your house or your Andrew Wyeth drawing), your consumption will change—even though your income does not. Feeling wealthier will affect your spending in a positive direction. Price level changes also produce changes in the *real* value of money or bonds (denominated in money terms). A doubling of the price *level* (not the price of, say, broccoli) will cut the purchasing power of these assets in half, and consumption spending will fall.

Expectations of higher or lower prices or incomes will also affect consumption spending. For example, an expectation of higher prices in the future will ordinarily increase current consumption. Moreover, as interest rates rise or fall—other things such as credit terms being equal—consumers will reduce or increase their present consumption expenditures. Taxation and government transfers also have direct effects on spending. Higher income taxes will reduce consumption and saving, whereas increases in Social Security benefits will increase spending and saving. Finally, population, age distribution, and geographic location all have an impact on consumption and saving. Middle-aged individuals are more likely to save—that is, they tend to save a greater proportion of their income—than are the young and the old. Urban dwellers, other things equal, tend to spend more of their incomes than rural families; a declining rural population will tend to increase overall consumption.

A change in *any* nonincome factor will shift the consumption function either upward or downward. A single consumption function, however, is constructed by holding all of the factors constant and by varying income. (How well does the data on actual consumption fit Keynes's theory? The answer to that question can be found in the Focus "Does Keynes's Consumption Theory Stand Up to the Facts?".)

Investment Expenditures

So far, we have looked at household consumption and its relation to income. Private spending in the economy also includes investment spending. In a macroeconomic context, **investment spending** means spending by the private sector—mainly businesses—on capital goods. Public investment in goods such as schools, water reclamation projects, or dams is not included in private investment expenditures. Public investment expenditures are categorized as government spending and will be covered later in this chapter. Private investment refers to the national income category gross private domestic investment, defined previously as including fixed investment in plant and equipment, all private-sector residential and nonresidential construction, and changes in business inventories (increases or decreases in stocks of finished goods, semifinished goods, or raw materials).

Clearly, there are two effects on the capital stock of the nation at any given time: Some of it is being used up or depreciated, and new net investment is creating additions to it. Businesses usually replace their worn-out capital stock and add to their stock of capital with new investments. Keynes argued that in the short run, investment expenditures could be viewed as autonomous—that is, independent of the level of income, profit expectations, the interest rate, and all of the other factors possibly affecting investment. The idea that investment could be autonomous

Investment spending
Expenditures made by businesses on capital goods plus any change (positive or negative) in business inventories.

f⊕cus   Does Keynes's Consumption Theory Stand Up to the Facts?

Unlike the classical economists, John Maynard Keynes believed that consumption was a direct and predictable function of income (given, of course, nonincome determinants such as those discussed in the text). How well, and in what way, does this notion stand up to the actual data?

Data on consumption and income are replicated in Figure 8.5 in such a manner that the two categories may be compared for the period 1972–1995 (in constant 1992 dollars). Here we abstract from the impact of taxes on income. Consumption spending (shown on the vertical axis in Figure 8.5) in the United States remains at about 60 percent of gross domestic product (depicted on the horizontal axis).

From even a casual examination of the data, it would appear that Keynes was exactly right: There appears to be a clear and predictable relation between income and consumption. As income rises, consumption rises; as income falls, consumption falls. But we must look a little more closely at the data. It appears, as later followers of Keynes argued, that although consumption rises with increases in income, it does not increase at the same rate as the rise in income. The same is true of declines in income (such as the 1982 and 1990–91 recessions, for example). People reduce consumption during recessions (periods of income declines), but not at the same rate as the reduction in their incomes. Consumers will save when incomes are disproportionately high and "dissave" (spend out of savings) when incomes are disproportionately low.

There are a number of explanations for the latter phenomenon. Consumption may, in effect, be "conditioned" by increases in income so that we become

FIGURE 8.5

Consumption and Income in Real Terms, 1970–1995

Just as Keynes predicted, real consumption expenditures are related to real income, although the correspondence is not perfect. Specifically, consumption rises as income rises, but not at the same rate.

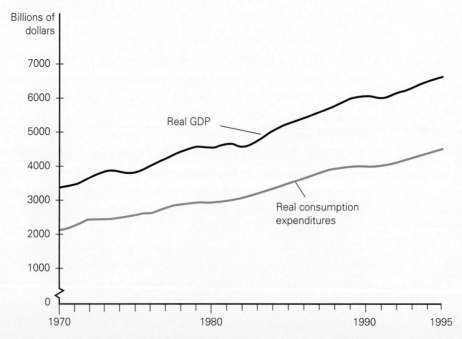

SOURCE: Council of Economic Advisers, *Economic Report of the President* (Washington, D.C.: U.S. Government Printing Office, 1996), p. 282.

accustomed to high levels of consumption spending. When income falls, we dissave in order to maintain that higher level of spending. Alternatively, we may consume in the present on the basis of some idea of our expected permanent income over our entire lifetime. According to the second theory, consumption in the present is conditioned by today's value of income received in the future. Some medical, law, or MBA students buy Infinitis, Porsches, and fine wardrobes. These people are dissaving out of current income, but they may also be seen to be consuming in response to expected income over their life cycles. Whatever the explanation for longer-term effects on consumption, however, it is clear that Keynes was on the mark with his major insight into macroeconomic theory: Current consumption does depend in an important manner on current income.

in the short run stems from the fact that most investment expenditures in any current period have been determined by past investment decisions.

Businesses, in fact, make investment decisions from a long-run perspective. The building of new plants and the installation of sophisticated equipment typically take a number of years to complete. During the investment period, planned investment expenditures are often carried out regardless of current business conditions. Planned investment expenditures are those that businesses desire to undertake. (Planned investment expenditures may not be the same as actual expenditures, as we will see later in this chapter.) These investment expenditures are then independent of the level of income.

Autonomous investment
Investment expenditures that are independent of the level of income.

The concept of **autonomous investment** spending can be analyzed within the framework of the simple Keynesian model of private spending. If I stands for investment spending by businesses, autonomous investment is simply described as some constant level, I_0, or

$$I = I_0,$$

where the subscript 0 means that expenditures are constant at some specified level—$20 billion, $50 billion, $100 billion—during a given period. This means that investment is independent of whatever the level of income happens to be.

LONG-RUN FACTORS AFFECTING INVESTMENT   While investment is considered autonomous in the Keynesian context, it is subject to a number of rapidly changing factors, including the rate of interest, the cost of capital, and current and expected sales.

Rate of Interest and the Cost of Capital.   Ultimately, profitability—or expectation of future profits—determines the amount of investment that businesses will undertake. Profitability is, in simple terms, the difference between a firm's revenues and its costs.

The cost of capital investment is heavily dependent on the rate of interest. Whether a business uses its own internal funds or borrows to make an investment, it incurs an opportunity cost in the form of interest lost. An increase in the interest rate, other things being equal, will reduce the amount of investment;

a reduction in the interest rate will increase investment. The cost of the capital equipment itself is also important in determining the amount of desired investment. An increase in costs, other things being equal, reduces the amount of investment.

Current Sales and Expected Sales.   The other side of the profitability of business investment is sales. If a large capacity to produce already exists, an increase in current sales will not encourage new investment expenditures very much. If businesses are operating close to the limits of their ability to produce, an increase in current sales will cause current investment spending to rise.

Expectations are also a central feature of Keynes's theory of investment. Sales expectations require estimates of future business conditions and tend to vary greatly and quickly over time. Optimism concerning future sales and business conditions will mean increases in capital investment in the present. Pessimism will have the opposite effect.

As we will see in later chapters, the volatility of profit expectations is a principal cause in the creation of unstable income levels, unemployment, and cycles of business activity. Before turning to these issues, however, we must first understand how income equilibrium is defined in a purely private economy.

PRIVATE INCOME-EXPENDITURES EQUILIBRIUM

The classical economists argued that full employment would be achieved automatically simply through the activity of supplying goods in an essentially private economy, an economy theoretically free of government intervention. Should difficulties in adjustment to this full-employment equilibrium take place, prices, wages, and interest rates would change to bring the aggregate output of goods in line with aggregate expenditures.

For reasons already outlined, Keynes did not agree that wages, prices, or interest rates would change in any predictable way to bring the demand for goods in line with the supply of goods. How could a depression economy reach equilibrium with high unemployment? Keynes argued that levels of private spending (consumption and investment) determine the output of goods produced in the economy. In other words, businesses react to any level of total expenditures by producing the quantities demanded. If households want more kitchen appliances, they are produced; if businesses demand less computer software, less is produced. Since it obviously takes more or less labor and other resources to produce more or less total output, the level of employment is also affected.

Keynes's theory of output and income determination can be expressed in symbolic terms using the tools of private spending analysis developed previously. Since total private expenditures are a function of income, and since these total private expenditures consist of consumption and investment spending, we can express the Keynesian equilibrium as follows:

$$Y = C + I = \text{total expenditures.}$$

TABLE 8.2

Planned Total Expenditures Determine Total Output and Equilibrium Income

For equilibrium in the private economy, planned total expenditures, $C + I$, must equal total income or output, Y. In this example, equilibrium is reached at a national income (or output) level of $300 billion. At national incomes less than $300 billion, total expenditures exceed total income. At national incomes higher than $300 billion, total expenditures are less than total income.

National Income or Output (Y)	Planned Consumption Expenditures (C)	Planned Investment Expenditures ($I = I_0$)	Desired or Planned Total Expenditures ($C + I_0$)	Difference Between Total Expenditures and Total Output ($C + I_0 - Y$)
100	120	20	140	+40
200	200	20	220	+20
Equilibrium 300	**280**	**20**	**300**	**0**
400	360	20	380	-20
500	440	20	460	-40

Private-sector equilibrium

A situation of equality between total private expenditures and output. In this equilibrium, there is no unplanned investment and no tendency for the level of output to change.

Private-sector equilibrium, or equilibrium output, occurs when $C + I$ equals income. In other words, equilibrium output in the economy exists when total expenditures equal what is produced.

An alternative way to define the establishment of equilibrium output involves the relation of income to expenditures. We know that income received by all factors of production may be disposed of in two ways, or

$$Y = C + S.$$

That is, income may be used for consumption spending or for savings, the residual of consumption spending. Equilibrium will occur when income received is equal to total expenditures:

$$C + S = C + I, \text{ or } S = I.$$

Total Expenditures Equal Total Output

Keynes's theory—that equilibrium income (or, its mirror image, equilibrium GDP or output) is a function of total expenditures—can be expressed numerically and graphically using tools already at our disposal. All of our previous consumption, investment, and income figures are reproduced in Table 8.2. Total expenditures, shown in the fourth column, are equal to the sum of consumption and investment expenditures. Recall that planned consumption depends directly on the level of national income, reported in column (1). According to the circular flow model, the first column represents both the total output of goods and services in the economy as well as national income. Total planned expenditures may be greater or less than total production or output. The amount by which income or output exceeds planned expenditures is shown in the last column.

As Table 8.2 shows (and we have already suggested), there is a difference between planned expenditures and actual expenditures. Unless we are speaking of equilibrium income and spending, all references to consumption, saving, and

FIGURE 8.6

Private-Sector Equilibrium

The equilibrium level of income exists when total private expenditures are just great enough to purchase the total output of the economy. At equilibrium, expenditures and output will meet at the point along the 45-degree line where they are exactly equal. At income level $Y = 300$, the economy is at equilibrium, E. At an income or output level of 400, desired total private expenditures at point B are insufficient to purchase the total output generated at point A. Inventories of goods will pile up, causing reductions in the rate of output and a lowering of income. These reductions will take place until income and output again equal the equilibrium level of 300. At this level, total expenditures equal total output produced in the economy. The opposite is true for income and output levels that are less than the equilibrium level.

investment are schedules of intentions or desires. Only one of these will be realized and that is the *equilibrium* value for these variables. Hereafter we typically omit the adjective "planned" or "desired" in front of consumption or saving, but the adjective "equilibrium" always refers to actual values.

At an income level of $100 billion, for example, total expenditures are greater than total output by $40 billion. This situation is possible only if businesses draw down on inventories of goods. Producers react to such a situation by producing greater quantities of goods and services, thus generating additional income to workers and to the other factors of production. The resulting increases in income will change consumption plans. At incomes higher than $100 billion, households will spend greater amounts on goods and services, indicated in the second column of Table 8.2 and Figure 8.6, which merely reproduces the information of Table 8.2 graphically. (Note in Figure 8.6 that investment is added vertically to the consumption function at an autonomous level of $20 billion in order to obtain the $C + I$ line.)

A new, higher level of output produced and income received at $200 billion creates higher total spending, but there is still an excess of total expenditures over

**Equilibrium level of
national income**
In the income-expenditures
model, the level of income at
which total private expenditures equal total output.

output (amount *FG* in Figure 8.6). Inventories continue to be drawn down and
production stepped up until an **equilibrium level of national income** of $300 bil-
lion is reached. Only at this level of income will production plans be in line with
the plans of households and businesses to consume and invest.

What would happen at an income level greater than $300 billion, say $400 billion? If an income level of $400 billion were temporarily established, total output
would temporarily exceed total expenditures by $20 billion, or *AB* in Figure 8.6.
Unwanted inventories of goods would pile up unsold, and producers would cut
back the rate of production. Since a cutback in production would reduce income,
consumption plans of households would be revised downward. Equilibrium would
again be achieved when the level of income dropped to $300 billion.

It is always worth remembering that the simple Keynesian model of total private spending is a short-run model. Prices, wages, and interest rates do not adjust
as they do in long-run classical theory. The only factors that are adjusting are the
real quantities of goods and services produced in the economy.

Unlike the classical economists, who believed that the economy would self-
adjust until full employment was reached, Keynes thought that the economy could
adjust to an equilibrium level with widespread unemployment. In terms of the situation depicted in Figure 8.6, the $300 billion level of income is not necessarily
the full-employment level of income. Moreover, fluctuations between unemployment and inflation would normally be experienced if the private economy was left
to itself. This unfortunate state of affairs, in Keynes's view, either was permanent
or would last a long time. In either case, some action was demanded in the economy. That action, as we will see, formed the basis for a role for the government.

FLUCTUATIONS IN THE PRIVATE SECTOR

Before turning to the role of government in the Keynesian macroeconomic system,
consider the source of fluctuations in the economy. In the Keynesian model, output
and income can increase or decrease in response to any change in the components
of total expenditures. For example, if autonomous consumption or investment increases, income will increase. If the economy-wide marginal propensity to consume increases, income will increase.

To see how changes in these factors actually affect income and output, consider
an increase in autonomous investment spending. Recall that autonomous investment spending is independent of income and depends instead on factors such as
the cost of capital, expected sales, and business profits. What happens to income
when investment spending increases? In the example illustrated in Figure 8.7, the
initial level of income of $300 billion is determined by the private spending level
$C + I_0$. Assume that investment spending then increases by $20 billion because of
an increase in expected future profits. The total spending curve shifts upward to
$C + I_1$ by the amount $\Delta I = \$20$ billion. Desired spending then exceeds the output
of goods and services by $20 billion (distance *AB* in Figure 8.7). To meet the de-
mand, inventories are drawn down, producers step up the rate of output, and income rises. The question is: What effect does a $20 billion increase in autonomous
investment spending have on equilibrium income? Does income increase by $20

FIGURE 8.7

The Effects of an Increase in Investment Expenditures

When the level of autonomous investment increases by $20 billion, from $60 billion to $80 billion (*AB*) in the figure, and the marginal propensity to consume is 0.8, equilibrium income rises by $100 billion—in this case, from $300 billion to $400 billion. The multiplier effect causes the level of income to rise by more than the amount of the increase in investment.

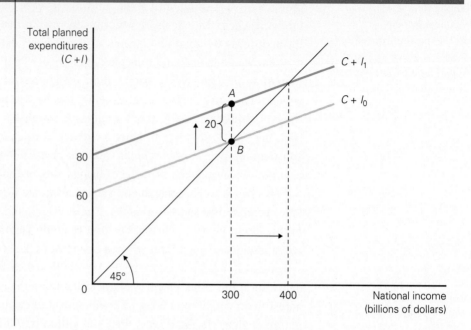

billion exactly or by a greater or lesser amount? As you may have noticed in Figure 8.7, income increases by $100 billion with an investment spending increase of $20 billion. Why does such a relatively small increase in investment result in such a relatively large increase in income?

Instability in the Economy: The Expenditure Multiplier

The answer to this question is given by the value of the multiplier, a number found by dividing the change in income by the change in autonomous spending that caused the change in income. In Figure 8.7, we are looking at a change in autonomous investment spending. Thus the **investment multiplier** is found by dividing $100 billion by $20 billion or, if k_I represents the investment multiplier,

Investment multiplier
The multiple by which equilibrium income will change given a change in autonomous investment expenditure; $1/MPS$.

$$k_I = \Delta Y/\Delta I = 100/20 = 5.$$

If autonomous investment spending increases by ΔI, or $20 billion, the initial expenditure first generates an addition to income of $20 billion ($\Delta Y$) because expenditures on investment goods create returns (or income) to resources. However, the process does not end here, for all resource owners, laborers, holders of capital or land, and so on, are consumer-savers. New income will cause the consumer-saver to spend some and to save the rest. The *MPC*—the marginal propensity to consume—and the *MPS*—the marginal propensity to save—will always add up to 1 out of total income. (What is consumed is not saved; what is saved is not consumed.) Consumption expenditures on goods and services, then, create additional income out of which another set of income recipients spend a portion and save the rest. In this process, the initial increase of $20 billion is multiplied at each stage.

Autonomous consumption multiplier
The multiple by which equilibrium income will change given a change in autonomous consumption expenditure; 1/*MPS*.

The same principle applies to the autonomous portion of consumption spending. The **autonomous consumption multiplier** applies to the autonomous portion of consumption, that portion of consumption spending independent of income and determined instead by variables such as thrift attitudes and the rate of interest on savings.

If autonomous consumption increases, income also increases by some multiple. If, for example, the autonomous component of consumption increases from $40 billion to $50 billion in a society with a marginal propensity to save of 0.2, equilibrium income would rise to $450 billion from its previous level of $400 billion. The change in income can be expressed as follows:

$$\frac{\Delta \text{ Autonomous Consumption}}{MPS} = \frac{\$10 \text{ billion}}{0.2} = \$50 \text{ billion}.$$

Thus the autonomous consumption multiplier, like the investment multiplier, is the reciprocal of the *MPS* (in this example, 1/0.2 = 5). The higher the *MPC* (or, what is the same, the lower the *MPS*), the higher the consumption multiplier and the higher the income change from a given change in autonomous expenditures.

The value of the multiplier is determined by the *MPC* or *MPS*. A quick method of determining the multiplier, therefore, is to divide 1 by the *MPS*: $k_I = 1/(1 - MPC)$ = 1/*MPS*. Using an *MPC* of 0.8, $k_I = 1/(1 - 0.8) = 1/0.2 = 5$. Any change in income caused by a change in an autonomous expenditure may then be determined by multiplying the autonomous expenditure change by the multiplier or, in the example, $\Delta Y = k\Delta I = (1/MPS) \times (\Delta I) = 5 \times \$20$ billion = $100 billion.

A change in the *MPS*, which also means a change in the *MPC*, will obviously alter the value of *k*, the multiplier. The multiplier is the reciprocal of the *MPS*. If the *MPS* is 0.1, the multiplier is 10. Under these circumstances, a $20 billion injection of autonomous expenditures would increase income by $200 billion. Or, if Americans saved one-half of every additional dollar received in income, the multiplier would take on a value of 2. (On a piece of scratch paper, demonstrate to yourself why this is so.) In this case, a $20 billion increase in investment spending would raise equilibrium income by $40 billion.

To summarize, income will rise or fall by an amount greater than the expenditure change because of a multiplier process. The multiplier, which is simply the reciprocal of the *MPS*, magnifies the change in autonomous expenditures that creates the change in equilibrium income. Stated another way, changes in equilibrium income are calculated by applying the multiplier to changes in autonomous expenditures.

These concepts are of importance for practical policymaking. The most significant effect of the multiplier is that very small changes in spending may be greatly magnified in resulting income and employment changes. For example, a small change in private spending could precipitate a relatively large economic contraction or reduction in employment and business activity. As we will see later in this chapter, Keynes recommended that government's fiscal actions be used to counteract the instabilities generated by the multiplier effects of private spending on GDP, employment, economic growth, and inflation.

CONTRACTIONARY AND EXPANSIONARY GAPS

Failure of the private economy to provide stable growth and predictable, stable levels of full employment led to Keynes's fundamental criticism of classical economics. Though Keynes himself did not discuss a business cycle, in his view the private economy was erratic and subject to long-run periods of large-scale unemployment and low production levels. The contractionary phase of the cycle would engender more and greater pessimism about future business conditions, keeping the economy in a contractionary phase of the cycle for a very long period of time. Only accident, not dependable market forces as the classical economists had maintained, would produce a stable equilibrium at full employment with no inflation.

For our more familiar income-expenditures approach to the macroeconomy, Keynes envisioned the economy as reaching, and remaining in, either a contractionary gap or an expansionary gap. A **contractionary gap** (sometimes called a recessionary gap) exists when equilibrium output is less than full-employment output. This occurs when the level of total expenditures that would exist at full employment is insufficient to purchase total output. Inventories pile up, and the level of output adjusts to a lower equilibrium level as businesses cut back production. An **expansionary gap** (sometimes called an inflationary gap), the opposite situation, means that total private expenditures exceed those expenditures necessary to produce a full-employment level of income without inflation. Excess expenditures, in other words, put pressure on the employment of resources. Since the economy cannot push output beyond its production possibilities frontier, inflation is created.

Contractionary gap
The amount by which total planned expenditures at the level of full-employment income fall short of the level required to generate full-employment income; also called a recessionary gap.

Expansionary gap
The amount by which total planned expenditures at the level of full-employment income exceed the level required to generate full-employment income without inflation; also called an inflationary gap.

GOVERNMENT SPENDING AND TAXATION

Keynes believed that the invisible hand—those forces that would return the economy to full-employment equilibrium without inflation—was seriously arthritic. Even if such forces on private spending did exist, in Keynes's opinion they would probably be unendurably slow in restoring equilibrium. Keynes argued that society should not have to endure contractionary or expansionary gaps of long duration. Since automatic forces were unreliable, he saw discretionary government interventions as necessary. Keynes felt that macroeconomic management should be entrusted to the central government, which theoretically has the ability to adjust aggregate spending in line with national economic goals by the use of its two major budget weapons: government spending and taxation. Changes in one or both of these areas constitute fiscal policy, the object of which is the manipulation of total spending in the economy.

Government Expenditures

In the context of the basic Keynesian income-expenditures model, government spending (G) is an addition to total private spending, represented graphically by raising the $C + I$ curve to account for the new source of spending.

Once a government sector is incorporated into the model, the equilibrium production level is that at which output is equal to consumption (demand from households) plus investment (demand from businesses) plus government spending on goods and services (demand from the government sector). Previously, we had operated under the assumption that the level of government purchase of goods and services was zero. Then, total spending consisted of household spending (consumption) plus business spending (investment).

Government spending can take many forms and have many (sometimes conflicting) objectives. For example, in one sense the government behaves like a business, purchasing inputs used in its daily operations, such as labor, machinery, and buildings. In another sense, the government acts like a consumer, purchasing products for its own use, such as missile systems, tanks, ammunition, and airplanes. An extensive and controversial type of government spending does not result in the outright purchase of goods and services: namely, transfer payments that redistribute income among various groups in society—from rich to poor, from able to disabled, from healthy to sick, from employed to unemployed. These transfer payments are not included in our definition of government purchases of goods and services; government spending, which we will designate as G, thus includes only purchases of goods and services.

Keep in mind that a government's decision about how much to spend is somewhat different from private decisions to consume or invest. A major difference is that the government is a not-for-profit sector of the economy. Its decisions are often not motivated by private profit or economic efficiency. Furthermore, its spending is not constrained by its income in tax receipts. Congress can, and often does, spend far more than it raises in the form of taxes, issuing government bonds or creating money to cover the difference. Because government spending is not constrained by government tax collections, enormous budget deficits have built up in recent years, causing much concern among the electorate and in Congress. It is dangerous to ignore the consequences of budget deficits, but in the first approach we will do so to keep the model simple.

Autonomous government expenditures

Government expenditures that are independent of the level of income.

To further simplify the analysis, we will assume that government expenditures to purchase goods and services actually are **autonomous government expenditures**; in other words, they do not depend in any predetermined way on national income. Thus we may write, as we did previously for investment, $G = G_0$ to indicate that government expenditures are independent of income. Total spending can now be redefined as follows:

$$C + I + G_0 = \text{total expenditures.}$$

Graphically, the addition of autonomous government spending, G, results in a parallel upward shift of the total spending function. In Figure 8.8, the $C_0 + I_0 + G_0$ curve is higher than the $C_0 + I_0$ curve at each level of national income by whatever amount of G_0 the government decides to spend. Notice that the addition of government spending to the total expenditures curve has the effect of moving the total spending curve to an intersection point higher up the 45-degree line. In other words, government expenditure, taken by itself, is expansionary; it leads to a higher level of equilibrium income.

The Effects of Taxation

To introduce the concept and effect of government spending, we merely acknowledged the impact of an injection of new spending on the macroeconomy.

FIGURE 8.8

Effects of
Government
Expenditures on
Total Spending

The introduction of government spending increases total
spending and the equilibrium
level of income. With government spending of G_0 added to
autonomous consumption and
investment, $C_0 + I_0$, total income rises from Y_0 to Y_1.

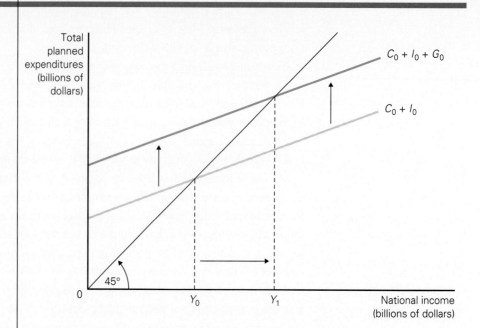

In fact, government spending decisions are rarely made in a budgetary vacuum. Decisions about taxes—both their level and their structure—often accompany decisions concerning government spending. We will disregard changes in tax structure and concentrate on the effects on output and employment of changes in the level of taxes. Taxes represent a leakage from the income-expenditures flow. In this respect they are like savings and for analytical purposes can be treated in the same way as savings. (You might think of taxes as "public saving" in conjunction with the private decision to withhold from spending a part of national income.)

To determine the effect of taxes on the macroeconomy we must ask: Who pays taxes? The answer, of course, is that consumers (and, to a lesser extent, businesses) do. The effect of taxes, therefore, is primarily to lower planned consumption insofar as taxes reduce the disposable income received by households, the income left after taxes. We must refine another assumption in light of government spending. As we saw earlier, when government is not a factor in the economy, several of the aggregate income measures are identical to each other. But once we subtract taxes from the national income, national income and disposable income are no longer the same. Disposable income is equal to national income minus the amount of taxes paid. Total spending is, therefore, a function of disposable aggregate income once taxes are admitted into the analysis. However, the purpose of the analysis is to determine equilibrium national income. As such, all of the figures and graphs we use measure national income on the horizontal axis. When the difference between national income and disposable income changes as a result of tax changes, the result is to alter consumption and saving at every level of national income (and therefore total spending). When taxes change, the consumption function shifts

FIGURE 8.9

Effects of a Lump-Sum Tax on Aggregate Household Spending and Saving

A lump-sum tax decreases both consumption and saving. The decrease in consumption from C_0 to C_1 is determined by the *MPC*. If *MPC* = 0.8, a lump-sum tax reduces consumption by 80 percent of each tax dollar paid. A lump-sum tax reduces equilibrium income—in this case, represented by the shift from income level Y_0 to Y_1.

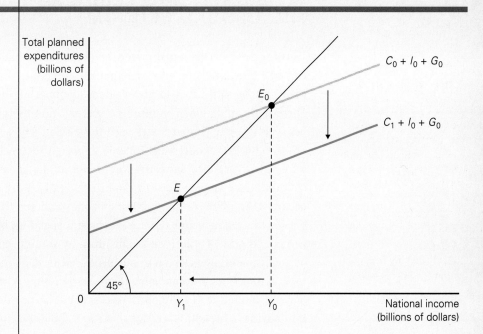

Lump-sum tax

A fixed level of total taxes; total taxes do not change as the level of income changes.

when it is plotted against national income. This same explanation is, of course, applicable to the saving function.

In order to concentrate on the effect that taxation has on equilibrium output, assume that the type of tax the government levies is a **lump-sum tax,** whose effect is straightforward: Every income earner is taxed the same amount, say $100. Each dollar increase in lump-sum tax revenue collected by the government results in a dollar lost from household and disposable income. An increase in the lump-sum tax therefore shifts the consumption curve downward, but the curve does not shift downward by the full amount of the tax because the saving schedule is also shifted downward. If *MPC* equals 0.8 and *MPS* equals 0.2, then every dollar increase in the lump-sum tax will reduce consumption by 80 cents and reduce saving by 20 cents. The downward shifts in the consumption schedule will be parallel; a lump-sum tax means that the tax amount is the same regardless of the level of income. Figure 8.9 shows the shifts in the consumption curve resulting from the imposition of a lump-sum tax.

In Figure 8.9, the imposition of a lump-sum tax on each household causes household consumption to decline by 80 percent of the tax because the *MPC* is 0.8. (Given any level of nominal income, disposable income, *DI*, falls by the amount of the tax. Since consumption is dependent on disposable income, consumption falls by $MPC \times \Delta DI$.) If the lump-sum tax is $100, the shift from $C_0 + I_0 + G_0$ to $C_1 + I_0 + G_0$ represents an $80 cut in household expenditures at every level of aggregate income.

The effect of a tax increase, taken by itself, is contractionary. It causes a reduction in aggregate income and output. This point is readily seen in Figure 8.9, where the effect of the tax is to reduce national income equilibrium from Y_0 to Y_1.

INTERNATIONAL TRADE AND
THE GLOBAL ECONOMY

Thus far, we have operated under the assumption that all goods produced in the United States are sold here and that all goods purchased by American households, business firms, and government agencies are made in the United States. There was a time when the foreign sector could be ignored without sacrificing believability; the United States used to be relatively self-sufficient. Now, any realistic economic model must include a foreign sector. Fortunately, incorporating a foreign sector into our basic Keynesian model is easy to do. First, the notion of equilibrium income must be modified slightly. With foreign trade, equilibrium occurs when domestic production of goods and services is equal to total spending for those goods and services, including spending by foreign buyers. In other words, **exports** (X), defined as spending by foreign households, business firms, or government agencies on goods produced in the United States, must be added to C, I, and G as a component of total spending. At the same time, the model must be altered to take imports into account. A portion of consumption spending, business spending, and government spending may be on goods produced abroad, and such expenditures do not represent demand for domestically produced goods. Therefore, if we define **imports** (M) as total spending on foreign goods, we must subtract M from total spending. Total spending, then, is equal to $C + I + G + (X - M)$, and the equilibrium level of national income is that level at which Y is equal to $C + I + G + (X - M)$.

Exports
Expenditures by foreigners on domestically produced goods.

Imports
Expenditures by domestic residents on goods produced in foreign countries.

The concept of a foreign trade component of total domestic spending is intuitive. The import of cashmere sweaters by consumers, computer chips by business investors, or titanium by the U.S. government replaces domestic spending by these groups and represents increased demands for *foreign* producers. Increased demand by U.S. consumers, investors, and by the U.S. government generates income in foreign countries. On the other hand, exports of American wheat, machinery, and airplanes represent demand for domestic products. These components of total spending (both positive and negative) must be compared before we can determine whether the trade sector contributes to or detracts from total expenditures in the United States. When imports exceed exports, total spending declines at home. The opposite occurs when our exports of goods and services exceed our purchases abroad.

In recent years, the United States has been a net importer of goods and services to the tune of over $100 billion per year. This means that Americans collectively spent over $100 billion more on goods and services produced abroad than foreigners spent on U.S. products. In terms of the Keynesian model, this means that total domestic expenditure on all goods and services was billions of dollars less than it would have been had our exports equaled our imports. This international trade deficit has a number of implications for the U.S. economy, but we postpone a more complete discussion of foreign trade and its effects until Chapters 16 and 17, where both real and financial aspects of international transactions are considered.

COUNTERCYCLICAL FISCAL POLICIES

Countercyclical fiscal policy
Changes in government expenditures or taxes that are designed to reverse changes in private expenditures or savings that produce unemployment or inflation.

Having reached an understanding of how the presence of a government sector influences the economy, we now move the discussion toward a fuller understanding of the Keynesian prescriptions for **countercyclical fiscal policy.** Fiscal policy, as we have already noted, means budget actions: government expenditure changes, tax changes, or a combination of the two. To say that a policy is countercyclical means that the policy seeks to correct whatever phase of the business cycle—contractionary or expansionary—the economy happens to be in. In a recession, for example, total spending, output, and employment are below the full-employment equilibrium level. In such circumstances, countercyclical fiscal policy would seek to raise the level of total expenditures to the full-employment level. During inflation, a countercyclical fiscal policy must try to induce a lower level of total spending. But knowing the appropriate direction of budgetary changes does not guarantee that the exact equilibrium target will be achieved. To do that, policy must be guided by knowledge of the relevant expenditure multipliers. Expenditure multipliers play a major role in the following analysis. Any autonomous expenditure is subject to the multiplier process; thus it is possible to identify consumption multipliers, investment multipliers, government spending multipliers, export multipliers, import multipliers, and so on.

Fiscal Policy to Deal with a Recession

To see how fiscal policies are used to change the direction of the business cycle, let us first suppose that the economy is in a recession. Imagine that government economic policymakers have determined that the actual level of aggregate income-output is $50 billion below the full-employment level. In Figure 8.10, the government's problem can be seen as that of moving the economy from an income level of $2.50 trillion to one of $2.55 trillion (an increase of $50 billion). What is required in this case is an increase in G or a decrease in T, either of which would lead to an increase in total spending, $C + I + G + (X - M)$. If government simply increases G by $50 billion, it will overshoot the desired target because the new additional expenditure of $50 billion will be multiplied through various rounds of spending into a much larger increase. What, then, is the appropriate fiscal stimulus?

The answer depends on the size of the contractionary gap, whether households or businesses are the ultimate recipients of government expenditures, and the value of the relevant multiplier. In the following analysis, assume (1) that only households will receive the government expenditures and (2) that MPC equals 0.8. Under these conditions we can determine the size of the contractionary gap, AB, and design a fiscal policy to eliminate it.

Since we know the value of MPC, we can compute the consumption multiplier (the only relevant multiplier in this case):

$$k = \frac{1}{1 - MPC} = \frac{1}{0.2} = 5.$$

FIGURE 8.10

Government Spending to Eliminate a Contractionary Gap in Income

If total spending, $C_0 + I_0 + G_0 + (X_0 - M_0)$, is not great enough to achieve full employment, then an increase in government expenditures may restore full employment. In this example, initial expenditures, $C_0 + I_0 + G_0 + (X_0 - M_0)$, are insufficient to create a full-employment level of income. Government expenditures are increased to $C_0 + I_0 + G_1 + (X_0 - M_0)$, and, through a multiplier process, the contractionary gap, AB, is eliminated.

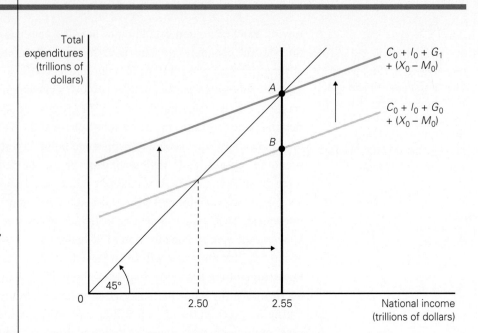

We know the size of the income gap ($50 billion), and we know that whatever increase in government spending occurs will be multiplied by 5. Therefore, we can determine the size of the contractionary gap, AB, by the formula

$$\text{Contractionary gap} = \frac{\text{income gap}}{k} = \frac{\$50 \text{ billion}}{5} = \$10 \text{ billion}.$$

In this case, an increase in total expenditures of $10 billion will, via the multiplier, produce an increase in aggregate income of $50 billion, thereby moving the economy to its full-employment equilibrium level.

There are two ways that fiscal policy could produce the additional $10 billion expenditure. The most direct way is to increase government expenditures, G, by $10 billion. We assume that this direct injection to the spending stream is not subject to any leakages. Therefore, the full $10 billion enters the expenditure flow at once.

An indirect way to accomplish the same thing is to cut taxes to stimulate consumption spending, as shown in Figure 8.11. Remember, however, that tax changes do not produce expenditure changes of the same dollar amount because taxes are paid partly at the expense of consumption and partly at the expense of saving. Against a contractionary gap of $10 billion, a lump-sum tax cut of $10 billion will only induce additional consumption of $8 billion ($MPC \times \Delta T$). To raise consumption spending by $10 billion requires in this instance a tax cut of more than $10 billion to offset the increase of saving that occurs when household disposable income increases. A lump-sum tax cut of $12.5 billion, given that $MPC = 0.8$, would be required to raise aggregate consumption by $10 billion and thereby eliminate the $10 billion contractionary gap.

FIGURE 8.11

Taxation to Eliminate a Contractionary Gap

If total spending, $C_0 + I_0 + G_0 + (X_0 - M_0)$, is not great enough to achieve full employment, then total expenditures may be increased by a tax cut. In this example, if taxes fall, then consumption increases from C_0 to C_1 to achieve full employment. A tax cut increases the disposable income of consumers, causing them to spend more.

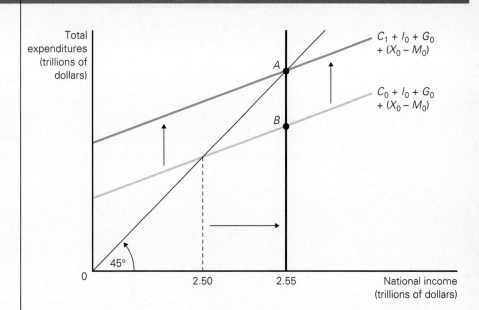

Government expenditure changes are more direct and more powerful, dollar for dollar, than tax changes of the same amount. This must be kept in mind when expenditures and taxes are changed simultaneously.

Fiscal Policy to Deal with Inflation

Once full employment is reached, further increases in total spending will tend to drive the price level upward, creating an expansionary gap. An expansionary gap develops because raw materials, labor, and inputs of all kinds become increasingly scarce. GDP, the economy's output, can be pushed only so far by excessive spending and only at the cost of causing inflation to accelerate. The reverse of a given policy that works in one phase of the business cycle works for the opposite phase of the cycle. If the economy is characterized by inflation and full (or "overfull") employment, the appropriate fiscal response would be a decrease in government expenditures or an increase in taxes.

An expansionary gap, as discussed earlier, is the difference between the existing level of total spending and the desired level. The trick is to bring the actual level of total expenditure, $C + I + G + (X_0 - M_0)$, in line with the desired full-employment level. As in the case of contractionary gaps, the correction can be achieved in one of two ways: either a change of government expenditures or a change of taxes.

Assume that the economy is operating at a level of nominal output-income too high for full employment. (We are talking about the effects of inflation, so the concepts of real and nominal come into play.) In what sense could the nominal level of income be too high? "More is better than less" when it comes to economic output, but there are two factors to consider. First, by definition, aggregate real output in the macroeconomy cannot increase after full employment has been reached because the economy is already at a point on the production possibilities frontier.

Second, income measures beyond the full-employment level mean that a constant amount of goods and services is valued at higher unit prices, showing the effect of inflation. When the newspapers say that the economy is "overheating," they mean that a lower level of national income is preferred to the present higher one. Too high a level of total spending produces inflation.

The problem posed by inflation, then, is how to reduce the level of nominal income by some amount, say by $50 billion. With a multiplier of 5, a reduction in spending of one-fifth the observed income gap will produce the desired effect. This result can be achieved by cutting government expenditures by $10 billion, leaving taxes unchanged. It can also be achieved by leaving government expenditures unchanged and raising lump-sum taxes by $12.5 billion (to reduce the consumption component of aggregate demand by $10 billion). The mechanics of these changes are exactly the reverse of those used in the contractionary-recessionary situation. Changes in taxes or government expenditures therefore composed Keynes's arsenal of methods for counteracting contractionary or inflationary swings of the business cycle.

The actual potential of Keynesian fiscal policy to deal with recession or inflation may, in reality, be severely limited. We must never forget that G and T are enacted within a political process. Within this process, other goals—such as balancing the budget—may receive priority. (See the Focus "How the Political System Helps Create Deficits".)

Keynesian Economics in Historical Context

Was Keynes right about the ability of government to use countercyclical fiscal policies to counteract extreme phases of the business cycle? Although the policy and theoretical issues are complex, it is probably the case that certain theoretical and political effects unforeseen by Keynes have inhibited the ability of government

Public works projects, such as the construction of this powerhouse and dam, are examples of how governments act as consumers. Keynes advocated such projects as a means of artificially stimulating the economy.

In Keynesian macroeconomic theory, surpluses are called for in an overheated inflationary economy, and deficits are called for when recession or depression (slow economic growth, low and falling employment rates) occur. The implication is that Congress and the president are able to read the economic tea leaves and are actually willing and able to raise or lower government spending and/or taxation at the appropriate time to ensure future economic growth and low unemployment rates.

The federal budget is *supposed* to be balanced over the business cycle according to the Keynesian theory. Unfortunately, things haven't worked out that way. Aside from the technical problems of judging the timing of economic cycles, lags in recognizing problems, and lags in implementing policies, political realities often hinder policy effectiveness. Self-interested politicians want to be reelected. Politicians who are under a reelection constraint will work very hard to improve their net chances of winning the next election. This means that policies whose lobbies and supporters can deliver the largest vote totals (and possibly other perks) have the best chance of being enacted. Similarly, other policies will not be enacted (unpopular tax increases, for instance) because there are insufficient incentives or even disincentives for politicians seeking reelection. Some call this process democracy in action. However that may be, the result has been a bias toward deficit spending at the federal level and an abridgement of Keynesian principles of discretionary fiscal policy.

Deficits occur when government expenditures exceed government income from taxation in any given fiscal year. The national debt is the sum at a certain point in time of all prior deficits. During the 1980s and early 1990s, huge deficits—some on the order of $300 billion per year—were incurred by the federal government, although they moderated somewhat between 1993 and 1996. These deficits pushed the national debt to right at $5 *trillion* in 1995. The point to be made is that these deficits were not primarily the product of conscious discretionary—that is, Keynesian—action to eliminate contractionary gaps. They were simply inevitable given the nature of the democratic political process.

The right to supply government products of all kinds—social services, welfare benefits, physical facilities—is temporary in a democracy. That right is subject to renewal at election time and is open to competition (Democrats versus Republicans versus Libertarians). Once in office, a politician is confronted with a choice between raising taxes or borrowing funds and creating deficits in order to finance the desired output of the public sector. Deficit finance may be preferred because it is less costly than the alternative—the decidedly unpopular tax increase.

The behavior of politicians with regard to the supply of deficits is understandable, but why would some voters reveal a preference for deficit finance? Those who earn little or no income and who receive large net benefits from the government have little incentive to demand restraint from politicians. Since taxes fall disproportionately on *human* capital in the form of income taxes in the United States, some voters have an incentive to support deficit finance over direct pay-as-you-go taxation to finance the activities of the federal government. In effect, these voters are electing to pass part of the burden of financing government expenditures on to succeeding generations of taxpayers. The success of further attempts to burden future generations with additional debt may be limited. The inequity of such an arrangement was the centerpiece of Ross Perot's 1992 presidential campaign. The success of Perot's bid (Perot received almost 20 percent of the vote) and his post-election surge in popularity indicate that many Americans are serious about deficit reduction. A bill passing a balanced budget amendment failed by only one vote in the U.S. Senate in 1995.

The plain fact is that politicians want to get reelected; and some voters would like to pass the bill for present enjoyment on to future generations. The economic effects of deficits (which will be discussed at length in Chapter 11) are less clear. What is obvious is that the lack of effective budget constraints on members of Congress and the president or on the financing process means that democracies have built-in tendencies to run deficits.

to control the business cycle and thereby guarantee continuous inflation-free levels of full employment and maximum economic growth.

Keynes was primarily concerned with the economic and human costs of economic depression (or, if you prefer, an extreme contractionary phase of the business cycle). His advice, though not fully implemented in Western democracies during the Great Depression of the 1930s and early 1940s, was at least partially responsible for the increased economic role of government at the time and, perhaps, for the absence of prolonged and serious depressions after World War II. But problems other than depression have been paramount in the U.S. economy since the late 1960s—particularly high rates of inflation combined with slowed economic growth and large budget deficits. Keynesian economics was not explicitly designed to deal with these problems.

How could actual fiscal policy have caused these problems? The use of Keynesian countercyclical fiscal policy means that balancing government expenditures and receipts—a balanced budget—takes on secondary importance. The cumulative effect of unbalanced budgets is ignored in this approach. As we have seen, anti-recessionary fiscal policy requires raising government expenditures or reducing taxes, either of which tends to produce a budget deficit. For reasons that will be explained more fully in Chapter 11, the history of fiscal policy in the United States has been one in which, since World War II, annual deficits have outnumbered annual surpluses by a margin of almost 20 to one, a policy that Keynes probably would not have supported. A deficit implies that government expenditures exceed revenues, further implying the need for creation of money and credit. Credit creation, in turn, has implications in the money markets of the macroeconomy. The most important of these implications is inflation.

A major deficiency of the income-expenditures model we have employed to this point is that it excludes monetary variables, particularly prices. Therefore, it does not tell all of the macroeconomic story. Prices affect both consumption and investment spending, which in turn affect macroeconomic activity. In other words, simple Keynesian economics leaves us ill-equipped to analyze adequately recent experience with unemployment and inflation. A more complete Keynesian theory of total expenditures, one including prices and other monetary factors, will help us better understand today's macroeconomic problems. This expanded theory will be presented in Chapters 9 and 10.

APPLICATION

Mortgaging Your Future: The Government and Your Incentive to Save

A great challenge facing the United States is reversing the decline in the national saving rate. This concern is based on the notion that the level of a country's savings determines how much it has to invest in new plant and equipment. A decline in the saving rate therefore leads to less investment, which in turn reduces the ability of the economy to produce goods and services.

Although there is some controversy concerning the importance of the saving rate as a determinant of economic growth, two things are clear: The saving rate in the

United States has declined sharply over the last 20 years, and this decline has brought the U.S. saving rate to a level far below that of other major economic powers (although it is worth noting that there are variations in the ways other countries measure savings). In 1973, Americans were saving about 10 percent of their disposable income; this percentage fell to under 3 percent in 1987. Since then, the trend has reversed somewhat, and the saving rate reached 4 percent by 1994.

In explaining the difference between the saving rate in the United States and in other countries, much attention has been paid to the way that interest income is taxed in the United States. In the United States, interest earnings are taxable income. If a family has accumulated, say, $20,000 in savings that yields 9 percent interest, the $1800 in annual interest is an addition to taxable income. Assuming the family to be middle income, each additional dollar of taxable income will lead to an increase of $0.28 in federal taxes owed by the family. In addition, this family probably would pay about $0.05 in state taxes for each additional dollar in interest earnings. When state and federal taxes are combined, $600 of the $1800 earned in interest will go to pay taxes—in effect reducing the interest rate to 6 percent. By taxing interest income, the tax system in this country reduces the returns to saving and presumably causes the saving rate to be lower than it otherwise would be.

In addition to discouraging saving, the U.S. tax system subsidizes borrowing. If a family in this country borrows $100,000 to buy a new home, any interest that the family pays is tax-deductible. Assuming mortgage interest payments of $9000 per year on the loan, this debt enables the family to reduce taxable income by $9000, which lowers state and federal taxes by about $3000. In effect, the loan costs the family only 6 percent in interest. Until recently, all interest paid on consumer loans was tax-deductible. However, this deduction has been phased out, explaining in part the recent upturn in savings. Nonetheless, U.S. tax policy (including the tax increases in President Clinton's 1993 budget plan) still reduces the return to saving.

What is the impact of a low saving rate for the U.S. economy? Other things being equal, anything that reduces the private saving rate will have a tendency to reduce private investment over time. (Other policies, such as the taxing of capital gains at the rate of ordinary income, also reduce individual investment.) One of the key factors in determining the level of private investment is the cost of making new investments in capital, equipment, labor training programs, and research and development. One of the major components in that cost is the rate of interest. A reduction in private savings for any reason will increase the rate of interest and raise the cost of new investment in the economy. Since, as Keynes noted, private investment (and investment volatility) is a prime determinant of the level of income over the short (and long) run, policies affecting private investment—such as taxes on savings and subsidies to borrowing—are of great importance to economic and employment growth.[a]

In addition to tax policies and to the natural inclination of individuals to value the present more than the future (which helps explain why higher interest rates in the present yield more present savings), other more subtle long-run factors affect the saving rate. While the consumption stream is roughly constant or slightly rising over time, the average individual's income flow is much lower in early age and in old age than in middle age. This means that individuals (and households) consume more of the value of their (expected) lifetime income flow in early age and in old age and less in middle age. When birth rates are constant, this poses no problem for a country's savings. But significant changes in the age distribution of the population may have important impacts on the distribution of long-term savings.[b] In the United States, the aging of the "baby-boomers"—the large group born between the end of World War II and 1964—may well have a negative impact on private saving and investment.

Finally, we need to mention the way recent trends in finance have tended to reduce private investment. Government borrowing has resulted from high federal deficits in the public accounts (when current government spending exceeds tax revenues). In order to finance all of its activities the government must in effect compete with private businesses for private savings. As we have seen, a lower supply of private savings tends to drive up interest rates. Increased government demands have the same effect, which means that politically determined spending and tax policies at the federal level will have huge implications for economic growth rates in the economy. Annual budget deficits and the resulting debt (about $5 *trillion* in 1996)—and the necessary payments of interest or "service" on the debt—play a major role in capital formation, economic growth, and growth in employment in the U.S. economy.

QUESTIONS:

What could the federal government do to encourage private saving? What does a low saving rate imply about the future prospects of the U.S. economy?

[a]Remember, however, that for short-run analytical purposes, Keynes thought that private investment was "autonomous," or independent of the level of income, as shown in Figure 8.6. Keynes believed, however, that the relation between consumption, saving, and the interest rate was inexact over the short run—in contrast to the direct relation between interest rates and saving identified by classical economists (see Figures 7.4 and 7.6).

[b]This feature of saving and consumption is called the "life-cycle" saving hypothesis.

SUMMARY

1. In the 1930s, John Maynard Keynes criticized classical theory as being an inadequate description of events in the real world. He based macroeconomics on a model of total expenditures. In the simple private-sector model, consumption and investment spending determine equilibrium output and income.

2. Keynes argued that consumption was primarily a function of current income and that the marginal and average propensities to consume were related to income in a stable and predictable manner. Investment, the other kind of private spending, was related to expectations and to a number of factors but could, in the short run, be considered autonomous of income.

3. The income-expenditures model of equilibrium output/income determination employs Keynes's arguments concerning the relationship of certain macroeconomic variables. The level of consumption spending is positively related to the level of income. The marginal propensity to save (MPS) measures the change in saving that results from a $1 change in income. Other factors, such as the price level, wealth, and taxation, help determine consumption and saving. Investment spending is assumed to be autonomous.

4. In the income-expenditures approach, the equilibrium level of income exists when total expenditure equals total income or output in the economy ($Y = C + I$). Whenever total expenditure does not equal total income or whenever desired saving does not equal desired investment, unintended investment in the form of inventory change exists. The unintended investment will drive income or output toward its equilibrium level. However, the equilibrium level of income may not be a level of income at which full employment occurs.

5. A multiplier is calculated by dividing a change in income by the change in autonomous expenditures that caused the change in income. The multiplier is the reciprocal of the marginal propensity to save, or $1/MPS$. A multiplier may be applied to *any* change in autonomous expenditures. For example, if the autonomous portion of consumption expenditures increases, income changes by the value of the expenditures multiplied by the reciprocal of the MPS.

6. Fiscal policy consists of budgetary action taken by the central government. More specifically, fiscal policy means action to adjust either the level of taxes or the level of government expenditures to achieve a stable level of growth.

7. An increase in government expenditures, G, or a decrease in taxes, T, is expansionary. A decrease in government expenditures or an increase in taxes is contractionary. Insofar as tax changes affect private spending only indirectly, a tax change is less effective than the same dollar amount of change in government expenditures. Output effects from changes in G or T are multiplied. Although the value of the consumption multiplier ($1/MPS$) is the same in both cases, the output effects are different because a $1 change in taxes affects consumption less than a $1 change in government expenditures does.

8. Exports and imports also have an impact on total expenditures. When imports exceed exports, total spending declines in the United States. Total spending increases when exports to other countries exceed our imports from abroad.

9. Keynes's macroeconomic theory and his remedies for macroeconomic ills, while probably appropriate for periods of contraction and widespread unemployment, omitted crucial monetary variables, especially prices, from primary consideration. More inclusive theories are able to explain inflation and other contemporary macroeconomic problems.

KEY TERMS

income-expenditures model
marginal propensity to consume
  (MPC)
marginal propensity to save (MPS)
average propensity to consume (APC)
average propensity to save (APS)
dissaving
autonomous consumption

consumption function
saving function
investment spending
autonomous investment
private-sector equilibrium
equilibrium level of national income
investment multiplier
autonomous consumption multiplier

contractionary gap
expansionary gap
autonomous government
  expenditures
lump-sum tax
exports
imports
countercyclical fiscal policy

QUESTIONS FOR REVIEW AND DISCUSSION

1. How does Keynes's view of saving differ from the classical view of saving? How does Keynes's view of wage-price flexibility differ from the classical view?
2. Define marginal propensity to consume and average propensity to consume. What is the essential difference between the two?
3. If the *MPC* is 0.75 and national income increases by $200 billion, then by how much will consumption expenditures increase?
4. Can you think of any nonincome factors not listed in the text that might affect consumption decisions?
5. What is autonomous investment spending? Does it change as the level of income changes?
6. When does equilibrium occur in the income-expenditures model? What adjusts to obtain equilibrium?
7. Define the consumption function and explain its relationship to the 45-degree line.
8. Juan spends an additional $20 a week in response to a $30 per week raise. What is Juan's *MPC*? His *MPS*?
9. What effect does a $30 billion decrease in autonomous investment have on total expenditures when the *MPC* is 0.9?
10. What is the essential implication of the investment multiplier? What is multiplied when autonomous investment changes?

11. Suppose autonomous consumption expenditures are $50 billion, autonomous investment expenditures are $20 billion, and the *MPC* is 0.8. What is the equilibrium level of income? What happens to the equilibrium level of income if autonomous consumption falls to $20 billion?
12. What was Keynes's basic dispute with the classical economists? What were his recommendations for smoothing out the business cycle?
13. What fiscal policy would Keynes recommend for large-scale unemployment? What would he recommend for inflation?
14. What effect does a lump-sum tax of $20 billion have on total expenditures if the *MPC* is 0.9? Would it have a greater effect if the *MPC* were 0.8?
15. Describe a contractionary gap and an expansionary gap and show each graphically.
16. What happens to the level of national income if consumption increases by $20 billion, investment increases by $5 billion, government expenditures decrease by $10 billion, and net exports increase by $15 billion?

PROBLEMS

1. Consider a basic income-expenditures model (with no government sector and where $Y = C + I$) in which Y is real national income, C is real consumption expenditures, and I is real autonomous investment expenditures. Let $C = \$40$ billion $+ (MPC)Y$ and let $I = I_0$. If $I_0 = \$50$ billion and $MPC = 0.5$, compute the equilibrium levels of national income, Y; consumption, C; and saving, S.
2. Suppose that an increase in national income from $200 billion to $350 billion increases consumption expenditures from $180 billion to $255 billion, or by $75 billion. Given this data, calculate the marginal propensity to consume and the average propensity to consume before and after the change in national income.
3. Suppose that in private-sector equilibrium, consumption expenditures are $50 billion and that investment expenditures are $10 billion. What is the *APC*? The

   APS? If the *MPC* is 0.75 and consumption expenditures increase by $40 billion as a result of an increase in income, what happens to the level of savings?
4. Suppose that total expenditures are $250 billion short of the full-employment level of income and that $MPC = 0.7$. In the Keynesian framework, by how much would government expenditures have to increase to bring the economy to full employment?
5. Suppose that a wave of optimism spreads through the business community, causing autonomous investment to increase by $60 million. As a result, the equilibrium level of national income increases by $500 million. Find k, the *MPS*, and the *MPC*.
6. Assume that a consumption function is given as $C = 400 + 0.80Y$. Let all of the other variables be autonomous as follows: $I_0 = 80$, $G_0 = 120$, $X_0 = 75$, and $M_0 = 60$. Determine the equilibrium level of income.

AGGREGATE DEMAND AND AGGREGATE SUPPLY

A fter World War II, a moderate inflation rate in the United States held off a doubling of the price level for 25 years. Less than ten years later, however, the price level doubled again. The acceleration of the inflation rate slowed between 1981 and 1996, but many economists believe there is a prospect of higher inflation in the future. By international standards, the United States has an enviable record of avoiding inflation. Peru, Mexico, and Brazil have experienced annual inflation rates in excess of 100 percent in recent years. In each case, runaway inflation devastated the country's economy. Such experiences should teach us the importance of avoiding economic policies that lead to excessive inflation.

When we began our discussion of macroeconomics in Chapter 5, we included price stability in our list of primary macroeconomic goals. (The other two were full employment and economic growth.) Subsequent chapters developed a model that explained how the level of national income was determined. This model was used to explain unemployment and inadequate economic growth. However, in that model the price level remained unchanged; the model did not address the problems of inflation and deflation. This chapter develops a model of aggregate demand and aggregate supply in which the interaction of these two forces determines both the level of national income and the price level. We will show how shifts in either aggregate demand or in aggregate supply can cause inflation or deflation. After you complete Chapter 9 you should understand

- how price level changes cause changes in total real expenditures by consumers and businesses.

- how the aggregate demand curve relates national income and output to price level changes.

- how the aggregate supply curve is constructed and how its shape is determined by production and capacity levels.
- how shifts in aggregate demand and supply affect output and price levels.

PRICE CHANGES AND AGGREGATE DEMAND

We have defined the function $C + I + G + (X - M)$ as total expenditures. But an important distinction must be made between total expenditures and aggregate demand once the price level is explicitly recognized. The term *aggregate demand* refers to the relation between the price level of all output and the total quantity of all goods and services demanded. In other words, from here on, as we discuss contractionary and expansionary phases in the economy and proper macroeconomic policies to remedy such phases, we will be tying total real expenditures to a specific price level, a composite index of all prices in the economy. We will then vary the price level to see how such changes affect equilibrium output or income, since price level changes will affect total real expenditures.

Price Changes and Changes in Purchasing Power

Chapter 8 defined the difference between nominal, or money, income—the income we receive in dollar terms—and real income—the purchasing power of those dollars. In times of inflation, nominal incomes may increase, yet real incomes may remain the same or even fall. For example, if you receive a 5 percent raise in a year in which the annual rate of inflation is 6 percent, you have actually lost ground in terms of the goods and services your salary can purchase. Since inflation erodes the purchasing power of each dollar received, real income, or income adjusted for changes in the price level, is a more accurate measure of how the economy is performing.

Inflation affects more than income, unfortunately. It also affects wealth. The term *income* is usually taken to mean the sum of weekly, monthly, or annual earnings. **Wealth,** on the other hand, is the sum of all assets. Income is a flow variable; wealth is a stock variable. Flow variables are measured per unit of time. Speed, for example, is a flow variable—it is measured in feet per second or miles per hour. By contrast, weight is an example of a stock variable; it is defined independently of time. It is meaningful to say that someone weighs 120 pounds without making any reference to time.

Wealth may be pecuniary (dollar-denominated, such as a savings account) or nonpecuniary (non-dollar-denominated, such as a house, auto, or Persian rug). The distinction between pecuniary and nonpecuniary wealth is important because the value of each type of wealth is affected differently by changes in the price level. Compare a $10,000 Persian rug with a $10,000 deposit in a savings account. When the price level doubles under 100 percent inflation, what happens to the real value of these two kinds of wealth? Dollar-denominated assets such as the $10,000 deposit in a savings account or a bond with a face value of $10,000 have a fixed dollar value. With a 100 percent increase in the price level, the value of a

Wealth
The total value of monetary plus nonmonetary assets in existence at a point in time; a stock variable.

dollar-denominated asset has been cut in half, in terms of purchasing power. However, the higher price level implies that the nominal value of all non-dollar-denominated assets, including the Persian rug, has increased, assuming that prices of collectibles keep pace with the general price level. But the rug is still a rug: In real terms it is worth as much as it was before. It would now fetch $20,000 in the marketplace instead of $10,000, but the higher dollar amount would merely purchase the same amount of goods and services as $10,000 would have previously. In other words, the real value of many nonpecuniary assets (real estate, paintings, jewels) is unaffected by changes in the price level.

Now contemplate the unfortunate effects of the same degree of inflation on the $10,000 savings deposit. Except in the unlikely case that the interest rate has kept pace with the 100 percent rate of inflation, the real value of the deposit will have declined. Assuming no interest rate return, the same $10,000 that would have purchased $10,000 worth of goods and services before inflation will purchase only $5,000 worth of goods and services now. In other words, price level changes bring about changes in the real value, or purchasing power, of pecuniary assets.

The Real Balance Effect

As inflation erodes the purchasing power of the money in our bank accounts and of our holdings of other dollar-denominated assets, we have to economize—buy fewer books, try to keep the old car running instead of buying an expensive new one. This change in consumption behavior that results from a change in the price level is sometimes called the **real balance effect**.

Real balance effect
The effect on investment and consumption spending of a change in the price level that alters the real value of pecuniary assets.

If we let MS stand for society's entire stock of pecuniary, or dollar-denominated, assets and P for the aggregate price level, then the value of real balances can be expressed as MS/P. The level of real household consumption expenditures will be determined by the value of real balances as well as by the level of disposable income.

The relation between consumption and real money balances is positive, just as the relation between consumption and income is positive. If prices fall, assuming that MS remains the same, the value of real balances rises and consumers experience an enhanced wealth effect; that is, their money assets will purchase more goods and services than before. Thus, consumption will rise in response to greater real wealth. Graphically, the consumption function will shift upward, establishing a higher equilibrium level of output and employment. Conversely, if prices rise, the value of real balances declines, the consumption curve subsequently falls, and lower output and employment result. Changes in real balances are capable of inducing the same kinds of changes in total expenditures as fiscal policy manipulations (ΔG and ΔT).

We have already encountered this important concept. Recall that classical economists before Keynes generally believed the wage-price flexibility would automatically bring about total expenditure changes that would correct the cyclical swings of the macroeconomy. The logic behind this self-correcting view was as follows: If the economy slides into a recession and unemployment occurs,

FIGURE 9.1

How Price Level Changes Alter Consumption Spending and Real Income

Any change in the price level, from the initial level P_0, will create a real balance effect on consumption, shifting the total spending curve upward or downward. A lower price level, P_1, is associated with a higher level of equilibrium real income, Y_1, and the total spending curve shifts upward to $C_1 + I + G + (X - M)$. A price level P_2 higher than the initial price level would, for similar reasons, be associated with a lower level of equilibrium income, Y_2, and a spending curve that shifts downward to $C_2 + I + G + (X - M)$.

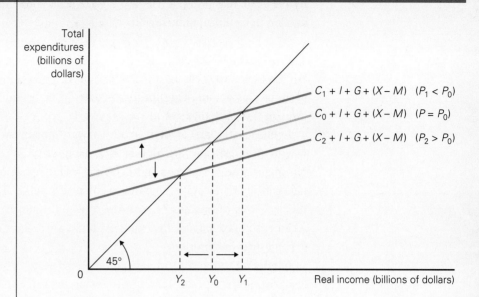

labor markets will be faced with an excess supply of workers. In competitive labor markets, this excess of workers will create downward pressure on wages. As wages fall, so will the unit costs of production; prices will therefore decline as well. The general decline in prices will sooner or later raise the real value of money balances, thus inducing consumers to spend more. The increased spending will thereby stimulate output and employment, lifting the economy out of the recession. In a similar fashion, the presence of inflation will eventually lead to a reduction in real balances and a consequent decline in total spending, thereby eliminating the inflationary tendencies. For the classical economists, the real balance effect on consumption helped explain the self-adjusting nature of the economy.

This important process can be fixed more precisely in graphical terms. In Figure 9.1, three total spending functions are shown for three alternative price levels. Given some price level P_0 and some constant level of pecuniary assets in the economy, real balances will produce some level of consumption, C_0. Consumption function C_0 and given levels of investment, government, and net foreign expenditures, I, G, $(X - M)$, produce an equilibrium level of real income Y_0.

What happens in the event of a price decline? A price reduction will increase the real value of pecuniary balances, causing an increase in the consumption component of total spending. In Figure 9.1, the original total spending function shifts upward to $C_1 + I + G + (X - M)$ at the new, lower price level. This new, higher total expenditures function is associated with a higher level of equilibrium income, Y_1. By the same reasoning, a rise in the price level above the initial level brings a reduction in equilibrium income to Y_2.

The Interest Rate Effect

We have seen that changes in the price level affect the purchasing power of our pecuniary assets and equilibrium income. Price level changes also affect income through the mechanism of interest rates.

Interest rates are always in the news. Consumers are highly interested in whether interest rates are high or low, rising or falling. Interest rates to some extent determine the purchasing decisions made by consumers—whether to buy a new car or to mortgage the purchase of a new home. Interest rates also influence the decisions of businesses. Businesses watch interest rate levels when deciding whether to make capital investments—build a warehouse, acquire new machinery, expand their inventories.

In general, interest rates depend on changes in the price level. When the price level rises, interest rates tend to rise; when the price level falls, interest rates tend to fall. As with all other goods, individuals will want to hold equilibrium quantities of real money—balances for transactions, for investments, or simply as a precautionary ("rainy day") measure. In other words, people are interested in the real value, or purchasing power, of their money balances, not in their nominal holdings of money. The value of dollar-denominated assets is inversely related to the price level, since these assets are fixed in money terms. The real supply of money is also altered by price level changes. The purchasing power of each dollar we hold rises when the price level falls and declines when the price level rises. In part, interest rates are the product of the demand for real money balances and their supply in real terms. Thus, as the real supply of these balances increases with reductions in the price level, the interest rate tends to fall. And, as the real supply of money balances declines with increases in the price level, the interest rate tends to rise. It is important to recognize that these interest rate changes affect the investment and consumption components of expenditures.

Figure 9.2 shows the effect of changes in the price level on interest rates. Investors react to these changes because the interest rate change alters the cost and profitability of investment projects; consumers react by changing expenditure plans, especially for durable goods (such as refrigerators or homes). These changes in expenditures in turn cause changes in income and employment. As prices rise (and the value of real money falls), output and real income decline; as prices fall, output and real income increase.

The **interest rate effect** can be viewed in the income-expenditures model depicted in Figure 9.3. With the price at some initial level, P_0, total expenditures equal $C + I_0 + G + (X - M)$. A decrease in the aggregate price level to P_1 will lower interest rates. Other things being equal, lower interest rates will lower the cost of all new investment projects. The consequent effect in the total expenditures model is to raise the investment function, thus stimulating the economy to a higher level of output and employment, Y_1.

Interest rate effect
The effect on investment spending that results from a change in the interest rate produced by a change in the price level.

FIGURE 9.2

The Interest Rate Effect

An increase in the price level may be related to a decrease in real income and employment via the process of investment and consumption spending. Conversely, a decrease in the price level can lead to an increase in income. The lower half of the diagram shows that declines in the price level tend to lower the interest rate and expand investment and consumption expenditures. Increased production and jobs result.

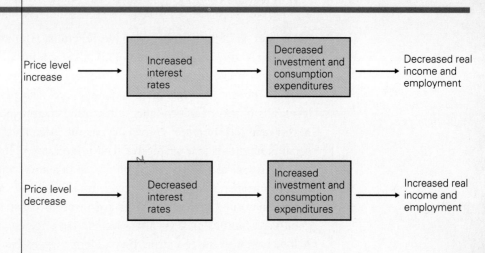

Conversely, higher aggregate price levels tend to drive up interest rates. Now all new investment projects will be more costly than before, so a decline in the investment schedule can be predicted. In Figure 9.3, the total expenditure schedule will shift downward to $C + I_2 + G + (X - M)$ and establish a lower level of income at Y_2.

To summarize, changes in the aggregate price level are likely to affect aggregate consumption (the real balance effect and the interest rate effect) and aggregate investment (the interest rate effect). The macroeconomy, viewed realistically, is a complex structure of relations in which the level of total expenditures is determined by the aggregate levels of income, wealth, and prices.

FIGURE 9.3

The Price Level and Investment Spending

Decreases in the price level from P_0 to P_1 lower interest rates and increase investment from I_0 to I_1. The higher level of investment increases real income from Y_0 to Y_1. Increases in the price level to P_2 increase interest rates and decrease investment to I_2 and income to Y_2.

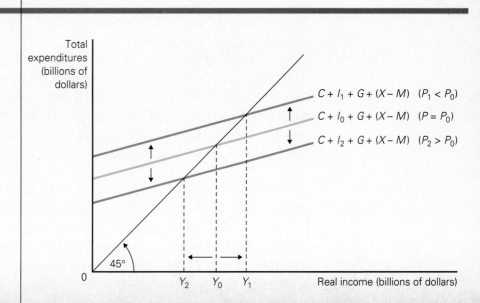

AGGREGATE DEMAND

Aggregate demand curve
Graphical relation showing the different levels of national income that exist at different price levels.

In Chapter 4, we saw that all demand functions relating prices and quantity demanded are downward-sloping. This also applies to the **aggregate demand curve**, which captures the relation between the aggregate price level and real national income. The aggregate demand curve basically tells us that as the price level falls in the macroeconomy, other things being equal, households and businesses tend to buy more. Conversely, as the price level rises, other things being equal, households and businesses tend to decrease their spending. Again, a contrast between microeconomic supply and demand relations and the macroeconomic concepts is instructive. Recall from Chapter 4 that the demand curve for a particular good or service slopes downward because a price decrease for some good—say, football tickets—alters its *relative* price compared to all other goods. A lower relative price causes the student to substitute football tickets for all other goods in her budget; this substitution explains the negative slope of the demand curve. The negative slope of aggregate demand in macroeconomic theory does not depend on changes in relative prices but on changes in the price level—a relation that can be shown with the Keynesian income-expenditures model.

Deriving the Aggregate Demand Curve

Examine Figure 9.4, in which the macroeconomy is assumed to be in equilibrium at Y_0. The $C_0 + I_0 + G + (X - M)$ curve in Figure 9.4a is constructed for a given price level, P_0 in Figure 9.4b. Starting from this point, we can hypothetically vary the price level up and down in Figure 9.4b and observe the corresponding income level produced. Matching pairs of P and Y will trace out the aggregate demand curve. For example, assume the price level falls from P_0 to P_1. The effect of this price decline will be to raise household consumption (the real balance effect) and to raise business investment (the interest rate effect). Thus, total expenditures will shift upward, establishing a higher income level at Y_1. A lower price level, P_1, therefore, matches a higher level of real income, Y_1. This matched pair of variables is plotted in Figure 9.4b as point F.

We can continue the conceptual experiment by raising the price level from P_0 to P_2. Inflation causes the consumption function to shift downward (the interest rate effect), moving the equilibrium income to Y_2. The combination (P_2, Y_2) is shown in Figure 9.4b as point B. The aggregate demand curve (*AD*) is the locus of all points generated in the manner of points B, A, and F. The curve is downward-sloping, as stated at the beginning of this section.

The Shape of the Aggregate Demand Curve

Both the real balance effect and the interest rate effect cause the level of aggregate demand to increase as the price level falls and to decrease as the price level rises. The shape of the aggregate demand curve depends on the magnitude of the two effects. If in Figure 9.4 a price level reduction from P_0 to P_1 causes a large increase in consumer wealth (perhaps because consumers have large holdings of dollar-denominated stocks), the total spending function will shift upward by a large

FIGURE 9.4

Derivation of Aggregate Demand from Total Expenditures

A decrease in the price level from P_0 to P_1 creates an increase in consumption and investment spending. (a) A decrease from P_0 to P_1 increases real income from Y_0 to Y_1. Increases in the price level decrease C and I, so real income falls from Y_0 to Y_2. (b) The price and income combinations trace out the aggregate demand curve: Greater quantities of goods and services are demanded at lower prices.

amount. This in turn will result in a level of aggregate demand much greater at a price level P_1 than at P_0. Accordingly, income level Y_1 will lie far to the right of Y_0, causing the aggregate demand curve to be flat. On the other hand, if consumers have few dollar-denominated assets, a fall in the price level will have little effect on total spending and the aggregate demand curve will be steep. In a similar fashion, the stronger the interest rate effect, the flatter the aggregate demand curve.

The shape of the aggregate demand curve is important. With flat aggregate demand curves, shifts in aggregate supply will primarily affect the level of output, having little impact on the equilibrium price level. With steep aggregate demand curves, a shift in aggregate supply will have a large impact on price level but little impact on the level of production.

TABLE 9.1

Shifts in the Aggregate Demand Function

A change in any of the listed variables will shift the aggregate demand function rightward or leftward, depending on whether the variable increases (↑) or decreases (↓).

Rightward Shift	Leftward Shift
Autonomous consumption ↑	Autonomous consumption ↓
Autonomous investment ↑	Autonomous investment ↓
Government expenditures ↑	Government expenditures ↓
Net exports ($X - M$) ↑	Net exports ($X - M$) ↓
The money supply ↑	The money supply ↓
Saving ↑	Saving ↓
Taxes ↑	Taxes ↓

Shifts in the Aggregate Demand Curve

In tracing out the relation between the aggregate price level and the aggregate level of income, certain variables other than price are assumed constant. These constants are numerous. They involve all of those things that shift the demand function either rightward or leftward. The following list of factors that are capable of shifting aggregate demand is representative but not exhaustive.

household consumption (C): autonomous component

business investment (I): autonomous component

government expenditures (G)

saving (S): autonomous component

net exports ($X - M$)

the money stock (MS)

taxes (T)

A change in any of these factors will result in a different level of national income at the same level of prices. Graphically, a change in any of these factors will create a rightward or leftward shift in the aggregate demand function. Table 9.1 summarizes the effects on aggregate demand for each change listed, and Figure 9.5 shows the shifts graphically.

To test our understanding of the principles involved, assume some change in total expenditures, such as an increase in the net export balance. Spending increases at every price level, creating higher real income for every possible price level. In Figure 9.5, the aggregate demand curve shifts to the right from AD_0 to AD_1, illustrating that the real income at each price level increases. The same effect would occur with an increase in consumption (a reduction in saving), investment expenditures, or government expenditures.

Leftward shifts in the aggregate demand curve are likewise caused by both private-sector and government-controlled factors. Reductions in consumption (in-

FIGURE 9.5

Shifts in Aggregate Demand

Any change in a nonprice factor affecting total expenditures will shift the aggregate demand curve rightward or leftward. An increase in savings, for example, will reduce total expenditures and aggregate demand at each price level, causing a leftward shift from AD_0 to AD_2. A decrease in taxes or an increase in government expenditures will shift the curve rightward from AD_0 to AD_1, reflecting greater spending on goods and services at every price level.

creases in saving), investment, or net exports would cause a leftward shift in the aggregate demand curve, from AD_0 to AD_2 in Figure 9.5, for example. An increase in taxes or a reduction in government spending would also shift the function leftward. These shifts occur due to a reduction in spending at every possible price level, meaning that the level of real income associated with any given price level falls.

As we have seen, many economic variables are capable of altering aggregate demand in the macroeconomy, thereby also altering the equilibrium levels of output, income, and employment. Some of these variables—such as household consumption and business investment—are determined by millions of decentralized, individual decisions. Others are determined by highly centralized government directives—decisions such as the appropriate level of government expenditures and taxes and the money supply. Among the latter decisions are various policy actions to combat the ups and downs of the business cycle.

The point of discretionary budget policies—manipulating taxes or government spending—is to stimulate the economy during periods of economic contraction and unemployment and to cool down the economy during periods of rapid expansion and inflation. Such efforts by the government to steer the economy are known as **discretionary fiscal policies.**

Discretionary fiscal policies
Government policy actions that attempt to influence aggregate demand.

Before we can discuss the possible effects of fiscal policy on aggregate demand, however, we must look at aggregate supply, the other major force determining the quantity of goods and services produced in the economy. We cannot determine the actual quantity of output produced through demand factors alone; we must also know what all businesses in the economy are willing to produce at alternative price levels.

AGGREGATE SUPPLY

Aggregate supply curve
A graph showing the different levels of aggregate output produced at different price levels.

Although higher price levels reduce the level of aggregate demand, they tend to have the opposite effect on aggregate supply. When producers receive higher prices for output, their profits rise, giving them an incentive to increase production. Furthermore, when producers attempt to increase production levels, they use existing resources more intensively, which drives up production costs. Producers are forced to charge higher prices to recover increased costs. The **aggregate supply curve** traces the relation between the price level and the aggregate level of production.

The Shape of the Aggregate Supply Curve

As noted in Chapter 7, the shape of the aggregate supply curve depends on the state of the economy. When the economy is operating far below capacity with large quantities of unemployed resources, production can be increased without having much effect on input prices. Not only is it possible to employ workers of nearly all types, but productive inputs such as land and machinery are also readily available. This means that firms can hire more inputs without having to compete for them and that output can be expanded without much of an increase in average production costs. Therefore, small increases in the price level will lead to large increases in the level of production. This portion of the aggregate supply curve is called the Keynesian range, reflecting Keynes's concentration on large-scale unemployment in an economy.

When the economy is producing fairly close to capacity, the aggregate supply curve will be much steeper. In this range, attempts to increase production lead to shortages of certain inputs. Average production costs will rise, as firms are forced to pay more for scarce inputs. While it is possible to expand production, additional output can only be obtained at substantially higher price levels.

In the classical range—named for the classical economists, who described a full-employment economy—resources are fully employed and the economy is producing at some point on the production possibilities frontier. Since all available resources are employed, an individual producer can expand production only by bidding resources away from competing producers. The effect is to drive the price level up without increasing overall production. In this range, the aggregate supply curve becomes vertical.

Shifts and "Shocks" in the Aggregate Supply Curve

In drawing an aggregate supply curve, certain variables other than price level are held constant. Should any of these variables change, the entire aggregate supply curve will shift. A complete list of variables that *might* cause aggregate supply to shift would be lengthy, but a relatively small number of variables have the greatest impact on aggregate supply—in particular, productive resource supply, technology, tax rates, and freedom to respond to economic incentives. Table 9.2 shows the effects of changes in these four factors.

TABLE 9.2

Shifts in the Aggregate Supply Function

Any change in any of the factors listed in the table will cause aggregate supply to shift. These supply shifts are called shocks if they occur quickly and without warning.

Rightward Shift	Leftward Shift
Technological advance	Destruction of capital
Increase in human resources	Decrease in human resources
Increase in natural resources	Decrease in natural resources
Decrease in taxes	Increase in taxes

Resource supply often affects aggregate supply in obvious ways. For example, the discovery of new energy resources will cause energy prices to fall and productive capacity to rise; at all price levels, firms will have an economic incentive to increase output. Increases in resource availability, then, shift the aggregate supply curve to the right; decreases cause a leftward shift. (Sudden changes in resource or capital supply are sometimes called supply "shocks.") Now consider a less obvious example—the recent criticism of the educational system in the United States and the many proposals for educational reform. Proponents of reform argue that improved education is necessary for the country to remain competitive in world markets. In terms of aggregate demand and supply, this proposal is an economic policy to increase the stock of human capital and, therefore, aggregate supply. (For an analysis of the effects of a decrease in the supply of both human and nonhuman resources, see the Focus "Black Death and Black Gold: Aggregate Supply Shifts Throughout History.")

An improvement in technology affects aggregate supply in a way similar to an increase in resource availability. It also reduces production costs and increases the economy's capacity, shifting the aggregate supply curve to the right.

To understand how a change in tax rates affects the aggregate supply curve, it is necessary to keep in mind that in a free society aggregate supply is determined by the willingness of producers to produce, not just by the ability to produce. With high marginal tax rates, producers must pay a substantial portion of their incomes in the form of taxes, and this reduces the incentive to produce. Workers in high tax brackets may choose to work shorter hours or to retire earlier. Reductions in tax rates remove disincentives to work and shift the aggregate supply rightward. Similarly, many economists believe that certain governmental regulations form a barrier between individuals and the business activities in which they have economic incentives to engage. Removal of regulations would increase the incentive to produce and cause aggregate supply to shift to the right. Much of the deregulation policy initiated during the Carter and Reagan administrations attempted to increase aggregate supply by reducing government red tape and, in Reagan's case, taxes. Since the Reagan administration, however, deregulation has taken a backseat to other concerns, such as deficit reduction and health care reform.

f Ocus

Black Death and Black Gold: Aggregate Supply Shifts Throughout History

A change in the supply of a resource or the level of technology will cause the production possibilities of an economy to expand and the economy's aggregate supply curve to shift. Supplies of resources, both human and nonhuman, can change dramatically in a number of ways. Here we consider two supply shocks—the first resulting from a natural disaster and the second resulting from the deliberate actions of humans.

One of the greatest natural disasters ever visited upon the Western world was the bubonic plague—the so-called Black Death. Between 1347 and 1350, rats infested with plague-ridden fleas spread death throughout Europe; between 33 percent and 65 percent of the population perished. Since labor had been cheap and plentiful relative to other resources before the plague, agricultural methods had been oriented to the large untrained labor supply. The scarceness of labor

following the plague (even with fewer mouths to feed) meant that society had to devote a large portion of its resources to food and other consumption goods in order to survive. This situation is represented in Figure 9.6 by the sudden leftward shift in the aggregate supply curve (from AS_0 to AS_1).

For our second example we consider a more recent case. In the late 1970s, the Organization of Petroleum Exporting Countries tried to hold Western economies hostage by reducing oil supplies (and increasing prices). Labor and other productive factors suddenly had less energy to work with, which led to a reduction in the productive effects of labor and other resources. The final result: a reduced demand for labor. OPEC thus caused a shift in aggregate supply, shown as a shift from AS_0 to AS_1 in Figure 9.6.

Fortunately, both of these stories have relatively happy endings. Relatively expensive labor, brought about by the general population reduction in the fourteenth century, meant that businesses economized or rationed labor by trying to substitute capital and other resources for labor. In the process, many labor-saving devices—including some that made use of water power—were invented. Later, steam power sup-

FIGURE 9.6

Reductions in Human and Nonhuman Resources Shift the Aggregate Supply Curve Leftward

Reductions in population due to the Black Death and in oil and energy due to the OPEC cartel both caused a sudden leftward shift in the aggregate supply curve. As the economy "recovers," the aggregate supply curve shifts again to the right.

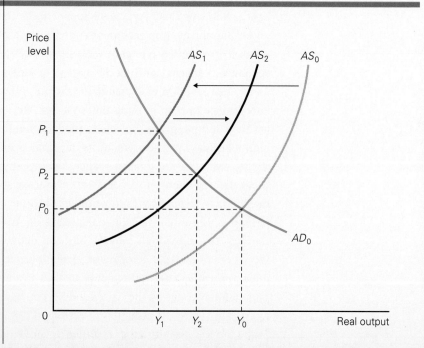

plemented or replaced water power. The Black Death may have ultimately sparked progress in European technology. The aggregate supply curve certainly shifted rightward over time (as from AS_1 to AS_2 in Figure 9.6).

Similarly, the 1980s witnessed a reversal of the OPEC supply shocks of the 1970s. Due in part to price cutting by OPEC members and an inability to maintain and police output restrictions, the cartel lost much of its power. As a result, U.S. producers and consumers had access to more oil at lower prices, a situation represented by the rightward shift in aggregate supply from AS_1 to AS_2 in Figure 9.6. To the extent that the formation of OPEC contributed to the inflationary and recessionary trends of the 1970s, its partial dissolution fostered lower inflation rates and higher output levels in the 1980s.

The critical point is this: An economy will tend to respond to supply shocks by developing alternative methods and resources. New resource development, such as solar energy, and alternative production techniques reduced the impact of the initial OPEC-induced supply shifts. Improvements in agricultural technology and methods following the Black Death paved the way for the advances that characterized the Industrial Revolution.

THE EQUILIBRIUM LEVEL OF PRICES AND PRODUCTION

Because both the aggregate demand curve and the aggregate supply curve are plotted with real output on the horizontal axis and the price level on the vertical axis, both curves can be plotted on the same graph. In Figure 9.7, we see that AD_0 and AS_0 intersect at price level P_0 and output level Y_0. At any price level above P_0, the quantity of goods producers are willing to supply will exceed the quantity demanded by households, business firms, and so on. The excess demand for goods will cause prices to fall and drive the price level down to the equilibrium level, P_0. Aggregate demand and aggregate supply jointly determine the level of prices and output. Furthermore, any change in the equilibrium price level or output level can be viewed as being caused by a shift in either aggregate demand or supply. If, in Figure 9.7, the aggregate demand curve were to shift to AD_1 because of a change in one of the variables affecting aggregate demand, both the price level and the level of production would increase—to P_1 and Y_1, respectively. Had the aggregate supply curve been in the Keynesian range, output would have risen with little effect on the price level. The same increase in aggregate demand would have led to inflation but no increase in real output if aggregate supply had been in the classical range. As depicted in Figure 9.7, an increase in aggregate supply would lead to an increase in equilibrium output and a decrease in the equilibrium price level. Decreases in aggregate supply have the opposite effects. Economists even note the possibility of "stagflation"—a combination of public and private effects on demand that could produce both unemployment and inflation at the same time. (See the Application "Uses of Demand and Supply Analysis: The Problem of Stagflation" at the end of this chapter.)

FIGURE 9.7

Equilibrium Price and Output Levels

With aggregate supply AS_0 and aggregate demand AD_0, the equilibrium price level will be P_0 and the equilibrium level of output will be Y_0. A change in any of the variables affecting aggregate demand that leads to increased aggregate demand shifts the curve rightward—in this case, to AD_1. This increase in aggregate demand increases the equilibrium price level to P_1 and raises the equilibrium level of real output to Y_1.

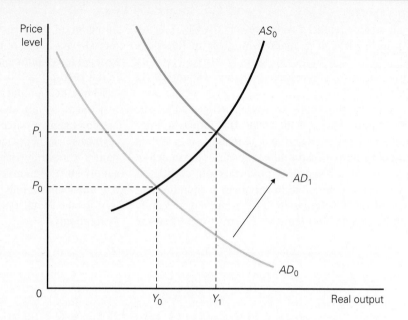

This chapter has focused on the construction of the aggregate demand and supply curves. In particular, we have emphasized the factors that determine aggregate demand and supply and, consequently, national income and the price level. It is only through an understanding of these factors that the problems of unemployment and inadequate economic growth can be addressed. Specific government policies—those designed to shift either the aggregate demand curve or the aggregate supply curve—are the subject of Chapter 10.

APPLICATION
Uses of Demand and Supply Analysis: The Problem of Stagflation

Aggregate demand and supply theory has an obvious advantage over the Keynesian total expenditures approach in explaining price inflation. Aggregate demand and supply theory helps predict what effects fiscal policy will have on prices. Assuming that the aggregate supply curve is in the intermediate or "upward sloping" range, aggregate demand changes will either increase prices along with increasing output and employment or they will decrease prices with accompanying decreases in jobs and production. In other words, there may be a built-in trade-off between inflation and employment. But consider another possibility—stagflation, inflation accompanied by unemployment or stagnation. This condition appears to have existed in the United States between 1969 and 1970, 1971 and 1972, 1973 and 1974, 1975 and 1976, and, most dramatically in terms of the inflation part, between 1979 and 1981. Could stagflation happen again?

Stagflation can be analyzed in terms of demand and supply curves such as those developed in this chapter. In Figure 9.8, point A represents a recessionary level of output and employment in the economy. In response to high unemployment, government increases spending or

FIGURE 9.8

Aggregate Demand Shifts and Stagflation

The phenomenon of stagflation is produced by an increase in aggregate demand from AD_0 to AD_1 caused by some fiscal action (government spending increase or a tax reduction) and a reduction in some component of private spending (autonomous investment, consumption, or exports). Prices, however, are sticky and fail to fall with the demand reduction (from AD_1 to AD_2), creating stagflation—inflation and unemployment at the same time.

decreases taxes in an effort to shift the aggregate demand curve rightward from AD_0 to AD_1. Prices rise, creating inflation, but output and employment also increase. Now assume that some other component of private expenditures—consumption, investment, or exports—decreases, causing a shift leftward in the aggregate demand curve from AD_1 to AD_2.

The result is that prices fall along with output to point F. But what if union or monopoly pressures mean that prices are too "sticky" to fall at all in response to the decreased demand? In this case, prices remain at high levels, and the full impact of the demand decrease falls on employment and output. Production falls as the economy stagnates, but inflationary pressures do not diminish. In terms of Figure 9.8, the economy would move to point C rather than to point F. Thus inflation and joblessness might go hand in hand.

While there are other interpretations of stagflation, the problem illustrates the usefulness of a macroeconomic theory—aggregate demand and supply analysis—that includes prices. In the post-Keynesian period, attention has focused on price inflation as well as on employment in considering aggregate demand management as a means for fine-tuning the economy. The fact that stagflation poses a possible trade-off between inflation and unemployment illustrates some of the problems associated with the use of fiscal policy to control demand and to stabilize the economy.

QUESTION

Does the apparent trade-off between inflation and employment observed in the United States in recent decades mean that fiscal policy is inadequate in controlling and stabilizing economic activity?

SUMMARY

1. The simple income-expenditures model is limited because it ignores monetary variables and price changes. These factors have become increasingly important since the late 1960s because of inflation.

2. Price level changes affect household consumption by changing the real value of money balances held by consumers. This real balance effect means that price increases will decrease consumption spending and that price decreases will increase consumption spending. These spending changes affect the level of real income and employment, meaning that price changes may be related to the aggregate demand for output.

3. Price changes also alter business investment expenditures via the mechanism of interest rates. Investment spending will increase with declines in interest rates and

decrease with increases in interest rates. The interest rate effect means that real income and employment are negatively related to prices through investment spending.

4. The aggregate demand function relates national income and output to changes in the price level; it is a downward-sloping function, like the demand curves discussed in Chapter 4.

5. Changes in both private and public nonprice variables (autonomous consumption, imports, government spending, taxation) cause the aggregate demand curve to shift rightward or leftward.

6. The aggregate supply curve relates the production of goods and services to the price level. It is a positively sloped function because higher prices increase the incentive to produce goods.

7. The shape of the aggregate supply curve depends on the level of production. At production levels that are low relative to capacity, the aggregate supply curve will be flat; its slope will increase until it becomes vertical as the production level reaches capacity.

8. The interaction of aggregate demand and aggregate supply determines the equilibrium level of output and the equilibrium price level, much like demand and supply for a particular good determine its equilibrium price and quantity.

KEY TERMS

wealth

real balance effect

interest rate effect

aggregate demand curve

discretionary fiscal policies

aggregate supply curve

QUESTIONS FOR REVIEW AND DISCUSSION

1. What macroeconomic goal does the simple Keynesian model of aggregate demand ignore? Why was this goal disregarded in the years immediately following World War II?

2. What effect does an increase in the price level have on the interest rate and, therefore, on the level of investment? Is this change in investment an example of the real balance effect?

3. Suppose that relatively small changes in the interest rate lead to large changes in business investment. Does this have any effect on the shape of the aggregate demand curve?

4. Moving from one point to another along the aggregate demand curve, what happens to exports? To government spending?

5. Can you think of two specific changes that would lead to a rightward shift of the aggregate demand curve? Two that would lead to a decrease?

6. As price level rises, what is likely to happen to business profits? To production levels?

7. Is it possible to solve major macroeconomic problems by inducing the aggregate supply curve to shift to the left?

8. If the government wanted to reduce the price level, would a reduction in aggregate demand be necessary?

9. What variable is likely to affect both aggregate demand and aggregate supply?

10. Under what circumstances is an increase in aggregate demand most likely to cause inflation? Least likely?

11. What is the real balance effect? Assuming the stock of money (MS) to be constant, what happens to the value of real balances if the price level in the economy increases? How does this affect people's wealth?

12. If the level of imports into the United States rises while the level of U.S. exports remains the same, what is the impact on aggregate demand?

13. What impact, if any, do you think time has on the shape of the aggregate supply curve?

14. If the economy is operating on the production possibilities frontier, what impact will an increase in the money supply have on economic output?

PROBLEM

Use the data in the following table for parts a and b.

AD₁		AD₂		AD₃		AS	
P	*Q*	*P*	*Q*	*P*	*Q*	*P*	*Q*
60	45	60	120	60	190	90	0
70	40	70	110	70	180	90	10
80	35	80	100	80	170	90	20
90	30	90	90	90	160	90	30
100	25	100	80	100	150	100	40
110	20	110	70	110	140	110	50
120	15	120	60	120	130	120	60
130	12	130	50	130	120	130	70
140	10	140	40	140	110	140	80
150	8	150	30	150	100	150	90
160	6	160	20	160	90	160	90
170	4	170	15	170	80	170	90
180	2	180	10	180	70	180	90
190	1	190	5	190	60	190	90

a. Graph aggregate demand curves AD_1, AD_2, and AD_3 and aggregate supply curve AS. Indicate the equilibrium price level and output for each aggregate demand curve.

b. Describe the prices and outputs that identify the Keynesian, intermediate, and classical ranges of the aggregate supply curve in part a.

CHAPTER 10

FISCAL POLICY AND THE SUPPLY SIDE: USING THE TOOLS

Contemporary macroeconomic theory and policy contain a large measure of both the classical and the Keynesian world views. The major Keynesian prescription uses policies designed to manipulate aggregate demand to correct imbalances of employment and income growth in the economy. But in the debate over policy today, more and more attention is being paid to the concerns first expressed by Adam Smith and other classical economists. Labor productivity and capital accumulation were major concerns of the classical writers—the supply side of the economy. Supply-side economics, popular early in the Reagan administration, is based on the idea that overreliance on aggregate demand management, in the form of taxation and spending policies, has had ill effects on the growth of aggregate supply and has fostered economic instability. This chapter considers the relation between aggregate demand and aggregate supply from both of these policy perspectives. When you complete Chapter 10 you will have insight into

- the role of government spending and taxing policies (fiscal policy) in Keynesian and new classical views of macroeconomics.

- using discretionary tools to affect the business cycle.

- how changes in fundamental factors affect the supply side of the economy and aggregate output and income.

- the interaction between policies designed to affect aggregate demand and the institutions and mechanisms that underlie aggregate supply.

POLICIES DESIGNED TO SHIFT AGGREGATE DEMAND

In large part, macroeconomic policy is an attempt to correct perceived failures in the private laissez-faire economy. When markets do not adjust automatically or adjust too slowly to correct imbalances in employment or economic growth, macroeconomic policies such as changes in taxes, government spending, or supply-side stimulation may be used as correctives. To assess the effects of macroeconomic policies, however, it is necessary to understand both the classical and Keynesian views of how the economy functions to correct imbalances.

Classical and Keynesian Perspectives

The classical economists had a long-run perspective on adjustments in the economy. Prices and wages were assumed to be flexible when there was an excess demand for or excess supply of labor in the labor market. These adjustments were not given an equivalent "clock time"; rather, classical theory assumed instantaneous adjustments. The result was a vertical supply curve.

This classical supply curve can be matched with an aggregate demand curve, as in Figure 10.1. The simplicity of the classical argument is revealed when aggregate demand is either increased or decreased from an initial equilibrium. Suppose, as in Figure 10.1, that the economy experiences a reduction in aggregate demand due to a fall-off in some component of private spending—the autonomous component of consumption, investment, or expenditures on exports. This reduction of aggregate demand is shown as a shift in the demand function from AD_0 to AD_1.

Equilibrium was established initially at E_0, where the economy was producing full-employment output (experiencing the natural rate of unemployment) at price level P_0. With the decrease in aggregate demand, we can think of the economy as

FIGURE 10.1

The Classical Long-Run Self-Adjustment Mechanism

In the classical view, when aggregate demand decreases, as from AD_0 to AD_1, the level of output temporarily falls from Y_F to Y_0, causing the level of employment to fall as well. The price level then falls from P_0 to P_1, and output rises back to Y_F. With flexible wages and prices, the economy returns to full employment.

FIGURE 10.2

Demand Deficiency Unemployment: Short-Run Keynesian and New Classical Views

If aggregate demand falls from AD_0 to AD_1, unemployment will result. If prices and wages do not adjust at all, the short-run Keynesian view, a movement from point E_0 to point A takes place. The economy will produce a level of output equal to Y_1. The difference in employment levels at Y_F and Y_1 is the measure of demand deficiency unemployment. In the classical view, prices will adjust quickly to point B. Demand deficiency unemployment will be less—the difference between unemployment levels Y_F and Y_0.

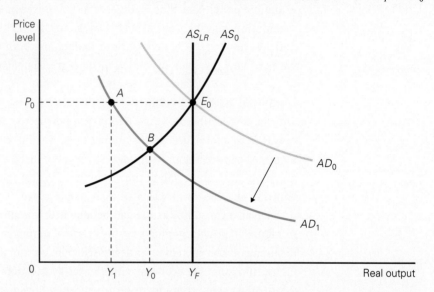

moving to point A, where supply ceases to create its own demand. Demand is insufficient to purchase Y_F worth of output at price level P_0. Contraction of production and employment temporarily sets in, since prices (and money wages) will not totally and immediately adjust downward. Once prices start to fall from P_0 to P_1, additional spending will increase output back to the full-employment level. As noted in Chapter 9, falling prices will increase consumption spending and investment spending through increases in real balances and decreases in the rate of interest.

When spending declines, unemployment is initially created. But in the classical version of events, wages also decline, so that all laborers seeking work find work, but at a lower nominal wage. In terms of Figure 10.1, prices and wages fall, so the economy rapidly ends up at a new full-employment equilibrium, E_1 at Y_F, but at a lower price level, P_1. In fact, the key to understanding the basically noninterventionist policies of the classical writers in macroeconomic affairs is the point that price, wage, and interest rate adjustments take place very rapidly.

Economists who adhere to modern versions of classical principles are called new classical economists. Keynesians and the new classical theorists differ on many policy issues. One of the central differences rests upon the time required for automatic macroeconomic adjustment to take place. This difference is conceptualized in Figure 10.2. Once more, assume that autonomous consumption, investment, or export expenditures decline, causing the aggregate demand curve to shift from AD_0 to AD_1. Demand is again insufficient to purchase the full-employment output Y_F and to sustain full employment at price level P_0. In this case, the economy is in disequilibrium; aggregate supply, represented by point E_0, exceeds aggregate demand at point A for

fOcus

"Did Keynesian Economics and World War II Save Us from the Depression?"

Keynes developed his famous theory in the midst of the Great Depression of the 1930s. Conventional wisdom has it that his ideas somehow "saved" Americans—especially through wartime spending on World War II—from continued economic ills. Was this the case?

In spite of monetary reforms, massive public works projects such as the WPA (Works Progress Administration), and new government regulations, the U.S. economy continued to falter throughout the 1930s. What appeared to be prosperity began to return as Americans anticipated more direct participation in World War II and as the government began to reorient production to war goods. The increases in government spending that occurred before and after the war are often served up by historians and others as a prime example of Keynesian economics at work, but not according to recent research into the so-called prosperity of the 1940s and into the theoretical explanation for it.

Economist Robert Higgs argues that both the economic measurement of the business cycle and the Keynesian "spin" given it for the 1940s are seriously flawed.[a] Higgs argues that the prosperity of the war

[a]Robert Higgs, "Wartime Prosperity? A Reassessment of the U.S. Economy in the 1940s," *Journal of Economic History* 52 (March 1992), pp. 41–60.

years was an illusion. While there was no *official* unemployment, a full two-fifths of the labor force was not being used to produce consumer goods or even goods that would increase U.S. capacity to produce consumer goods after the war was over. The index of real personal consumption per capita rose only two percentage points from 1939 to 1944. Business profits and the stock market prices lagged during the war years.

The United States became a command economy, as virtually all economies do in war. This means that massive reallocations of resources from private production to war goods was accomplished through artificial means such as price controls and quantity restrictions on consumer and other goods. The command economy performed well at turning out war goods and munitions, but it worked only because authoritarian controls made it work.

Not only do the data not tell the correct story of the so-called wartime prosperity, Higgs argues, but World War II itself did not *cause* the postwar boom in America. In Keynesian terms, the war did not create investments that would later be turned into income- and consumption-generative activities through a "multiplier." Rather, expectations were transformed and financial wealth was built up in America during World War II. These laid the groundwork for the genuine spurt of prosperity experienced in the second half of the 1940s, and in the decades that followed. World War II and "Keynesian principles" were not responsible for postwar prosperity.

Demand deficiency unemployment
A short-run situation in which the level of employment is less than if the full-employment level of output were produced; arises when aggregate demand is insufficient to purchase the full-employment output given the price level.

price level P_0. The degree and speed of wage and price level flexibility determines how quickly the economy will adjust to the excess supply at price level P_0. In the classical view, prices will quickly adjust downward to point B, but Keynesians believe that downward adjustments in prices and wages can be slow, unpredictable, and "sticky." Either drop—to A or to B—creates a certain amount of **demand deficiency unemployment**, unemployment that results whenever aggregate demand is insufficient to purchase the quantity of goods and services produced under full employment. Whether Keynesian principles were ever "tried" or not is debatable (see the Focus, "Did Keynesian Economics and World War II Save Us from the Depression?").

Under rigid Keynesian assumptions, prices and money wages are totally inflexible, meaning that the economy would move to point A with a relatively large amount of demand deficiency unemployment. Demand deficiency unemployment is measured as employment at the full-employment output, Y_F, minus the employment that will exist if the economy produces a level of output equal to Y_1. If prices and wages were somewhat flexible over a short period of time, however, a movement from E_0 to a point such as B on the short-run aggregate supply curve AS_0 would result. In this case, demand deficiency unemployment would equal the level of employment at Y_F minus the level of employment at Y_0.

Short-run unemployment of labor and reductions in real output are a fact of life both for modern Keynesians and for new classical theorists. But they differ widely in the kind of policies they would recommend. Keynesians favor the use of discretionary fiscal policy—the use of government expenditures and taxation or, to a lesser degree, discretionary monetary policy—to force the aggregate demand rightward from AD_1 back to AD_0 in Figure 10.2. According to Keynesian analysis, the economy is quasi-permanently stuck at point B, where unemployment exists. Government must do something about it.

By contrast, new classical economists believe that attempts to manipulate aggregate demand are doomed to fail. They feel that the discretionary actions of government—through fiscal and monetary policy—are unsettling and disruptive; they heighten fears about inflation and the economy in general, making the restoration of equilibrium even more difficult to achieve. New classical economists would prefer that government refrain from countercyclical fiscal policies except under certain conditions. Building on the simple concepts just outlined, we can describe some important aspects of the nature and practice of fiscal policy.

Fiscal Policy and Demand Management

Ordinarily, the economy's aggregate supply curve is positively sloped, meaning that, like the supply curves of individual products, higher levels for all output are associated with higher levels of production. The positively sloped aggregate supply curve is midway between traditional classical assumptions and rigid Keynesian assumptions about the speed of price and wage adjustments to changes in the aggregate economy. In Figure 10.3, such a supply curve is reproduced along with the negatively sloped aggregate demand curve.

FIGURE 10.3

Fiscal Policy Shifts the Aggregate Demand Curve to Combat Recession

Assuming a positively sloped aggregate supply curve, AS, an increase in government spending or a decrease in taxes will shift the aggregate demand curve rightward from AD_0 to AD_1. The increase causes prices to rise as real income and employment rise to the full-employment level.

Focus Politics and Fiscal Policy: How Brave Are Politicians Anyway?

In any discussion of government economic policy, some allowance must be made for the possibility that policymakers will not make the "right" response—that is, the policy change consistent with accepted counter-cyclical economic theory. Experience tells us that in the world of interest-group politics, economic considerations are not always uppermost in the minds of policymakers. There is every reason to believe that, like everyone else, elected politicians are self-interested individuals. What is it that the self-interested politician seeks to maximize? Is it the public interest or job security (the probability of future reelection by voters)? Many economists believe it is the latter, so they recognize that knowledge of economic theory on the part of government policymakers does not guarantee justifiable decisions. Political motives, in other words, frequently dominate fiscal policy decisions.

Consider the accepted "cure" for inflation, according to economic theory. In the Keynesian view, the appropriate fiscal response is a cut in government expenditures, an increase in taxes, or some combination of the two. But how many elected officials have the courage to vote for a tax increase in an election year? By the same token, reductions in government expenditures are politically unpopular with interest groups that receive these expenditures. What are politicians to do? If they wish to curry favor with the electorate—and what politician doesn't?—they will vote against unpopular

fiscal measures, even though such measures may be sound countercyclical actions. Proof of this principle is the fact that the United States has incurred budget deficits in every year but two since World War II. If economic theory had dictated the deficits, their existence would imply that the U.S. economy has been in a quasi-perpetual state of recession, with Congress continually trying to spend us out of the slump. We know that this has not been the case. For many of the postwar years, Congress has actually pursued procyclical rather than countercyclical policy because politicians were unwilling to pay the political price for an unpopular though analytically sound economic policy.

One possible solution to this dilemma is to reduce the degree of autonomy that politicians have over fiscal policy; to take decisions out of their hands to a degree by placing fiscal constraints on the executive branch and the Congress. One such fiscal constraint is a balanced budget rule imposed by a constitutional amendment. This would prevent Congress and the president from spending amounts larger than tax revenues allow. In other words, it would prevent them from creating budget deficits. While a legal balanced budget requirement (or the pegging of government expenditures to a percent of GDP) could be procyclical, some argue that there would be less inflationary bias than under the current political system. Some type of constraint, the argument goes, would force Congress and the president to choose more carefully how to spend a more limited source of funds. A legal fiscal constraint may prevent, during periods of inflation, pork-barrel spending legislation; it might remove some of the built-in incentives politicians have to cast economically unsound votes.

Equilibrium output occurs initially at the intersection of the aggregate demand curve AD_0 and the aggregate supply curve AS along the ordinary, upward-sloping intermediate range of the supply curve. A level of real output or income is produced within the economy in the amount of Y_0 at a price level P_0. However, aggregate demand level AD_0 is insufficient to provide a level of full-employment output Y_F. What kind of macroeconomic policy would be called for? For fiscal policy, the government would attempt to stimulate spending by reducing taxes and thereby increasing consumption, by increasing government spending, or by stimulating consumption and investment spending (see the Focus "Politics and Fiscal Policy: How Brave Are Politicians Anyway?"). Demand management consists of manipulation of these politically controlled variables (the tax system and government spending) to shift AD_0 to AD_1, or to move demand in the opposite direction to combat rapid expansion and inflation. Fine-tuning the economy by shifting aggregate demand either rightward (to stimulate economic activity) or leftward (to cool down economic activity), the government thus manages aggregate demand to achieve economic goals of full employment and maximum economic growth.

Many government policies other than tax or spending changes and practices affect aggregate demand. Federal policies relating to international trade, for example, can affect aggregate demand. As noted in Chapter 8, *net* foreign spending— the difference between exports and imports—is a component of aggregate demand. Anything that affects either imports or exports, such as the erection or elimination of trade barriers, will shift the aggregate demand curve either to the right or to the left. Trade agreements with Japan to limit the American importation of automobiles or computer components will, for example, increase domestic aggregate demand by increasing *net* foreign spending (exports *minus* imports). Likewise, policies that encourage exports of American products will shift the aggregate demand curve rightward.

Demand and Supply Interaction

Figure 10.3 shows a situation in which an increase in aggregate demand and an increase in real income and employment are accompanied by an increase in the price level. This is not always the case. Whether or not prices will rise with increases in aggregate demand depends on the shape of the aggregate supply curve, as we discussed in Chapters 5 and 9.

The economy performs within its production possibilities frontier when there is widespread unemployment of resources. An increase in aggregate demand through government fiscal policies will have the effect of increasing real output and employment *without* creating inflation by raising prices. Why? Widespread resource availability permits increased real output without putting pressure on resources and output prices. This situation is close to the one Keynes described for the Depression of the 1930s and 1940s. Under these extreme conditions, fiscal policy could achieve increases in output and employment without inflation.

The opposite extreme is also possible. When resources are fully and most efficiently employed, the economy is operating at or very near the production possibilities frontier. Given the state of technology, resources, and institutions, there is some maximum possible amount of real output and employment. If the economy is at this maximum point, the aggregate supply curve is vertical. With a vertical supply curve, an increase in aggregate demand created by monetary or fiscal policies will be inflationary. Demand management is unnecessary in the classical case because, as we saw in Chapter 6, the economy is self-adjusting and will produce full employment and maximum output automatically. Economists who adhere to classical principles or to modern versions of them argue that discretionary demand management by government is unnecessary and possibly harmful to the economy.

Between the two extremes lies an intermediate case. Increases in aggregate demand will put some pressure on prices along with causing some increase in real national income and employment. This situation was depicted in Figure 10.3. An increase in demand will create some increase in prices, but real output and employment will also rise. However, shortages will develop in some resource markets, creating production bottlenecks and price increases. As the economy approaches full employment and the production possibilities frontier, prices will ordinarily rise at a faster rate and output increases will be smaller and smaller as resource shortages become more acute.

In sum, the effectiveness of managing demand by monetary or fiscal means depends in part on the shape of the aggregate supply curve. In the Keynesian case, reflecting depression conditions, demand changes will have their full impact on real income and employment with no effect on prices. In the classical case, demand management is virtually useless in affecting employment or output: Its sole effects are on the price level. The intermediate case contains elements of both Keynesian and classical conclusions. Aggregate demand changes will change real output and employment as well as the price level. The government's ability to adjust spending and aggregate demand to contractionary or expansionary gaps—to control unemployment and inflation and to promote economic growth—is therefore partially limited by the shape of the aggregate supply curve.

Possible Limits to Discretionary Demand Management

In addition to extreme shapes of the supply curve, demand management by the government may be limited in its effectiveness by the realities of private decision making. About two-thirds of annual total expenditures in the economy come from the private sector—households and businesses. The private sector may have an ability to spend roughly equivalent to its income and wealth, and its desire to spend is not subject to direct government control. Thus it is possible for any governmental policy designed to accelerate or decelerate total expenditures to be thwarted by cumulative individual decisions to reduce or increase spending. In the context of the simple Keynesian model, for example, an increase in government spending could be partially or totally offset by a decrease in some autonomous component of private expenditures. By and large, the limits of discretionary demand management are related to expectations in the private economy and to the supply behavior of workers and other resource suppliers in the economy.

AGGREGATE SUPPLY POLICIES

Policies affecting the aggregate demand for goods and services in the U.S. economy are only one important part of macroeconomic policy. Beginning in the 1970s, academic economists began investigating the possibility that prolonged use of demand management might adversely affect aggregate supply. Many economists, for example, investigated the effects of tax rates on work incentives, the labor supply, and productivity. Some economists believe that tax rates, tax rate changes, and unpredictable changes in government spending affect the aggregate supply curve and thus employment and prices. Others emphasize the impact of institutional factors, such as minimum-wage laws and income maintenance programs, on raising the natural rate of unemployment. This means that discretionary aggregate demand changes brought about by altering tax rates (as well as legislatively mandated institutional changes) might be partially offset by adverse shifts in aggregate supply. In that event, macroeconomic policy might be self-defeating.

Aggregate Supply and Resource Employment

As we stressed in Chapter 9, aggregate supply in the economy is related to the cost and availability of resources, especially labor resources. To classical economists, **full employment** meant that everyone who wanted a job had one; in other words, there was no excess demand for labor. In this view, the real wage established by the interaction of supply and demand for labor is the full-employment wage. Some unemployed workers would work for wages higher than the equilibrium real wage, but they are not considered unemployed because they voluntarily take themselves out of the labor force. All who would accept lower than equilibrium real wages are employed.

Full employment
To the classical economist, a situation in which all workers willing and able to work at the current market real wage rate are employed.

Today, economists prefer to talk of a natural rate of employment or unemployment. A certain amount of unemployment is expected in an economy at any given time. Because of changing demand conditions, resources constantly shift among producers. As we explained in Chapter 5, a certain rate of unemployment arises from "friction" in the economic system, although the precise rate has changed over time and is a topic of debate among economists.

The **natural rate of unemployment** is easier to define than to measure: It is the rate of unemployment that exists when all unemployment is either frictional or structural unemployment. These two types of unemployment primarily result when there is imperfect labor market information, when job search requires time, and when there is no match between the skill and location requirements of job openings and those of unemployed workers. The natural rate of unemployment stems from fundamental market and institutional changes that affect the decisions of workers to supply and employers to demand labor. Specifically, changes in minimum-wage laws, tax laws (especially income tax laws), and the availability and scope of retirement benefits affect workers' incentives to supply labor and thus the natural rate of unemployment. Another important factor is the increased participation rate of women in the labor force since the 1960s.

Natural rate of unemployment
The rate of unemployment due to frictional unemployment plus structural unemployment; the rate of unemployment that will exist when expectations of inflation reflect actual inflationary conditions and all short-run macroeconomic adjustments have been made.

The business environment also affects the natural rate of unemployment on the demand side of resource markets. Taxes and tax laws affect business investments in capital and resources, including labor resources. Changes in tax laws or business regulations will affect the natural rate of unemployment in the economy.

Once these institutional factors are accounted for, the natural rate of unemployment may be interpreted as the rate of unemployment that occurs when full employment exists. This implies that the level of full-employment real output, Y_F, will be produced when the natural rate of unemployment exists. Any change in the institutional factors that affects either the supply of or the demand for resources will shift the aggregate supply curve either rightward or leftward. Supply-side economics, therefore, attempts to shift the aggregate supply curve rightward by changing policies and institutions that reduce the natural rate of unemployment. A rightward shift, for example, would enhance economic growth in terms of actual employment of resources and higher output.

The effects of supply-side or aggregate supply shifts may be shown utilizing the aggregate demand–aggregate supply apparatus from previous chapters. In Figure 10.4, long-run vertical aggregate supply curves are shown with an aggregate de-

FIGURE 10.4

The Effects of Increases in Aggregate Supply

If government policies such as tax cuts and deregulation reduce the natural rate of unemployment, the aggregate supply curve will shift rightward—in this case, from AS_0 to AS_1 to AS_2. As a consequence, the price level will fall (below P_0) and real output will rise, from Y_{F_0} to Y_{F_2}.

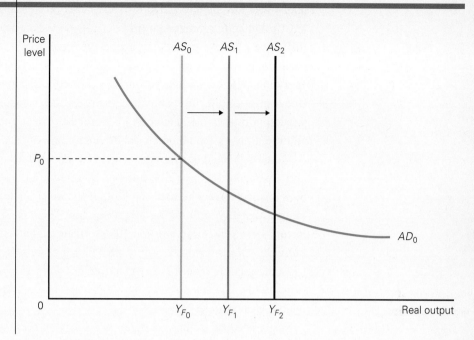

mand curve AD_0. Assume that initial equilibrium is associated with the intersection of the aggregate demand curve, AD_0, and aggregate supply curve AS_0. If the full-employment level of income produced by this intersection, Y_{F_0}, is insufficient, policymakers might choose policies to increase income and employment growth. Policies that affect the natural rate of unemployment and aggregate supply will shift the aggregate supply curve rightward to new equilibrium positions. Two of these positions are shown in Figure 10.4. Tax reductions or deregulation in labor or product markets will decrease the natural rate of unemployment and increase the equilibrium income potential in the economy. In terms of Figure 10.4, policies designed to increase aggregate supply would increase the output potential of the economy from Y_{F_0} to Y_{F_1} or Y_{F_2}. These supply-side policies have been the concern of politicians and policymakers in Congress for over a decade.

Supply-Side Economic Policies

Macroeconomic policy since the mid-1970s has been shaped by the recognition that excessive and prolonged use of demand management might have adverse effects on the economy. Some economists and policymakers believe that discretionary aggregate demand changes have produced offsetting shifts in aggregate supply. Specifically, they contend that certain fiscal and legislative measures, particularly tax measures and regulatory changes, alter incentives. Do businesses and workers respond to tax decreases by increasing investment in and production of goods and services? The Reagan administration made **supply-side economics**—the attempt to stimulate real production by providing new incentives to workers and businesses—a hallmark of its economic policy. In this section we consider the nature of some supply-side policies.

Supply-side economics
Policies designed to stimulate production by altering incentives of producers; policies designed to shift the aggregate supply curve to the right.

POLICIES TO INCREASE WORK EFFORT AND SAVINGS   Americans tend to save a smaller portion of their incomes compared to income earners in most other industrialized countries. However, Americans are not simply spend-thrifts who live only for the present: We have been encouraged by the design of fiscal policies to borrow more and save less. Interest income from savings is taxed as ordinary income, while for many years interest *payments* were tax deductible. Under present law, interest earnings are still taxed as ordinary income, although deducting interest payments on loans for consumer goods purchases is no longer allowed. (Interest on home mortgages and home equity loans remains deductible.)

Policies enacted during the 1980s were directed at upgrading American saving and work habits, especially among low-income groups. Interest rate restrictions paid to small savers by banks and other financial institutions were loosened or re-moved, thereby encouraging private saving. The largest income tax cuts in recent history were passed in 1981 and 1986 to increase both saving and work incentives. Individual Retirement Accounts (IRAs), which allowed income earners to shel-ter some income from taxes for retirement purposes, were also instituted in the early 1980s. IRAs clearly encourage private saving, especially among lower- and middle-class income earners.

Partly because of these policies, gross private personal savings did increase be-tween 1986 and 1992. However, the 1990 budget compromise reached by Congress and President Bush may have countered somewhat the impact of the earlier supply-side approach by raising a wide variety of taxes. Tax increases were also developed as part of the Clinton administration's deficit-reduction plan.

POLICIES TO ENCOURAGE BUSINESS INVESTMENT   Higher saving rates usually translate into higher investment rates by businesses. Institutional restrictions, such as high capital gains taxes and output-lowering regulations, have hampered productive investment in the past (and continue to do so today). Capital gains taxes are taxes on profits from the sale of stocks, real estate, and other investments. Prior to the Tax Reform Act of 1986, capital gains were taxed at a *lower* rate than ordi-nary income to encourage productive investment by small and large investors alike. (Purchasing stocks and bonds is similar to saving in that both allow businesses to make investments.) These investments are an essential vehicle for creating higher employment and output growth. Because such investments actually help create jobs, many economists believe that a reduction in the capital gains tax is justified.

The Tax Reform Act of 1986 increased the capital gains tax by treating capital gains from investments as ordinary income. That is, after 1986, capital gains were taxed at the same rates as earned income (15, 28, or 33 percent, and now 40 percent). Critics of this action claim that it had a chilling effect on investment—reducing the aggregate supply curve of the economy and thereby reducing economic growth potential. Institutional rigidities—in this case, a tax on investment—may have a neg-ative impact on aggregate supply and on economic performance.

DEREGULATION OF MARKETS   Red tape and unnecessary regulations ham-per economic performance in markets for goods and services or inputs, including labor. In the late 1970s, the federal government took steps to deregulate several industries, including the banking and financial services industry. The financial system that has emerged is more flexible and efficient, although the result has been tempered by widespread bankruptcies in the savings and loan industry, which may or may not be the result of deregulation.

Partial deregulation of transportation, including airlines, railroads, and interstate trucking, began under President Carter and continued through the Reagan administration. Deregulation of these industries gave consumers lower prices, larger output, and greater choice of services. Elimination of institutional restrictions on businesses by government agencies, including the Occupational Safety and Health Administration (OSHA), increased the productivity of business capital and encouraged new investment during the 1980s. Some changes in labor markets were also supply-oriented. For instance, modification of the minimum-wage law included a general increase in the minimum hourly wage but permitted the hiring of teenagers in need of job experience at lower-than-minimum wages for a limited "training period." The intended effects were enhanced aggregate supply and improved long-run labor productivity.

There are indications that such institutional changes have produced a more efficient use of resources, but this is not to say that all supply-oriented changes have been beneficial. Because of federal deposit insurance, taxpayers have had to bail out the savings and loan industry—at a cost of several hundred billion dollars. Also, certain Reagan-Bush supply-side policies—for example, the elimination of job training programs and cuts in educational grants and loans—may have adversely affected labor-market institutions and skill levels of workers.

TRADE POLICIES AND THE SUPPLY SIDE Protectionism has contradictory and self-defeating effects on the economy. The imposition of import tariffs or other trade restrictions may temporarily benefit the economy by providing a temporary increase in aggregate demand. However, the imposition of tariffs or other less formal trade restrictions will simultaneously reduce the long-run growth potential of the economy by reducing competition for domestic firms, input availability, and aggregate supply. While formal tariffs and quotas on goods and services are presently low (see Chapter 17), foreign cartels such as OPEC and "voluntary" trade agreements to restrict importation of foreign products or raw materials, which are more plentiful, have the same effects. As shown in a Focus in Chapter 9, the OPEC cartel created a negative supply shock in the U.S. economy in the 1970s, although its effects have been mitigated somewhat since. Likewise, import restrictions on imports to protect domestic industries such as the computer and textile industries reduce aggregate supply and the growth potential of the economy. Because it removed many of the restrictions on trade among the United States, Canada, and Mexico, the North American Free Trade Agreement (NAFTA) will enhance the growth potential of all three countries for several generations. Actual and potential changes in trade restrictions have an enormous impact on macroeconomic well-being and affect both aggregate supply and aggregate demand (see the Application, "The Impact of Freer Trade on the Macroeconomy," at the conclusion of this chapter).

The Impact of Supply-Side Policies

The results of supply-side policies enacted since the late 1970s have so far been mixed. A recession in the early 1980s, possibly precipitated by inflation-control measures, dampened enthusiasm for some such policies, although growth rates in real output and employment rose in 1983 and 1984. The economic growth rate in terms of real GNP was at a two-decade high in 1984 (6.8 percent); the rate has slowed to a little over 3 percent per year since 1984. Unemployment rates fell steadily after 1984. In 1988, Americans experienced the lowest unemployment rate (around 5 percent) since 1972. Inflation was brought down from 18 percent in 1979 to a little more than 6 percent in 1983 and has remained below that level—often significantly lower—since.

Many believe that the recession of 1990–1991 was the product of supply-side policies gone bad. Defenders of supply-side economics often blame the recession on the tax increase supported by Congress and President Bush in 1990. The 1990 budget compromise may have had demand-decreasing effects, but the causes of the downturn and slow recovery are likely complex and varied. Consumer perceptions and confidence undoubtedly played a major role. It is widely believed that President Bush's inaction—his decision not to invoke discretionary fiscal policy (which might have had growth-reducing long-term effects)—cost him the 1992 election. It is important to note that, albeit weakly, the economy did recover on its own. President Clinton raised taxes in 1992, and his era in government has been associated with lower deficits. As we approach the 1996 elections, economic growth is around 3 percent, inflation is low, and unemployment is about 5 percent.

DEMAND AND SUPPLY INTERACTION: PROBLEMS AND PROSPECTS

By the early 1980s, the ill effects of decades of countercyclical demand policies on aggregate supply were apparent to many economists. From the perspective of these economists, government at all levels tended to overspend and the increased taxation or inflationary tendencies created by deficit finance constrained work effort and private business investment. Aggregate demand policies by government may have worked faster than supply policies to alter inflation or unemployment, but their negative long-run effects on the economy's aggregate output of goods and services could no longer be ignored. Many economists now feel that quick-fix aggregate demand policies do not get at the long-run problems of economic growth and productivity. Aggregate supply policies—especially those relating to labor productivity, long-run business investment, and institutional change—will be more effective, but they also take more time. In this view, demand policies should receive consideration, but supply issues should be raised to equal importance.

Unfortunately, demand- and supply-side policies are enacted within a political process that often prevents or hampers coordination of macroeconomic policy goals. During the 1980s, tax cuts were enacted—a reasonable supply-side policy to enhance work effort, saving, and productivity. But at the same time, government expenditures were not reduced enough to cover increasing deficits in the federal accounts. These huge federal deficits were tantamount to an enormous Keynesian demand-side boost in total expenditures, which might explain the economic growth and general prosperity of the 1980s. But the federal deficit leads to uncertainty in private markets, which has a negative impact both on aggregate demand and aggregate supply. The deficit signals to potential savers and investors that inflation and/or government competition for private funds might soon be on the way. Deficits, then, have a dual impact: They increase the government portion of aggregate expenditures while reducing private expenditures through the creation of adverse expectations. Deficit reduction is an obvious macroeconomic good. However, as the bitter, highly partisan fight over the Clinton administration's $496 billion deficit-reduction plan demonstrated in the summer of 1993, it is difficult to achieve. The "Republican Revolution" based on their 1994 "Contract with America"—aimed at reduced spending and budget balance—was another bitter conflict that ended in federal government "shutdowns" in 1995 and 1996.

APPLICATION
The Impact of Freer Trade on the Macroeconomy

World trade totaled $8.5 trillion in 1994, up from $1.6 trillion in 1974. In the United States, exports now account for more than 10 percent of GDP—double the percentage of 20 years ago. These magnitudes illustrate the enormous potential trade has for increasing aggregate supply and demand in the United States over the long run. Aggregate supply will increase (shift rightward) whenever labor productivity rises, which is precisely what happens with a more efficient (lower cost) allocation of labor created by more open trade. Freer trade will also result in a rightward shift in aggregate demand if net foreign spending (exports minus imports) rises after trade restrictions are reduced or lifted.

Economists since David Ricardo (1772–1823) have emphasized the importance of economy-wide specialization and trade for economic growth in the macroeconomy. But special interests—industries and labor groups who gain from protection in the form of quotas or tariffs—have at times freely used the political process to reduce the volume of trade and to increase artificially the price of domestic wares to consumers. Such activities have reduced both aggregate supply and demand in the U.S. economy over time.

As Table 10.1 shows, the most protectionist legislation enacted in this century was the Smoot-Hawley Act, passed in 1930 at the onset of the Great Depression. Since that time, the trend has been toward freer trade. Tariffs have been systematically lowered, creating more exports and jobs. The trend, however, has been toward multilateral tariff reductions—those involving many countries.

Chiefly responsible for the modern liberalization of trade have been the multilateral trade negotiations conducted under the General Agreement on Tariffs and Trade (GATT), which was both an international charter designed to set out the rules of conduct in international trade (the General Agreement) as well as an international organization for oversight of the agreement and management of multilateral trade negotiations (the General Secretariat). Responsibilities for settling trade disputes and overseeing multilateral trade agreements shifted to the World Trade Organization (WTO) in January, 1995. Founded in 1947, the GATT currently has 93 member countries who account for over 80 percent of world trade. Another 31 countries have agreed to abide by the rules of GATT. The General Agreement has provided a forum for multilateral talks aimed at expanding trade by encouraging member countries to lower trade barriers and to eliminate discriminatory treatment.

Beginning in 1947 with the first round set in Geneva, there have been eight rounds of such negotiations, the most recent being the Uruguay Round. The formal negotiating process, involving representatives from 108 countries, began in late 1986 and concluded when the Final Act was signed in Morocco in April 1994 and ratified in the United States on December 8, 1994. The focus of this most recent round was not the reduction of tariffs but rather issues such as nontariff barriers, intellectual property rights, trade in services, trade in agriculture, and the functioning of the GATT system.

242   CHAPTER 10   FISCAL POLICY AND THE SUPPLY SIDE: USING THE TOOLS

TABLE 10.1

Major Trade Legislation in the United States

Since the end of the nineteenth century, trade legislation in the United States has promoted both protectionism and freer trade. Since the Depression era, and especially after the initial GATT agreement in 1947, legislation has generally moved in the direction of freer trade.

Legislation	Year	Type
Dingley Act	1897	Protectionist
Payne-Aldrich Act	1909	
Underwood Act	1913	Freer trade
Fordney-McCumber Act	1922	Protectionist
Smoot-Hawley Act	1930	Very protectionist
Reciprocal Trade Agreement Act (renewed 11 times between 1934 and 1962)	1934	Freer trade
GATT negotiations:		
Geneva	1947	
Annecy	1949	
Torquay	1950–1951	
Dillon-Round	1956–1961	
Trade Expansion Act	1962	Freer trade
GATT Kennedy Round	1964–1967	
Trade Act of 1974	1974	Freer trade
GATT Tokyo Round	1974–1979	
Trade Agreement Act	1979	Freer trade
GATT Uruguay Round	1986–1994	
New GATT Agreement		Freer trade
Omnibus Trade Bill	1988	Protectionist
North American Free Trade Association (NAFTA)	1994	Freer trade

SOURCE: Peter Moser, *The Political Economy of the GATT* (St. Gallen: Verlag Ruegger, 1990), p. 62.

It has always been the case that groups favoring tariff protection—most notably, large manufacturers and labor unions—have been both vocal and politically influential. In fact, protectionism in the past has warped resources to particular production processes as tariff protection became enshrined in law. Society earns a huge net benefit from free trade, but those benefits are spread among hundreds of millions of consumers whose individual share of these benefits is small. As a result, the interests of consumers—unlike the interests of groups such as textile manufacturers in the United States—are, almost always, underrepresented in congresses and parliaments around the world.

It has been suggested that no industry is farther from the ideal of free trade than farming. The price tag of the

taxes and higher prices that consumers around the world currently pay to support farmers has been estimated at $300 billion per year. The net welfare loss caused by the farm policies of industrial nations—the amount that exceeds the transfer of income to farmers—is thought to be approximately $100 billion per year. Especially in the European Community, recent efforts to reduce agricultural subsidies have been met with fierce resistance by farmers. The complex and emotional issue of agricultural subsidies and trade barriers proved to be a challenge for GATT negotiators.

GATT negotiators also confronted a well-organized environmental movement. Environmentalists have attacked both the North American Free Trade Agreement (NAFTA) and GATT (1994) on the grounds that freer trade promotes greater environmental hazards and costs along with economic growth. Many environmentalists are strongly opposed to agreements that limit national sovereignty because they fear that the relatively strong environmental measures currently in place in certain countries could be diluted.

GATT has also been threatened at times by the actions of participating nations. In the United States, for example, the Omnibus Trade Bill of 1988 contained the "Super 301" clause which was intended to automatize the process of retaliating against foreign trade practices deemed "unfair" by U.S. industries by threatening them with higher tariffs unless they altered their trade policies (this provision expired in 1990). This process has been likened to "prying open foreign markets with a crowbar." Such detours on the route towards trade liberalization directly undermine the foundation which has been set by the GATT.

Several studies concur that the increase in global real income from the Uruguay Round's full implementation in 2005 will be about 1 percent of the world's 1992 GDP. Merchandise trade is predicted to grow by more than 12 percent ($745 billion in 1992 dollars) over what would have occurred in the absence of such agreements. Some studies estimate the gains to less-developed countries from this stimulation of world trade to total $78 billion in 1992 dollars by the year 2005. Obviously, protectionist policies adopted unilaterally by GATT nations could significantly threaten the welfare- and productivity-enhancing capabilities of such agreements. In macroeconomic terms, freer trade—through multilateral agreements—is key to achieving dramatic long-term rightward shifts in both aggregate supply and aggregate demand.

QUESTIONS

Using graphs, show how trade liberalization through tariff and quota reductions might affect aggregate supply and demand (income and the price level) over time. If protectionist policies are known to have deleterious effects on economic growth and productivity, why do they remain so politically popular?

SOURCES: U.S. Bureau of the Census, *U.S. International Trade in Goods and Services,* series FT-900(94); Jadish Bhagwati, "It's the Process, Stupid," *The Economist* (March 27, 1993), p. 69; IMF, *World Economic Outlook 1994,* pp. 84–87.

SUMMARY

1. The interplay of aggregate supply and aggregate demand, in the long-run perspective of classical economists, produces full employment and economic growth at stable prices. Fiscal policy as a discretionary tool of government is largely unnecessary in the context of classical supply and demand interactions.

2. The Keynesian view of macroeconomics is that concerted discretionary policy is necessary to alleviate imbalances in aggregate demand and supply, since the private economy cannot produce an equilibrium at full employment with output growth.

3. Fiscal policy is the taxing and spending power of government. It can affect aggregate demand by increasing total government spending in the economy or by stimulating private consumption and investment spending (via tax cuts, for example). In the event of inflation, fiscal policy may also be used to reduce aggregate demand—that is, it can be contractionary as well as expansionary.

4. Policies other than tax and spending changes can also affect aggregate demand in the economy. Since net foreign spending is a component of aggregate demand, any policy change that affects imports or exports will shift the aggregate demand curve rightward or leftward.

5. The effects of fiscal policy by government depend on the shape of the aggregate supply curve. In the Keynesian range, demand increases cause increases in real income but not in prices; in the classical range, demand increases are inflationary, with no increase in income and employment; in the intermediate range, both prices and real income increase with increases in demand.

6. Supply-side economics is based on the idea that over-reliance on aggregate demand management, in the

form of tax policy, has had ill effects on the aggregate supply side of the economy.

7. Aggregate supply is related to the cost and availability of resources in the economy, especially labor resources. It is also related to the natural rate of unemployment, which exists when all unemployment is either frictional or structural in nature.

8. The natural rate of unemployment is dependent upon the institutions surrounding decisions to supply or demand labor. These institutions include but are not limited to tax policies on work and investment, the amount of government regulation, and trade policies.

9. Supply-side policies are designed to enhance work incentives, to increase productive investment, to eliminate regulations on businesses and workers, and to reduce formal or informal trade barriers.

10. Macroeconomic policies relating to both aggregate demand and aggregate supply have been hampered by the existence of huge federal deficits.

KEY TERMS

demand deficiency unemployment
full employment

natural rate of unemployment
supply-side economics

QUESTIONS FOR REVIEW AND DISCUSSION

1. Discuss the classical long-run adjustment mechanism with regard to a decrease in aggregate demand.

2. What is demand deficiency unemployment? How do short-run Keynesian and new classical views of this situation differ?

3. What, exactly, is demand management?

4. Why do modern Keynesians favor discretionary fiscal policies to address short-run unemployment problems?

5. In general, why do new classical or supply-side economists oppose demand management to address short-run problems of unemployment?

6. How would the elimination of all trade barriers with Japan affect aggregate demand and aggregate supply in the United States?

7. Suppose that demand management policies are effective in reducing aggregate demand. How will the price level be affected? Does your answer depend on the shape of the aggregate supply curve?

8. Define the natural rate of unemployment. How do market and institutional changes affect the natural rate?

9. How do policies related to saving and business investment affect output growth and employment in the economy?

10. Does the political process ever prevent or hamper the achievement of macroeconomic policy goals? How?

11. What are the three portions of the aggregate supply curve? How do increases in aggregate demand affect the price level in these different ranges?

12. During World War II, a large portion of the population left the work force in order to fight overseas. What impact would such an exodus have on the aggregate supply curve?

PROBLEM

Hurricane Andrew had devastating effects on local economies in Florida and Louisiana in the fall of 1992. Hurricane Opal blasted through North Florida in 1995. San Francisco experienced similar problems following the earthquake of 1989. Massive flooding along the Mississippi River in the summer of 1993 wiped out crops, homes, and businesses and disrupted transportation in the Midwest. Many billions of dollars of damages resulted from these natural disasters. Use graphs to show the short-run and long-run supply-side effects of such catastrophes.

CHAPTER 11

TAXES, DEFICITS, AND THE DEBT

In Chapter 10, we examined how fiscal policy could shift aggregate demand and supply curves to attain important macroeconomic goals. While fiscal policy may be a recommended stabilizing device, political pressures have led systematically to deficit spending. Since 1960, the U.S. government has run a surplus in only one year—1969. Government deficits exceeded $200 billion several times during the 1980s and topped $300 billion in 1991. Despite political promises to balance the budget, the national debt has risen more than tenfold since 1960, to about $5 trillion in 1996. The practice of fiscal policy involves the subject of public finance, or the role of government expenditures, taxation, and debt in the economy. Each of these areas of government policy are important and to some extent controversial. For example, the public, politicians, and economists are anxious about the effects of deficits and debt. This chapter examines the political foundation of federal deficits and debt. After reading Chapter 11 you should understand

- the proposed effects and the results of fiscal policy.

- features of government finance that automatically help control business cycles of recession and inflation.

- basic principles of public finance, especially as related to taxation.

- why deficits and debt concern economists and the public.

FISCAL POLICY IN PRACTICE

Fiscal policy is often difficult to implement—primarily because it must work through a political process. Inherent in this process are impediments to the smooth functioning of discretionary fiscal policy. It is often difficult to forecast economic downturns accurately or to implement appropriate fiscal policies in a timely fashion. In addition, political motives often cause politicians to favor certain fiscal measures.

Governments continually levy taxes and make expenditures on a variety of goods and services, and all taxes and expenditures have fiscal effects. But most government taxes and expenditures appear in the budget no matter what the particular phase of the business cycle happens to be. The *level* of these tax receipts and expenditures varies with phases of unemployment and inflation in the economy, however, and these changes, called **automatic stabilizers,** are a part of fiscal policy.

Automatic stabilizers
Taxes and government expenditures whose levels do not depend on decisions by policymakers for change but instead change countercyclically in response to changes in the level of economic activity.

Tax Structures

Before explaining the role of automatic stabilizers, we briefly consider three types of tax structure. (Although we use the example of income taxes here, these concepts can be applied to other kinds of taxes as well.)

Proportional income tax
A tax that is a fixed percentage of income for all levels of income.

PROPORTIONAL TAXES   A tax that requires individuals to pay a constant percentage of income in taxes is a **proportional income tax.** If the proportion is 10 percent, a taxpayer earning $50,000 per year would pay $5000 (or 10 percent) in taxes. If a taxpayer earned $5000, his or her tax bill would be $500 (or 10 percent). Some states, such as Michigan, Illinois, and Indiana, levy a proportional income tax (with deductions and exemptions allowed). Much of the current discussion of the so-called flat tax proposal involves the idea of proportional income taxation.

Progressive income tax
A tax that is a percentage of income and that varies directly with the level of income.

PROGRESSIVE TAXES   A **progressive income tax** requires that a larger percentage of income be paid in taxes as income rises. If the tax structure is based on this principle, an individual with a $15,000 income may pay only 5 percent of income in taxes, whereas an individual with a $30,000 income may pay 15 percent. The federal income tax system is based on the principle of progressive taxation.

Regressive income tax
A tax that is a percentage of income and that varies inversely with the level of income.

REGRESSIVE TAXES   With a **regressive income tax,** a lower percentage of income is paid in taxes as income rises. An individual with a $15,000 income may pay 10 percent in taxes, whereas an individual with a $30,000 income may pay 8 percent in taxes. While a regressive tax results in a lower percentage of income paid in taxes as income rises, people with higher incomes may pay higher taxes in absolute amounts. State and local sales taxes are good examples of regressive taxes, as are the more selective excise taxes on tobacco and alcohol.

How Much Is Discretion? How Much Is Automatic?

Prior to 1986, the personal income tax code in the United States was highly progressive (as opposed to proportional or regressive). The advantage of a progressive structure is that it can act as a built-in stabilizer against inflation and recession in the economy. As money income rises—pushing the economy against its production possibilities frontier and fully employing resources—rising money incomes would push people into higher and higher income tax brackets. This, in turn, would withdraw some inflation-producing consumption expenditures from the economy. (This effect assumes that government does not spend the increased tax revenues.) As income falls, the total tax bill of individuals declines with lower and lower tax rates placed on declining incomes, causing unemployment-reducing purchasing power to be automatically injected into the economy. (In this case, the tax bill will also fall with a proportional tax, but it will fall faster with a progressive tax.)

Certain types of government expenditures, such as transfer payments from entitlement (aid) programs, also constitute an automatic stabilizer in the economy. Social Security payments, Aid to Families with Dependent Children, food stamps, unemployment compensation, and other such income security programs automatically inject purchasing power into the poorer and older segments of the economy in case of recession and unemployment. At federal, state, and local levels—but especially at the federal level of government—larger amounts of support flow through these programs during periods of unemployment, and smaller amounts are paid out during periods of fuller employment (and often inflation). For example, the eligibility period for receiving unemployment benefits was extended several times during and after the 1990–1991 recession. Thus, both the tax structure and expenditure programs can be designed and set in place to act as moderating influences on adverse swings in the business cycle of unemployment and inflation.

What, then, is discretionary fiscal policy? If the Congress (with the help of the president) has previously decided the rules under which individuals will receive transfer payments and the rules under which individuals will be taxed, what is left to discretion? One obvious answer is that setting up the automatic stabilizers is itself an act of discretion. The U.S. tax system underwent significant changes in 1986 and in 1993. The Tax Reform Act of 1986 changed the automatic tax stabilizers that were part of the previous tax system, reducing the number of **marginal tax rates** from more than a dozen to two. (A third rate was added in 1991.) The Clinton administration's 1993 economic plan added two new marginal rates for upper-income Americans. (The marginal tax rate is the percentage rate that applies to some additional amount of taxable income; it is figured by dividing the change in taxes by the change in taxable income.) Welfare or entitlement program eligibility also may be changed periodically by Congress, as was recently the case when President Clinton signed welfare reform into law in 1996, and this has an impact on the countercyclical effectiveness of automatic stabilizers.

At any point in time, some expenditures (and tax sources) are controllable and some are not. Approximately 25 to 35 percent of federal expenditures are fully discretionary—that is, not tied to ongoing, in-place programs such as Social Security, unemployment compensation and other income security programs, and interest payments on the federal debt. The bulk of these fully discretionary expenditures includes a large portion of national defense expenditures, public works programs, and appropriations to federal agencies and to state and local levels of government. Without question, Congress has the power and the responsibility to set up all tax and expenditure programs over the long run, but once many of these programs are

Marginal tax rate
The tax rate, in percentage terms, that applies to additional taxable income; additional taxes divided by the additional income taxed.

set, room for short-run discretion is narrowed considerably. Over the short run, discretionary fiscal policy in the hands of Congress and the president is limited by the conditions attached to automatic stabilizers already in place. Some expenditures in the short run are controllable; some are uncontrollable.

Fiscal Policy and the Budget

Budget surplus
The amount by which government's tax revenues exceed government's expenditures in a year.

Budget deficit
The amount by which government's expenditures exceed government's tax revenues in a year.

Cyclically balanced budget
A long-term view of the budget, in which surpluses generated during expansions match deficits created during recessions over a period of years.

Federal debt
The total value of federal government bonds outstanding; arises from both current and past budget deficits.

As we have seen, discretionary fiscal policy suggests **budget surpluses** during periods of inflation and **budget deficits** over periods of unemployment and recession. While some classical economists advised strict balance in government accounts, the Keynesians argued that the budget should be balanced over the business cycle. A **cyclically balanced budget** in theory requires that budget surpluses run during periods of inflation match budget deficits run during periods of economic distress and unemployment. That is, economic contractions demand budget deficits that expand aggregate demand, and inflation demands a surplus in the federal accounts to reduce total spending on goods and services.

Unfortunately, the fiscal process has not worked exactly in this fashion over the past three decades. Deficits, which are supposed to be cyclically counterbalanced by surpluses, have been run by the federal government in all but one of the years since 1960. These deficits have fiscal ramifications of their own. As we will see later in this chapter, a pileup of deficits since 1960 pushed the **federal debt** over $5 trillion in 1996. It is most unlikely that such debt will bankrupt the United States, since the federal government has the power to tax and (unlike any individual or other unit of government) to create money. Economists do worry about other effects of deficits and debt, however. Such effects include adverse impacts on private spending in the present and potential reductions in economic growth and production possibilities in the future.

The Federal Budget: Process and Problems

Currently, federal government spending (including transfer payments) comprises nearly 25 percent of the United States's approximately $6 trillion GDP. The budget submitted to Congress by President Reagan in January of 1987 was the first ever to exceed $1 trillion and the size of the federal budget has increased every year since. Clearly, expenditures of such magnitude will affect aggregate demand. The process by which the level of federal government expenditures is determined each year is complicated. These expenditures are not simply set by the president and implemented immediately; they must be proposed, debated, and approved in a complex budget process.

In 1974, the Congress and President passed the Congressional Budget and Impoundment Control Act. The stipulations set out in this act are still in effect today. The major effects of the 1974 act are to deny the president the authority to refuse to spend congressionally appropriated funds and to establish a specific timetable for all the steps of the budgetary process (see Table 11.1). The act also established the Congressional Budget Office (CBO) to specialize in budgetary analysis for the Congress. The GAO by this time had acquired so many other duties, and federal budgets had become so very large and complicated, that Congress felt better economic analysis of federal spending could be provided by an office for which this was the sole task.

TABLE 11.1

Timetable for the Congressional Budget Process

To pass a federal budget for government expenditures, the Congressional Budget and Impoundment Control Act of 1974 requires that these specific legal actions be taken by the president and Congress each year. The act also sets deadlines for each step.

Deadline	Action to Be Completed	Deadline	Action to Be Completed
November 10	President submits current services budget	Seventh day after Labor Day	Congress completes action on bills and resolutions providing new budget
Fifteenth day after Congress meets	President submits budget	September 15	Congress completes action on second required concurrent resolution on the budget
March 15	Committees submit reports to budget committees	September 25	Congress completes action on reconciliation bill or resolution, or both, implementing second required concurrent resolution
April 1	CBO submits report to budget committees	October 1	Fiscal year begins
April 15	Budget committees report first concurrent resolutions to their houses		
May 15	Committees report bills and resolutions authorizing new budget authority; Congress completes action on first concurrent resolution on budget		

Though the reforms established by the 1974 act were intended to make the budget process more efficient and streamlined, they had the opposite effect. Deadlines are seldom reached, deficits have ballooned, and, frequently, special temporary budgets have been approved to prevent the government from running out of money and ceasing operations. A number of proposals have been suggested for overcoming these problems.

Among the most popular is the line-item veto, a power given to most state governors. This would allow the president to veto specific parts, or line items, of budgets passed by Congress. A major problem with the budget process, as some see it, has been that the president faces an all-or-nothing situation. Prior to 1996 the budget passed by Congress had to be accepted intact or vetoed. That provided an incentive to attach special-interest spending bills, known as riders, to major spending bills. With the line-item veto to go into effect in 1997, the president will be able to dispose of riders and leave the major budget legislation intact. The line-item veto, if it survives legal challenges, would also provide greater flexibility in pinpointing federal spending the president would prefer to cut. Opponents of the line-item veto point out that it would alter the balance of constitutional power between the president and Congress by giving the president effective total control over federal government spending.

Other proposals include implementing a two-year (instead of a one-year) budget and dividing the budget into a current expense budget and a capital budget. With a two-year budget, Congress would go through the budget process only once every two years, rather than annually. Since the budget process has become a costly, drawn-out affair, this proposal has some merit. Dividing the budget into a capital budget for public goods, investment outlay (for example, highways), and a current expense budget for yearly operating expenses also may provide for greater fiscal flexibility as well as greater opportunity for the president and Congress to agree on federal expenditures.

PUBLIC FINANCE

Government expenditures obviously require some means, such as taxation, to finance them. When government finances the production of public goods or services—a local sewer system, a research program looking into the cause of acid rain, a nuclear warhead, a presidential limousine—it uses taxes to help pay the bill. In the United States, about 82,000 governmental bodies at federal, state, county, city, school district, municipal, and township levels have the power to establish taxes. As we saw in Chapter 3, the market fails to provide the optimal amounts of public goods such as national defense, police and fire protection, and education. In response, federal, state, and local governments traditionally have taken an active role in providing or influencing the production of such goods and services. In macroeconomic stabilization, government expenditures and taxation (especially at the federal level) take on new roles and new significance. Since the impact of fiscal policy is felt in the economy through government expenditures and taxation, it is important to understand some of the history and foundations of **public finance,** which is the study of government expenditures and revenue-collecting activities. Each and every government expenditure, along with the various tax schemes to finance it, has fiscal effects in terms of helping or hindering economic stabilization.

Public finance
The study of how governments at the federal, state, and local levels tax and spend.

Government Expenditures

There are two basic types of government expenditures: (1) direct purchases of goods and services and (2) transfer payments, which are the redistribution of income from one group of people to another. Direct purchases involve spending on items such as defense, fire and police protection, and wages and salaries of government employees. Transfer payments include such expenditures as Social Security payments, Aid to Families with Dependent Children, and unemployment insurance.

The size of all government expenditures, adjusted for inflation, is shown in Table 11.2 for selected years from 1960 to 1995. Total government expenditures have increased dramatically since 1960 and are expected to rise even higher. These expenditures are ultimately determined by legislative decision, but about 70 to 80 percent are part of ongoing programs such as funds for police protection, water and sewer services (at the local level), military salaries, welfare entitlement programs, Social Security, and interest on the federal debt.

TABLE 11.2

Real Federal, State, and Local Government Expenditures,
1960–1995

All government expenditures increased during the period 1960–1995, with real state and local expenditures increasing at about the same rate as real federal expenditures. This increase was not totally due to population growth; per capita real expenditures more than doubled between 1960 and 1995.

EXPENDITURES (BILLIONS OF 1995 DOLLARS)

Year	All Governments	Federal Government	State and Local Governments	Total Per Capita Expenditures
1960	626.3	461.9	197.9	$3466
1965	814.5	591.3	276.3	4192
1970	1148.6	820.0	424.3	5602
1975	1458.1	1051.8	560.9	6751
1980	1554.2	1150.6	567.5	6825
1985	1857.9	1379.9	620.1	7791
1986	1941.2	1429.2	661.6	8066
1987	1979.2	1431.3	686.0	8151
1988	2000.9	1441.4	703.0	8166
1989	2039.6	1465.2	719.5	8246
1990	2099.0	1497.1	756.2	8399
1991	2125.3	1504.5	792.3	8412
1992	2242.3	1606.3	823.0	8779
1993	2264.1	1613.9	846.0	8771
1994	2281.6	1612.0	871.0	8753
1995	2326.4	1638.3	895.1	8844

SOURCE: Council of Economic Advisers, *Economic Report of the President* (Washington, D.C.: U. S. Government Printing Office, 1996), pp. 315, 371.

NOTE: Federal grants-in-aid to state and local governments are counted as federal government expenditures. The "All Governments" total has omitted the double counting. Dollar figures converted to 1995 dollars by the authors.

TRENDS IN GOVERNMENT EXPENDITURES   In Table 11.2, total expenditures are broken down into federal government expenditures and state and local government expenditures. Federal expenditures (which include grants-in-aid—cash distributions—to state and local governments) exceed state and local expenditures by a fairly constant proportion. Up to the early 1900s, local government expenditures exceeded the sum of federal and state expenditures. The Reagan administration attempted to return the provision and financing of many government goods and services to state and local entities, which caused many state and local governments to reorient their fiscal activities. This policy was dubbed the "New Federalism" because it sought a return to the fiscal system that existed prior to the 1930s in the United States.

Per household and per capita government expenditures at all levels have increased in the last few decades. Not only has the absolute level of expenditures increased, but the level of government expenditures as a percentage of GDP has simultaneously increased. Government expenditures at all levels increased from

FIGURE 11.1

Government Expenditures as a Percent of GDP, 1960–1995

Government expenditures at all levels have grown to over 30 percent of GDP, although they have fluctuated widely—especially during wartime; note for example the huge increase during the World War II era due to increased defense spending.

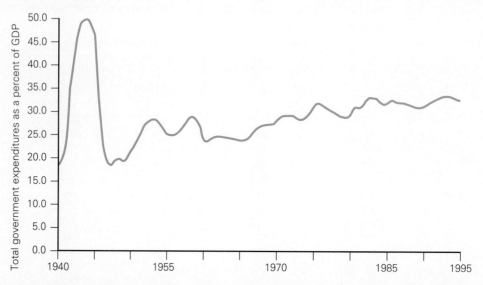

SOURCE: Council of Economic Advisers, *Economic Report of the President* (Washington, D.C.: U.S. Government Printing Office, 1979 and 1996), pp. 282, 371.

21.3 percent of GDP in 1950 to 23 percent in 1960, 28 percent in 1970, and 32 percent in 1986; the percentage declined slightly in the late 1980s before beginning to increase again at the present (see Figure 11.1).

Since the 1950s, federal government expenditures have increased most in the area of transfer payments, a trend that was sharply reinforced in the 1960s under the Great Society policies of the Lyndon Johnson administration. These Great Society policies expanded the welfare system, setting such expenditures at a sharply increasing rate of growth. As shown in Figure 11.2, the trend in federal expenditures on national defense declined as the percentage of outlays on social programs rose. Figure 11.2 also shows that the trend in these two broad expenditure classes reversed slightly under the Reagan administration, which emphasized defense readiness and military parity, or equality, with the Soviet Union. Further changes may be expected as the military is "downsized" in the post–Cold War era.

Direct purchases of goods and services by the federal government also have increased in absolute terms but have decreased as a percentage of total expenditures. Direct purchases at state and local levels exceed those of the federal government. Such a result is not surprising when you consider the programs offered. Most streets, roads, and highways, police and fire protection, hospitals, education, and sewage and garbage disposal are provided by state and local governments. Indeed, state and local governments probably have a greater fiscal influence on our daily lives than does the federal government.

FIGURE 11.2

Defense and Social
Programs as a
Percent of
Government
Expenditures,
1920–1992

Expenditures in these two categories of government finance
have fluctuated through time.
In percentage terms, social
programs have grown dramatically since the mid-1950s and
the Great Society programs of
the 1960s, while defense has
generally declined since 1950.

SOURCE: Council of Economic Advisers,
Economic Report of the President (Wash-
ington, D.C.: U.S. Government Printing
Office, 1993), p. 441.

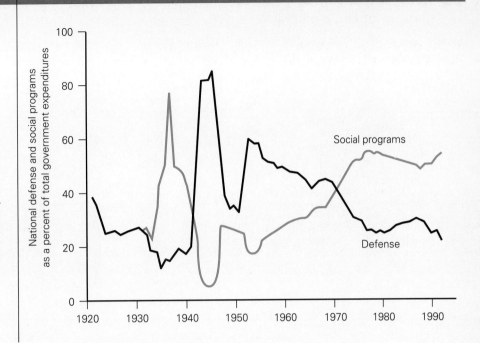

DISCRETIONARY POLICY AND THE LEVEL OF GOVERNMENT SPENDING

Aspects of government finance at the various levels are critical to understanding
the expenditure side of discretionary fiscal policy. Unquestionably, the expenditures of states, counties, townships, and cities have an impact on cycles of inflation and unemployment. Emphasis on the effectiveness of discretionary fiscal
policy must be placed on *federal* policies, however, and the reason is not hard to
understand. State and local governments, in most cases, *must* rely on tax sources
to finance government expenditures. Most states and lower units of government,
for example, are constitutionally forced to balance their budgets. (The predicament
of states is this: A state cannot use its fiscal policy to help the country out of a recession, and it is difficult for a state to recover from a recession while the country
is in one.) Although some governmental entities may borrow (largely through bond
sales) to finance longer-term projects and budget deficits, their ability to sustain
large debt is limited. Unlike the federal government, they do not have the power to
print money and to engage in massive levels of debt. The result is that budget policy at the state and lower levels of government tends to be procyclical in character—expenditures are reduced on the downswing due to reduced tax collections and
increased on the upswing when tax revenues are rising. In periods of economic distress and widespread unemployment, for example, these levels of government are
forced to cut back on all kinds of goods, purchases, and services. For example, the
weakening of OPEC in the early 1980s and the consequent fall in oil prices caused
recessions and reduced tax revenues in the oil-producing states of Texas,
Louisiana, and Oklahoma. These states' response was, at least in the short run, to
reduce expenditures on goods and services, such as road repair, public education,
and county and city services of all types. This response is said to be procyclical

FIGURE 11.3

Distribution of Government Revenue

Income taxes are the largest source of federal revenue. State and local governments receive most of their revenue from sales and property taxes.

<table>
<tr><td align="center">(a) 1995 Federal Government Revenue</td><td align="center">(b) 1995 State and Local
Government Revenue</td></tr>
</table>

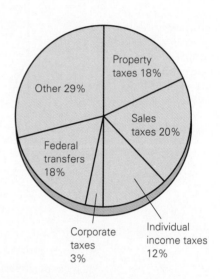

SOURCE: Council of Economic Advisers, *Economic Report of the President* (Washington, D.C.: U.S. Government Printing Office, 1996), pp. 370, 375.

rather than countercyclical in character because discretionary policy would call for increased government expenditures and/or reduced taxes in the face of recession and unemployment. Indeed, the fact that state and local fiscal policy tends to be procyclical in nature is itself important for the conduct of discretionary policy at the federal level.

Tax Revenues

Bonds

Financial instruments that create future obligations on the part of the issuers to make principal repayments and interest payments.

The two basic methods of financing public expenditures are taxing and borrowing. State and local governments usually borrow, as we have stated, by selling **bonds** to finance special projects such as highways, schools, or hospitals, but their access to such funds is limited by their ability to meet future obligations—that is, by their financial soundness and the faith that they will be able to pay off debt in the future. The federal government has come to use borrowing as a routine means of financing its burgeoning deficit, a practice that might eventually create economic problems of its own. Nevertheless, the largest portion of government expenditures is still financed by taxes. As shown in Figure 11.3a, the largest single source of federal tax revenues is the personal income tax, followed closely by Social Security taxes.

Property taxes and sales taxes are the two largest contributors to combined state and local government revenues. Figure 11.3b shows that sales taxes account for a larger percentage of tax revenues of state and local governments than any other tax. One thing is not apparent from Figure 11.3b: Property tax revenues have not been rising as rapidly as sales and income tax revenues. This indicates that property owners are being taxed relatively less over time than other groups.

EQUITABLE TAXATION: THEORIES ABOUT WHO SHOULD PAY   Given government's need for tax revenues, how should taxes be levied among the people? While voter-taxpayer resistance to specific forms of taxation is always a factor to consider since incumbent politicians must face voters after tax increases, the issue of tax equity is also important. Our society attempts to find an equitable way of distributing the tax burden, but there are no easy formulas for determining what is truly equitable. Theoretically, there are two basic methods by which we may determine who should be taxed and by how much: the benefit principle and the ability-to-pay principle. While these principles are not directly concerned with the impact of discretionary fiscal policy, they are worth mentioning briefly here.

Benefit principle
A method of determining individuals' tax burdens on the basis of the beneficiaries of the expenditures that are financed by taxes; an example is a gasoline tax.

Many taxes arise from the **benefit principle,** which means simply that individuals who receive the most benefits from government goods and services should pay the most for their production. Public transport facilities such as buses or subways, publicly owned electrical, water, and gas utilities, and toll roads charge users for the services provided. Many goods, such as national defense, interstate highways, and some educational facilities, provide indirect benefits to citizens that are not easily calculated. Some individuals receiving government benefits cannot always afford to pay an equitable share of taxes, even if the benefits they receive could be calculated exactly. For these reasons, most taxes are based on the ability-to-pay principle.

Ability-to-pay principle
A method of determining individuals' tax burdens on the basis of those most capable of paying taxes.

According to the **ability-to-pay principle** of taxation, those who are more able to pay should pay more taxes than those less able to pay. Under this principle, levels of an individual's income, wealth, or expenditures are measures frequently used for determining the level of tax obligation. There is general agreement that the wealthy should pay more taxes than the poor, but the question of how much more is not easily resolved.

FEDERAL TAXATION, TAX REFORM, AND FISCAL POLICY

All taxation at federal, state, and local levels alike has a direct impact on the overall economy through its effect on individuals. The very *fact* of taxation means that income is withdrawn from the private sector of the economy, reducing aggregate demand. On the other side, the very *fact* that governments at all levels spend means that governments affect aggregate demand. A *change* in government spending or taxation also will have effects on economic stabilization, *whether or not the effects are intended.*

When examining discretionary fiscal policy, however, we may provisionally ignore taxing and spending systems that are procyclical in nature and concentrate instead on those types of expenditures and taxes that may be used intentionally to affect aggregate demand. State and local spending and taxing policies certainly affect the economy. But such taxes and expenditures may be downplayed when discussing discretionary changes in fiscal accounts because they tend to be pro-cyclical in nature. Likewise, some taxes collected at the federal level, such as Social Security taxes, will clearly affect aggregate demand in the economy. But they are not, in the usual case, the taxes used to conduct discretionary policy in dealing with cyclical swings in unemployment and inflation.

Income and Corporate Taxes

Federal taxes on both individuals and on corporations were significantly altered in 1913 with the passage of the Sixteenth Amendment. This amendment allowed the federal government to levy income taxes on U.S. citizens. After its inception, the income tax system grew rapidly in size and complexity.

Beginning in 1966, the issue of tax reform was uppermost in political rhetoric. In 1976, President Carter called the U.S. tax system "a disgrace to the human race" due to its confusing and complex provisions. The major criticism of the tax system was the number and kinds of items allowed both individuals and corporations as deductions from income. Rather than viewing the tax system as primarily a means of generating revenue, federal taxation was used for a number of other purposes. Special breaks were given to individuals and to corporations, for example, for in-vestment purposes. The **investment tax credit** was instituted (in the early 1960s) on the principle that the tax code should encourage industrial modernization. Ac-celerated depreciation of business investments also was featured for the same pur-pose. Other deductions for both individuals and businesses were introduced, creating a tax code of incredible complexity and inequity.

Most economists believed that the tax code was inequitable and that it estab-lished counterproductive incentives for individuals and businesses. Tax "shelters" were sought and used to generate income losses to deduct from regular reportable income. The availability of tax shelters led to investments that generated loss po-tential rather than economic growth, which in turn weakened the economy. High marginal tax rates, moreover, may have caused individuals to work less or to work in the underground (untaxed) economy. Further, huge quantities of resources were employed in finding loopholes (tax provisions that generated tax-lowering deduc-tions) in the tax laws.

Investment tax credit
A percentage or amount of new investment expenditure that is directly subtracted from the investor's tax bill in calculating total taxes.

TAX CHANGES IN 1986 AND 1993   In the largest tax overhaul since World War II, Congress passed the Tax Reform Act of 1986. One major thrust of the reform was to scale down individual and corporate tax rates and to reduce tax complexity. (Figure 11.4 summarizes tax rates from 1913 to 1993.) Initially, two tax brackets replaced the 14 in place previously, and a maximum marginal tax rate of 28 percent replaced the old top rate of 50 percent. (For a time, a 5 per-cent surcharge was applied to certain income groups, effectively creating a maxi-mum rate of 33 percent.) Another major accomplishment of the act was the reduction and standardization of exemptions. While both individual and corpo-rate rates fell as a result of the 1986 law, more income was taxable, as many de-ductions were eliminated.

FIGURE 11.4

Summary of Individual and Corporate Tax Rates, 1913–1993

Individual and corporate tax rates have varied widely since 1913, with individual rates reaching a maximum marginal rate of 90 percent. The Omnibus Budget Reconciliation Act of 1993 set the maximum marginal rate on individuals at 39.6 percent and the maximum marginal rate on corporations at 35 percent.

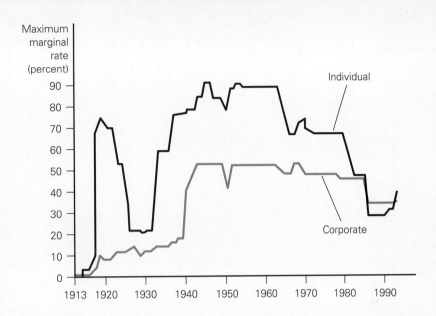

The Tax Reform Act of 1986 was also designed to provide more equity. Partly as a result of increased personal exemptions, millions of low-income families were completely removed from the tax rolls. In addition, the elimination of many tax loopholes forced more well-to-do Americans to pay their fair share of taxes.

The Omnibus Budget Reconciliation Act of 1993, the official name of the Clinton administration's deficit-reduction package, went a long way toward reversing the simplification of the U.S. tax system that was achieved in 1986. This piece of legislation added a marginal rate of 36 percent for individuals with incomes in excess of $115,000 and couples with more than $140,000 in annual taxable income. (Taxable income is the amount of income left over after subtracting personal exemptions and itemized deductions such as casualty losses and mortgage interest.) A new 10 percent surcharge on taxable income above $250,000 meant that the maximum marginal rate in 1993 was effectively 39.6 percent.

In addition to changing the personal income tax structure, the 1993 budget bill increased the corporate tax rate from 34 percent to 35 percent and raised the federal excise tax on gasoline. Another significant change was the repeal of the so-called "luxury tax" on purchases of boats, aircraft, jewelry, and furs, which was enacted during the Bush administration (the tax on purchases of luxury cars—those with a sticker price of $30,000 or more—remained in place, however).

Flat tax
A single tax rate levied on all income.

A FLAT TAX?   Today, the talk in the air is about a **flat tax**, a proposal that would radically simplify the federal tax system. There are several different flat tax proposals, but essentially the flat tax envisions a tax return that can be filled out on the back of a postcard. This system would feature *one* tax rate for all income levels and for *all* income. In other words, how much did you make last year? Multiply it by, say, 17 percent, and send it in. There would be no deductions or other complications. The

FIGURE 11.5

Deficits Over Time and as a Percentage of GDP

While the size of the federal deficit has grown over time, the deficit as a percent of GDP has remained fairly stable. This result is not surprising, since GDP is growing also.

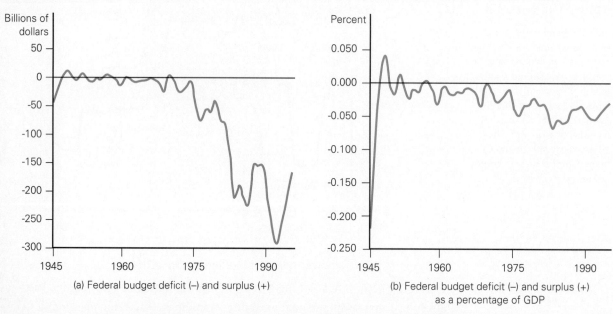

(a) Federal budget deficit (–) and surplus (+)

(b) Federal budget deficit (–) and surplus (+) as a percentage of GDP

SOURCE: Council of Economic Advisers, *Economic Report of the President* (Washington, D.C.: U.S. Government Printing Office, 1996), p. 367.

debate over such proposals has been intense. Proponents argue that it will stimulate economic growth and compliance with the tax laws. Opponents suggest that it is not fair and that it is a tax break for the wealthy. Taxpayers seem to love the idea of simpler taxes; tax preparers, such as H & R Block, are dead set against such proposals. It is difficult to tell at this point what the political fate of the flat tax will be.

DEFICITS, DEBTS, AND FISCAL POLICY

High deficits in the 1980s and 1990s alarmed voters, economists, and politicians. Just what are the effects of huge deficits and the growing federal debt they have created?

Growing Deficits

As we have shown, deficits are created when government expenditures exceed revenues from taxation. Figure 11.5 provides a disturbing portrait of the emerging deficit situation. Since local and state governments tend to have balanced budgets, the overall government deficit is created primarily at the federal level. Large deficits have been a feature of federal finance since 1960, but in the mid-1970s, their magnitude began to grow. In the 1980s, the federal deficit showed explosive growth. The deficit reached $200 billion in 1986 and has remained alarmingly high since then. Despite some recent progress (see Figure 11.5), the annual federal deficit remains a serious problem. Deficits of these magnitudes did not emerge overnight. The fiscal pressures of the Vietnam War, the social programs of the

**"Harry, she just said her first words!
She said, 'Why have you saddled my
generation with the huge national debt?'"**

© 1996 Joseph Farris from The Cartoon Bank™, Inc.

Great Society of the 1960s, the modernization of national defense by the Reagan administration, and so on—all added to contemporary deficit problems. There would be no deficit if Congress and presidential administrations were willing to tax in order to pay for government goods. Their unwillingness to do so means that the resulting deficits, or additions to the total federal debt, must be financed.

Deficits, Fiscal Policy, and Crowding Out

How else could the federal government finance a deficit in its accounts? Since the federal government is allowed to print money, it could simply create money to finance the shortfall between expenditures and receipts. The creation of money, discussed in the next few chapters, would erode the purchasing power of individuals' money holdings. The effect would approximate taxation, since resources are shifted to government from the private sector without the explicit consent of the governed.

The federal deficit is financed primarily through the sale of bonds to both individuals and privately owned commercial banks. Predictably, increases in the supply of bonds resulting from deficit financing lower bond prices. As the price of a bond declines, however, its interest rate rises. Thus, increases in the supply of bonds raise interest rates and channel private saving from private investment into government expenditures. When bonds are sold directly to individuals (EE or HH savings bonds, Treasury bills and notes, and such) or to commercial banks, pressure is placed on private investment if additional funds are not saved. This phenomenon, known as **crowding out**, means that, depending on the reaction of savers and investors to the rise in interest rates, government borrowing may crowd out private investment. If private investment is discouraged, the rise in the

Crowding out
The competitive pressure exerted on private investment by government expenditures.

interest rate may reduce the long-term growth prospects of the economy—unless individuals react to the increased deficit by saving more for future generations.

The high interest rates that result from government deficits may also lead to another type of crowding out—the displacement of domestically produced goods by foreign goods. As we will explain in more detail in Chapter 17, high interest rates in the United States make U.S. dollars attractive to foreign investors. This increase in demand for the dollar causes its price to rise in world markets; that is, the amount of a foreign currency that can be obtained for one dollar increases. For example, instead of getting 90 yen for a dollar, high interest rates in the United States may make it possible to obtain 100 yen. As a consequence, foreign goods become cheaper to Americans, but American goods become more expensive to foreign buyers. This leads to an increase in U.S. imports and a decrease in U.S. exports—both of which cause aggregate demand to shift to the left. In this way, an increase in the government's budget deficit crowds out private spending by both domestic and foreign buyers.

Often when the Treasury finances a government deficit, the Federal Reserve attempts to prevent interest rates from rising by simultaneously buying bonds on the open market. This might temporarily keep interest rates down and prevent crowding out, but it causes the money supply to rise, which ultimately leads to inflation and higher interest rates.

Deficits and the Federal Debt

Internally held debt
The amount of a country's total federal debt that is owned by the country's various governments, businesses, and individuals.

Externally held debt
The amount of a country's total federal debt that is owned by foreign governments, businesses, and individuals.

Large deficits have created a total federal debt of more than $5 trillion in 1996. In order to assess its importance, it is instructive to see who owns the debt.

Table 11.3 shows the composition of debt ownership in 1995. Ownership of the federal debt is dispersed among private individuals, banks, and foreigners. Most of the debt is thus **internally held debt,** with a sizable portion held by individuals and banks outside the United States. (The importance of this **externally held debt**—claims or IOUs against U.S. resources by foreigners—is discussed in the Focus "Who Bears the Burden of the Debt?".)

TABLE 11.3

Ownership of the Federal Debt in 1995

The federal debt is owned, or held, by various groups. This table shows the distribution of ownership of the federal debt in 1995. All numbers are in billions of dollars.

Type of Holder		Amount (billions of dollars)
Total federal debt:	4974.4	
Total U.S. government ownership:		1694.9
U.S. government agencies		1320.8
Federal Reserve		374.1
Total private ownership:		3279.5
Commercial banks		295.0
Other U.S. financial institutions		543.3
Individuals		345.9
Foreign ownership		847.8
Other, including state and local governments		1247.5

SOURCE: Federal Reserve Bulletin (May 1996), p. A30.

focus   Who Bears the Burden of the Debt?

Deficits occur when government expenditures exceed the taxes necessary to finance them. When the government borrows to finance these deficits, debt is created. The federal government has created debt from the very beginnings of the nation. Likewise, the debate over such policies is an ancient one among economists, politicians, and voters. In the nineteenth century and for part of the twentieth, sizable debt was issued before and during wartime, with repayment effected through taxation after war's end. Modern times have witnessed the explosion of bond-financed deficits and a federal debt reaching more than $5 trillion in 1996. Does the sheer size of the debt forebode disaster? Are we burdening our children, grandchildren, and more remote descendants with the disastrous prospect of having to pay our debts back?

As a way to begin answering these questions, we again point out that it is most unlikely that the federal government of the United States will ever have to declare bankruptcy. Since the federal government is permitted (by the Constitution) to print money, the debt could be covered, if necessary and perhaps with ill consequences, in this fashion. Further, since the rate of growth in GDP exceeds the growth rate of the debt, the economy is (in a real sense of productivity) able to "stand" the growth in the debt. But problems associated with bankruptcy are not what economists contemplate when discussing the burden of the debt.

Economists usually think in intergenerational terms when discussing the possible effects of debt. They are concerned with whether government debt is borne solely or only partly by present or future generations. One idea prevalent in the post-Keynesian period is that "we owe the debt to ourselves" and that, therefore, it is not a problem to be very concerned about. A simplified version of this view, attributed to economist Abba Lerner, asks the questions, "Who owns the debt?" and "Who owes the debt?" Since the answer in both cases is "Americans," Lerner concluded that we owe the debt to ourselves.[a]

While some of our children will inherit debt through taxation, others (or the same individuals) also will inherit claims (government bonds) to offset these debts.

However, a number of matters arise when we consider Lerner's proposition. In the first place, what if foreign individuals and governments hold some of our debt? Over $800 billion of the U.S. debt was so held in 1995. These foreign-held bonds represent real claims against the resources and output of the United States.

Another important matter is that the issue of debt by the federal government may have distributional effects over time. Bonds are usually purchased by high-income groups in our economy, but taxes are paid by all income ranges. Total economic well-being may be affected when a burden is placed on some Americans to the benefit of other Americans. Depending on propensities to consume, total private expenditures may be biased downward when debt is repaid from overall taxation to the upper-income groups over time.

Then there is the necessity of paying interest on the bonds that comprise the debt. Unless there is a declaration of bankruptcy, interest payments must be paid. They are, as Social Security has become, an untouchable area of the federal budget. During periods of high interest rates, this burden can become especially acute, putting demands on the tax system or on new debt finance. (In 1995, these interest payments were over $200 billion, a significant part of the total federal budget.)

Nobel laureate James M. Buchanan argues that the effects taxation and debt have on present and future generations are *not* equivalent due to the fact that interest payments place a burden on present and future taxpayers.[b] When debt is created, buyers and sellers engage in voluntary exchange and therefore cannot be made worse off. But when it becomes necessary to pay interest on government bonds, taxation is

[a]Abba P. Lerner, "The Burden of the National Debt," in *Income, Employment, and Public Policy* (New York: W.W. Norton and Company, 1948).

[b]James M. Buchanan, *Public Principles of Public Debt* (Homewood, Ill: Richard D. Irwin, 1958).

required, and it is not voluntary. Future generations, therefore, do bear at least a portion of the burden of the debt.

Economists disagree over the question of where the burden of debt should be placed. The issue of whether our grandchildren will bear a portion of the burden of present government expenditures is an open one, but at least some effects of debt are passed on.

The Effects of the Federal Debt

Many economists, citizens, and politicians argue that the growing federal debt is a grave present and future problem for the economy and for economic growth. Their concerns relate to (1) the supposed relation between the size of the debt, inflation, and interest rates and (2) the possible burden of the debt on present and future generations.

DEBT, INFLATION, AND INTEREST RATES   Depending on how government debt is financed, it tends either to raise interest rates or to cause inflation. When the U.S. Treasury places bonds up for sale, it has no control over who the purchaser will be—that depends on who is willing to pay the most for the bonds. When the highest bidders are individuals, business firms, or financial institutions, the deficit will drive up interest rates by the amount necessary to attract these buyers. At other times, the bonds will be purchased by the Federal Reserve, the central banking authority in the United States. (The details of such purchases will be made much clearer in Chapter 12.) Purchase by the Federal Reserve tends to keep interest rates down (at least in the short run), but it can lead to higher inflation in the future. (Again, Chapters 12–13 will make it clear why this is likely.) The upshot is that financing the deficit inevitably leads to higher interest rates, inflation, or both—something to consider when such deficits are recommended.

ARE DEFICITS AND DEBT A BURDEN ON FUTURE GENERATIONS? Economists are divided on the issue of whether the federal debt is a burden on future generations. The preponderance of opinion is that it is not, although the issue is far from settled.

How can this opinion be justified? First, the U.S. government will go bankrupt only if the government cannot meet all the debt claims that it issues. This is unlikely. If economic growth and the tax receipts that it brings continue at vigorous levels, the government will have no trouble meeting its obligations.

Other troublesome features of a large public debt are more subtle. Economic growth may be retarded if deficit and debt crowd out private investment expenditures. If private-sector expenditures are directed to more efficient and cost-effective investments, as they are under the revised tax system, productive expenditures might be crowded out by possibly less-productive government expenditures through government bond sales.

Ownership of the debt, moreover, might create other problems. A portion of the debt is owned by middle- to high-income families, although pension funds, which tend to be owned by low- to middle-income families, are also invested heavily in government bonds and notes. To the extent that future generations must finance present debt through tax payments, the burden of the debt will fall upon *all* future taxpayers. In other words, that portion of the debt owned by upper income groups will be paid for by all income groups in society in the future; some income will be intergenerationally redistributed from poor to rich.

Discretionary fiscal policy may be influenced in several ways by the existence of the large federal debt. In 1995, almost 15 percent of total federal expenditures was composed of interest payments on the federal debt. A growing proportion of interest payments to total federal expenditures creates a growing problem with both the size of the annual deficit and the ability of Congress to manipulate expenditures and taxes to control periodic swings in the business cycle. At times, growing interest payments may help create larger deficits, which, in turn, create larger debt, and so on. In other words, it is possible that the debt is self-perpetuating.

Can the Federal Deficits and Debt Be Controlled?
While it is easy to become unduly alarmed over deficits and the mounting federal debt, some real problems do exist. Economic growth and income distribution may be influenced in undesirable ways by growing debt and the problems (such as interest payments) that accompany it. Moreover, if discretionary fiscal policy is destabilizing, as some economists argue, efforts to balance the budget may bring some stability to the economy.

In late 1985, the U.S. Congress passed the Balanced Budget and Emergency Deficit Reduction Control Act (or Gramm-Rudman-Hollings) in an attempt to deal with growing deficits and debt. Gramm-Rudman-Hollings was supposed to "prorate," or automatically reduce, federal government expenditures when Congress did not come within preset deficit guidelines for the period 1986–1991. In the end, however, various political and legal challenges rendered the act ineffective at controlling deficits. In the early 1990s, the issue of deficit reduction rose to a position near the top of the national political agenda. In the 1992 presidential campaign, independent candidate Ross Perot focused on the issue and garnered nearly one-fifth of the vote. Perot's strong showing and post-election popularity suggested that many Americans were concerned about the effects of the federal government's huge budget deficits on their lives (see the Application, "Deficits, Debt, and the Average American"). In the spring of 1993, the Clinton administration responded to the growing concern about the federal debt by unveiling a controversial deficit-reduction plan. Opponents faulted the plan for relying too heavily on higher taxes and not enough on spending cuts. Still, by the narrowest of margins, a modified version of the Clinton plan gained congressional approval in the summer of 1993. All parties agreed, however, that this action represented only the first step in bringing the government's deficits under control. In 1995 and 1996 the Republican-led Congress pushed hard for a 7-year program to balance the budget—one that includes reductions in the rate of growth in many cherished programs including Medicare and Medicaid. The sheer size of the deficit and debt make some kind of actions to bring it under control inevitable. The implication of deficit-reduction efforts are far-reaching: The entire question of whether discretionary fiscal policy can be effective in controlling unemployment and inflation is intimately bound to tax, spending, and budget policies, as well as to constraints at the federal level of government.

Today, the argument has become not whether to balance the budget, but how? Some prefer a balanced budget amendment and others discretionary tax increases and expenditure reductions. This is an historic argument over the role and size of government in the economy, the outcome of which is not yet determined.

APPLICATION
Deficits, Debt, and the Average American

Deficits have long been part of the American political and economic scene; since 1960, the federal government has run a budget surplus only once, and federal expenditures have continued to grow as a percentage of gross domestic product. Since 1982, deficits have been more than $100 billion every year. Remember that annual deficits are simply added to previously incurred government debt. By early 1996, the federal debt had topped $5 trillion. That figure is perhaps easier to understand if it is given in terms of each American's share of the debt: about $19,000 in 1996.

Changes in the relative size of the debt are even more distressing. Outstanding federal debt was 34 percent of gross domestic product in 1980, but just ten years later it was a full 70 percent of GDP. Not since the World War II era have these levels of debt been reached in the United States. Moreover, for the privilege of incurring debt, government must service it annually. The interest payment on debt service is now the third largest expenditure in the federal budget.

Much of the credit for bringing the magnitude of the problem to the attention of average Americans goes to Texas billionaire and independent presidential candidate Ross Perot. Perot made deficit reduction the centerpiece of his 1992 campaign and effectively used charts and graphs to demonstrate the severity of the problem. But what do deficits and debt really mean to the average individual? In any given year, government spending is paid for by taxes and by borrowing (issuing government bonds to cover the deficit). Tax payments made to finance government spending reduce private spending on homes, movies, and vacations (and some saving as well) up to the total amount of the tax paid. Because tax payments to government have been insufficient to cover federal spending, the government has also been forced to issue bonds. The "excess spending" generated—that not covered by taxes—competes directly in markets for resources and drives prices up for consumers. There is thus an inflationary bias in deficit spending.

Deficits do the most overall harm in the area of investment and capital formation—the very heart of economic progress and job growth. When the federal government balances its budget, it does not intervene in the capital market. Savers lend money to borrowers, who, in turn, build houses, start businesses, install new equipment, and hire labor. The market sets the interest rate so that the amount saved is roughly equal to the amount borrowed. These productive investments help pay off the loans and interest.

When the federal government enters credit markets by issuing bonds, however, it crowds out private investment. Interest rates are forced higher because of the government's demand, with the result that fewer private loans make economic sense to lenders. Therefore, fewer productive investments are made for the future. There has been chronically low investment in capital in the United States since the early 1980s and sharply reduced productivity of labor (due to the fact that labor has less capital to work with). Lower investment due, in large part, to mounting debt since 1981 has also resulted in fewer new factories, less new machinery, and anemic growth in research spending. The government may also make productive investments, but it now most often borrows for consumption purposes or for "investments" of dubious value—such as the multibillion dollar supercollider or regional waterways. Many of these expenditures may be as productive as private sector investments, but others are simply unnecessary and occur solely for political purposes.

With $5+ trillion in federal debt to pay off and $300 billion or so coming due each year, the government has three basic options: (1) It can pay off deficit and debt by increasing taxes and/or slowing spending increases; (2) it can print money and create inflation; or (3) it can continue to borrow more money by rolling the debt over onto future generations. (On the latter point, see the Focus in this chapter.) What does all of this mean for the average American? If inflation is expected to increase dramatically, the average individual will want to borrow and buy real estate on fixed-rate mortgages and/or invest in such "hard" assets as fine art or gold. (Inflation has been the solution opted for by bankrupt governments from ancient Greece to modern-day Brazil.) If government continues to borrow heavily, the average citizen may count on lower taxes and a higher return on savings, but this will be accompanied by lower growth rates and job creation than previous generations of Americans have experienced.

The first option we mentioned—increasing taxes and/or decreasing spending—is perhaps the only long-term solution that is compatible with continued U.S. economic growth. This solution, however, is the most difficult to enact in a representative democracy, as demonstrated by the battle over the Clinton administration's tax-dependent deficit-reduction plan in the spring and summer of 1993 and in the ongoing political fight over how to balance the budget in 1995 and 1996. Tax increases and deep spending cuts both appear to be politically unpalatable. History tells us that the political process is unlikely to voluntarily control spending and deficits. Therefore, relatively unconstrained spending will likely remain a feature of the U.S. government without a law requiring Congress to balance the budget.

It is certain that tax increases and most spending cuts will continue to be unpopular. In the absence of attempts to reduce deficits, however, high rates of economic growth are unlikely as the United States enters the twenty-first century. Until the deficit-debt problem is resolved, many economists believe that long-term attempts to deal with poverty, health care, homelessness, and economic security of all kinds will be met with frustration.

QUESTIONS

Why haven't Congress and the president been able to balance the budget without running deficits? How would a constitutional amendment requiring a balanced budget work? What would happen in the event of a national emergency?

SUMMARY

1. Fiscal policy is the intentional manipulation of government expenditures and receipts to control cycles of unemployment and inflation in the economy. Its role is to help provide, along with monetary policy, stable growth in the economy without inflation.
2. While from a Keynesian perspective budgets are to be balanced over the business cycle, perennial deficits have been a feature of federal finance for more than 30 years. The mounting debt that these yearly deficits have produced has been a cause of concern.
3. Automatic stabilizers exist within the framework of government finance, wherein the levels of tax receipts and expenditures vary with rising and falling incomes in the economy, although they do not replace discre-

tionary actions on the part of the president and Congress. They are not sufficient to produce a cyclically balanced budget.
4. Taxing and spending policies of states, counties, townships, and cities have an impact on cycles of inflation and employment, but these entities have a limited ability to engage in deficit finance. Budgets at these levels tend to be balanced and procyclical in character.
5. There are two basic principles of taxation: the benefit principle and the ability-to-pay principle, where those who are more able to pay actually pay more in taxes.
6. With a progressive tax, individuals pay a larger percentage of their income in taxes as their income rises. A proportional tax takes a constant percentage of

income for taxes. A regressive tax takes a smaller percentage of income as income rises.

7. The Tax Reform Act of 1986 simplified many aspects of the tax structure, including reducing the number of income tax brackets and reducing the complexity of tax deductions. More recent changes have, in general, made the tax system more complex.

8. Many economists and politicians warn that allowing the federal debt to grow as it did throughout the 1980s and early 1990s will have serious consequences for economic growth and the distribution of income.

KEY TERMS

automatic stabilizers	budget deficit	ability-to-pay principle
proportional income tax	cyclically balanced budget	investment tax credit
progressive income tax	federal debt	flat tax
regressive income tax	public finance	crowding out
marginal tax rate	bonds	internally held debt
budget surplus	benefit principle	externally held debt

QUESTIONS FOR REVIEW AND DISCUSSION

1. Mention and discuss three automatic or uncontrollable expenditures in the federal budget. How large are controllable or alterable federal expenditures relative to those that are less easy to change?

2. Name the principles of discretionary budget policy.

3. If the federal government had both a capital budget and a current-expenses budget, which budget would contain federal spending on education?

4. Name and discuss two important trends in spending at the federal level and at the state and local levels of government.

5. What is public finance? Are the principles of public finance the same as those of personal finance? If not, how do they differ?

6. Clearly distinguish between progressive and regressive taxation, giving examples of each.

7. What are some of the economic advantages to society of the Tax Reform Act of 1986 over the previously existing tax code?

8. Economist Abba Lerner once observed that we owe the federal debt to "ourselves." Explain whether you agree or disagree with this proposition, and why.

9. How would you control deficits and debt at the federal level? Is a constitutional amendment the answer? Why or why not?

10. How do classical and Keynesian views on balanced budgets differ?

11. What are the methods used for financing government expenditures? How do state and local governments differ from the federal government in their reliance on these methods?

12. Politicians usually claim that they strive for "fairness" in determining the nation's tax structure. The concept of "fairness" usually implies taxing the wealthy at a much higher rate than the poor—in other words, imposing a progressive tax. Analyze excise taxes on tobacco and alcohol on the basis of fairness.

13. Do you think the ability-to-pay principle or the benefit principle is more appropriate for the following government expenditures?
    a. national defense
    b. fire protection
    c. public schooling
    d. drug enforcement
    e. foreign aid
    f. health care

PROBLEMS

1. George and James are two taxpayers with different incomes. George's annual income is $65,000; James earns $40,000 per year. The amounts each taxpayer would owe under three different income tax proposals are given below. Calculate the tax rates for each taxpayer and tell whether the tax would be proportional, progressive, or regressive.
   a. George—$5200; James—$3200
   b. George—$8450; James—$2400
   c. George—$4550; James —$4800

2. Suppose that the table shows the country of Macroland's annual fiscal standing for six recent years. Assume that interest payments on the debt are covered by government expenditures and that budget surpluses are used to retire the debt. (Amounts shown are in billions of dollars.)

Year	Government Expenditures	Tax Revenues	Deficit (-) or Surplus (+)	Debt
1	$1800	$1800	$——	$ 0
2	1180	1780	——	——
3	2200	——	-1500	——
4	——	2100	——	500
5	——	2400	+100	——
6	2500	2600	——	——

a. Calculate the missing data.
b. What factors might affect government expenditures and tax receipts from year to year?

JOHN MAYNARD KEYNES   JOSEPH A. SCHUMPETER

J. M. Keynes and Joseph Schumpeter: Intervention or Innovation?

John Maynard Keynes (1883–1946) was the son of John Neville Keynes, a famous logician and writer on economic method. Educated at Eton and later at King's College, Cambridge, the younger Keynes developed interests in literature, mathematics, and, later, economics. One of his teachers at Cambridge, the neoclassical economist Alfred Marshall, strongly urged Keynes to become an economist.

As an undergraduate, Keynes became an integral part of a small coterie of British intellectuals known as the Bloomsbury Group. Its members included novelist Virginia Woolf and biographer and literary critic Lytton Strachey. The group provided Keynes with an arena for intellectual debate, but he still had to decide on a career.

After a brief stint in a civil service job in London, Keynes returned to Cambridge and became editor of the prestigious *Economic Journal*, a post he held for 33 years. He joined the British treasury in 1915 as a monetary expert and became a key figure representing Britain at the Versailles Peace Conference at the end of World War I. In 1919, he wrote *The Economic Consequences of the Peace*, a condemnation of the Versailles Treaty, which brought him international recognition. He went on to write a *Treatise on Probability* (1921) and to amass a personal fortune in the risky game of speculating in foreign exchange markets.

In the late 1920s, Keynes's interest turned increasingly to the theory and practice of macroeconomics. His productivity was enormous: Major works of the period include the *Treatise on Money* (1930), *Essays in Persuasion* (1931), and *Essays in Biography* (1933). In 1936, Keynes published the work for which he is most famous, *The General Theory of Employment, Interest, and Money*. In this book, Keynes rejected the idea of automatic adjustment in the economy and maintained that public policy

and government expenditure are required for the prevention of economic stagnation and excessive unemployment. During World War II, Keynes negotiated lend-lease programs and was a leading figure in plans to restore the international monetary system. He died of a heart attack soon after the war ended.

Joseph A. Schumpeter (1883–1950) and Keynes were born only a few months apart. Schumpeter was raised in a provincial town in Austria (then Austria-Hungary) and studied law at the University of Vienna, where he also attended seminars on economics led by Carl Menger and Frederick von Weiser, two founders of the neoclassical Austrian school of economics. Schumpeter practiced law briefly before deciding to devote himself to economics. At the age of 28 he produced a brilliant doctoral dissertation, *The Theory of Economic Development* (1911), which brought him recognition as a first-rank theorist. After World War I, Schumpeter served as Austria's minister of finance. Throughout the 1920s, he lectured throughout Europe. In 1932, he emigrated to America and became the senior economics faculty member at Harvard, where he remained until his death.

Schumpeter stands out as an extremely innovative thinker. He rejected many contemporary approaches to macroeconomic theory partly because they were based on pure mathematical insight. Schumpeter preferred to base his theory of economic change on the creative force of the individual, whose social, historical, and psychological dimensions are largely ignored by strict mathematical formulas. Schumpeter is also known for his broadly historical views of the discipline itself, which are presented in the posthumously published *History of Economic Analysis* (1954). Another work, *Capitalism, Socialism, and Democracy* (1942), is famous for its prediction that capitalism will eventually destroy itself, not because of its failures (as a Marxist would contend) but because of its successes.

Fine-Tuning the Engine of Demand

Keynes's central work, *The General Theory of Employment, Interest, and Money*, shared one important characteristic with the work of economist Alfred Marshall: a love for abstraction. Robert Heilbroner calls the *General Theory* "an endless desert of economics, algebra, and abstraction, with trackless wastes of the differential calculus, and only an oasis here and there of delightfully refreshing prose."[a] Beneath the calculus, however, were ideas capable of influencing an entire generation of economists and affecting the economic fortunes of millions of people.

Keynes's great insight rested upon his central abstraction, aggregate demand—in shorthand, $C + I + G + (X - M)$. Unlike his classical and neoclassical predecessors, Keynes believed that insufficient demand, or spending, by consumers would leave the economy in disequilibrium, stagnating permanently below full employment. Accordingly, Keynes focused on means to increase demand through government policies and interventions in the economy.

In Keynesian terms, the economy is inherently unstable yet manageable. Guided by economic variables such as national income and business investment, government policymakers can rely on fiscal measures to increase or decrease aggregate demand in amounts sufficient to restore equilibrium. Individual, or microeconomic, decisions to spend, invest, or save would predictably follow whatever course the fiscal and monetary planners design.

Despite the increased role he recommended for government, Keynes was mistrustful of overreliance on central planning. He wrote the following in response to criticisms by economist Friedrich Hayek that an over-planned economy represents tyranny: "Moderate planning will be safe enough if those carrying it out are rightly oriented in their own minds and hearts to the moral issue (of tyranny)."[b]

Creative Destruction

Whereas Keynes could be said to honor the economist's role in rescuing a stagnant economy, Schumpeter honored the entrepreneur's role. In many respects Keynes viewed the economy from above, from the heights of abstraction. Schumpeter looked from below, from the vantage point of individuals whose risk-taking and profit-seeking behavior spurred innovations and new growth opportunities. Accordingly, Schumpeter looked for ways to ensure free enterprise, not manage it.

To Schumpeter, the tendency of an economy to fall below levels of full employment resulted from shrinking opportunities for profits. As breakthroughs in technology or production occur, inspiring new investment and greater opportunities for profit, the economy generates growth. Schumpeter called the process *creative destruction* of profit opportunities, the continual rebirth of production frontiers.

Schumpeter naturally argued against government intervention and central control of the economy. He was much more mistrustful of the results of fiscal management than Keynes and felt that governmental tyranny would be its inevitable result. The first victim of such tyranny, in Schumpeter's mind, would be the entrepreneurial spirit. As Schumpeter summarized the matter: "The problem that is usually being visualized is how capitalism administers existing structures, whereas the relevant problem is how it creates and destroys them."[c]

[b] Heilbroner, p. 244.

[c] Joseph A. Schumpeter, *Capitalism, Socialism, and Democracy*, 3rd ed. (New York: Harper & Row, 1950), p. 81. Also see the excellent article by Peter Drucker, "Schumpeter and Keynes," *Forbes* (May 23, 1983), pp. 124–128, on which some of the themes of this section are based.

[a] Robert Heilbroner, *The Worldly Philosophers*, rev. ed. (New York: Simon & Schuster, 1961), p. 235.

CHAPTER 12

MONEY, BANKING, AND THE FEDERAL RESERVE

As suggested in our discussion of macroeconomic theory, money is a vital factor in our economy. This chapter and the following explore the nature of money and its economic role. We look at how economists define money, how money functions within the economy, and the reasons people hold and use money. Further, we see how money is related to the banking system and how the banking system itself is regulated by the government.

Money and monetary control are intimately related to the major goals of economic stabilization. Conversely, lack of monetary control can contribute to a society's economic downfall. Before we delve into these issues, our goal in the present chapter is to lay the groundwork for an understanding of the role of money.

Economics is interested in the nature of money and its role in our individual and collective lives. When you complete Chapter 12 you should understand

- the definition of money and the role of commercial banking and other financial institutions in the monetary system of the United States.

- the structure and basic economic functions of the Federal Reserve System.

- how money is created through the banking system.

- how the Federal Reserve System controls money creation.

FUNCTIONS OF MONEY

Barter economy
An economy in which money is not used to facilitate exchange between individuals and firms; goods trade directly for other goods.

Double coincidence of wants
A situation in trading in which each party to the trade has what the other wants and wants what the other has.

Medium of exchange
An item that is generally acceptable as payment for goods and services.

Commodity money
An item that serves as a medium of exchange and that is also a good itself.

To understand the essential functions of money, try to imagine what a society would be like without it. Without the use of money all goods or services would be traded for other goods or services—a **barter economy** would exist. A visit to a psychiatrist, for example, would require a trade of some good or service for an hour on the couch. Suppose that you are the psychiatrist and three potential clients are waiting for your services, each with his or her own item of specialization to trade. Sam offers four hours of typing services, Bill offers three Persian kittens, and Judy, a farmer, offers one fully dressed hog. Will the demanders of psychiatric services be able to trade with you?

The result would depend on whether you, the psychiatrist, demand those goods or services in exchange for your own skills and on whether a price—a certain quantity of pork or kittens or typing services per hour of psychiatry—could be agreed on. In other words, a **double coincidence of wants**—a cat breeder wanting psychiatry and a psychiatrist wanting cats—would be required for a mutually beneficial exchange to take place. It may be that, although not a cat lover yourself, you know someone who would be willing to exchange cassette tapes for Persian cats. In that event, a more complicated set of exchanges might be arranged. But these sorts of trades would require either luck or a great deal of information gathering. Transaction costs—the costs of getting buyers and sellers together for mutually advantageous exchanges—are astronomical in a barter economy. Many mutually beneficial transactions in a money economy could never take place in a barter economy due to high transaction costs.

It is not surprising that where barter is practiced, specialization and trade tend to be at relatively low levels. The high transaction costs associated with barter inhibit specialization and trade. A modern free-trade economy could not be founded on a system of barter because of the system's limiting effects. Money emerged to overcome these limitations.

Money as a Medium of Exchange

The evolution of money as a **medium of exchange,** or means of payment, came about from the desire to avoid the transaction costs associated with barter and to achieve greater economic efficiency. The need for a coincidence of wants between traders is avoided by the introduction of money. Once money is generally accepted as a means of payment, hog or kitten owners sell their output in hog and kitten markets. They are willing to accept money in exchange for their products or services because they know that psychiatrists and sellers of all other items they consume are willing to do likewise. No longer is the psychiatrist required to search out demanders for psychiatric services who are simultaneously suppliers of goods or services that the psychiatrist demands. Use of money as a means of exchange fosters specialization and economic efficiency.

A huge variety of commodities have, throughout history, served as money.[1] Gold is perhaps the most familiar **commodity money.** The opportunity cost of

[1]These commodities have included horses, cowrie shells, elephants, stone wheels, cigarettes, colored beads, slaves, gold and other precious metals, cows, paper, and feathers. Obviously, the best commodity monies have been scarce relative to demands for them.

The use of money as a generally accepted medium of exchange greatly reduces transactions costs and fosters economic efficiency.

using gold as money is particularly important. Most societies have valued gold highly as decoration, as an object of possession, and, more recently, in industrial or medical uses such as dentistry. Gold that is used for money cannot simultaneously be used to produce jewelry or to serve any other purpose. The value of gold in nonmoney uses is precisely the value given up when gold is used as money. When this opportunity cost rises above the value of gold in use as a medium of exchange, gold will be converted—coins melted down—to the uses of higher value.

Two problems—the opportunity cost of using commodities as money and instabilities in the exchange value of the commodity used as money—contributed to the emergence of fiat money. **Fiat money** is paper (or some other inexpensive, low-cost item such as lead or nickel) that is certified by government decree, or fiat, to be money. Dollars, pesos, rubles, and yen are all fiat money. Fiat money is not backed by a commodity such as gold; that is, it is not freely and perfectly convertible into that commodity. A system of paper backed by a commodity functions exactly the same as commodity money: The commodity must be stored for instant convertibility, thereby incurring an opportunity cost.

Even though fiat money is not backed by a commodity, governments have various ways of giving the money a generally accepted value as a medium of exchange. Fiat money sponsored by government is issued under closely enforced monopoly restrictions by the state. As long as the state does not allow the quantity of fiat money to grow too rapidly, the public generally remains willing to accept the money. Each individual remains confident that any fiat currency received will be accepted by others as payment for goods and services. The government contributes to the general acceptability of fiat money by declaring that debts are forgiven if the creditor refuses to accept fiat money as payment and by accepting fiat money as payment for taxes.

Fiat money
Money, usually paper, that is made acceptable in exchange by law; usually not backed by any commodity such as gold.

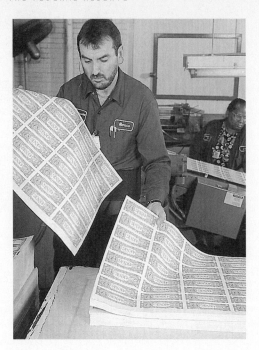

In the United States, responsibility for issuing government fiat resides with the Department of the Treasury.

Money as a Unit of Account

Money transactions are preferred to barter partly because money reduces the cost of economic transactions. Suppose that a leathersmith in a small-scale barter economy produces tanned leather in exchange for blankets, gunpowder, food, alcohol, and metal traps. Without money serving as a unit of account, the leathersmith (and anyone else who trades) must calculate relative prices of goods in terms of other goods in order to make rational trades. To allocate exchanges rationally, the leathersmith must consult separate markets to find out the leather price of blankets, of food, and so on. Each trader must do the same. As the number of traders and the number of goods rises, the number of calculations rises exponentially.

Unit of account
A standard measure, such as the dollar, that is used to express the values of goods and services; a function of money.

The use of money as a **unit of account** helps solve such problems. When money is introduced, all goods are valued in a common measure. Thus, if Jane knows that leather coats cost $4 each and that alcohol costs $2 a bottle, she will also automatically know that her can of gunpowder, worth $8, will trade for two leather coats or four bottles of alcohol or any other combination of goods equaling $8. The function of money as a unit of account means that the number of mental calculations required to determine the relative prices of all traded goods is vastly reduced.

Money as a Store of Value

Store of value
The ability to own wealth in the form of some item, such as money; a function of money.

Individuals who want to save must store wealth, and one way to store it is in the form of money. Money's role as a **store of value** is its least exclusive function. Virtually all commodities, including furniture, houses, stamps, Pekinese puppies, and money, serve as temporary storehouses of wealth or value. But there are better and worse keepers of value. Commodities such as perishable foods are used up relatively quickly. Other commodities, such as land, precious metals, works of art, or buildings, tend to change value relatively slowly.

While any commodity is a store of value, not all commodities are instantly salable. The salability of commodities is called **liquidity,** the ease or rapidity with which any commodity can be converted into a medium of exchange. Money is the most liquid asset—the one most readily accepted in exchange for other goods and services. All other commodities take varying amounts of time to be converted into money. When cash is needed, land or warehouses cannot easily be converted into cash, but stocks and bonds (which are not money) can. Land is therefore less liquid than stocks and bonds. Money has its own advantages and disadvantages as a store of value. It may retain its value over long periods, but during periods of inflation it may be a poor store of value.

THE OFFICIAL DEFINITION OF MONEY

Now that we have gained some understanding of money by examining its various functions, we can define more carefully what we mean by the word *money.* Of the various functions that money serves, its use as a medium of exchange is of greatest economic importance. Therefore, our definition of **money** is along these lines: Money is anything that is generally acceptable as a medium of exchange. Since coins and currency and checkbook money are widely accepted for payment, they must be considered money. To these, we want to add all close substitutes. Since how close a substitute certain assets are to currency is a matter of judgment, various official definitions of the money supply have emerged.

Possible confusion caused by the terminology surrounding checkbook money can be avoided by remembering that any accounts from which payments or funds transfers may be made are called **transactions accounts.** These include all demand deposits and checkable deposits managed by banks and other financial institutions. **Demand deposits** are those transactions accounts against which an unlimited number of checks may ordinarily be written. **Checkable deposits** often carry restrictions on transferability—a maximum number of checks may be written per month without penalty, for example. Both demand deposits and checkable deposits are "checkable" in the sense that either may be utilized as a medium of exchange.

Though the "general acceptability" definition is reasonably clear-cut, a number of assets, such as noncheckable savings accounts, may have important effects on the behavior of investors and consumers and, therefore, on the economy. These less-liquid assets, sometimes called "near-monies," are therefore included in some statistical compilations. Thus the nation's money supply is officially measured in a number of ways.

Two major measures of money developed by the Federal Reserve System, the nation's central bank, are described in Table 12.1. Notice that the M-1 measure corresponds to the definition of general acceptability. M-1 is composed of coins and currency in the public's hands and checkable deposits at many financial institutions including commercial banks, savings institutions, and credit unions. M-1 also includes interest-earning accounts on which the owner may write checks. Travelers' checks and money market accounts upon which checks may be written are also included in this most basic measure of money.

Liquidity
The ease with which any asset or commodity can be converted into money with little or no risk of loss to the holder.

Money
Anything that is generally acceptable as a medium of exchange.

Transactions accounts
Demand deposits or other checkable accounts that allow the transfer of funds by writing a check.

Demand deposits
A type of transactions account with virtually no restrictions as to the size, timing, or number of checks that can be written on the account.

Checkable deposits
Demand deposits plus other types of transactions accounts that pay interest but that may carry some restrictions on use, including minimum balance and limits on the number of checks that can be written per month.

TABLE 12.1

Measures of the Money Stock

Federal Reserve System classifications of money stock range from M-1 to L (only M-1 and M-2 are illustrated here), in order of decreasing liquidity. The most liquid measure is M-1, which includes currency in the public's hands, most checkable and demand deposits at financial institutions, and travelers' checks. Although L is many times greater than M-1, economists often identify money as only assets that are generally accepted as a medium of exchange—that is, M-1. The value of each measure in December 1995 is also given.

Measure	Components	Definitions	Amount (billions of dollars)
M-1	Currency, including coins and paper money held outside banks		
	Checkable and demand deposits at commercial banks, savings institutions, and credit unions		
	NOW and super-NOW accounts	NOW (negotiable order of withdrawal) account: Interest-earning account on which owner may write checks; super-NOW account; NOW account with higher interest and additional restrictions on withdrawals.	
	ATS accounts	ATS (automatic transfer savings) account: Interest-earning account, the contents of which are automatically transferred to an individual's checking account when the checking account falls to a minimum level.	
	Travelers' checks		
	Checkable money market accounts		1123.0

The M-2 measure of the money supply—one that has gained popularity in studies of the impact of money—includes M-1 plus a number of less liquid assets. These include small savings deposits (ordinarily more liquid than larger deposits) and some money market mutual funds (see Table 12.1). The M-2 measure includes those items which closely determine behavior of money holders on the basis of liquidity. Other measures are available for other purposes.[2]

You may be wondering why credit card balances have not been included in any of our definitions of the money supply. After all, if money is viewed as *anything* that is generally acceptable as a medium of exchange, credit card balances should qualify. Having $500 in unused credit card balances is as useful in making purchases as having $500 in a checkable account. Albeit indirectly, unused credit card balances are included in each of our money supply definitions. One component of M-1 (and therefore of the other money supply measures) is deposits in checkable

[2]The Federal Reserve arranges measures from M-1 to L in order of decreasing liquidity. Small savings deposits, included in M-2, are ordinarily more liquid than large-denomination time deposits, included in M-3, since convertibility of the latter into cash often requires advance warning to the financial institution. U.S. government securities, included in measure L but not in M-3, are less liquid still, and so on.

TABLE 12.1 (continued)

Measure	Components	Definitions	Amount (billions of dollars)
M-2	M-1		
	Savings deposits and small-denomination time deposits in both commercial banks and savings institutions	Time deposit: Large savings deposit requiring notification (usually 30 days) or interest penalties for early withdrawal.	
	Certain money market mutual funds	Money market mutual funds: Investment funds managed by banks or investment companies whereby investors' money is pooled and used to buy or sell bonds or other interest-earning investments; investors generally can write checks against their fund balances under some restrictions.	
	Overnight Eurodollars	Overnight Eurodollars: Short-term dollar-denominated deposits held in foreign banks.	
	Overnight repurchase agreements	Overnight repurchase agreements: Overnight loans of idle funds, in which Treasury bills serve as collateral.	3780.7

SOURCE: Council of Economic Advisers, *Economic Report of the President* (Washington, D.C.: U.S. Government Printing Office, 1996), p. 355

accounts. Credit cards operate this way: The issuing company maintains checkable balances that are transferred to the merchant's account whenever the merchant accepts one of the company's cards as payment. It would be double counting to include both these deposits and the unused balances held by cardholders.

Definitions of *money* and *near-monies* evolve with new developments, such as the recent emergence of checkable accounts at nonbank financial institutions such as credit unions. Various items in the Federal Reserve System's definitions are lumped together because they are more alike than other possible groupings. Each definition has its own strengths and weaknesses as a tool for measuring the nation's money stock. M-2, for example, may be used in analyzing economic problems where a broad view of liquidity is appropriate.

MONEY AND THE BANKING SYSTEM

Basically banks perform two essential functions: They accept deposits and make loans. Early goldsmith-warehousers originated the practice. Gold "warehouses" developed, often run by people whose job it was to certify the gold or silver content of coins and to stamp the coins accordingly. These warehouses were a primitive though essentially complete form of the modern bank. Goldsmiths stored the precious metal for traders, issuing a receipt representing the quantity of gold on deposit. These warehouse receipts, which were claims to gold, soon became acceptable as the medium of exchange in both local and international commerce.

A second major role of commercial banks is to make loans, a profitable but sometimes dangerous practice that was also devised by early bankers. In the beginning, the warehouser undoubtedly earned some income solely by guarding the deposited gold and charging a fee for risk and insurance. The warehouser's receipts were backed by 100 percent of the deposited gold. Soon, however, the primitive banker recognized that not all depositors presented receipts for payment at the same time. On the average, perhaps half the receipt holders demanded their gold during any given day or week. The ever-present profit motive took over. Gold (or gold receipts) could be lent to borrowers at some rate of interest, as long as some "safe" percentage of gold holdings was kept in reserve for conversion on demand. In this way, a **fractional reserve banking system**, in which banks maintain only a fraction of cash reserves against deposits, was born. The early goldsmiths issued more receipts than the actual value of gold in their vault. They kept a fraction of gold reserves in their vaults against the likelihood that depositors would demand their specie (gold and silver). The rest was lent at interest, creating another source of profit.

Fractional reserve banking system
A banking system in which banks hold only some percentage of deposits as reserves.

In performing the banking functions of accepting deposits and making loans, early goldsmith-bankers also encountered dangers similar to those inherent in modern fractional reserve banking. Lending too much money for profit—that is, underestimating the fraction of total gold reserves demanded by depositors at any given time—brought disaster. Bank runs occurred when customers became fearful that the goldsmith's deposits were not safe and immediately sought to withdraw their funds.

Two points related to early banking are central to understanding modern banking systems: (1) The practice of lending at interest in a fractional reserve system meant that goldsmiths could actually alter the money supply, expanding it by lending, reducing it by calling in loans; and (2) goldsmiths could place all deposits and banks in jeopardy by misjudging the fraction of depositors' liabilities that would be presented for payment at one time. The first matter—multiple expansion and contraction of checkable deposits by commercial banks in a modern fractional reserve system—is the next subject of this chapter. The second issue—the safety of the banking system and its regulation by the Federal Reserve System—is treated later in this chapter. First, we take a brief overview of the contemporary banking system.

The U.S. Banking and Financial System

There are currently about 11,000 commercial banks in the United States. A **commercial bank** is a privately owned but publicly regulated financial institution whose primary role is accepting checkable deposits and making business and consumer loans. For years, there was a clear distinction between commercial banks and other financial institutions: Only banks could issue checkable accounts. However, during the 1970s, other financial institutions found ways to circumvent rules preventing them from offering checking privileges. Since then, regulations have been changed so that checking services can now be offered by the 12,000 credit unions and the 2000 savings and loans in this country. Since 1980, regulatory changes have brought these nonbank institutions increasingly under the control of the Federal Reserve System. Today, the primary difference between banks and nonbanks lies in the types of loans in which they specialize. (Actually, functions of other institutions can take on the character of banks: see Focus, "Can a Pub Become a Bank? The Modern Case of Ireland.") However, it is still informative to focus on commercial banks in discussing the role of financial institutions in money and money creation.

Commercial bank
Chartered financial institution that accepts deposits of various types, especially demand deposits, and that makes commercial and consumer loans.

fOcus

Can a Pub Become a Bank? The Modern Case of Ireland

The proportion of hand-to-hand currency relative to checkbook money is low in most advanced societies. Historically, Americans' use of currency is only one-third the amount of checkable deposits, although the ratio does change over time. Other countries have even lower ratios of currency to demand deposits. Ireland's ratio, for example, was 18 percent in 1966, 15 percent in 1970, and 14 percent in 1976. But Ireland is unique in that its banks close frequently and for longer periods of time than banks of any other relatively advanced nation in the world. In fact, Irish banks closed for varying periods during 1966, 1970, and 1976 because of industrial disputes. For almost seven months (May 1–November 17) during 1970, citizens of the Republic of Ireland were deprived of the services of the Associated Banks, their branches, and their clearing facilities, which controlled virtually all of Ireland's demand deposits. Without 85 percent of its money supply, could Irish society function? Did the Irish resort to barter and the reduced economic activity associated with barter? In 1979, economist Antoin E. Murphy of Trinity College, Dublin, presented some intriguing evidence on all of the bank closures, especially the long 1970 closure.[a]

Money did not totally disappear after the bank closures. Irish currency and coin continued to circulate, and some major companies were provided with account facilities and clearing services by North American and non-Associated banks. The Central Bank of Ireland transferred currency to government departments at the beginning of the closure to pay wages and salaries of government employees and to continue welfare payments, but at the end of the closure there was only a net addition of 4 million pounds to the currency supply.

The increased demand for currency was partially offset by the summer tourist trade. Currency freely circulates in Ireland, and from April to November currency in circulation grew from £5 million to about £40 million. The North American and non-Associated banks provided some demand deposit transactions with means of alternative payment, but the aid was very limited because these banks had no branch facilities and were physically incapable of handling the volume of new business. By the end of May most of these banks refused to handle new accounts. In November 1970, according to Murphy's estimate, there was a total of £52 million in new demand deposits to facilitate consumers' money demands. This was less than one-twelfth of the closed Associated Banks' demand deposit accounts! How, then, did the Irish manage to transact?

People simply continued writing checks against pre-closure deposits and against checks received from other parties. During the bank closure, checks were written not against known accounts, but against the value of other uncleared checks along with the check receiver's assessment of the writer's creditworthiness. In such circumstances, default risk increased. Further, there was uncertainty about when the banks would reopen. Credit was therefore undated.

In this situation a personalized transaction system substituted for an institutionalized one. The nature of the Irish economy helped. A high degree of personal contact exists in the Irish population of about 3 million. Where personal information was lacking, credit information often existed at the 12,000 retail shops and at the more than 11,000 pubs in the Republic. One pub exists in Ireland for every 190 citizens over eighteen years of age. A pub keeper does not serve ale to a customer for years, as Murphy put it, "without discovering something of his liquid resources." Thus, pubs and shops provided goods, services, and currency for their customers against undated checks. They in fact formed the nexus of a substitute banking system.

Economic activity actually grew over the period at a somewhat reduced rate. There were no significant differences in retail sales and no significant deflationary trends. The important point is that information was the key to the emergence of a substitute medium of exchange. The Irish economy did not collapse or even cease growing when deprived of over 80 percent of its money. It simply and naturally fell back on old forms of transacting or invented new and alternative ones.

[a]Antoin E. Murphy, "Money in an Economy Without Banks: The Case of Ireland," *Manchester School of Economics and Social Studies* 46-47 (1978–1979), pp. 41–50.

Federal Reserve System
The central bank of the United States; regulates financial institutions and establishes and conducts monetary policy.

Federal Deposit Insurance Corporation (FDIC)
A government institution that provides commercial banks with insurance against default and protects bank customers up to $100,000 per deposit.

Both the individual states and the federal government charter, or license, privately owned commercial banks. National bank charters are issued by the Comptroller of the Currency (an official of the U.S. Treasury Department), while state banking commissions or similar bodies issue state bank charters. By law, all national banks must belong to the Federal Reserve System, whereas state banks may elect membership in "the Fed" subject to the approval of the **Federal Reserve System.** The basic role of the Federal Reserve System, a system of banks organized by geographic region, is to regulate member banks and other financial institutions. About two-thirds of all banks do not belong to the Federal Reserve System, but as we will see, this limited membership does not prevent the Federal Reserve System from overseeing and regulating the activities of all banks.

The **Federal Deposit Insurance Corporation (FDIC)** provides the commercial banks with insurance in case of default for a fee expressed in percentage terms. (Other financial institutions have similar government-sponsored insurance agencies.) Such insurance serves to add depositor confidence (up to $100,000 per deposit) against the possibility that imprudent bank managers may bring their institution to illiquidity or insolvency. It also greatly adds confidence in the banking system, which reduces the "panics" or runs on banks that characterized earlier banking in the United States.

Statistics on commercial bank assets and liabilities provide an idea of the overall importance of the commercial banking system in our economy. Table 12.2 shows the balance sheet (total assets equal total liabilities plus net worth) of all domestically chartered commercial banking institutions in the United States at the end of 1995.

A glance at Table 12.2 reveals that the major functions of the U.S. commercial banking system—accepting deposits and making loans—are identical to those of the early gold warehousers. Modern U.S. banking follows the same tradition, but it is far more complex in that many financial instruments—variants of the early bankers' warehouse receipts—have evolved. Regulations to prevent problems in the banking system have also evolved; in the United States the Federal Reserve System, which was created by the Federal Reserve Act of 1913, makes and enforces such regulations.

ASSETS   Many of the assets and liabilities of the commercial banking system are self-explanatory, but some require comment. As shown in Table 12.2, total commercial bank cash assets in December 1995 were $223.5 billion. This total includes vault cash, cash items in process of collection, demand balances due from other depository institutions, and deposits due from other Federal Reserve Banks.

Securities held by commercial banks constitute the second largest asset group. In December of 1995, commercial banks held $991.4 billion in securities. U.S. government securities made up a full 70 percent of the banks' security portfolio.

Loans to industrial and nonindustrial consumers constitute the largest asset of the commercial banking system. The commercial banking system had outstanding loans of $2,608 billion at the end of 1995. Loans for real estate and commercial and industrial uses make up more than half the total dollar amount loaned by commercial banks. Consumer loans, for that new car or high definition TV, amounted to $493.2 billion.

TABLE 12.2

The Balance Sheet of all Commercial Banks, December 1995

The aggregate balance sheet of all commercial banks highlights the major assets and liabilities of commercial banks. Major assets are cash and income-earning loans and securities. Major liabilities include demand and savings deposits (transaction and nontransaction deposits). Double-entry bookkeeping guarantees that total assets equal total liabilities plus capital or net worth.

Total Assets (billions of dollars)		Total Liabilities and Capital (billions of dollars)	
Total Cash	223.5	Deposits	2653.1
		Transaction	770.8
Securities	991.4	Nontransaction	1882.4
U.S. Government Securities	712.8		
other securities	278.6	Borrowings	687.8
Loans	2608.0	Net due to related foreign	
Commercial and Industrial	718.4	offices	263.4
Real Estate	1077.2		
Consumer	493.2	Other liabilities	227.6
Other	319.2		
Interbank loans	192.7		
		Residual	
Other assets	175.1	(assets less liabilities)	358.8
Total assets	4190.7	Total liabilities	4190.7

SOURCE: *Federal Reserve Bulletin* (May 1996), p. A18.

LIABILITIES   The major liabilities of commercial banks are deposits of several kinds. Transaction deposits are checkbook money—generally accepted orders by one business or individual depositor to pay another. Recall that such checkable deposits are included in M-1 and are therefore money as we have defined it. Savings and time deposits include passbook savings accounts; these are included in Table 12.2 under the heading Nontransaction Deposits. Most time deposits require notification of intended withdrawal or invoke interest penalties for early withdrawal. If savings accounts are checkable, or instantly transferable to checkable deposits, they are money in the M-1 sense.

The borrowing category includes borrowings from other banks, financial institutions, or the Federal Reserve System. Commercial banks often borrow from each other and from the Federal Reserve to invest in interest-earning assets such as loans or securities.

The Federal Reserve System

The Federal Reserve System is the basic regulatory agency in the business of commercial banking and other financial intermediaries.[3] The Federal Reserve System

[3]It should be noted that the Federal Reserve System shares some regulatory responsibilities with the U. S. Treasury Department's office of the Comptroller of the Currency and also with the Federal Deposit Insurance Corporation (discussed in the text).

FIGURE 12.1

The Federal Reserve and Commercial Banking Systems

The commercial banking system and other institutions issuing checkable deposits are regulated and controlled by the Federal Reserve System, which is composed of 12 Federal Reserve banks and 25 branch banks. Monetary control is exercised through the Board of Governors and the Federal Open Market Committee in Washington, D.C. The seven members of the board, including its chair, are appointed by the president, subject to Senate approval.

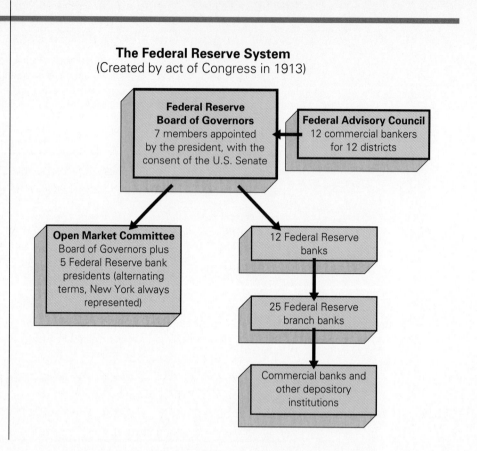

The Federal Reserve System
(Created by act of Congress in 1913)

Federal Reserve Board of Governors
7 members appointed by the president, with the consent of the U.S. Senate

Federal Advisory Council
12 commercial bankers for 12 districts

Open Market Committee
Board of Governors plus 5 Federal Reserve bank presidents (alternating terms, New York always represented)

12 Federal Reserve banks

25 Federal Reserve branch banks

Commercial banks and other depository institutions

has two essential functions. One is the older function of serving as a lender of last resort to commercial banks and other lending institutions—to respond quickly and adequately to bank runs, panics, or liquidity crises by providing currency or specie to meet withdrawals. The other, more modern function is to control the money supply to affect the business cycle and economic activity—to produce significant short-run effects on the rates of employment, inflation, and real income growth. This latter function developed slowly and has come into prominence only since the Great Depression of the 1930s, but it is now the major purpose of the Federal Reserve System. The Federal Reserve also conducts other service functions such as issuing currency and holding deposits of the federal government and its agencies.

Federal Open Market Committee (FOMC)
A committee of the Federal Reserve System made up of the seven members of the Board of Governors of the Federal Reserve System and five presidents of Federal Reserve district banks; directs open market operations (buying and selling of securities) for the system.

STRUCTURE   The structure of the Federal Reserve System is shown in Figure 12.1. The Federal Reserve System is composed of two basic units: the 12 Federal Reserve banks in different regions of the country and the central node of power, the Board of Governors in Washington, D.C. The Board of Governors consists of seven members appointed by the president, with six governors serving staggered 14-year terms; the chair of the board serves a four-year term. The board in general and the chair of the board in particular establish national monetary policy.

The **Federal Open Market Committee (FOMC)** consists of the seven members of the board plus five Federal Reserve bank presidents; the president of the New York bank is always on the committee because of the amount of major financial activity that takes place in New York City. Virtually all monetary policy is carried out by the board and the Open Market Committee. The board must approve any changes in regulations that directly affect the supply of money.

In contrast to the centralization of power and action in the hands of the board and the FOMC, the actual structure of the Federal Reserve System is elaborate and decentralized. The system is organized into 12 districts with one Federal Reserve bank and a varying number of branch banks for each district. The Federal Reserve bank for the sixth district is in Atlanta, for example, and branch banks for that district are in Miami, Jacksonville, New Orleans, Birmingham, and Nashville. The Federal Reserve banks and their branches are geographically dispersed to service and inspect member banks and other depository institutions in their areas.

MEMBERSHIP   Membership in the Federal Reserve System has fluctuated over the years. Assets and deposits of member banks declined between the mid-1960s and 1980, especially during the late 1970s. The major reason for this decline was the increasing regulatory cost of belonging to the federal system in contrast to looser regulations over banks at the state level. Shifts therefore occurred from national bank charters to state charters. In response, Congress gave the Federal Reserve System sweeping new powers over all banks and over nonbank depository institutions with the passage of the Depository Institutions Deregulation and Monetary Control Act of 1980. The Financial Institutions Reform, Recovery, and Enforcement Act of 1989 gave the Federal Reserve System additional regulatory powers over both banks and nonbanks. Despite declining membership in the Federal Reserve System, the system directly controls all checkable deposits in all U.S. financial institutions, the largest component of the money supply. This control enables the Federal Reserve System to control the overall money supply and greatly influence the course of economic growth.

HOW BANKS CREATE MONEY

The *fractional reserve banking system*—in which banks keep only a percentage of funds deposited with them available for withdrawals—is a vital aspect of banking behavior regulated by the Federal Reserve System. Why? Because banks are profit-maximizing institutions and will wish to make money by lending money. But, by making loans, banks expand checkable deposits and therefore the money supply.

Cash assets of commercial banks held in their own vaults or at the district Federal Reserve bank are called **cash reserves**. The Federal Reserve specifies that banks and other deposit-issuing institutions must keep a certain percentage of their cash reserves on hand or with a Federal Reserve bank at all times. These **required reserves**, sometimes called legal reserves, can be expressed as a percentage of checkable deposits or as a **reserve ratio**:

$$RR = r \times D,$$

where r is the reserve ratio, D is the amount of demand deposit liabilities, and RR is the amount of required reserves for demand deposits. (Different reserve ratios

Cash reserves
Commercial banks' and other depository institutions' holdings of vault cash or deposits at the Federal Reserve district banks.

Required reserves
Reserves against checkable deposits that banks and other depository institutions are required by the Federal Reserve to keep in the form of cash reserves; equal to the required reserve ratio times checkable deposits; also called legal reserves.

Reserve ratio
The percentage of checkable deposits that banks and other depository institutions hold as reserves.

apply to the various kinds of savings and time deposits.) If, for example, the deposit liabilities at a commercial bank are $1,000,000 and r is 10 percent, or 0.10, required reserves equal $100,000. If r is 5 percent, 0.05, required reserves are $50,000.

Depending on business conditions or expected loan demand, the bank may well decide to hold more than the required percentage of deposits as cash reserves. The total quantity of cash reserves held by a bank or the banking system consists of required reserves and excess reserves. **Excess reserves** are cash reserves over and above those reserves required by the Federal Reserve. If total reserves were $1,000,000, the required reserve ratio were 10 percent, and deposit liabilities were $1,000,000, excess reserves would total $900,000 ($1,000,000 − $100,000 = $900,000). Some of these excess reserves could be desirable for the bank; for one thing, they provide an extra cushion against the possibility of default—that is, the possibility that the bank will be unable to meet its depositors' demands for cash. Some excess, however, may be undesirable, for the bank is holding funds that it could use to earn profits through loans or purchases of securities. Generally, banks try to minimize the amount of excess reserves they keep on hand.

The ability of a single commercial bank to lend and create new checkable deposits (thereby increasing the money supply) is strictly limited by the amount of excess reserves it has. Why? This is because the deposits created can be "checked away" to other banks. But this limitation does *not* apply to the banking system *as a whole*.

Money Expansion in the Multibank System

The process of money creation within the banking system is not mysterious at all. Consider some simplifying assumptions. First, we assume that the entire banking system is initially fully committed with loans. There are initially no excess reserves in the system. Second, all borrowers at all commercial banks are assumed to want their loans in demand deposits rather than in currency. Third, as in the previous balance sheets, savings deposits are assumed not to exist. Fourth, we assume that banks are solely profit maximizers and do not wish to hold any excess cash reserves. In other words, banks do not hold any reserves in excess of legally required reserves. Finally, to simplify matters even further, we assume that in each transaction, the bank granting a loan lends its entire excess reserves to a single borrower who places the loan in another bank, which then does the same thing. We assume that excess reserves work their way through the banking system in this simplified manner.

Initially, we assume that Cut and Shoot National Bank and all other commercial banks are fully committed with loans. Suppose that Monica, a wealthy miser, deposits $1 million in cash in Cut and Shoot National Bank. The bank acquires cash reserve assets and demand deposit liabilities (to Monica) of $1 million. Cut and Shoot is now in a position to lend dollar for dollar with its excess reserves. Given the assumptions described previously and a legal required reserve ratio of 10 percent, excess reserves exist in the amount of $900,000: $(R − rD) = \$1,000,000 − (0.10 × \$1,000,000) = \$900,000$. With total reserves in the bank of $1 million, required reserves are $100,000.

Cut and Shoot finds a borrower, Jonathan, for the entire amount of its excess reserves. The asset category Loans is enhanced by $900,000, as are deposits of a

Excess reserves
Total reserves minus required reserves.

TABLE 12.3

Creating Money as Excess Reserves Work Their Way through the Banking System

The money multiplier, the reciprocal of the required reserve ratio, determines the amount by which the money supply can increase. With a required reserve ratio of 10 percent and initial excess reserves of $9,000,000, demand deposits and the money supply can be increased by $9 million.

Bank	Reserves and Deposits Acquired	Required Reserves	Excess Reserves	Bank Loans	Increase in Demand Deposits	Increase in Money Supply
Cut and Shoot	1000	100	900	900	900	900
Altoona State	900	90	810	810	810	810
Buffalo Bank and Trust	810	81	729	729	729	729
'	'	'	'	'	'	'
'	'	'	'	'	'	'
'	'	'	'	'	'	'
All other banks	7290	729	6561	6561	6561	6561
Totals	10,000	1000	9000	9000	9000	9000

NOTE: All numbers are in thousands of dollars.

like amount. Jonathan, however, does not let his demand deposit lie idle. He has been in debt to Yvonne of Altoona State Bank on a business deal and wishes to pay back $900,000 of the debt. Jonathan writes a check to Yvonne, who deposits it in her bank. When Jonathan's check is cleared through the Federal Reserve System's clearinghouse, Cut and Shoot loses cash reserves of $900,000 and Jonathan's deposit liabilities of the same amount. Simultaneously, Altoona State Bank gains cash reserves and deposit liabilities of $900,000. Cut and Shoot is left with an interest-earning asset (the loan to Jonathan), but its cash reserves have been checked away to another bank. At a 10 percent legal reserve ratio, Cut and Shoot is fully committed with loans.

Not so at Altoona State Bank. After Yvonne's deposit, Altoona State Bank has excess reserves in the amount of $810,000 [$900,000 − (0.10 × $900,000)]. These reserves may be lent to provide income for the bank. A borrower, Chris, wants the entire proceeds of the loan in the form of a demand deposit so that he can pay off a debt to Susan, a creditor who lives in Buffalo. Susan accepts Chris's check and deposits it in her bank (Buffalo Bank and Trust). After Chris's deposit is checked away to Buffalo, Altoona State Bank loses deposit liabilities of $810,000 and cash reserves of the same amount. Altoona State Bank is fully committed with loans when it holds $90,000 in legally required reserves against Yvonne's deposit of $900,000.

Excess reserves make their way through the entire banking system in this manner. Each individual bank can lend only an amount that is within its excess reserves, but part of these reserves become excess to some other bank in the system. Given our assumptions about the continuous movement of excess reserves through the system, the money creation process stops only when there are no more excess reserves within the commercial banking system. Table 12.3 summarizes this process.

The initial $1 million deposit of cash creates $9 million worth of new loans and deposits. As the individual commercial banks make loans, they are accepting something from borrowers that is not money—a private note payable to the bank—and are providing the borrower with a demand deposit that is money. Individual banks can only lend dollar for dollar with excess reserves because they face the possibility of losing both cash reserves and deposits, but reserves and deposits cannot be lost to the multibank system as a whole. Therefore, we may think of this system as closed. **Deposit expansion** is the total amount of money created above some initial amount of excess reserves.[4]

Money is expanded on the basis of excess reserves, and **money expansion** takes place at the same rate as the expansion of loans and deposits. In fact, money expansion is equivalent to demand deposit expansion. The process of money expansion can also work in reverse. In other words, contraction of the money supply is possible within the fractional reserve commercial banking system.

Money Supply Leakages

The money expansion process within the commercial banking system is limited by two important "leakages" from the system: cash withdrawals and idle reserves. In the example described in the previous section, if a depositor had withdrawn cash from his or her account in the Cut and Shoot Bank, a chain of deposit destruction could have been brought about. While the act of currency withdrawal by itself does not initially alter the money supply, the bank's cash reserves—the raw material that it draws on to make loans—would be depleted.

A normal demand for cash is to be expected, even in a modern system of electronic transfers and at-home computerized bill payment. Currency and coin are still necessary to accommodate day-to-day transactions—coins for a candy bar or soda from a machine or currency to pay for a subway ride or lunch. If this currency leakage continues to circulate and the cash does not find its way back into banks—a likely event—the deposit- and money-creating potential of the banking system is reduced.

A second "leakage" is the idle reserves that banks might wish to hold, especially during periods of high economic uncertainty. Banks are privately owned, profit-maximizing institutions, but they also tend to be prudent. As we indicated earlier, a bank totally committed with loans will fall below its legal required reserve if so much as $1 in cash reserves is withdrawn. Banks will not ordinarily let this happen because of the resulting embarrassment and possible repercussions from the Federal Reserve System or from other lenders or clients. Commercial banks therefore usually hold an additional amount in cash reserves. It should be clear that any holding of idle reserves by commercial banks further reduces the possibilities of money and deposit expansion. In other words, the holding of idle reserves, like the currency drain, acts as a brake to increases in the money supply as well as a cushion against decreases.

By now you may suspect a deeper theme to money creation and destruction than the simple mechanical exercises of this chapter. Another actor in addition to

Deposit expansion
The total amount of additional money or checkable deposits created by some given amount of excess reserves.

Money expansion
The increase in the money supply created by some given amount of excess reserves.

[4]The total amount of deposits that can be supported by cash reserves can be conveniently expressed as $D = R(1/r)$, where D is the total amount of deposits and demand deposit money created, R is the total amount of cash reserves, and r is the required reserve ratio. The reciprocal of the reserve ratio $(1/r)$ is sometimes referred to as the simple money multiplier—the number multiplied by reserves to obtain total deposit expansion. In the example of the multibank system, the money multiplier is 10 $(1/(0.10) = 10)$. The lower the required reserve ratio, the larger the money multiplier; the higher the ratio, the smaller the multiplier. For example, a value of 20 percent for r would reduce the value of the multiplier to 5 $(1/0.20 = 5)$.

the commercial banks and the public lurks backstage. The Federal Reserve System pulls the strings that control deposit and money expansion within the commercial banking system. We have only indirectly hinted at the tools of the Federal Reserve in manipulating the money stock.

Government Regulations

Banks are for-profit, privately owned institutions, but they are also regulated by government. Their major function of creating or destroying money is of the highest importance to economic society. The regulatory umbrella over the entire banking system includes a multiplicity of state and, particularly, federal regulations. These regulations have not always been totally effective. Some regulations over the financial system have sometimes been insufficient to stem particular problems in particular financial institutions (see the Application at the end of this chapter entitled "Moral Hazard and the Savings and Loan Crisis"). The maintenance of legally required reserves is but one of the Federal Reserve System's regulations. Indeed, the U.S. constitutional authority to print and control money is carried out through the Federal Reserve System.

HOW THE FEDERAL RESERVE CONTROLS MONEY CREATION

Basically, the Federal Reserve achieves control over the money supply by manipulating member institutions' reserves. As noted above, banks can lend by a multiple of their excess reserves, thereby expanding or contracting the money supply. By increasing assets, either through new loans to member institutions or by purchasing securities from members, the Federal Reserve makes additional reserve funds available to member banks.

While increases in Federal Reserve assets increase bank reserves, increases in liabilities other than commercial bank reserves reduce the banks' reserves. Increases in the Federal Reserve's stock of securities would increase bank reserves, for example, while decreases in loans to banks would decrease reserves. The difference between the value of the factors increasing bank reserves and those decreasing reserves is called **reserve bank credit** outstanding. This statistic is deemed so important that it is reported on a weekly basis in the *Federal Reserve Bulletin*. Changes are often viewed as an indicator of whether the Federal Reserve is increasing bank reserves (and therefore increasing the money supply) or limiting bank reserves (and therefore decreasing the money supply).

The Federal Reserve attempts to control the money supply by controlling the **monetary base**, the sum of banks' reserves (including the reserve in their own vaults as well as the reserves deposited with the Federal Reserve) and currency in the hands of the public. Controlling the monetary base is the object of Federal Reserve control because of the direct relation between the monetary base and M-1, the money supply. Naturally, the public decides how much currency it wishes to hold relative to demand deposits. To control the money supply, then, the Federal Reserve must control bank reserves—the stuff of demand deposit money creation—

Reserve bank credit
The total value of loans and securities owned or held by the Federal Reserve System. Changes in reserve bank credit affect member institutions' reserves.

Monetary base
The sum of depository institutions' reserves plus currency held by the public.

and adjust for the changes in currency holdings of the public, which also affect the ability of banks to create money.

Currency withdrawals limit the amount of money that commercial banks can create. Sharp increases or decreases in the public's currency demands could have far-reaching effects on the total quantity of bank reserves in the system and thus on the ability of such reserves to support a certain total money supply. Factors such as currency withdrawals are said to be outside the system's control, which does not mean, however, that the Federal Reserve cannot estimate and predict them. It does mean that overall Federal Reserve control of reserves and the money supply is a complicated business.

METHODS OF FEDERAL RESERVE CONTROL

The Federal Reserve can control the money supply in a number of ways. Some methods, such as open market operations (discussed below), affect the monetary base directly. Others, such as changes in the reserve requirement, affect the ability of depository institutions to lend and affect the monetary base indirectly. The major tools of the Federal Reserve, sometimes called **credit controls**, are the following:

1. Open market purchases and sales of securities;
2. Changes in the discount rate;
3. Alterations in the reserve requirement;

Open Market Operations

The most important and flexible tool available to the Federal Reserve in its attempt to control the monetary base is **open market operations**—the buying and selling of securities on the open market. The Federal Reserve uses this tool daily to directly affect member banks' reserves. Again, when the Federal Reserve increases its securities holdings by purchasing government-issued bonds, the reserves of banks are increased. With increased reserves, banks have greater capacity to lend money, which leads to an increased money supply. When the Federal Reserve sells its securities, the reserves of banks are decreased and the money supply contracts. Open market operations are used to correct short-run, predictable fluctuations in the money supply or to expand or contract the money supply over longer periods. If, for example, the Federal Reserve purchases government securities directly from the portfolio of commercial banks, the bank acquires reserve assets and loses securities assets in an equal amount. The bank will want to turn these reserves into interest-earning assets (loans), a process that creates deposits and expands the money supply. If the Federal Reserve purchases securities from nonbank individuals, the result is essentially the same: An individual receives the proceeds of the sale in a check and then deposits the check in a commercial bank, thereby providing the banking system new reserves on which to lend.

THE ROLE OF THE FEDERAL OPEN MARKET COMMITTEE (FOMC)

The Federal Open Market Committee is the principal operating arm of the Federal Reserve System. It is responsible for Federal Reserve Board decisions to buy or sell

Credit controls
The method or tools that the Federal Reserve System uses in efforts to control the monetary base and the money supply, including reserve requirements, open market operations, the discount rate, and other selective credit controls.

Open market operations
The purchase or sale of securities by the Federal Reserve System in order to affect the monetary base and the money supply; the major tool of monetary policy.

securities. This committee ordinarily meets every three or four weeks to set trading policies, which are kept secret to avoid upsetting the plans of buyers and sellers. In these sensitive, closed-door sessions, the FOMC considers such factors as the inflation rate, the economy's growth or real income (GDP or GNP), the unemployment picture, the size of excess reserves and borrowings from the Federal Reserve, probable currency drains, and the international balance of payments. It then decides on a monetary base, or reserve target, and a federal funds rate target to shoot for.

Federal funds rate
A market-determined interest rate on loans and borrowings of bank reserves among commercial banks and other depository institutions.

The **federal funds rate** is the interest rate commercial banks charge on overnight and short-run loans to other banks. Banks often lend excess reserves overnight and short term in order to earn interest returns; the rate is basically determined by the supply of and demand for these reserves. The key point here, however, is that the Federal Reserve attempts to influence this rate by altering the supply and demand for reserves through open market operations. When the Federal Reserve targets changes in the federal funds rate, it is attempting, in effect, to change all interest rates, such as the prime interest rate and mortgage rates.

After the FOMC decides how it would like to alter reserves, the money supply, and the federal funds rate, the decision is transmitted to the open market account manager, an officer of the Federal Reserve Bank of New York. This individual, who controls the open market desk at the New York Federal Reserve and deals directly with commercial securities and investment houses on Wall Street, then implements the intentions of the FOMC. According to 1979 rule changes, the account manager has only narrow latitude in affecting monetary aggregates (such as bank reserves, the monetary base, and the money supply), but the account manager is still given a specific target for the federal funds rate.

As of March 1995, the Federal Reserve System held almost $305 billion worth of securities on its balance sheet. In any given month, billions of dollars' worth of securities are bought and sold by the Fed. Let us see how these open market transactions affect the condition of the banking system, expanding or contracting the money supply. There are two open market channels through which the Federal Reserve can affect bank reserves and the money supply: It can deal directly with banks or with the nonbank public.

PURCHASE OF SECURITIES FROM BANKS   First consider a Federal Reserve purchase of securities (bonds, notes, or bills) from commercial banks. The effects of a $5 billion purchase are summarized in Table 12.4, which shows only changes in accounts. The Federal Reserve acquires $5 billion in assets (+ securities) but creates a new reserve liability to the banks to pay for the securities in exactly the same amount (+ reserves). On the other hand, the commercial banks lose a securities asset on the asset side of their balance sheet but gain an asset—reserves—of equivalent amount. The crucial point is that the monetary base rises as excess reserves—those above required reserves—are created in the banking system. Banks cannot lend on the basis of securities, but they can lend on the basis of excess reserves. After the Federal Reserve's purchase of securities, these excess reserves are ready to be lent. Given a specific reserve requirement, the banking system's desired reserve holdings, and a desired ratio of currency to deposits on the part of the public, money creation may proceed apace. In theory, as the Federal Reserve buys

TABLE 12.4

Purchase of Securities from Banks

When the Federal Reserve purchases securities from commercial banks or other depository institutions, it provides them with reserves on which the banks may make new loans, increasing the money supply. The Federal Reserve's purchase of $5 billion in securities from commercial banks changes those assets from a securities entry to a reserves entry in the commercial banks' aggregate balance sheet.

FEDERAL RESERVE SYSTEM		COMMERCIAL BANKS	
Assets (billions of dollars)	Liabilities and Capital Accounts (billions of dollars)	Assets (billions of dollars)	Liabilities and Capital Accounts (billions of dollars)
+ Securities 5	+ Reserves 5	- Securities 5 + Reserves 5	

securities and as the banks begin supplying new loan funds, interest rates tend to fall initially, encouraging consumers and investors to borrow. (A securities sale would have the opposite effect.) In reality, the monetary expansion also depends on general business conditions and expectations for the future.

PURCHASE OF SECURITIES FROM THE PUBLIC   Another method by which the Federal Reserve conducts open market operations pumps demand deposits in or out of the monetary system directly. Suppose that rather than purchasing $5 billion worth of securities from commercial banks, the Federal Reserve buys them directly from the nonbank public. The results of such a purchase are summarized in the balance sheets of Table 12.5.

When the Federal Reserve buys securities from the public and pays for them with, in effect, checks written on itself, the public gains demand deposit assets and loses securities assets in equal amounts. Note that the commercial banks gain new reserve assets and new deposit liabilities of $5 billion if the public deposits all of its proceeds from the sale into banks. In such a case, the money supply is increased directly by $5 billion by the very act of the public sale. Monetary expansion will depend on banks' desired idle reserves, the legal reserve ratio, the public's desired currency holdings, and, more broadly, general economic conditions. The extent of monetary expansion due to a securities purchase does not depend on the seller of securities to the Federal Reserve—commercial banks or the public.

These open market operations take place daily and are the most flexible and efficient tool in the Federal Reserve's arsenal. But how can the Federal Reserve be sure that banks or the public will be willing to sell or buy securities on demand? Simple supply and demand analysis provides the answer. When the Federal Reserve sells securities, it increases the supply of securities on the open market in quantities large enough to affect the interest rate. When the Federal Reserve buys securities, demand for them is increased. An increase in supply lowers the price and increases the interest return on securities, making security holdings an attractive investment for banks or the public. Likewise, when the Federal Reserve places an

TABLE 12.5

Purchase of Securities from the Public

When the Federal Reserve buys securities from the public and the public deposits the proceeds in banks, the public gains demand deposit money and commercial banks acquire new reserves. Banks may then lend additional money on the basis of their excess reserves.

FEDERAL RESERVE SYSTEM BALANCE SHEET

Assets (billions of dollars)		Liabilities and Capital Accounts (billions of dollars)	
+ Securities	5	+ Reserves	5

PUBLIC BALANCE SHEET

Assets (billions of dollars)		Liabilities and Capital Accounts (billions of dollars)	
– Securities	5		
+ Demand deposits	5		

COMMERCIAL BANKS' BALANCE SHEET

Assets (billions of dollars)		Liabilities and Capital Accounts (billions of dollars)	
+ Reserves	5	+ Demand deposits	5

order to buy on the open market, the demand increase causes security prices to rise and the interest return from holding them to fall. Selling securities to the Federal Reserve then becomes attractive to banks and the public because of the possible capital gains from selling and because of the reduced yield from holding the securities. Supply and demand conditions thus assure the Federal Reserve that there will be a response to its actions in the open market.

Who gets the interest return on the large quantity of securities held by the Federal Reserve? The Federal Reserve itself does. Congress permits the Federal Reserve to use this income to finance its operations. Historically, the Federal Reserve has been able to pay its own way out of its earning assets. Excess income is turned over to the U.S. Treasury. Remember, however, that the Federal Reserve is not supposed to be in business to make profits but to control the money supply for purposes of economic stabilization. The same is true of the other earning assets on the Federal Reserve balance sheet, such as loans to depository institutions. Like securities, these assets are used to affect monetary policy and are not for profit.

TREASURY OPERATIONS AND THE FEDERAL RESERVE   The role of the United States Treasury, a branch of the administrative arm of the President, must be sharply contrasted to that of the Federal Reserve System, especially with respect to the question of government securities. The Treasury administers the budget of the government by receiving and spending funds. In order to finance operations, the Treasury also issues government securities of several types (bonds and notes) to the public, to banks and other financial institutions and, occasionally, to the Federal Reserve. The Treasury uses the proceeds from the sale of securities to pay for the expenditures of government—public goods, transfers, and so on. These transactions are a "wash"—the Treasury receives money for the securities but pays the money out to defense contractors, welfare recipients, and others in receipt of government spending.

These Treasury operations do *not* have an impact on the money supply as does the buying and selling of securities described above (see Table 12.5). When the Federal Reserve buys or sells securities it is with the intent of affecting the reserves in the banking system—the raw material used to expand or contract the money supply for particular purposes of economic stabilization. The Treasury and the Federal Reserve system cooperate on a number of margins, but they are entirely separate institutions.[5]

Loans to Banks: The Discount Rate

Discount rate

The interest rate charged by the Federal Reserve to depository institutions on loans of reserves from the Federal Reserve.

The process of lending to banks at some interest rate, called a **discount rate**, is the oldest function of a central bank. The discount rate is an interest rate (expressed as a percentage) charged by the Federal Reserve to depository institutions for loans backed up by some form of collateral—securities, notes, or commercial paper. This loan process was originally related to the status of a central bank as a lender of last resort—an institution that provided liquidity and currency to the banking system in times of sudden currency demands. Many of these bank crises or panics took place in the United States prior to the establishment of the Federal Reserve System in 1913. Yet modern banks are not immune to crises. In 1984, the massive Continental Illinois National Bank and Trust Company of Chicago, the nation's largest business and industrial lender, narrowly avoided closing its doors. The Federal Deposit Insurance Corporation (FDIC) and the Federal Reserve came to the rescue, the latter through loans and through the discounting of notes for the bank. More recently, banks have been closed by the authorities (but with full payments to depositors).

Initially, the discount rate was perceived to be the Federal Reserve System's major tool to avert crises. In modern times, loans to member banks and other financial institutions have performed another function as well—to control expansions and reductions in money and credit. Several discount rates are charged by the Federal Reserve depending on the kind of collateral put up by the banks and the purpose and duration of the loans. The rate for short-run or seasonal credit is lower than that for extended credit to institutions whose loans extend beyond 150 days. These differential rates reflect the Federal Reserve's policy toward banks' motivations for borrowing. A commercial bank may borrow because of seasonal cash drains, to cover very short-run deficiencies in legal reserves, or because it sees the Federal Reserve discount loans as a source of profit. If there is a wide spread between the discount rate paid for borrowing excess reserves at the Federal Reserve and the interest rate banks receive on lending out these excess reserves, banks may

---

[5]We do not wish to imply that the Treasury has no economic effects. Many economists argue that the huge deficits of the early 1980s, which required the Treasury to issue large amounts of government bonds, helped raise interest rates over this period. We simply point out that Federal Reserve open market operations have an important and direct impact on the money supply whereas Treasury policy does not.

TABLE 12.6

Contemporary Reserve Requirements of Depository Institutions

Reserve requirements have been made uniform for all institutions issuing demand, savings, or time deposits. The total amount of reserves required for an individual bank or savings and loan, for example, depends on the type and amount of deposits issued by the institution.

Net Transactions Accounts	Nonpersonal Time Deposits
3% up to 52.0 million	1.5% on less than $1\frac{1}{2}$ years maturity
10% over 52.0 million	0% on more than $1\frac{1}{2}$ years maturity

SOURCE: *Federal Reserve Bulletin* (May 1996), p. A9.

seek to borrow from the Federal Reserve to enhance their profits. The Federal Reserve discourages borrowing for this reason by charging higher rates for longer-run credit. In fact, the Federal Reserve may stop this sort of borrowing entirely. Whatever the reason for borrowing, lending by the Federal Reserve swells the quantity of reserves at the disposal of the banking system.

The Federal Reserve has several ways of encouraging or discouraging borrowing: (1) it alters the rate or rates charged; (2) it changes the form of collateral required; and (3) it always retains the option to lend or not to lend. Loans to depository institutions and acceptances (another form of short-run lending with different collateral required) make up a relatively small percentage of the Federal Reserve's financial transactions compared to open market operations. But the ultimate importance of the discount rate hinges not so much on the quantity of loans as on the information the rate conveys concerning the intentions of the Federal Reserve. Commercial and consumer interest rates, such as the prime rate (the rate that banks charge to their lowest-risk commercial borrowers), tend to anticipate or follow the discount rate. Along with the Federal Reserve's changing monetary base targets, the discount rate is seen by the banking and business community as one indicator of whether the Federal Reserve is following an expansionary or contractionary monetary policy. A higher rate indicates a tightening of credit and a contractionary policy. A lower rate indicates the reverse. The stock market, for one, is apt to react sharply to changes in the Federal Reserve discount rate. Thus, while the discount rate is not the major mechanism of Federal Reserve control over the monetary base, it is often considered the principal messenger of the Federal Reserve's policy intentions.

Changing the Reserve Requirement

Changing the legal reserve requirement is potentially the most powerful tool at the disposal of the Federal Reserve, but it is seldom used. To understand this seeming contradiction, remember that an alteration in the legal reserve ratio affects the ability of any given amount of excess reserves to support new money, and it increases or decreases the amount of excess reserves held by depository institutions.

Reserve requirements limit the profitability of banking and depository institutions and so are regarded as a necessary evil by the financial system. Table 12.6 provides a summary of reserve requirements in force in May 1996. Changes in the requirements (especially increases) can cause massive disruptions and large-scale adjustments in the portfolios of member banks and other institutions required to hold legal reserves.

TABLE 12.7

Major Federal Reserve Controls and Their Probable Effects

Alterations in any one of the three major credit controls of the Federal Reserve will affect the monetary base of the financial system, bank reserves, and the money supply.

Federal Reserve System Tools	Bank Reserves	Money Supply	Monetary Base	Excess Reserves	Money Multiplier	Currency
Open market operations:						
Federal Reserve buys bonds	Increase	Increases	Increases	Increase	Remains same	Increases
Federal Reserve sells bonds	Decrease	Decreases	Decreases	Decrease	Remains same	Decreases
Discount rate:						
Raise rate	Decrease	Decreases	Decreases	Decrease	Remains same	Decreases
Lower rate	Increase	Increases	Increases	Increase	Remains same	Increases
Reserve requirement:						
Raise requirement	Decrease	Decreases	Remains same	Decrease	Decreases	Decreases
Lower requirement	Increase	Increases	Remains same	Increase	Increases	Increases

(EFFECTS header spans Bank Reserves through Currency)

Even small changes might create financial crises for some institutions, depending on their profitability. When banks are fully committed with loans—that is, have low amounts of excess reserves—an increase of only one-quarter or one-half percent in the legal reserve could reduce lending and money creation by billions of dollars, creating tight money and possibly bank failures. The Federal Reserve is therefore reluctant to make sudden large changes in the reserve requirement. Open market operations are far more flexible in operation and predictable in effect. The reserve requirement will always be a part of monetary control, but it will likely be used sparingly.

The Federal Reserve has other means for affecting the monetary base—including attempts to simply *persuade* banks that some course of action is desirable or undesirable.[6] But the Federal Reserve is always on sounder ground if it can affect the nature of banks' portfolios directly. Table 12.7 summarizes the Federal Reserve's major tools for money control and their likely effects.

MONETARY CONTROL: RESERVES, THE MONETARY BASE, AND THE MONEY SUPPLY

We have seen that the Federal Reserve has numerous means of altering the stock of reserves and the monetary base. It remains to be shown how the monetary base—the sum of bank-held reserves and currency in circulation—is related to the money

[6]This kind of policy is called moral suasion. The Fed also possesses controls over the margin requirement—the percentage of the total price of a stock that must be paid in cash when borrowing money for stock market transactions. The latter rate changes infrequently, and has been 50 percent since 1974.

supply. In December 1995, for example, the U.S. monetary base was $434 billion, while the M-1 measure of the money supply was $1.12 trillion. These figures indicate a money supply on the order of 2.6 times the value of the monetary base. The **M-1 money multiplier** is the number by which the monetary base is multiplied to obtain the M-1 measure of the money supply. This number can change over both short-run and long-run periods. We must understand why and how it changes because the very ability of the Federal Reserve to control the money supply through the monetary base depends on the predictability of the money multiplier.

M-1 Money Multiplier
The multiple by which the money supply will change given a change in the monetary base.

How the Money Stock Is Determined by the Fed

To understand the forces determining the money stock, M-1, we must consider the role of the money multiplier. In simplified terms the money stock is

$$\text{M-1} = \text{monetary base} \times \text{M-1 money multiplier}.$$

We have already seen that the Federal Reserve controls the monetary base by pumping reserves into or withdrawing them from the banking system through its credit control powers. But recall that bank reserves are only one part of the monetary base. Currency in public circulation is the other part of the monetary base, and currency holdings by the public are determined by the desires of the public. An individual may, at his or her discretion, convert demand deposits into cash by writing a check at the bank or some other place that cashes checks. The individual's decision to hold cash has an impact on the banking system's ability to expand the money supply. It would reduce the money-expanding capabilities of the system if an individual made a permanent decision to hold more cash than checkbook money.

The actual money multiplier is determined by a number of factors. We have seen that the reserve requirement is one important determinant, but there are others. As we have implied, determination of the money multiplier must take into account the desires of the public to hold currency and a host of other factors. The actual value of the money multiplier is often difficult to predict in the short run, but it is clearly an element in being able to calculate the money supply accurately. The monetary base—controllable by the Federal Reserve in general—is only one factor in determining the money supply.

Federal Reserve Controls

In practice, it is often difficult to tell what the Federal Reserve is attempting to control—the money supply or interest rates. Although the Board of Governors of the Federal Reserve has at various times in the past stated clear objectives concerning the *size* of the money supply or the *level* of interest rates, the board has often failed to hit its targets. These failures have raised the question of whether the Fed is able to control the money supply or—through controlling the money supply—interest rates.

Any change in the money supply is caused by either a change in the monetary base or in the money multiplier; if these remain the same, the money supply in the preceding example will remain at a level of $1.12 trillion. Can the Fed control the size of the monetary base? The answer to this question is yes, though with some difficulty. As we discussed earlier, the monetary base changes when the Fed engages in open market operations or when banks borrow additional reserves from the Fed or repay loans previously taken from the Fed. Since the Fed is in total control of open market operations, it can regulate any changes in the monetary base that originate from this source. However, the Fed has only indirect control over bank borrowing at the discount window. For example, the Fed may lower the discount rate to discourage banks from reducing their borrowed reserves, but the Fed cannot prohibit banks from repaying these loans, thereby reducing the monetary base. While this complicates the Fed's control over the monetary base, it does not make control impossible. If banks insist on repaying a certain amount (say $2 billion) in borrowed reserves, the Fed can counter this by purchasing exactly $2 billion in bonds on the open market. In this manner, the Fed can control the overall size of the monetary base regardless of independent action by banks.

Independent actions by banks or by the public can cause the money supply to change—perhaps in a way not desired by the Fed. However, by making appropriate changes in the required reserve ratio, the discount rate, or in open market operations, the Fed can offset these undesired changes in the money supply—which is another way of saying that the Fed does exercise some control over the money supply.

Despite short-run alterations in the money multiplier, the Federal Reserve is perfectly able to control the money supply within fairly narrow bounds by following monetary aggregate targets. The question that concerns macroeconomists is whether any discretionary control over the money stock would be adequate medicine for the macroeconomic ills of inflation, unemployment, and lagging growth in GDP. We further analyze this critical question in Chapter 13.

APPLICATION
Moral Hazard and the Savings and Loan Crisis

Prior to 1980, the savings and loan industry was subject to extensive government regulations. In particular, S&Ls were prohibited from offering checking services, they were not permitted to pay interest rates of more than 5.5 percent to depositors, and they were precluded from making speculative loans (such as loans to real estate developers). In addition, nearly all the S&Ls in the country were members of the Federal Savings and Loan Insurance Corporation (FSLIC), a governmental agency that insured deposits at member S&Ls. Member savings and loans were charged an insurance fee equal to one-twelfth of one percent of their deposits for insurance coverage protecting all depositors against loss on accounts containing up to $40,000.

In the early 1980s, regulations on maximum interest rates for S&Ls were gradually phased out. As a consequence, S&Ls began offering higher interest rates to attract depositors. At the same time, other regulations that

enabled S&Ls to make loans for a variety of risky ventures from which they previously had been excluded were lifted. In addition, insurance coverage by the FSLIC was expanded to cover deposits of up to $100,000.

As a consequence of these regulatory changes, managers of S&Ls found themselves operating in an environment totally different from the one to which they had grown accustomed. Aggressive institutions pursued new deposits by offering higher interest rates, which forced even conservative S&Ls to match the rates or risk losing business. In paying higher interest on deposits, the S&Ls put themselves in the position of having to generate higher interest rates on their loans in order to turn a profit. As a consequence, they turned from loans to local customers for the purpose of financing homes and autos to loans to high-risk ventures and to investors willing to borrow at high interest rates. Inexperience in making these kinds of loans was one of the factors that eventually led to insolvency.

The ability of S&Ls to attract deposits was greatly enhanced by the existence of federal deposit insurance. Had deposits not been insured, depositors would have become alarmed at the particularly risky loans S&Ls were taking on and would have protected themselves against loss by diverting deposits elsewhere. Because deposits were insured, however, depositors were indifferent about the financial status of the neighborhood S&L. S&Ls on the brink of financial disaster had no trouble attracting additional deposits—right up to the day they were finally shut down by FSLIC examiners. This enabled the S&Ls to run up debts of unprecedented magnitude.

The economic environment in which the S&Ls were operating was flawed. The incentives facing S&L managers and boards of directors led them to behave in an irresponsible and noneconomic fashion. The term *moral hazard* refers to a situation in which the presence of insurance leads individual decision-makers to use less care in making their choices than they otherwise would. For example, the homeowner who has fire insurance will be somewhat less careful with respect to fire prevention than the homeowner who does not have fire insurance. Because their deposits were insured by the federal government, depositors in S&Ls had little incentive to monitor the investment behavior of their S&Ls. Unfortunately, deregulation of interest rates coupled with guaranteed deposit insurance provided S&L decision-makers with incentives to misbehave—that is, to charge high interest rates and to make risky loans. The results were disastrous. If each S&L had had to provide its own (private) deposit insurance, the outcome would have been different, and American taxpayers would have been spared the enormous expense—perhaps as much as $500 billion—of bailing out insolvent S&Ls.

The ongoing financial difficulties of the S&Ls greatly complicate management for the Fed. The survival of many S&Ls has depended on their ability to repay delinquent loans. Such repayment is, in large measure, directly related to the health of the economy. With the exception of the brief recession of 1990–1991, steady (if slow) growth has added to the strength of the S&Ls prior to and after the recession. The Fed is therefore under some pressure to carry on a monetary policy that leads to continued economic growth (while guarding against inflation, of course).

The survival of many S&Ls also depends on interest rates. Many of the loans held by S&Ls are long-term loans at fixed interest rates; if interest rates were to rise rapidly, S&Ls would find themselves paying more on their deposits than they receive from their loans, endangering their financial strength and viability. Thus, low interest rates in the early 1990s have contributed greatly to the low failure rates in the S&Ls in recent years.

QUESTION

If the Federal Reserve's monetary policy raised interest rates by 2 to 3 percentage points in the next two years, would you expect the number of savings and loan failures to increase or decrease? Explain.

SUMMARY

1. Money was invented to avoid the transaction and information costs of barter, which required a coincidence of wants among traders and imposed limits on the division of labor and specialization.

2. Money serves as a medium of exchange, a unit of account, and a store of value. Money's most important function is its general acceptability among traders as a means of exchange or payment.

3. Money has a number of alternative official definitions, but the one most commonly used by economists is the classification M-1, which consists of all currency and coins in circulation and all checkable deposits at banks and other financial institutions, and M-2, which adds small saving and time deposits and certain money market mutual funds.

4. The Federal Reserve System was formed in 1913 to regulate and control the banking system. Its functions are to prevent bank collapse and to control the money supply to help promote full employment and economic growth and to prevent inflation.

5. Fiat money is paper or other low-cost money that is nonconvertible to gold or other commodities. Fiat money is certified by governments, and its general acceptability is fostered by its acceptance by the government as payment for taxes.

6. The structure of the Federal Reserve System includes 12 geographically dispersed Federal Reserve banks and 25 branch banks to serve the commercial banking and financial system. Decision-making power rests with the Board of Governors and the Federal Open Market Committee, both located in Washington, D.C.

7. Through double-entry bookkeeping, the deposit of cash by an individual or business means that the bank's cash assets are counterbalanced by a corresponding amount of demand deposit liabilities.

8. The Federal Reserve System requires that all banks and financial institutions accepting checkable deposits hold a certain percentage, called the required reserve ratio, of cash reserves against deposit liabilities.

9. An individual commercial bank can lend dollar for dollar with its excess reserves. The commercial banking system can lend and create money by a multiple of its excess reserves. The multiple of excess reserves by which the banking system can create money is called the money multiplier. Deposits and the money supply will expand or contract by an amount equal to the multiplier times the change in excess reserves.

10. The monetary base is the sum of banking system reserves and currency in the hands of the public. The Federal Reserve attempts to control the monetary base, which is the basis of expansions and contractions in the money supply.

11. The monetary base is controlled by the Federal Reserve's use of major credit controls: open market operations, loans or discounts to commercial banks, and changes in the required reserve ratio.

12. Purchases of securities from commercial banks or the public, lowering of the discount rate, and lowering of the required reserve ratio all have the effect of increasing bank reserves. Sales of securities, raising of the interest or discount rate charged to banks for loans, and increases in the required reserve ratio decrease bank reserves and the monetary base.

13. Federal Reserve control over the money supply is made trickier by changes in the money multiplier. A change in the money multiplier may be caused, in both the short run and the long run, by changing desires on the part of the public to hold currency relative to demand deposits.

KEY TERMS

barter economy
double coincidence of wants
medium of exchange
commodity money
fiat money
unit of account
store of value
liquidity
money
transactions accounts
demand deposits

checkable deposits
fractional reserve banking system
commercial bank
Federal Reserve System
Federal Deposit Insurance
   Corporation (FDIC)
Federal Open Market Committee
   (FOMC)
cash reserves
required reserves
reserve ratio

excess reserves
deposit expansion
money expansion
reserve bank credit
monetary base
credit controls
open market operation
federal funds rate
discount rate
M-1 money multiplier

QUESTIONS FOR REVIEW AND DISCUSSION

1. Explain why a money system of exchange is better than a barter system.
2. For money to lower the costs of transactions and to perform its other functions well, it must have certain physical characteristics. List and explain the desirable physical characteristics and also explain why paper makes better money than M&Ms or stamps.
3. Define money and then discuss why each of the following is not considered money: IRAs, savings accounts, certificates of deposit, and gold.
4. What is the major feature that distinguishes M-1 from M-2?
5. What are the options for a bank if it finds that its actual reserves have fallen below its required reserves?

6. By how much can a single bank increase the money supply from a deposit of $1 million of new cash? By how much can the entire banking system increase the money supply from such an injection?
7. If a bank purchases U.S. government securities from the Federal Reserve, does this purchase increase the money supply? Does the money supply change if an individual purchases a government bond from the Federal Reserve?
8. If $2 million were stolen from a bank's vault, would this theft increase or decrease the money supply?
9. "Banks do not like to hold excess reserves." Is this statement true? Explain.
10. How does the Federal Reserve System control the money supply through the banking industry? What

tools does the Federal Reserve use? How does it control the money supply without using the banking system?

11. What is the monetary base? Is this the same thing as the money supply?

12. Discuss the following statement: The Federal Reserve can control the minimum amount of reserves that the banking system holds but not the maximum amount.

13. If the statement in question 12 is true, does it mean that the Federal Reserve can limit increases in the money supply but cannot stop the money supply from falling?

14. In terms of the money supply, how do Federal Reserve purchases of securities from the nonbank public differ from purchases from the banking system?

15. "The Federal Reserve is just a big cartel that is operated by the government to make greater profits for the banking industry." Give some arguments that may support this view and some that may refute it.

PROBLEM

Use the following table showing the various components of a hypothetical money supply for the United States to answer the questions.

Component	Amount (in billions)
Paper currency	$301
Coins	9
Checkable deposits at commercial banks	980
NOW accounts	2
Savings deposits	624
Large-denomination time deposits	853
U.S. savings bonds	441
ATS accounts	3
Money-market mutual funds	260
Commercial paper	35
Traveler's checks	28
Short-term government securities	98
Eurodollar deposits held by U.S. individuals	30

a. What is the total amount of cash in the economy?

b. Using the M-1 measure, what is the value of the money supply?

c. Using the M-2 measure, what is the value of the money supply?

CHAPTER 13

MONEY AND INFLATION

Money clearly matters. The Federal Reserve Board announces weekly changes in M-1, the nation's basic money supply, and that announcement—which can suggest the possibility of loose or tight credit in the future—creates optimism or pessimism along Wall Street. Investors react by buying or selling stock. Buyers and sellers of home mortgages and all other financial instruments also anxiously observe the weekly changes in M-1 in an attempt to predict changes in interest rates and the future profitability of their financial investments.

The main reason for all of the attention paid to M-1 is the relationship between M-1 and price inflation. Inflation has been perhaps most aptly described as "too much money chasing too few goods," and although economists have constructed elaborate theories to explain inflation, it is still best understood in these simple terms. When the production of real output (bananas or personal computers or hair stylings) does not grow as fast as the money supply, inflation sooner or later is the result. And most people readily understand that when their nominal money income does not grow at the same rate that prices increase, they are worse off.

In this chapter we take a brief look at monetary theories, specifically at the relation between the money supply and the price level. After reading Chapter 13 you should understand

- the three components of the demand for money and their importance for monetary theory and policy.

- how classical, Keynesian, and modern monetarist writers interpret the relation between money, prices, and the real output of goods and services in the economy.

- who wins and who loses from inflation.
- some of the causes of and cures for inflation.

THE DEMAND FOR MONEY

How do economists explain the relation between M-1 and inflation? Economists argue that, like the value of other goods, the value of money—the price level of all output—depends on its demand and supply. However, when discussing how money supply and demand interact to determine the price level, we need to be particularly careful with the terms we use. When economists talk about the demand for money, they are implicitly talking about **real money demand.** Real money demand is a demand to hold or own purchasing power in the form of money (cash and checkable deposits), not just the demand to hold pieces of paper. Thus, real money demand should always be interpreted as a purchasing-power concept. (The purchasing power of a dollar changes with alterations in the price level.) The money supply, though, is a nominal variable unrelated to purchasing power. When economists speak of the supply of money, they simply mean the total current number of dollars that the amount of cash plus checkable deposits in the economy add up to. Throughout the remainder of this chapter, we will use these meanings for money demand and supply.

We have seen that the Federal Reserve controls the nominal money supply, but the Federal Reserve does not control real money demand. People in their roles as money holders determine what real money demand is and what specific quantity of real money they wish to hold. Economists have singled out three reasons or motives for holding purchasing power in the form of money—in other words, for the existence of real money demand. These motives, which may exist simultaneously, are described as the transactions, precautionary, and speculative demands for money.

Real money demand
Demand on the part of individuals and businesses to hold purchasing power in the form of cash and checkable deposits.

Transactions Demand

People hold or demand money, the medium of exchange, as a simple means of carrying out transactions—to buy chewing gum, dinner at a fancy restaurant, or a personal computer. Businesses demand money to pay for labor, materials, and other inputs. The amount of real money holdings that accommodates transactions of businesses and consumers is referred to as the **transactions demand** for money.

The transactions demand for money is related to the real income of consumers and businesses. As real incomes rise, the demand for more and more money to carry out transactions also rises. For example, a family with an income of $30,000 will have a greater transactions demand for money than a family with an income of only $15,000. This general relation is true of the economy as a whole as well. As real income rises throughout the economy, the transactions demand for money will also increase.

Transactions demand
Money demand that arises from the desire of businesses and consumers to facilitate exchange with the use of money.

Precautionary Demand

A second reason for holding money is the "rainy day" motive. People usually want to keep some money readily available to meet unforeseen emergencies such as illness or car repair. Likewise, firms generally exercise caution in how much money they hold.

Precautionary demand
Money demand that arises
from the desire of businesses
and consumers to hold
money in order to facilitate
unexpected purchases.

**Speculative motive
or demand**
Money demand arising from
the uncertainty of future interest rates and the fact that
people can substitute be-
tween holding money and
holding bonds.

Liquidity preference theory
A theory stating that the interest rate is determined by
the interaction of real money
demand and supply, and that
interest rate changes due to
real money demand or sup-
ply changes produce changes
in real economic activity.

The **precautionary demand** for money is simply the amount of money that
households and firms want to hold to meet unforeseen events. Ordinarily, the
amount of money that people wish to hold against unforeseen contingencies rises
with income. Precautionary demands may therefore be included with transactions
demands as being directly related to income.

Speculative Demand

A final explanation for money demand is the **speculative motive or demand.** Like
precautionary demand, the speculative motive for holding money is based on uncertainty: Some individuals will want to hold money to speculate in the markets
for bonds or other liquid assets whose price and interest rate vary. These speculators have to choose between holding money and holding interest-bearing bonds.
To make the choice, they consider the present interest rate and the degree of uncertainty about future conditions.

To money holders, the nominal interest rate is the opportunity cost of holding
money. It is the return we give up by holding money and not investing it in some
other asset (a savings account, a share of a firm's stock, or a bond) that would yield
interest. Holding money means keeping or owning some quantity of cash and/or
checkable deposits over a period of time. Economists theorize that high interest
rates make people want to hold bonds. The price of a bond and its interest yield are
inversely related; high interest rates mean relatively low bond prices, and vice versa.
When interest rates are high, bonds are a good deal for two reasons. One obvious
reason is the high interest return; in addition, if the price of bonds rises in the future, bond holders would experience a capital gain. A capital gain occurs when
bond buyers purchase bonds at a low price and then bond prices increase. In the
event of rising bond prices—which occurs with falling interest rates—selling bonds
becomes more attractive. With high bond prices and low interest rates, people generally prefer to hold more money and fewer bonds. Conversely, low bond prices and
high interest rates mean that people will hold less money and more bonds.

The speculative motive for holding money means that real money demand is inversely related to the interest rate. As the interest rate rises, bonds are a more attractive asset, and the real quantity of money demanded declines. As the interest
rate falls, bonds are less attractive and money is more attractive.

Figure 13.1 graphically expresses the preceding ideas. The curve labeled L_S is
the speculative demand for money (L is demand for money, or "liquidity"). At any
time, money holders have formed some expectations about what interest rates and
therefore bond prices will be in the future. Given expectations about future bond
prices and interest rates, a present interest rate of r_0 means that the real quantity
of money demanded for speculative purchases is L_{S_0}. A lower interest rate, such as
r_1, means that actual bond prices rise and, as discussed above, the amount of
money that individuals will want to hold for speculative reasons will rise. In Figure 13.1, the real quantity of speculative balances demanded rises to L_{S_1}.

The speculative demand for money is concerned with *liquidity preference*—how
liquid people want to be. The speculative motive for holding money also forms the
basis of the **liquidity preference theory,** which states that the rate of interest is determined by overall money demand and supply. As we will see later in this chap-

FIGURE 13.1

The Speculative Demand for Money

Individuals hold money for speculative purposes—that is, to take advantage of good deals in the bond market. A low interest rate, r_1, means relatively high bond prices and increased real money holdings. A higher interest rate, r_0, indicates higher bond holdings and lower holdings of money for speculative purposes, L_{S_0}.

ter, this theory implies that economic activity, including price changes, flows from changes in the rate of interest.

THE QUANTITY THEORY OF MONEY

Quantity theory of money
A hypothesis suggesting a predictable positive relationship between the money supply and the price level—specifically, that money supply changes cause price level changes.

One of the essential ingredients of classical economic theory and policy, developed toward the end of the eighteenth century, was the **quantity theory of money**. This theory maintains that there is a direct and predictable relation between the money supply, M-1, and prices, given a constant transactions demand for money. If the number of real dollars demanded to carry out everyday transactions (referred to by the classical economists as the income velocity) remains constant, then an increase in the nominal money supply will increase prices.

The Simple Quantity Theory

In economic shorthand, the simple quantity theory is written

$$MV = PQ,$$

where M = the nominal money supply, M-1, consisting of currency in the hands of the public and checkable deposits;

Income velocity
The average number of times that a unit of money (a dollar) is used, or changes hands, in purchasing nominal GDP.

V = the **income velocity**, or the average number of times dollars (the medium of exchange expressed in M-1) are used per year (or week or month) to finance the final purchase of goods and services;

P = the price level of all goods and services; and

Q = the final real output of all goods and services produced and sold in the economy over some period (a year, a month, a week).

One of the oldest commonsense macroeconomic propositions is that inflation is "too much money chasing too few goods." The quantity theory explains why that is true. First note that, in general, V and Q were assumed to be constant and predictable. Income velocity—the turnover of money—was thought to be relatively constant over the short run and predictable over the long run. Although the velocity of money, or its average turnover time, for money holders varied from individual to individual, its average remained constant and stable for all money holders taken together.

Why didn't early quantity theorists worry about the level of Q, the final output of real goods and services? They simply assumed that real output was at a maximum. In fairness to these early theorists, we should point out that theirs was a long-run view. Economic disasters created by financial panics, wars, famines, supply shocks, or other disruptions were certainly as much a part of their world as ours, as were beneficial economic events such as inventions and improvements in technology and labor productivity. These events obviously caused reductions or increases in real output. Early monetary theorists such as Adam Smith, David Ricardo, Alfred Marshall, and Irving Fisher neither were unattuned to real-world events nor were they fools. They knew that there would always be short-run fluctuations in output and in the employment of resources—what economists call business cycles. Adjustments were always taking place. The classical economists assumed that output and therefore income were at a maximum because they believed there is a persistent tendency to have economy-wide full employment of resources, implying maximum Q.

The significance of assuming V and Q to be constant or predictable is that the quantity theory of money becomes a theory of cause and effect. Money supply is the cause; prices are the effect. In a modern context, if velocity and real income are constant, increases in M-1 will increase prices; decreases in M-1 will decrease prices. But by how much do prices increase with increases in M-1? And, more pointedly, how exactly do "too many dollars" end up "chasing too few goods"? A feature of the relation between money and prices assumed by many early economists answers both questions.

Money and Relative Prices

Neutrality of money
A proposition stating that in the long run the relative prices of goods and services are not affected by changes in the money supply.

Early economists advanced a proposition called the **neutrality of money,** which means that the relative prices of all goods and services (how many computer games trade for concert tickets, for example) are independent of the overall price level.

The neutrality of money can be easily understood with a simple example. Suppose that, starting from some stable equilibrium money supply that produces an equilibrium price level—that is, where money demand equals money supply—the money supply is suddenly doubled. That is, we wake one morning to find that the banks will redeem every $1 bill with $2 and will double the value of all of our checkable deposits. The quantity theory predicts what will happen:

$$MV = PQ,$$

so

$$2MV = 2PQ.$$

If consumers' tastes remain the same, the price level will exactly double in the long run when the excess balances created by a doubling of the money supply are spent, but relative prices of goods and services will not change.

What does this mean in practical terms? At first, individuals perceive the increase in their money holdings to be a bonanza. Their new real money holdings exceed their real demand for money. What do they do to restore a balance between money demand and supply? They spend their excess money holdings in the attempt to acquire more goods. If their tastes do not change, their relative expenditures on shoes, candy, and gasoline do not change. But there are no more goods to be had. The neutrality of money assumes that changes in the money supply do not have significant effects on real variables such as employment and output; the economy is already at a full-employment level of real output. The only effect of these increased money expenditures is to drive all prices up. The price level doubles, but relative prices remain unchanged if money is neutral. Once the price level has doubled in response to the doubling of the nominal money supply, people find themselves with the same real holdings of money. Their attempts to spend excess real money stop because there no longer is excess real money. The process ends with the price level exactly doubled but no change in relative prices.

Thus, if money is neutral, relative prices are independent of the price level and of the nominal prices of all goods and services traded in the economy. Neutrality means that money is the oil of trade, not the wheel of trade.

The Simple Quantity Theory: Transmission Mechanism

The aggregate supply curve is vertical at full employment. If we now designate Y as real output of goods and services, Y_f represents the full employment of all resources. An increase in the money supply from M_0 to M_1 has the effect of shifting the aggregate demand curve rightward from AD_0 to AD_1. In the classical view of the macroeconomy, an increase in the money supply (assuming full employment at Y_f) has *no* effect on real output; for a time, the real supply of money is greater than the demand for it. People attempt to purchase more goods and services, but these attempts are thwarted by the fact that full employment exists. The result is a rise in the price level, as shown in Figure 13.2, from P_0 to P_1. At the new point of equilibrium—E_1 in Figure 13.2—money demanders are again holding actual balances equal to their desired balances. In the classical transmission mechanism, the only impact of a change in the money supply in the long run is to cause an increase in the price level. (The interesting question of how illegal money production, or counterfeiting, affects inflation is discussed in the Focus "Counterfeiting and the Quantity Theory of Money.")

SPECULATIVE MONEY DEMAND AND PRICES: KEYNES'S PERSPECTIVE

We now consider a second important theory about the relation between money supply and prices. The classical economists, as we have seen, emphasized the transactions and precautionary motives for holding money and related money

FIGURE 13.2

The Classical Transmission from Money to Prices

An increase in the money supply has no effect on any "real" variables in the economic system, such as real output or income. In the long run, prices rise as aggregate demand shifts upward from AD_0 to AD_1.

demand solely to real income. John Maynard Keynes emphasized a third motivation for holding money—to speculate in bond and other asset markets where price and interest rates vary. Recall also that this speculative demand for money varies inversely with interest rates: When interest rates rise, the quantity of money demanded for speculative purposes declines, and vice versa.

The Importance of Speculative Demand

In the Keynesian view of macroeconomics, speculative demand plays a special and important role. Assuming that transactions and precautionary demands are satisfied, the rate of interest is the product of the demand for speculative balances and their supply. This is called the liquidity preference theory of money and interest. More important, *economic activity is determined by changes in the rate of interest.*

The importance of the speculative demand for money becomes apparent when we examine the effects of increases in the money supply on the rate of interest and of changes in the rate of interest on economic activity. Figure 13.3a shows that the rate of interest is a product of the interplay of speculative balances demanded, L_S (reproduced from Figure 13.1) and the supply of money devoted to speculation, M_S. (Transactions and precautionary money demands are assumed to be satisfied.) The interplay of speculative demand and supply produces an equilibrium interest rate r_0 when supply is M_{S_0}. As Figure 13.3a shows, an increase in the supply of money available for speculative purposes—in this case, to M_{S_1}—drives interest rates down. The higher bond prices that result from lower interest rates cause asset holders to opt for fewer bonds and more speculative money balances. In other words, lower interest rates create a preference for the liquid asset, money, over the less-liquid asset, bonds.

fOcus

Counterfeiting and the Quantity of Theory of Money

Throughout history, counterfeiting has been a critical economic problem for both governments and private money issuers. Successful counterfeiting obviously takes the control over the quantity of money from the money producer. In order to increase costs to counterfeiters, governments have taken extraordinary measures over the years to make their currency and coin unique. Benjamin Franklin had some unusual suggestions for making early U.S. currency difficult to counterfeit: Reproduce an actual leaf with a unique and intricate pattern of veins and intentionally misspell words on the currency. Modern producers of money use unique papers, ink, design, and printing techniques to foil would-be counterfeiters.

The counterfeiting operations depicted in movies and on television usually consist of one or two small-time criminals printing small bills on a basement printing press. Therefore, most people have probably never considered the possibility that nations can use counterfeiting to wage economic warfare on each other. Because one of the principal advantages of using money is to help eliminate the transactions costs of barter, successful counterfeiting can quickly reduce an economy to the most primitive forms of exchange. As exchange breaks down, so does production and specialization. Goods are hoarded in anticipation of still higher prices; chaos reigns.

Many examples of such economic warfare may be cited. Both sides in the U.S. Civil War made stabs at replicating the other side's currency. The United States and allied governments were reported to have made attempts to disrupt the currency system of Nazi Germany. There are contemporary examples as well. For example, it has been alleged that the government of Iran has been printing and circulating (through Syria) U.S. $100 bills in an attempt to ease its budget deficit and to disrupt U.S. foreign exchange markets abroad. Iran is thought to be interested in issuing about $12 billion per year in $100 bills to help erase its foreign currency shortage.[a] Iran vigorously denies the charge, but counterfeit bills of excellent quality keep appearing outside the U.S. banking system in European markets. The same bills, often comprising up to 30 percent of given deposits of laundered drug money *within* the U.S. banking system, apparently even slip by commercial banks and the Federal Reserve System's sorting equipment as well. The bills are so good and the source so mysterious that the counterfeiters have eluded the Secret Service (the agency charged with rooting out counterfeiters). In Iraq, the United States and other Western nations may be using economic warfare to accomplish what their militaries could not (or were not allowed to) accomplish during and after the Persian Gulf War—namely, bring Saddam Hussein's regime to its knees. Western nations have apparently printed and introduced into Iraq's economy vast quantities of Iraqi currency. New U.S. $100 bills were introduced into circulation in 1996 with newer safeguards against counterfeiting. Other new bills are to follow. But warfare will continue.

Currency warfare is evidence that virtually all governments have an implicit understanding, however crude, of the quantity theory of money. Counterfeiting obviously creates "runaway" inflation—any overzealous use of the printing press does—and unrestrained increases in the money supply can eventually reduce an economy to primitive economic conditions and negative economic growth.

[a]"Iran May Be Printing Dollars," *San Francisco Chronicle* (July 2, 1992), p. A3.

The key to understanding the importance of speculative demand is to observe that investment and consumption might be affected by changes in the interest rate, as the classical economists had suggested. As discussed in Chapter 7, a rise in the interest rate reduces desired investment and increases desired saving, whereas a fall in the interest rate has the effect of increasing both investment and consumption. In the classical approach, lower interest rates ordinarily mean higher spending, higher output, and higher employment. In the event of unemployed resources, monetary policy—altering the quantity of money—could be used to lower interest

FIGURE 13.3

Money Supply, Interest Rates, and Investment Spending

In the Keynesian framework, an increase in the money supply for speculative balances *may* succeed in lowering the interest rate (a), which *may* increase investment spending in the economy (b). Keynes thought these events unlikely in a depression economy, however.

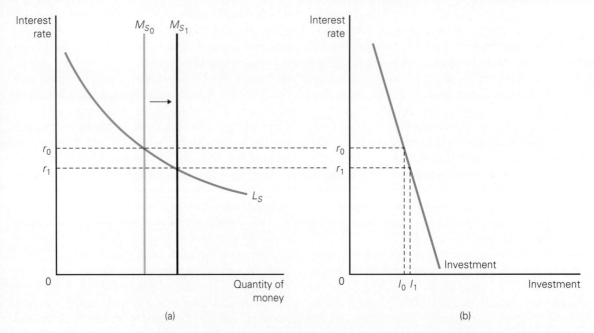

(a)   (b)

rates, to increase consumption and investment spending, and to help bring the economy back to full-employment equilibrium if it ever veered from that level.

Keynes rejected the classical assessment. He did not believe that interest rate reductions would necessarily have much impact on investment and consumption. In his view, consumption and investment were largely insensitive to interest rate changes, being autonomous or more responsive to changes in income. In Figure 13.3b, increases in the money supply from M_{S_0} to M_{S_1} produce a small reduction in the rate of interest from r_0 to r_1. These reductions in the interest rate may have an impact on investment, but this effect depends on the responsiveness of investment to changes in the interest rate. Keynes believed that individuals would be hesitant to invest in bonds (or in durable consumption goods—big-ticket items) in periods of economic distress. Uncertainty about economic conditions would cause people to hold money even though bond prices were falling (making bonds "a good deal"). Likewise, businesses would exercise extreme caution about investments in new capital in the midst of recessions or depressions. In short, investment would not be very responsive to reductions in the interest rate. Figures 13.3a and 13.3b show that interest rate reductions would increase investment only slightly, from I_0 to I_1. Monetary policy, in Keynes's view, would not be a very effective way to nudge the economy toward full employment.

Money and Prices: The Keynesian Transmission Mechanism

What does Keynes's view mean for the short-run relation between the money supply and prices? The addition of speculative demand to the transactions and pre-

FIGURE 13.4

The Keynesian Transmission Mechanism

Keynes did not have much faith that monetary expansion could increase real output and employment during recessions or depressions. As the money supply increases, investors (and consumers) *might* increase spending *if* the interest rate actually falls. Aggregate demand increases, however, would likely be insignificant.

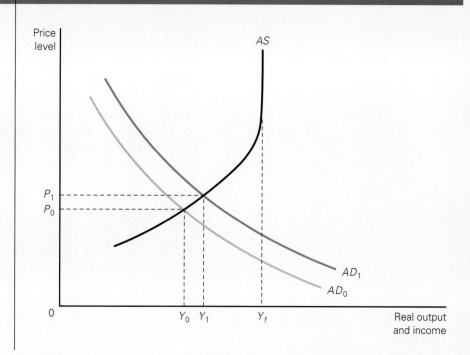

cautionary demand for money short-circuits the cause-and-effect relation between the money supply and prices. Increases in the money supply may have little or no effect on the price level if the spending generated by an interest rate decrease is small or nonexistent.

Keynes's view of the transmission from money to prices is depicted in Figure 13.4. *If* increases in M-1 actually do cause interest rates to fall and *if* the fall in interest rates causes investment and consumption to increase, total expenditures would increase and aggregate demand would shift rightward. As we have seen, Keynes believed that in the presence of uncertainty about economic conditions money holders, consumers, and investors would hold on to speculative money balances and postpone purchases of consumer and investment goods. We show these effects with a minimal increase in aggregate demand and small increases in real output in the economy for a change in the money supply from M_0 to M_1 in Figure 13.4. Clearly, the Keynesian prescription for economic recovery had to rely on other factors affecting total spending and aggregate demand—namely, increases in government spending and/or reductions in taxes.

MODERN MONETARISM AND INFLATION

Recall that inflation is a rate of increase in prices, not a simple rise in the price level. In a static framework, it is sometimes convenient to say, as we did using the simple quantity theory, that a doubling of M produces a doubling of P and to identify this once-and-for-all change as inflation. In a dynamic real-world setting, however, the money supply is constantly being increased or decreased by the Federal Reserve Board at some rate per week, month, or year. Likewise, prices are

**"I understand inflation is your
department. Congratulations!"**

rising or falling at some rate. Real income is also changing, by values typically expressed in terms of growth rates such as 3 percent per year, although in the present simple discussion of the inflation process we assume a constant income growth rate. To arrive at the modern conception of inflation, therefore, we must adapt the static quantity theory to a dynamic setting.

The Process of Inflation

The simple process of inflation is best understood by starting from a dynamic equilibrium position in the economy. In this initial position, the economy is characterized by the following conditions.

Rate of monetary expansion
The annual percentage by which the nominal money supply is changing.

1. There is a constant **rate of monetary expansion** (whether 3 percent or 50 percent growth in the money stock, M-1, per year—the actual percentage is not important as long as it is constant).
2. Expected and actual inflation rates are equal, and further, market participants will expect the inflation rate to be exactly what it has been in the present and recent past.
3. The nominal rate of interest equals the real rate of interest plus the constant inflation rate. Since the inflation rate has been constant in the most recent past experience, the inflation rate (and therefore the nominal rate of interest) is expected to be the same in the future.
4. People are actually holding real cash balances equivalent to their desired holdings of money balances. The quantity demanded of money is equal to the quantity supplied of money in real terms.
5. Real income or real GDP is growing at a constant rate.

FIGURE 13.5

How the Fire of Inflation Gets Fanned

The process of inflation begins with an increased rate of M-1 expansion by the Federal Reserve. Excess money holdings are spent, creating higher actual inflation and higher expected inflation. Higher expected inflation causes higher market interest rates, further increasing spending and inflation. The process continues until the Federal Reserve stabilizes the rate of growth in M-1.

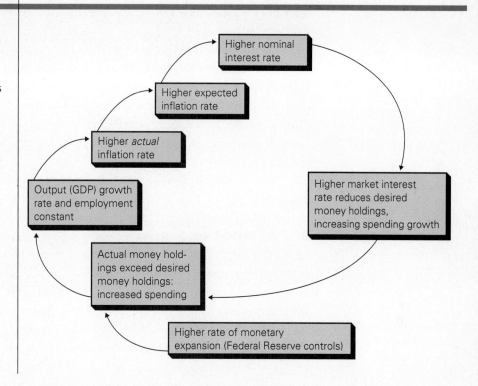

If we numerically express the percentage rates of change of the items in the quantity theory, we can calculate a rate of change in prices. If, for example, the monetary expansion rate, which we now designate with a dot on top of M, or $\dot{M}$, is 12 percent, and the constant growth rate in real income, $\dot{Q}$, is 4 percent, and velocity V is constant ($\dot{V}$ is thus zero), the inflation rate $\dot{P}$ is easily calculated. The dynamic quantity theory becomes

$$\dot{M} + \dot{V} = \dot{P} + \dot{Q},$$

or, given the hypothetical numbers,

$$12\% + 0\% = \dot{P} + 4\%,$$

$$\dot{P} = 12\% - 4\% = 8\% \text{ inflation rate.}$$

The inflation rate is thus calculated as 8 percent.

The exercise of casting the quantity theory into rates of change might seem mechanical so far, but it is invaluable in providing a simple understanding of inflation as a process. To initiate the inflation process we need simply to suppose that the Federal Reserve, through its powers over the monetary base, suddenly increases the rate of monetary expansion from 12 percent to 15 percent. Further, the Federal Reserve maintains the rate of monetary expansion at 15 percent from that point forward and forever.

Figure 13.5 illustrates what happens. The new, higher growth rate in the money supply initially creates disequilibrium among money holders. After the expansion, but before prices begin rising faster, money demanders find themselves holding more real money balances than they want to hold. Consumers and businesses will attempt to rid themselves of these excess balances by spending more on all goods and services.

What, however, is the long-term impact of the increased spending on real income and employment? Because output and employment were already growing at a constant full-employment rate, the attempt to purchase more goods will only drive up prices and money income more rapidly. Thus the actual inflation rate begins to rise. Because it takes time for higher actual inflation rates to be translated into expectations of higher inflation, higher expected inflation rates will lag behind the actual rate.

It is easy to predict what will happen next. Since the nominal interest rate equals the real interest rate (which we assume to remain constant) plus the expected inflation rate, nominal rates begin to climb. This rise in the nominal rate affects the desired real holdings of money. Since the real demand of money is partially a function of the nominal interest rate (the opportunity cost of holding money), the higher interest rate generated by higher inflation expectations leads to lower desired money holdings. This effect reinforces the attempt of money holders to rid themselves of cash balances. That is, the higher nominal rate further fans the rise in the inflation rate.

When does the process stop? When is a dynamic equilibrium reattained? The process will stop only if the Federal Reserve sticks to a constant rate of monetary expansion (15 percent in our example). The process of increasing inflation rates will continue only if the Federal Reserve continues to increase the rate of money creation. If the Federal Reserve holds the rate to 15 percent, for example, equilibrium will be reattained at a new constant inflation rate, a new nominal interest rate, and a new rate of price expectations equal to the actual inflation rate. In the numerical terms of our example, equilibrium will take place when

$$\dot{M} + \dot{V} = \dot{P} + \dot{Q},$$

or

$$15\% + 0\% = 11\% + 4\%.$$

Prices must rise, in other words, so that *actual* real money holdings are equivalent to *desired* real money holdings. Spending and the inflation rate will rise until real money demand equals money supply.

Some Preliminary Lessons About Inflation

The preceding explanation of inflation is a central tenet in an economic school of thought called **monetarism**. The monetarist view of inflation contains certain explicit and implicit lessons. First and foremost, monetarists argue that inflation is always a monetary phenomenon. Economists Milton Friedman and Anna Schwartz have supported this proposition with massive hundred-year empirical studies of the quantity theory in the United States and England.[1] The villain in the monetarists'

Monetarism

A theory that centers on money supply growth, real money demand, nominal and real interest rates, and inflationary expectations in explaining the process of inflation or deflation.

---

[1] See Milton Friedman and Anna J. Schwartz, *A Monetary History of the United States* (Princeton, N. J.: Princeton University Press, 1963).

inflation scenario is expansionist policies pursued by the monetary authority that controls the money stock.

In the monetarist version of events, for example, high interest rates do not cause inflation; rather, they are the *result* of inflation. What we did not mention in our simplified treatment is that one short-lived initial effect of the Federal Reserve's monetary expansion is a temporary decline in market interest rates. Of course, the market rates begin to rise as expectations of higher inflation take hold of borrowers and lenders. Observers and politicians often make the mistake of arguing that the money stock growth rate should be expanded to lower the interest rates. As we have seen, however, the monetarists show that such a shortsighted policy will have the opposite effect: Increasing the rate of expansion of the money supply will soon raise nominal interest rates. Higher interest rates follow higher inflation rates, but higher monetary expansion is necessary for both events to occur.

Many people also think that inflation is self-generating. Higher nominal interest rates do affect desired money balances and spending. But in the monetarist view, this process must come to an end if the central bank holds the money expansion to a constant rate. It may, of course, take time for inflationary expectations to adjust between consumers and producers, borrowers and lenders, and employers and employees, but when the market adjusts, a dynamic equilibrium will be attained.

It is very important to note that an increased rate of monetary expansion *will* have some short-run effects on the economy. Specifically, the Federal Reserve can temporarily lower both the nominal and the real rates of interest, thereby creating a *temporary* surge in total spending. This might have short-term effects on output and employment as well if employment is not growing at a full-employment rate (or if overfull employment is a temporary possibility). If the economy is at or near full employment, however, the inevitable result in the monetarist view is a higher rate of inflation. A contemporary school of macroeconomics called *rational expectations theory* goes one step further than monetarism on the matter of even the short-run possibility of monetary policy having any real effects on the economy. As discussed in Chapter 29, rational expectations theory is based on the belief that monetary policy can have no effects on real output or employment because all of the effects of policy are fully anticipated by market participants.

INFLATION

Several measures of inflation are used in the real world to guide policy-making. Both a consumer price index and a producer price index are calculated by the Bureau of Labor Statistics. A third major index is the implicit price deflator, which is a means of converting nominal GDP values into real GDP values. No matter what measure is used, the presence of higher indexes over time indicates a rising price level. Actual U.S. inflation rates between 1960 and 1995 are shown in Table 13.1.

The Effects of Inflation

The statistical presence of inflation in the economy tells us little about the costs and other distortions it inflicts there. Runaway inflation of 80 or 2000 percent per month or per year, such as that sometimes experienced in war-torn or developing

TABLE 13.1

Two Measures of Inflation, 1960–1995

Two popular measures of inflation used in the United States are the implicit price deflator, a means for converting nominal GDP into real values, and the consumer price index, which bases the inflation rate on price changes in some hypothetical market basket of consumer goods. The numbers given for both indexes are annual rates.

Year	INFLATION RATE AS MEASURED BY Implicit Price Deflator	Consumer Price Index	Year	INFLATION RATE AS MEASURED BY Implicit Price Deflator	Consumer Price Index
1960	1.5	1.7	1978	7.7	7.6
1961	1.3	1.0	1979	8.5	11.3
1962	1.3	1.0	1980	9.2	13.5
1963	1.2	1.3	1981	9.2	10.3
1964	1.5	1.3	1982	6.3	6.2
1965	2.0	1.6	1983	4.2	3.2
1966	2.9	2.9	1984	3.9	4.3
1967	3.1	3.1	1985	3.3	3.6
1968	4.3	4.2	1986	2.7	1.9
1969	4.7	5.5	1987	3.1	3.6
1970	5.4	5.7	1988	3.7	4.1
1971	5.2	4.4	1989	4.2	4.8
1972	4.3	3.2	1990	4.3	5.4
1973	5.7	6.2	1991	4.0	4.2
1974	8.7	11.0	1992	2.7	3.0
1975	9.6	9.1	1993	2.6	3.0
1976	5.6	5.8	1994	2.3	2.6
1977	6.3	6.5	1995	2.6	2.8

SOURCE: Council of Economic Advisers, *Economic Report of the President* (Washington, D.C.: U.S. Government Printing Office, 1996), pp. 286, 348.

countries with low or severely restricted stocks of goods and services, can reduce an economy to barter or cause it to collapse altogether. Milder inflation—3 to 15 percent per year—also creates economic costs in any advanced economy. The full effects of increases in inflation rates may take some time to be fully realized, so inflation has both short- and long-run effects.

INFLATION, FIXED INCOMES, AND ASSETS   The most publicized effect of inflation is the redistributive impact it has between specific groups in society. Inflation affects those who can least afford to pay for it—the sick, the poor, and especially the elderly and others on fixed incomes—through erosions of purchasing power. Congress, in recent years of inflation, indexed or "tied" Social Security and other welfare benefits to a price level index, thereby alleviating some of the problems inflation causes for the retired or the aged. Nevertheless, inflation is a constant threat to the most economically vulnerable groups in society.

Inflation also adversely affects holders of assets denominated in nominal, or money, terms as opposed to real terms. Suppose you purchase a house—a real asset—and hold it for five years, over which time the price level doubles because of inflation. What happens to the nominal value of your investment? Excluding the real factors of natural appreciation and depreciation that might take place over the five years (resulting from the location, deterioration of property, and so on), the money value of your house should closely follow the inflation rate over the period, doubling at the end of the five years.

While the value of real assets tends to follow inflation, the value of money-denominated assets may not. Suppose that you lend a friend $10,000, to be paid at the end of a five-year period, and that your friend issues you a promissory note attesting to the loan. Again suppose that the price level doubles over the five-year span because of inflation. Aside from any interest paid by your friend, what has happened to the real value of your asset? Although the nominal value of the note remains at $10,000, the real value is only half of what it was at the beginning of the five-year period. You will now be able to purchase only half the goods and services that you could have bought before you made the loan. Capital gains or losses—changes in real value—are always associated with holding any kind of asset in the face of unanticipated inflation. Real assets generally gain in value, whereas money assets—those expressed in fixed money terms—generally lose value.

DISRUPTIVE EXPECTATIONS   A second major effect of inflation is that it distorts expectations of inflation, wage rates, and interest rates. When the inflation rate is not perfectly anticipated, workers and employers, buyers and sellers of goods and services, and borrowers and lenders will be uncertain of future real values. Since these transactors will generally make mistakes in forecasting the effects of inflation in specific markets, there will be continuous and unanticipated transfers of wealth among workers and employers, buyers and sellers, borrowers and lenders.

Escalator clauses
Provisions of labor contracts that tie changes in nominal wages to changes in some price index.

Market participants try to protect themselves, of course. Workers belonging to labor unions often bargain for **escalator clauses** in their contracts, provisions that tie future wages to some index of the price level as a hedge against inflation.

Inflation and expectations of the rate of inflation also affect nominal interest rates. When the inflation rate fluctuates, so do expectations of inflation as well as nominal and real interest rates. These changes can have severe effects on the economic well-being of various groups and individuals in the economy by altering the real value of indebtedness. In the late 1970s, for example, unexpected inflation worked to the benefit of many homeowners by substantially reducing the real value of their mortgage payments, the real value of the indebtedness incurred when they borrowed money to buy houses. Of course, there is the other side of this coin. Lenders were being paid back, in real terms, much less from homeowners than they had originally agreed to. The presence of volatile inflation and interest rates not only transfers wealth among groups in society, but also will serve to make credit markets function less efficiently. Consider how unexpected inflation may affect individuals.

WHO WINS, WHO LOSES FROM UNEXPECTED INFLATION?   Just as price changes for a particular commodity can benefit one group and simultaneously harm another, the financial positions of debtors and creditors also can be modified by unexpected changes in the inflation rate. Expectations of the future inflation rate are built into nominal or money rates of interest. The nominal rate of interest at the time money is borrowed or lent not only reflects the real interest rate, but also the inflation rate that the borrower and lender expect will persist over the term of the loan. If, after the loan is made, the rate of inflation that actually occurs turns out to be different from that expected, the purchasing power of the interest and principal repayments turns out to be different from what both parties to the loan expected it to be. The result is an unexpected wealth transfer between the debtor and the creditor. The direction of the transfer depends on whether inflation was "overanticipated" or "underanticipated."

Consider the case of underanticipated inflation—when the rate of inflation that exists turns out to be higher than the rate the debtor and creditor expected when the loan was made. Assume that a student wishes to borrow $3000 from a rich aunt for one year to finance college expenditures. Both agree that the real interest rate on this family loan will be 0 percent. Suppose that both expect no inflation— an inflation rate of 0 percent—over the year. The student then promises (a loan contract) to repay $3000 at the end of the year. Since both parties to this agreement expect no inflation over the course of the year, they expect the $3000 repayment to have the same purchasing power at the end of the year that the $3000 loan had at the beginning of the year. The promise (or the loan contract) is to repay $3000 nominal dollars. The expectation implicit in the loan agreement is that the $3000 nominal dollars will purchase the same amount of goods and services at the end of the year as they were able to purchase at the beginning of the year.

At the end of the year, suppose that the price level had doubled; that is, suppose that the inflation rate had been 100 percent. The student would be obligated to pay back $3000, but each dollar would purchase only one-half as much as it did at the beginning of the year. In essence, the student would pay back only $1500 constant-purchasing-power dollars. The inflation rate was actually 100 percent, but the debtor and creditor expected 0 percent. Hence, inflation was underanticipated, and as a result, a wealth transfer of $1500 constant-purchasing-power dollars from the creditor (the rich aunt) to the debtor (the student) has taken place.

The direction of the wealth transfer is not always from creditors to debtors, however. It is quite possible for it to be in the opposite direction. Consider the fictitious student loan discussed above. Suppose, though, that both parties expect a 100 percent inflation rate over the year. The student will agree to pay back $6000 at the end of the year because it is expected that each dollar paid back will be worth half as much as each dollar borrowed. A constant-purchasing-power payback of 3000 beginning-of-the-year dollars is expected. If the actual inflation rate during the year turns out to be 0 percent, who wins? The rich aunt expected a purchasing-power repayment of $3000 ($6000, but at a doubled level of prices). But with zero inflation, she will receive 6000 nominal dollars that have a purchasing power of 6000 beginning-of-the-year dollars. The wealth transfer here goes from the student (debtor) to the rich aunt (creditor) because both overanticipated inflation when the loan was made.

INFLATION AS A TAX   Inflation also levies two different kinds of "taxes" on people, taxes that are not directly imposed through the traditional democratic

Pure inflation tax
The reduction in purchasing power of an individual's nominal money holdings due to inflation.

process of taxation by legislation. The first of these is the **pure inflation tax.** No one fills out an inflation tax form and writes a check, but the pure inflation tax is nonetheless very real. The taxpayers are those individuals and businesses who hold money. Anyone who holds money over, say, a month will see the purchasing power of that money decline due to inflation. The amount by which the purchasing power of an individual's money holdings declines is the pure inflation tax.

A second way in which inflation acts as a tax is more direct. In many countries, including the United States, a progressive income tax exists. Higher tax rates are applied to higher incomes. When the tax rate that a person is subject to depends on the person's nominal income, inflation pushes people into higher tax brackets even though their real incomes have not changed or have even fallen. The individual ends up paying a larger fraction of income in income taxes solely because of inflation, not because of any increase in real income or any direct change in the tax laws.

Tax indexation
Periodic adjustment of the tax brackets of a progressive income tax so as to base taxes on real, not nominal, income; eliminates bracket creep and increased income taxes due solely to inflation.

This phenomenon, sometimes called "bracket creep," became prevalent in the United States during the inflationary years of the 1970s. In 1981, however, the Congress voted to include **tax indexation** as a feature of the federal income tax code. Beginning in 1985, tax indexation eliminated bracket creep due to inflation by adjusting the income tax brackets yearly to account for any inflation that has occurred during the year. This makes the U.S. income tax a tax on real, rather than nominal or money, income.

The degree of inflation, both expected and unexpected, is also heavily influenced by politics. Inflation may be particularly affected by the degree of independence that the central bank of a country has from the political apparatus. In general, the more independent and further removed control over the money supply is from political manipulations, the lower the degree of inflation and, hence, the lower the tax on citizens. (See the Application, "Politics and Inflation: A Global Perspective" at the end of this chapter.)

THEORIES OF INFLATION

Theories about the cause of inflation can be broadly divided into two categories: cost-push and demand-pull. In brief, **cost-push inflation** results from monopoly or union power pushing prices up. Either unions may respond to rising monopoly output prices by demanding higher wages or monopolists may respond to union demands for higher wages by raising prices. A variant of the cost-push explanation is the supply shock theory of inflation, which explains inflation as the result of a sudden increase in production costs caused by some resource scarcity, such as that created by OPEC or by crop failure.

Cost-push inflation
Increases in the price level caused by monopoly and/or union power or by shocks to the economy that reduce aggregate supply.

Demand-pull inflation
Increases in the price level caused by increases in aggregate demand.

Demand-pull inflation is an increase in prices that results from increases in expenditures on goods and services. When actual holdings of cash balances exceed consumers' and investors' desired holdings, they begin to spend. Such spending drives prices upward until they rise enough to reduce actual real money holdings to desired real holdings. In other words, increases in demand pull prices up.

Monetarists adhere to the demand-pull explanation of inflation. In their view, long-run inflation is the result of the Federal Reserve's pumping the money supply above the level necessary to keep its growth in line with the growth in the public's desired real holdings of money. Most Keynesians view inflation as a combined result of demand-side and supply-side forces in the economy.

Cost-Push Theories of Inflation

Cost-push explanations place the blame for inflation on pressures from monopolies or unions or from sudden shortages of natural resources. Two theories of how these factors can cause inflation are the monopoly power/wage-price spiral argument and the supply, or resource, shock explanation.

THE MONOPOLY POWER/WAGE-PRICE SPIRAL THEORY   Some economists argue that one cause of inflation is that the prices of goods and services are pushed up by monopoly power. There are two variants of this argument, depending on the source of monopoly power—monopolies in product markets or monopolies, such as labor unions, in resource markets. Concentration of monopoly power in input or output markets causes rigid constraints on the ability of prices and wages to move downward in response to falling aggregate demand. Output monopolies are able to resist cutting prices by controlling output—by supplying lower quantities in an effort to maintain their revenues. Rather than accept lower wages, input monopolies such as giant labor unions curtail labor's supply in an effort to counteract falling demand for labor. The rigidities imposed by output and input monopolies mean that prices and wages are not freely adaptive to changes in demand. When aggregate demand falls, the result is lower output and employment rather than falling prices and wages.

Another version of this argument is that, at any point in time, the price demands of monopolies or the wage demands of unions will create a **wage-price spiral** of inflation. If monopolies can set prices and make higher prices stick, the wage demands of unions will escalate; erosions of real purchasing power will cause union members to demand higher nominal wages. Either increased monopoly price demands or union wage demands will reduce the short-run aggregate supply of output because both market activities have the short-run effect of temporarily reducing the hiring of labor.

Any wage-price spiral must ultimately be **accommodated** by the Federal Reserve. Unless the Federal Reserve validates price and wage increases by increasing M-1, unemployment and reduced output will occur. Monetary and fiscal authorities may stand their ground, forcing unions and monopolies to endure unemployment until prices and wages fall and the economy is brought back to equilibrium at full employment. Or the Fed may accommodate cost-push pressures by increasing the money stock, thereby validating inflation. At most, argue critics of the wage-price spiral, unions and monopolies can force a once-and-for-all increase in nominal wages and prices—unless the Federal Reserve accommodates these pressures in the economy. The rise in prices will not be continuous—that is, inflationary—unless the Federal Reserve permits it to be so.

THE SUPPLY SHOCK THEORY OF INFLATION   Another cost-push explanation of inflation is related to **supply shocks**—natural or artificial reductions in the supply of an input to a production process. The United States also experienced

Wage-price spiral
The process whereby increased prices of final goods cause increased wage rates and other resource prices, which in turn result in still-higher prices of final goods; for the spiral to continue, the money supply must continually increase or real output must continually fall.

Accommodation of cost-push inflation
Increases in the money supply designed to offset a decrease in aggregate supply caused by monopoly or union action or by an aggregate supply shock; increased aggregate demand results, preventing decreases in real output.

Supply shock inflation
Price level increases stemming from a decrease in aggregate supply; decreased aggregate supply usually occurs because of sudden increased scarcity of essential resources.

oil price shocks in the 1970s, when the OPEC nations progressively monopolized the oil export industry and raised prices. Since oil-based energy was an important input in U.S. manufacturing and other uses, some observers argued that increases in costs were passed on to consumers in the form of higher prices. OPEC's price demands were seen as ushering in a higher rate of inflation. (Between 1974 and 1980, the average inflation rate was approximately 9 percent.)

In determining who was to blame for the inflation of the 1970s, then, some economists might begin with the oil sheiks. Others believe that the supply shock scenario just described would have been impossible without the cooperation of the Federal Reserve's expansionary monetary policy. After all, not every OPEC-dependent country suffered the same inflationary consequences. Switzerland, for example, whose central bank followed a much more conservative policy than that pursued by the Fed, seemed to suffer less from the OPEC supply shock than the United States.

Demand–Pull Theories of Inflation

The theories we have discussed so far—monopoly power, wage-price, and supply shock—focus on the supply side of inflation. These theories predict inflation on the basis of shifts in the aggregate supply curve.

Inflation, of course, also has roots in the demand side of the economy. Any rightward shift in the aggregate demand curve, given an upward-sloping supply curve, will create or increase inflationary pressures. Monetary expansion on the part of the Federal Reserve will shift the aggregate demand curve and drive the price level up. (The effects of demand shifts depend on the shape of the aggregate supply curve.) Other factors that can shift the aggregate demand curve include increased government spending, investment spending, and consumer demand.

MONEY-SUPPLY GROWTH AND INFLATION   Monetarists and other economists believe there is a direct relation between expansionary monetary policy on the part of the Federal Reserve and inflation. In other words, inflation—a continuously rising price level—cannot take place without a continuously rising money supply.

This demand-pull theory of inflation is based on an updated version of the quantity theory of money. Briefly stated, the monetarist demand-pull model assumes that monetary expansion on the part of the Federal Reserve will merely increase the cash holdings of individuals without affecting output. If individuals rid themselves of excess money holdings by spending, but output is constant, then prices will go up. Price increases will fuel expectations of higher prices as well as higher nominal interest rates. Higher interest rates will increase pressure on the Federal Reserve to increase the money supply, and so on. Monetarists believe that this cycle of inflation can be halted only when the Federal Reserve maintains a steady growth rate in the money supply. Such a policy will stabilize money demand, price expectations, and interest rates and permit steady growth in output.

INFLATION AND THE DEFICIT   Politicians are fond of blaming high inflation on growing government deficits. Economists, however, are less sure of the effects of deficits on the inflation rate. For one thing, deficits are not always caused by increasing government expenditures. They may also result from decreasing revenues. Therefore, the deficit may be increasing at a time when the economy is in a recession and prices are not under inflationary pressure. Deficits can affect inflation, however, if the government finances them in certain ways. When the government borrows money from the Federal Reserve System, it spurs growth in the money supply, setting off the inflationary spiral. Reserves and deposits are added to the banking system with no withdrawals, which would have occurred with taxation. When the government borrows from private sources, it contributes to higher interest rates, another source of inflationary pressure.

CURES FOR INFLATION

Solutions to inflation—policies that might bring about price stability—are always being hotly debated. Just as there is no single agreed-upon cause for inflation, there is no single accepted cure. When policymakers attempt to resolve the inflation problem, moreover, they may bring about other, perhaps worse, consequences. Many blame the Federal Reserve's anti-inflationary policy of 1979–1980 for the severe recession that followed almost immediately. Strategies to combat inflation can be placed in two broad categories: nondiscretionary policies and discretionary policies.

Nondiscretionary Cures

Those who believe that inflation is directly attributable to monetary expansion urge restraint on the Federal Reserve. This restraint may take several forms. Monetarists urge that the Federal Reserve avoid policies that disrupt the price expectations of the public. Sudden expansions or contractions of the money supply, for example, usher in cycles of rising and falling prices. Such changes affect future prices and interest rates and require future discretionary actions. The roller-coaster path of high inflation followed by debilitating recessions is not caused by a destabilized economy but by a destabilizing stop-and-go policy on the part of the Federal Reserve. Monetarists urge that the Federal Reserve adopt a money supply growth rule. Such a rule, they believe, can allow the economy to reach a proper, long-run equilibrium rate of GDP growth with stable prices.

Discretionary Cures

Discretionary policies to combat inflation are varied. The first step in proper policy-making is accurate diagnosis: Is the inflation a supply-side or a demand-side phenomenon? If the inflation is caused by excessive demand, the proper fiscal cures involve budget cuts or higher taxes to dampen the growth in expenditures. Such policies are obviously not very popular with politicians or voters, so inflation-fighting measures are often left to the Federal Reserve. The Federal Reserve's proper monetary policies include reductions in M-1 growth rates and higher interest rates. Both actions tend to choke off consumption spending and investment, reducing the pressure on prices (and meanwhile risking a recession).

Policies to combat inflation caused by supply factors such as monopoly or union pressures and the wage-price spiral are also varied. We briefly look at two such policies: price and wage controls and tax-induced policies.

PRICE AND WAGE CONTROLS   **Gain Without Pain?** Under price and wage controls, price and wage increases are forbidden by Congress, with penalties for noncompliance. Direct price and wage controls are a familiar, staple policy of governments. From the time of the Roman emperor Diocletian (and probably earlier), governments have tried to put a ceiling on price levels by legal means or by the use of price and wage "guidelines," with means of enforcement ranging from fines to death by firing squad. The most notable experiment with the price and wage controls in the United States occurred during the Nixon administration. Two basic beliefs underlie the modern advocacy of price and wage controls: (1) Structural rigidities—monopolies and unions—are the cause of inflation, and (2) fiscal and monetary policies are at times insufficient for dealing with the inflation problem.

Price and wage controls usually fail because they cannot be enforced or because they are too costly to enforce. Black markets develop in both output and input markets where there is excess demand for goods or input services (see Chapter 4). Rationing output through coupons and other devices usually fails to overcome these problems. After the OPEC oil crisis, the Carter administration initiated plans for an emergency rationing program for gasoline. The program sparked much controversy and was eventually dropped.

Most economists are opposed to price and wage controls because they distort production and economic relations between transactors in the market. If the government is successful as an enforcer of controls, which is itself a costly and difficult job, short-run price expectations may be somewhat stabilized, helping to contain inflationary pressures. Most often, however, a simultaneous and politically popular increase in monetary expansion takes place along with the price and wage controls, turning expectations in the other direction and creating more difficulties. Many economists believe that announced and concrete action on the part of government to control money and fiscal growth has proved to be of greater benefit in containing and stabilizing expectations and, therefore, inflation. Most economists believe that wage and price controls attack the symptoms of inflation but not the cause.

APPLICATION   Politics and Inflation: A Global Perspective

The Federal Reserve System was created by Congress in 1913 to administer and manage the money supply as directed in the Constitution. As an agency of Congress, the Federal Reserve Board represents or is an extension of Congress, but Congress set up the Federal Reserve to be quasi-independent—that is, at some distance from the control of the president and from direct congressional involvement. For example, Federal Reserve Board members other than the chair are appointed for 14-year terms by the president, which means that they can remain on the job regardless of which party controls the White House. The chair is also appointed as a member of the Board for a 14-year term. The appointment as chair lasts four years but may be renewed. Independence is also reflected in the fact that the Federal Reserve is not dependent on congressional and administrative budget appropriations. The Federal Reserve finances all of its own operations, mainly through interest earned on government bonds.

Is the Federal Reserve too independent? Should it be brought under closer scrutiny of Congress or the president, or is its current position appropriate to its intended function? Critics argue that the loose connection between the president and the Federal Reserve System creates discoordination between fiscal and monetary policy. Monetary policy, in this view, should be under the direct control of the executive branch of government so that it is tied closely to the democratic wishes of voters. Such criticism is usually heard during periods of high interest rates and tight money.

Defenders of quasi-independence claim that control of the money supply and other aspects of monetary policy should be insulated from politics. Defenders of the Fed argue that quasi-independence permits monetary policymakers to have a longer-run perspective, to be able to see beyond the next election. They point out that the Federal Reserve is a creation of Congress and that it can be abolished at any time by an act of Congress. (During the 1980s, when many members of Congress actively opposed the Fed's tight monetary policy, Congress amended the Federal Reserve Act and limited the Fed's ability to change reserve requirements—an action widely interpreted as a symbolic gesture to remind the Fed that too much independence would not be tolerated.)

The Federal Reserve Board chair is required to present periodic reports to Congress, relating to the management of money measures and interest rates. To go beyond this level of accountability, some say, might tempt politicians into inflating the money supply to cover budget deficits, unwise government spending, or political ambition.

Table 13.2 provides evidence that central bank independence has beneficial effects in keeping inflation low. The World Bank has calculated (with an index expressed as a percent) the "legal" independence of central banks from political control, the turnover of central bankers at each central bank, and inflation rates between 1980 and 1989 for various nations.[a] Table 13.2 shows the relation

[a]*World Bank Policy Research Bulletin* (November–December 1992), vol. 3, no. 5, pp. 1–6. For further details see Alex Cukierman, Steven B. Webb, and Bilin Neyapti, "Measuring the Independence of Central Banks and its Effect on Policy Outcomes," *World Bank Economic Review* 6 (1992), pp. 353–398.

TABLE 13.2

Degree of Central Bank Independence and Inflation

In the table, a measure of the legal degree of central bank independence in 21 countries is shown with the average inflation rates in those countries. In general, during the period 1980–1989, the greater the degree of independence, the lower the inflation rate.

Economy	Legal Central Bank Independence (index)	Average Annual Inflation Rate (index)
Germany, Fed. Rep of	0.69	3
Switzerland	0.64	3
Austria	0.61	4
Denmark	0.50	7
United States	0.48	5
Canada	0.45	6
Ireland	0.44	9
Netherlands	0.42	3
Australia	0.36	8
Iceland	0.34	32
Luxembourg	0.33	5
Sweden	0.29	8
Finland	0.28	7
United Kingdom	0.27	7
Italy	0.25	11
New Zealand	0.24	12
France	0.24	7
Spain	0.23	10
Japan	0.18	3
Norway	0.17	8
Belgium	0.17	5

SOURCE: World Bank Policy Research Bulletin (November–December 1992), vol. 3, no. 5, p. 4.

between the World Bank's index of legal independence and the inflation rates in 21 industrial countries. While *legal* independence may differ from actual independence (especially in developing economies), the study concludes (a) that legal independence is a significant determinant of price stability in industrial nations and (b) that the turnover rates of central bank governors (not shown here) are significant in explaining the inflation rates of developing countries over the 1980s. Germany, for example, has had very low inflation rates since World War II, and its central bank (the *Bundesbank*) operates essentially unfettered by elected politicians. All but one of the countries in Table 13.2 with more central bank independence than the United States—Denmark—had lower inflation rates than the United States had over the 1980s. Thus it is reasonable to conclude that more independence from normal politics may result in better performance by central bankers.

QUESTION

It has been illustrated that countries with central banks operating independently of government typically have lower inflation rates than other countries. Why do you suppose a government would want to control a nation's central bank?

SUMMARY

1. There are three basic demands for money: transactions demands, precautionary demands, and speculative demands in the bond or securities market.
2. Transactions and precautionary demands are directly related to income. An increase in income, for example, would cause an individual to hold a proportionately greater amount of money for transactions and precautionary purposes.
3. The public also holds money to speculate on the bond market. Expectations of higher bond prices (lower interest returns) would mean that individuals would choose to hold money rather than bonds, whereas lower bond prices (higher interest returns) would mean that individuals would prefer to hold bonds rather than money. Speculative money demands are therefore inversely related to the interest rate.
4. The simple quantity theory of money is a macroeconomic theory of how the price level is formed. When transactions demands are considered proportional to income, velocity is assumed constant. Since real output and income are also assumed to be at a maximum, increases in money supply, M-1, cause proportionate increases in the price level.
5. The monetarists view inflation as a dynamic process originating with higher rates of M-1 expansion by the Federal Reserve System. Increased spending leads to higher actual and expected inflation rates (real GDP being constant) and therefore to higher nominal interest rates. Higher nominal interest rates lead to lower money demand, more spending, and more inflation.
6. In the monetarist explanation of inflation, the inflationary process does not end until the Federal Reserve stabilizes growth of the money supply.
7. Inflation is a process of price increases. Inflation redistributes income in society away from those on fixed incomes and those holding dollar-denominated assets. Inflation also disrupts expectations and amounts to a tax that is imposed without having been voted on.
8. Nonmonetary theories of inflation focus on structural problems in the economy such as the existence of or increases in monopoly and union power. In this view, unreasonable demands can create a wage-price spiral that can be stopped only through government intervention or through price and wage controls.
9. Monetarists argue that the ultimate cause of inflation is monetary expansion in excess of the economy's ability to produce goods and services. They feel that only rules pertaining to the conduct of both fiscal and monetary policy can create stability in the macroeconomy.

KEY TERMS

real money demand
transactions demand
precautionary demand
speculative motive or demand
liquidity preference theory
quantity theory of money
income velocity

neutrality of money
rate of monetary expansion
monetarism
escalator clauses
pure inflation tax
tax indexation
cost-push inflation

demand-pull inflation
wage-price spiral
accommodation of cost-push
   inflation
supply shock inflation

QUESTIONS FOR REVIEW AND DISCUSSION

1. Why do people hold money? What effect does the level of income have on the amount of money people hold?
2. What is the cost of holding money? If bond prices fall, does the cost of holding money rise or fall?
3. What is the quantity theory of money? How is it related to the neutrality of money?
4. What is the income velocity of money, V? How does V relate to the transactions demand for money?
5. If the rate of growth of the money supply is equal to 10 percent, the velocity of money is constant, and real output is falling by 2 percent, what will be the rate of inflation according to monetarist theory?
6. What effect does an increase in the rate of monetary expansion have on the total level of spending? The actual rate of inflation? The expected rate of inflation?

7. According to monetarists, what causes inflation? How is inflation stopped?
8. How does inflation decrease individuals' wealth? How can people protect themselves from inflation?
9. In what sense is inflation a tax? Do government tax revenues increase when inflation occurs?
10. How might monopolies or unions cause inflation? Can monopolies cause inflation without the assistance of monetary expansion?
11. Why do wage and price controls fail to stop inflation when monetary expansion continues?

PROBLEMS

1. Suppose that the rate of monetary expansion is 10 percent per year, the growth rate in real income is 3 percent, and velocity is constant. Calculate the inflation rate using the dynamic quantity theory. Now suppose that the rate of monetary expansion rises to 15 percent per year, all else remaining the same. What is the rate of inflation? Clearly explain the process by which the increase in monetary expansion changes the inflation rate.
2. The following table represents the prices and quantities of all the goods produced and purchased in an economy in a year.

Good	Price	Quantity
Tape rentals	$4.50	240
Shoes	$8.00	220
Shirts	$6.50	300
Pants	$7.00	350
Sardines	$1.20	750
Tequila	$3.00	400

Given the information in the table, what is the nominal GDP, the real output, and the price level? If the money supply equals $3.80, then what is the velocity of money? If the money supply rises to $5.70 and money is neutral, then what happens to the price level and the quantities of the goods produced?

POINT
COUNTERPOINT

MILTON FRIEDMAN

JAMES TOBIN

Milton Friedman and James Tobin: How Important Is the Money Supply?

Milton Friedman (b. 1912) is best known for his strong and eloquent defense of capitalism and the free market, for his support of monetarism, and for his arguments against government intervention in the economy.

Born in Brooklyn, New York, Friedman was the son of immigrant parents. His mother was a seamstress; his father, the owner of a small retail dry goods store. When his father died, 15-year-old Friedman and his mother were left with very little money. The teenager showed great aptitude in mathematics in high school and won a scholarship to Rutgers University in 1929. While a student at Rutgers, Friedman waited tables to support himself, passed exams to become an accountant, and then became increasingly interested in economics. His professor, Arthur Burns, who later became chairman of the Federal Reserve Board, taught him the importance of empirical research in economics, and another professor, Homer Jones, encouraged Friedman to apply for a scholarship to graduate school at the University of Chicago. Friedman went on to receive his M.A. from Chicago and, in 1946, a Ph.D. from Columbia University. During the 1930s he worked as a statistician for the National Bureau of Economic Research, and in 1938 he married economist Rose Director, a fellow graduate student at the University of Chicago. Friedman taught economics at Chicago until his retirement in 1977, when he moved his scholarly base to the Hoover Institute at Stanford University. Friedman was the winner of the Nobel Memorial Prize in Economics in 1976.

In *Capitalism and Freedom* (1962), Friedman argues that market forces are sufficient in both individual and aggregate markets to direct resources and to establish steady growth in the economy. Government fiscal policies, Friedman believes, often bring about results contrary to those that policymakers intend and disrupt planned expenditures in the private sector. In his classic work *A Monetary History of the United States* (1963), coauthored by Anna Schwartz, Friedman claims that money velocity—related to the demand for money—is stable enough to make the money supply an excellent barometer of inflation, output, and economic growth. His views provided the basis for modern monetarist theory.

James Tobin (b. 1918), winner of the 1981 Nobel Memorial Prize in Economics, grew up during the Depression with an awareness that many of the world's problems were economic in origin. He made the decision to become an economist while taking an introductory economics course during his sophomore year at Harvard University in 1936. One of his major influences at that time was his teacher, Spencer Pollard, who suggested he read Keynes's *The General Theory*, which had just been published. According to Tobin, *The General Theory* "was a difficult book, but when you are 19 you don't know what's difficult and what's not. You just plow into it."

Describing himself as a "very, very, shy, noncompetitive individual" during his undergraduate years, Tobin went on to obtain his Ph.D. from Harvard in 1947 and was appointed Sterling Professor of Economics at Yale University in 1957. He faithfully carried Keynesian principles into the public policy arena when he was appointed to President John F. Kennedy's Council of Economic Advisers in 1961. He was one of the architects of the Kennedy-Johnson tax cut of 1964 and has consistently advocated a loose rein on the money supply. He has also played a key role in the recent effort to join Keynesian macroeconomics and neoclassical microeconomics.

Tobin received the Nobel Prize primarily for his analysis of portfolio selection and financial markets. He was president of the American Economic Association in

325

1971 and continues to support modern activist economic policies.

Keeping Watch Over the Money Supply

Friedman and Tobin certainly represent different views on monetary and fiscal policies. For Friedman, control of the money supply is the main determinant of economic stability. For his part, Tobin emphasizes the effects of government spending, taxation, and stable interest rates on economic performance. Juxtaposed, the views of each man illustrate the difference between monetarist and Keynesian approaches to the economy.

Are money supply fluctuations a cause or an effect of changes in real income? This question may be impossible to answer definitely, but Milton Friedman has consistently argued that money supply growth is the best barometer we have of economic expansion and contraction. Friedman cites a variety of statistics to back his claim. For example, since the turn of the century, fluctuations in rates of growth in real GNP have strongly coincided with annual growth rates in the nation's money supply. Prior to recession and depression, the money supply growth rate has fallen dramatically; prior to expansions and a booming inflationary economy, the money supply growth rate has shown marked increases.

To explain this statistical marriage of money supply and economic activity, Friedman argues that money velocity is a stable variable. Therefore, interest rates, which may go up or down in response to government spending, do not contribute to economic fluctuations as many economists believe. They are merely a sideshow to the growth patterns in the money supply.

If Friedman's premise is correct, then the government's attempts to fine-tune the economy through spending and taxation policies are largely misdirected. For the sake of stability, Friedman argues, government should concern itself with a stable growth rate in the money supply. By doing so, he believes, the roller-coaster ride of business cycles, of temporary boom followed by temporary bust, can be leveled out and the economy can achieve consistent, measured growth for the future.

There are many complicated issues surrounding Friedman's proposal. For instance, can government officials afford to sit idly by in times of high unemployment, believing that over the long run a stable monetary policy will rescue the economy? Experience in the 1960s and 1970s suggests that Friedman's proposal is perhaps politically unfeasible. A second issue involves the definition of money supply. For Friedman, the only significant money supply definition is M-1—currency plus demand deposits. Recently, however, changes in the banking system have created uncertainties over what exactly constitutes money in the traditional sense of M-1. If the Federal Reserve policymakers cannot rely on a firm definition of the money supply, efforts to control its growth may be frustrating or even futile. Friedman strongly believes that the concept of M-1, for all its apparent weaknesses, is the Federal Reserve's best measure of money supply. Larger aggregates, such as M-2 or M-3, are far beyond the control of the Federal Reserve System.

Fiscal Activism and Stable Interest Rates

For James Tobin, the issue of what determines ups and downs in the economy is not nearly so straightforward. In essence, Tobin believes that consumption and investment activity are the true determinants of economic performance. Controlling or directing such activity, however, is much more complicated than simply monitoring the money supply. On the one hand, it involves spending and taxation policies to counterbalance the rise and fall of aggregate demand. On the other hand, it involves monetary policies to keep interest rates at acceptable levels.

Unlike Friedman, Tobin believes that the velocity of money is unstable. If this assumption is correct, then interest rates are much more important in economic policy than M-1 growth rates because interest rates determine the shifting demand between different kinds of money assets, leading to greater or lesser consumption and investment activity. Tobin argues that the "strict monetarist regime" he believes to have been in effect at the Federal Reserve between 1979 and 1982 was a failure. He blames the recession and high unemployment between 1981 and 1983 on the Fed's attempt to place limits on M-1 growth.[a] Rather than target M-1 or the money base, the Fed, according to Tobin, should target broader economic aggregates such as the growth rate in nominal GDP and adjust its monetary policy according to its best estimate of where the economy is headed. (Friedman disputes the idea that monetarism has ever been tried by the Federal Reserve System.)

Tobin's position not only admits the need for politicians to do something in times of high unemployment, but it argues for such action. His activist stance, however, can be a two-edged sword. Spending policies can adversely affect interest rates, and therefore fiscal and monetary policies can conflict with one another. The current debate over high government deficits reflects this conflict, for many economists argue that growing deficits drive up interest rates.

[a]For details on Tobin's position, see his "Monetarism: An Ebbing Tide?" *The Economist* (April 27, 1985), pp. 23–25.

PART 4

MACROECONOMIC POLICY AND ECONOMIC GROWTH

CHAPTER 14

MACROECONOMIC THEORY AND POLICY

A s we have seen in previous chapters, economists find it hard to agree on where the economy is heading and what, if anything, should be done about altering its course. How many times have you heard different predictions of future macroeconomic events by government economic advisers, academics, and business economists? Economists often are equally at odds over the proper policy to correct or sustain economic forces. These differences over policy often arise from differences in theory, particularly differing opinions regarding the inherent stability of the economy. Earlier we discussed how specific theories of the economy, such as early classical theory and Keynesian theory, have led to quite different policy prescriptions. In the view of most economists, these older theories have not fully explained events or predicted accurately. Over the past two decades new theories have arisen that build upon older ideas and that are currently being tested. After reading Chapter 14 you should understand

- how macroeconomic policy prescriptions designed to alleviate inflationary or unemployment situations depend on theories about how the economy functions.

- how new Keynesians and new classical writers—those who lean toward monetarist or "rational expectationist" theories—view fiscal and monetary policy.

- some of the elements in the debate among macroeconomists on the issues of discretionary versus nondiscretionary policies.

POLICY ALTERNATIVES

The purpose of macroeconomic policy is to ensure economic stability—full employment, price stability, and steady growth. There are, of course, various interpretations of exactly what full employment, price stability, and steady growth mean in percentage terms, but most economists and policymakers would agree, for instance, that persistent unemployment rates of 12 or 14 percent or inflation rates of 15 or 20 percent are unacceptable. Likewise, most economists and observers would agree that unemployment rates of 5 to 7 percent, inflation rates of 2 to 4 percent, and real GDP growth rates of 3 percent are "in the ballpark" as acceptable macroeconomic policy goals. These ballpark figures are about the right percentages for a well-functioning economy.

In previous chapters on macroeconomic and monetary theory, we saw that there are a number of interacting monetary and nonmonetary factors that affect prices, real income, and employment. Figure 14.1 summarizes these various forces. As the figure shows, the nonmonetary factors are consumption, investment, real interest rates, and net foreign trade expenditures on the private side and government spending and taxation on the public side. The monetary factors are money supply and money demand.

A subset of these variables can be manipulated through discretionary government policy. Fiscal policy—manipulation of government spending or taxation by Congress and the president—is one means of ensuring overall stability. (See the Focus, "The President's Council of Economic Advisers," for a discussion of one

FIGURE 14.1

Determinants of Price Stability, Full Employment, and Economic Growth

Both monetary and nonmonetary variables determine whether the goals of economic policy are achieved. Of these determinants only government spending, taxation, and the money supply may be directly altered in discretionary fashion (also see Figure 14.2).

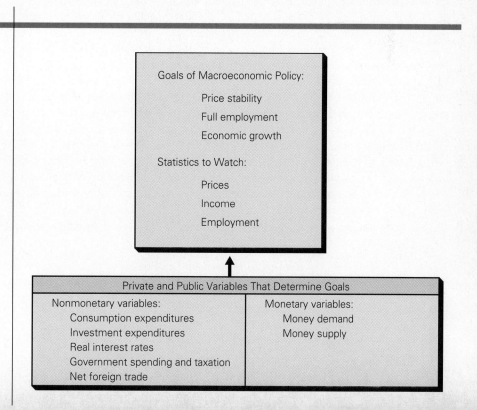

ƒOcus   The President's Council of Economic Advisers

President Harry S. Truman is reputed to have remarked that he would have been willing to pay a princely sum for a one-handed economist. After the Council of Economic Advisers gave their economic policy recommendations, Truman bemoaned, his economists always ended up saying, "But on the other hand. . . . "

What is the Council of Economic Advisers, and what exactly does it do? The Council of Economic Advisers (CEA) was established as an office in the executive branch of the federal government by the Employment Act of 1946. The CEA's basic duties are to supply the president with economic analysis and advice in order to assist in the development and implementation of national economic policy. Outstanding economists such as James Tobin, a Nobel laureate (1981) appointed by President John F. Kennedy, have served as members of the CEA.

The CEA consists of three members who are appointed by the president, with approval of the Senate, one of whom serves as chair of the CEA. The professional staff of the CEA is made up of 11 senior and 6 junior economists, as well as a statistician. The staff economists specialize in fields of expertise such as macroeconomics, international finance, labor, public finance, taxation, monetary policy, regulation, and agriculture. In most cases, the senior staff economists are on leave of absence from major universities, research institutions, or other government agencies.

By far, the CEA's most important duties are to provide the president with sound economic analysis concerning areas where policy decisions, either legislative or regulatory, are to be made. These areas include, of course, the broad area of national macroeconomic pol-

icy. The CEA not only assists the president in formulating macroeconomic policy but also assists in designing the necessary programs through which such policy is carried out. Forecasts and projections of critical macroeconomic variables such as the deficit, inflation, real GDP growth, and foreign exchange rates are all prepared by the CEA. In addition, the CEA has prepared economic analyses of such microeconomic issues as farm credit, airline and trucking deregulation, banking deregulation, space shuttle pricing, immigration, and antitrust legislation.

At the end of each January, the CEA submits an annual report to the president. This report, together with the president's own report, is then transmitted to Congress. These are then published yearly as the *Economic Report of the President*. The Report is not only an informative analysis of recent economic events and current problems, but it is also one of the better sources of economic statistics. Data on everything from budget deficits to farm income to unemployment are reported here, some going as far back as 1929. The CEA also is responsible for data contained in a more up-to-date monthly publication called *Economic Indicators*.

The Council of Economic Advisers does not decide economic policy. This is the duty of the president and Congress. However, the CEA is in a position to strongly influence economic policy. The CEA chair and members are usually chosen on the basis of shared philosophy with the president, as shown by President Bush's selection of Stanford University economist Michael Boskin, a moderate, and President Clinton's selection of Joseph Stiglitz, a liberal economist from Stanford University, to head their respective councils. Like other administration officials dealing with economic questions and problems—the Secretary of the Treasury, the head of the Office of Management and the Budget—CEA members influence decision making by force of personality, reputation, and personal relationship with the president.

organization used by the President to develop economic policy.) Monetary policy—actions of the Federal Reserve Board to alter the money supply or interest rates—is another means of achieving macroeconomic goals. Table 14.1 summarizes these two types of policy.

Fiscal and monetary policies differ according to the amount of time each takes to implement, the magnitude of their effects, and the direction of their effects. For example, by using one of its specific tools the Federal Reserve can act to alter the money supply when there is a perceived employment downturn or inflation up-

TABLE 14.1

Types of Macroeconomics Policies

Fiscal policy is controlled by the president and Congress. Monetary policy is directed by the Federal Reserve Board.

Type of Policy	Scope	Tools
Fiscal policy	Changes in government taxation, spending	Alterations in income tax rate or other tax rates
		Changes in government spending on goods and services or for transfer payments
Monetary policy	Changes in money supply, interest rates	Open market operations
		Changes in discount rates
		Changes in reserve requirements

surge, but Congress usually requires a bit more time to enact fiscal correctives. Fiscal policies, moreover, may have more immediate effects on the economy, but the effects of monetary policies may be longer lasting. In the following sections, we consider different views of these possible effects.

NEW KEYNESIAN THEORY AND POLICY

Early Keynesian economics, developed in the 1930s and 1940s, was a product of the era in which it was born: It was primarily oriented toward the problems of depression and unemployment. New Keynesians retain a belief that the economy, left

"On Wall Street today, news of lower interest rates sent the stock market up, but then the expectation that these rates would be inflationary sent the market down, until the realization that lower rates might stimulate the sluggish economy pushed the market up, before it ultimately went down on fears that an overheated economy would lead to a reimposition of higher interest rates."

Robert Mankoff ©1981 from The New Yorker Magazine, Inc.

FIGURE 14.2

The Keynesian Stand on Demand-Deficiency Unemployment

A decrease in real expenditures causes aggregate demand curve AD_0 to shift downward to AD_1, also causing a shift from full employment, Y_F, to Y_1. This gap in income caused by a shift in aggregate demand produces demand-deficiency unemployment. Keynesians suggest that this unemployment can be eliminated through the use of fiscal policy, returning aggregate demand, income, and employment to their original levels.

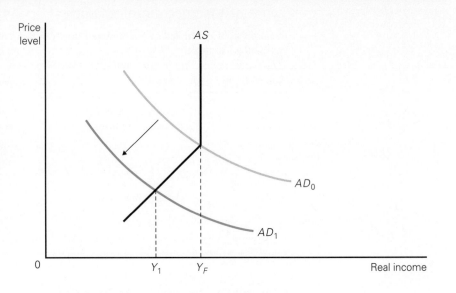

to itself, is unable to adjust to falling aggregate demand and to restore the equilibrium level of income and full employment. In this view, fundamental instabilities pervade the economic system. In the broadest sense, the role of policy is to overcome the forces of instability in the economy.

An Unstable Economy

Sharp fluctuations in GDP, unemployment, and inflation can occur for a variety of reasons. Investment spending can initiate cycles of rising and falling business activity. Supply shocks, caused by natural disasters or international upheaval, can disrupt domestic markets. Autonomous consumer spending, magnified by the multiplier, can drive GDP and unemployment up or down.

Our analysis of aggregate demand shifts in Chapter 10 helps illustrate graphically the effects of such disturbances. Figure 14.2 shows aggregate demand and aggregate supply of a hypothetical economy. Along curve AD_0, the economy reaches full employment, Y_F. Assume, however, that investment spending, in response to a sudden change in profit expectations, drops. As a result, unemployment increases and real output falls. Figure 14.2 shows the effect: a shift in aggregate demand from AD_0 to AD_1 and a fall in income from Y_F to Y_1. The gap in employment caused by the shift in aggregate demand is usually referred to as demand-deficiency unemployment. With resources idle and a gap in demand, policymakers must wrestle with these two questions: Will the economy be able to self-correct the deficiency? and How long will it take to do so? In the long run, as we have noted, theory predicts that prices and wages will fall in response to a shift in aggregate demand. But what about the short run? Can the economy or the unemployed afford to wait for natural market forces to restore full employment?

TABLE 14.2

Keynesian Prescriptions to Control the Business Cycle

In the fiscal arena, budget deficits should be employed to cure unemployment and lagging economic growth, while inflation should be controlled by budget surpluses. Throughout all phases of the cycle, stable interest rates should be maintained by the Federal Reserve in money markets.

Economic Problem	KEYNESIAN CORRECTIVE	
	Fiscal Policy	Monetary Policy
Recession (high unemployment and slow income growth)	Budget deficits ($G > T$) (government spending greater than taxation)	Increase M-1 and keep interest rates low and stable
Inflation	Budget surpluses ($G < T$) (taxation greater than government spending)	Reduce M-1

Countercyclical Fiscal Policy

In the Keynesian view, time is at the heart of the problem and, to Keynes, the short run could last a long time. While the economy might be self-correcting in the long run, the adjustment would be painful and time-consuming. In the short run, prices and wages would not fall sufficiently to restore full employment. Unnecessary economic disruption—in product and labor markets—would occur if the economy were allowed to establish its own natural rate of income and employment growth. The Keynesians' recommended cure for macroeconomic problems is to apply countercyclical fiscal policy. Proper macroeconomic policy in the event of recession and unemployment is to run budget deficits—that is, to keep government expenditures greater than tax revenues. And, though the advice has seldom been taken, inflation calls for budget surpluses—that is, for tax receipts to exceed government expenditures.

Table 14.2 simplifies and summarizes the Keynesian position. During recession or depression, Congress, the administration, and state and local governments should increase spending and/or reduce taxes. Inflation calls for the opposite policies.

Keynesian Monetary Policy

Note in Table 14.2 that monetary policy is also included in the Keynesian approach to economic instability. Most Keynesians advocate that the Federal Reserve Board respond to inflationary or recessionary pressures in the economy by keeping order in financial markets. That is, the Federal Reserve should use its discretionary power over the M-1 money supply to stabilize interest rates, which, left unchecked, can rise to levels that discourage or even choke off private spending.

As outlined in the discussion of the liquidity preference curve and the speculative demand for money in Chapter 13, the Federal Reserve might be unable to increase or decrease interest rates at will. Changes in the money supply can affect interest rates, but only if money demanders cooperate. If, for example, money demanders want to hold additional balances for speculative purposes due to dim expectations about bond prices or about the economy in general, an addition to the money supply will not have much effect on interest rates. Alternatively, if the Federal Reserve wanted to increase interest rates by lowering the supply of money, individuals might simply reduce their holdings of money for speculative purposes in roughly equal proportions, which again would result in little or no change in interest rates. Further, any change in interest rates—large or small—might not translate into changes in consumption or investment spending if expectations are that future investment profitability and economic conditions will not be good.

The use of an interest rate target, therefore, is an unpredictable method of changing total spending because the Federal Reserve is constrained by the liquidity preference curve. Because speculative demands for money are based on expectations, liquidity preference is likely to change without much notice. The role of the Federal Reserve, therefore, is to attempt to maintain order in financial markets and, if possible, to keep interest rates low to encourage consumption and investment spending.

DIRECT VERSUS INDIRECT POLICY   Given recurring short-run instabilities in the economy, Keynesians consider fiscal policy a more direct and more immediately effective tool to manage aggregate demand than monetary policy. In the Keynesian model, there is no solid link between changes in M-1 and changes in aggregate demand. If M-1 increases, the larger holdings of money by individuals and businesses might not all be spent on more goods and services; some of these funds will be channeled into speculative holdings.

PROBLEMS WITH M-1   In addition, the money supply is less suited to discretionary policy. The Federal Reserve is sometimes unable to keep interest rates within specified targets by manipulating M-1. One reason for this problem is the recent emergence of close money substitutes such as money market mutual funds (a type of checkable deposit not included in M-1), which have tended to blur the definition of M-1 money. Without a reliable measure of the money supply, the Federal Reserve is potentially unsure of the effects of its M-1 policy.

For these reasons and others, Keynesians believe that tax and spending policies can give policymakers greater discretionary control over the business cycle than can monetary policies. The effects of monetary adjustments, especially on interest rates, are a second, unpredictable line of defense to ensure economic stability.

More important, perhaps, than the issue of whether fiscal or monetary policy is the preferred tool of policymakers is the issue of whether such policy does what it is supposed to do—correct the instabilities caused by shifts in aggregate demand. Keynesians obviously believe that ignoring such instabilities in the short run would inflict greater potential harm on the economy. As we will see, however, not all economists believe that countercyclical discretionary policy is the best way to ensure stability.

NEW CLASSICAL ECONOMICS: MONETARIST THEORY AND POLICY

New classical economics (NCE) is an alternative view of the macroeconomy that predicts that, in the extreme, monetary policy will have no effect on real magnitudes of output and employment and that fiscal policy will not have the effects on output and employment that Keynes had predicted. It combines elements of a number of older theories—classical, supply-side, monetarist—to produce a theory of market behavior based on perceptions and learning by market participants. Much of new classical economics is based on the assumption of rational expectations—the assumption that rational market participants (investors, consumers, taxpayers) learn to anticipate the effects of monetary and fiscal policy changes and act to neutralize them. Because new classical economics takes monetarism one step further, let us again consider the monetarist policy position, aspects of which were treated in Chapter 13. The monetarist, like the classical economist but unlike the Keynesian, views the economy as inherently stable.

A Self-Stabilizing Economy

Figure 14.3 analyzes demand-deficiency unemployment from the monetarist perspective. Assume there is a reduction in autonomous consumption or investment, shifting the original aggregate demand curve from AD_0 to AD_1. The reduction in

FIGURE 14.3

Monetarist Policy on Demand-Deficiency Unemployment

According to monetarist theory, the economy will self-adjust to the natural rate of unemployment, Y_F, in the event of a decline in aggregate demand. Price and nominal wage reductions occur when aggregate demand declines from AD_0 to AD_1, creating increased real balances, which in turn increase consumption and investment spending. Such price reductions also create, through adaptive expectations, rightward shifts in short-run aggregate supply from $SRAS_0$ to $SRAS_1$. The economy finally readjusts to the full-employment level of output, Y_F, at equilibrium E_2 with lower price level P_1.

autonomous spending is accompanied by an increase in consumers' and businesses' holdings of real money balances. Initially, the economy is in equilibrium at point E_0. The price level is P_0, and the full-employment level of output, Y_F, is being produced. The rate of unemployment in the economy is the natural rate of unemployment that will exist when Y_F is produced. In the short run, the drop in aggregate demand moves the economy to a new equilibrium at point E_1, where the level of real income produced is Y_1—less than the full-employment level of income. The rate of unemployment is higher than the natural rate of unemployment, or, what is the same thing, the level of employment is less than full employment. Then the economy self-adjusts to a new long-run equilibrium at E_2. Real income rises back to Y_F. The level of employment returns to the full-employment level, and of course, the rate of unemployment falls back to the natural rate of unemployment.

Errors in Real Wage Perceptions

How might we explain the important process of movement from E_0 to E_1 and then from E_1 to E_2? When aggregate demand falls from AD_0 to AD_1, the level of prices and, to a lesser degree, nominal wages also fall. Employers correctly perceive an increase in real wages and respond by reducing the amount of labor employed. Although the price level has fallen somewhat, workers' price expectations have yet to adjust downward. They still perceive the price level as being P_0. This means that workers believe their real wage has fallen. They will consequently reduce their labor supply. The economy will move along the short-run aggregate supply $SRAS_0$ to point E_1, and real income will fall to Y_1. Temporarily, unemployment exists in the economy equal to the level of employment associated with real output level Y_F minus that associated with output level Y_1. This unemployment is demand-deficiency unemployment.

From the monetarist perspective, the demand-deficiency unemployment that occurs when the economy produces Y_1 cannot exist permanently. In the monetarist view of the macroeconomy, dynamic forces are at work assuring a return to the full employment of resources at some new equilibrium, E_2. If we assume that no fiscal or monetary actions are undertaken by Congress or the Federal Reserve to deal with unemployment, two sets of automatic changes will dominate. First, falling prices will affect the aggregate demand for goods and services through the real balance effect. A decline in the price level will increase real holdings of money, leading to increased consumption and, through lower interest rates brought about by the increased real money supply, to increased investment.

A second effect will act on the short-run aggregate supply curve. When workers' expectations adapt to the lower price levels, their perceptions of the real wage they receive will change. Specifically, they will adapt their expectations to falling actual prices, which signal an increase rather than a decrease in real wages. Time is required, in short, for workers to perceive the actual decline in prices. They will begin to supply more, not less, labor at every wage level. This adaptation in expectations has the effect of shifting the short-run aggregate supply curve rightward from $SRAS_0$ to $SRAS_1$.

Given pressures on prices, where will equilibrium finally reemerge? Downward pressure on nominal wages and prices will exist as long as there is unemployment in the system. As price expectations adjust to lower price levels, the *SRAS* curve shifts rightward because of unemployed workers' desires to regain work even at lower nominal wages. After effects from the drop in prices have taken place and after expectations have finally adjusted to the lower prices, equilibrium will reemerge at E_2. The economy moves along aggregate demand curve AD_1, and the relevant short-run supply function will be $SRAS_1$. Due to the initial decrease in consumption and investment spending, prices will fall to P_1, a level to which both employers and workers will again adjust.

In the monetarist view, the interplay between price changes and aggregate demand and between price-wage changes and short-run aggregate supply is sufficient to return the economy to full employment at E_2. However, the monetarist result hinges crucially on the *absence* of interventions by Congress or the Federal Reserve. In the monetarist view, such interventions interfere with the adjustment of price level expectations. As a result, they complicate and prolong the adjustment process.

Destabilizing Effects of Fiscal and Monetary Policies

Monetarists adhere to the belief that the market economy will stabilize at full employment. But alternating periods of recession and inflation have been, and continue to be, a feature of market economies. How do monetarists explain the facts of instability?

Like Keynesians, monetarists admit that shifts in aggregate demand can cause waves, or cycles, of unemployment and inflation. Monetarists, however, believe that the primary cause of aggregate demand shifts is not the movement of investment or consumption spending but the actions of government fiscal and monetary policymakers. According to monetarists, the destabilizing element in the macroeconomy is the shifting expectations of market participants—laborers, businesspeople, consumers, and producers—created by erratic alterations in government expenditures, taxation, and the money supply.

THE EFFECTS OF FINANCING GOVERNMENT EXPENDITURES   In the monetarist view, increases in government expenditures—one of the primary tools of fiscal policy—come at the expense of private expenditures. If government spending is financed through taxation, private consumption and investment spending are reduced by the amount of the tax. If government spending is financed through borrowing in private markets, the government's demand for loanable funds will likely raise real interest rates; higher interest rates will tend to choke off investment, depending on the responsiveness of investors to the increase. This competition for private funds is termed the crowding-out effect. If government spending is financed through the selling of Treasury bonds to the Federal Reserve, the result is potentially inflationary (Chapters 12 and 13 explain why this is so). In sum, the effects of financing government expenditures may offset any gain those expenditures offer a demand-deficient economy. In addition, such policies may create destabilizing effects.

LAGS IN FISCAL POLICY   Another problem with fiscal policy often cited by monetarists concerns legislative frailties. Given the nature of public policy and the competing demands of political interest, fiscal policymakers are often slow to

Recognition lag
The amount of time it takes policymakers to realize that a destabilizing economic event has occurred.

recognize and act on economic distress signals. **Recognition lags** are the time it takes the president and Congress to identify impending or existing economic conditions. Predicting economic events is both a science and an art. But an even larger problem for economic policymakers is that time-consuming data analysis is required before experts can comment conclusively on the health of the economy. All during the 1992 presidential campaign, for example, President Bush kept insisting that the economy was growing at a satisfactory rate—or would be very soon. Bill Clinton argued that the economy needed fiscal stimulus to get moving again after the recession of 1990–1991. Before the election, both the anecdotal evidence—people's perceptions—and the government's statistics tended to support Clinton's position. In December 1992, however, one month after Bush's defeat, the government released figures showing a growth rate in GDP of 4.6 percent for the third quarter of 1992—very respectable indeed, but too late to help Bush's reelection bid. Meanwhile, President Clinton's economic stimulus plan was defeated in Congress, largely on the basis of the 4.6 percent rate of growth in GDP for the third quarter of 1992.

Administrative lag
The amount of time between recognition of a destabilizing economic event and the implementation of a policy designed to correct it.

In addition to the difficulties of recognizing a problem in time, there are administrative lags with fiscal policy. **Administrative lags** are the length of time between politicians' recognition of a business cycle problem and their enactment of legislation to correct the problem. (The lag is even more properly called a *decision* lag—the time it takes to decide what to do.) We cite two examples of such lags. The Kennedy-Johnson tax cut of 1964 to stimulate economic growth was proposed as early as 1961 and 1962; its not being enacted until 1964 indicates an administrative lag. Likewise, a jobs bill passed in 1982 to deal with unemployment was debated for months and, when finally passed, was scheduled to go into effect more than a year later. Monetarists emphasize that economic conditions may change before the effects of these legislative acts take place. This would mean that fiscal policy could be procyclical rather than countercyclical in effect, buttressing inflation or recession as the case may be.

Once fiscal policy is enacted, it also takes time for its full impact to be realized—an impact lag, if you will. Estimates vary, but it is thought that tax or spending changes may take from one to two years to have their full impact on income and employment. Recognition and administrative lags make monetarists dubious about the effectiveness of fiscal policy. The unpredictability of how long it may take even well-intentioned fiscal policy to have an effect means that market participants' expectations about prices and future incomes are thrown into uncertainty in the meantime.

EFFECTS OF MONETARY POLICY   Discretionary monetary policy has its own problems in the monetarist view. Like fiscal policy, the attempt to control the money supply in countercyclical fashion is also subject to recognition and administrative lags. In the case of monetary policy, it is the quasi-independent Federal Reserve Board and its Federal Open Market Committee, not politicians, who must recognize macroeconomic problems and then enact and administer a change in policies affecting interest rates or the money supply. While problems of recognizing signs of recession or anticipating unemployment or assessing inflationary pressures may be as great as with fiscal policy, they are somewhat easier to handle because of the small number of Federal Reserve Board or Open Market Committee members. Concerted discretionary recognition and action is probably quicker than with the larger numbers of participants in the fiscal policy setting.

Despite the quicker response, the time between enactment of monetary policy and when it takes effect is as unpredictable as the time related to fiscal manipulations. Some economists believe that the lag between growth in the money supply and the rate of inflation is at least two years long. These same economists view the effects of monetary growth on income and employment as somewhat more immediate. Other studies appear to show that most of the effects of monetary growth on prices, income, and employment take place rapidly, perhaps within six months. A third body of evidence seems to indicate that changes in aggregate demand induced by monetary growth will first have an impact on employment and income and will affect prices later, when expectations catch up. Such competing evidence illustrates the present uncertainty over the effects of discretionary monetary policy. The short run, in other words, may be shorter than the lag time between the money supply and policy variables. Critics also argue that even the best-intentioned fiscal policy is unable to address certain kinds of economic problems (see the Focus "Homelessness and Unemployment: The Limits of Discretionary Policy").

The monetarist conclusion is that, on balance, discretionary fiscal and monetary policy will not be able to control swings of the business cycle. Indeed, in some regard, business cycle alterations are caused by destabilizing attempts to control cycles of inflation and unemployment. Stop-and-go policies that accelerate, decelerate, or otherwise interfere with private saving and spending are seen as the primary causes of aggregate demand instability, leading to prolonged recession and unemployment. The solution to the problems created by discretionary political or quasi-political attempts to control the business cycle is to establish rules through which fiscal and monetary policy is carried out.

Monetary rule
A monetary policy consisting of a fixed rate of growth of the money supply.

In general, monetarists advocate that both fiscal and monetary policy be taken out of the hands of discretionary authorities—Congress, the President, and the Federal Reserve Board. Indeed, monetarists advocate the use of a **monetary rule** that would replace stop-and-go Federal Reserve policies with a constant growth rate in the money stock. On the fiscal side, monetarists argue, government's budget should be balanced at all levels—local, state, and federal—through fiscal restraint or through a balanced budget amendment. (For a discussion of the pros and cons of a Balanced Budget Amendment to the Constitution, see the Application at the end of the chapter). Along with balanced budgets, the monetarists and other economists urge that government regulations supporting monopoly be eliminated or modified. Deregulation in some industries and some occupations would create greater price and wage flexibility. Greater price and wage flexibility would in turn encourage a faster adjustment to both demand-deficiency unemployment and to inflation when the economy is disturbed.

fOcus   Homelessness and Unemployment: The Limits of Discretionary Policy

Economists have identified two major types of unemployment: frictional and structural. Frictional unemployment—movement from job to job or from one kind of job to another—is a perfectly natural and necessary part of any market economy that has efficiency as its goal. With structural unemployment, adjustments to new kinds of work either never take place or take place very slowly. The unemployment that has resulted from the shift from coal to other (cleaner) types of energy is a case in point. Whether discretionary fiscal policies ever could have an impact on this type of "hard-core" unemployment is doubtful.

During the 1980s, another form of hard-core unemployment—utter homelessness—became a part of the lexicon of America's social ills. Although "street people" are found in virtually every major urban area in the United States, relatively little is known about the homeless. Estimates of their numbers ranged from 0.5 million to 1 million in 1993. Sociologists believe that about one-third of the homeless are afflicted with severe mental conditions and that more than 50 percent are addicted to drugs or alcohol. A relatively small proportion of the homeless are single mothers. Most of the homeless are virtually unemployed, meaning that they represent an opportunity cost of forgone production for the United States.

Economists have been unable to pinpoint the exact causes of homelessness, although several studies suggest that certain factors appear to be consistently important. There is some evidence that homelessness is positively related to local rent levels, rent controls, and unemployment rates.[a] Homelessness appears to be negatively related to higher levels of public spending on alcohol, drug, and mental health rehabilitation but not to increased federal expenditures on housing. This last point warrants some elaboration, for if true, it means that homelessness is not per se a housing problem!

How could homelessness not be a housing problem? Most observers would agree that areas such as New York, San Francisco, and Washington, D.C., harbor a large percentage of the nation's homeless.[b] These metropolitan areas also tend to provide high-quality resources to homeless persons. Therefore, many of the best resource opportunities for the homeless are found in areas where the opportunity of finding affordable housing is greatly reduced—large urban centers. In other words, the homeless are drawn to those areas in which they are least likely to find affordable housing. Many big cities have rent controls, which, as economic theory predicts, create a variety of local housing problems—including shortages. Local zoning restrictions and urban "renewal" projects may also create housing shortages in major metropolitan areas. There is no doubt that a lack of housing is a symptom of homelessness; a lack of housing may well not be a cause of homelessness, however.

Hard-core unemployment does not respond well, if at all, to aggregate fiscal or monetary policies. A tax cut or an aggregate spending increase will likely not affect hard-core unemployment or homelessness very much. More likely to have an impact are specific policies, such as providing subsidies to larger numbers of halfway houses for recovering addicts across the country. Employment problems—the province of macroeconomic policymakers—are not monolithic. Institutional considerations and rational analysis must be applied when designing policies that attempt to bolster employment or economic growth.

[a]See William Harris Troutman, John D. Jackson, and Robert B. Ekelund, Jr., "Homelessness and Housing Policy: An Empirical Study" (manuscript, Auburn University, 1996).

[b]William Tucker, "How Housing Regulations Cause Homelessness," The Public Interest (Winter 1991), pp. 78–88.

NEW CLASSICAL ECONOMICS: RATIONAL EXPECTATIONS

Some of the new classical economists are concerned with the ability of the economy to adjust to the policy actions of Congress or the Federal Reserve. In the opinion of traditional classical writers such as A. C. Pigou, market participants (buyers, sellers, consumers, investors) could not be consistently manipulated by government. Their "rationality" was based on an assumption of perfect information, although classical models did not formally take rationality into account. We have seen, however, that "adaptive" expectations are central to the monetarist view of the effects of policy. What is the difference between the monetarist conception and the newer theory of rational expectations?

The adaptive expectations theory holds that market participants form expectations about the future course of the inflation rate by tracking past rates of inflation. To use a simple example, suppose that people expect inflation this year to be what it was last year. If it was 10 percent last year, people expect it to be 10 percent this year, but if the inflation rate turns out to be 5 percent this year, people adapt and expect it to be 5 percent next year. At each period the public adjusts its expectations according to the differences between the actual inflation rate and the predicted inflation rate. It takes time and many readjustments of expectations for people to become convinced that any inflation rate (be it 6 percent or 106 percent) is permanent.

The Rational Expectations Hypothesis

Rational expectations theory
A theory of behavior that assumes that people make efficient use of all past and present relevant information in forming expectations; implies that people's reactions to policy may neutralize the intended effects of the policy.

Over the past two decades, a group of new classical economists has developed a new theory of expectations to challenge and amend the adaptive expectations hypothesis. It was founded on a pioneering contribution by economist John Muth in 1961.[1] Although much of this work—called **rational expectations theory**—is extremely technical, the major thrust of the idea is simple, straightforward, and intuitively appealing. According to the rational expectations view, people are rational in the sense that they make use of both past and present relevant information in forming expectations of the future. Here, information includes not only the current values of important policy variables such as government expenditure and money growth; it also includes knowledge of the structure of the relationships among variables such as that between the inflation rate and the nominal interest rates. It suggests that, after some learning, individuals begin to understand some of the fundamental workings of the economy. For example, they will learn through experience that increases in the rate of monetary expansion by the Federal Reserve are generally followed by increases in the inflation rate, which are then followed by

---

[1] See John Muth, "Rational Expectations and the Theory of Price Movements," *Econometrica* (July 1961), pp. 315–335. Other innovators in this area include macroeconomists Thomas J. Sargent, Neil Wallace, and Robert E. Lucas; see Thomas J. Sargent, "Rational Expectations, the Real Rate of Interest, and the Natural Rate of Unemployment," *Brookings Papers in Economic Activity* 2 (1973), pp. 429–472; Thomas J. Sargent and Neil Wallace, "Rational Expectations and the Theory of Economic Policy," *Journal of Monetary Economics* (April 1976), pp. 169–184; and R. E. Lucas, "An Equilibrium Model of the Business Cycle," *Journal of Political Economy* (December 1975), pp. 1113–1144. Lucas won the Nobel Prize in Economics in 1995 for this work.

higher nominal interest rates. Knowing something of the basic structure of the economy as well as the current values of key policy variables, individuals will be able to form expectations of likely future outcomes in the economy.

Does this mean that market participants will always be correct in their anticipations? In a world filled with uncertainty, outcomes will depend on an enormous number of random occurrences. Individuals will not always be right in their expectations about future economic events, but they will be correct on average.

If people can anticipate discretionary policy and its effects, they are in a position to neutralize the purpose of the policy. For example, if the Federal Reserve Board increases M-1 to increase employment but workers and firms perfectly anticipate the resulting increase in prices, then workers will instantly demand a proportionately higher nominal wage. Firms, anticipating higher nominal revenues, would be willing to pay the higher nominal wage, thus leaving the real wage and the level of unemployment unaffected. In this contest, policymakers are pitted against market participants; policymakers will not win continuously, and they certainly will not win over time. Policymakers may attempt to surprise the public, but they cannot do so forever. People catch on to, say, the effects of federal deficits on inflation, anticipate the change, and neutralize or counteract the effects of the change. In the long run, when a model of macroeconomic behavior is learned and actions are correctly anticipated, fiscal or monetary policy is totally ineffective in producing intended alterations on the demand side of the economy. Paradoxically, to have any purposeful effect, fiscal and monetary policy would have to be random. If it is not—if policymakers act in any systematic manner—learned behavior over time will neutralize the policy.

At base, the theory of rational expectations reinforces the classical-monetarist position: The private economy, while not perfect in providing full employment and maximum income at all times, is superior to fiscal and monetary authorities in providing a relatively stable economy. But rational expectations theory goes further and proposes that over time the effects of fiscal and monetary manipulations can be fully anticipated and therefore neutralized. Policies related to aggregate demand will either have no effect or in the longer run will actually produce reductions in aggregate supply. In short, there is little or no room for discretionary macroeconomic policy.

NEW KEYNESIAN CRITICISMS OF NEW CLASSICAL ECONOMICS

The rational expectations approach to policy has generated an enormous amount of interest. Much of the contemporary research has been devoted to the question of whether or not and under what conditions the policy-neutral implications of new classical economics hold. A good deal of sophisticated econometric testing has left open the answer to the question: Does discretionary policy work? Until testing yields consistent results, the matter of policy neutrality and the theoretical foundations of the new classical economics will form a lively debate between the rational expectationists and those with differing theoretical perspectives. Chief among the critics of new classical economics are the new Keynesians.

While many new Keynesians see value in more sophisticated theories of expectations, they retain a belief in the efficacy of discretionary government action in the economy. Policy, to the new Keynesians, is nonneutral and necessary in an economy that is inherently and endogenously unstable over nontrivial time periods. The basic dispute is over the form of the expectational assumptions of the rational expectationists and over the related issue of the efficiency of market functioning.

New Keynesians (and others) object that the new classical economics requires market participants to be more sophisticated than they really are in their abilities to predict. How might we expect buyers of VCRs and sellers of rental properties to utilize intricate and sophisticated theories of economic functioning in order to accurately predict prices, outputs, interest rates, or any other economic variable into the future and to act quickly and accurately on the prediction in the present?

Rational expectationists counter with the point that market participants are correct, *but only on average* and only after a "learning" period. If, in other words, policy itself is not random (which would be a peculiar manner of conducting it), those who consistently come up with inaccurate predictions would be severely punished in the market through losses on exchanges. Acting in their own self-interest, market participants would attempt to learn the probable effects of policy. Armies of economists in the "think tank" or "prediction service" business are hired by market participants to help them learn or to give them rational information about the future. It would be strange, indeed, for market participants not to react in this manner.

Importantly, new Keynesians argue that rational expectations theory fails to explain prolonged periods of unemployment and depression. New Keynesians regard the economy as inherently unstable (especially with regard to investment spending) and characterized by institutionalized sticky prices and wages (from monopolies and other imperfections in both product and labor markets). Rational expectationists do *not* believe, as the old classical writers did, that full production and employment *always* characterize the economic system. Unanticipated policy and price surprises cause real variables such as employment and income to diverge from their natural rates. Once market participants discover the "true" nature of the policy change, expectations catch up with actual economic magnitudes (such as prices) and the economy returns to the rational expectations equilibrium. An important question is: How long does this process take?

New Keynesians point to events such as the Great Depression of the 1930s, with its prolonged periods of unemployment and reduced growth rates in real GDP or GNP, as proof that market participants do not react in the manner described by the rational expectationists. To restate the question, even if expectations are "rational" and even if they eventually return the economy to the natural or full-employment level of output and employment, aren't the sacrifices unacceptable?

The question is, of course, a good one. The actual situation of the 1930s economy has proved difficult to gauge. New Keynesians believe that factors such as reduced aggregate demand and sticky nominal wages and prices due to effective rigidities in both product and labor markets are the essential explanation for the prolonged depression of the 1930s. Rational expectationists counter by arguing that that depression was prolonged, if not fostered, by wrongheaded government policies. Price changes failed to clear product and labor markets due to the *continuous* and *persistent* policy and institutional changes by the government. Discouragement of business investment and unanticipated policy "surprises" were the result of the government's increased participation in the private market system. Blame for the origins and length of the Great Depression is also placed at the door of the Federal Reserve System, which failed to perceive and correct for the precipitous decline in the real stock of money during the period.

The debate between the new Keynesian and the rational expectationist views of the proper role of policy will, of course, continue. Whether discretionary policy or "rules" give the best results will not be decided by theory or opinion, but by facts, illuminated by econometric testing.

THE MAJOR POLICY POSITIONS: A SUMMARY

We have now evaluated three major policy positions based on three theories of the functioning of the aggregate economy. Some theoretical or policy views are contrasting and some are complementary, as Table 14.3 reveals.

New Keynesians hold that the private economy is inherently unstable and unable to correct itself during periods of inflation and unemployment. In their view, government should take a primary role in managing fiscal and monetary policy for economic stabilization. Of the two major arms of policy, new Keynesians advocate discretionary fiscal policy as the primary weapon in controlling unemployment and inflation. Fiscal policies, they believe, have direct effects on spending in the private economy, whereas monetary policy (control of the money stock) has only indirect results. Monetary policy should maintain the order or stability of interest rates, keeping them low or moderate.

Monetarists and rational expectationists view the economy as essentially stable and self-correcting. Both views envision the private decisions of laborers, employers, money demanders, and consumer-savers and investors as producing a natural equilibrium constituting some natural rate of output and employment (or unemployment). In the monetarist view of this process, discretionary policy of any sort produces instabilities in private markets that distort, exaggerate, or accentuate any natural changes. In the monetarist view, discretionary fiscal or monetary policy contributes to instability in the private economy. That is, discretionary policy (consciously taken direct government action) either creates inflation and unemployment of itself or has erratic effects on the private economy's ability to establish economic stability. The solution: Conduct monetary and fiscal policy so as to minimize disturbances of private market participants' expectations and decisions. In the monetarist's policy views, such stability can be achieved by invoking a monetary rule, such as fixing the money supply growth rate, and insisting on balanced government budgets.

In the rational expectations variant of macroeconomic theory, the recommended role of fiscal and monetary policy is identical to that espoused by monetarists. Dif-

TABLE 14.3

Alternative Positions on Macroeconomic and Monetary Policy

A simplified menu of economic policy choices includes various recommended roles for fiscal and monetary policy. The new Keynesian position places primary emphasis on fiscal policy, while the monetarist defends a rule for monetary policy and balance in the budget. The rational expectations theory predicts that, over the long run, neither fiscal nor monetary policy will have a positive effect on the aggregate economy.

Policy Position	Role of Monetary Policy	Predicted Effects of Monetary Policy	Role of Fiscal Policy	Predicted Effects of Fiscal Policy
New Keynesian	Maintain orderly and low interest rates through discretionary adjustments in money supply	Possible destabilizing effects on interest rates if Federal Reserve only attempts to control money supply	Primary tool of macroeconomic stabilization; discretionary changes in government spending and taxation	Discretionary fiscal policy capable of ensuring full employment
Monetarist	Maintain a 3–5% growth rate in M-1	Discretionary policy will destabilize decision making in private markets; monetary rule will stabilize expectations	Provide stable environment for private economy through balanced budgets	Discretionary policy will bring erratic effects on income, employment, and prices; such policy creates an unstable economy
Rational expectations theory	Same as monetarist	In the long run, rational expectations will neutralize discretionary policy	Same as monetarist	Possible adverse long-run aggregate supply effects

ferences between these two positions lie rather in the rational expectationists' view of the probable effects of monetary and fiscal policy. As market participants gain sufficient information about the effects of economic policy through time, policy can have no effects on the private economy. Participants learn the effects of anticipated policy and act more and more quickly to counteract them. The rational expectations approach might be regarded as an extreme view within the monetarist position.

The important point is that *macroeconomists have not reached a consensus on exactly how the macroeconomy works.* Under such circumstances we expect to see a variety of policy views, as Table 14.3 shows. One of the problems with establishing a consensus among macroeconomists is the difficulty of proving one view with a statistical test that all would accept. The economist, like the meteorologist, is faced with a kaleidoscope of ever-changing conditions; hard-and-fast answers are difficult to come by.

APPLICATION   Should Congress Be Forced to Balance the Budget?

There is much grass-roots support for a constitutional amendment to balance the budget. Since 1977, thirty-two states (two short of the required number) have called for a constitutional convention to consider such an amendment. In addition, such an amendment was part of the House Republicans Contract with America in the 1994 elections, and the House passed such an amendment in 1995. The vote on the amendment fell one vote short in the Senate, securing 59 votes. So the country may be on the verge of passing a balanced budget amendment to the Constitution (a feature of many state constitutions). And, indeed, support for a constitutional amendment persists, fueled by frustration and anxiety over Congress'(and the President's) seeming inability to do anything about budget deficits.

Why not simply balance the budget in seven (or some other number) of years, as suggested in the political ruckus created in later 1995 and early 1996 between President Clinton and Congress? The real problem is that no future Congress is bound by the decisions of any past Congress. Why should future Congresses (or presidents) feel obliged to make the hard cuts that budget balancing must bring without huge increases in taxes? In so many of the proposals to balance the budget without a constitutional amendment, all of the pain of cuts in domestic welfare and other entitlement programs is pushed to the future. Budget agreements without legal constraints have all the solidity of quicksand.

The federal government has a clear record. In 1982 tax hikes were passed to relieve deficit pressures. They did not have that effect. Congress tried again in 1985 with the Gramm-Rudman-Hollings Deficit Reduction Act. It was soon avoided by Congress. Gramm-Rudman II was necessitated in 1987 because politicians would not live by the rules of the first one. Again, no effect. A bipartisan tax increase was designed to reduce the deficit in 1990 with

no impact. Finally, in 1993, the Clinton tax hikes were designed to reduce deficits. But all projections of effects to the future (including the Clinton Administration's) show a dramatic increase in deficits after 1996.

The problem is that budget agreements or tax increases will never balance the budget so long as politicians cater to the wishes of particular constituencies in order to be re-elected. Further, as mentioned above, there is no reason for one Congress to respect the laws or appropriations passed by Congresses of the past. Thus, those who argue for a balanced budget amendment stress that a legal constraint rather than simply a congressional-administration agreement would be required to bring budgets into balance.

Why is a balanced budget amendment so critical to the future of America? The answer is complex, but many believe budget balance to be the linchpin of the future of American democracy. There are the obvious economic reasons for putting absolute limits on aggregate spending and taxation. Budget balance and eventual debt reduction will bring stability to financial markets, lowering interest rates, increasing investment, and benefiting all Americans regardless of age, sex, ethnicity, and income class.

But there are reasons why some advocate a legal budget rule for the federal government—a return to a self-enforcing and self-sustaining "federalism" in our government which protects individual rights and economic growth. The key to this kind of federalism is a hierarchy and balance of power between national and state-local governments, with "regulation" (including taxation) primarily determined at the *lower* levels of government.

This balance underwent revision in only two instances in American history—after the Civil War and in the wake of the Great Depression. The lifting of the constraints on federal government growth in relation to lower levels of government—accepted in the norms of society after the 1930s—has resulted in an unrestrained federal government in terms of functions and effects in this view. Budget and debt problems are only a manifestation of this secular shift in the federal system. Incursions on the property rights of lower-level governments and on individual citizens through federal mandate are another. A balanced budget amendment would put a halt to or strictly limit such activity on the part of the federal government.

QUESTION

There has been much talk in recent years favoring a constitutional amendment to balance the federal budget. Given this, why do we still not have a balanced budget amendment at the federal level?

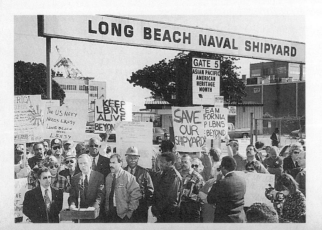

SUMMARY

1. Macroeconomic policies—those prescribed to solve macroeconomic problems such as inflation and unemployment—rest on alternative versions of macroeconomic theory.
2. The tools of policymakers include changes in taxes, government spending, and the money supply to effect changes in total spending.
3. The new Keynesians argue that fiscal policies—government spending and taxation policies—have direct and predictable effects on the private economy. Discretionary fiscal policies should be used to cure economic problems such as demand-deficiency unemployment and inflation. Money supply changes may affect spending indirectly through their impact on interest rates.
4. Monetarists advocate a stable, nondiscretionary fiscal and monetary approach to economic stabilization. Monetarists assert that lags in the recognition of economic problems on the part of both fiscal and monetary authorities, as well as lags between policy imple-

mentation and the effects of policies, are potentially disruptive in controlling the macroeconomy. Monetarists advocate a balanced budget on the fiscal side and a rule fixing money supply growth for the Federal Reserve's conduct of monetary policy.
5. Rational expectations theorists argue that, rather than ignore useful information, market participants use all learned information to predict the outcome of policymakers' discretionary decisions. Decision-makers with rational expectations are not always right, but they learn through time and are able to predict outcomes over the long run. The result is that when the discretionary decisions of policymakers are perfectly anticipated, monetary and fiscal policy will have no effect on aggregate demand. Unanticipated policy or events will have short-run effects, which are eventually overcome through natural adjustments. Fiscal demand-side policies, moreover, may result in long-run adverse shifts in aggregate supply.

KEY TERMS

recognition lag
administrative lag

monetary rule
rational expectations theory

QUESTIONS FOR REVIEW AND DISCUSSION

1. Explain how fiscal and monetary policies differ with respect to the amount of time necessary to implement them and the amount of time required for their full force to be realized.
2. Under what conditions is Keynesian fiscal policy most effective? What fiscal policies are called for during times of recession? During inflation?
3. What role do the monetary authorities play in Keynesian policies? In the monetarists' view, what is the proper role of the monetary authorities?
4. According to monetarists, what variables adjust to maintain full employment? What effect do discretionary demand management policies have on the economy?
5. According to monetarists, what effect does increased government spending have on aggregate demand? What effect do recognition and administrative lags have on the cycles of inflation and unemployment?
6. Why do monetarists suggest that monetary rules be followed rather than discretionary policies?
7. According to the rational expectations view, what are the probable effects of discretionary monetary and fiscal policies?
8. What theoretical conditions would have to exist before discretionary fiscal or monetary policies could completely eliminate the cyclical swings in inflation and unemployment?

PROBLEM

The figure represents aggregate demand and aggregate supply for some hypothetical economy Keynesland. Initially, the Keynesland economy is operating on aggregate demand curve AD_0 and short-run aggregate supply $SRAS_0$ at point A. Suppose that Keynesland's central bank increases the money supply, resulting in a shift in the aggregate demand curve to AD_1.

a. Describe what happens in the economy in the Keynesian view. What policy would a Keynesian recommend to eliminate the problem created by the increased aggregate demand in the economy? Explain.

b. Describe what happens in the economy in the monetarist view. What policy would a monetarist recommend? Explain.

c. Describe what happens in the economy in the rational expectations view. What policy would a rational expectationist recommend? Explain.

CHAPTER 15

GLOBAL ECONOMIC GROWTH AND DEVELOPMENT

Afull-employment economy without inflation is the major goal of macroeconomic policy. But achievement of this goal does not necessarily mean that an economy is growing over the long run. Full employment and price stability surely affect long-run economic growth prospects, but factors such as population, natural resources, capital growth, and improvements in technology also determine the economy's future.

Long-run growth has been the key to the United States' prosperity. The standard of living, usually defined as the quantity of real goods and services that the average citizen is able to consume per year, has risen by an average of 2 to 3 percent per year for more than 150 years in America. Other nations have not experienced such good fortune. Many developing nations in Asia, Africa, and Latin America, for example, are stymied in their growth prospects because of a lack of productive labor or capital equipment or because population is growing as fast as or faster than output of real goods and services.

Unfortunately, there is some evidence of a slowdown in long-run growth rates in the United States. (Slow economic and productivity growth was an issue in the 1992 presidential campaign.) Is the slowdown in U.S. growth temporary or is it a permanent state of affairs resulting from the fixed or dwindling supplies of some of our natural resources? Will future generations of Americans suffer the effects of a shrinking economy, or are there economic policies that might ensure steady prosperity? In a global economy, what impact do political institutions—especially those found in developing countries—have on international trade and worldwide economic growth? This chapter attempts to provide insight into such questions. After reading Chapter 15 you should understand

Standard of living
The real value of the quantity of goods and services consumed by the average member of the economy.

- how economic growth is defined and some of the factors that lead to growth.
- how aggregate demand and labor productivity are key elements in explaining economic growth.
- some of the features of U.S. economic growth, past and present.
- problems of economic growth in a global context, especially in the developing world.
- the role of international trade in U.S. and global economic growth.

THE MEANING OF ECONOMIC GROWTH

Economic growth
Increases in real GDP or real per capita GDP over time.

Economic growth actually has two definitions. It may simply refer to increases in real GDP, the value of the annual output of final goods and services in the economy adjusted for inflation. While this measure certainly tells us whether overall economic performance has improved, it does not tell us much about whether the average citizen is better or worse off than at some previous time.

Real per capita GDP
Real GDP divided by the population size; real output per person in the economy.

An increase in **real per capita GDP** is a more accurate measure of economic growth. If real GDP increases by 4 percent over some period and population increases by 2 percent, real economic growth per capita has taken place. By contrast, a population increase of 6 percent with 4 percent growth in real output means that the average citizen is worse off, that economic decline has occurred in per capita terms.

Both measures are useful for understanding growth processes. For example, a statement that Mexico's real GDP grew at a rate of 3 percent last year tells us that some of the prerequisites for growth exist in Mexico. Likewise, to say that per capita GDP grew at only 1 percent last year indicates that Mexico may be having population problems, since per capita income growth depends on population growth. Both measures, however, are merely statistical concepts; economists generally recognize that neither measure, no matter how useful for comparison purposes, can tell us definitively about the quality of life or the distribution of wealth in a society.

The Causes of Growth

The causes of economic growth are complex. We have already pinpointed some of the important short-run requirements of economic growth: Adequate employment of productive resources, price stability, efficient allocation of resources, and other such conditions generally ensure a rising standard of living.

To sustain long-run growth in real GDP, however, an economy must enjoy steady growth in population, natural resources, productivity of labor and resources, capital formation, human capital, and technological improvement, encouraged by a free-market environment and free-trade policies.

POPULATION   Population may be detrimental to growth in real per capita GDP in many modern nations, especially developing nations, but under certain conditions, an expanding population may be essential to growth. During the industrialization of the United States in the nineteenth century, rapid population growth, much of it achieved by immigration, fueled a phenomenal economic growth rate. On the supply side, growth in population and labor supply led to increased efficiency in production through higher productivity in the use of machinery and natural resources. Mass production such as assembly-line techniques greatly improved the productivity of labor through increased specialization. On the demand side, higher population led to increased demand for all goods and services, making possible mass production and greater consumption. Population growth is therefore an ingredient in growth, but increases in population by themselves are insufficient for sustained economic growth. As we will see later in this chapter, rampant or unrestrained population increases may retard, halt, or even reverse any progress in per capita GDP.

NATURAL RESOURCES   Every society is endowed with some quantity of land and natural resources such as fresh water, forests, and minerals. The United States, the former Soviet Union, and China, for example, have large quantities of both. Possession of land and natural resources may make growth easier, but it will not guarantee growth; nor will lack of natural resources prevent growth. Japan has a small quantity of land and natural resources, yet Japan's post–World War II growth rate has been greater than that of most other countries.

By themselves, natural resources are valueless. They must be developed by labor and capital. Improvements in technology, moreover, may make resources more productive—as in fertilizing land—or even contribute to the development and invention of new resources. Aluminum, for example, is an invented alloy. It is a common misconception that the quantity of certain natural resources is absolutely fixed in supply. For example, as technology develops, it becomes possible to tap oil reserves at previously unreachable depths. New technology also may create opportunities to extract oil profitably from shale. Should the supply of oil ever begin to run short, new technology would likely bring alternative fuel sources to the market. Technological change continuously alters the relative scarcity of natural resources.

Productivity of labor
Output per worker over any given period of time.

PRODUCTIVITY OF LABOR   Economic growth is very closely tied to the **productivity of labor**—how much output per hour, week, and so on, results from labor input. Labor's productivity depends on a number of factors, including the quantity (population size) and quality (degree of education and skill) of the labor supply, the stock of capital and other resources each laborer has to work with, and the technology available for production. Educational development and on-the-job training of laborers—growth in human capital—is a rather obvious requirement for productivity increases, but productivity increases are also closely linked to capital formation and technology.

CAPITAL FORMATION AND INFRASTRUCTURE   A fourth ingredient of economic growth is growth in the size and quality of the capital stock—productive assets like buildings, machinery, and equipment used in production and the infrastructure, the roads, bridges, and communications systems used in moving goods and disseminating information. (For a discussion of the importance of infrastructure as a determinant of economic growth, see the Application, "Infrastructure, Economic Growth, and Clintonomics" at the conclusion of this chapter.) Labor productivity—output per worker—is enhanced when the stock of capital available grows faster than the labor supply. When capital is growing faster than the labor supply, capital is said to be deepening. **Capital deepening** has occurred throughout most of the economic history of the United States. In contrast, many countries experience rapid population growth and little capital accumulation, which causes labor productivity to fall and adversely affects the growth potential of these countries.

Increases in capital stock are costly, however. Resources, including time, must be sacrificed to produce capital goods that are not directly consumable, so capital growth requires saving or abstention from current consumption. For new investments in machinery, buildings, and equipment to grow, society's ability to save must grow. The reward for saving is greater future growth in either consumable goods or in more capital stock. In the latter sense, economic growth is cumulative: It feeds on itself by using capital to produce more capital.

Capital deepening

Increases in the total stock of capital in conjunction with increases in the ratio of the capital stock to the labor force; occurs when the capital stock grows at a faster rate than the labor force.

IMPROVEMENTS IN TECHNOLOGY   Technological growth and invention—improvements in the methods by which goods and services are produced and sold—is another key to economic growth. The Industrial Revolution of the eighteenth and nineteenth centuries in Europe and the United States ushered in the age of mechanization, increasing the productivity of labor and natural resources. The result has been the highest standard of living for the greatest number of people in the recorded history of humanity. Such living standards would have been impossible to achieve without the invention of items such as the steam engine, the spinning jenny, assembly-line production, and indoor plumbing. Who could have imagined 30 years ago, for example, that a high-speed digital computer no larger than a breadbox would be within the reach of the average American to calculate income taxes, store recipes, or play games on? Technology and invention have been responsible for nothing less than the modern world.

THE MARKET ENVIRONMENT   Most Western economists believe that the market environment surrounding the growth in, among other things, natural resources, labor productivity, and capital formation is a large contributing factor to economic growth. A competitive market system, many believe, encourages invention and rapid innovation. Those holding this view generally argue that free-trade policies also enhance a country's ability to grow economically; such policies enable the country to specialize in the production of the goods and services at which it is most efficient. However, Japan's experience shows that growth can also occur in a restrictive environment; despite the Japanese government's elaborate system of barriers to internal and external trade, the country has achieved a remarkable record of economic growth since 1950 (see the Focus "The Japanese Economy: Model for Growth and Development?").

The Production Possibilities Frontier Revisited

All of the fundamental elements of long-run economic growth may be summarized in terms of a production possibilities frontier. A production possibilities frontier, as

Japan's industrial revolution began in the early twentieth century, and by the time of World War II, Japan was a leading industrial power. But after the war, the Japanese economy was in shambles; its people were poor, and its production processes were primitive. Japan was essentially a developing country.

The growth and development of the Japanese economy since 1950 has been astonishing. Between 1950 and 1993, real GDP per capita in Japan rose by a factor of twenty-four (from $843 to $20,523). In 1993, Japanese GDP per capita was about 85 percent of that of the United States; in 1950 it had been only 12.7 percent. Today the Japanese economy ranks with those of most European nations in terms of per capita GDP.

To put the Japanese economy in perspective, it must be noted that Japan is 10 percent smaller than California, has only about half the population of the United States, and of the major industrial countries is the poorest in nonhuman natural resources, importing virtually its entire supply of raw materials. Finally, Japan is one of the most densely populated countries on earth. Yet, despite these obvious disadvantages, Japan has an enviable development record.

Japan has a capitalist market economy characterized by an industrial policy and extensive import restrictions. The term *industrial policy* refers to government-led industrial consortiums, health-care plans, worker training, and tax policies. Despite such heavy and direct government involvement in the economy, virtually all productive resources are privately owned and operated. Lifetime employment contracts are still common in the case of larger firms, which partly explains the absence of national labor unions. Local unions in Japan, moreover, do not exert much power over labor allocation. The high degree of economic efficiency observed in Japan has been achieved in an atmosphere virtually free of labor market rigidity.

Two features of the Japanese economy are probably most responsible for Japan's rapid growth: historically low marginal and absolute tax rates and high rates of saving and investment. Taxes consume a much smaller share of GDP in Japan than in Western economies—although Japan is catching up. In 1989, for example, Japan's parliament levied a value added tax (VAT) of 3 percent. (A VAT is a tax on consumption that is levied on the value added to products at each stage of production.)

During the period 1960–1979, almost one-third of Japan's GDP was allocated to investment—a considerably larger fraction than could be found in other developed countries. Japan still saves a far greater percentage of its GDP than the United States—18 percent compared to 4 percent in 1992. The Japanese government increases investment by taxing businesses and capital gains at low rates and exempting from taxation capital gains derived from sales of securities. In contrast, the Clinton administration increased the top corporate tax rate in 1993 and kept the capital gains tax very high.

Another ingredient in Japan's amazing growth is worth mentioning—its unabashed copying of technology developed in the West. Extremely successful in this area, the Japanese have invested heavily in research and development. Approximately 3 percent of its GDP in the 1990s is devoted to research.

The Japanese have quickly achieved a high standard of living. In 1970, for example, only 17 percent of Japanese families owned an automobile; by 1992, that figure had climbed to more than 75 percent. In 1970, 26 percent of Japanese families owned a television set; that figure was 99 percent in 1992.

The Japanese economy experienced a sharp downturn in the 1990s, including Japan's worst recession in two decades. The 1990s have brought rising unit labor costs, shrinking employment, and plant closings. A number of observers believe that new taxes and the government's industrial policy are to blame for the economic slowdown. Many of Japan's weakest industries are heavily subsidized by government, and the strongest industries have developed without the government's help. Perhaps as important in explaining slower growth in Japan, however, are changing notions of company loyalty and the sacrifice of pleasure in order to work. Many young Japanese do not share their parents' work ethic. Perhaps the most that should be said about the Japanese economy at this point is that private initiative and relatively low government involvement created one of the great success stories of economic development in the twentieth century.

SOURCES: Steve Lohn, "The Japanese Challenge: Can They Achieve Technological Supremacy?" *New York Times Magazine* (July 8, 1984); and Paul Sperry, "Must We Copy Our Competitors?" and "Is the Grass Greener Abroad?" *Investor's Business Daily* (April 13–14, 1993), pp. 1–2.

FIGURE 15.1

Economic Growth and the Production Possibilities Frontier

Growth is assumed to result from increases in the stock of capital goods. (a) If one economy forgoes a relatively larger amount of consumption goods than another economy in order to obtain more capital goods, then its production possibilities frontier will shift outward by a larger amount. (b) Country Y's preference for consumer goods in year 1 results in significantly less growth by year 2.

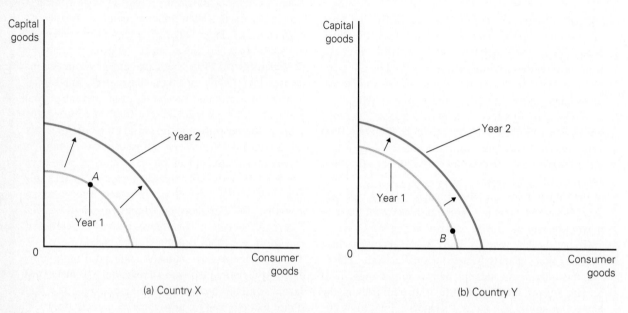

(a) Country X   (b) Country Y

explained in Chapter 2, shows the choices available to society in producing two goods, given a fixed quantity of resources—labor, capital, and natural resources—and assuming a given state of technology. If society is positioned on the production frontier, it is fully employing and efficiently allocating all resources and utilizing technology to its best advantage. However, most societies, even highly efficient ones, are at times positioned inside the frontier because of unemployment or underemployment of resources. Societies cannot advance beyond the frontier because of absolute limits at any given time in the quantity and quality of resources.

Figure 15.1 shows production possibilities frontiers for two economic societies—country X and country Y, respectively—both of which must choose production levels for consumption goods and capital goods. Each country is assumed to possess a similar resource base and the same technology. Country X's initial choice between capital goods and consumer goods is labeled *A* in Figure 15.1a; country Y's choice in Figure 15.1b is labeled *B*. Country X has devoted a higher proportion of its resources to capital goods production in year 1 than has country Y. The net result—and the key to understanding the principles underlying economic growth—is that country X's choice results in a higher production possibilities frontier in some future year, say, year 2. In year 2, societies X and Y will again choose some capital-consumer goods combination on a new frontier, but if both countries remain fully employed, country X's economy will have grown to a higher level of output and presumably to a higher level of real GDP per capita.

TABLE 15.1

Cumulative Effects of GDP Growth

Different growth rates applied to the same hypothetical GDP in 1996 will produce dramatic changes in real GDP in the future. GDP will double in 20 years with an approximate growth rate of 3.5 percent per year.

Country	Average Growth Rate of Real GDP, 1990–1995 (annual percent change)	Hypothetical Real GDP, 1996 (billions of dollars)	Projected Real GDP, 2000 (billions of dollars)	Projected Real GDP, 2005 (billions of dollars)	Projected Real GDP, 2010 (billions of dollars)	Projected Real GDP, 2015 (billions of dollars)
United States	2.2	500	545	608	678	756
Canada	1.3	500	527	562	599	639
Japan	1.8	500	537	587	642	702
France	1.5	500	531	572	616	663
Germany[a]	2.5	500	552	625	707	800
Italy	1.3	500	527	562	599	639
United Kingdom	1.1	500	522	551	582	615

SOURCE: Council of Economic Advisers, *Economic Report of the President* (Washington, D.C.: U.S. Government Printing Office, 1996), p. 402.

[a]Former West Germany

Economic growth, in other words, is determined by society's choice of future goods over present goods. This fact does not mean that the capital stock is the only element in growth. Capital combines with labor and natural resources to increase society's growth possibilities, even with a constant state of technology.

Comparative Growth Rates

Economies grow at different rates. Diminishing marginal returns when one or more resources are fixed or growing slowly is a major aspect of theories featuring limits to growth. For instance, bottlenecks may be predicted when all arable land and freshwater resources in a country are already being used intensively for food production. Whether the limits to long-run economic growth are absolute or relative, it is clear that growth is an extremely complex matter. Further, it is clearly the case that even small differences in growth rates matter a great deal over time.

Table 15.1 presents actual average growth rates in real GDP between 1990 and 1995 for seven nations. The growth rates varied from 2.5 percent (Germany) to 1.1 (in the United Kingdom).

In the rest of Table 15.1, we consider what would happen if each of the nine economies continued to grow at the actual average 1990–1995 rate. We begin in 1996, and, for the sake of simplicity, assume that each country has a GDP of $500 billion in that year. After five years of about 2.5 percent growth per year, Germany's GDP would be $800 billion, or about 6 percent higher than the U.S. GDP of $756 billion. It should be clear from Table 15.1 that relatively small differences in the growth rates of two countries will produce huge differences in real income in the not-too-distant future.

A warning about the determinants of growth in different nations: Many cultural and institutional factors heavily influence actual growth rates. Significantly different growth rates even in highly developed nations may ultimately be explained only in terms of a particular society's cultural, governmental, and institutional structures, areas where the economist may not be able to analyze key differences. To understand the economic development of any nation, we must look to cultural and institutional factors, as well as the quantifiable features of growth.

GROWTH AND MODERN MACROECONOMIC THEORY

Modern economic theory has much to say on the issue of growth. Foremost in current analysis is the importance of capital formation and improvements in technology. According to modern analysis, growth potential also depends on the ability of an economy to absorb growth.

The Demand Side of Growth

Growth absorption

Increases in total spending sufficient to purchase additional output generated by increases in productive capacity.

Growth absorption means keeping up with the expanding productive capacity of the economy through increasing total expenditures. Recall that aggregate demand must always be sufficient to create full employment at any point in time. The same must hold true to create full employment and maximum economic growth over time.

Figure 15.2 shows total expenditures on the vertical axis and the output capacity of the economy over time on the horizontal axis. Along the 45-degree line, total expenditures equal the total output capacity of the economy. A central requirement for sustainable economic growth is that total expenditures, private and public, must keep the economy on or near this 45-degree line through time; otherwise, unemployment and slower growth will result. If output capacity is Y_0 in the year 2000, total expenditures must be at the level of TE_0 to achieve maximum income and income growth. A given level of net investment and capital formation in 2000 creates a larger output capacity in 2010, Y_1, which in turn requires a rise in total expenditures in 2010 to realize the growth potential of the economy in 2010.

Ensuring adequate aggregate demand for maximum growth is one of the goals of short-run macroeconomic theory. New Keynesians argue that the economy should be managed in discretionary countercyclical fashion to keep aggregate demand at full-employment levels. Monetarists and new classical economists argue that adequate growth in aggregate demand can be achieved only through stable rules for Congress and for the Federal Reserve System. However one looks at the matter, policies to ensure adequate aggregate demand are essential in maintaining a sustained high rate of economic growth.

The Supply Side of Growth

The other facet of economic growth involves the factors that enhance or enlarge the productive capacities of the economy. All of the factors—capital growth, technological improvements, growth in natural resources—discussed earlier in this

FIGURE 15.2

Growth in Total Expenditures Required for Economic Growth

In this simple model, increases in total expenditures must keep up with expanding resources and population to bring about maximum economic growth from an output capacity of Y_0 in the year 2000 to Y_1 in 2010; the aggregate demand curve must shift from TE_0 to TE_1 by 2010 to keep resources fully employed. Total output equals total expenditures along the 45-degree line.

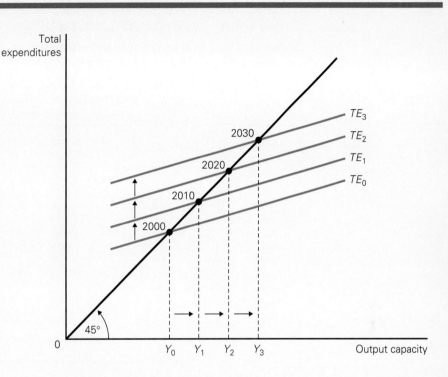

chapter create supply increases. We call these *supply-side* factors because they have the effect of shifting the aggregate supply curve of real output to the right.

In Figure 15.3, we assume that the economy's demand for goods and services will be sufficient to absorb the increased output of goods and services made possible by growth. The question we ask instead is: What factor or factors underlie rightward shifts in the aggregate supply curve? The long-run supply of goods and services is influenced by certain variables—capital accumulation, the productivity

FIGURE 15.3

Economic Growth and Rightward Shifts in Long-Run Aggregate Supply

Over time, the level of technology or the supply of resources may increase, shifting the long-run aggregate supply curve to the right and increasing full-employment income.

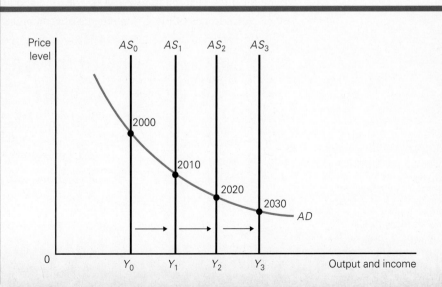

TABLE 15.2

Net Domestic Investment, 1970–1993

Net investment as a percentage of GDP remained fairly steady between 1970 and 1995, although there were significant dips in 1983, 1990, and 1992. (Net private domestic investment is in billions of 1987 dollars.)

Year	Net Private Domestic Investment	Percentage of Real GDP
1970	172	5.9
1980	194	5.1
1983	152	3.9
1984	302	7.3
1985	274	6.4
1986	248	5.6
1987	247	5.4
1988	255	5.4
1989	239	4.9
1990	192	3.9
1991	114	2.3
1992	130	2.6
1993	220	4.3

SOURCE: U.S. Bureau of the Census, *Statistical Abstract of the United States,* 1995 (Washington, D.C.: U.S. Government Printing Office, 1995), pp. 451, 560.

of labor, taxation, and so on. For purposes of discussion, however, there are two major economic factors to watch in predicting the growth rate in the productive capacities of any economy:

1. Growth in private saving and investment, which leads to capital formation; and
2. Growth in the number of laborers, in laborers' participation in the work force, and in labor's productivity.

Any variable, policy, or institutional factor that affects these two factors will affect economic growth through its effect on the long-run aggregate supply curve. Consider some recent trends of these components of economic growth in the United States.

RECENT U.S. ECONOMIC GROWTH AND PRODUCTIVITY

The various growth rates in real GDP in industrialized nations shown in Table 15.1 have numerous causes. Short-run economic stabilization—the ability of an economy to provide full employment of resources—will naturally affect long-run growth prospects. But the supply-side features of economic growth are of greatest importance in explaining U.S. growth trends.

Capital Formation

A useful measure of **capital formation** is net investment as a percentage of GDP. This figure shows the fraction of total output being put into new plant and equip-

Capital formation
The process whereby the stock of capital in an economy increases.

FIGURE 15.4

Personal Saving Rate in 1980–1995

The personal saving rate stood at just above 4 percent in 1995. This rate is well below the average savings rate of 7 percent for the period 1959 to 1995.

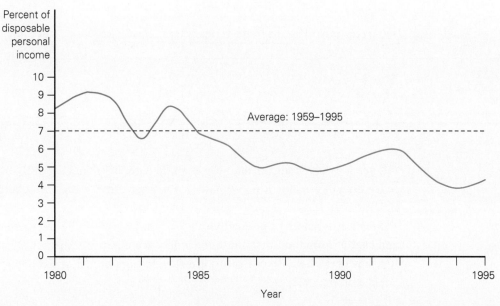

SOURCE: Council of Economic Advisers, *Economic Report of the President* (Washington, D.C.: U.S. Government Printing Office, 1996), p. 310.

ment—an indicator of future productivity. As Table 15.2 shows, net investment fell to $114 billion in 1991, barely 2 percent of GDP. Since then, the investment rate has risen sharply—to levels more in line with historical norms.

Saving

Personal savings are the primary source of new investment and capital formation in the United States. However, corporations also engage in saving when they retain earnings, as do governments when they run government surpluses. In recent years, foreign capital has flowed into the United States, providing an additional source of savings. Figure 15.4 shows that while, historically, Americans have saved about 7 percent of their disposable income, the rate in the late 1970s and for most of the 1980s was lower—at times, significantly so.

The dip in personal savings coincided with an era of enormous government deficits. To finance these deficits, the government has been forced to compete with private investors. Accumulated savings drained to finance government deficits greatly reduce the funds that are available for private capital formation.

Productivity

The declines in net investment and saving combined to reduce U.S. productivity in the early 1980s (see Table 15.3). After 1982, total output and output per hour rose dramatically; the 7.9 percent rate of output growth in 1984 was the highest since 1950. Since 1984, the growth rate has moderated somewhat, and while the

TABLE 15.3

Output and Productivity Growth Rates in Nonfarm Business Sector, 1980–1991

The output growth rate fluctuated throughout the 1980s and into the 1990s, with growth in productivity (output per hour) lagging stubbornly behind.

	GROWTH RATES (PERCENT)															
	1980	1981	1982	1983	1984	1985	1986	1987	1988	1989	1990	1991	1992	1993	1994	1995	1980–1995 (average)
Output per hour	−.4	1.2	−.9	4.2	1.8	1.0	2.7	−.2	.6	.5	.9	−1.8	3.2	.2	.5	.9	0.9
Output	−1.2	1.9	−3.3	6.1	7.9	3.6	3.4	3.0	4.1	3.2	.7	−1.8	3.0	2.9	4.0	1.9	2.56

SOURCE: Council of Economic Advisers, *Economic Report of the President* (Washington, D.C.: U.S. Government Printing Office, 1996), p. 33.

rate remains much higher than it was in the late 1970s and early 1980s, productivity growth remains low compared with what it has been throughout most of U.S. history.

Small differences in productivity growth rates and in the rates of investment and capital formation that cause them may seem inconsequential. Over the long run, however, they are critical to growth. As the Council of Economic Advisers pointed out in 1983,

> The consequences of reduced productivity growth for our standard of living over the long run are greater than those of any other current economic problem. In 1981 the American economy produced approximately $12,780 worth of output per capita. Had productivity growth continued at the 1948–67 rate during the 14 years subsequent to 1967, output per capita would have reached $16,128 in 1981, 26 percent higher than the actual value.[1]

Small changes in productivity, investment, and capital formation growth rates can have a major impact on overall economic growth. Increasing the annual productivity growth rate by only 2 percentage points, for example, would more than double the standard of living in terms of goods and services by the year 2020.

The somewhat disappointing picture of growth in the U.S. economy in recent years has many interrelated causes. Unfortunately, economists have not been able to pinpoint the exact causes of the slowdown. Even if they could, however, economists and policymakers alike would be unlikely to agree on a plan to reverse the trend.

The slowdown in labor productivity has been attributed to, among other things, lower research and development expenditures; a transition to a high-technology economy; higher energy prices; swings in the business cycle; increased regulation affecting saving, investment, and labor markets; changing composition of the labor force; and changing attitudes of workers. Discrimination against private capital formation has taken a number of forms, including tax policies, destabilizing

[1]Council of Economic Advisers, *Economic Report of the President* (Washington, D.C.: U.S. Government Printing Office, 1983), p. 13.

inflation created by expansionist monetary policies, and the competition for investment funds by the federal government through government budget deficits.

A more comprehensive accounting for productivity declines and for slower overall growth can be found in the identification of the sources of economic growth itself. Economist Edward F. Denison has sought to account for the relative importance of all of the major ingredients of economic growth by using index numbers. Denison converted trends in total output (national income) and in various factor inputs (labor, capital, legal and human environment, and so on) for the period 1929–1982 into index numbers.

According to Denison's estimates, U.S. national income rose at an average annual rate of 2.9 percent per year over the period 1929–1982. Of the factors contributing to this rise, increases in factor inputs—labor and capital combined—were most significant. The increase in the labor supply consisted partly of increased education and partly of an increased rate of employment. Recall that new net capital growth is the result of growth in savings and in net investment expenditures. The remaining major factors contributing to growth, in order of importance, are advances in technology (knowledge), economies of scale, and improvements in resource allocation.

Denison found that changes in the legal and human environment actually *reduced* economic growth. The latter statistic makes sense because investments in environmental protection, for example, do not increase the quantity of the output of goods and services but do increase the quality. To the extent that quality is important in assessing economic growth and well-being, output per worker understates productivity, because capital investments in environmental and pollution production do not ordinarily result in more real salable output but simply in output with fewer by-products.

ECONOMIC GROWTH AND ECONOMIC DEVELOPMENT

Why do some economies grow at brisk rates while others grow slowly, if at all, in terms of per capita income? In order to better understand growth prospects for the United States in the future, it is instructive to study the process of economic development. In economic terms, development is not quite the same as growth. Economic growth usually refers to the increase in per capita GDP in an economy; **economic development** is the process of capital formation, improvement in entrepreneurial and labor skills, and growth in economic productivity that causes rates of economic growth to rise. The U.S. economy provides a model of successful economic development, in that the United States has succeeded at combining a growing population with high and sustained rates of economic growth. In 1776, however, the United States was in many respects an underdeveloped economy. The transition from a low state of development to a high one occurred rapidly during the nineteenth century. The critical question is whether the United States can maintain high levels of growth in the future, and the experiences of some developing nations may be instructive.

Economic development
The process through which an economy achieves long-run economic growth; involves capital formation, the development of markets, productivity growth, and the improvement of entrepreneurial ability and labor skills.

An identifying characteristic of developing economies is the dominance of the agricultural sector.

In the modern world, the developed nations are the relatively rich economies, and the developing nations are the relatively poor economies. Many developing countries are relatively stagnant economically, while others are gaining rapidly in terms of per capita income, productivity, and output. Most developing nations are experiencing high rates of population growth. Why do they differ in growth experience? It appears that the form of economic institutions plays an important role in determining the extent to which economies, both developed and developing, grow.

The Characteristics of Developing Countries

Developing countries
Countries with relatively low levels of per capita real GDP; generally characterized by a large subsistence agricultural sector, low saving rates, and high population growth.

Most countries of the world are considered less-developed countries, or **developing countries;** three-quarters of the world's population lives in developing countries. But there is an amazing amount of diversity among these countries; the only thing they have in common is their less-developed status. Economically, what characteristics are associated with the low development rates of less-developed countries?

In describing less-developed countries, there is general agreement that four features stand out: low per capita income, a dominant agricultural-household sector, relatively low saving rates, and rapid population growth.

A less-developed country is a poor country in the sense that its per capita GDP is low. Compared with poverty in developed countries, poverty in less-developed countries is more severe. In many less-developed countries, the plight of the lowest income group has not changed dramatically in hundreds of years. The second defining characteristic of less-developed countries is a dominant agricultural-household sector. In a way, this is merely another way of saying that less-developed countries are poor—a large proportion of their population is engaged in subsistence agriculture. Nearly two-thirds of the labor force of the low-income countries of Asia, Africa, and South America are employed in agriculture. In contrast, only 2 percent of the U.S. labor force is employed in agriculture. The size of the household (or nonmarket) sector in less-developed countries is generally much larger than in developed nations. Most households in less-developed countries are engaged in subsistence production in the sense that they raise their own food, make their own clothes, and construct their own homes. The degree of specialization in production in these economies is limited compared to the more-developed economies. With the degree of specialization limited and a large amount of time devoted to subsistence production, the opportunities for welfare-enhancing exchange and trade with others in the society becomes relatively limited also.

The other two characteristic features found in most less-developed countries (although there are important exceptions) are low saving rates and high rates of population growth. Many poor economies have low saving rates because saving is very difficult (or even impossible) when income is at or near the subsistence level. Low saving rates mean that very little income is set aside each year for investment in capital goods for increased production. This inability to save, in turn, contributes to continuing low rates of development. The term sometimes used for this problem is the **vicious circle of poverty.**

Vicious circle of poverty
An attempt to explain why some countries remain less developed that centers on low savings and investment as the cause of low real incomes, which in turn lead to low saving and investment rates.

Rapid population growth is another condition commonly associated with less-developed countries. The population of the poor countries of Asia, Africa, and South America has been expanding at an average rate of about 2.5 percent per year. At this rate, the populations of these nations double every 25 or 30 years. In contrast, the populations of developed nations grow less than 1 percent per year on average. The difference is often taken to mean that rapid population growth is a major contributor to low rates of development because such growth imposes an increasing burden on the limited resources of less-developed countries. The more people, the greater the need to provide education, health care, and other basic services—which require resources that would otherwise be available for capital investment. To the extent that rapid population growth represents more mouths to feed, per capita income will decline as population grows, other things being equal.

Like wealth and poverty, development and underdevelopment are relative concepts. In 1750, England was probably the richest and most-developed country in the world, but by modern standards mid-eighteenth-century England was relatively poor and undeveloped. Moreover, we cannot judge reliably whether any given country should be counted as a developed or less-developed economy on the basis of secondary characteristics—such things as the rate of population growth, degree of literacy, or degree of industrialization. There are, for example, some developed countries that have high rates of population growth and a lesser degree of industrialization than do some less-developed countries. A more reliable way to distinguish quantitatively between the developed and less-developed countries is by per capita income—that is, the level of a country's GDP divided by its population. On these grounds, according to calculations by the World Bank, per capita income in the industrial market economies in 1995 was estimated to be on the order of 12 times greater than that in less-developed countries. Not all developing countries are experiencing slow growth, however, and economic institutions may provide some explanations for the differences.

Property Rights Arrangements and Economic Growth

Can differences in economic institutions be pinpointed as a major cause of under-development and slow growth? It is often pointed out that economists are not able to bring societies into the laboratory and use the experimental method to test their theories. While this is certainly true, economists are able to observe the effects of different economic institutions on economic performance. In this section we look at some countries that, despite their common culture, similar climates, and common ethnic-religious origin, have taken radically different routes to economic development. This comparative analysis will shed some light on the causes of underdevelopment and growth.

MAINLAND CHINA, HONG KONG, AND TAIWAN   Until fairly recently, the People's Republic of China (mainland China) had one of the strictest, and least flexible, systems of central economic planning anywhere in the world. Unlike some other communist countries, for example, China before the late 1970s apparently did not have a legally sanctioned private sector in the economy; in other words, economic activity was even more tightly controlled by the state than in the Soviet Union. China apparently also had very little in the way of an underground economy; in the Soviet Union, the black market helped restore some degree of flexibility to the centrally planned system. Therefore, prereform China can serve as a good example of the effect of communist institutions on economic development.

It is instructive to compare the level of economic development in China in 1980—before most of the current economic reforms had been instituted—with development in the neighboring countries of Taiwan and Hong Kong. In 1995, GDP per capita in mainland China was about $2,000. Although the people of Taiwan and Hong Kong are ethnically identical to the people on the Chinese mainland, Taiwan and Hong Kong have market economies, with relatively small public sectors. In fact, both countries have considerably less government regulation than the United States. Of the two, Taiwan has the greater endowment of natural resources. Hong Kong is very poor in natural resources; it has little level land for agriculture and must import both food and water from the mainland. Yet each of these economies has enjoyed successful economic development. Estimated 1995 GDP per capita for Taiwan was $13,000; for Hong Kong, $21,000. The standard of living in each economy is high and visibly improving. Largely unrestricted by government, entrepreneurship thrives. Although China's per capita GDP still lags far behind those in Taiwan and Hong Kong, the extensive market reforms undertaken in China since 1980 are allowing the huge population of China to enjoy the development advantages of markets, too.

THE TWO KOREAS   The experiences of North Korea and South Korea—neighboring countries with vastly different institutions—offer additional evidence that differences in social, political, and economic institutions may be a major cause of differences in economic development and growth.

The two Koreas were one nation for hundreds of years. When the two separated in 1950, they adopted diametrically opposed paths to economic development. The Democratic People's Republic of (North) Korea has adhered strictly to the central planning model. It has one of the world's most highly socialized and centrally planned economies. All industrial enterprises are either directly owned by the state or are cooperatives owned indirectly by the state. Agriculture is carried out on either collective or state farms. Following the old Soviet model, the central planning system has allocated priority to investment in heavy industry at the expense of the consumer and agricultural sectors. Despite this emphasis, the performance of the industrial sector has been disappointing. Productivity is low, and virtually all plants and equipment are obsolete, although North Korea has recently begun to purchase Western equipment and technology, including complete plants. Nominal per capita income in 1995 was approximately $1500 per year. There is little variety in consumer goods, and quality is uniformly low. Shortages are common, and standing in long lines to purchase basic necessities is a way of life. Consumer durables such as appliances are usually unavailable.

Although the land, climate, and people of South Korea are similar to those of North Korea, there are dramatic differences between the two countries. The Republic of (South) Korea has an economy based on private enterprise and a market economy. In a little over 20 years, South Korea transformed itself from an economy dominated by subsistence agriculture (which is characteristic of most poor nations) to a modern economy with an emphasis on light industry. A thriving export market has led to South Korea's surge of development, and exports increased annually between 1974 and 1995. This growth reflects, in part, the improving quality of its exports, including finished goods such as Hyundai automobiles and trucks and Reebok shoes. The standard of living is among the highest in modern Asia; per capita income for South Koreans in 1995 was about $10,000, with a diverse array of high-quality consumer goods available. Interestingly, South Korea has only 10 to 20 percent of the Korean peninsula's deposits of mineral resources.

Such real-world examples suggest that different systems of property rights and incentive structures play a vital role in relative economic development. In other words, economists believe that many differences in economic development between North and South Korea can be explained on the grounds of different institutions. These institutional differences, especially those relating to political controls or to regulation of markets and economic processes, are often more important than the endowment of resources in determining economic progress.

DEVELOPMENT AND TRADE LIBERALIZATION   At times, developing countries have made the task of development more difficult by following ill-advised policies designed to restrict the flow of foreign trade. Such policies prevent the international economy from taking full advantage of the law of comparative advantage, thereby reducing global economic efficiency. Perhaps worst of all, the developing countries that have adopted restrictions on foreign trade have usually reduced the rate of growth of their own economies in the process. Recently, however, many developing countries have modified their trade policies in the direction of greater liberalization.

A major aim of recent trade reforms has been the elimination of quantitative restrictions (for example, trade quotas) in such countries as China, Colombia, Gambia, Ghana, Indonesia, and Mexico. At the same time, many developing countries

TABLE 15.4

Developing Countries: The Degree of Openness and Economic Performance

Developing countries can use the law of comparative advantages to accelerate their rates of economic development. Countries with relatively open foreign-trade policies experience higher rates of economic growth and lower rates of inflation than countries with restrictive trade policies, although they may have slightly lower investment rates.

	Number of Countries	Growth (in percent per year)	Inflation (in percent per year)	Investment (in percent of GDP)
Average Degree of Openness[a]				
Less than 25	28	3.5	244.6	24.8
25 to 40	23	5.2	50.7	24.3
More than 40	23	5.7	5.0	20.9
Openness by Exports[b]				
Less than 25	38	3.5	247.6	24.7
25 to 40	16	5.3	14.4	23.4
More than 40	20	6.2	3.1	22.0

[a]Defined as the average of exports and imports as percent of GDP.

[b]Defined as exports as percent of GDP.

have replaced quantitative restrictions on trade with tariffs. This makes the degree of protection "transparent," which allows voters to easily see how a protectionist trade policy increases the costs they must pay for imported consumer goods. As a result, tariffs have already been substantially reduced in many countries, and political pressure is building for further reduction. Falling tariffs in developing countries are leading to more international trade and greater economic efficiency in the use of resources.

Trade reform tends to increase economic efficiency by increasing competition in domestic markets and by reducing distortions in the prices of traded versus non-traded goods. One measure of the degree of openness in a country's trade policy is the ratio of average exports and imports to GDP. Table 15.4 shows that the rate of economic growth in 74 developing countries tended to increase with the degree of openness in trade policies.

Even when the size of the economy and other factors that affect growth—such as the investment rate, terms of trade, and domestic inflation—are taken into account, there is a statistically significant relationship between the degree of openness and growth. In Asia, for example, an increase in the degree of openness of 10 percent is associated with an increase of nearly 1 percent in the growth rate. In other parts of the world, especially in Africa, the correlation between openness and growth is not as strong, however. It may be that the relatively greater flexibility of the Asian economies—the direct result of rapid capital formation in the last 20 years—allows resources to flow more rapidly into expanding sectors.

LOOKING AHEAD: EXPLAINING ECONOMIC GROWTH AND DEVELOPMENT

Why do economies, developed and less developed, grow at different rates? Why do many, but not all, less developed countries have difficulty matching the levels of development found in Europe, Japan, and North America? In terms of economic growth, how will the United States fare, comparatively, in the global economy in coming years? We explore these controversial issues in the following sections.

U.S. Growth

Careful studies of the sources of growth (such as those done by the late Edward Denison) suggest the complexities involved in trying to identify causes of growth and then trying to stimulate them. Factor growth and, with it, technological change—the importance of which was downplayed in classical economics—are the two essential causes of growth. The long-run benefits and the possible short-run costs of rapid technological change have received a great deal of attention from politicians, economists, and the media in recent years, creating a rather muddy picture.

It is clear that the United States is experiencing a transformation from traditional smokestack industries (coal, steel, heavy machinery) to high-technology industries (computers, communications). The political blame for much of this economic change has been placed on foreign competition. The United States is no longer a self-sufficient economy; it imports more than twice as many goods now as in 1970. According to Commerce Department statistics, the United States imported $51.3 billion of petroleum products, $184.4 billion of capital goods, and $113.6 billion of industrial supplies and materials in 1994. Total U.S. imports for 1994 were $668.6 billion—$166 billion more than exports.

The two major reasons for heightened foreign competition are the lower wage rates and the swift spread of technology to foreign countries. Labor costs in South Korea and Taiwan are about one-fifth those in the United States. Japan, relying greatly on automation, uses approximately six times as many industrial robots as the United States. Some economists and business leaders fear that more automation in the United States will lead to higher unemployment, while other economists feel there will be a shift into other jobs.

New jobs are being created in the service industries. According to Labor Department statistics, about 20 million people were employed in manufacturing industries in 1995, while more than 43 million people were employed in **service industries**—those offering teaching, health care, financial services, and food service, for example. McDonald's now employs more workers than USX (formerly U.S. Steel).

The United States is not alone in its transition from heavy industry to high-technology and service industries. European industrial nations are also having difficulty with changing economies. Even Japan is experiencing some decline in heavy industry, but Japan, unlike Western countries, encourages changes in the economy. Japanese companies diversify greatly in areas of production. One

Service industries
Those industries whose major, or sole, output is a consumer service, such as banking, entertainment, and health care.

company produces products ranging from foodstuffs to nuclear power plants. This diversity allows workers whose jobs become unnecessary to move into other branches of production within the same company, but it requires large-scale retraining programs within the companies.

Rather than following the Japanese model, politicians, businesspeople, and workers in the United States have demanded protection for the old smokestack industries against foreign competition. During the late 1970s and through the mid-1980s, the United States experienced its worst outbreak of protectionism (the establishment of legal artificial trade barriers and restrictions such as tariffs and import quotas) since the 1930s. The United States has tried to reduce imports and place quotas on autos, steel, and many other products, as we will see in Chapter 16. However, trade restrictions could well do more harm than good to the United States. The United States now exports more than twice the quantity of products it exported in 1980, and retaliation (in the form of trade restrictions on U.S. goods set in place by foreign governments) by other nations in response to U.S. restrictions is always a possibility. Such reactions inevitably reduce economic growth and well-being among all traders. The fate of U.S. growth may ultimately lie in successful implementation of free-trade agreements, especially the North American Free Trade Agreement and those negotiated under the General Agreement on Tariffs and Trade.

Contrary to popular belief, the United States has not fallen behind its major competitors in terms of economic growth. According to the Organization for Economic Cooperation and Development, average unemployment in 1994 was 6.0 percent in the United States, 11.1 percent in Europe, and 10.3 percent in Canada. Inflation was also lower in the United States (3 percent) than in all of the OECD countries (4.0 percent). Per capita GDP in the United States for the period was $17,200, compared to $14,984 in Canada, $12,948 in Europe, and $12,806 in Japan.

Some economists believe that rigid government regulation in other countries—including industrial policies consisting of government-directed technology, targeted investment strategies (favorable or unfavorable tax treatment), and mandated job training and health insurance programs—has retarded economic growth. Many international businesses, especially German and Japanese firms, have located in the United States because costs are lower here. Institutions matter to employment and economic growth, and government policies in both developed and less-developed countries affect institutions.

U.S. Growth and Global Development

Clearly, the causes for economic growth in nations around the world are complex. For developing nations, there are special problems, such as the "vicious circle of poverty" and high population rates. But it appears that neither of these problems has prevented economic development in Hong Kong, Taiwan, and South Korea. These nations have developed rapidly by attracting foreign investment, not relying primarily on foreign aid.

The level of technology in most developing countries is low. But this is an effect, not a cause, of low levels of development. Poor countries are unable to afford the sophisticated equipment and techniques found in rich countries. The technology itself—inventions, and new processes and techniques—is widely available to less-developed countries as is the knowledge necessary to improve productivity. What less-developed countries lack are the property rights arrangements and institutions that reward economic efficiency, consumer choice, and entrepreneurship—the things that make the acquisition of technical knowledge worthwhile.

There is a lesson for the United States in the experiences of developing nations. It is not likely that the United States will meet the challenge of economic growth by increasing restrictions and regulations on competition or on capital formation. Rather, the United States can sustain growth only by adapting to new technology through competition and human capital development. The management of change in a complex economy is a difficult matter. It often amounts to a balancing of the present interests of workers and other resource suppliers against the overall interests of consumers and economic growth. American prosperity is clearly the result of earlier technological challenges that were met head-on within the context of vigorous and open competition, with due regard for the temporary distortions that new trade and technology might create.

APPLICATION

Infrastructure, Economic Growth, and Clintonomics

Discussions of economic growth typically focus on the impact of private investment and capital formation, but the size and condition of government's capital stock are also critical to growth. What is the society's capital stock? In the United States, society's share of the capital stock is approximately one-quarter of the total and is composed of highways, schools, streets, bridges, sewers, and other public goods. The bulk of the nonmilitary government capital—or infrastructure—is owned by state and local governments, although some of the original investments were federally provided. Often, as in the case of highways, maintenance and upkeep expenditures are shared by federal and the other government entities.

The value of infrastructure in economic growth tends to be undervalued and underappreciated in the United States; government investment in goods such as highways, schools, and airports is not generally subject to a market test of profitability, as are investments in the private sector. The value of an investment in computer chip production or in building new privately provided student apartments soon becomes apparent, as investors make or lose returns on the difference between revenues taken in and costs incurred. Such measures of profitability are difficult or impossible to apply to new investments in public university buildings or city streets. It would be a mistake, however, to take the absence of a market test for these kinds of goods to mean that infrastructure is not critical to private sector productivity and economic growth.

That this nation's infrastructure is deteriorating is undeniable. Water main breaks are an almost daily occurrence in New York City, and bridge closures (or, worse, collapses) are common everywhere. According to the President's Council of Economic Advisers, there has been a dramatic decline in the growth in state and local infrastructure investments since 1970.[a] Growth in infrastructure investments at state and local levels fell from an average rate of 4.9 percent per year in the 1950s and 1960s to 2.2 percent in the 1970s and to only 0.9 percent in the 1980s. Completion of the interstate highway system and a decline in the size of the school-age population (the petering out of the post–World War II baby boom) explains some of the decline in infrastructure investment, but certainly not all of it. To many observers, failing local

[a]Council of Economic Advisers, *Economic Report of the President* (Washington, D.C.: U.S. Government Printing Office, 1990), pp. 122–123.

government services, underinvestment in real education plant and equipment, outmoded airport facilities, and overcrowded streets and poor or failing rapid transit systems suggest that there is an infrastructure crisis in America and that investments are far from adequate. Critics also point out that rapidly growing countries such as Japan and Taiwan are devoting huge amounts of resources to infrastructure to complement increased productivity in the private sector.

As usual, the issue of infrastructure provision comes down to this: Who pays? In general, the federal government shifted the financial burden for infrastructure provision to state and local governments under the Reagan and Bush administrations. (Indeed, when state and local expenditures are added to the federal government's expenditures, U.S. spending on infrastructure is comparable to that of other major world nations—about $140 billion in 1991.) State and local governments complain that access to new taxes for infrastructure items is limited and that the federal government is acting irresponsibly by refusing to shoulder more of the tab for maintaining and expanding facilities. The void left by slashes in federal funding has largely been filled with a mix of privatization schemes and user fees. It is clear, in fact, that private enterprise is fully capable of providing certain types of infrastructure. In April 1993, for example, Tele-Communications Inc. (TCI) announced that it would invest $2 billion to install fiber-optic cable in its cable television systems between 1993 and 1998. TCI's fiber-optic network closely resembles the "information superhighway" that President Bill Clinton discussed during his presidential campaign. Private enterprise will lead the way here, however, not the federal government.

Economists, generally, do agree that there is a link between federal, state, and local government policies to increase economic growth and infrastructure investment. They warn, however, that maintenance priorities as well as new projects must be carefully weighed according to costs and benefits. Since governmentally provided infrastructure does not have to meet a market test, detailed estimates of the net benefits of any project (new or continuing) are critical if waste is not to be incurred. There are some classic cases of government miscalculation. Anxious to encourage movement of its population westward from coastal urban cities such as Rio de Janeiro, Brazil built a new inland capital—Brasilia. The problem has been that few people want to live there; billions of dollars' worth of infrastructure and facilities lie grossly underutilized and deteriorating. While these kinds of costly miscalculations are possible in infrastructure provision or in maintenance priorities wherever market signals cannot be used, maintenance and expansion of the nation's capital stock is indisputably a necessary condition for increased productivity in any nation that aspires to higher economic growth.

QUESTION

Can the investment returns on the privately financed construction of a new movie theater and the publicly financed construction of a new school building be compared? Why or why not?

SUMMARY

1. Economic growth is defined as growth in real GDP or in real GDP per capita.
2. The causes of economic growth are complex, but they certainly include growth in population, labor productivity, capital accumulation, and technology.
3. Economic growth requires increases not only in the productive capacity in the economy but also in aggregate demand, which must keep pace with increases in potential output.
4. An essential feature of slower U.S. economic growth in the 1980s was the decline in the growth rate of the productivity of labor—in output per worker. Though numerous factors caused the decline, the major factor appears to be a reduction in capital formation.

5. A lower saving rate, which has led to a lower growth rate in investment expenditures, is a major factor in explaining the lower rate of capital formation in the United States.
6. The United States is faced with a high-technology challenge to economic growth—a movement away from heavy industries such as steel, automobiles, and shipbuilding to industries based on electronics and other advanced technologies and to service industries. America's response to this challenge will determine growth prospects for many decades to come.
7. The less-developed countries of the world are characterized by low per capita income, large and growing

populations, low saving and investment rates, and slow economic growth.

8. The vicious circle of poverty refers to the fact that there is little saving in a poor economy and, therefore, little chance for future development. Economies are thus said to be poor tomorrow because they are poor today. This idea has some merit in explaining underdevelopment, but it must be applied carefully.

9. Institutions matter to economic growth and development, as illustrated by the experiences of economies such as Hong Kong, Taiwan, and South Korea.

KEY TERMS

standard of living
economic growth
real per capita GDP
productivity of labor

capital deepening
growth absorption
capital formation
economic development

developing countries
vicious circle of poverty
service industries

QUESTIONS FOR REVIEW AND DISCUSSION

1. What is the difference between growth in real GDP and growth in real GDP per capita? Would it be accurate to suggest that the percent change in real GDP per capita is equal to the percent change in real GDP minus the percent change in the population?

2. Would it be accurate to suggest that a developing country with an abundance of natural resources has the potential for a high growth rate? What must occur in such countries before a high rate of growth can occur?

3. What is the cost of capital? What happens to real GDP per capita when the number of machines increases?

4. What changes occurred during the Industrial Revolution that resulted in large increases in real GDP per capita? Are similar changes necessary to obtain growth in developing countries?

5. Explain what economic growth means in terms of production possibilities curves. What causes this growth? Is this identical to increases in aggregate supply?

6. Suppose that 1000 tractors were added to a nation's stock of capital every year. Would total farm output

rise by the same amount every year? Why or why not?

7. If growth causes an increase in aggregate supply, what must happen to the price level to achieve the higher level of output? Does this suggest that increases in aggregate demand must accompany increases in aggregate supply to maintain price level stability and full employment?

8. What has happened to the rate of growth in real GDP per capita in the United States since the late 1960s? What has caused or accompanied this trend?

9. If you had to choose between price and employment stability and sustained growth in real GDP per capita, which would you choose?

10. What are the primary characteristics of a less-developed economy?

11. Evaluate the following statement: Less-developed countries are poor today because they were poor yesterday.

12. Evaluate the following statement: To achieve economic growth, an economy requires lots of resources, including land, and a low rate of population growth.

PROBLEM

Draw a production possibilities curve for the economy of Macronesia for the year 1996. Place consumer goods on one axis and capital goods on the other. Suppose that in 1996 net investment of $20 billion in new capital occurs, with no change in technology levels or in any other resources.

    a. Show the new production possibilities curve for 1997.

b. If additional (new) net investment of $20 billion occurs in 1997, 1998, and 1999 with no change in the level of technology or other resources, what happens to the production possibilities curve for 1998, 1999, and 2000? Why?

c. Do your results change if the initial and subsequent net investment increases are in government infrastructure spending financed by taxation? Explain.

PAUL SAMUELSON

ROBERT E. LUCAS, JR.

Paul Samuelson and Robert Lucas: Do We Need Discretion or Discipline in Policy?

Paul Samuelson (b. 1915) "has done more than any other contemporary economist to raise the level of scientific analysis in economic theory." So announced the Swedish Academy of Sciences in 1970, when Samuelson became the first American recipient of the Nobel Prize in economics. Although he has been called on frequently by presidents and Congress for his advice on economic matters, Samuelson has never held an official policy role in any administration. He has worked principally in the service of his profession: as a professor of economics at M.I.T., as president of the American Economic Association, and as a frequent contributor to journals and magazines. Born in Gary, Indiana, Samuelson received his Ph.D. in economics from Harvard in 1941. His doctoral dissertation, *Foundations of Economic Analysis*, was published in 1947 and became one of the definitive technical treatises on neoclassical economics. Today, Samuelson is one of the most widely respected Keynesian economists.

Robert E. Lucas, Jr. (b. 1937), credited with introducing rational expectations theory into macroeconomics, has helped change the way economists view the role of macroeconomic policy. Born in Yakima, Washington, Lucas received his Ph.D. in economics in 1964 from the University of Chicago, where he gained a firm background in Keynesian economics. One of the texts he found particularly influential at that time was Paul Samuelson's *Foundations of Economic Analysis*.

After graduate training, Lucas became increasingly disillusioned with Keynesian interpretations of the macroeconomy. His article "Econometric Testing of the Natural Rate Hypothesis," published in 1972, is one of many that discuss the implications of rational expec-

tations theory. This theory assumes that people will make economic decisions based on their knowledge of economic policy, their past experiences, and their expectations of future events. In theory, such rational behavior can distort or even neutralize the effects of well-publicized fiscal and monetary policies. According to Lucas, he and his early followers were initially regarded as "very far out" by colleagues for their nontraditional views. However, appreciation of rational expectations theory earned Lucas the Nobel Prize in 1995. Lucas has held academic posts at Carnegie-Mellon University, the Ford Foundation, and the University of Chicago, where he currently teaches.

The Case for Activism

In 1964, the unemployment rate stood at 5.2 percent and GDP was $638 billion. The economy was near the end of a bitter recessionary period. Government policy advisers, following Keynesian theory, called for direct intervention in the form of a massive tax cut. Congress responded by passing the 1964 Revenue Act, which slashed personal income taxes by almost 20 percent and corporate taxes by almost 8 percent.

The tax cut, aided by a surge in the money supply, ushered in several boom years. Over the next four years, GDP grew over 11 percent and unemployment dropped to 3.8 percent. Policy activists cite the 1964 tax cut as evidence of the usefulness of well-planned fiscal and monetary actions. Although the evidence since the 1960s has been less clear-cut, the case for activism rests on the assumption that the economy cannot easily readjust to full employment without some form of countercyclical policy, whether in the form of monetary growth, monetary restraint, fiscal cutbacks, or fiscal spending. The fiscal actions are generally preferred by activists because they can exert a direct impact on the flow of expenditures. Monetary policy works more slowly and less directly on expenditures, through the mechanism of interest rates.

Defending the need for activism, Samuelson and other economists focus on the terrible social costs of economic downturns and sudden shocks to the system. Left to correct itself, a shrinking economy could inflict insufferable damage on millions of people before prices and aggregate demand readjust to full-employment levels.

The record of policy activism gives some support for this view. Since World War II, the United States has suffered several recessions, but depressions seem to be a thing of the past. "Another depression on the order of the 1930s just doesn't seem possible," says Samuelson. The government nowadays "will do what it has to do" to avert economic disorder. "There's no longer the sense that we must somehow sweat these things out."[a]

Although activist policy has eased the severity of business cycles, it has not found a means to avoid them altogether. Indeed, there are many who argue that the economy's boom-and-recession pattern since World War II has been more the effect of discretionary policy than the cause. Also, there are many economists who point to the accelerating inflation suffered over these years and the failure of government to apply the appropriate countercyclical fiscal medicine: budget surpluses.

The Case Against Activism

For Robert Lucas, attempts to unbend the business cycle through discretionary, countercyclical policy are based on some unexamined assumptions. For such a policy to work, individuals and firms must respond cooperatively; when the government tries to close a recessionary gap, they must respond as if such actions will have no effect on prices.

Lucas believes that expectations about prices will always direct behavior, whether one is speaking in micro-

economic or macroeconomic terms. If individuals and firms believe that government policy will drive up prices, they will act to protect themselves: Wage earners will demand higher wages, investors will seek higher interest rates, and so on. When such expectations are considered, Lucas deems most countercyclical policy to be futile and counterproductive. For instance, if policymakers try to reduce unemployment through deficit spending, wage earners who have experienced the effects of such spending in the past will anticipate higher inflation. They will naturally try to keep the wages they have and to increase them. In the face of such demands, employers will find it more and more difficult to hire additional labor, and unemployment will remain despite the increase in aggregate demand. Rather than bend the recessionary cycle, the policymakers will have managed to foster inflationary pressures, perhaps ushering in high unemployment and high inflation.

The checkered performance of macroeconomic policy in the early 1980s provided Lucas plenty of ammunition to blame discretionary policy for a variety of economic ills. To Lucas, appropriate macroeconomic policy would try neither to fool nor to ignore the expectations of individuals and firms. Instead, Lucas calls for some fixed limits for policy that recognize the long-run patterns of growth in the economy, which have been in the range of 3 to 4 percent for GDP over the past 100 years. He also advocates a monetary rule that would keep the growth rate of the money supply to approximately 3 percent.

Many economists find the rational expectations model extreme in its assumptions. How is it, they ask, that citizens can adopt an accurate set of expectations about the effects of policy when even competent observers of the economy are often misjudging the rate or even direction of economic change? Moreover, what happens when fiscal or monetary policies are overwhelmed by a supply shock? Will government then be required to overcome the instability? Questions such as these have brought lively debate over the future course of activism in policy.

[a] Quoted in "Economists Don't See Threats to Economy Portending Depression," *Wall Street Journal* (October 12, 1984), p. 1.

PART 5

THE GLOBAL
ECONOMY

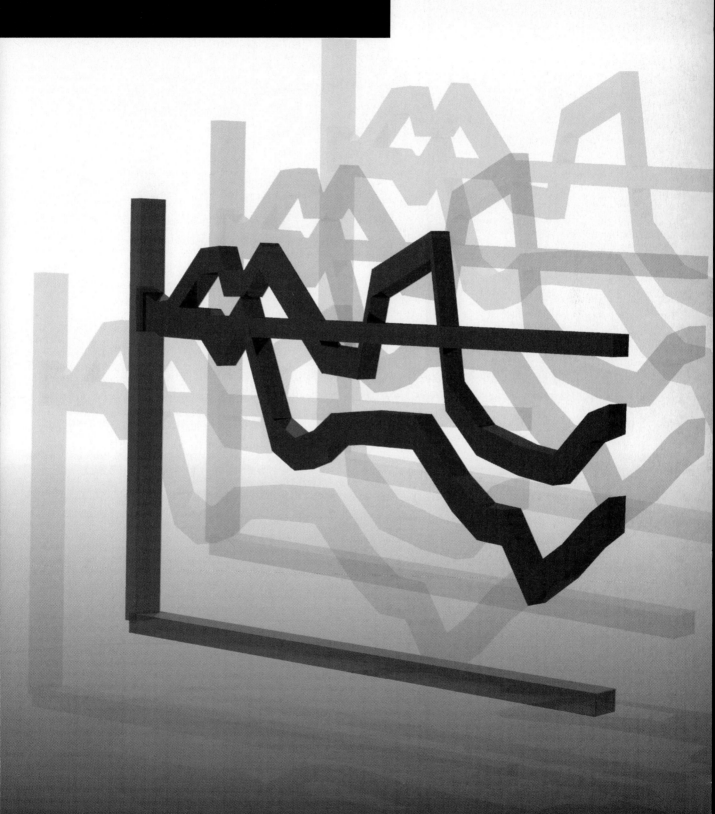

CHAPTER 16
INTERNATIONAL TRADE

We do not often stop to ponder all the ways in which imported goods enrich our lives and improve the material well-being of all nations of the world. On a typical day, for example, an American student's consumption patterns are clearly global. She awakes on sheets made in England and prepares breakfast on a hot plate made in Taiwan. Donning a cotton dress made in India and shoes made in Mexico, she catches the morning news on a TV with components manufactured in Japan. She drives to campus in a Japanese-made car.

The desirability of a diverse array of available goods and services and the interrelation of the U.S. economy with the economies of other nations present us with issues and problems we have left unexamined until now. The issue of the competitiveness of U.S. firms in world markets may have directly affected you or your family. The large foreign trade deficit that arose in the 1980s and 1990s spawned much debate in business, labor, and government circles on the desirability of a new U.S. trade policy with countries such as Japan, Canada, and Mexico. Large swings in the value of the U.S. dollar overseas can alter not only vacation plans but consumption patterns and employment as well.

New technology has enabled nations to become more economically interdependent. In a sense, the whole world is now an economic system. Our entire study of economics has highlighted the role of global factors in U.S. economic functioning. In particular, we have emphasized the impact of free markets and trade on U.S. competitiveness and economic growth and on global development. In this chapter and the next, we focus closely on international trade and finance in order to make clearer the role the United States plays in the global

In many ways, importing automobiles from Japan into the U.S. economy in exchange for corn is no different from residents of Hawaii and California trading pineapples for oranges.

economy. We will demonstrate that the familiar concepts of supply and demand and production possibilities are extremely useful in discussing international trade (Chapter 16) and the financial system that supports it (Chapter 17).

International economics is composed of both microeconomic and macroeconomic elements. This chapter focuses on the microeconomics of trade. After reading Chapter 16 you should understand

- the reasons for and the advantages of specialization and trade.
- the factors that determine actual amounts and directions of trade between countries.
- how artificial interferences with trade, such as tariffs and quotas, affect the prices and quantities of goods and services sold in importing countries.
- how historical and contemporary trade policies and international integration, such as that contemplated by Western European nations, affect world trade.

THE IMPORTANCE OF INTERNATIONAL TRADE

All nations have particular talents and resources; like individuals, whole nations can specialize in one or many activities. For example, the islands of the Caribbean have abundant sunshine and good weather year round, and so these islands specialize in tourism. **Specialization** enables nations to emphasize the activities at which they are most efficient and at the same time gain certain advantages through trade.

Specialization
An economic entity's (an individual's or a nation's) producing only one good or service, or the performance of a single task in a production process by an individual.

Examples of international specialization and trade abound. France has a favorable climate and specialized land for wine growing, so it exports wine to Colombia and the United States and imports Colombian coffee and U.S. machinery. Likewise, both Colombia and the United States specialize and trade products that best utilize their qualities and quantities of resources.

TABLE 16.1

World Trade: Exports and Imports, 1994

Area	Exports (billions of dollars)	Imports (billions of dollars)
Industrial countries	2886.0	2881.3
Developing countries	1315.3	1443.6

SOURCE: International Monetary Fund, *International Financial Statistics Yearbook* (Washington, D.C.: IMF 1995), pp. 125, 129.

Trade and specialization take place within a given economy as well as among economies. The former type of trade is called intranational or interregional trade; the latter is called international trade. In principle, the two types of trade are the same. As we saw in Chapter 2, Canada may specialize in lumber production and Mexico may specialize in silver production. Each meets its wants for the commodity it does not produce through international trade. Likewise, Texans import potatoes from Idaho, while residents of Idaho import beef produced in Texas. Such intranational or interregional trade is common—so common in fact that most of us do not even think of it as interregional trade. The trade of Idaho potatoes for Texas beef is not fundamentally different from the trade of U.S. wheat for Japanese television sets.

In practice, important differences exist between interregional and international trade. Resources—climate, fertile land, and work forces with specialized skills—cannot easily be moved between countries or regions. What distinguishes international trade from interregional trade is *lower* factor mobility between nations than within countries. A nation generally trades with the products and services of its resources, not with the resources themselves. Beyond this basic point, countries have different currencies and political systems and values. For such reasons, international trade is different from interregional trade and therefore merits special study by economists.

National Involvement in International Trade

The overall magnitude of international trade and countries' shares in this trade can be measured in a variety of ways. The value of goods in international trade is given in Table 16.1 by major areas of the world. In 1990, world trade totaled over $3 trillion, measured in exports or imports.

Table 16.2 lists the foreign trade of 11 nations as a percentage of gross domestic product for 1994; the percentages vary widely. Exports accounted for over 30 percent of Germany's total output but less than 10 percent of Argentina's output. Imports were about one-fourth to one-third of the real consumption of such countries as South Africa, Germany, Sweden, and Switzerland.

Percentage figures do not tell the whole story, of course. In absolute terms the United States was the world's largest trader in both exports and imports in 1994. The value of merchandise exports totaled $832.9 billion, and the value of merchandise imports was over $954.4 billion. (The values of both exports and imports have doubled in a generation.) The United States trades with virtually every nation of the world, the primary sources of imports being Canada and Japan (both with about 19 percent in 1994). The main destinations of U.S. exports in 1994

TABLE 16.2

Exports and Imports as a Percentage of GDP in 1994

Country	Exports as a Percentage of GDP	Imports as a Percentage of GDP
United States	10.7	12.1
United Kingdom	26.0	27.0
Switzerland	35.9	31.1
Sweden	36.7	32.4
Japan	9.5	7.3
Italy	23.0	20.3
Germany	33.1	30.3
Canada	33.2	32.5
Argentina	6.8	9.2
South Africa	23.7	21.8
Venezuela	30.8	20.9

SOURCE: International Monetary Fund, *International Financial Statistics Yearbook, 1995* (Washington, D.C.: International Monetary Fund, 1995).

were Canada (22 percent), Japan (10 percent), and Western Europe (27 percent). In terms of products, the three main U.S. imports are crude oil, motor vehicles, and food, and the three main exports are machinery, motor vehicles, and grain.

The United States is far and away the biggest exporter of products in the world, although exports were only 10.6 percent of GDP in 1991. Some countries' economies—Venezuela, Germany, and Switzerland, to name just three—depend very heavily on exports; economic business cycles in other (importing) countries can have a dramatic effect on these countries' macroeconomies.

Why Trade Is Important: Comparative Advantage

The reason for all this trading is that all nations benefit from some degree of specialization and trade. Suppose two nations produce computer components and food with an equal expenditure of time and resources. Trade between the two countries will likely emerge because each can specialize at what it does better—emphasizing the production at which it is more efficient—and trade with the other country for the other good. As we will see, both countries will be better off because specialization and trade lead to increases in production and therefore to increases in the attainable consumption levels of both goods in both countries.

Comparative advantage
An economic entity's (an individual's or a nation's) ability to produce a good at a lower marginal opportunity cost than some other entity.

According to the principle of **comparative advantage,** countries will specialize in producing those goods and services in which they have relatively lower opportunity costs than their trading partners. For example, a hilly, rocky country will not be able to raise as many sheep per acre as a country with fertile grasslands, but the rocky land cannot support any production other than sheep raising, whereas the grassland will support more lucrative cattle production. Even though the grassland is absolutely more productive at raising both sheep and cattle, the rocky land has a comparative advantage in sheep growing because the opportunities forgone are very small. The rocky country will therefore tend to specialize in sheep; the grassy country, in cattle.

TABLE 16.3

U.S. and Japanese Production Possibilities Schedules for Food and Computer Components

Within the United States, 2 units of food cost 1 unit of computer components. Within Japan, 2/3 unit of food costs 1 unit of computer components. The relative opportunity cost of food production is lower in the United States, and the relative opportunity cost of computer component production is lower in Japan.

	PRODUCTION POSSIBILITIES (AT FULL EMPLOYMENT)			
	1	2	3	4
United States				
Food	0	20	40	60
Computer components	30	20	10	0
Japan				
Food	0	10	20	30
Computer components	45	30	15	0

Consider the simplicity and power of the idea that each country produces those products that it can produce with relatively greater efficiency—that is, at a lower relative opportunity cost. Countries that have relatively lower opportunity costs of producing certain goods and services have a strong incentive to produce those goods and services. Production across the world will thus come to reflect the principle of comparative advantage at work. The large amounts of fertile U.S. farmland combined with advanced farm technology have made the American farmer the most productive in the world. America has a clear comparative advantage in certain farm products and raw materials. America's skilled labor force and high rate of technological advance through huge investments in private and public research and development have helped make the United States relatively efficient in producing highly sophisticated machinery and equipment. Trading partners of the United States, especially Japan, have specialized in routinized productions such as automobiles and steel. Energy regulations and increased demand have forced the United States to import immense quantities of petroleum. The pattern of U.S. imports and exports therefore shows the process of economic specialization and comparative advantage at work. (For an example of the idea of comparative advantage, see the Application, "NAFTA: Free Trade or Free-for-All?" at the end of this chapter.)

PRODUCTION POSSIBILITIES BEFORE SPECIALIZATION   To demonstrate more precisely how all trading partners benefit by exercising their comparative advantages, we must look at what happens in each country before and after specialization and trade. Suppose that both the United States and Japan, in isolation, produce just two goods: computer components and food. Further assume that the production possibilities schedules facing the United States and Japan are depicted in Table 16.3, which gives the alternative combinations of food and computer components that could be produced in the United States and Japan if resources are fully employed. The United States, for example, may choose to produce

60 units of food and no computer components, 40 units of food and 10 units of computer components, 20 units of each, or 30 units of computer components and no food. With fully employed resources, Japan may choose between 45 units of computer components and no food at one end of the production spectrum and no computer components with 30 units of food at the other, or combinations between these extremes, as shown in Table 16.3.

These production alternatives are merely the trade-offs that are implicit in the countries' production possibilities curves. For the United States, the extreme choice is between producing 60 units of food (F) or 30 units of computer components (CC). That is, if the United States produces 60F, it will have to forgo 30CC. Within the United States, then, the opportunity cost of producing 1F will be $\frac{1}{2}$ a unit of CC. Alternatively, the cost to the United States of producing 30CC is 60F, or 1CC costs 2F. In summary, within the United States,

> 60F costs 30CC to produce, or
>
> 1F costs $\frac{1}{2}$ CC to produce, or
>
> 1CC costs 2F to produce.

These costs measure how many units of food must be given up to obtain a unit of computer components, or how many units of computer components must be given up to get an additional unit of food. In either case, what is being measured is the relative opportunity cost of producing food or computer components in the United States—that is, what must be given up to increase the production of food or computer components.

Exactly the same analysis can be applied to Japan. For Japan, the production possibilities schedule indicates that, in the extreme, either 45 units of computer components and no food or 30 units of food and no computer components can be produced. The opportunity cost of producing 1F in Japan is then $1\frac{1}{2}$ CC. Likewise, 1CC costs $\frac{2}{3}$ a unit of F. In Japan, the opportunity cost of production is summarized as

> 30F costs 45CC to produce, or
>
> 1F costs $1\frac{1}{2}$ CC to produce, or
>
> 1CC costs $\frac{2}{3}$ F to produce.

Therefore, in this example, the United States has a comparative advantage in producing food and Japan has a comparative advantage in producing computer components.

GAINS FROM SPECIALIZATION AND TRADE   The concepts of production possibilities and opportunity costs provide a perspective for understanding the benefits of trade. Continuing our example of trade between the United States and Japan, first look at the U.S. and Japanese production possibilities curves in Figure 16.1. Notice that these production possibilities curves are straight lines. In practical terms, this means that resources can be transformed from food production to computer component production at constant opportunity cost, that resources are perfectly adaptable to one production process or the other in both economies. The

FIGURE 16.1

Prespecialization Production Possibilities Curves

The straight-line production possibilities curves for the United States and Japan indicate that resources can be transferred from computer component production into food production at constant opportunity cost. The different slopes of the two curves indicate that different opportunity costs provide the basis for both countries to benefit from specialization and trade. The United States has a comparative advantage in food production, whereas Japan is relatively more efficient at producing computer components.

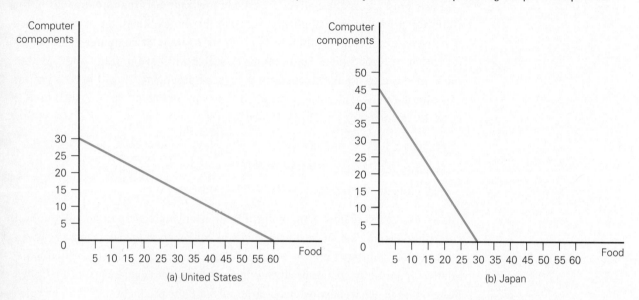

(a) United States   (b) Japan

simplicity of this assumption does not compromise the argument for specialization and trade.

The important part of the argument for gains from specialization turns on the pretrade opportunity costs of producing the two goods that face Japan and the United States. Before trade, consumers in the United States must sacrifice 2 units of food to produce 1 unit of computer components, while Japanese consumers must sacrifice only $^2/_3$ unit of food to produce the same amount of computer components. Or, American consumers must sacrifice $^1/_2$ unit of computer components to obtain 1 unit of food, while their Japanese counterparts must give up $1^1/_2$ units of computer components to get 1 unit of food.

Both countries can gain from trade. Since the United States produces food at an opportunity cost of $^1/_2$ CC and Japan produces computer components at an opportunity cost of $^2/_3$ F, we know that the Americans would gain if trade gave them more than $^1/_2$ CC for 1 unit of food, and the Japanese would gain from $^2/_3$ F for a single unit of computer components. These differences in relative opportunity costs of producing food and computer components yield a basis for specialization and trade between the two countries.

Terms of trade
The number of units of one good that exchange in the market for one unit of some other good; a relative price.

At what price will trade take place? The **terms of trade**—the ratio at which two goods can be traded for each other—will settle somewhere between the relative opportunity cost ratios for each country. For example, terms acceptable to both Japan and the United States will fall between $^2/_3$ F = 1CC (Japan) and 2F = 1CC (United States). We might say that the two countries bargain to set the terms of trade, and the bargaining range is determined by each country's internal opportunity cost

FIGURE 16.2

Production and Consumption Possibilities Curves

The United States specializes in food, producing 60 units; Japan specializes in computer components, producing 45 units. Once trade can take place at the terms of trade of 1F for 1CC, the consumption possibilities curves become relevant. The United States exports 25F and imports 25CC, increasing its consumption (over the pretrade situation) of food by 15 units and computer components by 5 units. Japan exports 25CC and imports 25F, increasing its consumption (over the pretrade situation) of food by 5 units and computer components by 5 units.

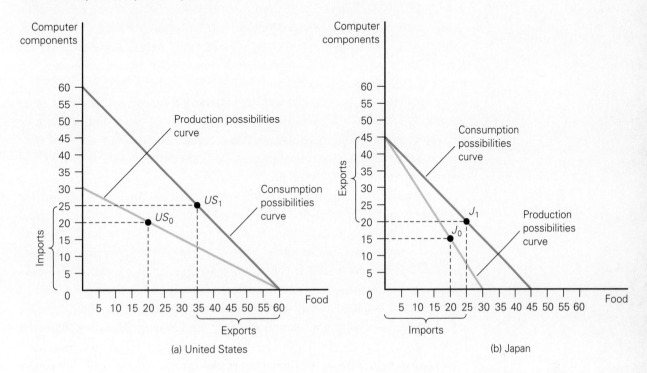

(a) United States   (b) Japan

Consumption possibilities curve
All the possible combinations of two goods that could be consumed by first specializing according to comparative advantage and then trading at the terms of trade.

trade-off. Let us assume that the terms of trade settle at 1 unit of food for 1 unit of computer components, or 1F=1CC.

Figure 16.2 illustrates the potential outcomes of this agreement in terms of the production possibilities curves and each country's posttrade **consumption possibilities curve.** If the countries choose to specialize totally according to comparative advantage, the United States produces 60 units of food and Japan produces 45 units of computer components. Each country can now trade for the product it no longer produces; each country is no longer restricted to consuming a combination of goods on its production possibilities curve. Without trade, a country is restricted to consuming whatever it produces. In the absence of trade, its production possibilities curve and its consumption possibilities curve would be one and the same.

With trade, however, each country's consumption opportunities are determined by how much of its specialized output is produced and the terms of trade. A country's consumption possibilities curve shows all the possible combinations of the two goods that could be consumed if production were specialized (according to comparative advantage) and trade could take place at the given terms of trade. Of course, only one combination can actually be consumed, so the consumption possibilities curve should be viewed as a menu of alternatives open to the country. The consumption possibilities curve with trade will always lie beyond the production possibilities curve, indicating that specialization and trade will leave the country economically better off. Remember, without trade, the country's consumption and production opportunities are identical.

Given that each country specializes and can now trade (at a price or terms of trade of 1F = 1CC) for the product it no longer produces, the consumption possibilities curves in Figure 16.2 become relevant. In contrast to a domestic opportunity cost of 60F for 30CC, the United States now enjoys a situation in which production of 60F could be traded for 60CC. (Naturally, Japan's resource base will not allow production of 60CC—only a maximum of 45CC. Only part of those 45CC will be traded.) Japan enjoys a similar expansion of consumption opportunities with specialization and trade. By specializing and trading, both countries are made economically better off. Each has the ability, with trade, to consume a bundle of goods beyond its production possibilities curve. This would be impossible, given each country's resources and technology, without trade. Specialization does not even have to be complete for the two countries to gain from trade. We have used the example of complete specialization here for simplicity.

If we assume that U.S. consumers originally consumed the bundle of food and computer components labeled US_0 in Figure 16.2a, we can note the improvement in their well-being by considering a new, posttrade consumption bundle, US_1, on their consumption possibilities curve. More of both goods are consumed after specialization and trade. A similar conclusion arises for Japan if we compare hypothetical pre- and postspecialization and trade consumption bundles, J_0 and J_1, respectively. Specialization and trade enlarge the consumption possibilities of the trading nations so that both countries can consume more of both goods after trade occurs.

Note that trade between the United States and Japan in this example takes place according to the principle of comparative advantage. Figure 16.3 shows the explicit pattern of trade. The United States exports food (25 units) because it has a comparative advantage over Japan in food production. This is so because 1F costs the United States only $1/2$CC to produce, whereas 1F would cost Japan $1\frac{1}{2}$CC to produce. Japan exports computer components for the same reason. It has a comparative advantage in producing them over the United States. Each country imports the good for which it is at a comparative disadvantage—that is, the good for which its trading partner possesses a comparative advantage. Gains from trade accrue to producers and consumers. In this example, American consumers of computer components benefit from the lower prices made available by imports, while American food producers benefit by obtaining a price for the food they export higher than the price they could obtain by selling it in the United States—which is not to suggest that no one is harmed by free trade. U.S. food consumers must pay higher food prices as a result of the decision to export some U.S. production. Similarly, U.S. producers of computer components are harmed when Japanese suppliers enter the market and cause prices to fall. On balance, however, gains from free trade exceed losses; free trade leads to improved standards of living.

Our discussion has been based on a simple example of how the principle of comparative advantage works. In discussing two-good trade between Japan and

FIGURE 16.3

The Pattern of U.S.–Japan Trade

Japan has a comparative advantage in computer component production; the United States, in food production. This means that Japan will export computer components and import food, whereas the United States will export food and import computer components. The terms of trade, 1F for 1CC in this example, must be between the two countries' opportunity costs of production.

the United States, we assumed that each country was absolutely more efficient than the other at producing one of the two goods. What if one country is absolutely more efficient in producing both goods? Suppose that productivity in the United States tripled—production of computer components increasing to 90 units and production of food increasing to 180 units. U.S. production capacity in this case would outpace Japan two to one in computer components and six to one in food. Nonetheless, the opportunity cost to the United States of producing each computer component would still be 2 units of food, which is higher than Japan's opportunity cost. It would still be mutually advantageous for the United States to specialize in food and to obtain computer components from Japan through trade. Remember, the argument for free trade is based on the principle of *comparative* advantage. Trade between two countries is mutually beneficial whenever the countries bear different opportunity costs of producing goods. This is true even if one of the countries is absolutely more productive at producing both goods.

Tariffs and Quotas

Despite the advantages of specialization and trade, certain barriers to trade exist in the real world. Some are natural costs of exchanges, such as negotiating and transportation costs, and cannot be avoided. Other barriers to trade are artificial, contrivances of governments designed to raise revenues or protect domestic producers from foreign competition. The major examples of artificial trade barriers are tariffs and quotas. A **tariff,** or import duty, is simply a tax levied on particular imported goods. For example, the United States imposes a tariff on imported shoes and steel. A **quota** is a partial or absolute limitation on the quantity of a particular good that can be imported. For example, until 1972, the United States imposed a quota on the importation of foreign oil and permitted oil refiners to import only the allowed amount of oil. Both tariffs and quotas reduce the extent of specialization and trade and, therefore, the gains that consumers obtain from free trade. Both raise the

Tariff
A tax or levy on imported goods.

Quota
A restriction or limit on the quantity of an imported good.

FIGURE 16.4

Domestic Producers' Supply Schedule for Automobiles

Imposition of an import tariff on imported automobiles allows U.S. producers to raise the prices of their automobiles from the free-market world price, P_w, to P_{w+t}. The higher prices encourage them to increase the quantity of automobiles they produce from Q_0 to Q_1. Their profits are therefore increased by the shaded area $P_{w+t}E_1E_0P_w$. This increase in profits is also referred to as an increase in producer surplus. Employment of domestic resources increases because domestic production rises from Q_0 to Q_1.

prices of imported and domestically produced goods and restrict imports. In these respects, tariffs and quotas are similar.

THE EFFECTS OF ARTIFICIAL TRADE BARRIERS

Free trade
The exchange of goods between countries without the presence of artificial trade barriers such as tariffs and quotas.

With very few exceptions (to be discussed later in the chapter), **free trade**—trade without artificial barriers—leads to maximum economic welfare among nations. Free trade and specialization expand consumption possibilities and deliver goods to consumers at the lowest possible costs. Yet given all the benefits of free trade, the world does not often seem to allow it to work, at least not completely. The reason is that some parties are harmed by free trade. Pressures are brought to bear on governments by producer groups for protection from foreign competition. Sometimes these groups win political favors, such as tariffs or quotas, to reduce the competitive threat. In this section we use economic theory to show how these interferences with free trade reduce the overall economic welfare of a country.

Trade and Tariffs: Who Gains? Who Loses?

To understand who really gains and loses from a tariff, consider Figure 16.4. It shows two possible prices facing domestic suppliers of automobiles: the free-market world price of autos, P_w, and the free-market world price plus some per unit tariff on autos imported to the United States, P_{w+t}.

Imposition of a tariff on imported autos clearly benefits domestic automobile manufacturers. Since imported cars are now more expensive, domestic suppliers

FIGURE 16.5

Effects of Tariff on Consumer Demand

A tariff on imported automobiles causes the price to increase from P_w to P_{w+t}, which in turn causes a reduction in the quantity of automobiles demanded by consumers from Q_0 to Q_1. Benefits to consumers are reduced by the amount represented by the shaded area $P_{w-t}E_1E_0P_w$. This loss is referred to as a reduction in consumer surplus.

can raise their prices without any increase in costs. The higher price P_{w+t} encourages domestic auto producers to increase output from quantity Q_0 to quantity Q_1, which has the effect of increasing domestic suppliers' profits by the shaded area $P_{w+t}E_1E_0P_w$. This increase in profits is often described as an increase in producer surplus. Naturally, because the tariff increases domestic production, it also increases domestic employment in the industry producing the good that is subject to the tariff. We must be careful, though, not to generalize that a tariff on a specific good or set of goods will increase the overall level of employment in a country. The tariff is likely to have economic repercussions that are felt in the markets for other goods and services and that tend to reduce employment in those markets.

What if the auto tariff were reduced? A reduction in the tariff would reduce producers' profits (their producer surplus) as well as domestic employment in the auto industry. But before we can present an overall economic assessment of tariffs, we must investigate their effects on consumers.

The effects of a tariff on consumers are shown in Figure 16.5. The figure shows an initial price, P_w, and an initial quantity of autos, Q_0, purchased by consumers. Imposition of a tariff on imported cars increases the price to P_{w+t} and reduces consumption of autos from Q_0 to Q_1. A reduction in benefits to consumers accompanies the increase in price. (Previously, we have equated these benefits with consumer surplus.) The shaded area $P_{w+t}E_1E_0P_w$ in Figure 16.5 represents the reduction in consumer surplus caused by the tariff on automobiles. We will elaborate on this concept in the following sections.

The Benefits of Free Trade

Using the concepts of consumer and producer surplus, we can now see the benefits of free trade. We will first examine an industry in which the United States is an

FIGURE 16.6

The Benefits of Importing Freely

The total supply curve S_T is the horizontal summation of domestic (S_{US}) and foreign (S_F) supplies of automobiles. In the pretrade situation, when consumers purchase only domestic automobiles, equilibrium E_0 is established at price P_D and quantity produced Q_D. Under free trade, imports lower prices from P_D to P_T and increase quantity consumed in the domestic market from Q_0 to Q_T, with equilibrium established at E_1. Free trade improves the welfare of consumers by $E_0 E_1 E_2$.

importer—the automobile industry. Then we will look at the effects of free international trade on an industry in which the United States is an exporter—the wheat industry.

Consider Figure 16.6, which shows the U.S. domestic supply curve for automobiles, S_{US}, the curve S_F, which shows the supply of cars to the U.S. market by foreign producers, and the American demand curve, D. The domestic supply curve and the foreign supply curve for automobiles are added together horizontally to produce S_T, a curve showing the total supply of cars to the U.S. market by domestic and foreign producers.

If no cars were allowed to be imported, the domestic price of cars would be P_D, and the quantity bought and sold would be Q_D. However, if cars were imported without restriction, the market would clear at E_1, where the price is P_T and the quantity is Q_T—the point at which domestic demand for cars equals total supply of cars. If we compare the equilibrium under free trade with the equilibrium under no trade, we see that the consumer surplus is larger by an amount $P_D E_0 E_1 P_T$. However, under free trade and a price of P_T, domestic producers produce only Q_2 cars and receive a producer surplus that is smaller by the amount $P_D E_0 E_2 P_T$ than the surplus they previously received. In other words, domestic car producers are harmed by free trade, since they sell fewer cars (Q_2 instead of Q_D) at a price of P_T. However, the gain that consumers receive by moving to free trade, $P_D E_0 E_1 P_T$, is larger than the cost of free trade to U.S. producers by an amount equal to $E_0 E_1 E_2$.

Figure 16.7 shows the effects of free trade in an industry like the wheat industry, in which the United States is an exporter. In Figure 16.7, D_{US} and S_{US} show

FIGURE 16.7

The Benefits of Exporting Freely

The total demand curve, D_T, is the horizontal sum of domestic demand (D_{US}) and foreign demand for U.S. wheat (D_F). In the pretrade situation, the equilibrium is at E_1. If exports are permitted, the price rises from P_D to P_T. Domestic producers increase sales from Q_D to Q_T, but domestic consumers reduce purchases from Q_D to Q'. As a consequence, the increase in the producer surplus of domestic producers is larger than the decrease in the consumer surplus for domestic consumers.

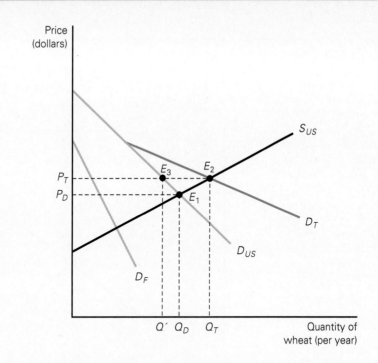

the domestic demand and supply of wheat, respectively. D_F shows foreign demand for U.S. wheat, and D_T shows the horizontal total of U.S. and foreign demand for wheat. If wheat is not permitted to be sold abroad, the wheat market in the United States will clear at E_1, with a price of P_D and with Q_D units bought by U.S. consumers from U.S. producers. However, if the United States and other countries allow free trade, the market will clear at E_2. The equilibrium price of wheat will rise to P_T and the equilibrium quantity will rise to Q_T. Of the Q_T units sold by domestic producers, Q_1 will be sold to domestic consumers, and the remainder ($Q_T - Q'$) will be exported. As a consequence of free trade, U.S. producers will experience an increase in producer surplus of $P_T E_2 E_1 P_D$. U.S. consumers will find that their surplus has fallen by $P_T E_3 E_1 P_D$. The gain to producers exceeds the loss to consumers by $E_3 E_2 E_1$.

We see that, as a group, consumers and producers benefit from free trade. Although some parties are harmed, the gains by others more than offset these losses. There are net gains from trade for import and export industries.

Welfare Loss from Tariffs

We have now seen how trade creates net benefits to domestic consumers and producers. Let us now look at the effects of a protective tariff on the society as a whole, using a hypothetical market for television sets.

Figure 16.8 represents the domestic market for TV sets, including the domestic supply of the product and the U.S. demand. Prior to the imposition of a tariff, American consumers buy Q_4 units at the world price P_w. Of this quantity purchased, Q_1 are sold by domestic manufacturers and $Q_1 Q_4$ are imported from abroad.

FIGURE 16.8

The Effects of a Tariff

Gains in producer profits and government revenue do not equal consumer losses from tariff-imposition. Net consumer losses are shown in the shaded triangles in the figure. Before a tariff on TV sets, consumers purchase Q_4 units at price P_w. The tariff causes the price to rise to P_{w+t}, imports to decrease from Q_1Q_4 to Q_2Q_3, and the total number of TVs sold to decrease to Q_3. Consumers' total loss is represented by $P_{w+t}E_3E_4P_w$ but producers gain $P_{w+t}E_2E_1P_w$, and government tariff revenues are E_2E_3AB. The net loss to society is therefore the sum of the areas E_2BE_1 and E_3E_4A.

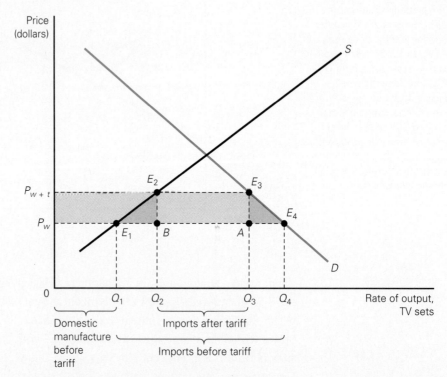

Assume that a tariff is imposed in the amount t, causing the price of TVs to American consumers to rise to P_{w+t}. (For clarity, we have assumed that the foreign TV supply curve is horizontal. A totally elastic supply curve would exist if TV production in the world was a constant-cost industry or if the United States bought such a small share of total world TV output that it was a price-taker country.) American TV producers gain additional profits or producer surplus in the amount represented by $P_{w+t}E_2E_1P_w$ because of the increased domestic output permitted by the higher price. Imports are reduced to Q_2Q_3, and the total number of sets sold decreases to Q_3. Consumers lose total benefits in the amount of $P_{w+t}E_3E_4P_w$. At the same time, the tariff on imported TV sets creates government revenues. These revenues are composed of the per unit amount of the tariff multiplied by the units of TV sets imported after the tariff is imposed (area E_2E_3AB in Figure 16.8).

Economists typically assume that the government revenue is used in a manner that produces benefits equivalent to those lost by consumers of TV sets. However, the tariff causes a net loss in benefits to society, of which TV consumers are a part, represented by the sum of the two areas E_2BE_1 and E_3E_4A. The sum of these triangles represents a loss that is not counterbalanced by the sum of producers' gains and government revenue resulting from the tariff. Economists call this loss a **welfare loss to society** due to the imposition of a tariff.

Welfare loss to society
The net loss to an economy resulting from the imposition of an artificial trade barrier.

Why Are Tariffs Imposed?

If tariffs create a welfare loss to society, why are they imposed? Certainly tariff revenue to the federal government is minuscule when compared to other sources of government revenue.

The source of tariff protection is to be found in the urgings of "merchants and manufacturers" as well as from labor in domestic import-competing industries. Consumers of TV sets and of any goods that actually bear a tariff could conceivably convince both producers and the government not to impose tariffs because, as we have shown, consumers lose more than producers and government gain from tariffs. Practically, however, the world does not work this way. Consumers, the gainers from free trade, are widely dispersed and costly to organize in any fight for free trade. Interest in fighting a tariff or quota is also apt to be low among consumers because their pro rata share of losses from artificial barriers to trade is generally small. To an individual consumer, for example, the tariff is a small proportion of the total price of an automobile. The incentive to organize and fight protective tariffs is therefore small.

Not so for producers. The pro rata, or proportionate, share of the effects of tariff protection is much higher among manufacturers, for they are far fewer in number than consumers. Manufacturers thus have stronger incentives than consumers to form an interest group, and, being fewer in number, their costs of organizing are lower. For such reasons, the consumer interest in free trade is often thwarted.

Nontariff Barriers to Trade

Nontariff trade barriers
Alternative (to tariffs and quotas) means of restricting trade; examples include domestic content legislation and health and safety regulations.

Historically, tariffs and quotas have been the most important types of artificial trade restrictions. In recent years, other types of restrictive practices, which are generally called **nontariff trade barriers** (NTBs), have taken on increased importance. Examples of nontariff trade barriers include domestic content legislation (laws that require a certain portion of goods sold in a country to be produced there) as well as safety or health regulations designed to discriminate against foreign products. NTBs have grown rapidly in recent years because many countries have enacted trade legislation that forbids tariffs or quotas; NTBs represent an alternative form of protectionism. The use of NTBs varies greatly among countries. In the United States, NTBs exist for about 25 percent of imported goods. The corresponding percentage for Japan is about 12 percent. Within the European Community, percentages vary but average about 20 percent.

Although it is difficult to determine the specific effects of nontariff trade barriers, the general effects are quite similar to those of tariffs. Figure 16.8 shows how a tariff artificially raises the price of imported goods and causes the quantity of imports to fall. NTBs have similar effects. If, for example, the United States were to enact legislation requiring that cars sold in this country have a 50 percent domestic content, the Japanese could continue exporting cars to the United States only if at least half of the parts and the assembly were American. The cost of compliance would be higher production costs to the Japanese, but it would be very difficult to determine how much costs would rise. The effect therefore would be identical to the imposition of some specific tariff. Without knowing by how much this legislation would increase production costs, it would be impossible to determine what an equivalent tariff would be.

Nontariff trade barriers have become a major issue in the United States, particularly with regard to the economic unification of Europe. There is some concern that the European Community will implement technical standards that discriminate against foreign firms. Some observers have suggested that U.S. exports to Europe would fall sharply as a result of any such barriers. Although it is impossible to predict what economic policies the European Community will pursue, the complete economic unification of Europe is sure to present certain advantages to U.S. exporters. For one thing, U.S. firms will no longer have to contend with different NTBs in each of the European countries. Also, it will no longer be necessary for U.S. companies to produce a different product for each country in order to meet different standards.

A Quota Is a Quota Is a Tariff

Quota agreements between two countries to voluntarily limit exports from one country to the other have become a popular alternative to tariff controls. One form of quota agreement is called the Voluntary Export Restraint (VER). In 1990, for example, President Bush used the device to restrict imported steel through 1992, but a precedent for this had been established during the Reagan administration with VERs on automobiles. In 1995 and 1996 the Clinton Administration continued to use threats of unilateral import restrictions in trade talks with particular nations. On April 1, 1981, an international trade agreement between the governments of Japan and the United States was put into effect. Under the VERs, the government of Japan would prevent Japanese automakers from exporting as many cars as they would like to the U.S. market. Japanese car manufacturers were restricted to shipping only 1.68 million cars to the U.S. market per year from 1981 to 1984. What was the economic effect of the VERs on U.S. automobile producers and consumers?

In order to answer this question, we must first recognize that this "voluntary" restraint was nothing more than a quota of 1.68 million cars. The U.S. government effectively restricted imports from Japan to a level of 1.68 million cars. The next question to answer is: What effect did the imposition of an import quota have on the domestic U.S. market for automobiles?

Figure 16.9 will help answer this question. In Figure 16.9, *PW* is the price of a car in the United States before imposition of a quota. Domestic producers sell Q_1 cars, and imports equal Q_4 minus Q_1 autos. Once the quota, equal to Q_3 minus Q_2, is imposed, how does the domestic market move to a new equilibrium? Recall that an equilibrium price is one at which quantity demanded equals quantity supplied. Part of quantity supplied is supplied by foreign producers, the amount of the quota in this case. To find what equilibrium price will be under the quota, we need only find a price at which the horizontal distance between the demand and supply curves equals the quota. At price P_{W+Q}, domestic output, Q_2, plus the quota, Q_3 minus Q_2, equals total quantity demanded, Q_3. Thus, at price P_{W+Q}, quantity demanded equals total quantity supplied. P_{W+Q} will then be the domestic price of a car if a quota of Q_3 minus Q_2 is imposed.

Figures 16.8 and 16.9 are similar in many respects because tariffs and quotas are similar in many respects. They both raise domestic price and reduce imports, but the tariff works initially by affecting price and letting quantity adjust, whereas the

FIGURE 16.9

The Effect of a Quota on the Domestic Market

When the quota is imposed, it is still necessary for quantity demanded to equal quantity supplied for the domestic market to be in equilibrium. Only at price P_{W+Q} will total quantity demanded, Q_3, equal total quantity supplied. Total quantity supplied equals quantity supplied domestically, Q_2, plus imports, Q_3 minus Q_2. The quota raises price, increases domestic producers' profits, and produces welfare losses—just as a tariff does.

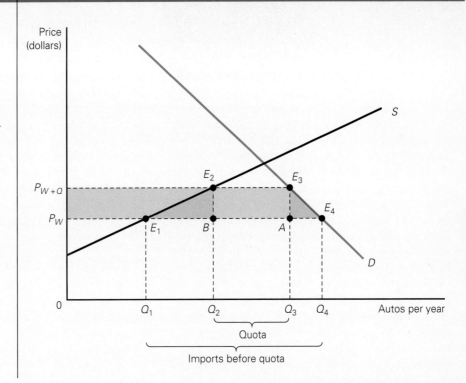

quota directly affects quantity with the result that prices adjust. Whichever method is used to restrict trade, higher domestic prices and fewer imports result.

There are some differences between tariffs and quotas, however. In Figure 16.9, if a tariff had driven domestic price up to P_{W+Q}, the U.S. government would have collected tariff revenue in the amount of area E_2E_3AB. However, under the VERs, no tariff revenue was collected from Japanese automakers. In fact, the United States government merely allowed the Japanese government and Japanese automakers to decide for themselves which companies would fill the quota of 1.68 million units. With the import rights left specifically unassigned (and not charged for) by the U.S. government, the area E_2E_3AB became revenue to Japanese producers (and their U.S. dealers) rather than tariff revenue for the United States. Some analysts have estimated this area to have been on the order of $10 billion over the 1984–1985 period. This is one of the wealth transfers, from American consumers to Japanese producers, of a quota designed in this fashion. (For a further discussion of "voluntary" export restraints, see Focus, "Autos, Peanuts and Politics: How Quotas Affect You".)

THE CASE FOR PROTECTION

Throughout history numerous arguments have emerged in defense of protection from free trade. Most of these arguments are but thin veils for producers' interests. All the arguments—both the well-constructed and the questionable ones—deserve careful scrutiny.

Quotas, like tariffs, raise the prices of the products you buy. While trade has been liberalized through the reduction of tariffs—and through free trade zones such as NAFTA—quotas may be even more insidious at increasing the prices of consumer goods in the United States. Consider some examples. Economist Robert Crandall of the Brookings Institution in Washington, D.C studied the Reagan administration's VERs in an attempt to gauge the economic effects on consumers and producers of automobiles.[a] He estimated that in 1984 the price of a Japanese car sold in the United States was about $2500 more than it would have been without the VERs. Additionally, the higher prices of Japanese imports allowed U.S. automakers to charge about $1000 more per car than they would have been able to in the absence of quotas. The stockholders of U.S. auto companies and the employees of these companies clearly benefited from the VERs. Crandall also estimates that American auto consumers paid approximately $16 billion more for cars in 1984–1985 than they would have in the absence of the quotas.

An interesting alternative study expands on the effects of U.S.–Japanese VERs on autos by calculating the impact of third parties on American consumers. Producers in Germany, Sweden, and France, though *not included* in the VER arrangement, were very much affected by it. These European auto exporters also were able to increase prices—by about one-third over the pre-VER level, according to economists Elias Dinopoulos and Mordechai Kreinin. This price hike, which is a direct transfer from U.S. consumers to Eu-

ropean producers, added considerably to the total welfare loss in the United States. Dinopoulos and Kreinin reveal a threefold welfare loss: "the loss to Japan (estimated at $2.3 billions in 1982 and $2.4 billions in 1984); the loss to Europe (estimated at $1.5 billions in 1982 and $3.4 billions in 1984); and a small social loss within the United States, over and above the pure internal transfer from consumers to producers ($208 millions in 1982)." Further, they put the total cost of the auto VER in 1982 at $4 billion. The automobile VER may have saved 22,358 auto-related jobs in 1982, but American consumers had to pay $181,000 for each of those jobs, many times each autoworker's average annual compensation.[b]

Quota and tariff concessions to special interests who pressured politicians for favors were a part of the Bush and Clinton administrations' trade policy. Such protection is often a cover for outright protection of favored industries, however. For example, in 1992 the Congressional Budget Office calculated the cost to American consumers of maintaining protection on textiles as $9000 to $38,000 per year over and above the wages of textile workers. The United States Department of Agriculture (USDA) estimates that peanuts cost $491 per metric ton to produce in the state of Georgia, although the world market price is about $300 per ton. The USDA peanut price support program permits U.S. farmers to sell peanuts in the U.S. market for more than $600 per ton. American consumers pay more because there is a virtual ban on the importation of the legumes. In a period of growing deficits, a huge federal debt and relatively slow economic growth, it does not seem reasonable that the economy and U.S. consumers should endure such artificially high costs.

[a]Robert W. Crandall, "Detroit Rode Quotas to Prosperity," *Wall Street Journal* (January 29, 1986), p. 30.

[b]Elias Dinopoulos and Mordechai E. Kreinin, "Effects of the U.S.–Japan Auto VER on European Prices and on U.S. Welfare," *Review of Economics and Statistics* 70 (August 1988), pp. 484–491.

National Interest Arguments for Protection

The two oldest and best-formed arguments in defense of protection and against free trade are the national defense argument and the "infant industries" argument. Both arguments contain a grain of truth, but each should be closely scrutinized before serving as a base for protectionist policies.

NATIONAL DEFENSE   The oldest argument for protection—and the one with superficially the best justification—is that such restrictions are necessary for national defense. As military technology has changed, steel, gunpowder, manganese, uranium, and a host of other inputs have all been commodities essential to making war and they have all been the subject of tariffs and quotas to keep domestic production of these commodities strong.

The logic of protection for defense is clear: Since the ultimate function of government is national defense, any possible threat to national defense, such as the unavailability of some resource during a crisis, must be avoided. A loss in consumers' benefits from protection is thus justified for a greater benefit—the availability of essential materials to be prepared for war. Artificial barriers to trade in these materials are used to protect domestic industries considered essential for national defense.

The national defense argument is plausible for some industries and some products, but consider that cheese, fruit, and watch manufacturers and other, non-defense-related industries have all resorted to the argument. History seems to prove that patriotism is the last and best refuge of a producer seeking protection from foreign competition. The national defense argument has seen double duty as an argument for maintaining unprofitable routes on railroads and protecting truck, air, and railroad companies by setting legalized cartel rates. The telephone industry was long protected on similar grounds.

The imposition of tariffs and quotas is not the only way to handle the national defense issue. A tariff is nothing but a hidden subsidy or cash grant to domestic producers. Thus, if an industry is to be protected for national defense reasons, an explicit subsidy may be more straightforward than tariff protection. That way, the national defense issue is made clear, and voters know how much defense actually costs them. If, for example, it is deemed vital to national security that the United States have a certain capacity to produce iron and steel, an alternative public policy would be to subsidize domestic iron and steel producers rather than to protect them against foreign competition with a tariff or quota.

Infant industry
A new or developing domestic industry whose unit production costs are higher than those of established firms in the same industry in other countries.

PROTECTION OF INFANT INDUSTRIES   Possibly the most frequently heard argument for protection, especially in developing nations, is the so-called **infant industries** argument. Discussed by Adam Smith and supported by Americans such as Alexander Hamilton, the infant industries argument reached its highest expression in the mid-nineteenth-century writings of German nationalist Friedrich List (1789–1846). List sought to unify and develop the German states against the incursions of British imports. He argued that protective tariffs were necessary in the transition from an agricultural-manufacturing to an agricultural-manufacturing-commercial stage of development. His reasoning was clear: Specific tariffs were necessary to maintain fledgling industries until they could compete with foreign imports on their own. After the "infancy" period of industrial development was over, protective tariffs would be lifted, forcing the businesses to meet the rigors of competition.

The infant industries argument is related to the idea of economies of scale. Economies of scale exist when, as plant size increases up to a point, long-run unit costs decline. This occurs because individual workers become more proficient at narrowly defined tasks, and machines are more closely tailored to individual processes. Scale economies may also occur because both workers and managers "learn by doing" and acquire more experience as output grows. Often, moreover, production of certain manufactured goods results in an enormous initial setup cost. As firm and industry output grow larger, these setup costs are spread over larger and larger numbers of units produced. A number of developing nations use this economies of scale or infant industries argument today in their quest for unilateral tariff protection. One-crop economies, whose foreign earnings are heavily dependent on a single export, seek to use an umbrella of protectionist policies to buy time for diversification.

As much as one might be concerned for the economic plight of poor nations, great care must be exercised in applying the infant industry argument to them. At best, the argument is one for allowing domestic industry to gain a foothold in international competition. Protection for any reason, as we have seen, means lost benefits for consumers. Obviously, any gains from ultimate independence must be balanced against the costs of lost consumer benefits over the period of protection.

A final question that should be applied to the infant industries argument concerns the vagueness of the goal of removing protection when the industry "grows up." It is hardly legitimate to apply the infant industries argument to the present-day steel industry in the United States and Western Europe, but the argument is still being used. Entrenched protectionist interests will always attempt to prolong the "infancy" of any industry. The dangers of giving protectionists a general legal foothold negate any merit the argument might have in limited and specific cases.

Industry Arguments for Protection

A number of other arguments for protection crop up from time to time, usually put forward by domestic firms and industries seeking protection for protection's sake. We characterize these arguments as wrong because they are assaults on the very principle that gains may be realized from trade. They are all variations on the theme that special-interest groups deserve protection from international competition.

THE "CHEAP FOREIGN LABOR" ARGUMENT   A common argument for tariff or quota protection is that labor or some other resource is cheaper abroad, enabling foreign manufacturers to sell goods at lower prices than U.S. manufacturers. This argument is usually heard from producers and workers who fear displacement by imports and foreign competition. Most recently, it has been the argument used by Ross Perot and others to urge the defeat of the North American Free Trade Agreement. Opponents of NAFTA claim that a massive loss of jobs will result as U.S. firms relocate to take advantage of lower-cost labor in Mexico.

While the argument may be correct—foreign producers may be more efficient combiners of resources—this truth in no way denies the benefits to free trade. The *absolute* level of wages in any other country does not matter. As we have seen, gains from trade derive from *comparative* advantage. Indeed, the request for protection from cheap labor turns the gains from trade position on its head: The reason for trade becomes a reason to limit or restrict trade. Open trade is beneficial precisely because resources may be cheaper or combined more efficiently elsewhere. The opening or extension of trade creates a temporary disruption of markets, including the unemployment of resources. To impose tariffs or quotas on the grounds that some groups of U.S. laborers are temporarily thrown out of work or that some U.S. stockholders are losing wealth is to subsidize special interests at a greater cost to all U.S. consumers of the subsidized product or service. Moreover, the domestic economy may actually gain from the movement of domestic resources into new fields of comparative advantage. For example, resources released from domestic steel production may be reallocated to computer production.

Side issues arise in the cheap foreign labor argument. One common complaint is that foreign governments subsidize the production of exported goods to shore up their domestic industries and prevent unemployment. This complaint is used as a plea for protection from cheaper imports. But to argue for tariffs on these grounds is to look a gift horse in the mouth. The benefits from trade are independent of the reasons that imports are cheaper. If governments choose to subsidize their exports, they in effect tax their own citizens to benefit foreign consumers.

Dumping

The selling of goods in foreign markets at prices lower than those charged in domestic markets.

Dumping, selling goods abroad at a lower price than in the home market, is also related to the cheap foreign labor argument for protection. The practice, an example of price discrimination, means that foreign buyers gain greater benefits from consuming the commodity or service than domestic consumers. In practice, it is often difficult to determine whether goods are being dumped. As defined by U.S. trade policies, dumping occurs when a foreign producer sells in the American market either below costs or at a price below that charged to the foreign producer's domestic customers. In real-world cases, then, a producer could be selling to his or her own customers at monopoly rates and be prohibited from selling to American consumers at lower rates (even though they more than cover costs). Such restrictions, if enforced by trade authorities, could work against American consumers.

Special interests in the favored country often complain that dumping constitutes "unfair competition," but the argument for free trade remains intact nonetheless. Consumers in the favored nations are able to purchase goods at lower prices, and overall welfare in the consuming country is enhanced.

It should not matter why foreign prices are low, as long as the foreign supplier who is dumping goods in U.S. markets has no monopoly power. If the producers of Japanese television sets undersell U.S. producers with an eye to putting them out of business and subsequently raising price to a monopoly level, dumping does pose an issue for public concern. More often, "dumping" by foreign producers is a reflection of their lower costs of production and puts competitive pressure on U.S. producers.

THE "BUY AMERICAN" ARGUMENT   The "buy American" argument, a call to patriotism, is based on the notion that Americans will be better off by keeping their money at home. More specifically, "buy American" means that imports should be restricted so that high costs or inefficient producers and their employees may be protected from foreign competition.

This well-known argument is fallacious on several counts. First, it asks consumers to pay higher prices for goods and services than are available to them through trade, thereby negating the potential expansion of trade benefits. Second, when money is kept at home, foreign consumers are unable to purchase domestic exports, reducing the welfare of domestic export producers and their workers and other input suppliers.

"TERMS OF TRADE" ADVANTAGE   A final argument applies to countries that have monopoly power in international markets. It suggests that a country employ its power to increase its share of the gains from international trade. Thus, if the United States is the world's largest supplier of computers, putting restrictions on computer exports will drive up the price of computers in the international market. Although the United States will then sell fewer computers, it will get a higher price per computer and possibly higher computer sales revenues. In effect, by restricting computer exports, the United States would alter the terms of trade in international transactions in its favor.

The **terms of trade argument** suggests that countries exercise monopoly and monopsony power where possible. Doing so is a means for a country to increase its revenues from international trade. The argument founders, however, on a simple point: the possibility of retaliation by other countries. If all countries seek terms of trade advantages, the trading nations of the world *collectively* may be made worse off. The exercise of monopoly or monopsony power to improve the terms of trade for all countries could mean a shrinking of total world production for exports. This negates the gains from comparative advantage and from the division of labor and reduces specialization within nations.

Perhaps the greatest flaw in all arguments for protection lies in the implicit assumption that other nations will lose export markets and will not retaliate. It is improbable that a country could win permanent terms of trade advantages on a unilateral basis while its trading partners sit idly by. U.S. history is peppered with examples of tariff wars. One of the fiercest tariff wars in history took place in the midst of the Great Depression of the 1930s, discussed in the next section. Tariffs or other forms of trade barrier retaliation can only create a reduction in worldwide economic welfare and massive and inefficient allocations of resources. Whatever the initial reasons for protective tariffs, consumers ultimately suffer the costs.

Clearly, the reduction or removal of tariffs or quotas benefits consumers as a whole, producing a *net* benefit to society. But against these gains must be set the losses that occur to laborers (and other input suppliers) in businesses and industries that no longer are protected. Many economists support *temporary* retraining and assistance programs for workers and industries that suffer hardship as a result of freer trade.

U.S. TARIFF POLICY

U.S. tariff history has been punctuated by cycles of less-restricted and more-restricted trade, with a move toward free trade in the past 50 years that may be more apparent than real. The average tariff rates for the years between 1821 (the

Terms of trade argument Defending the use of artificial trade barriers, combined with monopoly or monopsony power in international markets, in order to produce an improvement in a country's terms of trade.

FIGURE 16.10

Level of Tariffs

The United States today has lower tariffs, as measured by the ratio of tariff fees collected to the value of imports, than at any other time in its history. Since the establishment of the General Agreement on Tariffs and Trade (GATT) in 1947, tariffs have followed a downward trend.

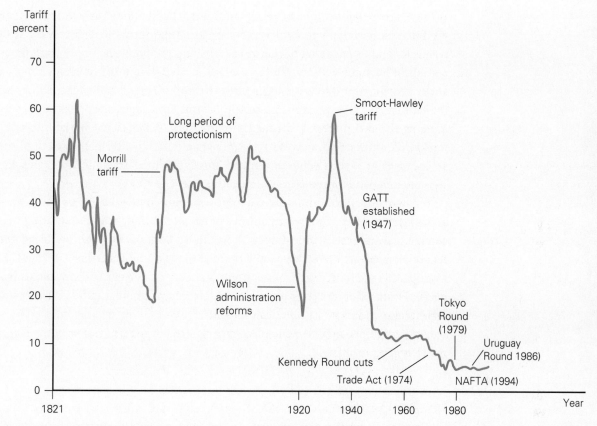

SOURCE: U.S. Bureau of the Census, *Historical Statistics, Colonial Times to 1970* (Washington, D.C.: U.S. Government Printing Office, 1975), p. 888. U.S. Bureau of the Census, *Statistical Abstract of the United States, 1995* (Washington, D.C.: U.S. Government Printing Office, 1995), p. 824.

year of the first good statistics) and 1995 are shown in Figure 16.10, along with some highlights of our tariff history. In the twentieth century, import duties as a percentage of the value of all imports subject to duty have ranged from almost 60 percent in the early 1930s to about 3 percent in the early 1990s.

Why has the average tariff fluctuated so widely during U.S. history? Before turning to a specific analysis of changing conditions, one broad issue will help us answer the question. With the minor exception of tariffs imposed for revenues to fight wars or to apply foreign policy pressures, the average tariff has varied with business conditions, falling in periods of prosperity and rising during prolonged recessions or depressions. During periods of rising prosperity, manufacturers and workers displaced by free trade find little political support for the imposition of tariffs. When general business conditions turn downward, creating reduced demand for products and increased unemployment, the cry for protection grows louder in the political arena.

Early Tariff Policy

Tariffs were a major source of revenue for our republic in its early years, as they are for some developing countries today. Post–1820 tariffs tended to vary with business conditions, rising during recessions and falling during more prosperous periods of business activity. On the eve of the Civil War, tariff revenues stood at about 19 percent of the value of imports, the lowest level in American history up to that time. In 1861, Congress passed the Morrill tariff under the pretext of generating much-needed revenue for the Union treasury. Whatever the initial intention, the Morrill tariff set off a wave of protectionism in U.S. policy that lasted until the second decade of the twentieth century. Tariffs declined dramatically during the Wilson administration, standing at only 16 percent in 1920.

The dramatic downturn in the economy beginning in the late 1920s had a stark and lingering effect on protectionism in the United States. Manufacturing and commercial interests, coinciding with a willing political climate, produced the Smoot-Hawley Act of 1930, which legislated the highest peace-time tariff in U.S. history. Average tariff levels were raised to almost 60 percent of the value of imports, setting off a frenzy of protectionist retaliations in other nations. The result of what was perceived as American self-interest was falling real incomes, sharply reduced consumer welfare, and a deepened and prolonged depression in the major world-trading countries.

Modern Tariff Policy

Contemporary tariff policy may be viewed as an attempt to overcome the disastrous effects of protectionism embodied in the Smoot-Hawley Act. The first Roosevelt administration, under the aegis of Secretary of State Cordell Hull, acted swiftly to counteract the protectionism of the Smoot-Hawley tariff. In 1934, the Reciprocal Trade Agreements Act was passed, giving the president power to negotiate bilateral tariff reductions of up to 50 percent with other countries. This act was the important first step in establishing the character of modern U.S. tariff policy. It established a framework within which free trade is envisioned as a policy goal and to a large extent it stripped Congress of its tariff-making power (but not the power to set nontariff barriers). While Congress could legally remove the tariff-setting powers of the president, these powers have been renewed and strengthened a number of times since 1934.

In the post–World War II era, the powers of the president have been expanded to include multilateral negotiations for tariff reductions—that is, negotiations with many nations simultaneously. A manifestation of America's multilateral policy was its support of the General Agreement on Tariffs and Trade (GATT) in 1947. GATT sets rules and conditions for tariff reductions and oversees bargaining with all participating nations simultaneously. Modern U.S. trade policies evolve through GATT, and tremendous gains and an expansion of world trade have occurred since the first GATT talks. Moreover, Congress has expressed some willingness to move toward free trade. In 1962, a Trade Expansion Act was passed, permitting the president to negotiate tariff reductions on all commodities simultaneously rather than commodity by commodity. This act led to the so-called Kennedy round of tariff reductions (1964–1967), which produced huge concessions on manufactured and industrial products, with special concessions for developing countries. Subsequent GATT rounds have produced additional tariff reductions. A new GATT tariff agreement was reached in 1994.

Where Does the United States Stand in the Battle for Free Trade?

Given the rhetoric of recent U.S. administrations and changes in U.S. tariff policy, one can be forgiven for concluding that the United States unabashedly supports free trade. Beyond a doubt, there has been movement toward free trade in recent years. The United States has forcefully worked toward lowering tariffs worldwide in a series of GATT negotiations and, through these same channels, has actively supported measures to free up trade in agricultural products. In addition, the United States and its largest trading partner, Canada, removed all trade barriers between the two countries in 1989, the first step in the creation of a combined North American market (including Mexico) under the North American Free Trade Agreement which went into effect on January 1, 1994. Finally, the disintegration of the Soviet bloc made longstanding trade and finance restrictions against Eastern European countries obsolete—virtually overnight.

The United States is a long way from having completely free trade, however. With three exceptions—Canada, Mexico, and Israel—no country escapes having certain of its imports taxed by the United States. The U.S. tariff policy for the European Community is uncertain, but creation of a free trade zone with the member countries appears unlikely. In fact, many observers foresee trade restrictions on the European Community greater than those used against members of the European Common Market.

In terms of nontariff barriers, the United States has been moving away from a policy of free trade. Since the authority to enforce laws against dumping was transferred to the Department of Commerce in 1980, the number of dumping cases has risen sharply. In the last ten years, the United States initiated about 30 percent of all the antidumping cases worldwide—a percentage exceeded only by Australia. The United States has applied pressure on other countries to enter into "voluntary" agreements to limit exports of various products to the United States. In addition to the well-known agreement with Japan to limit the number of cars sold in the United States, voluntary export agreements have been negotiated with other countries to limit the amounts of textiles, steel, and various agricultural products that enter the United States. In short, the United States is actively protectionist in its use of nontariff barriers to trade.

APPLICATION   NAFTA: Free Trade or Free-for-All?

The North American Free Trade Agreement (NAFTA), which was signed December 10, 1993, is a new, improved version of the Canada-U.S. FTA. The agreement passed the U.S. House against bitter resistance by a close vote of 234 to 200 and went into effect January 1, 1994. In large part, the agreement involves commitments by Mexico to implement the degree of trade and investment liberalization promised between its northern neighbors in 1988, creating the largest free trade zone in the world. However, the NAFTA goes further by including protection of intellectual property rights and other business left unfinished by the FTA.

What is a free trade zone, and what are the benefits of NAFTA for the United States? NAFTA provides for the phased elimination of tariff and most nontariff barriers to regional trade within 10 years, although a few "import-sensitive" products will have a 15-year transition period. United States-Canada bilateral tariffs will continue to be phased out according to the FTA schedule (by 1998). Tariffs are basically taxes on imports, so lowering tariffs will lower the costs of imports. Nontariff barriers include measures such as quotas, the elimination of which will have the effect of increasing trade among the member nations. Along with trade creation, free trade zones, by vastly increasing the size of the market, increase competitive pressures which, in turn, lead to greater efficiency in production and lower prices for consumers.

In reality, NAFTA is not without its shortcomings. On the U.S. side of the issue, complaints have arisen that Mexico has not moved fast enough in particular areas—express-mail delivery, tires, and wine—to open up its markets to U.S. imports as required under the agreement. For example, United Parcel Service (UPS) has cried "foul" with respect to Mexico's restriction that delivery vehicles be no bigger than four tons, a regulation which the firm argues makes it much less efficient and, hence, less competitive in that market. Mexican officials, facing domestic unrest due to a sharp recession in the economy, have acknowledged their fear of political retaliation from domestic delivery services if these restrictions are lifted.

Wine appears to be another sticking point in the implementation of NAFTA. On this issue, President Clinton has been fervid in his attempt to appease California's wine lobby by pressuring Mexico to hasten the phasing-out of tariffs on U.S. wine—a position on which Mexico appears to be holding firm. These disputes illustrate how special interests which would be hurt by trade liberalization can be very successful in keeping barriers in place.

The ability of special interests to influence the political process became apparent in the bitter debate which occurred over the ratification of NAFTA in the U.S. Congress. Industries and their employees who will benefit from increased specialization and growth in the volume of trade had every incentive to support the agreement through the political process. However, some industries and workers will be displaced in the move toward freer trade and could, therefore, be expected to oppose the agreement. A fierce opponent of NAFTA was organized labor in the United States, including the AFL-CIO, arguing that "cheap Mexican labor" would take high-paying union jobs as a result of reductions in tariffs on automobiles, textiles, and other goods. This claim denies the operation of the principle of comparative advantage in directing trade and specialization. Mexico will specialize according to its own comparative advantage in low-tech, low-pay industries due to a relative abundance of low-skill labor. As such industries move south, valuable resources will be freed up in the U.S. economy for investment in high-tech, high-pay industries, where our nation enjoys a comparative advantage arising from a relative abundance of high-skill labor.

It is important to keep the advantages of free trade firmly in mind. The increased value to consumers resulting from higher outputs and lower prices in all three nations will dwarf the costs to certain workers and particular industries with the free-trade area. Some studies estimate that the agreement will create about 170,000 new jobs in its first five years of implementation. Because any job creation that results from NAFTA is likely to occur in new, more efficient industries, the challenge for the United States is to help displaced workers make the transition to new jobs. Over the long term, the primary impact of increased trade will be higher incomes made possible by greater efficiency and faster growth. Efficiency in the United States, Canadian, and Mexican economies will be boosted by the tendency of each to export those goods and services in which it enjoys a comparative advantage.

NAFTA is a noteworthy achievement, but its implications for Mexico, Canada, and the United States should not be exaggerated. By widening the scope of the market and enlarging the range of available skills, the NAFTA enables North American firms and workers to compete more effectively against foreign producers both at home and in world markets due to *gains associated with specialization and trade*. But the ability of NAFTA partners to gain maximum benefits from the pact with minimum adjustment costs depends importantly on maintaining domestic economic policies that ensure growth. Firms will still look first and foremost at the macroeconomic climate in each country in setting their investment policies. As former U.S. trade negotiator Ambassador Carla Hills observed: "If low wages were the only factor in economic growth, many developing countries would be economic superpowers."

QUESTIONS

If the economic case for free trade is so strong, why did so many politicians fight the ratification of NAFTA? What implications do protectionist demands hold for the future and effectiveness of such free trade agreements?

SOURCES: See "North American Trade: Skidmarks," *The Economist*, October 14, 1995, pp. 78–79; Gary C. Hufbauer and Jeffrey J. Schott, *NAFTA: An Assessment* (Washington, D.C.: Institute for International Economics, 1993).

SUMMARY

1. All individuals possess talents that give them advantages in trade. Nations, like individuals, benefit from specialization and trade. Nations trade not resources but rather the products and services created with resources. Differing resource endowments are the basis for trade in products because products are ordinarily more mobile than the resources that produce them.

2. Specialization and trade may take place between countries of vastly differing degrees of economic development. The reason for this is the law of comparative advantage, which states that trade is possible when the relative opportunity cost of producing two goods differs between two countries.

3. Specialization according to the law of comparative advantage permits the production possibilities and hence the rate of sustainable consumption of nations to expand. That is, the parties to trade may obtain more of both traded goods after specialization and trade.

4. There are both natural and artificial barriers to trade. Natural barriers are all exchange costs, including transportation costs of moving goods from one country to another. Artificial barriers include taxes on imports of goods, or tariffs, and limitations or prohibitions on imported items, or quotas.

5. Tariffs on imports increase the profits of domestic producers and the revenue of government, but consumers lose more than producers and governments gain. This net welfare loss is the reason most economists oppose protectionist policies.

6. Although tariffs carry a net loss to society, they are imposed whenever domestic producer-competitors are strong enough to supply gains to politicians. Consumer groups may oppose tariffs but are seldom well enough organized or vocal enough to oppose them successfully.

7. Two substantive arguments are made for protection: the national defense and infant industries arguments. Most economists, however, question the adequacy of these arguments in actual operation. Other arguments—such as "cheap foreign labor" or "buy American"—are regarded by most economists as only thinly veiled protectionist fallacies.

8. U.S. trade policies have historically waxed and waned with prosperity and depression, becoming more protectionist during economic downturns. Although import tariffs have been reduced dramatically in the past 50 years, freer trade has not necessarily resulted. Protectionism lives on in the form of quotas and nontariff trade barriers.

KEY TERMS

specialization	tariff	nontariff trade barriers
comparative advantage	quota	infant industry
terms of trade	free trade	dumping
consumption possibilities curve	welfare loss to society	terms of trade argument

QUESTIONS FOR REVIEW AND DISCUSSION

1. Evaluate and discuss the following statement: Trade across international boundaries is essentially the same as trade across interstate boundaries.
2. How can two countries simultaneously gain from trade? Under what circumstances can two countries not gain from trade?
3. What is the difference between natural barriers and artificial barriers to trade? Was the development of the Panama Canal an artificial encouragement of trade?
4. What does a tariff do to the terms of trade? Are consumers in both countries hurt by a tariff?
5. How are tariffs and quotas similar? How are they different? Would consumers prefer one of these barriers to the other?
6. Who is hurt by a tariff? Who is helped? Who encourages government to impose tariffs?
7. What is the purpose of protective tariffs? Who or what is protected?
8. Evaluate the following statement: Tariffs discourage the movement of goods between countries; therefore, they encourage the movement of resources such as capital and labor between countries.
9. What are the effects of trade on a country's consumption possibilities? After trade, what is the relationship between the consumption and production possibilities curves and what does this imply for the country?
10. What are nontariff trade barriers? Compare the effects of nontariff barriers and the effects of tariffs.

PROBLEMS

Nations Alpha and Beta have the following production possibilities for goods X and Y.

Alpha	X	0	3	6	9
	Y	12	8	4	0
Beta	X	0	4	8	12
	Y	15	10	5	0

1. Draw the production possibilities curves for both countries. What does 1 X cost in Alpha before trade? What does 1 Y cost in Beta? If these countries traded, which would export X and which would export Y?

2. If some country Omega can produce 100 units of X with all its resources or 60 units of Y, how much does 1 unit of Y cost? If another country, Gamma, can produce 60 X or 40 Y, what does 1 unit of X cost in Gamma? Which country has a comparative advantage in the production of X?

CHAPTER 17

INTERNATIONAL FINANCE

When a car dealer in Virginia buys cars from a Detroit manufacturer to sell in Virginia, both use the same medium of exchange—U. S. dollars. Suppose, however, that the dealer buys cars from Japanese or German manufacturers to sell in Virginia. The Japanese firm will likely want payment in yen; the German firm, in marks. The car dealer thus confronts an international monetary problem. Are the prices stated in yen and marks acceptable? This question brings up others. How are dollars converted into yen and marks? Is there a fixed rate for currency exchange or does it vary? How would changes in exchange rates affect import prices in the United States? American manufacturers sell to citizens in foreign countries and seek payment for their goods and services in U.S. dollars. They must be careful, therefore, to pay attention to exchange rates because these rates can determine the prices and profits of their foreign sales.

The monetary, or financial, side of international trade concerns the ways in which countries pay for the goods and services they exchange. In this chapter we examine many aspects of the relations among the currencies of the world, relations that reflect a kaleidoscope of changing conditions in each country, from interest rates and inflation rates to exports and imports of goods and capital. When you finish Chapter 17 you should understand

- how international trade takes place when transactions must be made in terms of other countries' currencies.

- how currency transactions are determined when governments fix their respective currencies' value and when the market determines the relative value of currencies.

The worldwide volume of trade on foreign exchange markets exceeds $500 billion per day.

- how macroeconomic fiscal and monetary policies both affect and are affected by foreign trade and international exchange rates.
- the meaning of the balance of payments, its relation to exchange rates, and its importance for economic growth.

THE FOREIGN EXCHANGE MARKET

International sellers and buyers usually prefer to deal in the currency of their own country. American sellers prefer U.S. dollars for their products, and Japanese sellers prefer yen. The currency of another country that is required to make payment in an international transaction is called **foreign exchange.** Foreign exchange is bought and sold in **foreign exchange markets**—typically, large brokers and banks scattered about the globe.

Sometimes consumers demand foreign exchange; for example, when American travelers arrive at a foreign airport, they often exchange dollars for the local currency. Large firms dealing in international transactions simply keep bank deposits in foreign currencies to cover their foreign transactions. An American importer of French wine will likely pay for its purchases by writing checks on an American bank that holds an account in a French bank. The American bank will use the importer's dollars to purchase the francs needed for payment.

The demand for foreign exchange arises because a country's residents want to buy foreign goods. Conversely, the supply of foreign exchange arises because foreign customers want to buy U.S. goods. For example, we have a demand for francs by the U.S. importer who wishes to purchase French wine and a supply of francs by French customers who wish to purchase U.S. personal computers.

Exchange Rates

An **exchange rate** is the price of one country's money in terms of some other country's money. It is a relative price, much the same as the relative price concept

Foreign exchange
The monies of countries that are used to facilitate international trade in goods, services, and financial assets.

Foreign exchange markets
The interaction of the suppliers and demanders of foreign exchange, through which exchange rates are determined in a flexible exchange rate system.

Exchange rate
The (relative) price of one national currency in terms of another national currency.

discussed in Chapter 4, except that it is the relative price of one national currency expressed in terms of another national currency. Like the relative prices of goods, exchange rates can be expressed in one of two equivalent ways. We can talk about one concert ticket "costing" five pizzas, or we can say that one pizza costs one-fifth of a concert ticket. Either way, the relative price of one good in terms of another good (one concert ticket in terms of pizzas or one pizza in terms of concert tickets) is expressed. Which expression we choose is simply a matter of choice or convenience.

So it is with exchange rates. Because they are relative prices of one money in terms of another money, the way we choose to express the exchange rate is a matter of choice and convenience. For example, in June 1995, one U.S. dollar traded on the foreign exchange market for about five French francs (ff), the national currency of France. One U.S. dollar cost about five French francs to buy, or one U.S. dollar sold for about five French francs. This exchange rate is the relative price of the U.S. dollar in terms of French francs. Alternatively, it would be just as accurate to say that one French franc cost, or would buy, about 20 cents. This would be the relative price of the French franc in terms of the U.S. dollar. One is nothing more than the inverse or reciprocal of the other. Exchange rates are often expressed both ways. An American in France must use French francs to make purchases. Starting out the vacation, the traveler may have a budget, say $500, that she wishes to spend on meals. By using the U.S. dollar in terms of French francs exchange rate (5 per dollar), she can calculate that she will have 2500 ff (5 ff per dollar × $500) to spend on meals in France. Once in France, if our tourist pays 100 ff for a lunch, she may wish to know how many dollars the lunch cost. A quick calculation using the French franc in terms of the U.S. dollar exchange rate will provide a good estimate ($0.20 per ff × 100 ff = $20).

Of equal importance are changes in exchange rates, for such changes can alter the prices of imports and exports. Suppose that a bottle of French wine sells for 100 ff. Ignoring transportation costs and any tariffs, with a dollar-franc exchange rate of $0.20 per French franc, the wine will cost $20 in the United States. But suppose the exchange rate were to change to $0.25 per French franc. The same bottle of wine would still cost 100 ff in France, but its cost in the United States would rise to $25. Changes in the exchange rate alter the prices of foreign goods in home markets and of domestic goods in foreign markets.

Just as tourists must pay attention to exchange rates in order to make plans and informed decisions, so must businesses and governments. International trade, like interpersonal trade, requires the use of money. The prices of these monies relative to one another are important economic variables. A sudden change in an exchange rate can alter the actual values of any business transaction, making it more or less profitable than at first thought. Such changes influence business decisions and can alter the volume of international trade. At issue, then, is what determines exchange rates. Why, in 1995, did a dollar buy (cost) about five French francs and not four or ten French francs? What has caused the U.S. dollar price of French francs, or for that matter German marks, English pounds, Japanese yen, Mexican pesos, or any other country's money, to change from day to day, month to month, and year to year?

Knowledge of current exchange rates is crucial to tourists traveling in foreign countries.

Exchange Rate Systems

Exchange rates, like any other price, are determined in markets by the forces of supply and demand. However, exactly who suppliers and demanders are, and under what constraints the market operates, determines the type of system within which the exchange rate will be determined. One type, the **flexible, or floating, exchange rate system,** is a system whereby the exchange rate is determined solely by the interaction of private demanders and suppliers of foreign exchange. This is the type of system most major trading countries employ today to determine the world market value of their respective currencies. Of course, government fiscal and monetary policies can help determine the exchange rate under such a system by influencing the behavior of private market participants. But government policies usually are not specifically designed to influence the exchange rate directly.

A second system of exchange rate determination is called a **fixed exchange rate system.** A fixed exchange rate system was in existence from the late 1940s until 1971. A few countries today still fix the value of their currencies on world markets in terms of U.S. dollars. Under a fixed exchange rate system, government intervenes directly in the foreign exchange market, either as a buyer or as a seller, in order to fix the exchange rate at some level. Some European countries combine elements of both the fixed- and flexible-rate systems. The values of these European currencies are fixed relative to one another, but all float against the U.S. dollar.

Since 1973, the exchange rate system determining the relative prices of national currencies has been a blend of these two systems. By and large, the flexible-rate system is in use for the currencies of the United States and other major industrial countries. No country, however, allows its exchange rate to float freely all the time. Wide swings in the exchange rate are controlled by government intervention in the

Flexible, or floating, exchange rate system
An international monetary arrangement in which exchange rates are determined by private suppliers and demanders without government intervention.

Fixed exchange rate system
An international monetary arrangement in which exchange rates are set by the government, which then must intervene in the foreign exchange market in order to maintain the pegged exchange rate.

foreign exchange market. For this reason, the present international monetary system is called a **managed flexible-rate system.** In the next two sections we analyze how floating exchange rates and fixed exchange rates work.

FLEXIBLE EXCHANGE RATES

As we pointed out earlier, U.S. demand for foreign currency arises because U.S. citizens wish to buy foreign products, travel in foreign countries, invest in foreign companies, and carry on other international activities. The supply of foreign currencies to the United States arises because foreigners want to buy U.S. goods, travel in the United States, send their children to school in the United States, invest in this country, and so on. All of these forces of supply and demand affect the exchange rate between the U.S. dollar and other currencies. In effect, they form the basis of the supply and demand schedules in the foreign exchange markets.

Exchange Rates between Two Countries

We begin our analysis with a simple model of the determination of floating, or flexible, exchange rates. For simplicity, we assume that international trade takes place only between two countries, the United States and Switzerland. The U.S. demand for foreign exchange is thus a demand for Swiss francs; the supply of foreign exchange is a supply of Swiss francs.

SUPPLY, DEMAND, AND THE MARKET FOR FOREIGN EXCHANGE   Before beginning our analysis of the factors that determine and change exchange rates, some preliminaries are in order. The exchange rate is determined in the foreign exchange market; it is the relative price of one money in terms of another. As we have indicated, the actions of both the Americans and the Swiss are manifested in this market. But any action on the part of residents of one country is mirrored in the actions of residents of the other. Swiss exports are American imports, and vice versa. This means that technically we would want to look at both the supply and demand of dollars and the supply and demand of Swiss francs to the foreign exchange market in order to examine exchange rate determination. But because the dollar-franc exchange rate is just the inverse of the franc-dollar exchange rate (so that changes in one are mirrored by changes in the other), and because Swiss imports are American exports, we can simplify matters. We need only examine the supply and demand for either francs or dollars on the foreign exchange market in order to be able to discuss exchange rate determination. We will look at the supply and demand for Swiss francs, the foreign exchange in our discussion.

Figure 17.1 depicts the supply and demand for foreign exchange, Swiss francs. What establishes the supply and demand for francs on the foreign exchange market? Consider the demand for franc foreign exchange first. American importers of Swiss goods must pay Swiss producers with francs. Thus, American imports from Switzerland are the basis of foreign exchange demand. The demand for foreign exchange slopes downward because, other things constant, a higher exchange rate

FIGURE 17.1

A Two-Country Foreign Exchange Market

The exchange rate—in this case, the dollar price of one Swiss franc—is measured on the vertical axis. The quantity of francs is measured on the horizontal axis. The equilibrium exchange rate is $0.50 per Swiss franc because this is the only exchange rate that equates quantity demanded with quantity supplied. At the exchange rate of $0.90 per franc, there exists a surplus of francs, and the exchange rate will fall. At the $0.50 exchange rate, a shortage of francs on the forcign exchange market exists, which will drive the exchange rate back to $0.75

(more dollars per franc) implies higher import prices, fewer imports, and a smaller quantity demanded (by Americans) of foreign exchange.

The supply of foreign exchange arises from Swiss import activity and, therefore, American export activity. Swiss importers must pay for goods produced in the United States (American exports) with dollars. In order to obtain dollars, they must buy them with francs in the foreign exchange market. The supply of foreign exchange originates with Swiss imports or, what is the same thing, American exports. It is upward-sloping because, other factors considered, a rise in the dollar price of the franc (the exchange rate measured on the vertical axis) means that one franc now buys more dollars, making American goods cheaper to the Swiss. This implies an increase in the desire of the Swiss to import from the United States. They will then offer more francs for sale at the higher exchange rate to obtain additional dollars. The additional dollars are then used to purchase the larger quantity of imports.

The equilibrium exchange rate, like any other price, is one that equates quantity demanded with quantity supplied. In Figure 17.1, this equilibrium exchange rate is $0.75 per Swiss franc. Suppose that the exchange rate were below equilibrium, at $0.50 per franc. The quantity demanded of foreign exchange would then exceed the quantity supplied of foreign exchange. There would be a shortage of francs on the foreign exchange market. As in any other market, a shortage in the foreign exchange market will tend to drive price back toward equilibrium.

Given the fundamental economic factors determining exports and imports in both countries, an exchange rate below the equilibrium exchange rate ($0.50 per franc in Figure 17.1) creates a situation in which Americans wish to import much more from Switzerland than the Swiss wish to sell. At this exchange rate, Swiss goods are "too cheap" to Americans because the dollar price of the franc is "too low." On the other side of the coin, American goods are "too expensive" to the Swiss. Swiss imports are too low, and thus the quantity supplied of foreign exchange is also too low. To stimulate the quantity of Swiss imports and increase the quantity supplied of foreign exchange, as well as to reduce the quantity of U.S. imports and reduce the quantity demanded of foreign exchange, an increase in the exchange rate is necessary. The movement to equilibrium from $0.50 to $0.75 results from the bidding up of the dollar price of francs by American consumers eager to obtain Swiss goods. (Americans demand Swiss francs and *simultaneously* supply U.S. dollars.) The actions of American consumers tend to elevate the price of Swiss francs in terms of dollars, returning the dollar-franc market to equilibrium. Naturally, the rise in the dollar price of francs reduces the quantity demanded of Swiss goods and services by Americans as equilibrium is approached. (The Swiss are willing to supply the additional francs because of the higher price of their currency expressed in dollars.)

Likewise, the exchange rate of $0.90 per franc is too high for equilibrium, creating a surplus of foreign exchange. At $0.90 per franc, Swiss products are very expensive for Americans and American products are relatively inexpensive to the Swiss. As the Swiss demand dollars to get American goods, the price of dollars in terms of francs rises and the price of francs in terms of dollars falls. Simultaneously, with Americans wanting to import less than the Swiss wish to export to the United States, a surplus of franc foreign exchange exists. A fall in the dollar price of the franc will increase American imports and the quantity demanded of foreign exchange. This same fall will also make American goods more expensive in Switzerland, reduce imports, and thus reduce the quantity supplied of francs to the foreign exchange market. Equilibrium is restored, as shown in Figure 17.1, when the dollar price of francs returns to $0.75.

Changes in Flexible Exchange Rates

The foreign exchange market is like any other market studied in economics. Supply and demand determine price, whereas surpluses and shortages of foreign exchange will move the exchange rate toward its equilibrium value. We now examine why the supply of or demand for foreign exchange might change, producing a change in the equilibrium exchange rate in a flexible exchange rate system.

APPRECIATION AND DEPRECIATION   The dollar price of the Swiss franc, or any other currency, fluctuates from day to day and even minute to minute. Trying to explain every small fluctuation in the exchange rate would be a fruitless exercise. However, broad and significant changes in exchange rates have occurred since the collapse of the fixed-rate system and subsequent inception of the managed flexible-rate system in 1973. The late 1970s and the early 1990s were periods of dollar **depreciation**. A depreciation of a country's currency on world markets means that the equilibrium exchange rate has changed such that it requires more of the currency to purchase other money. An increase in the equilibrium dollar price of the Swiss franc from $0.75 to $0.90 constitutes a depreciation of the

Depreciation
A decrease in the equilibrium exchange market value of a country's currency in a flexible-rate system; an increase in the number of units of a country's money required to purchase one unit of a foreign country's money.

FIGURE 17.2

Price Level Changes in the Flexible Exchange Rate System

S and D are the initial foreign supply and demand curves. In Figure 17.2a, an increase in the U.S. price level, holding the Swiss price level constant, causes the supply of foreign exchange to shift to S_1, while the demand for foreign exchange shifts to D_1. This causes the Swiss franc to appreciate from e_0 to e_1. This can also be described as a depreciation of the dollar. If the Swiss price level increased while the price level in the United States remained unchanged, the supply and demand curves would shift to S_2 and D_2 in Figure 17.2b. This would cause the exchange rate to fall from e_0 to e_2.

(a)

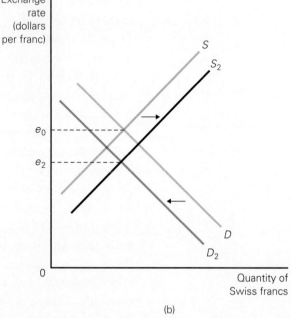

(b)

Appreciation

An increase in the equilibrium exchange market value of a country's currency in a flexible-rate system; a decrease in the number of units of a country's money required to purchase one unit of a foreign country's money.

dollar. It takes more dollars to buy a franc than previously, or equivalently, one dollar buys fewer francs. Another term used frequently by the financial press to describe a depreciation is a "weakening" of the currency on the foreign exchange market. The early 1980s was a period of dollar **appreciation**. An appreciation is the opposite of a depreciation; less of the money is required to buy other monies on the foreign exchange market. A fall in the equilibrium exchange rate from $0.75 to $0.50 per franc signifies a dollar appreciation (and a franc depreciation). A currency that has appreciated is said to have "strengthened" on world currency markets or is a "strong" currency. The basic reasons and fundamental causes of currency appreciations and depreciations are addressed in the following sections.

PRICE LEVELS, MONEY SUPPLIES, AND INFLATION RATES   One factor that can cause the exchange rate to change is a change in the price level of either country. Suppose that the price level in the United States were to increase by 20 percent while the general level of prices in Switzerland was stable. Figure 17.2a depicts the effects this would have on the foreign exchange market and the exchange rate. Other things equal, higher U.S. prices would reduce Swiss import demand for American goods. This would, in turn, cause a decrease in the supply of foreign exchange, shown as a shift of the supply curve of francs from S to S_1. The rise in the prices of U.S. goods also would make Swiss goods relatively more

FIGURE 17.3

Real Income Changes
and the Exchange
Rate

An increase in real income in
Switzerland has the effect of
shifting the supply of foreign
exchange from S to S_1. This
appreciates the dollar in the
foreign exchange market,
causing the exchange rate to
fall from e_0 to e_1. Should U.S.
real income rise, the effect will
be to increase the demand for
foreign exchange to D_1 and
depreciate the dollar, moving
the exchange rate from
e_0 to e_2.

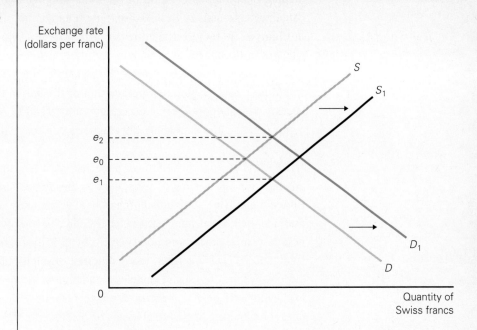

attractive to Americans. American import demand would increase, and the demand
for foreign exchange also would then increase. In Figure 17.2a, the demand for
foreign exchange shifts from D to D_1.

The effect is to increase the dollar price of the franc. The equilibrium exchange
rate rises from e_0 to e_1, or the dollar depreciates on the foreign exchange market.
Of course, one could also say that the franc has appreciated. Had the price level in
Switzerland risen by 20 percent with the price level in the United States constant,
just the opposite would have occurred. Swiss goods would have become more expensive to Americans, reducing American import demand and the demand for foreign exchange from D to D_2 in Figure 17.2b. Swiss import demand would increase
as American goods become cheaper in Switzerland, causing the supply of foreign
exchange to increase from S to S_2. The equilibrium exchange rate would fall from
e_0 to e_2, and a dollar appreciation (franc depreciation) would have taken place.

REAL INCOME, EXPORTS, AND IMPORTS   Other factors also can cause a
currency to appreciate or depreciate on world currency markets. Consider the effect
of an expansion in the Swiss economy that results in an increase in Swiss real income. As Swiss real income increases, the demand for imports from the United States
also increases. More francs are supplied to the foreign exchange market at any given
exchange rate, and the supply of foreign exchange increases. In Figure 17.3, the foreign exchange supply curve shifts from S to S_1 and the equilibrium exchange rate
falls from e_0 to e_1. The increase in Swiss real income has caused the dollar to appreciate on the foreign exchange market or, equivalently, the franc to depreciate.

Should real income in the United States rise, the dollar would depreciate on the
foreign exchange market. Larger U.S. real income would cause a desire for greater
imports from Switzerland. The demand for francs would increase in Figure 17.3

from D to D_1. Given the initial supply of foreign exchange, S, the rise in U.S. real income causes a depreciation of the dollar (appreciation of the franc) on the foreign exchange market. In this case, the exchange rate rises from e_0 to e_2.[1]

Changes in factors that directly affect exports and imports can also cause changes in exchange rates. Should consumer tastes in the United States change in favor of goods produced at home, for example, the demand for foreign exchange would decrease, causing an appreciation of the dollar. Government policies aimed at restricting imports or encouraging exports tend to reduce the demand for foreign exchange and appreciate the country's currency on world markets.

INTEREST RATES   So far, we have discussed the supply of foreign exchange as arising from the desires of foreigners to buy goods and services produced in the United States. But foreigners purchase real estate and financial assets in the United States as well; for instance, Rockefeller Center in New York was purchased by Japanese investors. Stocks and bonds issued by U S. businesses and governments (state, local, and federal) are other, less-publicized examples of such purchases by foreign businesspeople. Both such examples are foreign investments in the United States. Just as the purchase of U.S. goods by foreigners creates a supply of foreign exchange, so does the purchase of financial assets or real assets such as automobile or computer assembly plants. Likewise, U.S. citizens purchase the financial assets of other countries, adding to the demand for foreign exchange. Our next task is to determine how changes in the purchases of financial or real assets may affect the exchange rate.

An increased desire on the part of the Swiss to invest in the United States, to buy more U.S. financial or real assets, signals an increased supply of foreign exchange. More francs are supplied to the foreign exchange market to purchase the dollars necessary to buy U.S. assets. In Figure 17.4, the supply of foreign exchange increases from S to S_1 and the exchange rate falls from e_0 to e_1. What would cause this to happen?

Investors everywhere look at many different variables in deciding how to allocate their investment funds among particular firms, industries, or countries. Such factors as risk, liquidity, and the degree of political stability are all important. However, a primary factor that goes into any investment decision is the real rate of interest those funds earn.

The real interest rate, recall, is the rate of interest earned adjusted for inflation. Suppose that the real interest rate in the United States rose. That would make U.S. financial assets more attractive to own and would increase the demand by foreigners to purchase U.S. financial assets. This increase in the U.S. real interest rate would have caused the increase in the supply of francs to the foreign exchange market depicted in Figure 17.4. The effect of a rise in the real interest rate in the United States is dollar appreciation, or, in terms of Figure 17.4, a decline in the dollar price of the Swiss franc on the foreign exchange market from e_0 to e_1.

Alternatively, should the real interest rate increase in Switzerland, the demand for francs on the part of Americans would increase, from D to D_1 in Figure 17.4.

[1]We are assuming that as real income rises, the money supply increases enough to accommodate the extra demand for money.

FIGURE 17.4

Real Interest Rate Effects on the Exchange Rate

When the U.S. real interest rate rises the Swiss wish to invest more in the United States, to buy more financial assets. The supply of foreign exchange increases to S_1, and the exchange rate falls to e_1. Higher U.S. real interest rates cause dollar appreciation. When the real interest rate in Switzerland rises, Americans wish to buy more Swiss securities, and the demand for foreign exchange increases. The exchange rate moves from e_0 to e_2, and the dollar depreciates.

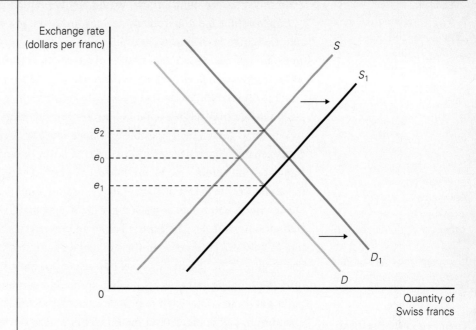

Given the supply of franc foreign exchange of S, the exchange rate would rise to e_2. An increased Swiss real interest rate causes the dollar to depreciate, or the franc to appreciate, on the foreign exchange market.

FIXED EXCHANGE RATES

As we have seen, a system of flexible exchange rates allows the foreign exchange market to determine the prices at which currency will change hands. By contrast, a fixed exchange rate system does not allow exchange rates to float in a free market. Government intervenes in the foreign exchange market to fix or "manage" the international price of its currency. Once fixed exchange rates are established, governments stand ready to protect the rates through intervention in the foreign exchange market.

The Operation of a Fixed Exchange Rate System

Although the United States and Switzerland no longer trade on the basis of a fixed exchange rate, imagine what would happen if they did. Figure 17.5 illustrates what happens when a fixed exchange rate between francs and dollars does not happen to correspond to ever-shifting market conditions. If the current market equilibrium rate is e_0, but the U.S. government seeks to maintain an exchange rate of e_1, the official or fixed rate is above the equilibrium rate. In this case, the dollar is said to be undervalued relative to the Swiss franc. The dollar is **undervalued** because at exchange rate e_1 each dollar will buy fewer francs than it would at the lower equilibrium exchange rate, e_0. Of course, if the dollar is undervalued, then the franc is overvalued. Similarly, if the government were to fix the exchange rate at e_2, each

Undervalued

A term describing the foreign exchange market value of a country's money; occurs when the number of units of a country's money that purchases one unit of a foreign currency is greater than the equilibrium exchange rate.

Overvalued
A term describing the foreign exchange market value of a country's money; occurs when the number of units of a country's money that purchases one unit of a foreign currency is less than the equilibrium exchange rate.

Foreign exchange market intervention
Purchases or sales of foreign exchange by government, usually a central bank, with the goal of maintaining a fixed exchange rate or influencing the exchange rate in a flexible-rate system.

Foreign exchange reserves
The stock of a foreign exchange held by a central bank that is available for use in exchange market intervention.

dollar would purchase more francs than it would at the equilibrium exchange rate, e_0. In this case, the dollar (franc) would be **overvalued** (undervalued).

Suppose that the government decides to fix the price of its currency in the foreign exchange market at e_1. In order to do so, the government must not merely decree that all currency trades take place at an exchange rate equal to e_1. The government, usually the central bank, must also become a big enough player in the market to make the exchange rate e_1. To do this, the central bank must continuously engage in **foreign exchange market intervention.**

When the government fixes the exchange rate at e_1, even though fundamental foreign exchange market forces dictate an equilibrium exchange rate of e_0, a surplus of francs on the foreign exchange market is created. At the high dollar price of the franc, quantity supplied of francs will exceed quantity demanded. Without exchange market intervention, as described earlier, the exchange rate would fall back to its equilibrium value, e_0. The central bank can prevent this fall, and maintain exchange rate e_1 only if it intervenes in the exchange market by buying up the franc surplus. The buying of francs, in this case, by the central bank builds up the central bank's **foreign exchange reserves,** its holding of foreign currencies. Such an intervention is not a one-time affair. Each month or year that the exchange rate is fixed above its equilibrium value, the central bank must purchase the surplus of francs in order to maintain the fixed rate. Fixing the rate above equilibrium tends to make a country's exports cheaper and its imports more expensive. Hence, such a policy may be used by governments in an attempt to reduce imports and encourage exports.

Sometimes central banks fix the exchange rate below the market equilibrium exchange rate, such as rate e_2 in Figure 17.5. This creates a shortage of foreign exchange, since quantity demanded at exchange rate e_2 is greater than quantity supplied. Again, without continuous exchange market intervention, the exchange rate would move back toward its equilibrium level, e_0. In this case, foreign exchange market intervention takes the form of sales of foreign currency (Swiss francs) from the central bank's foreign currency reserves. Setting such an exchange rate, one that deliberately overvalues the country's currency in world markets, is not a policy that most countries could pursue indefinitely. Sooner or later the central bank would run out of reserves and be unable to support the fixed exchange rate. Fixing the exchange rate below equilibrium tends to encourage imports and discourage exports.

Fixed Exchange Rates

The fixed exchange rate set by government can stray significantly from the equilibrium exchange rate. A country will therefore experience persistent problems in international trade; namely, it will confront persistent surpluses or deficits in its foreign trade. In the balance of trade between exports and imports, a country whose exports have greater value than its imports is said to have a **balance of trade surplus;** one whose imports' value exceeds its exports' value has a **balance of trade deficit.** What are the options under a fixed-rate system for alleviating such situations?

Balance of trade surplus
Occurs when the value of a nation's exports exceeds the value of a nation's imports; also called a trade surplus.

Balance of trade deficit
Occurs when the value of a nation's exports is less than the value of a nation's imports; also called a trade deficit.

CHANGES IN DOMESTIC MACROECONOMIC POLICY   Consider first the example of Figure 17.5, where the dollar price of the franc is maintained at e_1 while the equilibrium price is e_0. The dollar is undervalued, and the United

FIGURE 17.5

Fixed Exchange Rates above and below Equilibrium

If the government sets an exchange rate below equilibrium, such as e_2, a shortage of foreign exchange develops, and the central bank must continuously sell foreign exchange from its exchange reserves to keep the rate at e_2. If the rate is set at e_1, a surplus of foreign exchange is created, and the central bank must continuously buy foreign exchange, adding to its exchange reserves, in order to maintain the fixed rate.

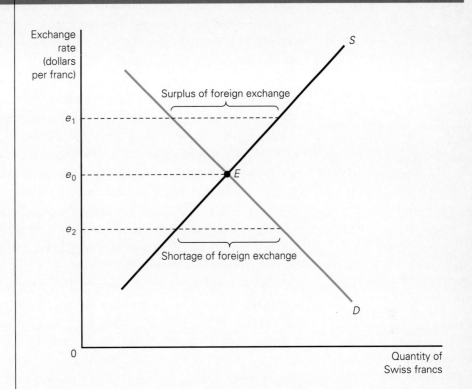

States experiences a balance of trade surplus, while Switzerland runs a persistent deficit, importing more than it exports. The Swiss will demand that something be done.

One option is to change domestic macroeconomic policies in the two countries. Suppose the United States allows its money supply to rise and Switzerland lets its money supply fall. In the United States the increase in money supply will lead to higher prices and costs. In Switzerland the opposite effects will occur: There will be lower prices and costs. Thus, U.S. exports will fall because they are now relatively more expensive on world markets, and U.S. imports will rise because foreign goods are now cheaper and income is higher. In Switzerland exports will rise because Swiss goods are now relatively cheaper, and imports will decline because U.S. goods are more expensive and Swiss GDP has fallen. The basic tendency in both countries, then, is toward adjustments that erase the surplus of exports over imports in the United States and the corresponding deficit in Switzerland.

An important point emerges from this discussion. In a fixed exchange rate system, where the government chooses to defend the fixed rate at all costs, imbalances in foreign trade must be resolved through macroeconomic adjustment of entire domestic economies. To keep one price—the foreign exchange rate—fixed, the United States and Switzerland manipulate the level of all the other prices in their economies. A flexible-rate system, by contrast, changes one price—the foreign exchange rate—to resolve balance of trade problems.

DEVALUATION AND REVALUATION   The second option facing two fixed-rate countries with a trade imbalance is to change the official exchange rate. In this way, the two governments can avoid costly manipulation of their domestic economies to restore foreign trade equilibrium. There are two possible changes in this regard.

Devaluation

An official change in a country's exchange rate in a fixed-rate system; the number of units of a country's money that purchases one unit of another country's currency is increased by the government.

One is **devaluation** of one country's currency. When the dollar is overvalued (e_2 per franc in Figure 17.5), the United States suffers a trade deficit and Switzerland a trade surplus. With Switzerland's agreement, the United States can lower the official exchange value of its currency. In this case, we say that a devaluation has occurred. In terms of Figure 17.5, this means that the dollar price of francs is moved upward, closer to its equilibrium value. This change in the exchange rate changes the relative prices of each country's imports and exports so as to help erase the U.S. deficit and the Swiss surplus without each country's having to resort to costly deflation and inflation of its domestic economy.

Where the official rate is above the equilibrium rate (such as e_1 per franc in Figure 17.5), the opposite process can be applied. In this case, the United States has a trade surplus and Switzerland a deficit. The two countries can support this exchange rate if the United States buys francs or if Switzerland sells dollars or some combination of both. However, to avoid inflation in the United States and deflation in Switzerland to correct the balance of trade situation, the two countries might agree to revalue the dollar. A **revaluation** occurs when the official price of a currency is raised. This means that the dollar price of francs would move downward in Figure 17.5, closer to its equilibrium value. The value of the dollar is thus raised, or revalued, and the corresponding value of the franc is lowered, or devalued.

Revaluation

An official change in a country's exchange rate in a fixed-rate system; the number of units of a country's money that purchases one unit of another country's currency is decreased by the government.

Adjustments in official exchange rates seem less costly than the manipulation of whole economies. However, as we will see later, such adjustments are not always easy to accomplish. The Swiss may reap advantages from a balance of trade surplus and may resist efforts to devalue the dollar or to implement a domestic economic policy that chips away at their surplus. Complex international negotiations are inherent in a fixed-rate system.

CHANGES IN TRADE POLICY   A third option for resolving balance of trade difficulties under a fixed-rate system is for a deficit country to erect barriers to international trade. Tariffs, quotas, and other barriers to the free movement of people and goods across international borders can be established to try to solve a trade problem. This is not an option that would find much favor among economists, however. As detailed in Chapter 16, such impediments to international trade cost the worldwide economy economic efficiency and gains from specialization.

Instead of erecting trade barriers, another policy is pressuring trading partners to abolish current import restrictions. This strategy has been advocated as a means of reducing the persistent trade deficit between the United States and Japan.

Both floating and fixed exchange rate systems have been used in the past. The most economically powerful countries presently operate essentially on a floating system and have done so since early 1973. Before that, starting shortly after World War II, a fixed exchange rate system governed international monetary relations. For an analysis of the balance of trade problems as they persist in the 1990s, see the Application, "Trade Deficits, Flexible Exchange Rates, and the Competitiveness of the U.S. Economy," at the conclusion of this chapter. We will discuss the historical evolution of the international monetary system later in the chapter.

MACROECONOMIC POLICY, EXCHANGE RATES, AND TRADE BALANCE

Foreign trade can have dramatic effects on a government's macroeconomic policy. We consider briefly how monetary policy and fiscal policy are affected by foreign trade.

Monetary Policy

The link between the foreign exchange market and monetary policy depends on whether trade takes place under a system of fixed or floating exchange rates. In the former case, the central bank fixes the exchange rate and allows the money supply to be determined by the economic system; in the latter case, the central bank lets the exchange rate be determined in the market for foreign exchange and manipulates the domestic supply of money.

THE CASE OF FIXED EXCHANGE RATES   To support a fixed exchange rate, the central bank must be prepared to buy and sell whatever foreign exchange is necessary to keep the exchange rate at the fixed level. Suppose that there is a surplus in the balance of trade: At the current exchange rate, the quantity of foreign exchange supplied by exporters exceeds the amount of foreign exchange demanded by importers. In this case, the central bank must purchase foreign exchange by an amount equal to the excess supply to eliminate the tendency for the exchange rate to fall. The central bank purchases foreign exchange by printing more domestic currency, and this increase in the supply of money sets forces in motion that tend to restore equilibrium. Other things being equal, domestic prices rise with a larger money supply, and these higher prices will discourage exports and encourage imports, thus diminishing the trade surplus. In the case of a trade deficit, the central bank will be selling foreign exchange (in effect decreasing domestic currency) to keep the exchange rate from rising. This action will lower the domestic money supply, and the accompanying lower domestic prices will tend to discourage imports and encourage exports. The important point is that to fix one price—the exchange rate—the central bank must give up other money supply controls and allow all other prices to adjust. (The fixed exchange rate system operates like the old gold standard, which is described in the Focus "Should We Return to a Gold Standard?")

THE CASE OF FLEXIBLE EXCHANGE RATES   If the government is using a flexible exchange rate system, the central bank can use its domestic monetary policy tools, allowing the exchange rate to be determined by the market. Starting from equilibrium, an increase in the domestic money supply tends to raise prices, and these higher prices tend to encourage imports and discourage exports. Thus, there is

f0cus

Should We Return to a Gold Standard?

The relatively high inflation rates experienced by the United States during the late 1970s and early 1980s led to a variety of proposals for a return to a gold standard. Proponents of the gold standard argued that linking the nominal money supply to gold would prevent large increases and decreases in the money supply that lead to inflations and deflations. Congress established a U.S. Gold Commission to study the question, and the members not only debated the desirability of again tying the dollar to gold but also considered how to implement a new gold standard.

Proponents of a return to the gold standard argue that the Federal Reserve has neither the willingness nor the ability to follow monetary policies that promote price stability and that some constraint on excessive monetary expansionism is necessary. What are the advantages and disadvantages of gold-backed dollars?

Under a gold standard, currency is freely convertible into gold at some fixed rate, such as $35 per ounce, which was for many years the official U.S. price of gold. Thus, a nation's currency supply is directly related to its supply of gold. The supply of currency can be expanded relative to the supply of gold only by devaluing the dollar in terms of gold—that is, by raising gold's dollar price. A gold standard therefore enforces monetary discipline. In the absence of devaluation, the currency supply can be increased only at a rate equal to the increase in the output of gold, an expansion that has occurred historically at about 1.5 to 2 percent annually. Such a monetary policy would foster price stability with little or no inflation in the economy.

There are several major drawbacks to a gold standard. Real resources are tied up in money production— gold must be mined, stored, and transported. Also, the supply of gold is relatively inelastic. Expansion in the demand for money as economic growth occurs will generate downward pressure on the general price level. If the supply of gold rises more slowly than the demand, a gold standard will bring about persistent deflation. Discovery of new gold sources or improvements in the technology used to extract gold from existing mines would likely bring about rapid inflation.

Even though the dollar price of gold is fixed, a variety of demand-side factors can cause the market price of gold to diverge from its official price. Indeed, it would be sheer coincidence for the two prices to be equal. Cooperation among nations is required to maintain the official price in such circumstances. For instance, during the late 1960s, a two-tier system evolved in which a world price of $35 per ounce was supported through sales among Western central banks and by an agreement between governments not to buy or sell gold in the open market. Prior to that time, a group of countries had formed a gold pool for the purpose of using their gold reserves to intervene periodically to stabilize the open market price at the official price.

Finally, incentives to engage in monetary expansionism are not completely eliminated by a gold standard. Increases in the stock of currency can be purchased for a time by a willingness to suffer a drain on gold reserves. That is, domestic inflation tends to create a trade deficit, which under a gold standard is balanced by shipments of gold to trade surplus nations. However, the inflating country's currency becomes overvalued, and pressures to devalue gradually become irresistible. In fact, persistent monetary expansion by the United States ultimately led to the collapse of the earlier world gold standard.

In the United States, the Federal Reserve System has amply demonstrated its willingness to gradually reduce the inflation rate during the 1980s and 1990s. This would appear to take some of the steam out of the argument for a return to the gold standard. But gold standard advocates point out that the Fed's work could easily be undone at any time with a greater degree of political participation in directing the decisions of the U.S. central bank.

a trade deficit (an excess demand for foreign exchange) at the old exchange rate. For individuals to be willing to supply the extra foreign exchange to finance these trade movements, the exchange rate must rise by whatever amount is necessary to eliminate the excess demand. The result of an increase in the domestic money supply is therefore a rise in the exchange rate by exactly the same proportion.

Fiscal Policy

The effects of a government's fiscal policy initiatives on exchange rates depend largely on how the changes in government spending are financed. If we assume, for simplicity, that all increases in government expenditures are financed by borrowing, then expansionary fiscal policies stimulate aggregate demand, including the demand for imports on the one hand, and raise government borrowing on the other. The increased demand puts upward pressure on the exchange rate because of the additional foreign currencies required to finance the increased imports. But the increased government borrowing tends to raise interest rates, attracting foreign capital and placing downward pressure on the exchange rate. The net change in the exchange rate resulting from the expansionary policy depends on which of the two effects dominates.

Similarly, contractionary fiscal policies may raise or lower the exchange rate. A lower level of government spending will reduce aggregate demand, reduce the demand for imports, and, at the same time, lower government borrowing. The lower import demand will tend to lower the exchange rate by fostering an excess supply of foreign currencies. But with less government borrowing, interest rates tend to fall. Capital outflows increase, putting upward pressure on exchange rates. Again, the net change of the exchange rate depends on which event—the fall-off in imports or the decline in interest rates—has greater effect.

THE BALANCE OF PAYMENTS

Balance of payments
An official accounting record of all the foreign transactions of a nation's residents, businesses, and governments.

Countries keep track of the flow of international trade and periodically publish a report of their transactions, called the **balance of payments**. The balance of payments is essentially an accounting record of a nation's foreign business. It contains valuable information about the level of exports, imports, foreign investment, and the transactions of government such as purchases and sales of foreign currencies.

The balance of payments, as an accounting statement, is kept according to the principles of double-entry bookkeeping. The concept of double-entry bookkeeping is simple: Each entry on the credit side of the ledger implies an equal entry on the debit side. Thus, each international transaction creates both a debit (–) and a credit (+) item in the balance of payments ledger.

There is a simple rule to follow in classifying debits and credits: Any foreign transaction that leads to a demand for foreign currencies (or a supply of dollars) is treated as a debit, or a minus, item. The act of importing is a debit entry in the balance of payments. Any foreign transaction that leads to a demand for dollars (or a supply of foreign currency) is entered as a credit, or a plus, item. The act of exporting is a credit entry in the balance of payments.

Suppose that a U.S. firm exports computers to France, and the French importer of the computers pays for the purchase with an IOU. The French IOU is entered on the credit side in U.S. balance of payments bookkeeping because the French importer must ultimately demand dollars to pay off its IOU to the U.S. firm. The sale of computers is entered on the debit side as the offsetting part of the transaction. The U.S. firm must give up a computer in return for the French importer's payment.

TABLE 17.1

U.S. Balance of Payments, 1994

U.S. exports enter the balance of payments with plus signs because buyers of these exports must pay U.S. firms with dollars. Dollars thus flow into the United States and are recorded as a plus, or credit, in the balance of payments. U.S. imports receive a minus sign, indicating that to pay for foreign goods U.S. buyers must supply dollars to foreign countries. Dollars thus flow out of the United States, and imports are then treated as a minus, or a debit, in the balance of payments. Similarly, outflows of U.S. capital and inflows of foreign capital are treated as debits and credits, respectively. To classify an item as a debit or a credit, think of whether dollars are leaving or entering the country. If they are leaving, the item is a debit; if they are entering, the item is a credit.

Item		Amount (billions of dollars)
1. Exports of goods and services		832
a. Merchandise, excluding military	503	
b. Services and other	329	
2. Imports of goods and services		-954
a. Merchandise, excluding military	-669	
b. Services and other	-285	
3. Unilateral transfers		-34
4. U.S. assets abroad, net (capital outflow)		-125
5. Foreign assets in U.S., net (capital inflow)		+314
6. Statistical discrepancy		-33
7. Total		0

SOURCE: U.S. Bureau of the Census, *Statistical Abstract of the United States, 1995* (Washington, D.C. U.S. Government Printing Office, 1995), pp. 802–803.

Since each transaction implies an equal debit and credit, the balance of payments must always balance. In this respect, the balance of payment is like any other accounting balance sheet.

Of course, although the total balance of payments of a country must always balance (debits minus credits equal zero), its component parts need not balance. For example, the imports and exports of specific merchandise such as automobiles do not have to balance. But overall, surpluses in one part of the balance of payments must be canceled out by deficits in other parts. This is not to say, of course, that countries do not experience balance of payments problems. Problems arise, as we will see, from persistent surpluses or deficits in the component parts of the balance of payments.

Exports and Imports: The Balance of Trade

Table 17.1 presents the data on the U.S. balance of payments for 1994. Items 1 and 2 represent exports and imports of goods and services. The difference between the sums of these aspects of the balance of payments—exports contrasted with imports—is the balance of trade. Note that trade in merchandise is only one facet of this balance. Merchandise trade figures are the result of a country's international trade in physical goods, such as books, cars, planes, and computers—the visible exports and imports. The data in Table 17.1 show that in 1994 merchandise exports (1a) were less than merchandise imports (2a) by $166 billion. This figure is sometimes called the merchandise trade balance and is equal to merchandise exports minus merchandise imports. If the figure is positive, there is a merchandise trade surplus. It was negative in 1994, so there was a merchandise trade deficit.

Many imports and exports are invisible. U.S. citizens and firms supply various services to foreigners, such as transportation, insurance, and telecommunications. Payments are received for these services just as in the case of visible exports. Items lb and 2b represent invisible exports and imports in the balance of payments. When both visible and invisible exports and imports are considered in Table 17.l, U.S. exports were still substantially less than U.S. imports, yielding a trade deficit of $122 billion.

Net Transfers Abroad

Net unilateral transfers abroad are one-way money payments from the United States to foreigners or United States citizens living abroad. Included in this category are such items as foreign aid and pension checks to retired U.S. citizens living abroad. Nothing tangible comes back to the United States for these transfers, but they do give rise to a demand for foreign exchange. They thus are entered as a debit item in the balance of payments. In 1994, the United States made $34 billion worth of such transfers.

Current Account Balance

The balance on current account is equal to exports of goods and services minus imports of goods and services minus net unilateral transfers abroad. The United States had a deficit on current account in 1994 of $156 billion.

Net Capital Movements

When U.S. residents purchase foreign stocks and bonds, they obtain a claim to foreign capital (buildings, factories, future foreign government payments, and so forth). Funds that would otherwise be invested in the United States are exported, or, to put it another way, capital is exported. When foreign citizens purchase the stocks and bonds of U.S. businesses and governments, foreign capital is imported into the United States. In 1994 capital outflows were $125 billion, whereas capital inflows were $314 billion.

Note what happens in bookkeeping terms when capital flows into and out of a country. Capital outflows are treated as a debit item in the balance of payments because they constitute a payment; they give rise to a demand for foreign exchange with which to make foreign investment. Capital inflows are a credit item because they consist of receipts by U.S. residents from foreigners; they generate a supply of foreign exchange necessary to obtain dollars with which to purchase U.S. financial assets.

Statistical Discrepancy

Item 6 in Table 17.1 is called statistical discrepancy, an accounting fudge factor. When all the data were collected and debits and credits computed, the credits outweighed the debits by $33 billion. The negative statistical discrepancy is added to make the balance of payments balance by compensating for imperfections in data gathering. (Some debits have apparently gone unrecorded in computing the balance of payments. These could include hidden imports or unrecorded capital outflows. Most experts think that the former is the source of most of the discrepancy, which can be quite large.)

The Balance of Payments and the Value of the Dollar

The last entry in Table 17.1 is zero, indicating that the balance of payments must balance. This is the way any double-entry accounting system works. The balance of payments, however, is an aggregate record of a country's international payments for one year. Behind this record are the myriad transactions of U.S. citizens and firms with foreign citizens and firms. These transactions determine how the U.S. dollar fares in the foreign exchange market.

THE EVOLUTION OF INTERNATIONAL MONETARY INSTITUTIONS

Major world trading nations today rely on floating exchange rates. These governments will occasionally intervene in the foreign exchange market when exchange rate changes are significant, but generally currency prices are free to adjust according to the forces of supply and demand. We briefly review the developments over the past hundred years that led the major trading nations to adopt floating exchange rates in 1973.

The Decline of the Gold Standard

In the period before World War I, dating back to the 1870s, most currencies in the world economy were tied to gold. This means that each country was prepared to redeem its currency at a fixed price in gold to both its own citizens and foreigners. The United States, for example, stood ready to exchange an ounce of gold for $20.67 over this period. In addition, countries on the **gold standard** linked their money supplies to their holdings of gold bullion.

The gold standard worked reasonably well in eliminating balance of trade surpluses and deficits over the period 1870–1914. Nonetheless, for a variety of reasons the gold standard broke down after World War I. There were attempts to return to the gold standard in the 1920s, but the shock to the international economy caused by the Great Depression in the 1930s brought the gold system down once and for all.

Bretton Woods and the Postwar System

Not until after World War II were the problems of the international monetary system addressed in a concerted way. Negotiators for the free-world countries met in Bretton Woods, New Hampshire, in 1944 to develop a new international monetary order. The **Bretton Woods system**, which was in place for almost 30 years, was characterized by fixed exchange rates and an international central bank, called the **International Monetary Fund (IMF),** to oversee the new system.

We have already discussed the economics of fixed exchange rates. The basic idea of the Bretton Woods system was that, over time, countries would obtain or

Gold standard
An international monetary system in which currencies are redeemable in gold at fixed rates or prices.

Bretton Woods system
The fixed exchange rate system established among Western countries after World War II.

International Monetary Fund
An international organization, established along with the Bretton Woods system, designed to assist in the efficient functioning of the Bretton Woods fixed exchange rate system.

pay for their imports with their exports. There might be temporary periods over which a country might wish to run a trade deficit to obtain more imports than its current level of exports allowed it to obtain. Under the Bretton Woods system, it could do so by borrowing international reserves from the IMF. Over time, the country was expected to return to a trade surplus and pay back the earlier loan of reserves.

The IMF was the bank that held the reserves that allowed the system to operate in this way. When the IMF was formed, each member country was required to contribute reserves of its currency to the bank. The bank thus accumulated substantial holdings of dollars, marks, francs, pesos, and so on, and when member nations ran into balance of trade deficits, the bank would lend them reserves. Each time a loan was made, the debtor nation was encouraged to reform its economic policies to avoid future deficits. Sound economic management might also lead to a trade surplus and a source of funds to repay the IMF loan.

The Bretton Woods system sounds fine in principle, and indeed it functioned tolerably well for a number of years. However, as we saw earlier, fixing the price of a currency is like fixing the price of any other good or service—it is very likely to cause surpluses and shortages in the market. As the conditions affecting imports and exports across countries change, the demand and supply of currencies will shift. Countries can find themselves with overvalued fixed exchange rates, which means that they will face persistent balance of trade deficits. Under the IMF system, the deficit country could draw on its IMF reserves to settle the deficits, but it could not do this forever because it would exhaust its reserves. Chronic deficit countries with overvalued exchange rates were thus said to be in fundamental disequilibrium.

In our discussion of the theory of fixed exchange rates, we reviewed the various courses of action that a country in fundamental disequilibrium could take. First, it could devalue its currency as a step toward restoring equilibrium in its balance of trade. Once its currency was devalued, the exchange rate would again be fixed and defended. Second, the country could attempt to improve its trade balance by imposing tariff and quota barriers to imports and perhaps by subsidizing exports. In other words, the country could move away from free trade to balance its imports and exports. Third, the country could behave as if it were on the gold standard. This would mean adopting restrictive monetary and fiscal policies designed to promote domestic deflation and high interest rates in the hope that such changes would restore the balance of trade to equilibrium. This, of course, is a problematic course of action for any country. For example, if the country's unemployment rate were already high, it is hard to believe that the nation's leaders would be sufficiently disciplined to undertake a deflationary course of action.

Speculation by buyers and sellers of currencies also undermines a fixed exchange rate system. Suppose Great Britain is running chronic trade deficits, and everyone, including speculators, expects that the pound will be devalued (even though British central bankers will deny such rumors vehemently). In effect, speculators are in a no-lose position. Will they continue to hold pounds? Clearly, they will not; pounds are about to become less valuable relative to other currencies. Speculators will sell their pounds for other currencies, increasing the supply of pounds to the foreign exchange market and putting additional downward pressure on the pound. By selling the weak currency and buying a strong currency,

Speculation
The buying and selling of currencies on the foreign exchange market with the intent of profiting from possible devaluation or revaluation in a fixed-rate system or from possible future movements in the exchange rate in a flexible-rate system.

speculators make it difficult for authorities to find a new fixed value for the pound. This is why speculation in a fixed exchange rate system is often termed destabilizing.

In the early period of the Bretton Woods system, the United States ran a large trade deficit, and this deficit provided a means of supplying dollar reserves to the rest of the world. It was thought that this deficit was a temporary problem that would soon be replaced by a U.S. trade surplus. This was the premise of the Bretton Woods system. Yet the dollar was overvalued, and the U.S. deficits continued and grew larger into the 1950s and 1960s. The United States was in a difficult position. It was hard for it to devalue the dollar because the dollar was held by virtually every nation as an international reserve asset. A U.S. devaluation would have decreased the wealth of all those countries holding dollars. Several times, the United States tried to impose a restrictive macroeconomic policy to correct its balance of trade. However, when unemployment rose as a consequence, such policies were rapidly abandoned, as political pressures were brought to bear on policymakers. U.S. deficits continued to grow, and foreign holdings of dollars rose.

Speculators entered again. Many holders of dollars became concerned about what the United States was going to do. There were various runs on the U.S. gold stock, as dollars were traded in by foreigners. In 1950, the United States had 509 million ounces of gold; by 1968, this stock had fallen to 296 million ounces. Confidence in the dollar fell further, and the stage was set for a drastic change in the international monetary system.

The Current International Monetary System

The present international monetary system was born in 1971. In the face of continuing large trade deficits and mounting speculation against the dollar, President Nixon broke the link between the dollar and gold in August 1971. No longer would the United States stand ready to exchange gold for dollars at $35 an ounce. In effect, the dollar was set free to fluctuate and seek its own level in the foreign exchange market. As a result, the overvalued dollar depreciated substantially against other major currencies. There were interim attempts to fix the price of the dollar again, but they failed. By early 1973, all the major currencies were floating.

The international monetary system that has been in effect since 1973 is a managed flexible-rate system. Exchange rates are allowed to seek their free-market values, as long as fluctuations are within an acceptable range. If fluctuations fall outside this range, governments may intervene with their reserve holdings to dampen the fluctuations in their currencies. Thus, exchange rates are not completely free; government intervention in the foreign exchange market will be forthcoming if a country's currency falls dramatically in value. In 1978, for example, the dollar fell sharply, and the Carter administration intervened to restrict this decline with international reserves and loans from West Germany and Japan. The central banks of major trading countries also have stepped up intervention activity since September of 1985. It should be remembered, though, that under the managed flexible-rate system, the ranges within which governments consider exchange rate fluctuations acceptable are not well defined as a matter of policy. As a result, it is difficult to tell how far a nation's currency would have to appreciate or depreciate before central bank interventions would occur.

Although the new system abandoned fixed exchange rates, it did not abandon the IMF, which still exists as an international monetary organization. The role of the IMF under the managed flexible-rate system is still evolving, and to this point it has consisted of helping countries that have persistent balance of payments problems by giving them loans and policy advice about how to conduct domestic macroeconomic policy to overcome these problems. The World Bank, which is part of the IMF system set up by the Bretton Woods agreement, has also played an increasing role in the new system. This sister institution of the IMF makes long-run development loans to poor countries.

ADVANTAGES OF THE CURRENT SYSTEM   The consensus view seems to be that the new system has worked very well under difficult circumstances. The following are the major advantages of the flexible-rate system.

1. It allows countries to pursue independent monetary policies. If a country wants to inflate its economy, it can do so by letting its exchange rate depreciate, thereby maintaining its position in international markets without sacrificing its preferred monetary policy.

2. Under the fixed-rate system, a country sometimes had to deflate its economy to solve a balance of trade deficit. With floating rates it only has to let its exchange rate depreciate. Clearly, it is easier to change one price than to change all prices to resolve balance of trade difficulties.

3. The current exchange rate system has proven capable of handling large economic disturbances. When the OPEC countries dramatically raised the price of oil in 1973–1974, the world economy experienced a tremendous shock. The greatest achievement of the flexible-rate system is the way it handled this shock. Oil-importing countries developed large trade deficits; huge trade surpluses built up in OPEC countries. These deficits and surpluses were accommodated by floating rates. Moreover, the huge oil revenues of the OPEC countries were recycled into Western investments. Though exchange rates changed significantly over the period, the new system weathered the storm and got the job done.

DISADVANTAGES OF THE CURRENT SYSTEM   The flexible-rate system is not, however, without its critics. Some of the major disadvantages of the current system are discussed in this section.

1. Some observers point out that flexible rates can be very volatile, and this volatility creates considerable uncertainty for international trade. Thus, exchange rate flexibility leads to conditions that can retard the amount of international trade and therefore the degree of specialization in the world economy.

2. A second criticism of floating rates is that they promote increased world inflation rates. Under a fixed-rate system, countries experience a balance of trade deficit if they inflate their respective economies. This link is severed under a flexible-rate system. Hence, domestic political authorities can more easily give in to interests that benefit from inflation.

3. Some countries that have relied primarily on adjustments in exchange rates to resolve trade imbalance problems have found that the solution has been a

long time in coming. For example, despite depreciation of the dollar, the U.S. trade deficit with Japan has persisted for years, causing some observers to conclude that dollar depreciation never will solve the problem.

In sum, there are pros and cons with respect to the present international monetary system, but in general the system seems to have worked well over a difficult period in the international economy. Growing problems in the international payments system, however, call for the prospect of further reform of the system.

APPLICATION
Trade Deficits, Flexible Exchange Rates, and the Competitiveness of the U.S. Economy

Two of the concepts explored in this chapter cropped up again and again in the financial news during the early 1990s. The value of the dollar abroad during the flexible exchange rate period has fluctuated significantly. Depreciation was the order of the day during the late 1970s, whereas the early 1980s saw a record strengthening of the dollar. (In general, the dollar has depreciated since 1985, although there was some appreciation between 1988 and 1989.) The United States has experienced merchandise trade deficits in every year since 1976; this deficit reached an all-time high of approximately $180 billion in 1995. These events have provoked much debate concerning the worldwide competitiveness of U.S. producers, the desirability of new tariffs and quotas to stem the deficit, and suggestions to return to a fixed exchange rate system. A clearer focus on the concepts involved in the debate, as well as a review of their behavior in the 1970s, 1980s, and 1990s, can lead to a better understanding of the current problem.

The merchandise trade balance is, for most people, the most familiar international economic statistic. This is the number that is usually reported in the media as the trade deficit (or surplus). As pointed out in this chapter, however, the merchandise trade deficit only measures the amount by which the value of imported goods exceeds that of goods exported.

A truer measure of trade flows and imbalances includes trade in services along with trade in goods. Both goods and services are traded among nations, and trade in both goods and services is subject to the same fundamental economic forces. In discussing trade, there is little reason to exclude trade in such services as travel and telecommunications, just as there would be little reason to exclude the value of services consumed by an indi-vidual from a measure of the individual's economic well-being.

Figure 17.6 shows both measures of the trade balance for the period 1971–1995. While the balance on merchandise trade was in deficit in every year after 1975, once trade in services is included (military transactions have been excluded), serious balance of trade deficits did not appear until 1983. In fact, as Figure 17.6 shows, the balance on goods and services was in surplus for some of the flexible exchange rate period.

After 1983, however, large deficits have appeared in the overall trade balance. What has caused such large deficits, however measured, in the last few years? Unfortunately, no simple answer exists, much less a cure. Economists have focused attention on a number of possible causes and have offered suggestions for possible cures.

One explanation for trade balance movements is the exchange rate. From 1980 through 1985, the dollar appreciated significantly vis-à-vis other major currencies. As the average dollar price of foreign currency fell, imports became less costly to Americans, while the prices of American-produced goods and services abroad rose. This strengthening of the dollar in the early 1980s, some economists believe, was a major factor in explaining the burgeoning trade deficit. The balance on goods and services responded to dollar appreciation with a lag of about one year.

As the trade deficit ballooned, the issue of American "competitiveness" in international markets arose. Merchandise exports of the United States actually decreased from 1981 to 1987, while imports climbed steadily. A popular explanation was that American industry could no longer compete with more efficient foreign manufactur-

FIGURE 17.6

Trade Balances, 1970–1995

Both the balance of merchandise (goods) trade and goods and services trade are shown. As can be seen, the balances move together over time. The difference between the two lines is a surplus in services traded. Both measures exclude military purchases and are reported in nominal dollars.

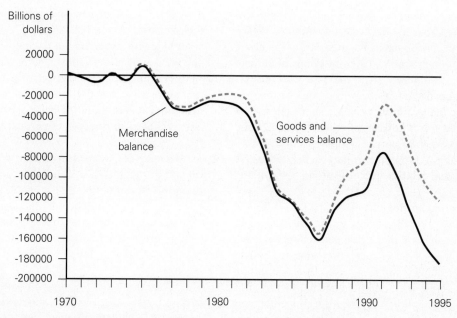

SOURCE: Council of Economic Advisers, *Economic Report of the President* (Washington, D.C.: U.S. Government Printing Office, 1996), p. 392.

NOTE: The trade numbers for 1995 are an extrapolation based on the first three quarters of 1995, calculated by the authors.

ers, resulting in high prices of U.S.-made goods. Opponents of this argument noted that between 1980 and 1985, unit labor costs rose by 11 percent in the United States but by 16 percent in other major countries.

Thus, it does not appear that U.S. firms lack the ability to compete on world markets. Smaller increases in unit labor costs imply production efficiency gains. However, the reduction in the world relative prices of U.S. exports that would have occurred from these relative productivity gains were more than wiped out by appreciation of the dollar. As a result, the prices of U.S. exports on world markets rose, while the prices of foreign goods in the United States fell or did not rise as much. American firms did not lose their ability to compete; they were instead the victims of exchange rate appreciation.

Large government budget deficits undoubtedly contributed to the continued strength of the U.S. dollar on world markets during the 1980s. In 1982, the budget deficit rose to over $100 billion, and it has not been lower than that amount since. Throughout the 1980s, actions by the U.S. Treasury to finance these deficits kept real interest rates high in the United States compared to other countries. As we saw in this chapter, a rise in the real interest

rate in a country will lead to an appreciation of the currency of that country on world markets. Therefore, we can see that there is a link between the "twin deficits"—the trade deficit and budget deficit. The large budget deficit brought about high interest rates, which led to an appreciation of the dollar. With the dollar remaining strong, American business firms found it difficult to compete in world markets, so the large U.S. trade deficit persisted.

During the early 1990s, real interest rates in Germany and Japan rose relative to those in the United States. As a result, there has been a depreciation (weakening) of the dollar, against a number of major currencies. Unfortunately the U.S. trade balance has not yet turned around.

QUESTION

With trade deficits come foreign capital inflows into the United States—that is, investment in U.S. plant and equipment by foreigners. In the long run, is this good or bad, economically, for the United States?

SOURCE: Council of Economic Advisers, *Economic Report of the President* (Washington, D.C.: U.S. Government Printing Office, 1993), p. 462.

SUMMARY

1. Foreign exchange is the currency of another country that is needed to make payment in an international transaction.
2. Foreign exchange can be obtained in the worldwide foreign exchange market. The demand for foreign exchange arises from the desire to buy foreign goods. The supply of foreign exchange arises from the desire of citizens of one country to buy the goods of another country.
3. A foreign exchange rate is the price of one currency in terms of another. A currency's value appreciates when its purchasing power in terms of other currencies rises. It depreciates when its purchasing power falls.
4. The demand for foreign currency depends largely on income and relative price levels in the trading countries.
5. Under a floating, or flexible, exchange rate system, a country allows its exchange rate to be set by the forces of supply and demand in the foreign exchange market. Flexible exchange rates change in response to changes in countries' money supplies, price levels, inflation rates, real interest rates, and fundamental factors such as technology, consumer rates, and government export and import policies. Under a flexible-rate system, exchange rate movements act to alleviate balance of trade surpluses and deficits.
6. Under a fixed exchange rate system, governments intervene in the foreign exchange market to set and defend the value of their currency. When a country's

currency is overvalued relative to the equilibrium rate, the country will run a balance of trade deficit. It can seek to cure this deficit by deflating the domestic economy, establishing trade barriers, or devaluing its currency to a new, lower, fixed rate of exchange. When the fixed exchange rate is below its equilibrium value, a country will experience a balance of trade surplus and will sometimes revalue its currency upward.
7. An important difference between floating- and fixed-rate systems is that the former changes one price to maintain equilibrium in the balance of trade, while the latter changes all prices in the economy to maintain a fixed exchange rate.
8. The balance of payments is a record of the international transactions of a country's economy. It follows the principles of double-entry bookkeeping and must therefore always balance in an accounting sense. Transactions that give rise to a demand for foreign exchange are entered as debits; transactions that give rise to a supply of foreign exchange are treated as credits.
9. The modern history of the international monetary system began with the gold standard, followed by a system of fixed exchange rates managed by the International Monetary Fund. The present international monetary system is a managed floating-rate system. Exchange rates are set by supply and demand, but governments can and have intervened if exchange rate movements are too large.

KEY TERMS

foreign exchange
foreign exchange markets
exchange rate
flexible, or floating, exchange rate system
fixed exchange rate system
managed flexible-rate system
depreciation

appreciation
undervalued
overvalued
foreign exchange market intervention
foreign exchange reserves
balance of trade surplus
balance of trade deficit

devaluation
revaluation
balance of payments
gold standard
Bretton Woods system
International Monetary Fund
speculation

QUESTIONS FOR REVIEW AND DISCUSSION

1. Suppose that the British pound is worth $1.50, and that $1 is worth about 6.5 Swedish krona. How much would a Jaguar automobile cost in U.S. dollars if the British price is 20,000 pounds? How much would a

Volvo cost in U.S. dollars if the Swedish price is 84,000 krona?
2. Suppose that the United States and Sweden are on a floating exchange rate system. Explain whether the

following events would cause the Swedish krona to appreciate or depreciate.

a. U.S. interest rates rise above Swedish interest rates.

b. American tourism to Sweden increases.

c. Americans fall in love with a newly designed Volvo, and Volvo sales in the United States skyrocket.

d. The U.S. government puts a quota on Volvo imports.

e. The Swedish inflation rate rises relative to the U.S. rate.

f. The United States closes a military installation in Sweden at the urging of the Swedish government.

3. How would you treat the following items in the balance of payments? In other words, would you enter them as debits or credits?

a. An American travels to Canada.

b. A U.S. wine importer buys wine from Italy.

c. A California wine grower sells wine to England.

d. An Austrian corporation pays dividends to American stockholders.

e. General Motors pays dividends to French investors.

f. Several Japanese visit Hawaii on an American cruise ship.

g. A Swedish citizen invests in a U.S. company based in Houston.

4. Explain why capital inflows are a credit entry in the balance of payments and capital outflows are a debit entry.

5. When we say that the fixed exchange rate system requires that all prices but one be changed to overcome a balance of trade deficit, what do we mean?

6. What are the primary advantages and disadvantages of the present international monetary system?

7. Use the exchange rate tables to answer the questions.

U.S. DOLLAR PER CURRENCY UNIT		
	Thursday	Wednesday
Swiss franc	0.7978	0.8003
Italian lira	0.0006480	0.0006474

CURRENCY PER U.S. DOLLAR		
	Thursday	Wednesday
Swiss franc	1.2535	1.2495
Italian lira	1543.30	1544.55

a. Did the Swiss franc rise or fall from Wednesday to Thursday?

b. Did the Italian lira rise or fall from Wednesday to Thursday?

c. What happened to the dollar value of the franc?

d. What happened to the dollar value of the lira?

PROBLEM

What happens to the floating exchange rate of a country that has a higher inflation rate than other countries? Show your answer graphically.

POINT
COUNTERPOINT

PETER TAMAS BAUER

GUNNAR MYRDAL

P.T. Bauer and Gunnar Myrdal: Third World Development and Trade

Peter Tamas Bauer (b. 1915) is a distinguished critic of development theory. Bauer's studies of the rubber industry and West African trade paved the way for his works on development—*Dissent on Development* (1972) and *Reality and Rhetoric: Studies in the Economics of Development* (1984). Bauer struck his central theme concerning economic development in earlier works: Economic growth, Bauer argued, is the product of voluntary responses and efficient domestic and international markets—not of state intervention or central planning by governments.

Born in Hungary, Bauer was a fellow of Gonville and Caius College at Cambridge (England) between 1946 and 1960 and again from 1968 and 1984. He was also professor of economics in the University of London at the London School of Economics from 1960 until his retirement in 1983. While in these academic posts, Bauer launched attacks on the conventional wisdom regarding economic development, including theories relating to the widening gap of income differences within and between countries, the vicious circle of poverty, the operation of marketing boards and commodity agreements in developing countries, and the operation of foreign aid. Principally, Bauer targeted the economic development theories of Gunnar Myrdal.

Gunnar Myrdal (1898–1987), sociologist and economist, was a joint recipient of the Nobel Memorial Prize in economics with Friedrich A. von Hayek in 1974. Myrdal is best known for his work on racial discrimination and social problems. His most famous work, *An American Dilemma: The Negro Problem and Modern Democracy*, began as a study commissioned by the Carnegie Corporation in 1938 and had an enormous impact on American attitudes toward integration. His later works explored trade and economic development: *The Political Element in the*

Development of Economic Theory (1935) focused on the philosophical foundations of classical free-trade doctrine to the problems of economic development.

Myrdal was born in the Gustaf parish of Sweden. He studied law as an undergraduate at the University of Stockholm and received his Ph.D. in law from the university in 1927. In 1924, he married Alva Reimer, with whom he researched and wrote a study of Sweden's decreasing population, which was published in 1934. After graduation, Myrdal taught economics, traveled abroad, and served the government of Sweden both as a representative of the Social Democratic party and as cabinet minister. In 1947, he was appointed executive secretary of the United Nations Economic Commission for Europe, a position he retained for the next ten years. In 1960, he became a professor of international economics at the University of Stockholm.

What Is the Problem?

Both Bauer and Myrdal pursued answers to timeless questions regarding the economic development of Third World nations. Does free trade promote or impede economic development in poor nations? Which is more conducive to economic growth and progress in developing nations—central planning or free markets? What is the nature and what are the effects of economic aid from industrialized nations to poor and developing nations of the world?

Bauer and Myrdal occupy opposite ends of the philosophical spectrum; they could not agree on what the problem of economic development is, much less any solution. Myrdal, for example, would center the investigation around the causes of poverty, while Bauer would have economists investigate the causes of prosperity and development. In other words, the burden of any theory of development is either to explain how certain nations and people got rich (Bauer) or why certain nations remained poor (Myrdal).

Not only are Myrdal and Bauer worlds apart on the definition of the problem of development, they stand apart on the philosophical nature of equality and power. Of great importance here is the concept of "equality," which both economists support, but in vastly different forms. As an important modern commentator on their views has remarked, "Whether Myrdal or Bauer is more in favor of equality depends entirely on whether equality is conceived as equality of economic results or equality of political process. Myrdal clearly believes more in equality of economic results—and Bauer equally clearly prefers equality of social processes."[a] In other words, the goal of economic development, in Myrdal's view, is to promote economic equality—similar levels of development and equitable income distributions—between rich and poor nations. Economic power exemplified by concentrations of monopoly power, Myrdal believed, is the root cause of inequalities. Bauer, on the other hand, believes that economic development requires that social processes and access to economic activity be open to all and be free and unfettered. In Bauer's view, power restricts the choices of others, most often exemplified by government planning and regulation. The rich, according to Bauer, most often get that way by expanding the choices and opportunities of others.

Trade, Central Planning, and Economic Aid

Not surprisingly, the philosophical differences between Bauer and Myrdal show very different views of key elements in economic development. Here we consider only three of these key elements.

Trade

In Myrdal's view, the principle of comparative advantage and free trade works in favor of rich nations and keeps poor nations locked within a vicious cycle of poverty. The low saving rates of poor countries mean low investment, which means low economic growth, which means low savings, and so on. To Myrdal, trade with other countries does not unlock this vicious cycle. In *Rich Lands and Poor: The Road to World Prosperity*, he writes, "The forces in the market tend to increase, rather than to decrease, the inequalities between regions." Myrdal points to the so-called banana republics, underdeveloped nations that specialize in one product. In Myrdal's view, such overspecialization leaves a country vulnerable to changes in demand and puts its economy in continuous peril. He suggests that tariffs and subsidies would provide the impetus for developing nations to diversify production and to reduce dependence on one or a few exports.

In Bauer's analysis of trade, these views are wrongheaded and counterproductive. In the first place, Bauer denies that there is a vicious cycle of poverty in underdeveloped countries. Saving and investment take place even where people are poor and illiterate. In his classic study of the rubber industry, Bauer showed that very rapid growth was possible as a consequence of voluntary responses by peasants to expanded opportunities and contacts of developed countries in the West.[b] Further, Bauer argued that trade restrictions and attempts to substitute domestic production for goods that can be obtained more cheaply abroad were a certain path to welfare reductions and to lower growth and development. Development could be maximized only with free interaction between *all* trading nations.

Central Planning and Aid

Myrdal urged central planning as an extension of his belief that unequal distribution of power and property was the principal obstacle to equitable economic growth. Institutional planning, production goals, and price planning are all parts of the system that Myrdal urged on developing nations as prerequisites to growth and changing attitudes. He had faith that, with enough information and competent managers, planning would be superior to any other method of achieving growth and human development. Further, he believed the role of industrialized countries was to provide aid to poor nations.

Sentiments expressed by Bauer more than two decades ago have a very contemporary feel. Bauer pointed out then that planning, if it works at all, does not maximize an economy's opportunities. All investment undertaken for political motives is wasted. Bauer likewise criticized foreign aid as intergovernmental grants of taxpayers' money. While such aid augments resources in recipient countries, Bauer believes there is no reason to expect that, in the hands of politicians, bureaucrats, and administrators, it will be put to productive uses. With few exceptions, foreign aid promotes centralized and closely controlled economies (factors that choke growth), and it sometimes generates resentment and suspicion toward the donor.[c] Of far greater effect is aid provided on a commercial basis, direct foreign investment in developing nations, and—of ultimate importance in Bauer's view—free and open trade between rich nations and poor.

[a]Thomas Sowell, *A Conflict of Visions* (New York: William Morrow and Company, 1987), p. 159.

[b]A.A. Walters, "Peter Tamas Bauer," *The New Palgrave: A Dictionary of Economics*, edited by John Eatwell, Murray Milgate, and Peter Newman (London: The Macmillan Press Limited, 1987), vol. I, p. 207. For further information on Myrdal, see Paul Streeten, "Gunnar Myrdal," *The New Palgrave*, vol. III, pp. 581–583.

[c]For more on economic aid, see P.T. Bauer, *Dissent on Development: Studies and Debates in Development Economics* (Cambridge: Harvard University Press, 1972), pp. 114–135.

GLOSSARY

ability-to-pay principle A method of determining individuals' tax burdens on the basis of those most capable of paying taxes. (p. 255)

accommodation of cost-push inflation Increases in the money supply designed to offset a decrease in aggregate supply caused by monopoly or union action or by an aggregate supply shock; increased aggregate demand results, preventing decreases in real output. (p. 318)

accounting costs Actual money expenditures associated with any activity; payments a firm actually makes to resource suppliers; out-of-pocket costs or explicit costs. (p. 8)

administrative lag The amount of time between recognition of a destabilizing economic event and the implementation of a policy designed to correct it. (p. 338)

aggregate demand The total spending that occurs in an economy at various price levels during a specified period of time. (p. 131)

aggregate demand curve Graphical relation showing the different levels of national income that exist at different price levels. (p. 216)

aggregate supply The total output that will be produced by an economy at various price levels during a specified period of time. (p. 131)

aggregate supply curve A graph showing the different levels of aggregate output produced at different price levels. (p. 220)

antitrust policies Regulations established by laws and government agencies that attempt to preserve business competition. (p. 101)

appreciation An increase in the equilibrium exchange market value of a country's currency in a flexible-rate system; a decrease in the number of units of a country's money required to purchase one unit of a foreign country's money. (p. 412)

artificial barriers to trade Restrictions created by the government that inhibit or prevent trade; includes import quotas and tariffs. (p. 45)

automatic stabilizers Taxes and government expenditures whose levels do not depend on decisions by policymakers for change but instead change countercyclically in response to changes in the level of economic activity. (p. 246)

autonomous consumption Consumption expenditures that are independent of the level of income. (p. 182)

autonomous consumption multiplier The multiple by which equilibrium income will change given a change in autonomous consumption expenditure; $1/MPS$. (p. 195)

autonomous government expenditures Government expenditures that are independent of the level of income. (p. 197)

autonomous investment Investment expenditures that are independent of the level of income. (p. 189)

average propensity to consume (*APC*) The percentage of a particular level of income that is spent on consumption; total consumption divided by total income. (p. 181)

average propensity to save (*APS*) The percentage of total income that is saved; total saving during any given period divided by total income in the same period. (p. 181)

balance of payments An official accounting record of all the foreign transactions of a nation's residents, businesses, and governments. (p. 421)

balance of trade deficit Occurs when the value of a nation's exports is less than the value of a nation's imports; also called a trade deficit. (p. 416)

balance of trade surplus Occurs when the value of a nation's exports exceeds the value of a nation's imports; also called a trade surplus. (p. 416)

barter Direct exchange of one good or service for another without the use of money. (p. 13)

barter economy An economy in which money is not used to facilitate exchange between individuals and firms; goods trade directly for other goods. (p. 272)

benefit principle A method of determining individuals' tax burdens on the basis of the beneficiaries of the expenditures that are financed by taxes; an example is a gasoline tax. (p. 255)

bonds Financial instruments that create future obligations on the part of the issuers to make principal repayments and interest payments. (p. 254)

Bretton Woods system The fixed exchange rate system established among Western countries after World War II. (p. 424)

budget deficit The amount by which government's expenditures exceed government's tax revenues in a year. (p. 248)

budget surplus The amount by which government's tax revenues exceed government's expenditures in a year. (p. 248)

business cycles Recurrent, systematic fluctuations in the level of business activity; usually measured by changes in the level, or rate of growth, of real GDP over time. (p. 125)

capital deepening Increases in the total stock of capital in conjunction with increases in the ratio of the capital stock to the labor force; occurs when the capital stock grows at a faster rate than the labor force. (p. 352)

capital formation An increase in the stock of capital due to roundabout production; the process whereby the stock of capital in an economy increases. (p. 358)

capital stock The amount of nonhuman resources available in the economy. These include tools, land, machinery, equipment, and so on; the total amount of capital goods that exists in an economy at any point in time. (p. 35)

cash reserves Commercial banks' and other depository institutions' holdings of vault cash or deposits at the Federal Reserve district banks. (p. 283)

ceteris paribus The Latin phrase for "all other things held constant." (p. 61)

change in demand A shift of the entire demand curve to the right or left. (p. 63)

change in quantity demanded A change in the amount of a good a consumer is willing and able to purchase that is caused by a change in the price of the good or service. (p. 61)

change in quantity supplied A change in the amount of a good a producer is willing and able to produce and sell that is caused by a change in the price of the good or service. (p. 68)

change in supply A shift of the entire supply curve to the right or left. (p. 69)

checkable deposits Demand deposits plus other types of transactions accounts that pay interest but that may carry some restrictions on use, including minimum balance and limits on the number of checks that can be written per month. (p. 275)

choices at the margin Decisions based on the additional benefits and costs of small changes in a particular activity. (p. 31)

classical long-run equilibrium The hypothetical adjustment of an economy to full employment given an actual supply of resources, population, technology, and degree of specialization. (p. 159)

classical macroeconomic theory A view of the macroeconomy as being self-adjusting and capable of generating full employment and maximum output in the long run without government intervention; dominant from the late eighteenth century through the early twentieth century. (p. 157)

classical process of economic growth A process based on the division of labor, but also involving increases in saving, investment, capital accumulation, and, ultimately, growth in real GDP. (p. 157)

classical self-adjustment mechanism The theory that, through Say's law, full employment will be reached given interest rate flexibility and price-wage flexibility. (p. 170)

commercial bank Chartered financial institution that accepts deposits of various types, especially demand deposits, and that makes commercial and consumer loans. (p. 278)

commodity money An item that serves as a medium of exchange and that is also a good itself. (p. 272)

comparative advantage An economic entity's (an individual's or a nation's) ability to produce a good at a lower marginal opportunity cost than some other entity. (pp. 39, 379)

competition A market which functions under two conditions—no collusion among sellers or buyers (which occurs with a large number of buyers and sellers) and freedom to enter and exit the market. Competition results in prices equal to the costs of production plus a normal profit for sellers. (p. 91)

competitive labor market A labor market in which the wage rate is determined by the interactions of a large number of sellers (suppliers) of labor and a large number of demanders (buyers) of labor. Neither group acts in a collusive manner. (p. 306)

complements Products that are related such that an increase in the price of one will decrease the demand for the other or a decrease in the price of one will increase the demand for the other; two goods whose cross elasticity of demand is negative; $\varepsilon_c < 0$. (p. 64)

consumer price index (CPI) A price index that uses the prices of goods and services consumers generally buy to calculate the price level and the rate of inflation. (p. 150)

consumers' surplus The difference between what consumers are willing to pay for a given quantity of a good or service (the total consumer valuation) and what they have to pay (their total expenditure). (p. 93)

consumption function The positive relationship between levels of consumption expenditures and levels of income, holding all other relevant factors that determine consumption constant. (p. 182)

consumption possibilities curve All the possible combinations of two goods that could be consumed by first specializing according to comparative advantage and then trading at the terms of trade. (p. 383)

contractionary gap The amount by which total planned expenditures at the level of full-employment income fall short of the level required to generate full-employment income; also called a recessionary gap. (p. 196)

cost-push inflation Increases in the price level caused by monopoly and/or union power or by shocks to the economy that reduce aggregate supply. (p. 317)

costs An implication of scarcity; the necessary sacrifices associated with making any choice. (p. 4)

countercyclical fiscal policy Changes in government expenditures or taxes that are designed to reverse changes in private expenditures or savings that produce unemployment or inflation. (p. 201)

credit controls The method or tools that the Federal Reserve System uses in efforts to control the monetary base and the money supply, including reserve requirements, open market operations, the discount rate, and other selective credit controls. (p. 288)

crowding out The competitive pressure exerted on private investment by government expenditures. (p. 259)

cyclically balanced budget A long-term view of the budget, in which surpluses generated during expansions match deficits created during recessions over a period of years. (p. 248)

deflation Sustained decreases in the average level of prices. (p. 120)

demand curve A graphic representation of the quantities of a product that people are willing and able to purchase at all possible prices. (p. 59)

demand deficiency unemployment A short-run situation in which the level of employment is less than if the full-employment level of output were produced; arises when aggregate demand is insufficient to purchase the full-employment output given the price level. (p. 231)

demand deposits A type of transactions account with virtually no restrictions as to the size, timing, or number of checks that can be written on the account. (p. 275)

demand-pull inflation Increases in the price level caused by increases in aggregate demand. (p. 317)

demand-side policy Fiscal or monetary policy intended to alter the overall level of spending, or aggregate demand. (p. 134)

deposit expansion The total amount of additional money or checkable deposits created by some given amount of excess reserves. (p. 286)

depreciation The wearing out of capital goods that occurs with usage over time; a decrease in the equilibrium exchange market value of a country's currency in a flexible-rate system; an increase in the number of units of a country's money required to purchase one unit of a foreign country's money. (p. 411)

devaluation An official change in a country's exchange rate in a fixed-rate system; the number of units of a country's money that purchases one unit of another country's currency is increased by the government. (p. 418)

developing countries Countries with relatively low levels of per capita real GDP; generally characterized by a large subsistence agriculture sector, low saving rates, and high population growth. (p. 362)

discount rate The interest rate charged by the Federal Reserve to depository institutions on loans of reserves from the Federal Reserve. (p. 292)

discretionary fiscal policies Government policy actions that attempt to influence aggregate demand. (p. 219)

discretionary policy A policy or change in policy that is determined by choices or decisions of policymakers. (p. 133)

disposable personal income Personal income minus taxes; income available to spend. (p. 148)

dissaving Occurs when consumption is greater than income; the use of previous years' savings or borrowing to finance consumption expenditures that are greater than current income. (p. 182)

division of labor An economic principle whereby individuals specialize in the production of a single good, service, or task, thus increasing overall productivity and economic efficiency; the result of specialization. (pp. 26, 157)

double coincidence of wants A situation in trading in which each party to the trade has what the other wants and wants what the other has. (p. 272)

dumping The selling of goods in foreign markets at prices lower than those charged in domestic markets. (p. 397)

econometrics The combined use of economic theory and formal statistical techniques to analyze, explain, and predict economic phenomena. (p. 126)

economic development The process through which an economy achieves long-run economic growth; involves capital formation, the development of markets, productivity growth, and the improvement of entrepreneurial ability and labor skills. (p. 361)

economic efficiency The allocation of resources that allows maximum benefit to be achieved at minimum cost. (p. 87)

economic goods and services Goods and services that are scarce. (p. 4)

economic growth A sustained or permanent increase in the overall productive capacity of an economy over time; increases in real GDP or real per capita GDP over time. (pp. 36, 122, 350)

economic indicators Important data, or statistics, such as the money supply, investment spending, unemployment, and inventories that are used to help forecast economic activity and business cycles. (p. 127)

economic stabilization A situation in which the price level and the unemployment rate vary from desired levels only temporarily and by small amounts. (p. 124)

economic system The part of the social system determining what, how, and for whom goods and services are produced. (p. 87)

equilibrium level of national income In the income-expenditures model, the level of income at which total private expenditures equal total output. (p. 193)

equilibrium price The price at which quantity demanded is equal to quantity supplied; other things being equal, there is no tendency for this price to change. (p. 72)

escalator clauses Provisions of labor contracts that tie changes in nominal wages to changes in some price index. (p. 315)

excess reserves Total reserves minus required reserves. (p. 284)

exchange costs The opportunity costs of the resources used in making trades; includes transaction costs, transportation costs, and artificial barriers to trade. (p. 43)

exchange rate The (relative) price of one national currency in terms of another national currency. (p. 406)

expansionary gap The amount by which total planned expenditures at the level of full-employment income exceed the level required to generate full-employment income without inflation; also called an inflationary gap. (p. 196)

explicit costs Accounting costs. (p. 8)

exports (X) Total spending by foreigners on domestically produced goods and services. (pp. 145, 200)

externality Benefits or costs of an individual's actiivty that the individual does not receive or bear. (98)

externally held debt The amount of a country's total federal debt that is owned by foreign governments, businesses, and individuals. (p. 260)

factors affecting demand Anything other than price, such as consumer income and preferences, that determines the amount of a product or service that consumers are willing and able to purchase. (p. 60)

factors affecting supply Anything other than price, such as technology or input costs, that determines the amount of a product or service that sellers are willing and able to offer for sale. (p. 69)

federal debt The total value of federal government bonds outstanding; arises from both current and past budget deficits. (p. 248)

Federal Deposit Insurance Corporation (FDIC) A government institution that provides commercial banks with insurance against default and protects bank customers up to $100,000 per deposit. (p. 280)

federal funds rate A market-determined interest rate on loans and borrowings of bank reserves among commercial banks and other depository institutions. (p. 289)

Federal Open Market Committee (FOMC) A committee of the Federal Reserve System made up of the seven members of the Board of Governors of the Federal Reserve System and five presidents of Federal Reserve district banks; directs open market operations (buying and selling of securities) for the system. (p. 282)

Federal Reserve System The central bank of the United States; regulates financial institutions and establishes and conducts monetary policy. (p. 280)

fiat money Money, usually paper, that is made acceptable in exchange by law; usually not backed by any commodity such as gold. (p. 273)

final goods Goods sold to the final consumers of the goods. (p. 139)

fiscal policy The use of government spending and taxation to effect changes in aggregate economic variables. (p. 133)

fixed exchange rate system An international monetary arrangement in which exchange rates are set by the government, which then must intervene in the foreign exchange market in order to maintain the pegged exchange rate. (p. 408)

flat tax A single tax rate levied on all income. (p. 257)

flexible, or floating, exchange rate system An international monetary arrangement in which exchange rates are determined by private suppliers and demanders without government intervention. (p. 408)

flow of earnings Total income received by resource suppliers during any given time period. (p. 141)

flow of expenditures Total spending of consumers, businesses, and government on final goods and services during any given time period. (p. 141)

foreign exchange The monies of countries that are used to facilitate international trade in goods, services, and financial assets. (p. 406)

foreign exchange market intervention Purchases or sales of foreign exchange by government, usually a central bank, with the goal of maintaining a fixed exchange rate or influencing the exchange rate in a flexible-rate system. (p. 416)

foreign exchange markets The interaction of the suppliers and demanders of foreign exchange, through which exchange rates are determined in a flexible exchange rate system. (p. 406)

foreign exchange reserves The stock of a foreign exchange held by a central bank that is available for use in exchange market intervention. (p. 416)

fractional reserve banking system A banking system in which banks hold only some percentage of deposits as reserves. (p. 278)

free enterprise Economic freedom to produce and sell or purchase and consume goods without government intervention. (p. 90)

free goods and services Things that are available in sufficient amounts and provide all that people want at zero cost. (p. 4)

free trade The exchange of goods between countries without the presence of artificial trade barriers such as tariffs and quotas. (p. 386)

full employment A situation in which unemployment exists only because of normal market adjustments to changing people got rich (Bauer) or why certain nations remained poor (Myrdal).

Not only are Myrdal and Bauer worlds apart on the definition of the problem of development, they stand apart on the philosophical nature of equality and power. Of great importance here is the concept of "equality," which both economists support, but in vastly different forms. As an important modern commentator on their views has remarked, "Whether Myrdal or Bauer is more in favor of equality depends entirely on whether equality is conceived as equality of economic results or equality of political process. Myrdal clearly believes more in equality of economic results—and Bauer equally clearly prefers equality of social processes."[a] In other words, the goal of economic development, in Myrdal's view, is to promote economic equality—similar levels of development and equitable income distributions—between rich and poor nations. Economic power exemplified by concentrations of monopoly power, Myrdal believed, is the root cause of inequalities. Bauer, on the other hand, believes that economic development requires that social processes and access to economic activity be open to all and be free and unfettered. In Bauer's view, power restricts the choices of others, most often exemplified by government planning and regulation. The rich, according to Bauer, most often get that way by expanding the choices and opportunities of others.

Trade, Central Planning, and Economic Aid

Not surprisingly, the philosophical differences between Bauer and Myrdal show very different views of key elements in economic development. Here we consider only three of these key elements.

Trade

In Myrdal's view, the principle of comparative advantage and free trade works in favor of rich nations and keeps poor nations locked within a vicious cycle of poverty. The low saving rates of poor countries mean low investment, which means low economic growth, which means low savings, and so on. To Myrdal, trade with other countries does not unlock this vicious cycle. In *Rich Lands and Poor: The Road to World Prosperity*, he writes, "The forces in the market tend to increase, rather than to decrease, the inequalities between regions." Myrdal points to the so-called banana republics, underdeveloped nations that specialize in one product. In Myrdal's view, such overspecialization leaves a country vulnerable to changes in demand and puts its economy in continuous peril. He suggests that tariffs and subsidies would provide the impetus for developing nations to diversify production and to reduce dependence on one or a few exports.

In Bauer's analysis of trade, these views are wrongheaded and counterproductive. In the first place, Bauer denies that there is a vicious cycle of poverty in underdeveloped countries. Saving and investment take place even where people are poor and illiterate. In his classic study of the rubber industry, Bauer showed that very rapid growth was possible as a consequence of voluntary responses by peasants to expanded opportunities and contacts of developed countries in the West.[b] Further, Bauer argued that trade restrictions and attempts to substitute domestic production for goods that can be obtained more cheaply abroad were a certain path to welfare reductions and to lower growth and development. Development could be maximized only with free interaction between *all* trading nations.

Central Planning and Aid

Myrdal urged central planning as an extension of his belief that unequal distribution of power and property was the principal obstacle to equitable economic growth. Institutional planning, production goals, and price planning are all parts of the system that Myrdal urged on developing nations as prerequisites to growth and changing attitudes. He had faith that, with enough information and competent managers, planning would be superior to any other method of achieving growth and human development. Further, he believed the role of industrialized countries was to provide aid to poor nations.

Sentiments expressed by Bauer more than two decades ago have a very contemporary feel. Bauer pointed out then that planning, if it works at all, does not maximize an economy's opportunities. All investment undertaken for political motives is wasted. Bauer likewise criticized foreign aid as intergovernmental grants of taxpayers' money. While such aid augments resources in recipient countries, Bauer believes there is no reason to expect that, in the hands of politicians, bureaucrats, and administrators, it will be put to productive uses. With few exceptions, foreign aid promotes centralized and closely controlled economies (factors that choke growth), and it sometimes generates resentment and suspicion toward the donor.[c] Of far greater effect is aid provided on a commercial basis, direct foreign investment in developing nations, and—of ultimate importance in Bauer's view—free and open trade between rich nations and poor.

---

[a]Thomas Sowell, *A Conflict of Visions* (New York: William Morrow and Company, 1987), p. 159.

[b]A.A. Walters, "Peter Tamas Bauer," *The New Palgrave: A Dictionary of Economics*, edited by John Eatwell, Murray Milgate, and Peter Newman (London: The Macmillan Press Limited, 1987), vol. I, p. 207. For further information on Myrdal, see Paul Streeten, "Gunnar Myrdal," *The New Palgrave*, vol. III, pp. 581–583.

[c]For more on economic aid, see P.T. Bauer, *Dissent on Development: Studies and Debates in Development Economics* (Cambridge: Harvard University Press, 1972), pp. 114–135.

GLOSSARY

ability-to-pay principle A method of determining individuals' tax burdens on the basis of those most capable of paying taxes. (p. 255)

accommodation of cost-push inflation Increases in the money supply designed to offset a decrease in aggregate supply caused by monopoly or union action or by an aggregate supply shock; increased aggregate demand results, preventing decreases in real output. (p. 318)

accounting costs Actual money expenditures associated with any activity; payments a firm actually makes to resource suppliers; out-of-pocket costs or explicit costs. (p. 8)

administrative lag The amount of time between recognition of a destabilizing economic event and the implementation of a policy designed to correct it. (p. 338)

aggregate demand The total spending that occurs in an economy at various price levels during a specified period of time. (p. 131)

aggregate demand curve Graphical relation showing the different levels of national income that exist at different price levels. (p. 216)

aggregate supply The total output that will be produced by an economy at various price levels during a specified period of time. (p. 131)

aggregate supply curve A graph showing the different levels of aggregate output produced at different price levels. (p. 220)

antitrust policies Regulations established by laws and government agencies that attempt to preserve business competition. (p. 101)

appreciation An increase in the equilibrium exchange market value of a country's currency in a flexible-rate system; a decrease in the number of units of a country's money required to purchase one unit of a foreign country's money. (p. 412)

artificial barriers to trade Restrictions created by the government that inhibit or prevent trade; includes import quotas and tariffs. (p. 45)

automatic stabilizers Taxes and government expenditures whose levels do not depend on decisions by policymakers for change but instead change countercyclically in response to changes in the level of economic activity. (p. 246)

autonomous consumption Consumption expenditures that are independent of the level of income. (p. 182)

autonomous consumption multiplier The multiple by which equilibrium income will change given a change in autonomous consumption expenditure; $1/MPS$. (p. 195)

autonomous government expenditures Government expenditures that are independent of the level of income. (p. 197)

autonomous investment Investment expenditures that are independent of the level of income. (p. 189)

average propensity to consume (*APC*) The percentage of a particular level of income that is spent on consumption; total consumption divided by total income. (p. 181)

average propensity to save (*APS*) The percentage of total income that is saved; total saving during any given period divided by total income in the same period. (p. 181)

balance of payments An official accounting record of all the foreign transactions of a nation's residents, businesses, and governments. (p. 421)

balance of trade deficit Occurs when the value of a nation's exports is less than the value of a nation's imports; also called a trade deficit. (p. 416)

balance of trade surplus Occurs when the value of a nation's exports exceeds the value of a nation's imports; also called a trade surplus. (p. 416)

barter Direct exchange of one good or service for another without the use of money. (p. 13)

barter economy An economy in which money is not used to facilitate exchange between individuals and firms; goods trade directly for other goods. (p. 272)

benefit principle A method of determining individuals' tax burdens on the basis of the beneficiaries of the expenditures that are financed by taxes; an example is a gasoline tax. (p. 255)

bonds Financial instruments that create future obligations on the part of the issuers to make principal repayments and interest payments. (p. 254)

Bretton Woods system The fixed exchange rate system established among Western countries after World War II. (p. 424)

budget deficit The amount by which government's expenditures exceed government's tax revenues in a year. (p. 248)

budget surplus The amount by which government's tax revenues exceed government's expenditures in a year. (p. 248)

business cycles Recurrent, systematic fluctuations in the level of business activity; usually measured by changes in the level, or rate of growth, of real GDP over time. (p. 125)

capital deepening Increases in the total stock of capital in conjunction with increases in the ratio of the capital stock to the labor force; occurs when the capital stock grows at a faster rate than the labor force. (p. 352)

capital formation An increase in the stock of capital due to roundabout production; the process whereby the stock of capital in an economy increases. (p. 358)

capital stock The amount of nonhuman resources available in the economy. These include tools, land, machinery, equipment, and so on; the total amount of capital goods that exists in an economy at any point in time. (p. 35)

cash reserves Commercial banks' and other depository institutions' holdings of vault cash or deposits at the Federal Reserve district banks. (p. 283)

ceteris paribus The Latin phrase for "all other things held constant." (p. 61)

change in demand A shift of the entire demand curve to the right or left. (p. 63)

change in quantity demanded A change in the amount of a good a consumer is willing and able to purchase that is caused by a change in the price of the good or service. (p. 61)

change in quantity supplied A change in the amount of a good a producer is willing and able to produce and sell that is caused by a change in the price of the good or service. (p. 68)

change in supply A shift of the entire supply curve to the right or left. (p. 69)

checkable deposits Demand deposits plus other types of transactions accounts that pay interest but that may carry some restrictions on use, including minimum balance and limits on the number of checks that can be written per month. (p. 275)

choices at the margin Decisions based on the additional benefits and costs of small changes in a particular activity. (p. 31) used for calculating the inflation rate and for converting nominal into real values. (p. 149)

price stability A situation of no inflation or deflation in the economy; no change in the overall level of prices of goods, services, and resources. (p. 119)

price–wage flexibility An economic principle whereby prices and wages can fluctuate with changing economic conditions; thus the economy will be self-adjusting toward full employment even in response to shocks in supply and demand. (p. 167)

prices The market-established opportunity costs of goods and services obtained through exchange. (p. 11)

private choice Choices made through the private (non-governmental) markets. (p. 12)

private property Property that an individual (as opposed to a government) holds the right to control. (p. 88)

private-sector equilibrium A situation of equality between total private expenditures and output. In this equilibrium, there is no unplanned investment and no tendency for the level of output to change. (p. 191)

producers' surplus The difference between the total revenue to producers from selling a given quantity of a good or service and the total cost to them and to society of using the scarce resources in that particular production. (p. 95)

production possibilities frontier The curve that graphs all the possible combinations of two goods that an economic entity can produce given the available technology, the amount of productive resources available, and the fact that these resources are fully utilized. (p. 32)

productivity of labor Output per worker over any given period of time. (p. 351)

products market The forces created by buyers and sellers that establish the prices and quantities exchanged of goods and services. (p. 55)

progressive income tax A tax that is a percentage of income and that varies directly with the level of income. (p. 246)

property rights Any legal and/or enforceable rights to the use of resources of any kind. (p. 7)

proportional income tax A tax that is a fixed percentage of income for all levels of income. (p. 246)

public choice The economic analysis of political decision making, politics, and the democratic process. (p. 12)

public finance The study of how governments at the federal, state, and local levels tax and spend. (p. 250)

public good A good such that, once produced, one individual's consumption of the good does not reduce or exclude the ability of other individuals to consume the good. (p. 100)

pure capitalism An economic system in which most resources are owned, and most relevant decisions are made, by private individuals. (p. 87)

pure communism An economic system in which most productive resources, both human and nonhuman, are publicly owned. (p. 87)

pure inflation tax The reduction in purchasing power of an individual's nominal money holdings due to inflation. (p. 317)

quantity demanded The amount of any good or service consumers are willing and able to purchase at all various prices. (p. 59)

quantity supplied The amount of any good or service that producers are willing and able to produce and sell at some specific price. (p. 67)

quantity theory of money A theory stating that in the long run with output and velocity fixed, changes in the money supply cause proportional changes in the price level. (pp. 168, 303)

quota A restriction or limit on the quantity of an imported good. (pp. 45, 385)

rate of monetary expansion The annual percentage by which the nominal money supply is changing. (p. 310)

rational expectations theory A theory of behavior that assumes that people make efficient use of all past and present relevant information in forming expectations; implies that people's reactions to policy may neutralize the intended effects of the policy. (p. 341)

rational self-interest The view of human behavior espoused by economists. Given circumstances and preferences, people weigh the costs and benefits of choices in order to do the best they can for themselves. (p. 9)

rationing The allocation of goods among consumers with the use of prices. The equilibrium price rations the limited amount of a good produced by the most willing and able suppliers, or sellers, to the most willing and able demanders, or buyers. (p. 73)

real balance effect The effect on investment and consumption spending of a change in the price level that alters the real value of pecuniary assets. (p. 212)

real GDP The total production of final goods and services within a country measured in monetary units that have been adjusted for changes in the price level. (p. 123)

real income The buying power of a consumer's budget; determined by the consumer's money income and the prices of goods and services; the quantity of goods and services that money income can buy. (p. 121)

real money demand Demand on the part of individuals and businesses to hold purchasing power in the form of cash and checkable deposits. (p. 301)

real per capita GDP Real GDP divided by the population size; real output per person in the economy. (p. 350)

real rate of interest The nominal interest rate minus the inflation rate; the interest rate that measures the true incentives and costs that savers and investors face; the interest measured in terms of real buying power. (p. 164)

recognition lag The amount of time it takes policymakers to realize that a destabilizing economic event has occurred. (p. 338)

regressive income tax A tax that is a percentage of income and that varies inversely with the level of income. (p. 246)

relative price The price ratio or "trade-off" in consumption between one product (or service) and another product (or service) or between one good and other goods taken as a whole. (p. 58)

required reserves Reserves against checkable deposits that banks and other depository institutions are required by the Federal Reserve to keep in the form of cash reserves; equal to the required reserve ratio times checkable deposits; also called legal reserves. (p. 283)

reserve bank credit The total value of loans and securities owned or held by the Federal Reserve System. Changes in reserve bank credit affect member institutions' reserves. (p. 287)

reserve ratio The percentage of checkable deposits that banks and other depository institutions hold as reserves. (p. 283)

resources Those things used to produce goods and services. These include land, machines, energy, and human labor and ingenuity. Resources are also called factors of production. (p. 3)

resources market The forces created by buyers and sellers that establish the prices and quantities exchanged of resources such as land, labor services, and capital. (p. 55)

revaluation An official change in a country's exchange rate in a fixed-rate system; the number of units of a country's money that purchases one unit of another country's currency is decreased by the government. (p. 418)

saving function The positive relationship between levels of current saving and levels of income, holding constant all other relevant factors that determine saving. (p. 184)

Say's law A proposition of the classical economists that the production of goods and services will generate incomes sufficiently large that those goods and services will be purchased. (p. 163)

scarcity The condition whereby the resources, goods, and services available to individuals and society are limited relative to the wants and desires for them. (p. 3)

service industries Those industries whose major, or sole, output is a consumer service, such as banking, entertainment, and health care. (p. 367)

services All forms of intangible but useful activities that are valued by people. (p. 3)

shortage The amount by which quantity demanded exceeds quantity supplied at a price below the equilibrium price. (p. 72)

socialism An economic system in which most nonhuman productive resources are owned by the state. (p. 87)

specialization An economic entity's (an individual's or a nation's) producing only one good or service, or the performance of a single task in a production process by an individual. (pp. 26, 377)

speculation The buying and selling of currencies on the foreign exchange market with the intent of profiting from possible devaluation or revaluation in a fixed-rate system or from possible future movements in the exchange rate in a flexible-rate system. (p. 425)

speculative motive or demand Money demand arising from the uncertainty of future interest rates and the fact that people can substitute between holding money and holding bonds. (p. 302)

standard of living The real value of the quantity of goods and services consumed by the average member of the economy. (p. 350)

store of value The ability to own wealth in the form of some item, such as money; a function of money. (p. 274)

substitutes Products that are related such that an increase in the price of one will increase the demand for the other or a decrease in the price of one will decrease the demand for the other; two goods whose cross elasticity of demand is positive; $\varepsilon_c > 0$. (p. 64)

supply curve A graphic representation of the quantities of a product or service that producers are willing and able to sell at all possible prices. (p. 67)

supply shock inflation Price level increases stemming from a decrease in aggregate supply; decreased aggregate supply usually occurs because of sudden increased scarcity of essential resources. (p. 318)

supply–side economics Policies designed to stimulate production by altering incentives of producers; policies designed to shift the aggregate supply curve to the right. (p. 237)

supply–side policy Fiscal or monetary policy intended to alter the incentives to produce output; policies designed to shift aggregate supply. (p. 134)

surplus The amount by which quantity supplied exceeds quantity demanded at a price above the equilibrium price. (p. 71)

tariff A tax or levy on imported goods. (pp. 45, 385)

tax indexation Periodic adjustment of the tax brackets of a progressive income tax so as to base taxes on real, not nominal, income; eliminates bracket creep and increased income taxes due solely to inflation. (pp. 122, 317)

technology Knowledge of production methods associated with producing a particular good. (p. 6)

terms of trade The number of units of one good that exchange in the market for one unit of some other good; a relative price. Although not expressed in terms of money, it is a price nonetheless. (pp. 41, 382)

terms of trade argument Defending the use of artificial trade barriers combined with monopoly or monopsony power in international markets in order to produce an improvement in a country's terms of trade. (p. 398)

total consumer valuation The total amount that consumers are willing to pay for a given quantity of a good or service rather than go without it. (p. 93)

transaction costs The opportunity costs of the resources directly associated with trade; includes time costs, brokers' fees, and so on. (p. 43)

transactions accounts Demand deposits or other checkable accounts that allow the transfer of funds by writing a check. (p. 275)

transactions demand Money demand that arises from the desire of businesses and consumers to facilitate exchange with the use of money. (p. 301)

transportation costs The value of resources used in the transportation of goods that finalize any trade. (p. 44)

undervalued A term describing the foreign exchange market value of a country's money; occurs when the number of units of a country's money that purchases one unit of a foreign currency is greater than the equilibrium exchange rate. (p. 415)

unemployed A labor-force status characterized by an individual who is actively seeking employment but is not working. (p. 116)

unemployment of resources A situation in which some human and/or nonhuman resources that can be used in production are not used. (p. 34)

unemployment rate The percentage of the labor force without jobs. (p. 116)

unit of account A standard measure, such as the dollar, that is used to express the values of goods and services; a function of money. (p. 274)

velocity The average number of times a unit of money changes hands per year in financing the purchases of GDP. (p. 169)

vicious circle of poverty An attempt to explain why some countries remain less developed that centers on low savings and investment as the cause of low real incomes, which in turn lead to low saving and investment rates. (p. 363)

wage–price spiral The process whereby increased prices of final goods cause increased wage rates and other resource prices, which in turn result in still-higher prices of final goods; for the spiral to continue, the money supply must continually increase or real output must continually fall. (p. 318)

wealth The total value of monetary plus nonmonetary assets in existence at a point in time; a stock variable. (p. 211)

welfare loss to society The net loss to an economy resulting from the imposition of an artificial trade barrier; government revenues plus producer gains minus consumer losses. (p. 390) demand or supply or to outmoded skills of workers; also a numerical federal government goal for the unemployment rate; to the classical economist, a situation in which all workers willing and able to work at the current market real wage rate are employed. (pp. 117, 236)

full price The total opportunity cost to an individual of obtaining a good; includes money price and all other costs, such as transportation costs or waiting costs. (p. 57)

gold standard An international monetary system in which currencies are redeemable in gold at fixed rates or prices. (p. 424)

goods All tangible things that satisfy people's wants and desires. (p. 3)

government purchases (*G***)** Total spending by federal, state, and local governments on final goods and services. (p. 145)

gross domestic product (GDP) A measure of the final goods and services produced by a country with resources located within that country. (pp. 17, 122, 139)

gross national product (GNP) The value, measured at market prices, of all final goods and services produced in an economy in one year. (pp. 17, 139)

gross private domestic investment (*I***)** Total spending by private businesses on final goods, including capital goods and inventories. (p. 144)

growth absorption Increases in total spending sufficient to purchase additional output generated by increases in productive capacity. (p. 356)

human resources All forms of labor and skill used to produce goods and services. (p. 5)

implicit costs Nonpecuniary costs associated with the consumption of a good or service; the opportunity costs of resources used in production for which no explicit payments are made. (p. 8)

implicit price deflator A price index that uses the most comprehensive set of prices to calculate the level of prices and the rate of inflation facing households, businesses, and government; also called the GDP deflator. (p. 151)

imports (*M***)** Total spending by domestic residents on foreign-produced goods and services. (pp. 145, 200)

income velocity The average number of times that a unit of money (a dollar) is used, or changes hands, in purchasing nominal GDP. (p. 303)

income-expenditures model A theory suggesting that private expenditures

are basically determined by the level of national income and that these expenditures in turn determine the levels of output and employment in the economy. (p. 179)

infant industry A new or developing domestic industry whose unit production costs are higher than those of established firms in the same industry in other countries. (p. 395)

inferior good A good that a consumer chooses to purchase in smaller quantities as income rises or in larger amounts as income falls. (p. 63)

inflation A sustained increase in the general level of prices; inflation reduces the purchasing power of money. (p. 14)

inflation rate The percent by which the average level of prices in an economy rises; usually expressed as a percent per year. (p. 120)

information A scarce and important element in the process of economic exchange and growth. (p. 6)

institutions The sum total of the traditions, mores, laws, and governmental structures of an economy. (p. 7)

interest groups Collections of individuals with one or more common characteristics, such as occupation, who seek collectively to affect legislation or government policy so as to benefit members of the group. (p. 104)

interest rate effect The effect on investment spending that results from a change in the interest rate produced by a change in the price level. (p. 214)

internally held debt The amount of a country's total federal debt that is owned by the country's various governments, businesses, and individuals. (p. 260)

International Monetary Fund An international organization, established along with the Bretton Woods system, designed to assist in the efficient functioning of the Bretton Woods fixed exchange rate system. (p. 424)

investment multiplier The multiple by which equilibrium income will change given a change in autonomous investment expenditure; $1/MPS$. (p. 194)

investment spending Expenditures made by businesses on capital goods plus any change (positive or negative) in business inventories. (p. 187)

investment tax credit A percentage or amount of new investment expenditure that is directly subtracted from the investor's tax bill in calculating total taxes. (p. 256)

law of demand The price of a product or service and the amount purchased are inversely related. If price rises, then quan-

tity demanded falls; if price falls, quantity demanded increases, all other things held constant. (p. 59)

law of increasing costs As more scarce resources are used to produce additional units of one good, production of another good falls by larger and larger amounts. (p. 33)

law of one price In perfect markets, the market forces of supply and demand produce a single, equilibrium price for a good or service. (p. 71)

law of supply The price of a product or service and the amount that producers are willing and able to offer for sale are positively related. If price rises, then quantity supplied rises; if price decreases, then quantity supplied decreases. (p. 67)

liquidity The ease with which any asset or commodity can be converted into money with little or no risk of loss to the holder. (p. 275)

liquidity preference theory A theory stating that the interest rate is determined by the interaction of real money demand and supply, and that interest rate changes due to real money demand or supply changes produce changes in real economic activity. (p. 302)

logrolling The exchange of votes by legislators, usually in order to gain support for particular legislation. (p. 102)

lump-sum tax A fixed level of total taxes; total taxes do not change as the level of income changes. (p. 199)

M-1 money multiplier The multiple by which the money supply will change given a change in the monetary base. (p. 295)

macroeconomics Analysis of the behavior of an economy as a whole. (p. 17)

managed flexible-rate system Primarily a flexible exchange rate system, but with occasional government purchases or sales of foreign exchange intended to influence the exchange rate. (p. 409)

margin The difference between costs or benefits in an existing situation and after a proposed change. (p. 10)

marginal analysis Looking at changes in the costs and benefits of a change from the status quo to a proposed new situation. These marginal changes in the costs and benefits are the basis for rational economic choice. (p. 10)

marginal opportunity production cost The number of units of one good that do not get produced when one additional unit of another good is produced. (p. 38)

marginal private benefit curve A curve, equivalent to a demand curve, which represents the value that consumers place on marginal units of the good or service. (p. 92)

marginal private cost curve A curve showing the marginal or additional cost to society—the opportunity cost of scarce resources—of producing additional units of a good or service. (p. 95)

marginal propensity to consume (*MPC***)** The percentage of an additional dollar of income that is spent on consumption; change in consumption divided by change in income. (p. 180)

marginal propensity to save (*MPS***)** The percentage of an additional dollar of income that is saved; change in saving divided by change in income. (p. 181)

marginal tax rate The tax rate, in percentage terms, that applies to additional taxable income; additional taxes divided by the additional income taxed. (p. 247)

market A collection of buyers and sellers exchanging resources, goods, or services; prices tend toward equality in a market through the continuous exchange between suppliers and demanders. (pp. 11, 71)

market demand The total amount consumers are willing and able to purchase of a product at all possible prices, obtained by summing the quantities demanded at each price over all buyers. (p. 65)

market failure A situation in which the socially optimal (most economically efficient) amount of a good or service does not get produced by the private market; usually stems from unclear property rights assignments. (p. 98)

market supply The total amount producers are willing and able to offer for sale of a product at all possible prices, obtained by summing the quantities supplied at each price over all producers. (p. 70)

measure of economic welfare (*MEW***)** A concept of social and economic well-being that accounts for the production of all goods and services, not just those transacted for in markets. (p. 141)

medium of exchange An item that is generally acceptable as payment for goods and services. (p. 272)

microeconomics Analysis of the behavior of individual decision-making units, including individuals, households, and business firms. (p. 16)

model A simplified abstraction of the real world that approximates reality and makes problems easier to analyze; also called a theory. (p. 15)

monetarism A theory that centers on money supply growth, real money demand, nominal and real interest rates, and inflationary expectations in explaining the process of inflation or deflation. (p. 312)

monetary base The sum of depository institutions' reserves plus currency held by the public. (p. 287)

monetary policy The use of money supply changes to effect changes in aggregate economic variables. (p. 133)

monetary rule A monetary policy consisting of a fixed rate of growth of the money supply. (p. 339)

money A generally accepted medium of exchange. (pp. 13, 275)

money expansion The increase in the money supply created by some given amount of excess reserves. (p. 286)

money price The dollar price that sellers receive from buyers; a price expressed in terms of money, not in terms of an amount of another good. (p. 57)

national income (NI) Total earnings of resource suppliers during a given period of time. (p. 146)

national income accounting The process of statistically measuring the nation's aggregate economic performance. (p. 139)

natural rate of unemployment A theoretical concept; the unemployment rate that coexists with macroeconomic stability or labor-market equilibrium in the long run; the rate of unemployment due to frictional unemployment plus structural unemployment that will exist when expectations of inflation reflect actual inflationary conditions and all short-run macroeconomic adjustments have been made. (pp. 117, 236)

net exports (*X - M***)** Total spending by foreigners on domestically produced goods and services minus total spending by domestic residents on foreign produced goods and services. (p. 145)

neutrality of money A proposition stating that in the long run the relative prices of goods and services are not affected by changes in the money supply. (p. 304)

nominal GDP The total production of final goods and services within a country measured in monetary units that have not been adjusted for changes in the price level. (p. 123)

nominal income Income measured in terms of money, not in terms of what the money can buy. (p. 121)

nonhuman resources All resources other than human resources, such as machines and land. (p. 5)

nontariff trade barriers Alternative (to tariffs and quotas) means of restricting trade; examples include domestic content legislation and health and safety regulations. (p. 391)

normal good A good that a consumer chooses to purchase in smaller (larger) amounts as income falls (rises). (p. 63)

normative economics Value judgments based on moral principles or preferences about how economic life should be. (p. 16)

open market operations The purchase or sale of securities by the Federal Reserve System in order to affect the monetary base and the money supply; the major tool of monetary policy. (p. 288)

opportunity cost The highest-valued alternative forgone in making any choice. (pp. 8, 26)

overvalued A term describing the foreign exchange market value of a country's money; occurs when the number of units of a country's money that purchases one unit of a foreign currency is less than the equilibrium exchange rate. (p. 416)

perfect market A market in which there are enough buyers and sellers that no single buyer or seller can influence price. (p. 71)

personal consumption expenditures (*C***)** Total spending by households on final goods and services. (p. 144)

personal income (*PI***)** Total earnings resource suppliers actually receive during a given period of time plus transfer payments. (p. 148)

personal saving Disposable personal income less personal consumption expenditures. (p. 149)

policy trade-off A situation in which a policy that promotes the attainment of one macroeconomic goal necessarily implies that the attainment of another macroeconomic objective becomes more difficult. (p. 133)

positive economics Observations, explanations, or predictions about economic life; scientific economics. (p. 16)

precautionary demand Money demand that arises from the desire of businesses and consumers to hold money in order to facilitate unexpected purchases. (p. 302)

price ceiling A form of regulation in which a maximum legal price is established by government above which exchange between buyers and sellers is illegal. (p. 79)

price control The setting, by government, of a price in a market different from the equilibrium price. (p. 78)

price floor A form of regulation in which a minimum legal price is established by government below which exchange between buyers and sellers is illegal. (p. 80)

price index A statistic used to calculate the price level and the rate of inflation. (p. 150)

price level The average of the prices of all goods and services in the economy;

used for calculating the inflation rate and for converting nominal into real values. (p. 149)

price stability A situation of no inflation or deflation in the economy; no change in the overall level of prices of goods, services, and resources. (p. 119)

price-wage flexibility An economic principle whereby prices and wages can fluctuate with changing economic conditions; thus the economy will be self-adjusting toward full employment even in response to shocks in supply and demand. (p. 167)

prices The market-established opportunity costs of goods and services obtained through exchange. (p. 11)

private choice Choices made through the private (non-governmental) markets. (p. 12)

private property Property that an individual (as opposed to a government) holds the right to control. (p. 88)

private-sector equilibrium A situation of equality between total private expenditures and output. In this equilibrium, there is no unplanned investment and no tendency for the level of output to change. (p. 191)

producers' surplus The difference between the total revenue to producers from selling a given quantity of a good or service and the total cost to them and to society of using the scarce resources in that particular production. (p. 95)

production possibilities frontier The curve that graphs all the possible combinations of two goods that an economic entity can produce given the available technology, the amount of productive resources available, and the fact that these resources are fully utilized. (p. 32)

productivity of labor Output per worker over any given period of time. (p. 351)

products market The forces created by buyers and sellers that establish the prices and quantities exchanged of goods and services. (p. 55)

progressive income tax A tax that is a percentage of income and that varies directly with the level of income. (p. 246)

property rights Any legal and/or enforceable rights to the use of resources of any kind. (p. 7)

proportional income tax A tax that is a fixed percentage of income for all levels of income. (p. 246)

public choice The economic analysis of political decision making, politics, and the democratic process. (p. 12)

public finance The study of how governments at the federal, state, and local levels tax and spend. (p. 250)

public good A good such that, once produced, one individual's consumption of the good does not reduce or exclude the ability of other individuals to consume the good. (p. 100)

pure capitalism An economic system in which most resources are owned, and most relevant decisions are made, by private individuals. (p. 87)

pure communism An economic system in which most productive resources, both human and nonhuman, are publicly owned. (p. 87)

pure inflation tax The reduction in purchasing power of an individual's nominal money holdings due to inflation. (p. 317)

quantity demanded The amount of any good or service consumers are willing and able to purchase at all various prices. (p. 59)

quantity supplied The amount of any good or service that producers are willing and able to produce and sell at some specific price. (p. 67)

quantity theory of money A theory stating that in the long run with output and velocity fixed, changes in the money supply cause proportional changes in the price level. (pp. 168, 303)

quota A restriction or limit on the quantity of an imported good. (pp. 45, 385)

rate of monetary expansion The annual percentage by which the nominal money supply is changing. (p. 310)

rational expectations theory A theory of behavior that assumes that people make efficient use of all past and present relevant information in forming expectations; implies that people's reactions to policy may neutralize the intended effects of the policy. (p. 341)

rational self-interest The view of human behavior espoused by economists. Given circumstances and preferences, people weigh the costs and benefits of choices in order to do the best they can for themselves. (p. 9)

rationing The allocation of goods among consumers with the use of prices. The equilibrium price rations the limited amount of a good produced by the most willing and able suppliers, or sellers, to the most willing and able demanders, or buyers. (p. 73)

real balance effect The effect on investment and consumption spending of a change in the price level that alters the real value of pecuniary assets. (p. 212)

real GDP The total production of final goods and services within a country measured in monetary units that have been adjusted for changes in the price level. (p. 123)

real income The buying power of a consumer's budget; determined by the consumer's money income and the prices of goods and services; the quantity of goods and services that money income can buy. (p. 121)

real money demand Demand on the part of individuals and businesses to hold purchasing power in the form of cash and checkable deposits. (p. 301)

real per capita GDP Real GDP divided by the population size; real output per person in the economy. (p. 350)

real rate of interest The nominal interest rate minus the inflation rate; the interest rate that measures the true incentives and costs that savers and investors face; the interest measured in terms of real buying power. (p. 164)

recognition lag The amount of time it takes policymakers to realize that a destabilizing economic event has occurred. (p. 338)

regressive income tax A tax that is a percentage of income and that varies inversely with the level of income. (p. 246)

relative price The price ratio or "tradeoff" in consumption between one product (or service) and another product (or service) or between one good and other goods taken as a whole. (p. 58)

required reserves Reserves against checkable deposits that banks and other depository institutions are required by the Federal Reserve to keep in the form of cash reserves; equal to the required reserve ratio times checkable deposits; also called legal reserves. (p. 283)

reserve bank credit The total value of loans and securities owned or held by the Federal Reserve System. Changes in reserve bank credit affect member institutions' reserves. (p. 287)

reserve ratio The percentage of checkable deposits that banks and other depository institutions hold as reserves. (p. 283)

resources Those things used to produce goods and services. These include land, machines, energy, and human labor and ingenuity. Resources are also called factors of production. (p. 3)

resources market The forces created by buyers and sellers that establish the prices and quantities exchanged of resources such as land, labor services, and capital. (p. 55)

revaluation An official change in a country's exchange rate in a fixed-rate system; the number of units of a country's money that purchases one unit of another country's currency is decreased by the government. (p. 418)

saving function The positive relationship between levels of current saving and levels of income, holding constant all other relevant factors that determine saving. (p. 184)

Say's law A proposition of the classical economists that the production of goods and services will generate incomes sufficiently large that those goods and services will be purchased. (p. 163)

scarcity The condition whereby the resources, goods, and services available to individuals and society are limited relative to the wants and desires for them. (p. 3)

service industries Those industries whose major, or sole, output is a consumer service, such as banking, entertainment, and health care. (p. 367)

services All forms of intangible but useful activities that are valued by people. (p. 3)

shortage The amount by which quantity demanded exceeds quantity supplied at a price below the equilibrium price. (p. 72)

socialism An economic system in which most nonhuman productive resources are owned by the state. (p. 87)

specialization An economic entity's (an individual's or a nation's) producing only one good or service, or the performance of a single task in a production process by an individual. (pp. 26, 377)

speculation The buying and selling of currencies on the foreign exchange market with the intent of profiting from possible devaluation or revaluation in a fixed-rate system or from possible future movements in the exchange rate in a flexible-rate system. (p. 425)

speculative motive or demand Money demand arising from the uncertainty of future interest rates and the fact that people can substitute between holding money and holding bonds. (p. 302)

standard of living The real value of the quantity of goods and services consumed by the average member of the economy. (p. 350)

store of value The ability to own wealth in the form of some item, such as money; a function of money. (p. 274)

substitutes Products that are related such that an increase in the price of one will increase the demand for the other or a decrease in the price of one will decrease the demand for the other; two goods whose cross elasticity of demand is positive; $\varepsilon_c > 0$. (p. 64)

supply curve A graphic representation of the quantities of a product or service that producers are willing and able to sell at all possible prices. (p. 67)

supply shock inflation Price level increases stemming from a decrease in aggregate supply; decreased aggregate supply usually occurs because of sudden increased scarcity of essential resources. (p. 318)

supply–side economics Policies designed to stimulate production by altering incentives of producers; policies designed to shift the aggregate supply curve to the right. (p. 237)

supply–side policy Fiscal or monetary policy intended to alter the incentives to produce output; policies designed to shift aggregate supply. (p. 134)

surplus The amount by which quantity supplied exceeds quantity demanded at a price above the equilibrium price. (p. 71)

tariff A tax or levy on imported goods. (pp. 45, 385)

tax indexation Periodic adjustment of the tax brackets of a progressive income tax so as to base taxes on real, not nominal, income; eliminates bracket creep and increased income taxes due solely to inflation. (pp. 122, 317)

technology Knowledge of production methods associated with producing a particular good. (p. 6)

terms of trade The number of units of one good that exchange in the market for one unit of some other good; a relative price. Although not expressed in terms of money, it is a price nonetheless. (pp. 41, 382)

terms of trade argument Defending the use of artificial trade barriers combined with monopoly or monopsony power in international markets in order to produce an improvement in a country's terms of trade. (p. 398)

total consumer valuation The total amount that consumers are willing to pay for a given quantity of a good or service rather than go without it. (p. 93)

transaction costs The opportunity costs of the resources directly associated with trade; includes time costs, brokers' fees, and so on. (p. 43)

transactions accounts Demand deposits or other checkable accounts that allow the transfer of funds by writing a check. (p. 275)

transactions demand Money demand that arises from the desire of businesses and consumers to facilitate exchange with the use of money. (p. 301)

transportation costs The value of resources used in the transportation of goods that finalize any trade. (p. 44)

undervalued A term describing the foreign exchange market value of a country's money; occurs when the number of units of a country's money that purchases one unit of a foreign currency is greater than the equilibrium exchange rate. (p. 415)

unemployed A labor-force status characterized by an individual who is actively seeking employment but is not working. (p. 116)

unemployment of resources A situation in which some human and/or nonhuman resources that can be used in production are not used. (p. 34)

unemployment rate The percentage of the labor force without jobs. (p, 116)

unit of account A standard measure, such as the dollar, that is used to express the values of goods and services; a function of money. (p. 274)

velocity The average number of times a unit of money changes hands per year in financing the purchases of GDP. (p. 169)

vicious circle of poverty An attempt to explain why some countries remain less developed that centers on low savings and investment as the cause of low real incomes, which in turn lead to low saving and investment rates. (p. 363)

wage–price spiral The process whereby increased prices of final goods cause increased wage rates and other resource prices, which in turn result in still-higher prices of final goods; for the spiral to continue, the money supply must continually increase or real output must continually fall. (p. 318)

wealth The total value of monetary plus nonmonetary assets in existence at a point in time; a stock variable. (p. 211)

welfare loss to society The net loss to an economy resulting from the imposition of an artificial trade barrier; government revenues plus producer gains minus consumer losses. (p. 390)

INDEX

Note: Page numbers in boldface type indicate pages on which definitions of key terms appear; those followed by n indicate footnotes.

INDEX